SUPREME COURT UPDATE
Search & Seizure Decisions after January 1, 2002

Kenneth R. Evans

"The right of the people to be secure in their persons, houses, papers, and effects, against unreasonable searches and seizures, shall not be violated, and no warrants shall issue, but upon probable cause, supported by oath or affirmation, and particularly describing the place to be searched, and the persons or things to be seized."
—*The Fourth Amendment*

U.S. v. Arvizu, 122 S.Ct. 744 (2002)

The Ninth Circuit used what the Court called a divide-and-conquer approach in assessing articulable suspicion under **Terry v. Ohio** rather than using the totality approach. The Ninth Circuit isolated each factor and decided which factors, standing alone, were positive and which were negative. The Court said this is not a totality of the circumstances approach. This decision is perhaps the most important decision written on the analysis required by suppression judges when assessing articulable suspicion.

U.S. v. Drayton, 122 S.Ct. 2105 (2002)

This decision reaffirms the Court's position in **Florida v. Bostick,** 501 U.S. 429 (1984) that drug interdiction officers do not seize passengers on buses by merely walking the aisles. The Court also reemphasized that asking for a consent to search does not require the officer to inform the citizen of the right to refuse consent. This overruled decisions of the Eleventh Circuit by a majority of 6-3.

Kirk v. Louisiana, 122 S.Ct. 2458 (*per curiam* 2002)

A Louisiana court failed to follow the threshold crossing case of **Payton v. New York,** 445 U.S. 573 (1980) which held consent, warrant, or an exigency is needed to enter and arrest a person in his or her own home. The appellate court felt any felony permitted an in-home arrest and cited the Fourth Amendment. Since the Louisiana Supreme Court denied review, this non-action made the case ripe for U.S. Supreme Court action.

Board of Education of Independent School District No. 92 of Pottawatomie County v. Earls, 122 S.Ct. 2559 (2002)

The Court extended the reasoning and rule of **Vernonia School District 47J v. Acton,** 515 U.S. 646 (1985) that permitted drug testing of student athletes to any student involved in a school sponsored extra-curricular activity. The Court found an "…important interest in preventing and deterring drug use among its school children." Five justices joined the opinion, one concurred and three dissented.

THE NATIONAL JUDICIAL COLLEGE

Est. 1963

Search & Seizure
Sourcebook for State Judges

Kenneth R. Evans

THE NATIONAL
JUDICIAL COLLEGE

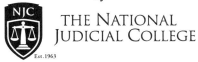
For any inquiry contact:

NJC Press Order Fulfillment
The National Judicial College/MS 358
Reno, Nevada 89557

Tel: 800-255-8343
Fax: 775-327-2161

E-mail: njcpress@judges.org

ACKNOWLEDGMENTS

This book is the product of significant support by the New England School of Law, its dean, Dean John F. O'Brien, the Chairman of the Board of Trustees, Judge James R. Lawton and the fine library staff, especially Barry Stearns. A very special thanks must be extended to Mrs. Patricia Gresham, the head of faculty services and my "word processor mentor." Revision after revision, she never gave up on me. Finally, this book was inspired by a need to be prepared as a lecture for The National Judicial College and the American Academy of Judicial Education. My inspiration came from the faith shown in me by Felix F. Stumpf. He has been a guiding hand in my career since 1975. Through his efforts and those of the College, I have had the honor of lecturing in over 16 states on search and seizure. Also, my thanks for their technical support to Patricia Knighten, Nickie Gunstrom, Margaret Walz-Yates, and Jenny Jones. Finally, and most of all, I appreciate the patience of my wife, Jo Anne, who has tolerated the hours needed to read, research, write, and grumble.

With gratitude,

Ken Evans

ABOUT THE AUTHOR

Professor Emeritus and former dean of Boston's New England School of Law, Kenneth Evans was also Director of Training and State Law Libraries, Supreme Court of Appeals of West Virginia; professor of law and director of the Criminal Justice Research Service and the University of Mississippi Judicial College; the Mississippi Prosecutors' Association; the Judicial Council of Georgia, and the Georgia prosecuting Attorneys' Council. He is a graduate of Stetson University College of Law, and the author of the *Mississippi Prosecutors' Handbook*. He has co-authored *Criminal Law for Policemen, Handbook of Criminal Law,* and *Introduction to Criminal Justice*. Professor Evans is an alumnus of The National Judicial College and has been on the faculty since 1976.

PREFACE

The Fourth Amendment to the United States Constitution is composed of 54 words that define the constitutional procedural limits of searches and seizures. Countless distinguished jurists and law professors have dissected, examined, deconstructed and interpreted the Fourth Amendment within the halls of The National Judicial College since its inception. Professor Kenneth Evans has been a faculty member at NJC since 1976, teaching judges ways to approach Fourth Amendment issues.

Professor Evans presents a unique book designed to illuminate the intricacies of the United States Supreme Court and state Supreme Court decisions on search and seizure issues. His treatment of the states' cases sets Professor Evans' book apart from the many other treatises which explicate the Fourth Amendment only in terms of U.S. Supreme Court decisions.

Professor Evans correlates state Supreme Court decisions with those of the United States Supreme Court in a coherent and meaningful way. Each of the book's chapters addresses a specific aspect of the law on search and seizure; checklists and an annotated search warrant are innovative, practical aids.

The National Judicial College is grateful to Professor Evans for making available to state court judges his years of scholarship and remarkable insights into the complexities of the Fourth Amendment.

We are deeply appreciative of the support of the Bureau of Justice Assistance, United States Department of Justice, who provided financial assistance for the publication of this book.

William F. Dressel
President
The National Judicial College

FOREWORD

With Mapp V. Ohio, the U.S. Supreme Court took the lead in determining the minimum rights of all citizens under the Fourth Amendment. Subsequently, through a series of decisions, the Court encouraged the states to use their own constitutions to determine if their state gives greater protection. This policy is called "The New Federalism." Each state can grant its citizens greater protection "in their right to be secure from unreasonable searches and seizures." The last three decades have produced significant diversity among the states. Each state has had to determine how it would react to each Supreme Court decision. This sourcebook attempts to demonstrate those reactions and the choices made by the states. Not since our founding have the state constitutions, statutes, folkways and mores been more important.

Significant cases on each topic from the several states have been chosen to demonstrate how each search doctrine has been treated across the nation. Not all states are represented in each chapter but every state in the Union is represented. Some states have not yet reacted to every decision of the Supreme Court, but every chapter has decisions from every geographical region to help the judge find a "sister state's" opinion to use as secondary authority. Several checklists have been included in the book. Some are directly from the state decisions. Others have been prepared by this author to aid as reminders and to help in running a better suppression hearing and in making a better record and findings of fact.

The cases cited are illustrative of the problems. Some are older and every judge should make sure they are still the law. The citations to some cases refer to the Criminal Law Reporter and to opinions reported in Westlaw (WL) including some unpublished or unavailable opinions. These cases are intended to familiarize judges with as many myriad factual permutations as possible because the faxts are the important factor and should be kept in mind when deciding a motion to suppress. Recent changes on many appellate courts have brought new faces and new philosophies to those courts. Some courts have become more defense oriented while others have become more oriented toward the prosecution. The author is not responsible for these changes. (Authorities cited as of July 1, 2001.)

AMENDMENT IV.

The right of the people to be secure in their persons, houses, papers, and effects, against unreasonable searches and seizures, shall not be violated, and no Warrants shall issue, but upon probable cause, supported by Oath or affirmation, and particularly describing the place to be searched, and the persons or things to be seized.

CONTENTS

CHAPTER ONE

THE FOURTH AMENDMENT AND THE EXCLUSIONARY RULE

I.   Introduction

Before the Fourth Amendment exclusionary rule can apply there must be:

1.   governmental action;

2   that invades a person's reasonable expectation of privacy;

3   that society is willing to recognize which leads to the viewing of or the capture of or both of either the person or his effects or both.

If the government proceeds correctly, the evidence yielded by the search or seizure is admissible in a criminal case. If the government proceeds improperly the evidence is inadmissible in the government's case-in-chief but it may be admissible to impeach the defendant's testimony. This book addresses the issues inherent in the foregoing complex statement. It explains that the Fourth Amendment does not apply to:

1. Routine searches along the border of the United States or its functional equivalent;
2. Property that people abandon freely and voluntarily;
3. "Open Fields" outside the curtilage of the home;
4. Conduct or things exposed to public view and the other senses; and
5. Property possessed illegally.

This book also shows the Fourth Amendment recognizes some necessary and well-defined exceptions to the warrant requirement and the "taint removers:"

1. Consent,
2. Exigent circumstances,
3. Independent source,
4. Inevitable discovery,
5. Attenuation, and
6. Good faith reliance.

When a government agent conducts an illegal search and seizure, and when no exception applies, and no taint remover can be used, what do we do then? We rule the evidence inadmissible. This is the Exclusionary Rule. Hated by police, misunderstood by the public, not preferred by many trial judges currently serving on the courts, the exclusionary rule is constantly being re-evaluated. The exclusionary rule was first announced by the U. S. Supreme Court in **Weeks v. U.S.**, 232 U.S. 383 (1914) and made applicable to the states through **Mapp v. Ohio**, 367 U.S. 643 (1961). In a retreat from that guardianship, the Court took a bold step in **Stone v. Powell**, 428 U.S. 465 (1976) in the hope of reducing the docket of the federal court system. A consideration of these cases follows.

Why is there an exclusionary rule? It was hoped that it would act as a deterrent to arbitrary police action. That it has not does not make it the "wrong" rule. It works better than proposals to allow recovery in damages against law enforcement agencies and their officers. Under what circumstances would a jury be so outraged as to award more than nominal damages when the police unearth what is in fact absolute evidence of criminal activity? How often would one find a jury willing to convict an officer who was trying to "protect and serve?" Until someone creates a system that will guarantee the Fourth Amendment better than the exclusionary rule, it is the rule that the courts must apply. The Fourth would have no meaning at all without the exclusionary rule. The only way to neutralize illegal activity by law enforcement agencies is to nullify the use of the "fruits" of that illegal activity.

"The Fourth Amendment has principles of humanity and civil liberty which were secured in England after years of struggle. We adopted these principles in a form not subject to the whims of legislators." **Weeks v. U.S.**, 232 U.S. 383 (1914). The courts and the police are subject to limitations and restraints. These are necessary to secure the people (and that which they call their own) against unreasonable searches and seizures. Everyone is entitled to the benefit of the Fourth Amendment. Courts should not sanction a "watering down" of these rights. The applicability of the Fourth Amendment does not depend on whether there is a personal remedy against the wrongdoer. It provides that illegal governmental action should not be countenanced by the government which includes the courts. **Weeks** (*supra*) at 398.

A dual standard was obvious. Many, if not most, state courts tolerated infringements not permitted to the federal officials. It was not until 1961 that the next step would be taken to assure uniform application of the Fourth Amendment. The exclusionary rule of **Weeks** was made applicable to the states in **Mapp v. Ohio**, 367 U.S. 643 (1961). The Court felt they could no longer tolerate disobedience to the U.S. Constitution by allowing state prosecutors to use evidence that would not be admissible in Federal courts. Without the exclusionary rule the Fourth Amendment would be an empty promise. **Mapp** at 660. They expressed the hope that three goals would be accomplished:

1.   The guarantee to the individual is assured;
2.   More honest police officers; and
3.   A higher level of judicial integrity.

Whether these goals have been accomplished is left to the judgment of history. There are still hundreds of cases each year involving illegal police activity and there are still judges willing to admit the "fruits of the poisonous tree."

With the advent of **Mapp's** directive came a flood of challenges to state action in the federal courts through the extraordinary writ of *habeas corpus*. The fear of the destruction of an independent state judiciary was decried by some. Thus it appeared that the warning of George Mason was about to come true when he said: "*The judiciary of the United States is so constructed and extended, as to absorb and destroy the judiciaries of the several states.*" (A letter by George Mason on the

4

objections to the proposed federal constitution (1789)). The real effect of the exclusionary rule was that the federal courts were inundated with writs based on real and pretended violations of Fourth Amendment rights. But the federal courts had to entertain and reach a conclusion on every writ presented. When remands were required, or new prosecutions necessary, the costs in terms of money and manpower at all levels were indeed staggering. Everyone felt something had to be done.

The U.S. Supreme Court took a very bold step in 1976, which was hailed as a return to federalism and recognition that the states were in fact capable of preserving individual rights. That step was the decision in **Stone v. Powell**, 428 U.S. 465 (1976). The issue in **Stone v. Powell** was stated as follows:

"The question presented is whether a federal court should consider, in ruling on a petition for habeas corpus relief filed by a state prisoner, a claim that evidence obtained by an unconstitutional search or seizure was introduced at his trial, when he has previously been afforded an opportunity for full and fair litigation of his claim in the state courts." The Court gave the following answer: "The question is whether state prisoners who have been afforded the opportunity for full and fair consideration of their reliance upon the exclusionary rule with respect to seized evidence by the state courts at trial and on direct review may invoke their claim again on federal habeas corpus review. The answer is to be found by weighing the utility of the exclusionary rule against the costs of extending it to collateral review of Fourth Amendment claims...the focus of the trial and the attention of the participants therein, are diverted from the ultimate question of guilt or innocence that should be the central concern in a criminal proceeding. Moreover, the physical evidence sought to be excluded is typically reliable and often the most probative information bearing on the guilt or innocence of the defendant. Application of the rule thus deflects the truth-finding process and often frees the guilty. The disparity in particular cases between the error committed by the police officer and the windfall afforded a guilty defendant by application of the rule is contrary to the idea of proportionality that is essential to the concept of justice. Thus, although the rule is thought to deter unlawful police activity in part through the nurturing of respect for Fourth Amendment values, if applied indiscriminately it may well have the opposite effect of generating disrespect for the law and administration of justice. These long-recognized costs of the rule persist when a criminal conviction is sought to be overturned on collateral review on the ground that a search-and-seizure claim was erroneously rejected by two or more tiers of state courts... More importantly, over the long term, this demonstration that our society attaches serious consequences to violation of constitutional rights is thought to encourage those who formulate law enforcement policies and the officers who implement them, to incorporate Fourth Amendment ideals into their value system... The additional contribution, if any, of the consideration of search-and-seizure claims of state prisoners on collateral review is small in relation to the costs... There is no reason to believe, however, that the overall educative effect of the exclusionary rule would be appreciably diminished if search-and-seizure claims could not be raised in federal habeas corpus review of state conviction... The view that the deterrence of Fourth Amendment violations would be furthered rests on the dubious assumption that law enforcement authorities would fear the federal habeas review might reveal flaws in a search or seizure that went undetected at trial and on appeal... In sum, we conclude that where the State has provided an opportunity for full and fair litigation of a Fourth Amendment claim, a state prisoner may not be granted federal habeas corpus relief on the ground that evidence obtained in an unconstitutional search or seizure was introduced at his trial...." Reversed.

As a footnote to the case, Chief Justice Burger, in his special concurring opinion, and Justice White called for reform of the exclusionary rule. Both had been calling for reform for years but neither had come up with a workable alternative that the five justices necessary for a change could accept.

The Court was not entirely clear in defining "full and fair opportunity." Shortly after the decision, the Sixth Circuit indicated that the state court needed do more than "take cognizance of the constitutional claim and rule in light thereof." **Moore v. Cowan**, 560 F. 2d 1298 (C.A. 6th 1977). Does this mean that **Stone** contemplates a full evidentiary hearing when a claim is raised? This is evidently the position of the Tenth Circuit as noted in **Gamble v. Oklahoma**, 583 F. 2d 1161 (C.A. 10th 1978).

The Sixth Circuit was not willing to go that far, however. It held that federal habeas relief is available when a criminal defendant is not allowed to fully present his Fourth Amendment claim in the state courts because of unanticipated and unforeseeable application of a procedural rule which prevents state court consideration of the merits of the claim. **Riley v. Gray**, 674 F. 2d 522 (C.A. 6th 1982). In this case, the appellate court said Riley lacked standing; a point not raised at the trial and not briefed or argued on appeal. The opinion failed to cite the reason for its ruling and did not base it on any U.S. Supreme Court decision. Failure to remand was thus a violation of the "full and fair" doctrine of **Stone v. Powell** 428 U.S. 465 (1976).

Thus, as the law stood before **Stone v. Powell**, federal courts had to do a *de novo* suppression hearing retracing the entire process even if that had already been done in the state court. After **Stone v. Powell** the federal court merely reads the record and determines if "full and fair opportunity" was observed. This, of course, speeded up the process of getting to finality in the case. The *de novo* review must be done by the state appellate court of first review. When that has been done, the federal district court can review that record and in most cases routinely reject the habeas petition.

One final issue must be addressed. Does an illegal arrest prevent the use of illegally obtained evidence in civil or administrative matters or does the exclusionary rule only impact criminal proceedings? This issue was before the Connecticut court in **Fishbein v. Kozlowski, Comm'r of Motor Vehicles**, 743 A. 2d 1110 (Conn. 1999). The court held that due process does not require the exclusionary rule be used at administrative hearings on the suspension of driver's licenses for driving under the influence. They looked at their own decisions involving those on parole and probation and noted that, like those areas, the purpose of the exclusionary rule is "not likely to be furthered." Thus the legality of an investigative stop is not within the scope of a license suspension hearing. The local law enforcement official is already punished by the exclusion of the evidence at the criminal trial. Therefore, the exclusion at the license suspension hearing would have been only of minimal value.

II.   What Constitutes a Search? A Seizure?

What is a search? A search occurs when an expectation of privacy that society deems reasonable is infringed. **Illinois v. Andrews**, 463 U.S. 765 (1983). Could it be a sensate impression formed by a government agent? Basically the answer is yes. This was the issue examined by the Court in **Arizona v. Hicks**, 480 U.S. 321 (1987). The police were in the defendant's house, under the authority of a search warrant, looking for evidence of a specific crime. They had completed their search, but because they had seen several pieces of boxed and un-boxed stereo equipment, they decided to move the un-boxed stereo equipment to get a view of the serial numbers. If in order to gain a sensate impression (in this case to see certain serial numbers on the back of a stereo, which view had nothing to do with seeking guns, victims and the shooter of guns), the police had to turn the stereo around, was this a search? Justice Scalia, writing for the six-member majority said: "A search is a search even if it happens to disclose nothing but the bottom of a turntable," and "…moving it a few inches is much more than trivial for Fourth Amendment purposes."

I would like to believe Scalia's position would hold up in the suitcase puff cases. At airports everyday suspect luggage, in non-border areas, is subjected to "plain smell" by the use of sniffing dogs. The sensate impression found is of no concern. What is of concern is the fact that the bags often have to be squeezed so that the dog will have something to smell. How does that differ from turning the stereo equipment to see the serial numbers? The standard current wisdom is that puffing is not a search. The **Bond** case (*infra*) may provide the answer to this.

The **Hicks** case is allowing courts to take a new look at what conduct amounts to a search. In a California case the officer had probable cause to believe a car was crime involved but that it had recently been painted to hide its identity. The officer scraped the fresh paint to reveal the under-color. Was this a search? Yes, said the court. Why? The officer was "engaged in an intentional act which had as its purpose the acquisition of physical control over the paint sample." This was equated to the act of turning of the stereo equipment in **Hicks** which was also found to be a search. **People v. Robinson**, 257 Cal. Rep. 772 (Cal. Dist. Ct. App. 1989). This court properly recognized that control to determine the nature of an item and not destruction is the key to determining what constitutes a search. Control, standing alone, is a seizure.

If turning a stereo around to see the serial number to determine ownership is a search, is the insertion of a key into a lock to determine ownership or control a search? One would think so, but the First Circuit disagrees. They held that a person does not have a reasonable expectation of privacy in a key used by police to "merely" determine ownership. Only the dissenting judge saw the **Hicks** issue. **U.S. v. Lyons**, 898 F. 2d 210 (C.A. 1st 1990). Unlike California, this court missed Scalia's point.

Two more recent U.S. Supreme Court cases further define what constitutes a search. The key word in both cases is "manipulation." One case involved a good case of articulable suspicion the other involved no suspicion at all. The articulable suspicion case involved a valid **Terry** seizure of the person and the scope of the permitted frisk. **Minnesota v. Dickerson**, 508 U.S. 366 (1993), (better remembered as the plain feel case). In this case, the Court ruled that the manipulation of the item went beyond the scope of a valid frisk. However, the Court did not specifically address, by rule, **mere manipulation**.

Bond v. U.S., 529 U.S. 334 (2000) is a pure manipulation case not connected to any suspicion at all nor to any safety concern. A Border Agent boarded a bus some distance beyond the border and its functional equivalent. The purpose was to check the immigration status of the passengers. After everyone "checked out" O.K., the agent, then at the back of the bus, moved forward touching every bag. He felt a brick-like

8

object in the bag above Bond's head in the luggage rack and he squeezed it. This was an unreasonable search. Breyer and Scalia dissented. Travelers, said the Court, expect that bus personnel and even passengers may touch their bags, but that does not permit government agents to believe that all right to privacy is lost. Travelers do not expect their belongings to be manipulated by anyone. Scalia's position appears to be inconsistent with his position in **Hicks**.

The latest definition of what constitutes a search also comes from the "pen" of Justice Scalia. The use, without a warrant, of a thermal imaging device was found to be a search. In **Kyllo v. U.S.**, 121 S. Ct. 946, (2001), he wrote for the five member majority that "obtaining by sense-enhancing technology any information regarding the home's interior that could not otherwise have been obtained without physical intrusion into a constitutionally protected area...constitutes a search at least where (as here) the technology in question is not in general public use."

What is a seizure? A seizure occurs when there is some meaningful interference with an individual's property or person. **U.S. v. Place**, 462 U.S. 696 (1983). Here we have to be very careful because we must not confuse detention or custody with arrest. Seizure should not be limited to physical capture because some things can be seized without the physical capture of it; a house can be seized; a car can be seized. People can be detained, but not in custody; detained and in custody; and can be arrested thus seized. Custody and arrest are different but both are seizures.

In **Michigan v. Chesternut**, 486 U.S. 567 (1988) the Court was called on to define seizure. The state said no seizure (arrest) unless the police are successful in apprehending the individual. The defendant said any and all police chases are Fourth Amendment seizures. Choose one? Not this court. Married as they are to "totality" dogma it said: "Rather than adopt either rule proposed by the parties and determining that an investigatory pursuit is or is not necessarily a seizure...we adhere to our traditional contextual approach, and determine only that in this particular case, the police conduct in question did not amount to a seizure." The opinion goes on to list what criteria must be applied:

1.   was there physical force or show of authority that has **restrained the liberty** of a citizen;
2.   would a reasonable person have believed that he was **free not to leave** when all circumstances are taken into account; and
3.   no room for subjective analysis – from either side – **objective analysis** only may be used.

Thus merely **dogging the trail** of a person without more **is not a seizure**. **Michigan v. Chesternut**, 486 U.S. 567 (1988). Obviously denying a person access to his home would constitute a seizure of the home. Impounding a car is a seizure. Keeping the defendant's wallet at booking is a seizure of that wallet. Both of these definitions will be twisted and turned. But that is not critical. More critical is that it is understood that search and seizure are separate concepts, separately defined. This point is of utmost importance. A lawful seizure and arrest of a person creates a right to search incident to that arrest which in turn creates the right to seize such evidence for use at the subsequent trial. Each type of seizure, from the command of the stop sign to the full arrest carries with it well-defined incidents of search for the type or level of seizure involved. The balance of this book deals with those issues.

The **Chesternut** opinion relied for much of its reasoning on the "reasonable person test." Would a reasonable person have felt he was not free to leave, if so, then a seizure had taken place. This type of analysis fits in nicely with the custody analysis we must make with regard to **Miranda** issues. Both Kennedy and Scalia thought it inappropriate for a Fourth Amendment inquiry and preferred a discussion of whether an unmistakable show of authority can result in a seizure and they felt that the Fourth Amendment is not implicated until a restraining effect had taken hold. Is the Court saying, since they did not specifically address the issue, that there may be a different standard for Fifth Amendment issues of custody and Fourth Amendment concerns? If so are they also saying that the wrong standard has been employed in the airport stop cases or that consents to search arising from airport stops should use the **Miranda** standard but that abandonment cases arising from airport stop cases should use a Fourth Amendment standard and not the **Miranda** custody standard? To be sure Kennedy and Scalia saw the danger of mixing the two standards.

The standard for seizure, hinted at by Scalia and Kennedy, may have been adopted by five members of the court in **Brower v. County of Inyo**, 489 U.S. 593 (1989). This opinion, written by Scalia, does not address seizure from the point of view of the reasonable person test. Rather the focus is on the announcement of authority plus the intentional acquisition of physical control. Scalia says that is when a Fourth Amendment seizure takes place. The case involved the police wanting to stop a person suspected of driving a stolen car. The driver decided not to stop upon the announcement of authority. He was stopped when he crashed into the physical roadblock that was set up for this purpose. Citing **Tennessee v. Garner**, 471 U.S. 1 (1985), Scalia said a gun pointed at a person by a police officer was found to be a seizure and he said this case is no different than that. The gun in **Garner**, he said, served the function of the acquisition of physical control and a roadblock "...is designed to produce a stop by physical impact if voluntary compliance does not occur."

The concurring justices would have preferred the reasonable person context analysis. What they did not address was whether they saw the difference between the spheres in which both operate. The difference is subtle and in fact when applied to **Mendenhall** (*infra*) one ends up with the same result but not in the context of the nonsensical finding that Mendenhall should have felt free to leave but based on the fact that although there was an announcement of authority there was no show of authority that could be said to be the intentional acquisition of control. The **Royer** case (*infra*) comes out as it did before because the keeping of Mr. Royer's license and ticket was a show of control that could be said to be the intentional acquisition of the control of Mr. Royer.

In fact, the test works very nicely even in a **Miranda** context in all but the defendant personality cases (low I.Q.; suffering D.T's; inexperienced first offenders) where we generally provide for exceptions to the **Miranda** rule and custody often abounds, but the waiver is found to be ineffective. Also provided in the **Miranda** area are exceptions where there is custody (spontaneous statements, on-the-scene and public safety).

The "show and tell" or rather tell (announce authority) and show (intentional acquisition of control) would work well in the consent to search cases and in fact have very little impact since a valid consent can be given in a valid seizure context. The focus of consent is on voluntariness in a totality of the circumstances sense. Consents given during an illegal seizure are affected by attenuation and if there is no attenuation then the consent is found to be involuntary. None of the foregoing rules would be altered by the Scalia analysis. In any event, if Scalia meant what he wrote and those who joined him accepted the theory, then Stevens, Brennan, Marshall and Blackman had more to worry about.

The reasonable person test allows for significant court discretion and allows the courts to chastise police when they do not like the result of their activity. The show and tell rule is more of a black and white rule and anything short of gun-pointing, property-keeping, body-holding, road- blocking, *etc.*, will not be a seizure. Courts thus lose their supervisory control in a Fourth Amendment context and instead will have to use a due process-outrageous conduct approach more directly. However, the exclusionary rule was adopted to avoid the inconsistency of result created by the use of the egregious conduct standard of due process. The due process standard is too dependent on the personal views of the judge or judges reviewing the police conduct.

In fact, Scalia says that merely blue lighting, or the act of the officer in holding up a hand to stop is not a seizure. He says that merely chasing a car by police is not a seizure even when the pursued crashes his car because he loses control. However, a seizure occurs when the officer pulls the cruiser alongside and sideswipes the pursued or puts a road block in his way. The Scalia approach makes good sense. Standstill orders by police while lawful searches are conducted of premises certainly tell the person he is not free to leave. That is a Fourth Amendment seizure and reasonable but it is not an arrest thus whether a frisk can be conducted turns on reasonableness as outlined in **Ybarra** and **Summers** (*infra* at Chapter Twelve). An arrest, as a form of seizure, is dependent on probable cause in the felony context or the "committed in presence" in the misdemeanor context. Thus the traffic stop is a seizure because, as Scalia put it, the announcement of authority as a show of authority "was the very means that the government selected and a Fourth Amendment seizure... occurred." In the traffic stop no one can seriously argue that the citizen feels free to leave any time he wants after the stop.

Is it an arrest? It can be, but when the car is stopped because the officer suspects drunken driving he is stopped for a misdemeanor for which there is no probable cause but only the "in the presence" rule. At best there is articulable suspicion. A carefully circumscribed seizure upon articulable suspicion was permitted in **Terry** (*infra*) based upon fear for the safety of the officers and others. If the fear was dispelled the actors were allowed to move on; if the fear was not dispelled a limited intrusion by way of frisk was permitted. By analogy the failure to dispel fear in the DUI suspect case would arise when the officers smell the inebriated defendant or hear a slur in his speech. The frisk analogy occurs when the driver is asked to perform field sobriety tests which, if not performed well, can lead to the formal arrest. Thus Scalia's test also works in this context.

How does **Berkemer v. McCarty**, 486 U.S. 420 (1984), measure up against the Scalia view? In fact the Court would merely have to continue the **Miranda** exception created there and find no custody for **Miranda** purposes in the ordinary routine traffic stop until a full-fledged arrest occurs. No change would be required. It would operate either as an on-the-scene exception or as a part of the public safety exception. Yes, there is a seizure in the routine traffic stop, but the officer is permitted to ask routine questions associated with the reason for the stop without the "bother" of giving the **Miranda** warnings.

That the dual decisions of **Chesternut** and **Brower** would produce controversy would be no surprise to anyone. A California court said, in agreeing with

Chesternut, that the mere fact that a police officer followed a fleeing individual did not amount to a seizure. They noted that the officer did not pull his gun and never ordered the defendant to stop. Thus the abandoned drugs were properly admissible. **People v. Nickleberry**, 270 Cal. Rep. 269 (Cal. Dist. Ct. App. 1990). But Texas felt that the action of two officers who merely approach a defendant (one from the front; the other from the rear) constitutes a seizure. **Hawkins v. State**, 758 S.W. 2d 255 (Tex. Ct. Crim. App. 1988). Maryland held that under **Chesternut**, when an officer asks a person to stop there is a seizure even though no gun is pulled nor other force used. **Jones v. State**, 572 A. 2d 169 (Md. 1990). But does this comport with the **Brower** case? It does not appear to if one accepts Scalia's chase-without-touching analogy.

Because of growing confusion among the several state and federal courts, the Supreme Court chose a case from California to hopefully resolve the **Chesternut-Brower** dispute. **In Re Hodari D.**, 265 Cal. Rep. 79 (Cal. App. 1 Dist. 1989) (withdrawn from publication March 15, 1990) was chosen. In **Hodari D.** police approached a group of youth on a street. The group broke up with some driving away and some running. An officer got out of the cruiser and circled the block. Hodari D. running, while looking over his shoulder, nearly ran into this officer. They were about eleven feet apart when Hodari D. threw a rock of cocaine away. The California court felt that by running toward the defendant there was an illegal seizure. Arguments were held on January 14, 1991 by the U.S. Supreme Court. The decision should resolve the unanswered questions. **Hodari D.** was decided April 23, 1991. Scalia, writing for the seven justice majority, said ":..the only issue presented is whether, at the time he dropped the drugs, Hodari had been 'seized' within the meaning of the Fourth Amendment." The answer: no seizure had taken place when the drugs were abandoned. Why?

First, the Court applied the dictionary approach coupled with an historical analysis. Citing 1828, 1856, and 1981 dictionaries the Court said seizure means taking possession. Historically seizure "...connoted not merely grasping, or applying physical force to, the animate or inanimate object in question, **but actually bringing it within physical control**". It also noted that an arrest took place at common law upon touching or application of physical force even if the arrestee got away.

Second, since it raised the issue of an unsuccessful seizure or arrest, the Court had to determine whether the arrest/seizure is a single or continuous act. If a single act the fugitive who disposed of evidence after an unsuccessful act of seizure or release from a seizure would not be seized or under arrest at the time of the abandonment. If a continuous act, such property would be the "fruits" of the seizure and then the seizure would have to be tested for "poison." The Court chose the "single act" approach.

Third, it said Hodari's case did not involve the application of physical force at the moment of the act of abandonment. The chase was a "show of authority" or better yet a telling of authority. They then held that a person who does not yield to a stop order or, for that matter, a chase, is not seized. A "fleeing form" who does not stop when ordered to stop **cannot be, even remotely, seized**. "An arrest requires either physical force... or, where that is absent, submission to the assertion of authority." Words alone will not do it. Thus the exclusionary rule is to be used only on successful unlawful seizures. In footnote 2, the court said: "But neither usage nor common-law tradition makes an attempted seizure a seizure. The common law may have made an attempted seizure unlawful in certain circumstances; but it made many things unlawful, *very few of which were elevated to constitutional proscriptions.*" To hold otherwise would be a return to a due process analysis rather than a Fourth Amendment analysis.

Finally, how does the Court handle the "reasonable person" test? The Court continues it in the one circumstance to which it must apply – the submission cases. Those cases where the police ask a person to stop and the person stops are to be found seized, objectively, *only if* "in view of all the circumstances surrounding the incident, a reasonable person would have believed that he was not free to leave." Or as the Court said it is "not whether the citizen perceived that he was being ordered to restrict his movement, but whether the officer's words and actions would have conveyed that to a reasonable person." This protects the officer's right to seek to engage a person in a dialogue as seen in the airport cases.

The Court did not decide the flight or furtive gesture in the case because it did not have to, but footnote 1 presaged the rule to come. The Court there said: "California conceded below that Officer Pertoso did not have the reasonable suspicion required to justify stopping Hodari, see **Terry v. Ohio**, 392 U.S. 1 (1968). That it would be unreasonable to stop, for brief inquiry, young men who scatter in panic upon the mere sighting of the police is not self-evident, and arguably contradicts proverbial common sense. See Proverbs 28:1 ('The wicked flee when no man pursueth'). We do not decide that point here, but rely entirely upon the State's concession." **California v. Hodari D.**, 499 U.S. 621 (1991).

Indeed the "wicked flee." That issue came before the U.S. Supreme Court in a case from Illinois. The right to stop a person requires at a minimum articulable suspicion and at the most probable cause (and anything higher such as a crime committed in the officer's presence). Can articulable suspicion arise by the act of mere flight? Yes, said the Court, in the *right circumstances* using *common sense*. **Illinois v. Wardlow**, 528 U.S. 119 (2000). Police and courts were given permission to use common sense (at least five justices say so).

Wardlow ran after he spotted police patrolling an area known for heavy narcotics trafficking. He was caught and the pat-down revealed a.38 caliber handgun. He was then arrested. This is a most common scenario in every city and large town in the nation. The trial judge refused to suppress but the appeals court and Supreme Court of Illinois said the gun should be suppressed. The Illinois high court thought Wardlow was merely "going his own way" citing **Florida v. Royer**, 460 U.S. 491 (1983), an airport stop case. As in **Brown v. Texas**, Royer was merely walking and neither of these men bolted at the mere sight of the police. A distinction with a big difference. The U.S. Supreme Court noted that some states (Wisconsin, Indiana and Georgia) say unprovoked flight is enough but that (Nebraska, New Jersey, Michigan and Colorado) say it is not. (See Footnote 1 of the **Wardlow** opinion for cites.)

Brown v. Texas was cited to demonstrate that mere presence in a high crime area without more is not enough for a **Terry** seizure, but that it is relevant in context. That context is high crime area **plus** unprovoked flight. Whether there is reasonable suspicion must be based on commonsense judgments and inferences about human behavior because there is no scientific certainty out there. Flight that is not provoked is "by its very nature, is not 'going about one's business'." Wardlow had the choice of walking and if stopped, remaining silent in the face of police questioning. The Court agrees that there are innocent reasons for flight but **Terry** was created to resolve such ambiguities. The court somewhat suggests that everyone read **Terry's** facts again.

The game warden in **Keller v. Franks**, 745 F. Supp. 1428 (S.D. Ind. 1990) suspected a van contained a dead carcass and shot at the van to later identify it. Unfortunately his bullet hit an occupant. The vehicle stopped and everyone was formally arrested. The wounded man sought money damages. Citing **Brower**, the district court judge said the court is not permitted to assess subjective intent because that is irrelevant. The judge said: "This case turns on **Brower's** third prong – whether the stop occurred through means intentionally applied." There was a seizure here.

Relying on **Chesternut** and the reasonable person test rather than **Brower's** "show and tell" rule, the Illinois Supreme Court said a motorist who was pulled over, met by two officers, asked to go to the stationhouse to "clear up" something, had his driver's license held, was escorted in his own car to the stationhouse, and taken to an interrogation room where he made incriminating statements, was under arrest when he made the statements. It felt a reasonable person would not have felt free to leave. Since there was only suspicion and not probable cause for the arrest the statements were the fruits of the poisonous tree. The court also noted that the defendant was never told he was free to leave at any time. **People v. Holveck**, 565 N.E. 2d 919 (Ill. 1990).

The **Keller** case (*supra*), was decided before **Hodari D.** There was force applied followed by submission. No evidence was gathered after the gun shot and before the stop, but incriminating evidence was gathered after submission to the stop. If then the stop (a seizure under **Hodari D.**) was without lawful authority the evidence was fruits of the poisonous tree. **Holveck** also appears to be correctly decided as a submission case under **Hodari D.**

When is a command not an order to submit to detention? In **Hodari D.** the U. S. Supreme Court indicated that a seizure occurs when, without touching, a defendant submits to a command. If the command was lawful the seizure is lawful; if the command was unlawful the seizure is unlawful.

Virginia takes the position that not all orders to "come here" are **Hodari D.** commands. In their case an officer did not have articulable suspicion to order a suspected drunk to "come over here." The officer had a radio call that there were some drunks in a general area of town. While in that section of town the police saw two men. The car was stopped with the floodlight focused on the two men. The two men began walking away when the officer commanded them to "come over here." The defendant approached the officer. The basic question of "have you been drinking" was answered yes. Coupling that admission with clearly viewed evidence of public drunkenness the defendant was arrested, searched, and drugs were found. Relying on "totality" the Virginia court held there was not a "showing of authority" by a "threatening presence" of police because floodlights are not weapons. Without the "threatening presence" or real show of force, an order to "come over here" and acquiescence to that does not constitute a seizure. **Com. v. Baldwin**, 413 S.E. 2d 645 (Va. 1992). However, does this appear to comport with **Hodari D.**? Virginia may be wrong.

The U.S. Supreme Court further clarified the reasonable person test as it relates to police-citizen confrontations where there is no order to stop by their opinion in **Florida v. Bostick**, 501 U.S. 429 (1991). When the police board a bus and approach passengers no seizure takes place. Asking questions of seated passengers does not constitute a seizure. The Court noted, so there would be no question on the point, that the officers in **Bostick** had neither probable cause for an arrest nor articulable suspicion for a **Terry** stop. Police do not need either before being permitted to ask questions. A seizure occurs only when the police convey a message that compliance with the request is required; that they order the conduct requested. The Court said,."..the mere fact that Bostick did not feel free to leave the bus does not mean that the police seized him. His confinement was.".. the natural result of his decision to take the bus..." It also emphasized that a refusal to cooperate, without more, does not supply grounds to seize. In this case no guns were pulled, no threats made and Bostick was even told he did not have to consent to the search. Critical was the point made that a reasonable person "...presupposes an *innocent* person." An innocent person is one who does not carry drugs. The Court thus rejected Bostick's argument that no reasonable person would freely consent to a search of luggage that he or she knows contains drugs. Thus, if Bostick has any relief coming it comes from the nature of the consent, whether voluntary or involuntary.

Distinguishing a Search from a Seizure

Remember: Both searches and seizures involve control of the thing, place or person by a governmental agent by use of the tactile senses or by submission of a person to governmental command.

Seizure: Governmental activity that:
1.   controls access to an item; or
2.   controls the mobility of the person or thing; or
3.   controls the ability to move, destroy or otherwise alter the thing

Searches: Governmental activity that controls a person or thing to determine, by tactile impression, its:
1.   condition;
2.   nature;
3.   contents; or
4.   status for the purpose of resolving the legal issues raised by the facts and circumstances of the incident in question.

III.   Standing to Object to the Fruits of a Search

Who can complain about an unlawful search and seizure? Obviously the person must have been the victim of the search. To be a victim one must demonstrate two factors. First, it must be shown that the defendant had some legitimate interest in the thing or place searched. Second, it must be shown that an expectation of privacy that is tolerated by society as reasonable was invaded. This has always been the rule.

The problem has been that there has been wide disagreement of the scope of the first requirement – the problem of standing.

Consider the facts of **Jones v. United States**, 362 U.S. 257 (1960). Jones had been given a key to his friend's apartment. He admitted he did not live there, but that he kept a pair of pants and shirt there. The police were in the apartment searching for narcotics under an invalid search warrant. Jones had been seen with his hand on the awning. Drugs were found when the awning was searched. The defendant admitted these were his. He was charged with possession. The government said that since he was not a possessor of the apartment he could not challenge the warrant or search because he did not have standing. The Supreme Court disagreed. They distinguished between those lawfully on premises from those wrongfully on such premises. Since Jones was given a key and permission to be in this apartment they held that he had standing and his motion to suppress should have been given a full hearing. Thus, the defendant need not have a traditional possessory interest in the searched premises in order to have standing. It was sufficient that he was legitimately on the premises when the search occurred. This was called the "legitimately on the premises" rule. If the defendant was the "target" of the search then the defendant had sufficient interest to complain.

However, in subsequent cases the "right is personal and not to be vicariously asserted" rule was announced but it did not seem to affect the **Jones** rule. 1978 and 1980, however, saw a redefinition of the rules. Re-emphasizing that Fourth Amendment rights are personal and may not be asserted vicariously, the U.S. Supreme Court upheld the conviction of two passengers in an automobile. **Rakas v. Illinois**, 439 U.S. 128 (1978). The Court warned against reading **Jones** too broadly and said the "target" theory presented there was mere *dicta* and was rejected in **Alderman** (discussed below). The Court pointed out that, if properly examined, it can be seen that Jones had an expectation of privacy in the premises he was using. It said that was true even if the "interest" was not a property interest recognized at common law. The defendant must make a showing that he had a legitimate reasonable expectation of privacy and not merely be legitimately present.

A California court had to assess whether the defendant had a right to privacy in utility poles, wires, transformers and meters through which electricity was transmitted. The police suspected marijuana growing. The police used a surveillance meter to nab the defendant in **People v. Stanley**, 86 Cal. Rep. 2d 289 (Cal. App. 2d Dist. 1999). The court said there was no standing or right of privacy under the holdings of **Katz**, **Smith v. Maryland**, **Karo**, **Knotts**, **Dow Chemical** and **California v. Greenwood** (all discussed in subsequent chapters).

Obviously a defendant cannot confer standing on himself with regard to property he has stolen. Thus, the search of a car or bag that was stolen would yield no violation of a privacy interest that society is willing to protect. But, what if the police stop a car not knowing or believing the car to be stolen. Can the subsequent discovery that the car is stolen justify the seizure and the search incident of the individual? It should not be justified and that is the conclusion that the Florida court came to in **Nelson v. State**, 578 So. 2d 694 (Fla. 1991). The seizure of the individual may always be challenged even if that person was in a stolen car not believed or known to be stolen at the time of the arrest. The concurring judges said any other ruling would mean police would go fishing in the "...hope of occasionally finding a stolen one." The court is, of course, correct for if the evidence in **Rakas** had been taken from Rakas' person the result would have been quite different because the illegal stop (the poisonous tree) would have yielded evidence from his person (fruits of the poisonous tree). But if the car was stolen by Nelson how can he complain if the evidence that it was stolen had an independent source? Courts should not write so broadly.

The place searched in **Rakas** was an automobile and not Rakas himself. Before anyone could throw this case in the "automobiles are different" category, the Court said Rakas' argument would fail even in an analogous situation "...in a dwelling place...." More must be shown. The Court noted that Jones had the key to the apartment and could exclude others; an element of control that demonstrated an expectation of privacy. Whereas, merely being a guest, without control or some semblance of control, gives the guest nothing to show as an expectation of privacy and that is all Mr. Rakas could show. This conclusion was modified, slightly, in **Minnesota v. Olson** (discussed *infra*).

Rather than follow broadly the "control right" aspect of **Rakas** and **Jones**, the Oklahoma Court of Criminal Appeals used an agency theory to say that an employee's right to bar others was derivative and not his own right. They interpreted **Rakas** and **Jones** narrowly by holding that the employee was unable to show a personal right to exclude others from the back room where stolen goods were stored in this pawn shop. It did not help his cause when he told the police at first that he did not work there. If the Oklahoma court would hold that he could not consent then there would be logical consistency to their holding. **Whitehead v. State**, 546 P. 2d 273 (Okla. Ct. Crim. App. 1988). This is an interesting "twist" to justify a conviction.

Two fairly recent cases from Pennsylvania illustrate a lack of standing. One thief thought that by asking his lady friend to put the stolen money somewhere safe he acquired standing in the lady friend's mother's safe deposit box. Without a key or permission to get into the box he had no standing. **Com. v. Whiting**, 2001 WL 79979 (Pa. Super.). The second case involved mail. The mail was addressed to a third party at these defendants' address. This gave them enough standing to challenge the warrant for the search of the house to find the package. But did they have a reasonable expectation of privacy in the package to challenge the validity of the warrant since the package was not addressed to them and neither of them admitted they were the addressee? No. **Com. v. Black**, 758 A. 2d 1253 (Pa. Super. 2000).

The Connecticut Supreme Court was faced with a more traditional standing issue in **State v. Reddick**, 456 A. 2d 1191 (Conn. 1988). The police had a search warrant for two units of a two-family home but the warrant did not cover the basement area of the building. As usual the police went into the basement area anyway and found a sawed-off shotgun that belonged to the adult son of the owner. He lived in his mother's apartment. He claimed standing and the Connecticut court agreed. They felt that under **Rakas** one does not have to show exclusive control or use of an area to have a reasonable expectation of privacy. The fact that this was a two-family building rather than a large apartment complex made the expectation of privacy in the laundry area where the gun was discovered reasonable. This is a fair interpretation, under the totality, of the standing rule.

The control issue and when it is lost came up in **U.S. v. Barry**, 853 F. 2d 1479 (C.A. 8th 1988). Unlike the man who leaves a bag of drugs at a roadside point to be picked up, a person who checks a bag at a public baggage claim counter in the name of the proposed buyer does not lose his reasonable expectation of privacy. Thus his standing to object to a warrantless search before he turns the claim check over to the other person, said the Eighth Circuit, is not lost. The claim check, which was the control device for possession, thus, whoever had it had the possession of the bag. This is not "nit-picking;" it represents a reasonable interpretation of the standing rules.

If one wants standing in an automobile under **Rakas**, the right of control by the person driving must be demonstrated by the person claiming standing. In this case the defendant was driving a cocaine laden truck that was not owned by, nor registered to him. The defendant produced no one to establish that he had lawful possession of the truck. The court said **mere possession** in this case without proof of lawful authority to drive the truck or have its possession causes this defendant's standing argument to fail. Legal documentation is, of course, not required, but there must be some evidence of lawful possession or control shown. **U.S. v. Arango**, 47 Crim. L. Rep. 1476 (C.A. 10th 1990). Without an automatic standing rule, the person must prove his expectation of privacy once the government overcomes the presumption of lawful possession.

One can lose the right of control as illustrated by a decision from the Eighth Circuit. In this case a failure to renew a rental contract on a locker (even though the failure to renew was caused by his arrest) caused the defendant to lose his expectation of privacy in the rented locker. **U.S. v. Reyes**, 908 F. 2d 281 (C.A. 8th 1990). A like result was reached in a Pennsylvania case. There is a distinct difference between the privacy rights of a hotel guest who is merely late in checking out and one who has abandoned a room with regard to the personal property left behind. In either event, it is likely that the hotel guest loses an expectation of privacy in the room itself. However, if the hotel continues to bill the guest, then the hotel clearly recognizes a continuing right of occupancy in the guest. If the hotel does not bill for the additional time the hotel may treat the occupancy as ended and the occupancy right has returned to the hotel. As for the property left behind, the guest retains the right of privacy in the merely overdue context but not when he has abandoned the room. In the merely overdue situation, the hotel (and not the state) assumes an obligation of safekeeping which may include a right to inventory the goods. But it certainly does not give the hotel the right to consent to a police search of the property. Unless **Walters** and **Jacobson** (*infra*) are applicable, the police may not search such items in a hotel room (if not abandoned) unless the items meet the "immediately apparent" standard of the plain view doctrine (*infra*). **Com. v. Brundidge**, 583 A. 2d 450 (Pa. Super. Ct. 1990).

As already noted, it is not enough to have a reasonable expectation of privacy. One must also show that society is willing to protect that expectation. Squatters and other trespassers may well have an expectation of privacy in certain premises. But is society willing to protect their unauthorized use of such premises against warrantless activity based upon probable cause? This issue was met head-on by the Pennsylvania Supreme Court in **Com. v. Peterson**, 54 Crim. L. Rep. 1204 (Pa. 1993). Peterson had taken trespassory possession of a vacant store front, installed a security door, and ran a "gate house" drug operation. The police broke the door down after seeking permission to enter. Drug evidence was found. The defendant admitted the police had probable cause. His argument was that police did not determine that he was not a lawful possessor before they entered. Like the U.S. Supreme Court had in **Rakas,** the Pennsylvania court distinguished between a mere expectation and a legitimate expectation of privacy. If no right exists then no right is diminished by the warrantless entry.

The **Rakas** decision left some doubt about the "automatic standing" rule in **Jones**. Any doubts were wiped away with this statement: "The automatic standing rule of **Jones v. U.S.**, (*supra*), is therefore overruled." The Court announced this in **U.S. v. Salvucci**, 448 U.S. 83 (1980). The rule announced in **Salvucci** said that defendants charged with possessory crimes may claim the benefits of the exclusionary rule only if their own Fourth Amendment rights have in fact been violated. The stolen mail in the **Salvucci** case was found in a co-defendant's mother's apartment. In rejecting **Jones** the Court saw automatic standing as a "windfall to defendants whose Fourth Amendment rights have *not* (emphasis by the Court) been violated." Thus the Court puts the burden on the defense to establish their own expectation of privacy. This decision and others like it should come as no surprise since the Court served notice of its Fourth Amendment policy in **Stone v. Powell**, (*supra*). The reader is urged to re-read that quotation as a guide for this Court.

Soon after **Rakas** came down, the Kentucky Supreme Court was faced with a standing problem. Police entered the defendant's friend's house to execute an arrest warrant. The officers smelled marijuana and observed seeds on the mantle. A search warrant was then sought while everyone was detained. The warrant was brought back. The police decided to search everyone present. In the purse of another friend, drugs belonging to the defendant were found. The lady with the purse said they were the defendant's and the defendant admitted this. The Kentucky Court found the search of the purse illegal as to the woman who owned it. But did the defendant have standing to object? That court held that the illegal search did not violate the defendant's legitimate or reasonable expectation of freedom from government intrusion. **Rawlings v. Commonwealth**, 581 S.W. 2d 348 (Ky. 1979). The **Rawlings** case went to the U.S. Supreme Court. The Court agreed that **Rawlings** had not made a sufficient showing that his reasonable expectations of privacy were violated. Once the police found his drugs in her purse, his arrest was legal and thus also legal was the subsequent search of him incident thereto. Therefore, the Court upheld the Kentucky decision. **Rawlings v. Kentucky**, 448 U.S. 98 (1980).

In order to establish standing, however, a defendant has to testify to show a legitimate presence. Can such testimony at a suppression hearing be used as a waiver of the Fifth Amendment right to remain silent? The Court, in **Simmons v. United States**, 390 U.S. 377 (1968), said no. The Court said, "...we find it intolerable that one constitutional right should have to be surrendered in order to assert another." This point was stressed in **Salvucci**.

Suppose three fellows are in the stolen clothing business. Suppose that the "takers" are in jail while the store of the "fence" is searched with a defective search warrant. Could the "takers" use the "fence's" standing and defective warrant argument? The Court said no. There was no standing because: (1) the defendants were not on the premises at the time of the search; (2) they had no proprietary or possessory interest in the premises; and (3) they were not in possession of the seized evidence at the time of the search and (4) possession was not an essential element of the offense charged. **Brown & Smith v. United States**, 411 U.S. 223 (1973). The Court went on to say the Fourth Amendment rights are personal and cannot be vicariously asserted: a point re-emphasized in **Rakas**. Point one would no longer be germane under both **Rawlings** and **Salvucci**.

For this last rule the Court cited its decision in **Alderman v. U.S.**, 394 U.S. 165 (1969). **Alderman** presented a somewhat unique situation. A bug had been planted in Alderman's house. A conversation between two persons other than Alderman implicated Alderman in a crime. This evidence was used against Alderman at his trial. The security of his home had been illegally invaded, but the evidence secured was not his property or personal effects in the physical sense. The Court said that the right to be secure in one's house is not limited to protection against a policeman viewing or seizing tangible property. Otherwise, they said, the express security of the home provided by the Fourth Amendment would approach redundancy. The Court said the fruits of such an illegal search are not admissible.

Despite the fact that **Katz** holds that "people not places" should control the issue of a reasonable, societally protected expectation of privacy, the truth is that "place" does matter and nowhere is this better illustrated than it is in **Minnesota v. Olson**, 495 U.S. 91 (1990). Olson was an overnight guest in another's home and that threshold was crossed without a warrant, consent and without exigency. The state urged that Olson had no standing since he did not have a right of control as apparently required by **Rakas**. Citing **Rakas** (and *not* overruling the control language) the Court held that one's status as an overnight guest is alone enough to show a societally protected reasonable expectation of privacy. The Court concluded that was the holding in **Rakas** as it regarded the **Jones** case. So, if one is an overnight guest in a home there is a **Katz** expectation; if one is a guest in a car there is not a **Katz** expectation unless control is shown.

Clearly the **Olson** protection applies to a guest while the guest is present. Otherwise the **Jones-Rakas** analysis must apply. An illegal search of another's apartment when the person against whom the evidence is found is not an overnight guest, should be admissible if **Jones-Rakas** is not satisfied as raising a privacy interest. This concept and distinction was recognized by Nebraska in **State v. Cortis**, 465 N.W. 2d 132 (Neb. 1991). However, there will be dispute over the "end-of-guest" status and the "mere-temporary-interruption-of-guest" status. Courts should be able to resolve those disputes. It should also be noted that **Olson, Rakas** and **Jones** only apply to the search of the guests' property during an illegal search of the host's home. An Illinois court has held that if an overnight guest in a house gets standing, then so should an overnight guest in another's hotel room also get standing. **People v. Olson**, 556 N.E. 2d 273 (Ill. App. Ct. 1990). This is consistent with the **Stoner v. California** case discussed in the Chapter Six on consents,

If an overnight guest has a reasonable expectation of privacy and if a guest like **Jones** has independent privacy rights due to the possession of a key, should a baby-sitter also have privacy rights even though the duration of the sitting arrangement is short term? This was the issue presented in **People v. Moreno**, 3 Cal. R. 2d 66 (Cal. App. 1992). Moreno, the baby-sitter and brother of another defendant, was home alone with the child when the police did a warrantless search of the home and found a large quantity of cocaine. The trial judge refused to find standing since Moreno was not an overnight guest. The appellate court said that Moreno was not an overnight guest but that in itself does not end the standing inquiry. The critical issue was whether Moreno had sufficient control to meet the **Rakas** standing test. The court then went into the function of the baby-sitter when the parents leave the house. It found that the general rule is that the baby-sitter is in exclusive charge of the child and the premises. This exclusive control exists to give the sitter the right to decide who may or may not enter the home while the parents are absent. Such control then satisfies **Rakas** concerns because the right to exclude is central to a control analysis. "Indeed the baby-sitter has responsibilities the overnight guest never encounters," the court noted. Even though the duration of this right is short term, there is for the normal brief period involved, an "otherwise legitimate expectation of privacy..." during that period.

Do all "guests" get privacy protection in another's house at all times of the day? That was the question left unanswered by **Olson**. Another case from Minnesota was chosen to address a day-time guest who was in the apartment to help package drugs. An officer with plain view through open Venetian blinds sees Carter and others sitting around a table packaging drugs. The officer gained entry and arrested everyone. Carter challenged the entry saying he had standing under **Olson**. He lost in the trial court and in the court of appeals but won at the Minnesota Supreme Court. The state petitioned and was awarded certiorari review since Minnesota relied on the Fourth Amendment. The U.S. Supreme Court reversed the Minnesota high court saying Carter had no standing under the circumstances of this case. **Minnesota v. Carter**, 525 U.S. 83 (1998).

Why? Seven judges concurred and five agreed with the rationale. So what did the five agree to? They found that: (1) these were not overnight guests; (2) they were there to transact business; (3) it was only a dwelling for the leasehold tenant; (4) they were not workers in the sense of **O'Connor v. Ortega**, 480 U.S. 709 (1987) (an administrative search case); (5) it was not their home; and (6) merely being legitimately on premises, without more, gives no spatial right of privacy from police intrusion.

So the home is secure for owners and overnight guests. Are the defendant's offices secure? How private does the office have to be? Consider the case of **Mancusi v. De Forte**, 392 U.S. 364 (1968). DeForte was a vice-president of a union local. Before he was indicted on extortion and other charges a subpoena was issued for the union's records. The union would not comply, so the officers searched the files from an office DeForte shared with several other union officials. There was no warrant. This evidence was used against him over his objection. These papers were not his so the right he urged had to come from the "to be secure in their houses" provision of the Fourth Amendment. The word "house" is not to be taken literally. It is extended to commercial premises. Thus, one can object to a search of his office as well as his home as long as the tests of **Rakas** are met. This does not change even though a man shares an office. Therefore, DeForte had standing. See also **O'Connor v. Ortega**, 480 U.S. 709 (1987) as discussed in Chapter 10 on Administrative Searches.

When a person is convicted of a felony that person loses most civil rights and his constitutional expectations are reduced except the one that prohibits cruel and unusual punishment. He certainly loses the bulk of the Fourth Amendment's protection and the expectation of privacy. When a person escapes from prison he does not bestow upon himself an expectation of privacy and, thereby, standing. Such was the problem in Stanley's case. He escaped and was traced to a house that was forcibly entered by police without a search warrant. **Commonwealth v. Stanley**, 401 A. 2d 1166 (Pa. Super. Ct. 1979).

If an escaped prisoner does not have standing would a parolee have standing to object? Does a parolee have a reasonable expectation of privacy? If a parolee has a reasonable expectation of privacy does this also apply when the person searching is his parole officer? One commentator noted that "in all but one reported case, warrantless searches by parole officers, acting on their own knowledge or suspicion have been held to be reasonable...." **Comment** 30 So. Car. L. Rev. 813, 815 (1979). And this was true until the Fourth Circuit's decision in **U.S. v. Bradley**, 571 F. 2d. 787 (C.A. 4th 1978). In **Bradley,** the court held that "unless an established exception to the warrant requirement is applicable, a parole officer must secure a warrant prior to conducting a search of a parolee's place of residence...." The court rejected the idea that the special relationship between parole officer and parolee did away with the need for a warrant. Nor was it willing to accept the idea of an exception based upon the public's need to have the parolee properly supervised. Under a state action theory this decision is sound.

There was one question that the **Bradley** court did not answer. Would the probable cause standard be as high as it is in normal contexts? They indicated that standard may not be as demanding as that required in a normal criminal investigation. Therefore, at least two courts agree that the exclusionary rule applies to evidence acquired without a warrant by a parole officer when its introduction is sought at a trial on criminal charges. However, does the rule apply to non-trials? Does the defendant, as a probationer or parolee, have standing to object to warrantless evidence sought to be introduced at a probation or parole revocation hearing? A revocation hearing is not a trial, thus the due process rights are not as fully granted as in a trial on charges. Most courts have held that the exclusionary rule does not extend to revocation hearings. **Dulin v. State**, 346 N.E. 2d. 746 (Ind. App. 1976).

How does the Supreme Court view the area? Persons who have been placed on probation and assigned a probation officer are in a unique category. In order for the system to work there must be more than periodic meetings at the probation office. To assure that all terms and conditions are followed, unannounced appearances and even searches should be conducted of the person, effects and home of the probationer. A Fourth Amendment full-probable cause requirement would hinder the process. In fact some of the things sought are not illegal if held by the average person but are contraband in the hands of the probationer. The Supreme Court, therefore, agreed and approved a Wisconsin program that allowed unannounced searches on reasonable grounds after approval by the probation officer's supervisor. **Griffin v. Wisconsin**, 483 U.S. 868 (1987). This decision would be applauded. The only disaster it spells is the possibility of police pressure on probation officers and the further problem of bootstrapping. Police would love to go along while such a search is being conducted or in fact, conduct it themselves.

In its latest decision, the U.S. Supreme Court held that the exclusionary rules only apply to criminal trials. State parole boards are not federally required to exclude evidence found in violation of the Fourth Amendment. **Pennsylvania BD. of Probation and Parole v. Scott**, 524 U.S. 357 (1998). The court held the exclusionary rule is *prudential* and not constitutionally mandated. That means it was judicially created to deter illegal searches and seizures. It felt that in this context the rule's benefits do not outweigh the social costs.

The Supreme Court in Montana adopted **Griffin** in **State v. Burke**, 766 P. 2d 254 (Mont. 1988). The terms and conditions of Burke's probation were that he submit to reasonable cause based warrantless searches by a probation or by police officers. Upon getting "plain smell" the police officer called the probation officer to get permission to continue the search. That permission was given by the probation officer. Drugs and paraphernalia were found. This involvement of a police officer was not an exigency presented in **Griffin**. The Montana court approved the search because of Montana's unique situation. It is a very large state geographically, but it is primarily rural with a very dispersed population which causes probation officers to have to serve several counties. They felt that to only allow probation officers to search would be unworkable and would cripple the system. They did conclude their opinion by saying that such search rights should not be used as an instrument of harassment or intimidation. Time will tell.

If **Griffin** means a statute as well as a warrant can establish reasonableness for a probationer's search can a judicial order to the same effect be held to be reasonable? Yes, said the Eighth Circuit in **U.S. v. Schoenrock**, 868 F. 2d 289 (C.A. 8th 1989). The case involved a search condition under the Probation Act 18 USC Sec. 3651 as imposed by the judge. They held that the condition was necessary for rehabilitation and protection goals even though it subjected the probationer to random searches with or without a warrant. Though not totally comfortable with such a broad provision, the court held that the way the searches were conducted in this case was reasonable. Besides, they said, the judge in this case knew what this man's needs were and that is why this provision was made one of his terms and conditions.

One California court sees probationers search consent provisions as a complete waiver of Fourth Amendment rights except the retained right to complain of harassment or searches conducted in an unreasonable manner. This is a broader way of viewing things than the **Griffin** case. **People v. Madrid**, 256 Cal. Rep. 338 (Cal. Dist. Ct. App. 1989). One district court adopted the reasoning of **Griffin** for the federal system in its area. The court said reasonable suspicion and not probable cause was needed by the probation officer who seized the documents in plain view. **U.S. v. Giannetta**, 711 F. Supp. 1144 (D.C. Me. 1989).

Though not specifically a Fourth Amendment case, **Turner v. Safley**, 482 U.S. 78 (1987) gives state and federal courts guidelines to follow when an inmate suggests that his constitutional rights have been violated. The Court in an earlier case, **Procunier v. Martinez**, 416 U.S. 396 (1974) said prison walls do not separate prison inmates from the protection of the Constitution. But the Court there noted that "courts are ill equipped to deal with the increasingly urgent problems of prison administration and reform." However, the Court did not set a standard to be applied in trying to determine whether the prison's response to a problem was rational especially when confronting a security problem. In cases subsequent to **Martinez** a "reasonably related to penalogical objectives or exaggerated response test" was used. In such a test the courts must inquire whether there was:

1. a valid rational connection between the regulation and the governmental interest put forward to justify it;

2. alternative means of exercising the rights that remain open to inmates;

3. the impact of the accommodation of the asserted constitutional right will have on the guards and other inmates and on the allocation of prison resources generally; and

4. the absence of ready alternatives is evidence of the reasonableness of a prior regulation.

If an inmate claimant can point to an alternative that fully accommodates the prisoner's rights at a *de minimus* cost to valid penological interests a court may consider that alternative as evidence on the issue of reasonableness.

Thus when looking at prison shakedowns for weapons and drugs it is hard to envision a reasonable rule that would require announcement of such shakedowns. Unannounced searches (and lockdowns while they are conducted) are reasonably related to safety and health concerns of both the staff and other inmates. Strip searches of inmates after contact visits seem reasonable in most contexts. Strip and body cavity searches are reasonable when a new inmate is being introduced into the general population. Thorough searches after riots and attempted escapes seem highly reasonable in any event.

The Ninth Circuit approved, under **Safley**, the Nevada State Prison's use of strip searches on maximum security prisoners every time such a prisoner returns to the unit and even after times when they have been free within the unit. In fact, that court approved the use of "tasers" to force prisoners to comply with this search policy. The reasonableness of searches is determined by reference to the prison context. Citing **Bell v. Wolfish**, 441 U.S. 520 (1979), which upheld visual body cavity searches without probable cause of pretrial detainees, the Ninth Circuit said a balancing test is applied. In a maximum security unit, they felt, there is a need for elevated security precautions. When looking at alternatives the only one seriously considered was whether doing the search in the privacy of the prisoner's cell was better than conducting it in the hallway. Private cell searches required more officers and posed a threat to officer safety, therefore, the prison's choice of place was not unreasonable under **Safley**. The fact that from time to time female officers might be required to do the visual search was also found to be reasonable under the circumstances. **Michenfelder v. Summer**, 860 F. 2d 328 (C.A. 9th 1988).

In its 1980 "standing" opinion the Court was faced with a totally illegal search of a person's briefcase which search revealed a list of people having secret foreign bank accounts. Defendant was one of those on the list. He was convicted of falsifying his 1973 income tax return. Citing **Rakas**, the Court acknowledged that the defendant's constitutional right was not violated. He had no privacy interest in this briefcase. The significance of the decision is that they rejected the lower court's theory that when a gross illegality occurred, the court should be able, under general supervisory powers, to exclude such tainted evidence. The U.S. Supreme Court did not agree because they feared the exercise of standardless discretion in applying in the Fourth Amendment. **U.S. v. Payner**, 447 U.S. 727 (1980). See also the full opinion in **Salvucci**. Do these cases represent a retreat from the intent of **Weeks**? No, the intent of **Weeks** was to get away from due process types of analysis.

A number of states are slowly accepting the fact that there is no such thing as automatic standing in search cases. New York has all but abolished all of their automatic standing rule in **People v. Wesley**, 540 N.Y.S. 2d 757 (N.Y. 1989). Just because the Supreme Court has declared that there is no automatic standing does not mean that the battle is over. As already noted and as more fully discussed later in this chapter, states can find that their own constitutions grant defendants more rights. But that is not the only approach. In states that follow **Rakas** and **Salvucci** defense attorneys have continued to attempt to sell two more theories of standing. Namely they are the "target" theory of standing and the "derivative" theory of standing. However, some states cling tenaciously to automatic standing. See **State v. Bullock**, 901 P. 2d 61 (Mont. 1995).

The target theory is based on the "little fish/big fish" approach. That is, constitutional rights of a lesser criminal are violated to get evidence against the greater criminal – that the bigger fish was the "target" of the unconstitutional search; the purpose of the unconstitutional search. This, however, was rejected in **Rakas** and a state would have to find that their own constitution gives more rights to deter such action. The derivative standing approach is argued when all "fish," big and small are joined as co-defendants. The argument is that all such defendants should have standing to challenge the lawfulness of the police conduct.

In **Com. v. Manning**, 406 Mass. 425 (1990) the Supreme Judicial Court remanded the case to allow the trial court to determine and use the "target" theory but rejected the "derivative" theory. The issue of automatic standing was not fully resolved in **Manning**. In fact, when postured against **Com. v. Santoro**, 406 Mass. 421 (1990) and decided the same day as **Manning,** the court found a defendant without standing with regard to a search of a friend's house. Santoro's failure to show a privacy interest caused his appeal to fail. One month later the same court would rule that in "possession" crimes a defendant does have automatic standing, but then by footnote, limited the adoption of the rule to "possession" crimes and automobile searches and left for another day the question whether the rule should be applied to other "possession" situations. **Com. v. Amendola**, 406 Mass. 592 (1980). As can be seen the battle regarding standing goes on.

Clearly the Ninth Circuit had been straying from the Supreme Court's standing rules. Nowhere is this more evident than in **U.S. v. Padilla**, 960 F. 2d 854 (C.A. 9th 1992). In **Padilla** the Ninth Circuit said that a co-conspirator had standing in an automobile not owned or controlled by the co-conspirator merely because the co-conspirator was a member of the conspiracy. Just as clear was the need for the Supreme Court to "rein in" the Ninth Circuit. In its **Padilla** decision, the Supreme Court condemned the Ninth's reasoning and rejected the co-conspirator standing rule that had developed in the Ninth. Privacy rights do not arise merely by conspiratorial association. Without an invasion of a privacy or property interest there is no Fourth Amendment issue. **U.S. v. Padilla**, 508 U.S. 77 (1993).

Observations Regarding Standing

1.   What is Standing?

The ability to complain about police or other governmental Fourth Amendment activity that yields tangible incriminating evidence against the complaining defendant.

<u>Note:</u>   Though most standing cases involve warrantless state action it also is inherent in every warranted search case when property of a non-owner, controller or possessor is searched within the place or thing described in the warrant.

2.   How does "standing to sue" differ from "standing under the Fourth Amendment?"

A person may be personally and economically affected by improper state action in the Fourth Amendment context yet have no right to complain about the invasion of the property so seized or searched when offered as evidence. Thus, Fourth

Amendment standing is in fact a physical property concept and not a police conduct connected concept; involving due process considerations.

3.   **What types of standing theories are possible?**

A.   *Automatic standing* – to be used when any search or seizure is conducted without a warrant or upon an invalid warrant.

B.   *Vicarious standing* – the right to complain about the invasion of anyone else's property that yields evidence against the complainant.

C.   *Target (object) (big fish-little fish) standing* – could also be called ulterior or pretextual motive standing.

D.   *Personal-non-vicarious standing* – complainant must show a lawfully held object or place was invaded in which the complainant had some right of control or reasonable expectation of privacy.

4.   **Why is personal-non-vicarious standing (and not other forms) logically consistent with Katz?**

The exclusionary rule was intended to replace the due process analysis of Fourth Amendment issues and to prevent the judiciary from becoming the supervisors of police conduct.

The **Katz** rule says that the Fourth Amendment protects people and not places (or objects) and tells us that when a person has a reasonable expectation of privacy that society is willing to protect, then and only then will the power of the exclusionary rule be applied. Thus personal standing is the only standing rule consistent with **Katz**. *Note*: Standing requires the defendant to demonstrate a subjective expectation of privacy *but* requires the court to apply an objective test as to whether the expectation was reasonable *and* then determine if society is willing to protect this expectation.

5.   **How does a person waive standing?**

A.   consent (Voluntary, Knowing, and Intelligent: **VKI**) to a search or seizure,

B.   abandonment of property,

C.   use of a depository not covered by the **Katz** rule,

D.   by using the border of the nation,

E.   by using the open fields.

6.   **Under what circumstances can "full-blown" standing take a "back seat" to compelling state interests?**

    A.   Under the highly regulated industries doctrine of the administrative search doctrine, and

    B.   Under the exigent search doctrine.

IV.   The State Action Requirement

After its adoption of the exclusionary rule in **Weeks**, U.S., 232 U.S. 383 (1914) and before it had an opportunity to apply it to the states, one significant question had to be answered. Does the exclusionary rule apply only when government agents violate the Fourth Amendment or should the rule be applied where the expectation of privacy is intruded upon by a private citizen? The Court had its first opportunity to answer this question in **Burdeau v. McDowell**, 265 U.S. 465 (1921). The Court held that the Fourth Amendment's protection applied to governmental action. It was intended as a restraint upon the activities of sovereign authority and was not intended to be a limitation on private activity. If the record shows that no governmental official had anything to do with the wrongful seizure, then the defendant is left to his or her remedy against those who unlawfully took the items. Brandeis and Holmes tersely dissented. It felt that this decision would not further the goal of respect for law as this conduct was a shock to the average citizen's sense of decency and fair play.

After the exclusionary rule was made applicable to the states, the states all appeared to have adopted the rule of **Burdeau**. The significant problem in applying **Burdeau** by both state and federal courts centered on whether the person taking the evidence was acting as an agent for the government. The following decisions illustrate the variations encountered in determining agency.

In Wisconsin, a teacher was found to be a state agent. Thus her search of a student was state action. **In re L.L. v. Circuit Court**, 280 N.W. 2d. 343 (Wis. Ct. App. 1979). This appeared to be a proper rule because governmental action is not limited to law enforcement officers. Otherwise, there could be great abuses by directing non-enforcement personnel to do what police cannot do.

The Territorial Court of the Virgin Islands found certain searches by teachers to constitute state action and in violation of the Fourth Amendment despite the fact

32

that teachers act under the "*in loco parentis*" doctrine. The standards for teacher initiated searches can be lessened by application of a three part test. The government would have to show: (1) unique danger exists; (2) solution cannot be found within the confines of the probable cause requirement; and (3) search conducted more limited than police type search. The court compared this to the reasonable suspicion/articulable suspicion standard. **In re M.S.**, 30 Crim. L. Rep. 2015 (Vir. Is. Terr. Ct. 1981).

A few states had taken the position that unless directed by the police a search by a public school teacher would not constitute state action. The stage was set for an answer from the Supreme Court and it finally came in **New Jersey v. T.L.O.**, 469 U.S. 325 (1984). The factual scenario was simple and typical. The school prohibited smoking at the school. Two girls were discovered smoking in the restroom by a teacher who took them to the assistant principal's office. T.L.O.'s denial of the "offense" was not believed by the assistant principal who grabbed her purse and began to search for the cigarettes. To his surprise he found drugs, paraphernalia, money, and a list of buyers in the girl's purse. Ultimately the New Jersey Supreme Court found the search illegal.

What did the U.S. Supreme Court hold? First, children do have a legitimate expectation of privacy. Second, schools have a legitimate need to maintain a learning environment. Balancing these two legitimacies the school gets a reduced Fourth Amendment burden but they do not get the advantage as surrogates of the parents nor the parent's immunity. They are, after all, representatives of the state. Third, the warrant requirement is unsuited to the school environment; to obtain a warrant before a search of a child suspected of an infraction of rules or of criminal law would interfere with the main tenet of swift and informal disciplinary procedure needed in the schools. Fourth, the legality of a search of a student should depend simply on the reasonableness, under all the circumstances, of the search. Reasonable searches are justified at the inception and reasonable as related in scope to the circumstances. The search in this case was reasonable.

The question often arises regarding the status of private security guards. Unless directed by the police, such guards have been deemed private parties and not state agents. **People v. Holloway**, 267 N.W. 2d 454 (Mich. Ct. App. 1978). However, if the security guard is an off-duty or auxiliary police officer, the result might be different. **Com. v. Eshelman**, 383 A. 2d 838 (Pa. 1978). Unless there is that connection or some police direction, private security guards are private citizens. **People v. Moreno**, 64 Cal. App. 3d 23, 135 Cal. Rep. 340 (Cal. Super. Ct. App. Dept. 1976).

Some courts go even further in defining state action and the role of the security guard in a department store. Consider the decision of the D.C. Court of Appeals in **Lucas v. U.S.**, 411 A. 2d 360 (D.C. Ct. App. 1980). The case involved the monitoring of a microwave sensor by security personnel. Before the court addressed the issue of whether microwave sensors were subject to a reasonableness test, it had to be determined whether there was any state action that raised the reasonableness issue. The court said that for there to be state action, two criteria must be met. First, the special police must have been acting as agents of the state. Second, the involvement by the special police must have been significant. The court held that because of the nature of their duties these special police were acting as agents of the state. Of course, they said, for all other purposes they were private employees. However, when they are performing their police function they are acting as public officers and assume all the liabilities of public officers. As a result, the court found the Fourth Amendment applicable.

It must be noted that the phrase "special police," as used here, has a specific meaning. The District of Columbia Code provides that special police are licensed to carry guns, use handcuffs and generally have the same powers as D.C. police. In the **Lucas** case, the special police were in fact licensed private investigators. Thus the **Lucas** decision is based upon the state's involvement in licensing these two security people. A decision announced just two months after **Lucas** indicates that where the security officers are not special police and are not being directed by local police, their actions do not bring the Fourth Amendment into play. Ordinary security guards are, when acting alone, merely employees and private citizens. **U.S. v. Lima**, 424 A. 2d 113 (D.C. Ct. App. 1980). The question also arises whether a public utility, which is granted a monopoly and often given the power of condemnation, is a private citizen or quasi-governmental. Generally, they are private citizens and unless directed by the state to do something in the nature of a search, their actions are non-governmental. **Lusch v. State**, 387 A. 2d. 306 (Md. Ct. Spec. App. 1978).

The jurisdiction of a police officer is limited by statute and in all instances a state officer has no jurisdiction beyond his own home state. Thus when an officer goes into another state and secures evidence, he is acting (unless done with the prior approval of local authorities) as a private citizen. **Stevenson v. State**, 403 A. 2d. 812 (Md. Ct. Spec. App. 1979).

So one looks for active police involvement even though the police did not do the actual physical taking. **Pomerantz v. State**, 372 So. 2d. 104 (Fla. Dist. Ct. App. 1979). If the citizen acts independently, no state action. **People v. Heflin**, 376 N.E. 2d.

1367 (Ill. 1978). Thus where a doctor takes a blood sample for a blood test before any arrest and for the sole purpose of diagnosis and treatment, the results would be admissible in a subsequent trial; **State v. Jenkins**, 259 N.W. 2d. 109 (Wis. 1977); dorm advisor finds a stolen tape recorder on his own, **State v. Keadle**, 277 S.E. 2d 456 (N.C. Ct. App. 1981).

However, there are times when the citizen is so tied up with the police that state action has to be found. Consider the case of **State v. Anonymous**, 379 A. 2d. 946 (Conn. 1978). "In the present case it appears that the state police had been in contact with the informers for some time before the cocaine theft occurred. The informer had been encouraged to continue his surveillance of the defendants' activities and to furnish such information as he might acquire. There is no indication that the police suggested that the informer take anything from the home of the defendants. Obviously, they must have realized that the substance handed to them by the informer had been stolen from the defendants." There can be no question but that an express request or authorization by the police that a private individual engage in an illegal seizure would be sufficient to attribute the wrongful conduct to the police. A passive acquiescence by a police officer in an illegal search when the officer was present at the scene and aware that an illegal search was being conducted by a private individual has also been deemed to make the officer a participant in the unlawful activity.

One should not get the impression that state action through private parties is only an issue when there is police initiation, order or request. Illustrative of the joint venture or citizen initiative approach is the case of **State v. Abdouch**, 434 N.W. 2d 317 (Neb. 1989). The citizens in this case asked for police help to enter their deceased father's house. The surviving spouse had been preventing their entry and the heirs wanted police help. The officers agreed and went along and helped in the search for personal items of the deceased. Evidence of drug dealing was uncovered. The court held that state action may occur when it is a joint endeavor between a private person and a state or governmental official.

There is a fine line between joint endeavors and purely private action as illustrated by **U.S. v. Koenig**, 856 F. 2d 843 (C.A. 7th 1988). If Federal Express has a policy that suggests opening packages that appear suspicious and if drugs are discovered the policy requires company security to report such discoveries to the government. Would that constitute state action? If this policy was not compelled, urged or even requested by the government then there is no state action. Would it make a difference if a government memo were sent out saying that it would respond to calls for assistance when drugs were found? Not unless there was a request, urging or compulsion would there be state action. Does Federal Express have a right to protect its employees from all types of criminal activity without becoming a government agent? Yes. Thus the search of the defendant's package by a security officer who was not paid or directed by the government was the act of a private party and not state action despite the fact that this security officer had been involved in several of these types of cases over an extended period of time.

Thus, until 1979, it seems that no state was willing to heed the advice of the dissenters in **Burdeau**. All apparently accepted the theory of private versus state action. All, that is, until the decision of the Montana Supreme Court in **State v. Helfrich**, 600 P. 2d 816 (Mont. 1979). Using their own constitution, the court held "...the right of individual privacy explicitly guaranteed...is inviolate and the search and seizure provisions...apply to private individuals as well as law enforcement officers." Therefore, the evidence gathered through illegal invasions by anyone are not admissible in Montana. No other state, however, has been willing to go that far.

However, just because a state court is unwilling to find a broader constitutional right does not mean that the state action inquiry is at an end. Legislatures can by legislation selectively put limits on what is acceptable in the evidence gathering activity whether that activity is private action or state action. Such was the dilemma faced by a California court in **People v. Murtha**, 50 Crim. L. Rep. 1231 (Cal. App. 1991). In **Murtha**, without police direction, a private citizen taped a telephone conversation. This citizen turned the tape over to police who in turn applied for a search warrant. The warrant was issued. Clearly, unless such activity is prohibited by statute, the information may be used to obtain a warrant. Unfortunately, 18 U.S.C. §2511 prohibits interception by "any person" and "any person" means "any individual," 18 U.S.C. §2510 (6), **Murtha** at 1252. Deciding to follow the First Circuit's opinion in **U.S. v. Vest**, 813 F. 2d 477 (C.A. 1st 1987) and to reject the Sixth Circuit's opinion in **U.S. v. Underhill**, 813 F. 2d 105 (C.A. 6th 1987), this California court said the information gathered in violation of the Congressional act could not be used even when it can be proven that the state was an "innocent recipient of the recording." The warrant and conviction in this case were saved under **Leon** and the good faith exception announced in **Leon** (*infra*).

Perhaps the real test is: Does it appear that the police were trying to accomplish indirectly, by using a citizen, that which the police could not do directly? Courts which suspect this will find state action when the evidence is uncovered by a private citizen. This was the conclusion reached by a California court. A police officer accompanied a burglary victim to the suspect's car. The police officer did not get near the car but stood some distance away while the victim entered the car to search for his property. The court viewed this as state action by giving great weight to the official participation. The court would not give any weight to the motives of the private citizen. **People v. North**, 629 P. 2d 19 (Cal. Dist. Ct. App. 1980). Of course, had the citizen broken into the car on his own and then turned the property over to the police, the evidence would have been admissible.

The **Burdeau** case was not sufficient to handle most modern day problems. The Court was seeing a number of cases involving private carriers who, for some reason, had come upon packages containing suspect items. The first case was **Walter v. U.S.**, 447 U.S. 649 (1980) in which the private person had opened a misdirected carton and found rolls of motion picture films which appeared to be obscene, thus contraband. The private party opened one of the cans of the films and tried to view them merely by holding them up to the light without the aid of a viewer, magnifying glass or projector. The private party turned the film over to the F.B.I. The F.B.I. went one step further than the private citizen and got a projector, thus confirming the well grounded belief that the films were indeed obscene. The Court, through a plurality opinion, seemed to agree to a rule that the government search could not exceed the private party's intrusion. Therefore, a warrant should have been secured to use the projector. All prior conduct by the F.B.I., however, was lawful.

How far would the court take the "not exceed" rule? Would they distinguish between items that are more obviously contraband and those that are only merely inferentially contraband? Yes, they would. The refinement of the rule came in **U.S. v. Jacobsen**, 466 U.S. 109 (1984). The Court said the Fourth Amendment is implicated only if the authorities use information with respect to which the expectation of privacy has not already been frustrated. This was to be the key to limiting and distinguishing **Walters**. Jacobsen had sent or was sent (it is not clear, nor important) a well-wrapped package by way of Federal Express. The fork-lift punctured it and while inspecting it and its contents for claims purposes the FedEx people saw that it contained a silver taped tube which they cut open. In the tube were "zip-lock" bags of white powder. They hurriedly put the package back together and called the D.E.A. D.E.A. repeated the FedEx routine and went one step further. The D.E.A. agent "field tested" for cocaine and it was cocaine. The defendant urged **Walters** and its "not exceed" rule. There was no search in the repeat of the FedEx steps, the Court held. The agent's dominion and control over the package and its contents did constitute a seizure, but not an illegal one because there is no reasonable expectation of privacy in contraband, and, of course, the D.E.A. had ample probable cause to believe this was contraband. Did the field test infringe an expectation of privacy that society is prepared to consider reasonable? No, such a test does not compromise any legitimate privacy interest. Cocaine is an illegal substance. The amount destroyed was minimal. Therefore, a warrant was not required. **Walters** was distinguished because of the nature of the items found and their obvious nature or lack thereof as being contraband.

For our purposes the bottom line is as the Court agreed: "It is well settled that when an individual reveals private information to another, he assumes the risk that his confidant will reveal that information to the authorities, and if that occurs the Fourth Amendment does not prohibit governmental use of the information."

If **Jacobsen** approves field testing for drugs at the site of the discovery can it be read broadly enough to allow field testing away from that site? North Dakota felt that where the field testing took place was not the key issue in **Jacobsen** but rather the complexity of the testing (or lack thereof) was the core in **Jacobsen**. Therefore, taking the substance to a police facility did not destroy rights gained by the police to do a "limited-in-scope" field test. **State v. Rode**, 456 N.W. 2d 769 (N. D. 1990).

The state action cases can arise in a more subtle form. The **T.L.O**. case in essence recognized that a public employee of any kind can be imbued with state action status, but as **T.L.O**. recognized, these employees are not held to the same Fourth Amendment standards when acting within the scope of their duties unless directed by police. However, **T.L.O.** should not be read to mean all public employees are always acting as Fourth Amendment agents.

Consider the Kansas case of **State v. Smith**, 763 P. 2d 632 (Kan.. 1988), in which the Kansas Supreme Court held that a state park employee's entry of a house trailer on park property to investigate a mysterious "hissing" sound was not a government search for purposes of the Fourth Amendment. This man was a trash collector. The court found that he entered as a private citizen. There was no connection of the trash collector with any police agency and his entry had no connection with his duties as a state employee. Therefore, the evidence was admissible.

The Tenth Circuit had a case where a special delivery messenger of the post office opened a piece of mail containing cocaine and he seized some for his own personal use. The court held that the messenger's conduct did not amount to a governmental search or seizure of the package within the meaning of the Fourth Amendment. **Smith v. U.S., 810** F. 2d. 996 (Cir. 10th 1987), cert. denied 488 U.S. 218 (1988) Both the Kansas and Tenth Circuit decisions appear to be based on sound grounds because neither employee was acting in their official capacity. Neither employee was acting at the direction or control of the police. Neither case involved an off-duty police officer. And it is the last point where such cases may be read and applied too broadly. To this date when an officer is within his jurisdiction and if "off-duty," he is still considered to be a police agent when he engages in search and seizure activity. The "outside the scope" language of these cases should not be applied to police officers who are off-duty within their jurisdiction.

Airlines are often responsible for hiring the people who monitor carry-on luggage. The FAA has issued screening profiles as directives that require "white tagging" of bags of persons who meet a profile of a bomber or a hijacker. The ticket agent "white tagged" Ms. Schaffer's carry-ons; a purse and a backpack. This directed the x-ray security people to hand search her bags. At first she said okay but she may have withdrawn the consent during the search. The thorough search found cocaine in a sock. Was this a private search or was it State action? Since it was ordered by a government official through the "directive" it was found to be a governmental search. **Schaffer v. State**, 988 P. 2d 610 (Alaska App. 1999).

A doctor employed by the government at a government owned hospital who takes a blood sample for medical reasons was not intending to assist the government in its prosecution of the defendant according to the Ninth Circuit. They did not say the doctor was a private citizen but decided that the doctor was acting in a non-law-enforcement capacity. **U.S. v. Attson**, 900 F. 2d 1427 (C.A. 9th 1990). As both of the foregoing cases forcefully illustrate, state or government employees who are not law enforcement officers will not be considered law enforcement officers unless they are acting under the direction or control of the police.

But does this mean that the police can stand by and let the state employee act like a police officer and then accept the benefits of the activity? Consider this case from New Mexico. The defendant was taken to the emergency room to be treated. A nurse and a police officer are on either side of the treatment table. The nurse proceeds to interrogate and the officer does nothing to stop it. Although finding no collusion her questioning was found to be governmental action. **State v. Ybarra**, 804 P. 2d 1053 (N.Mex. 1990). *Contra*: **Com. v. Allen**, 395 Mass. 448 (1985), no state action by this public employee nurse in a similar situation.

V.   The End of The "Silver Platter Doctrine"

Simply stated, the "silver platter doctrine" allowed federal officers to use evidence illegally seized by state officers as long as the federal officer did not participate in the illegality. With their decision in **Elkins v. U.S.**, 364 U.S. 206 (1960), the U.S. Supreme Court did away with the "silver platter doctrine." In **Elkins**, state officers illegally seized some evidence which was suppressed in the state action.

Elkins was then tried in the federal system for the federal violation that arose out of the incident. His motion to suppress the same evidence at his federal trial was denied and he was convicted. The Court said that by admitting the unlawfully seized evidence, the federal court served to defeat the state's efforts to assure obedience to the Constitution. Federal-state cooperation is hardly promoted by a rule that implicitly invites the federal officers to withdraw from such association, at least tacitly, to encourage state officers to disregard constitutionally protected freedoms. The Court observed that if they said it cannot be used then there can be no inducement for subterfuge. Finally, the Court noted, the decision must be based on judicial integrity and to do otherwise undermines that concept.

That is the end of "silver platter" – correct? Not according to the dissenters in **U.S. v. Janis**, 428 U.S. 433 (1976). An invalid state search yielded some evidence of tax evasion by the defendant. The state was denied the use of this evidence in his gambling violation trial. The I.R.S. used the evidence in a federal civil trial. The issue, as the majority saw it, was whether evidence seized in good faith by an officer under an invalid warrant could be used in a U.S. civil proceeding. The majority said yes, it could be used. Noting the history of the exclusionary rule, the Court did not find a case that required exclusion in a civil case. They did not see the exclusion from a civil case as an effective deterrent to future police action. The Court was unwilling to extend the rule any further. They did appear to hold that the rule announced in this case would apply only to intersovereign cases and not intrasovereign cases. Thus the I.R.S. could not use such evidence if turned up by the F.B.I., for example. Accord see: **Vanderlinder v. U.S.**, 502 F. Supp. 693 (D. Iowa 1980).

Would a corollary rule to the one adopted be effective? Suppose the I.R.S., under an invalid inspection, comes up with evidence of a state crime? Could the state use that evidence in its case against the defendant? There is no clear – cut answer, yet it would be a logical extension of the "intersovereign rule" adopted by the Court in **Janis**.

The difficulty with a doctrine as old as "silver platter" and its demise is that the further we get from the date of such decision, the more likely it becomes that the bench and bar will not consider its constraints. If, as the Court said in **Elkins**, the subterfuge of federal agents seeking to avoid more strict federal constitutional or statutory constraints by utilizing state illegally derived evidence simply by appearing not to be involved in its seizure is to be avoided, should not the same rule apply to states using legally obtained federal evidence that the state prohibits? Consider **Basham v. Commonwealth**, 675 S.W. 2d 376 (Ky. 1984). Kentucky had a statute prohibiting electronic surveillance. At the state trial, properly seized federal evidence under Title III was admissible. The court expressed concern that if they had found collusion between the federal and state authorities to circumvent the state law, then it would have been inadmissible. In **U.S. v. One Parcel of Real Property**, 873 F. 2d 7 (C.A. 1st 1989), the court held that evidence taken by a state officer in violation of state law could be admitted in federal court as long as its taking did not offend federal constitutional and statutory law.

To be sure, **Elkins** put to an end the use of **constitutionally** illegally seized evidence by one sovereign in the trial courts of another sovereign. But the Court did point out the collusion concern. If, as Kentucky says, the potential for collusion exists even where the evidence seized by one sovereign was legally done, was not that the exact reason why **Elkins** was decided as it was? At least an argument can be so made. That officers do work together is well illustrated by **U.S. v. Van Horn**, 579 F. Supp. 804 (D. Neb. 1984). The federal officers worked with the state officers on an investigation using a state issued surveillance order. Title III does not prohibit this and it appeared the state statute also did not prohibit such cooperation.

This whole question of "silver platter" is further complicated by the fact that more and more we are seeing "piggyback" searches. These searches occur where one enforcement agency has probable cause and the other does not. The jurisdiction without probable cause is invited along to help execute a valid warrant. A Florida appeals court said the Supreme Court approved such practices in **Scott v. U.S.**, 436 U.S. 128 (1978), and it held that such piggyback searches are constitutional. **Frazier v. State**, 44 Crim. L. Rep. 2374 (Fla. Dist. Ct. App. 1989). The Florida court's reliance on a wiretap case and the issue of minimization is not well placed. The issue whether an officer, without probable cause, can physically accompany an officer with a proper warrant has not yet been specifically addressed. Piggyback searches by intergovernmental agents must come within the "silver platter" context. This is not to say that the "in-aid-thereof" search statutes are unconstitutional *per se*, but when an officer asks others from other agencies and from another government to assist in the search, a "red flag" should go up in the mind of the judge whether such aid was needed, or whether it was used to avoid probable cause for the officer giving the assistance.

New Jersey has faced the modern "Silver Platter" era "head-on" in their decision in **State v. Mollica**, 554 A. 2d 1315 (N.J. 1989). The state had created a right of privacy in telephone numbers called that the federal government, through **Smith v. Maryland**, 442 U.S. 735 (1979), does not recognize. The defendant, Mollica, was using his hotel telephone for illegal gambling operations. Without getting a warrant, the FBI obtained the list of numbers called. The FBI turned this information over to state authorities who used the information to obtain a search warrant that led to Mollica's conviction. New Jersey approved the use of this "reverse silver platter" subject to one condition. That condition they call vital and significant. "It is essential," the court said, "that the federal action deemed lawful under federal standards not be alloyed by any state action or responsibility." They felt there must be an examination of the entire relationship between the two sets of government actors. Mutual assistance may sufficiently establish agency as well as planning, joint cooperation or joint operations. Mere contact or mere awareness may not. This fact-sensitive exploration should be made in all such cases.

A Washington Court has joined with other courts finding that evidence seized legally by federal agents but illegally by state rules can be used in the state trial. The court cited **Mollica** from New Jersey approvingly saying that state constitutions do not control federal action. It too requires that the federal agents must not have acted under the direction or control of state officers. Mere knowledge of an on-going investigation is not prohibited, however. **State v. Gwinner**, 796 P. 2d 728 (Wash. Ct. App. 1990).

Nebraska, on the other hand, rejected "reverse silver platter" in **State v. Harms**, 449 N.W. 2d 1 (Neb. 1989) where an illegal federal search produced evidence that was in no way a product of state action. The illegality was not of constitutional proportions and did not violate state law. Failure, however, of the state to prove the legality of the U.S. Marshal's action and even whether the arrest warrant used by the marshal was properly issued required the suppression of the evidence gathered.

The cases continue to grow regarding searches invalid under state constitutional or statutory law that are proper under federal law. A district court in Washington, following **U.S. v. Chavez**, 844 F. 2d 1368 (C.A. 9th 1987), said that as long as the federal agents did not involve themselves in the state search the evidence is admissible. **U.S. v. Brady**, 734 F. Supp. 923 (D.C. Wash. 1990).

New Jersey's next Reverse Silver Platter case also involved gambling, but this time the seizure was made by a sister state, Illinois, and not federal authorities, as had been the case in **Mollica**. However, Illinois illegally seized the evidence under Illinois law due to an involuntary consent and an insufficient affidavit used to secure the warrant that was used. Can New Jersey use this evidence relative to the pyramid gambling scheme that began in New Jersey? New Jersey's answer was yes. **State v. Curry**, 532 A. 2d 721 (N.J. 1987). Since the New Jersey police had absolutely nothing to do with the Illinois search the court said this was not a "pure" silver platter type case. New Jersey, in other words, did not have Illinois "do any dirty work for them." But it is, at the first level, a choice of law problem, they said. The evidence gathering would have been upheld by New Jersey contrary to the Illinois position. Which law did they use? Is this evidence, in Justice Holmes' words, "sacred and inaccessible?" **Silverthorne Lumber Co. v. U.S.**, 251 U.S. 385 (1920). In this case New Jersey authorities had subpoenaed these records before the Illinois seizure. Thus an independent source existed for them and the state was not to be put in a "worse position" because of Illinois acts. No matter how you say it. New Jersey did not feel compelled to rule this evidence inadmissible even though it was illegally obtained by Illinois and even their own standards if judged by New Jersey standards. Is this case thus only slightly different than **Mollica**?

New Jersey's next case is **State v. Knight**, 678 A. 2d 642 (N.J. 1996). This case involved interrogations. The officer in this case was a federal officer who observed federal guidelines regarding interrogations. However, he did not observe a more stringent New Jersey standard. Under the federal rules the statement would have been admissible. But the **Knight** case points out that a federal officer may act as a state agent and when that happens he or she must follow state interrogation guidelines. **Mollica** was reaffirmed. The close cooperation between the state and this FBI agent saddled this agent with state responsibility.

Georgia noted that the rejection of Silver Platter Evidence does not apply when the searching entity or sovereign properly observed all of its own laws. This, of course, is much like the rationale of **Mollica. Rowe v. State**, 352 S.E. 2d 813 (Ga. App. 1987). Hawaii had an electronic surveillance case where California gathered evidence properly under California law but would have been "illegal" under Hawaiian law. Hawaii used the "deterrence" analysis and, like New Jersey in **Mollica**, found no Hawaii/California conspiracy and therefore they admitted the evidence. **State v. Bridges**, 925 P. 2d 357 (Haw. 1996). Nebraska properly held that the **Elkins** rejection of "silver platter" evidence flows both ways. Illegally seized evidence by federal officers is not admissible in a Nebraska court. But, they also said evidence seized lawfully by federal agents, independent of state action, would be admissible in Nebraska. **State v. Harms**, 449 N.W. 2d 1 (Neb. 1989).

Although reversed on failure to provide timely discovery, New York's high court held that interception in Canada by Canadian authorities of a telephone conversation between a Canadian suspect and a New York defendant who, of course, was speaking from his New York phone, did not violate New York law. Had New York given this defendant proper notice of the intercept the evidence would have been admissible. Of course, like **Mollica**, proof of a law enforcement cooperation conspiracy would dictate a different result. The fact that no Canadian law was violated also played a prominent role in the court's reasoning. **People v. Capolongo**, 623 N.Y.S. 2d 778 (N.Y. 1995).

A federal warrant executed in a timely manner for federal purposes, but not for Tennessee purposes, was at the center of the controversy in **State v. Hudson**, 849 S.W. 2d 309 (Tenn. Crim. 1993). The key to this court was whether the "cooperation conspiracy" existed. If none, then Tennessee should admit the evidence if the federal agents were not acting as agents for the state. The case was remanded for this determination. **Mollica** was cited and analyzed. See also **State v. Toone**, 872 S.W. 2d 750 (Tex. Crim.1994) and the federal use of an anticipatory warrant which Texas officers cannot use. But one Texas court feels reverse silver platter does not apply to private searches because of a very specific statute (Vernon's Ann. Tex. Code Crim. Proc. Art. 38.23 (3)). A Vermont case only cites **Mollica** for its standing analysis and not for reverse silver platter. **State v. Welch**, 624 A. 2d 1105 (Vt. 1993).

Texas continues their recognition of "reverse silver platter" doctrine by the decision in **Gutierrez v. State**, 22 S.W. 3d 75 (Tex. App. Corpus Christi 2000). A border patrol agent on duty at a fixed check-point, lawfully under U.S. Supreme Court decisions and Congressional acts, intercepted and ultimately arrested the defendant for transporting marijuana. The agent released the defendant and the evidence into the custody of Texas authorities. The state charged, tried and convicted the defendant. The defendant said his motion to suppress was wrongly denied. Citing **Toone**, this court noted that, "Evidence obtained by federal officers acting lawfully and in conformity to federal authority is admissible in state criminal proceedings."

Washington **Miranda** law requires an interrogated defendant be notified that his responses are being recorded. California's law does not have such a provision. Can Washington use the California derived statements? Yes, they are admissible held the court in **State v. Brown**, 940 P. 2d 546 (Wash. *en banc* 1997). **Mollica** was used and this court stressed the "non state agency" acts of the federal authorities. They noted that without mutual planning, joint operations, cooperative investigations or mutual assistance there is no "color of state agency." Thus, as in **Mollica**, mere contact or awareness of an investigation does not taint the evidence because "agency" Wyoming's case was very much like **Mollica** and the pen register created by the federal authorities. A dissenter bemoaned the fact that "silver platter" was resurrected by this decision. **Saldana v. State**, 846 P. 2d 604 (Wyo. 1993).

In a Massachusetts case the defendant complained that his admissions to Massachusetts police officers during an in-cell interrogation in a New Hampshire jail violated his **Miranda** rights to counsel. Why? The defendant's attorney called the New

Hampshire police and told them he was not to be interrogated. The local officers did not tell the Massachusetts police. The Massachusetts police secured a valid waiver of **Miranda** rights. No New Hampshire case was cited that New Hampshire law was violated. Thus, Massachusetts decided the case under the Fifth Amendment and under Massachusetts law. Since Massachusetts follows **Moran v. Burbine** and the "it's a defendant's right, not an attorney's right, to invoke" rule no violation of Massachusetts law was found. The court did note that there appeared to be no "more than minimal" involvement by the New Hampshire police with the Massachusetts police other than merely informing the Massachusetts police that New Hampshire had Mr. Cryer in their jail. But the court clearly pointed out that they were not endorsing in this case, as they had said in **Com. v. Gonzalez**, 688 N.E. 2d 455 (Mass. 1997), the "reverse silver platter" doctrine. **Com v. Cryer**, 689 N.E. 2d 808 (Mass. 1998).

Indiana indicates an unwillingness to embrace "reverse silver platter." In their case a juvenile's statement was taken by Illinois authorities very properly under Illinois law but since there was no interested adult present at that interrogation such a statement, if taken in Indiana, would be inadmissible. Citing **Mollica, Toone** and other "reverse silver platter" cases they said "we reject their authority." However, because one of the statements used in Indiana appeared to be a voluntary and spontaneous statement, this juvenile's conviction was remanded for a new trial without the interrogation derived statement. **Stidham v. State**, 608 N.E. 2d 699 (Ind. 1993).

One of the questions not yet answered in the "reverse silver platter" area is whether the Supreme Court will accept in the federal courts criminal evidence taken in violation of a state statute, rule, or state constitutional decision granting a defendant more rights where the search does not violate federal provisions. Does the Supreme Court have a duty under **Elkins** to teach state officers respect for their own law by prohibiting the admission of such evidence in the federal courts that is otherwise relevant and admissible? Narrowly interpreted **Elkins** only prohibits state seized evidence taken in violation of the federal constitution. Evidence that is not seized in a shocking or outrageous manner is fully admissible. The First Circuit, concerned that *dicta* in one of their earlier decisions left the impression that a silver platter defense existed concerning the use in their court of state gathered evidence, clearly rejected the silver platter defense. In **U.S. v. Sutherland**, 929 F. 2d 765 (C.A. 1st 1991) the court said they wanted to "curb that speculation." Under the supervisory power there might be an extreme case of federal officers capitalizing on a flagrant abuse by state officers. But that does not create a silver platter defense, they noted. It held: "there is no such exception."

State officers approached two corn-on-the-cob vendors and asked for their business license. They did not have a license so the police arrested them for violating the city code and, upon search incident, found several counterfeit $20 bills. The federal agents were called and the defendants were charged with possession. They sought suppression. California law prohibits arrests for this type of city code violation. Since there was no arrest-search authority, can the federal government use the evidence seized? Though the general rule is that admissibility depends on federal and not state law, **Welsh v. Wisconsin,** (*infra* at Chapter Thirteen) seems to indicate that the state classification of an offense is germane to the Fourth Amendment analysis. And so held the Ninth Circuit in **U.S. v. Mata,** 52 Crim. L. Rep. 1353 (C.A. 9th 1993) in suppressing the use of the counterfeit bills. The decision is dangerous only because it sweeps too broadly. Under federal law the city code violation was not a crime. No general custodial arrest rights exist for non- crimes under **Robinson** and **Gustafson,** both fully discussed in Chapter Eleven.

The state rules are also commands and standards for state law enforcement. State courts also sit to enforce state law. The officer of the state also has an obligation to obey state rules. State policy would also be defeated if the state officer could flout the policy and use the fruits in federal court. If a state actively participates in a federal search and if the determination of its legality is dependent on credibility, is a state foreclosed from using, federally suppressed evidence in the state court action? This was the issue in **People v. Meredith,** 52 Crim. L. Rep. 1354 (Cal. App. 1992). This court felt that since a federal court could make a fresh analysis, a state court has that same right. Thus the state officer who made the arrest and search could testify in the state court action and, if believed, the evidence could be found admissible without violating any principle of *res judicata* or collateral estoppel despite the fact that a federal judge has determined the evidence inadmissible for federal purposes.

SILVER PLATTER REMINDERS

Silver Platter Doctrine
- federal use in federal criminal case
- of state evidence
- illegally gathered
- the gathering of which did not involve the federal officers
- doctrine overruled in **ELKINS**
- *caveat*: some federal courts say if federal law or
- constitution not offended it can be used
- a strict reading of **ELKINS** Intersovereign Silver Platter Doctrine

- **JANIS**
- good faith illegally seized evidence
- by state officers
- usable in federal civil case

Reverse Silver Platter #1

- illegally seized evidence
- by federal office
- no state participation? open question some courts
- sought to be used in state criminal action
- most courts will not allow where seizure
- also violates state law
- some courts allow where non-constitutional violation of Federal law involved

Reverse Silver Platter #2

- legally seized evidence under federal law
- seizure invalid under state law
- use is sought in state criminal action
- split of authority
- some states do not allow in any circumstances
- some states allow as long as state officers are not
- connected with search and seizure (collusion issue)

"Piggy Back" searches

- either federal officer asks state officer to accompany or state officer asks federal officer to accompany
- "piggy back" officer has no independent probable cause and
- search violates that sovereign's search statutes but other sovereigns laws not offended
- many courts permit
- "in aid thereof" statutes complicate area.

VI.   Fruits of the Poisonous Tree

The "fruits of the poisonous tree" doctrine concerns itself with derivative evidence. Evidence derived as the result of governmental exploitation of an independent violation of a substantive constitutional rule. Therefore, exploitation of a prophylactic rule, such as the **Miranda** rule, does not prevent the use of physical evidence or testimony found as a result of the mere failure to properly advise the defendant of his or her rights or even if the police fail to scrupulously honor invoked rights.

However, evidence found as a result of the exploitation of a violation of the Sixth Amendment right to counsel, the Fourteenth Amendment's due process protection against coerced confessions and the Fourth Amendment's privacy protection against illegal searches and seizures, are the focus of the FRUITS doctrine. Evidence so derived, even though "once removed" from the primary illegality is presumed inadmissible. The burden is thus put on the prosecution to overcome this presumption by proving that the tainted evidence (FRUITS) is subject to some approved "taint remover." Tainted evidence may be used in most instances by the prosecutor as impeachment evidence when the defendant chooses to testify. It must also be remembered that only one with standing get the "fruits" protection. Standing, under Supreme Court rules, is personal and may not be asserted vicariously and there is no automatic standing in warrantless search cases. Local rules may change this result.

In a Mississippi case an arrest warrant was issued for Mr. Conerly accusing him of a home burglary. The defendant was arrested and, after being held *in communicado,* he was interrogated after waiving Miranda and he immediately confessed. However, it appears that the arrest was illegal as the warrant appears to have been issued on rumor. If that arrest was illegal then the formal confession, immediately after total isolation, would be fruits of the poisonous tree. The case was remanded to determine the legality of the arrest. **Conerly v. State**, 760 So. 2d 737 (Miss. 2000).

To understand this concept a close reading of **Wong Sun v. United States**, 371 U.S. 471 (1963) is required. Police illegality may directly yield evidence; that is the "poisonous tree." Parlaying that illegality to gather indirectly other evidence is "fruit of the poisonous tree." Thus an illegal arrest of a person is the "poisonous tree" and the evidence taken as a result of the search incident to that illegal arrest is "fruits." Verbal evidence taken as the result of an illegal arrest is also "fruits." Illegally obtained statements are "poisonous tree" and the use of the statements to justify a search is the "fruits" thereof. And, as the Court said in **Wong Sun,** there is "no logical distinction between physical evidence and verbal evidence."

The doctrine is being subjected, like so many others, to re-examination. The Michigan Court of Appeals was faced with a totally illegal vehicular stop. As the police approached the car, the officers recognized for the first time that the driver of the car was one who had several outstanding warrants against him. They arrested him on the prior charges and the defendant consented to a car search and made an inculpatory statement. The court took the logic of illegality and fruits and totally disregarded the theory. Saying that finding this defendant was totally unforeseeable and the subsequent arrest was without the taint found in the average "fruits" case, thus, the evidence gathered was admissible. **People v. Lambert**, 436 N.W. 2d 699 (Mich. Ct. App. 1989).

While searching for drugs upon probable cause, a police officer went outside the scope of such a search and began reading some personal papers. By reading these papers the officer suspected alien-smuggling and began an immediate interrogation that yielded the inculpatory statement "fruits." The Ninth Circuit held that the statements were not saved by any taint remover thus they were inadmissible. **U.S. v. Ramirez-Sandoval**, 872 F. 2d 1392 (C.A. 9th 1989).

But further clarification is needed lest a simple rule be created. Not all "fruits" are inadmissible. Is the evidence the result of the exploitation of that illegality or did it come by means sufficiently distinguishable to be purged of the primary taint? That is the standard to be applied. Unless there is some form of "taint remover" the evidence must be considered inadmissible. The next section deals with the recognized "taint removers."

Clearly a coerced confession that is inadmissible should also be the poisonous tree for any physical evidence derived there from. A coercively or involuntarily taken statement in violation of **Miranda's** voluntariness prong should also yield the same result. Evidence derived from a **Roberson** or **Edwards** violation should be treated the same way. Likewise, failing to scrupulously honor a **Mosely – Miranda** request should also condemn derivative physical evidence. However, because of **Elstad**, it appears that not all violations of **Miranda** where only a prophylactic rule is violated, should cause suppression of derivative evidence. In **Elstad** unwarned statements given, followed by proper warnings and waiver, make all statements made after the proper warnings admissible and not "tainted" by the presumptively compelled pre-waiver statements. The pre-warning and pre-waiver statements are only presumptively compelled and in fact may not, in a pure due process sense, be a result of compulsion.

What **Elstad** does not answer is the role of pre-waiver statements that are not repeated in the post-waiver confession. May those pre-waiver statements be used to secure warrants to search and seize or would they authorize and otherwise validate warrantless search and seizure? If there is an answer from the Supreme Court it must be found in **Michigan v. Tucker**, 417 U.S. 433 (1974) where **Wong Sun** was directly addressed. Tucker was interrogated before **Miranda** was decided but tried after **Miranda** was decided. Police had given all the warnings subsequently required by **Miranda** except that portion dealing with indigency and appointed counsel. The trial court excluded the statement because of **Miranda**. The Supreme Court reversed because the police only violated the prophylactic standards and did not violate the privilege against compulsory self-incrimination. Thus "genuine" compulsion, at 440, was distinguished from presumed compulsion. As a result of Tucker's statement a witness who was supposed to bolster Tucker's story turned out to be a witness that discredited Tucker's version of the day's events. Henderson testified and Tucker was convicted and the fruits of the poisonous tree were at issue. Since there was no genuine compulsion but only **Miranda's** presumed compulsion the Court determined that there was no error in admitting Henderson's testimony. The court felt that the deterrent purpose of the exclusionary rule could not be served by excluding such evidence voluntarily derived. The court, through Rehnquist, said: "Where the official action was pursued in complete good faith, however, the deterrence rationale loses much of its force." **Tucker** at 447. It went on to say: "For when balancing the interests involved, we must weigh the strong interest under any system of justice of making available to the trier of fact all concededly relevant and trustworthy evidence which either party seeks to adduce." **Tucker** at 450.

Broadly read, any violation of **Miranda** can be viewed as merely a prophylactic rule violation and does not require the suppression of derivative evidence. This is the "flag" which all prosecutors should try to capture when the facts do not indicate overreaching by the police. Unless a state court had decided otherwise, a state trial judge who finds a lack of genuine compulsion is well within his or her discretion to rule in favor of admission of the derivative evidence even though the statement itself may not be admissible. However, with the protection given under the Sixth Amendment right to counsel and since that right itself is direct and not derivative, the broad **Tucker** analysis should not be applied to those violations. **Tucker** should only apply to **Miranda's** Fifth Amendment concerns.

Two courts have had occasion to address the **Tucker – Elstad** issue. New Hampshire indicated that it is not deterrence of illegal Fourth Amendment activity that should be the focus. Rather it is deterrence of illegal **Miranda** activity that should be the focus. The defendant told the trooper in the New Hampshire case he was going to need a doctor. The trooper asked why and the defendant indicated he was going to be "coming down" from "coke." The officer asked if he had anymore on him and the defendant said "No." The officer, still without observing **Miranda**, asked the defendant where he did his drugs and the defendant said "I do everything in my bedroom" and admitted that was where he "did" the drugs on this day. The trooper used the "bedroom admission" to secure a warrant. Suppression was denied. New Hampshire's Supreme Court felt there was custodial interrogation without the aid of **Miranda**. It said the issue of physical evidence was left open in **Tucker.** The court

50

also recognized a general reluctance to apply **Wong Sun** in this area citing both **Tucker** and **Elstad**. It said **Elstad** is not applicable because that is a successive-confession case. The court then went on to adopt the position taken by Maine in **State v. Preston**, 411 A. 2d 402 (Me. 1980) that police misconduct in the **Miranda** area will only be deterred if physical evidence derived therefrom is suppressed. This court, therefore, rejected the "mere" violation position taken by the U.S. Supreme Court and invoked New Hampshire's constitution and held that mere violations of **Miranda** require the suppression of derivative physical evidence. **State v. Gravel**, 601 A. 2d 678 (N. H. 1991).

The second case to address the issue came from Illinois and involved a failure to scrupulously honor a Fifth Amendment invocation of counsel under **Miranda**. They took the position that failing to allow the defendant to contact his lawyer before interrogation was no "mere" Miranda violation. Through this conduct police secured a "live" witness used to convict the defendant. This Illinois court, unlike New Hampshire, left rooms for "mere" prophylactic violations and saw the police conduct as being closer to "genuine compulsion" because their facts were more like **Escobedo** and less like **Elstad. People v. Winsett**, 583 N.E. 2d 589 (Ill. App. 1992).

VII. The "Taint Removers" and Other Exceptions: Use of Illegally Seized Evidence in the Government's Case-In-Chief

This section covers the following doctrines which overcome shortcomings in a state's case where police activity affects someone with standing. These doctrines are: (1) Attenuation; (2) Independent source; (3) Inevitable discovery; and the (4) "Good faith exception." If one of these doctrines applies, the government is permitted to use the evidence in its case against the defendant directly. Defense counsel must, therefore, prepare for the suppression hearing as thoroughly as he or she would for trial because it is at the suppression hearing that the case will most likely be lost or won from the defense perspective. The police conduct of the case is not a jury triable issue in the Fourth Amendment context. Once the judge deems the evidence admissible, it comes in, in that condemnatory manner without explanation as to the "taint."

The **first** taint remover is that of **attenuation**. Though not the first case in the area, the decision that most clearly states the attenuation doctrine is **Taylor v. Alabama**, 475 U.S. 687 (1982). Basically, attenuation answers the question whether and under what circumstances a prior illegality can be erased causing what would normally be considered "fruits" to be admissible. Simply stated if a combination of the passage of time and a break in the flow or stream of events is sufficient, then information or evidence acquired after the initial illegality will be deemed admissible. **Taylor** emphasized the concept of "break in the flow" that had been overlooked by several courts, including the Alabama court. There is no clear point in time which can be said to be enough, thus, the most significant factor has to be the "break in flow." When can it be said that the police have provided "breathing space?" Depending upon the totality of the circumstances, including the intelligence and sophistication of the defendant, that time may be minutes or it may be hours.

I am not positive that the U. S. Supreme Court would agree with the New York Court that an illegally arrested defendant, put in the back seat of a patrol car and within 3 to 5 minutes of the initial arrest could make a voluntary and knowing decision to abandon a gun. There was obviously no "break in the flow." But when it involves confessions, New York's analysis is on target. **People v. Harris**, 72 N.Y. 2d 614 (N.Y. 1988). Though **Taylor** focused on arrest and confession, as can be seen from the New York case the attenuation issue can be encountered in any context. For example where a **Miranda**-violation obtained statement is used to provide probable cause for a warrant or where an illegally arrested person gives consent to be searched are but other examples of "fruits" cases.

The Court has not strayed far from the attenuation doctrine first announced in **Nardone v. U.S.,** 308 U.S. 338 (1939), and most recently upheld in **Hayes v. Florida**, 470 U.S. 811 (1985) where fingerprints of the defendant were ruled inadmissible because there was an arrest without probable cause, no consent, no hearing. A somewhat unusual case of attenuation is that of **U.S. v. Ceccolini**, 435 U.S. 268 (1978). A live witness was discovered as the result of an unintentional search. The witness' existence was not revealed to the F.B.I. until the next day. It was considerable time before the F.B.I. contacted the witness and it was three years before this willing witness appeared on the stand. The Court upheld the admission of the witness' testimony.

In **Com. v. Gallant**, 381 Mass. 465, 410 N.E. 2d 1021 (1980) a defendant's right to remain silent was violated when the police showed him an accomplice's statement. That defendant signed a statement of his own. This illegally obtained statement rather than the first legally obtained statement was shown to a third defendant. This defendant had not specifically waived nor had he invoked his rights. The court said the use of the invalid statement on this third defendant was "fruits" but, using both attenuation and independent source, the Supreme Judicial Court disagreed with the trial judge that had suppressed the third defendant's statement by citing **Ceccolini** saying that his constitutional rights were not violated.

The South Dakota Supreme Court recognized a separate ground other than attenuation, etc., to cut off the taint of the poisonous tree. In their view an independent, efficient, intervening cause can supersede the taint. Police in this case had an arrest warrant and violated statutory "knock and announce." The defendant heard the police coming down the stairs. Thinking they were other than police, he grabbed a loaded shotgun. The uniformed officer approached and the defendant threatened to shoot and kill the officer. The second officer arrived and disarmed the defendant. Since the first officer had made no threatening moves, defendant's reaction in resisting an unlawful arrest was excessive, thus, the court held the claim of causation was broken and his words and actions for this charge were properly admissible. **State v. Miskimins**, 435 N.W. 2d 217 (So. Dak. 1989). The use of an illegal road block that yields, without attenuation, a consent to search causes the consent to be invalid. **State v. Williamson**, 772 P. 2d 404 (Ore. 1989).

The North Dakota court does an excellent job of explaining attenuation to its courts. In **State v. Gregg**, 615 N.W. 2d 515 (N. D. 2000), the police searched the motel room of the defendant without a warrant and without consent. Drugs were discovered, but the police did not arrest Gregg nor did they take the drugs. The police left the premises. Gregg, not long after, left his room, got into his car and began to drive. Some distance from his motel, the officer who had determined that Gregg and another had suspended licenses, stopped the car. Gregg was seized for the suspension. A hypodermic needle was seen on the floorboard. It was determined no one was a diabetic. A quick search revealed a clear plastic bag with white powdery contents. Gregg was then arrested. A full search followed. Gregg gave the officers a second crack at the motel evidence by driving on a suspended license. That was an act of free will. The heart of attenuation is, that despite an earlier police illegality, the defendant, often of his own free will chose to act. In this case the illegal search was not the "but for" cause of the discovery of the evidence in the car. The "but for" in this case was driving under suspension.

Can we agree with the court? To be sure, the officers obtained the names while an illegal search was in progress. Of the three men in that room, two had suspended licenses. But that information was not volunteered by the men. That information came from a database to which the police had lawful access. The police did not inform the men of that discovery but left the motel in the hope that the men would leave the motel and the driver would be one of the two men who had suspended licenses. In this posture, the three men had survived an illegal search. They, without a police presence, had a chance to formulate a plan. They could have flushed the evidence. They did not do that. They could have stayed put. They did not do that. They could have chosen the one licensed driver to drive the car. Sufficient time had passed to form a plan. The plan they chose was the wrong plan but it was not a police plan. There was sufficient time intervening between the illegal act and their chosen path to qualify under attenuation.

The **second** "taint" remover is the **inevitable discovery** doctrine. First, the doctrine acknowledges illegal police activity. Second, the heart of the rule is that the state must prove that the evidence would have been found without the unlawful activity and how that discovery would have occurred. Many see the rule in these terms: "The defendant is entitled to be as well off as if there was no unlawful seizure but he is not entitled to be any better off." **State v. Byone**, 595 S.W. 2d 301 (Mo. Ct. App. 1979). Official constitutional recognition came in **Nix v. Williams**, 467 U.S. 432 (1984). In doing so the Court rejected LaFave's position that the state must prove no bad faith in the attempt to accelerate the discovery of the evidence in question. This, the Court said, is not required.

The Court said if the prosecution can establish by a preponderance of the evidence that the information ultimately or inevitably would have been discovered by lawful means then the deterrence rationale has little meaning. The state should not be put in a worse position than it would have occupied without any police misconduct. Exclusion of physical evidence that would inevitably have been discovered adds nothing to either the integrity or fairness of a criminal trial. When inevitably discovered, without reference to the police error or misconduct, there is no *nexus* sufficient to provide a taint and the evidence is admissible.

The preponderance standard alluded to above would only be provable, as LaFave indicates, by the prosecution showing how the discovery would have been made. He tracks the philosophy of the New York Court of Appeals where it refused to accept the proposition that every warrantless non-exigent seizure automatically would be legitimized by assuming the hypothetical alternative. It felt that without the deterrent effect of the exclusionary rule constitutional protection would be in shambles. **People v. Knapp,** 439 N.Y. S. 2d 871 (N.Y. 1981).

Does the following case represent a hypothecated discovery case? Assuming the trial court was correct in disbelieving the officer's plain smell story of probable cause to search the car, the Missouri Supreme Court also found that the officer had sufficient reason not to allow the defendant to drive his car and also had reason to custodially arrest the defendant and impound his car. With such an impoundment would have come an inventory which would have yielded the marijuana found in this case. They felt the evidence should not have been suppressed because the trial court should have applied the inevitable discovery doctrine. In so deciding, Missouri became one of the first courts to apply inevitable discovery to an inventory case. **State v. Milliorn**, 45 Crim. L. Rep. 1402 (Mo. 1990).

From January 1, 1999 to December 1, 2000, no fewer than 21 opinions discussing inevitable discovery were written by appellate courts. Eight defendants won. The first defendant was Mr. Robb. The Minnesota court talks in terms of eventuality; that despite the disputed police conduct the evidence would eventually have been discovered. An arrest took place away from the vehicle searched and not "from the vehicle." Therefore, there were no grounds for a **Belton** search incident and it was not consented to. There were no grounds to impound the car thus an inventory would have been out of the question. Finally, denial of consent to search is never grounds for probable cause. Therefore, no case of inevitable discovery was present here. **State v. Robb**, 605 N.W. 2d 96 (Minn. 2000).

Without properly addressing the **Bostick** issue, a Washington court seems to say police cannot peacefully approach a person, state their suspicions, and ask for a consent to search. The consent in this case was done in an open area and not even in close confines, as in **Bostick**. While asking for consent, the other officer performed a wants and warrant check and it came up positive. Thus, the state argued inevitable discovery. The court said no to that argument. Why? There was no evidence that the police would have followed "predictive police behavior." This is a very questionable decision. **State v. Reyes**, 993 P. 2d 921 (Wash. App. 2d 2000).

The third winner comes from Indiana. This defendant complained that the inventory of his car was improper and the handgun found should have been excluded. Bartruff was stopped for going 57 m.p.h. in a 55 m.p.h. speed zone. Before a warning was issued, the driver told police he had a suspended license. The officer confirmed this with his computer. Bartruff was asked for a consent but refused to sign the consent form. The officer decided to impound the car, disregarding the right of a citizen to refuse to give a consent and because the car was a hazard to traffic. The passenger also did not have a valid driver's license. The officer started the inventory before the tow truck arrived and the handgun was found and it also was "unlicensed." So what is wrong? Pretext! Since the driver was at the scene of the inventory, locally mandated procedures would call for allowing the owner to retrieve his personal property. Since those procedures were not followed, the inventory was bad. It was also improperly conducted because it was done at the scene without an exigency (also a locally mandated rule). Since both men were sober and capable of retrieving their property there would not have been an inevitable, proper inventory. **Bartruff v. State**, 706 N.E.

2d 225 (Ind. App. 1999). This is a well reasoned opinion based on the state's particular inventory rules.

The next case comes from Ohio where blood samples were drawn without a warrant. The trial court used inevitable discovery doctrine to allow admission because probable cause preexisted the intrusions. Be that as it may, there was no exigency to bypass the standard procedure. But the error was harmless beyond a reasonable doubt. **State v. Coyle**, 2000 WL 283073 (Ohio App. 4th) (unpub. op.). As this case ably points out, even when a taint remover is not available, the prosecution should explore the ultimate fail-safe device: the constitutional harmless error doctrine.

In an Arkansas case, the police had a warrant to search the defendant's house. As they arrived at the house they saw the defendant driving away. They followed and stopped him to ask him to return to his house and told him why. He was ordered from his car and a substance fell from the car when he got out. This warrantless stop was not authorized. The evidence from the car was not inevitably discovered and it was not harmless error. The car was not included in the warrant and the alleged drug sale took place in the house and not from the car. No **Terry** basis existed for the stop. **Colbert v. State**, 12 S.W.3d 162 (Ark. 2000).

Police in Mississippi responded to a report that a truck was blocking the travel lane and the officer responded. As the officer arrived he saw a person, not the driver, take an open bottle of an alcoholic beverage from the bed of the pickup truck and toss it in the cab. The driver was ordered out and frisked. Nothing was discovered. The officer then searched the cab and found a gun. That led to a more thorough search whereupon drugs were found. The lower court used inevitable discovery to save the evidence which was upheld by the appeals court. The Mississippi Supreme Court was unable to figure out how drugs inside a pill bottle inside a passenger compartment underneath a jacket would have been legally discovered, inevitably. The court apparently does not follow **Belton v. N.Y.** (discussed in Chapter Thirteen). The **Terry** frisk and the **Long** frisk of the car gave probable cause. The **Belton** issue was not addressed except by way of saying that handcuffing both men prevented evidence from being destroyed. **White v. State**, 735 So. 2d 221 (Miss. 1999).

The California high court has also decided an inevitable discovery case. A warrantless search of the defendant's garage turned up a stolen car. Why were the police at his address? They were there to conduct a search of a co-tenant's rooms pursuant to the probation terms of that co-tenant. A probationer cannot consent to searches of areas he does not control – he has no standing. Thus there were no grounds for the inevitable discovery search. **People v. Robles**, 3 P.3d 311 (Cal. 2000). This reasoning is unassailable.

In another case, a gun (discovered during a legal search) was found inadmissible because there was no evidence to lead the police to believe that probable cause existed. **State v. Garza**, 1999 WL 562111 (Minn. App.) (unpub. op.). A gun, by itself and with no other facts, is not automatically evidence of a crime.

The following decisions found inevitable discovery:

1. UTAH: **State v. James**, 2000 WL 1459715 (Utah) Accepts but has not yet filled in all the blanks.
   M.V. v. State, 977 P. 2d 494 (Utah App. 1999) Knife felt during an improper pat-down would have been discovered at the juvenile detention facility.
   State v. Topanotes, 2000 WL 1677217 (Utah App.) Invalid stop (no articulable suspicion) but wants and warrants check would have and did turn up outstanding warrants – remand to trial court for inevitable discovery analysis.

2. WISCONSIN: 2000 WL 1292691 (Wis. App.) (unpub. op.) Unconsented to search during a consented-to search, because of circumstances of all the other drugs found in the room, because the police had probable cause to arrest and search incident to that search.

3. MAINE: **State v. St. Yves**, 751 A. 2d 1018 (Me. 2000). D was convicted of manslaughter. Remains of the body were found due to un-**Mirandized** statements but the body would have been found by lawful means.

4. ARKANSAS: **Miller v. State,** 27 S.W. 3d 427 (Ark. 2000) Marijuana growing in a backyard that could be seen from any neighbor's house meant that the arguably illegal presence of police in backyard would have been inevitably discovered evidence.

5. NEW JERSEY: **State v. Hinton**, 754 A. 2d 576 (N.J. Super. 2000). Trooper illegally entered car and found a wallet showing that the driver and passenger had given a false name. This would have been revealed upon a wants and warrants check when the plate and the names were "run."

6.   <u>MINNESOTA</u>: **Tracht v. Comm. Pub. Safety**, 592 N.W. 2d 863 (Minn. App. 1999). Illegal entry of home by police following an auto accident participant revealed nothing that would not have been found upon "running" his address and vehicle plate.

7.   <u>OHIO</u>: **State v. Reddish**, 1999 WL 819575 (Ohio App. 2) (unpub. op.). Evidence known before illegal search would have been enough, on its own, to justify the issuance of a warrant and thus no "fruits" under **Nix**.

8.   <u>HAWAII</u>: **State v. Silva**, 979 P. 2d 1137 (Haw. App. 1999). An inventory search at stationhouse after a legitimate arrest would have led to the discovery of drugs found upon earlier pre-P.C. search.

9.   <u>DISTRICT OF COLUMBIA</u>: **Hicks v. U.S.**, 730 A. 2d 657 (D.C. App. 1999). Finding the shot gun during an illegal stop before eyewitness arrived did not taint the evidence.

10.   <u>ALASKA</u>: **Smith v. State**, 992 P. 2d 605 (Alaska App. 1999). Court does not have to use the doctrine unless an illegal search or seizure has taken place.

11.   <u>MARYLAND</u>: **Wilson v. State**, 752 A. 2d 1250 (Md. App. 2000). Even assuming the prior warrant was invalid; DNA characteristics would inevitably be discovered by virtue of new search warrant for D's blood.

12.   <u>MICHIGAN</u>: **People v. Stevens**, 597 N.W. 2d 53 (Mich. 1999). This is perhaps the most important decision by a state court to date. The police have a warrant but do not have an exigency to avoid "knock and announce" statute but enter anyway, without knocking and announcing. Should the exclusionary rule bar the evidence? No, although the entry was illegal, the search and why they were there were not the product of that illegality. The exclusionary rule, the court reminds us, was not meant to put the prosecution in a worse position than if the police improper conduct had not occurred–the prosecutor cannot be put in a better position. Unless the "knock and announce" statute itself demands suppression, which in this case it did not even mention the issue, suppression is *not* the remedy.

The **next** "taint" remover to be considered is that of **independent source**. The first case to be considered is **Silverthorne Lumber Co. v. U.S.**, 251 U.S. 385 (1920). An illegal search produced information that led to the issuance of some subpoenas which the Silverthorne's refused to obey. It was in this case that the doctrine of "independent source" was introduced. The Court said:

> "Of course this does not mean that the facts thus obtained become sacred and inaccessible. If knowledge of them is gained from an independent source they may be proved like any others, but the knowledge gained by the government's own wrong cannot be used in the way proposed."

The doctrine did not receive much attention until the end of the Burger era. In **Segura v. U.S.**, 468 U.S. 796 (1984), the Court had to decide whether an earlier illegal entry required suppression of evidence. The police entered, arrested the persons present, and secured the premises while awaiting a warrant that did not come until 19 hours later. The Court held that the subsequent search of the apartment the following day under the valid search warrant issued wholly on information known to the officers before the entry into the apartment need not have been suppressed as "fruit" of the illegal search because the warrant and the information on which it was based were unrelated to the entry and therefore constituted an independent source under **Silverthorne**.

The next major development of independent source came in the 1988 Supreme Court decision of **Murray v. U.S.**, 487 U.S. 533 (1988). The court held that independent source can save evidence discovered by police during an illegal search if rediscovered during the execution of a valid search warrant. The warrant, to be valid, must be unrelated to the prior illegality, from the viewpoint of both the magistrate who issues it and the officers who seek it. This is the fruition of the "no worse position" rationale of the independent source doctrine. Nothing illegally gained can be presented to the magistrate and the police officer's decision to get the warrant must not be influenced by what they learned during the illegal entry. The Court thus took **Segura** to its next level – no indicia of proper conduct can even be ascribed to the earlier entry in this case whereas in **Segura** they were at least waiting for a warrant.

A close reading of **Murray** would indicate a "what the magistrate doesn't know won't hurt him" rule. What if the police inform the magistrate of the prior illegal entry? This was the issue faced by a California Appeals Court. A residential search warrant obtained after an illegal entry and "walk-through" of the premises may be upheld, the court said, even if the police have told the issuing magistrate about what they saw during their improper intrusion. The key for the California Court was not the "telling" but rather that the police present enough information from legitimate independent sources to provide probable cause. **People v. Angulo**, 244 Cal. Rep. 819 (Cal. Dist. Ct. App. 1988).

In a Utah case, the appeals court said that evidence observed in plain view during an illegal entry and later seized pursuant to a valid warrant based upon independent information may be admissible under either the independent source or inevitable discovery doctrine. **State v. Van Holten**, 43 Crim. L. Rep. 2231 (Utah Ct. App. 1988). The Colorado case adopting **Murray** was **People v. Schoondermark**, 717 P. 2d 504 (Colo. 1988).

Another California court has held that it is not enough merely to excise illegally obtained information from a warrant. Even if independent probable cause exists without the taint, the court said there is a burden on the state to show that first, the officers would have sought a warrant even if they had not earlier entered the premises; and second, that the magistrate would have issued the warrant had the tainted information not been presented to the magistrate. The second step may be satisfied by calling the magistrate as a witness or the state may argue from the facts and circumstances that it is unlikely that the magistrate was influenced in favor of issuing the warrant by the tainted information. **People v. Koch**, 257 Cal. Rep. 483 (Cal. Dist. Ct. App. 1989).

A few cases involving the independent source doctrine came down from state high courts in 2000. They are: **People v. Morley**, 4 P.3d 1078 (Colo. *en banc* 2000); **State v. Thibodeau**, 747 A. 2d 596 (Me. 2000); **State v. Shively**, 999 P. 2d 259 (Kan. 2000); **State v. Therriault**, 2000 WL 1728702 (Mont.); and **State v. Gregg**, 615 N.W. 2d 515 (N. D. 2000).

The **Morley** case involved an "awaiting warrant-early entry" case. They entered five minutes too early. The court held that the rule announced in **Murray v. U.S.**, 487 U.S. 533 (1988) was the case to use. The suppression order should have been reversed by the court of appeals and no remand was needed for further fact-finding. In the **Thibodeau** case, probable cause already existed but an officer was sent to get the address perfect for the warrant. For some reason he knocked on the door. When he received no answer he twisted the door knob and the door opened. He saw the marijuana plants. He closed the door and called in the exact address and reported he saw the marijuana plants. Like Colorado, Maine relies heavily on **Murray** and emphasizes that nothing seen was used by the officer seeking the warrant. The **Shively** case addresses the issue whether a bad no-knock entry poisons a warrant based on information unrelated to that entry. The second warrant was upheld under **Murray**. In the Montana case it was determined that despite the unlawful entry the officer received independent incriminating information from Therriault's sister which was enough to receive a warrant for a proper independent source entry and search. Finally, in the case from North Dakota the issue concerned drugs and drug paraphernalia found in the defendant's car. The problem, however, was whether the source was the earlier illegal entry of D's motel room or not. It could have been but the stop of the car was lawful, the arrest was lawful and the inventory was lawful. Therefore, there was an independent source.

The **final** doctrine to be considered in this section is **"good faith."** Probable cause cases tell us that we must give the police "fair leeway" when judging probable cause. If we are already giving the police leeway is there any need to add a "good faith" exception to the mixture? If good faith has a place should it be the good faith of the police in determining probable cause or should it be limited to reliance based conduct? **Stacey v. Emery**, 97 U.S. 642 (1878) taught us that neither malice nor good faith is relevant. That static position would change as to reliance but not as to probable cause. Why? Reliance is an act of faith; probable cause is a matter of motive.

First, consider **Giordenello v. U.S.**, 357 U.S. 480 (1958). Typical of cases of the time, the Court focused not on the issuance of the warrant by the magistrate. The whole case turned on inadequacy. Next came **Beck v. Ohio**, 379 U.S. 89 (1964). The good faith issue was brought up. They said: "We may assume that the officer acted in 'good faith' in arresting petitioner. But 'good faith' on the part of the arresting officer is not enough...If subjective good faith alone were the test, the protection of the Fourth Amendment would evaporate and the people would be secure...only in the discretion of the police." Therefore, the Court was unwilling to engraft a "good faith-motive" exception onto the Fourth Amendment.

Next, consider **Michigan v. DeFillippo**, 443 U.S. 31 (1979). The officer relied on an ordinance that was not facially invalid but turned out to be declared invalid at a subsequent time. The Court said the officer was not required to anticipate that a court would later hold the ordinance unconstitutional. This law was not so grossly and flagrantly unconstitutional that any person of reasonable prudence would be bound to see its flaws. This case, of course, comported with the first good faith-reliance case of **Pierson v. Ray**, 386 U.S. 547 (1967); see also **U.S. v. Peltier**, 422 U.S. 531 (1975) (reliance on prior consistent U.S. Court of Appeals decisions) and most recently **Illinois v. Krull**, 480 U.S. 340 (1987) affirming **DeFillippo**.

The stage of development not covered by the Court was good faith-reliance and warrant issuance. This would come in **U.S. v. Leon**, 468 U.S. 897 (1984). Here there was a warrant that was supported by an affidavit that was more detailed than the one in **Giordenello**. The warrant issued, the search was conducted, and then the warrant was later determined to be invalid. Can the police rely in good faith on the judgment of a neutral and detached magistrate? Yes. The Court said the Fourth Amendment's exclusionary rule was intended to prevent official misconduct; substantial and deliberate misconduct. But not all evidence so obtained is kept out even under a rule without a good faith exception (standing, impeachment, and grand jury use of excludable evidence).

If the magistrate has not relied on reckless falsities (done to uphold **Franks v. Delaware** [*infra*]), nor acted as a rubber stamp (**Aguilar** and **Lo Ji Sales**), and has not relied on mere conclusions, (**Spinelli**), then the police should be able to rely on the magistrate's determination of probable cause as long as the police acted within the scope of the warrant so issued. Once the warrant issues, the Court noted, there is literally nothing more the police can do in seeking to comply with the law. Police reliance, however, must be objectively reasonable. Finally the Court said, "In the absence of an allegation that the magistrate abandoned his detached and neutral role (**Lo Ji Sales** [infra]) suppression is appropriate only if the officers were dishonest or reckless in preparing their affidavit or could not have harbored an objectively reasonable belief in the existence of probable cause." See also **Massachusetts v. Shepard**, discussed in the warrant materials of Chapter Three. Thus the Court has determined that the probable cause standard is enough leeway in the warrantless situation but close calls plus good faith and reasonable reliance on a magistrate's decision can be used in the warrant area.

The court that may best understand the goal of **Leon** is the high court of Maryland. They understand that the goal is to encourage police to use the process and not to discourage warrant seeking. This court well understands that in fact the warrant in such cases does not state probable cause even though the police fairly believed in it. When the issuing magistrate misses the call and issues a warrant why punish the police? The Maryland court points out a little used or understood passage from **Illinois v. Gates** where the Supreme Court said: " A grudging or negative attitude by reviewing courts toward warrants is inconsistent with the Fourth Amendment's strong preference for searches conducted pursuant to a warrant; courts should not invalidate warrants by interpreting affidavits in a hyper-technical   rather than a common sense manner." They echo **Ventresca** where Justice Douglas said "call close plays" in favor of the magistrate's decision. Only clear errors or clear abuses of discretion should be attacked.

What defense attorneys want and do not get is the ability to use the lack of probable cause as proof of bad faith. It does not work that way if **Leon** is properly applied. The lack of probable cause is the reason **Leon** is the next step. The focus in **Leon** is on the neutrality of the judge, the lack of intentional falsehoods (or critical omissions), and more than a merely conclusory affidavit. If a bad warrant passes the **Franks, Lo Ji Sales** and **Spinelli** tests then the call goes to the police. **Leon** puts teeth into **Ventresca's** mouth, so to speak. For those who do not understand **Leon** this decision is an excellent textbook on the subject. **West v. State**, 2001 WL 220238 (Md. App.).

Colorado, though more briefly, echoes Maryland and it lists the four key factors surrounding the **Leon** call. It says **Leon** does not save warrants: (1) Based on deliberately false affidavits; (2) Issuer wholly abandoned the neutral and detached role; (3) The warrant is so facially deficient that the executing officer cannot reasonably determine the warrant is valid; and (4).That the affidavit is so lacking in indicia of probable cause that official belief in its existence is unreasonable. **People v. Gall**, 2001 WL 209780 (Colo.).

The Ninth Circuit was faced with a case of reliance where "knock and announce" was waived and a surreptitious entry was approved. The magistrate did some crossing out on a standard warrant form but he went too far. Would good faith be applicable? Yes. The magistrate told the officers he made the necessary changes and the fault was his not that of the police. **U.S. v. Freitas**, 856 F. 2d 1425 (C.A. 9th 1988).

The Arkansas Supreme Court saved an invalid warrant under good faith in **Starr v. State**, 759 S.W. 2d 535 (Ark. 1988). The warrant was signed by a court clerk rather than the magistrate as was required by state law.

A Missouri appellate court tersely sums up **Leon** by saying: "Because we encourage law enforcement officers to obtain warrants before conducting searches, it would be inappropriate for us to undermine such encouragement by requiring the second guessing of a magistrate's determination." **State v. Pattie**, 2001 WL 205989 (Mo. App. E.D.).

Saying that "We simply cannot accept the **Leon** court's conclusion," Connecticut rejected outright the good faith exception. This court felt that **Leon** does nothing to encourage good police work; in fact, it encourages sloppy police work and said it would not accept a "close-enough-is-good-enough" rule. **State v. Marsala**, 579

A. 2d 58 (Conn. 1990). But of course Connecticut does not appear to understand the true function of **Leon**.

If properly read, **Leon** and the good faith exception has no application when the magistrate issues a warrant on a facially invalid affidavit as seen in **Spinelli**. Such was the conclusion of the Pennsylvania Supreme Court in **Com. v. Melilli**, 555 A. 2d 1106 (Pa. 1989). This is one of the tests the affidavit must pass for **Leon** to apply.

The good faith doctrine has been involved in "omitted list or items" cases. In a California case the affidavit listed things which unfortunately did not get duplicated in the warrant. The officer read both documents but failed to realize the lack of incorporation. The court called this an understandable mistake based on good faith. **People v. Alvarez**, 257 Cal. Rep. 445 (Cal. Dist. Ct. App. 1989). Nebraska, on the other hand, said a B-B gun listed in the warrant but omitted from the affidavit could not be saved by the good faith exception. This, of course, makes sense since the warrant had no factual basis to include the B-B gun. **State v. Parmar**, 437 N. W. 2d 503 (Neb. 1989).

The Tenth Circuit refused to extend the **Leon** good-faith exception to a warrantless search saying that **Leon** clearly applied only to searches with a warrant. **U.S. v. Scales**, 903 F. 2d 765 (C.A. 10th 1990). Such a request should not be surprising not only because police want such an extension of the exception but also because several courts, in warrant cases, have said that the focus in good faith cases is on the police information and not the judge's reasonableness. This court faithfully follows **Leon's** limits.

In the "reliance on the past status of appellate rules of courts" context, two significant cases came down from Wisconsin and Iowa. Both states had U.S. Supreme Court decisions that impacted their Fourth Amendment jurisprudence. Wisconsin's high court had taken the position that police were never required to knock and announce when executing a drug search warrant. That policy was struck down by the U.S. Supreme Court in **Richards v. Wisconsin**, 520 U.S. 385 (1997). However, for the brief period that **Richards** was the law of Wisconsin police departments relied on that announcement. How should those no-knock cases be handled regarding suppression? The other taint removers require remands and hearings (independent source or inevitable discovery). The easiest solution to Wisconsin's problem is to use the good faith reliance exception created in **Illinois v. Krull**, 480 U.S. 340 (1987). The exclusionary rule is a Court created rule and not a personal right created by the Fourteenth Amendment due process clause. It is thus intended to prevent police abuse not repair it. Competing policies must be evaluated because the rule is not absolute.

Thus, Wisconsin says, there is nothing to prevent; there is no valid remedial objective to be served by not using the **Krull** decision. **Krull** requires good faith reliance upon statutes and appellate decisions. The officers relied on "our pronouncement" the court noted. How can an officer be charged with unlawfulness if they faithfully followed our rule, the court asks. They closed by saying that law enforcement officers and magistrates must be allowed to reasonably rely upon "the pronouncements of the court."

The issue in Iowa was whether the law the police supposedly relied upon was indeed the law. The Iowa case was centered on the practices condemned in **Knowles v. Iowa,** 525 U.S. 113 (1998). An Iowa statute gave a search incident right to the police officers to conduct a search upon the issuance of a mere civil citation for a traffic violation. **Knowles** reminds everyone that search incident only applied to arrests for crimes. The prosecution in **State v. Scott**, 2000 WL 1714565 (Iowa), just as the Wisconsin prosecutor, argued good faith reliance. The Iowa court dealt the prosecutor a double-blow knockout punch. First, it said the law relied on in **Knowles** was never the law and second, we do not follow **Krull** and its good faith exception and said read our decision in **State v. Cline**, 617 N.W. 2d 277 (Iowa 2000). But did they go further and reject all good faith exceptions? It said: "We hold that searches and seizures cannot be upheld on a good-faith basis, and on retrial, the defendant shall have an opportunity to challenge them." What does such a holding say? It says police will need a lawyer or two at their side whenever they would like to rely on a statute that is not facially invalid. Iowa's court has gone from the court that gave us the inevitable discovery exception to a very pro-defendant court. Time will tell what impact that has on law enforcement and crime rates in Iowa. The court is taking a due process approach and has abandoned an exclusionary rule approach. Who is right? Wisconsin or Iowa?

During the routine traffic stop the police will conduct a "wants and warrants" check on the car and its driver. The modern era connects the officer with a computer data bank that will yield information that contains all forms of warrants that are outstanding and this will not be limited to vehicular crimes. Suppose an officer gets information indicating that an outstanding arrest warrant exists as to the driver. Is the officer justified in making the arrest and conducting the search incident of both the arrestee and the passenger compartment of his car? If the warrant was and remains valid the answer is yes. However, what is the result if the warrant was no longer valid? The answer is that the arrest was unlawful and therefore the search incident is unlawful. Can the "good faith" doctrine of **Leon** be applied?

The **Leon** "good faith" issue presents a more difficult problem. Maryland's highest court addressed this issue and they provide a well reasoned answer. It felt that **Whiteley v. Warden**, 401 U.S. 560 (1971) as applied through **U.S. v. Hensley**, 469 U.S. 221 (1985) provides that answer. As the court noted, **Whiteley** held that "an arrest predicated on a warrant of which the arresting officer learned by radio was invalid because the warrant was not supported by probable cause" and that **Hensley** says the arresting officer acts at his own risk whether the information he relied on was valid and that **Whiteley** was not affected by **Hensley**. In the Maryland case a valid warrant indeed had been issued. However, it had already been served and the problem was cleared up before this arrest. The police had failed to "clear" the warrant from the computer database. That, however, was not the end of the problem. Reality is a part of the process. The reality is that there will be gaps in processes. When can it be said that an officer is negligent in relying on the radio or computer report? When can it be said that the department becomes negligent in failing to remove such information? The Maryland court recognized these realities. The state put on no evidence that this seven day delay was required or, at least, not negligent. The court cited a case from the District of Columbia where a four day delay (with a two day weekend) was not negligent and **Leon** therefore applied. **Ott v. State**, 600 A. 2d 111 (Md. 1992). See also **Childress v. U.S.** 381 A. 2d 614 (D.C. Ct. App. 1977).

The most recent "good faith" reliance decision from the U.S. Supreme Court is **Arizona v. Evans**, 514 U.S. 1 (1995). In this case, during a lawful traffic stop, a "wants and warrants" check was run that revealed an outstanding arrest or bench warrant. The defendant claimed he "cleared that up" but the officer did not believe him. Evans was arrested and evidence of a crime was discovered. In fact, the warrant had been "cleared" but not from the computer maintained by the local court. Since the police had no control over that data bank they were permitted to reasonably rely on the information and act appropriately.

Clearly then, **Arizona v. Evans** only addresses database s controlled by non-law enforcement agencies and *only* because the primary purpose of the exclusionary rule was created to defer Fourth Amendment violation by the law enforcement community. As the Court notes, courts and court clerks are "not adjuncts to the law enforcement team..." as they are not "engaged in ferreting out crime..." since they "have no stake in the outcome of particular prosecutions." Unless it can be proven that the court's system is so bad that no officer could be found to have acted reasonably when relying on the computer record the seizure and its fruits should be admissible.

More recent cases have indicated a willingness to accept the *court database* feature of **Evans**. Colorado accepted **Evans** in **People v. Blehm** *et al*, 983 P. 2d 779

(Colo. *en banc* 1999). A co-defendant of Blehm, James Saint-Veltri, was arrested on a warrant that was invalid due to a mixup between the county and district courts. A warrant had been vacated but this was not communicated to the police and no evidence existed that the police were unreasonable in relying upon the warrant. Thus **Evans** and its rule were adopted.

A more perplexing case comes from Ohio through **State v. Silcott**, 1999 WL 100072 (Ohio App. 2) (unpub. op.) A bench warrant was issued April 25, 1996 and that was entered by the court clerk into court and police computerized records. The matter was resolved on May 15, 1996. The clerk removed the item from the court computer but did not remove it from the police records "as should have been done." Eighteen months later, responding to a child abuse call the police took control of the scene, got everyone's names and they ran a computer check which reveals the warrant of April 25, 1996. Silcott was arrested and searched and cocaine was found. The trial court used *Evans* and did not suppress. On appeal the defense argued there was a duty to verify the information in its computerized records. The appellate court answered this by stating: " The State was not required to rebut the suggestion that its failure to verify the information that the clerk provided rendered the seizure and subsequent search of Silcott unreasonable, absent some showing that such information was on prior occasions to be inaccurate for similar reasons. No such showing was made." The court relied heavily on that portion of **Evans** that dealt with the issue of court negligence. See **Arizona v. Evans**, 514 U.S. 1 at page 15 and 16 where the court discusses the evidence presented by the court clerk to the effect that such errors only occur one every three or four years.

Another judicial branch database case arose in **People v. Downing**, 40 Cal. Rep. 2d 176 (Cal. App 4th 1995) . It agreed that the focus of the exclusionary rule is to deter police misconduct, not to correct judicial error. This case involved a search waiver signed by Downing when he accepted a probated sentence. When the police conducted this search the probation had expired but still "existed" in the court supplied database because clerks failed to "clear it." A year had gone by since the expiration. The court held that the error here was solely caused by the superior court. The "log" told the officer that the probation had two more years before expiration. Nothing told the officer to check further. The court made one interesting observation where they wrote: "In this fast-paced, computerized society, it is absurd to require a police officer to exhaust all avenues of investigation and corroboration when he had no objective reason to question facially valid computer data produced by other than the collective law enforcement department in front of him." In fact in this case even if the officer called the court clerk he would have obtained the same information.

Yes, this is a "fast-paced, computerized society." Several state agencies feed information from their data banks to police, prosecutors and even into national data banks such as the NCIC. Are these agencies law enforcement agencies – that they "ferret out crime?" Consider **Bunse v. State**, 661 So. 2d 389 (Fla. App. 5th 1995) and its conclusion that the Missouri Motor Vehicle Bureau was not a law enforcement agency under **Evans**. The case is quite simple. An officer made a stop of a pick-up truck because no tag was displayed on the rear of the truck. Bunse said it was registered in Missouri and that no tag was required on the rear but on the front as permitted under Missouri law. To check this out the officer accessed Missouri through the FCIC/NCIC computer. Missouri indicated no record of that tag as assigned. The VIN was checked revealing a totally different tag than the one displayed. The arrest ensued and cocaine was found upon the search incident. Florida's first reaction to **Evans** was **State v. White**, 660 So. 2d 664 (Fla. 1995) which adopted a "collective knowledge" rule that holds police accountable for computer errors *if* the computer is under the control of law enforcement but not those compiled by non-law enforcement agencies. Thus in this case the appeals court had to decide whether the motor vehicle bureau was a law enforcement agency. The court in **Bunse** held that it was not a law enforcement agency? Why? It felt that such clerks "have neither the opportunity nor inclination to ignore or subvert Fourth Amendment rights, and the exclusion of evidence in the instant case would do nothing to speed up the process of updating records at the motor vehicle bureau." In fact the license and registration in this case was valid as of January 15 but not updated until January 29. The stop in this case occurred between those two dates.

But this case would not end the debate in Florida. The function of the agency would become the focal point in **Shadler v. State**, 761 So. 2d 279 (Fla. 2000). The agency involved was the Florida Department of Highway Safety and its driver's licensing division. The court noted that the "maintenance of records of revocations and suspensions clearly relate directly to the enforcement of the laws relating to driving privileges." Heavy reliance was placed on these records thus as an agency "it is a vital part of the law enforcement infrastructure of the entire State of Florida." Thus as a law enforcement agency the rule of **White** applies to exclude this evidence. Only one of the seven justices dissented.

The NCIC database was the subject of a case from Texas and one of its intermediate appellate courts. In **Brown v. State**, 986 S.W. 2d 50 (Tex. App. Dallas 1999), the police stopped a car because it appeared on the officer's "hot sheet" as a stolen car. The NCIC was accessed after the stop and it was still listed as stolen. Cocaine residue was found. There was no other reason for the initial stop. The court, though not unsympathetic to such defendants trapped by computer "garbage," held the

NCIC database was reasonably trustworthy and that it established probable cause for this arrest. In a footnote it was pointed out that 80,000 agencies can access the 17 databases containing one ten million records and handles 2 million transactions a day.

Of course a database maintained by a prosecutor's office does not enjoy the benefits of **Arizona v. Evans** as found by **People v. Boyer**, 713 N.E. 2d 655 (Ill. App.3d 1999). The duty to recall warrants in this region of the state fell on the shoulders of the prosecutor due to a "local practice" and not state law. But that was enough to deny the use of **Arizona v. Evans.**

The one rejection of **Evans** that yet upheld an arrest on an unrecorded recalled warrant comes from a Texas appeals court. It refused to "engraft" the **Evans** distinction between errors committed by judicial personnel because a Texas statute, Article 38.23(b) of the Code of Criminal Procedure only prevents "bad faith" evidence from being used.

The question not addressed by **Evans** is the status of staleness or freshness of information in police maintained databases as discussed in the cases discussed at the beginning of this section. The **Evans** ruling is quite limited to non-law enforcement databases. At least one court in the post-**Evans** era had a chance to discuss the issue but did not. That case is **State v. Williams**, 1998 WL 248839 (Wis. App.) (unpub. op.) The issues thus surrounding erroneous police databases is not one of good faith reliance but is one of mere reliance. If officers rely on what appears to be fresh information do they automatically forfeit search incident evidence if the information was not "true" at the time of the seizure. The police in **Williams** received a very fresh "hot sheet" at 6:30 a.m. At 2:30 p.m. the stolen car noted in the "hot sheet" appeared before them. They did not know the driver was the owner who very recently had his car returned to him. By the time they discovered this they had arrested the owner on a concealed weapons charge. A straight forward **Leon** – like approach was taken *but* not as a matter of federal law. The court here specifically says the state constitution demands it. The court said the officers acted in good faith reliance on the information, which if true at the time, would have provided reasonable suspicion to make the stop.

I disagree with the analysis, but not with the outcome. This is more like a **Terry** – stop case. Though the report of the stolen car is not "gospel" and could be stale; it certainly was enough to create an ambiguity serious enough for a brief detention of the vehicle. Sadly, the owner did not have enough respect for the law to avoid driving around with a concealed weapon. The behavior of the police was eminently reasonable and not brutal. If a case like this is "lost" then we might as well destroy all communication devices. The information in this case *was* reliable at some point – when can it be said it becomes unreliable – when the car was recovered – whether it was recovered or not? Some common sense should be allowed.

VIII. Back Door Uses of Illegally Obtained Evidence

Can the prosecution use illegally obtained evidence when it cannot be used in the case-in-chief? Several U.S. Supreme Court decisions illustrate the parameters of the use of illegally obtained evidence. The first is **Walder v. U.S.**, 347 U.S. 62 (1954). Walder was successful in obtaining suppression of illegally obtained narcotics. Walder took the stand on his own behalf. On cross-examination Walder was asked whether he had ever purchased, sold or possessed narcotics. Walder said never. Then, over defense objection, Walder was asked about the heroin capsule taken from his home. Walder denied that it was his. The government put the officer on the stand who had seized the evidence. The judge admitted the evidence for impeachment purposes only and cautioned the jury to that effect. The Court said the government cannot violate the Fourth and use the fruits. Nor can it make indirect use of such evidence. But, the Court added, neither can the defendant turn the illegal method used to seize the evidence to his own advantage. We cannot let the defendant "affirmatively resort to perjurious testimony in reliance on the Government's disability to challenge his credibility." Thus if the defendant opens the door on cross-examination he or she runs the risk of the use of the "fruits" by impeachment.

The second decision concerning this topic is **Harris v. N.Y.**, 401 U.S. 222 (1971). Harris took the stand and said he sold baking powder and not heroin because it was his intent to defraud the buyer. On cross-examination, a prior signed statement of Harris was used for impeachment purposes. Its use for this purpose was approved. The court said: "Having voluntarily taken the stand, petitioner was under an obligation to speak truthfully and accurately...." "The shield provided by **Miranda** cannot be perverted into a license to use perjury...." The defendant risks confrontation with his prior utterances. This rationale was reaffirmed in **U.S. v. Havens**, 446 U.S. 620 (1980).

There is another side to this problem as illustrated by **U.S. v. Hickey**. One of the defendants claimed that the car used in a robbery had been stolen and the ski masks and hair brush found in the car were not his. When this defendant was arrested he was given the **Miranda** rights and he said he would not answer any but the most routine questions without an attorney. The police had learned the identity of the third man as Bubba. The agent asked defendant if he was known as Bubba and defendant said he was known as Booboo. Defendant got his statement suppressed. The trial court ruled that defendant could be cross-examined on the alias problem and the police could even testify for impeachment purposes as to the previously suppressed statement. Because of this, the defendant decided not to take the stand. Did the judge err in this advance ruling on impeachment? As the appellate court viewed the advance ruling, they felt the court authorized impeachment even if the defendant did not bring up the subject on the direct examination. This they felt was improper. They said that illegal evidence should not be used as a trump card to keep the defendant off the stand. Had the trial court in its advance ruling made clear that impeachment could not be used unless the defendant brought up the subject of aliases, would that have passed muster? It should have. **U.S. v. Hickey**, 596 F. 2d 1082 (C.A. 1st 1979).

The Nevada Supreme Court was not willing to let **Harris** apply where the statements used to impeach the defendant were taken during plea negotiations. They felt that when an accused plea bargains he waived his right to remain silent. But, when the plea "falls through" the waiver dies and his statements are protected. **Mann v. State**, 605 P. 2d 209 (Nev. 1980). This is currently the majority position taken by state courts.

Massachusetts has taken the position that evidence gained from an illegal wire tap cannot be used to impeach. Their position is that the ban on "one party consent" in that state requires flat bans on such evidence. **Com. v. Fini**, 531 N.E. 2d 570 (Mass. 1988).

However, the Supreme Court had put one limit on the "back door" use of an illegally obtained statement from a defendant. In **James v. Illinois**, 493 U.S. 307 (1990), defendant was illegally arrested and a non-attenuated statement concerning his hair color on the day of the crime was taken. That statement was used to impeach a defense witness who testified as to the defendant's hair color. The Court refused to allow this impeachment to stand more from the point of view that it would tend to deter the defense from calling witnesses and saw possible prosecutorial use in this context as a "sword" to dissuade defendants from presenting a meaningful defense through other witnesses.

Fruits of the Poisonous Tree Doctrine

WEEKS, KATZ, MAPP,
RAKAS, BURDEAU,
SALVUCCI, OLSON,
CARTER

I.   If evidence or information is gathered by police or their agents or those acting under police direction or control [STATE ACTION] and that conduct does not meet 4th, 5th or 6th Amendment substantive standards the evidence gathered is inadmissible in the state's case-in-chief.[BASE EXCLUSIONARY RULE] [POISONOUS TREE]

WONG SUN, BROWN, ELSTAD

II.   If a substantive right under the U.S. Constitution is violated and if police incidentally gather further evidence as a result of an exploitation of the first violation that evidence is inadmissible as [FRUITS OF THE POISONOUS TREE]:

Examples:

FULMINANTE

A.   *Involuntary confession* – the words – *Poisonous Tree* further physical evidence found as a result of those words – Fruits

BREWER V.
WILLIAMS

B.   *Interrogation of defendant* who has been formally charged and has "hired" a lawyer – words *Poisonous Tree* further physical evidence found as a result of the words – *Fruits*

SIBRON V. N.Y.

C.   *Illegal seizure of defendant* the seizure is thus *Poisonous Tree* evidence gathered as a result of the search incident – Fruits

PAYTON,
N.Y. V. HARRIS,
MILLER, SABBATH,
KER, STEAGALD,
OLSON, WELSH,
CHRISMAN, CARTER

D. ***Entry of Privacy Area*** without warrant, consent or exigency to make a probable cause based arrest – the entry is ***Poisonous Tree***. Any evidence gathered within the wingspan of defendant ***or*** seen in ***plain view*** whether immediately seized or later seized by warrant or unattenuated consent is ***Fruits***.

ILL. V. LAFAYETTE

E. ***Illegal Seizure and Incarceration*** and defendant immediately consents to search of premises.
Seizure – POISONOUS TREE
Consent – FRUITS
Booking and Jailing inventory items – FRUITS
Immediate interrogation – FRUITS

WALDER,
HARRIS V. N.Y.,
HASS, TUCKER,
HAVENS

III. Thus if evidence is the product of a substantive constitutional violation such product is FRUITS of the POISONOUS TREE and inadmissible as direct evidence ***BUT*** in most instances can be used to impeach a testifying defendant's testimony if that defendant brings up the *FRUITS* and judge gives standard cautionary instruction.

IV. TAINTED FRUITS – removing the taint – use of evidence in state's case-in-chief.

TAYLOR V. ALA.

A. *ATTENUATION* – the "quality time" issue – for consents/interrogations.

SILVERTHORNE, MURRAY, SEGURA

B. *INDEPENDENT SOURCE* – knowledge of evidence gained from a source independent from violative police activity.

NIX V. WILLIAMS

C. *INEVITABLE DISCOVERY* – evidence would have been found without the unlawful/unconstitutional activity.

D. *GOOD FAITH RELIANCE* – police reasonably rely on others.

PELTIER
DEFILLIPPO
LEON

1. court appellate decisions;
2. facially valid statutes;
3. issuing magistrate's probable cause finding on a warrant;

ILL V. RODRIGUEZ

4. consenter's standing to permit a search of a place or thing;

ARIZ. V. EVANS

5. relying on court generated and maintained wants and warrant computer program.

IX. U.S. Constitutional Rights versus State Constitutional Rights.

The United States Supreme Court determines the scope of U.S. Constitutional rights. In a case where the states apply U.S. Constitutional rights they are to apply them as determined and they are neither to expand nor retract such rights. Thus any attempt to give a defendant more rights or to limit the defendant's announced rights by a state interpreting the U.S. Constitution is an invalid exercise of judicial power. It is clearly understandable why states may not shrink such announced rights but is it as clear why the court will not allow states to use the U.S. Constitution to give a defendant more rights than an announced Supreme Court opinion? It should be because in either event there can only be one final arbiter of the United States Constitution and that power is vested in the United States Supreme Court (a point forcefully made by the Court most recently in **Arkansas v. Sullivan**).

But does this mean that the state courts have no jurisprudential policy setting function in the criminal constitutional arena? No, it does not. Our federal system and its dual sovereignty function (state and national) invites a slightly different package of rights from each government. How different may each of these packages be? States are free to interpret their own constitution as long as they do not shrink the rights of defendants. Though diversity is permitted, the citizens and residents of the states and United States are entitled to know the absolute minimal rights they are guaranteed. In this context then, the U.S. Constitution through Supreme Court decisions preempts the field of minimal rights. Uniformity at this level is not only preferred, it is essential to an orderly society. Thus no state may, for example, reject the exclusionary rule of **Weeks** or **Miranda**.

Do United States Supreme Court decisions set maximum rights? Qualifiedly, yes they do, but only insofar as the United States Constitution. The U.S. Supreme Court may not dictate what the states allow as maximum constitutional rights under state constitutional interpretations. This was the heart of **Oregon v. Hass**, 420 U.S. 714 (1975). There the Supreme Court said the state may impose greater restrictions on state action than the federal constitution as long as that decision is based on its own laws or constitution. To have decided otherwise would have in itself created a constitutional crisis. Any other decision would have been a denial of the federal system created by the Constitution of 1789. By deciding to uphold federalism the court allows diversity and non-conformity to be a continuing part of our national heritage. But such diversity and lack of uniformity causes confusion among the citizenry and its law enforcement personnel in the basic area of social conduct.

When the so-called criminal law revolution began with **Mapp**, state courts were seen in a pro-police and pro-prosecution light while the federal system was seen as pro-defendant. Whether that vision was correct is left to others to debate. Suffice it to say that it was for the most part the striking down of state decisions that labeled the Warren Court as the creators of the revolution. Much has changed since then. The Burger Court and now the Rehnquist Court are labeled as pro-police. The expansion of defendant rights has certainly ended. Whether it is totally fair to say that defendant rights have been shrunk, it is clear that restrictive interpretations of prior decisions have increased.

To be sure, the U.S. Supreme Court's "floor of rights" theory is somewhat consistent with early American theory of the sovereign states of America united for a common set of limited purposes but independent of each other for all other purposes. The Bill of Rights, prior to the Fourteenth Amendment was intended only to circumscribe the conduct of federal agents acting within each of the other sovereignties. Whether the Fourteenth Amendment was truly intended to do what the Warren Court said it does is still open to debate (an exercise in futility to be sure). But even the Warren Court felt uncomfortable, thus, with **Mapp v. Ohio**, the Fourteenth Amendment was not used as the incorporator. Instead, state citizens, also being U.S. citizens, must be given the right to enjoy the exclusionary rule but not be saddled with an egregious conduct rule that due process requires.

The seeds for a "new federalism" were sown. When the so-called "new federalism" was announced it was clear that there could and would be different packages of rights that arose above the floor established by the U.S. Supreme Court. Today when the Supreme Court announces a decision most states will follow it but one must "shepardize" each case. When pulling a case on West Law one will sometimes see a blue H which indicates general acceptance. We do not see that often. Instead a yellow flag most often appears. Click that yellow flag and you will see those states that either harshly criticize the opinion or outright reject it based on state law constitutional grounds.

It is interesting to note that some of this activity has been applauded by some state courts and legislatures; others have, for various reasons, disagreed. Their disagreement is demonstrated by the increasing use of **Oregon v. Hass** and the reliance of state courts on their own constitutions. However, not all such decisions are based on the idea of rejecting a Supreme Court decision. Some states grant greater rights for purposes of simplicity and to limit discretion. By limiting discretion and by taking a "rules jurisprudence" approach they not only increase a defendant's rights but more importantly they increase judicial efficiency. It takes less of a judge's time to determine a "yes" or a "no" than it does to do a full "totality of the circumstances" suppression hearing.

The Arkansas Supreme Court somehow thought it could grant its citizens more rights under the U.S. Constitution than what the U.S. Supreme Court's "own federal precedents provide." **Oregon v. Hass** was cited in refutation of that thinking. The Court, quoting from **Hass**, repeated their stance where they said: "...a State is free as a matter of its own law to impose greater restrictions on police activity than this Court holds to be necessary upon federal constitutional standards..." and that states "...may not impose such greater restriction as a matter of federal constitutional law when this Court specifically refrains from imposing them." **Arkansas v. Sullivan,** 2001 WL 567705 (U.S.).

The federalism protection given recognition by the Court in **Oregon v. Hass** has an unfortunate side to it. Diversity has a tendency to encourage political polarization in an area where liberal versus conservative should have no place. At the very basic level of human conduct society's rights to protect itself and the right of the citizen to be free from discretionless police conduct should not be played out in the broader arena of politics.

Over 200 years ago we decided that we could prohibit certain society-threatening conduct while at the same time secure the right of all to be free of a police state. That decision creates a tension that is not always easy to keep in balance. Putting the political question aside, what messages are we sending to the people? In the criminal law area it has long been the primary rule of construction that of all the laws, this area should be the easiest to understand; that clarity is a virtue so that people may adjust their conduct accordingly. We are now seeing greater disparity and are faced with the fact that our rights may be more determined by geography rather than constitutional precepts. State courts should carefully consider whether this proper exercise of states rights is worth more than simplistic national uniformity. If that has been considered against the states unique cultural heritage, then the decision may well be worth the cost. Otherwise it might be better to wait until the pendulum begins to swing in the other direction (for surely it will); the law is not static. In any event, throughout these materials mention will be made of these decisions which have been accepted and which have been rejected. Since not all states have yet reacted to all decisions the reader is encouraged to consult local sources to determine the status of each case in his or her own jurisdiction.

It is interesting to note that in one year Wyoming chose to break ranks with the Supreme Court in two areas. By interpreting its own constitution it held that a warrant must be obtained to search an automobile unless it is impracticable to obtain a warrant. **Perry v. State**, 50 Crim. L. Rep. 1223 (Wyo. 1991). In another case the Wyoming high court said police violate state due process by coercing an individual into "knotting her own noose" by securing a confession. The problem was the police were not using anything other than **Miranda** permitted custodial interrogation on a pregnant woman who knew her husband was cooperating in the investigation. **Black v. State**, 820 P. 2d 969 (Wyo. 1991). In both cases vigorous dissents were filed.

Just how does a state trial judge determine whether the state gives more rights in areas not yet addressed by the local high court? No one knows for sure but hints such as, "We have consistently not felt bound by decisions of the U.S. Supreme Court" or some such language says watch out! Language that indicates a general willingness to follow the Supreme Court or "our constitution is just like theirs" type language points generally in the opposite direction.

More importantly, when the defense counsel asks for a fresh look and more protection, it is counsel's duty to demonstrate historical, language, cultural or statutory differences from those faced by the U.S. Supreme Court in its decision. For example, when **Mapp v. Ohio** came down the Supreme Court acknowledged that several states had already adopted an exclusionary rule. Nothing in **Mapp** changed those decisions. Perhaps some were more restrictive defense rights but it is also possible it was more liberal than the Warren, Burger, and Rehnquist courts. Those decisions can be used where the state has not created more restrictive constitutional rules.

The debates that surrounded the adoption of the local constitution can add to the meaning of the language as adopted (even if it's the same). A fair opportunity must be given defense counsel to develop an argument of greater rights.

The research should also be aided by what we see in **Mapp**, 367 U.S. at page 651 where the Court notes that several courts had adopted or adhered to some form of the **Weeks** exclusionary rule. They then send us to **Elkins v. U.S.**, 364 U.S. 206 (1960), at pages 224-232 and the appendix to that opinion. The chart reveals that 20 states before **Weeks** were undecided whether to exclude or not after **Weeks** and before **Wolf v. Colorado** 18 states excluded and one was undecided. Then after **Wolf** and before **Mapp**, 24 would admit and 26 would exclude, thus none were undecided. However, the exclusion decisions of Alaska and Hawaii were territorial decisions and not statehood decisions.

The appendix to **Elkins** that continues on pages 226 through 232 cites the seminal exclusion cases that predate **Mapp** and **Elkins**. It is through these cites that one can begin to see if one's state granted more, less or the same rights set out in **Weeks**. For example, Iowa's rule predated Weeks. Rules from Alabama, Maryland, Michigan and South Dakota gave only partial exclusionary relief. Also note that most states before **Mapp** also had (and still have) statutes making it a crime to violate Fourth Amendment-like rights. However, these statutes, as noted **Mapp,** had little or no impact on the decision to admit evidence at the defendant's trial.

The Connecticut appeals court decided to accept the guidelines of **Greenwood**, the garbage at the curbside case. Its rationale centered on the fact that the citizens of Connecticut had not been accustomed to a more protective rule governing garbage. However the decision did not give significant guidance to the bench and bar regarding future decisions of the U.S. Supreme Court. See **State v. DeFusco**, 606 A. 2d 1 (Conn. App. 1992). That guidance came in two other opinions. The issue in these cases focused on the rules of **Franks v. Delaware** and the veracity challenge to the search or arrest warrant issuing process. **Franks** was accepted without local modification. These two courts suggest that the hearing judge apply the following criteria: (1) compare the text of the state and federal constitutions; (2) look at related state precedents (if any) regarding the specific area of the current case and other local precedents; (3) federal precedents in the area or region; (4) precedents of other state courts, especially the bordering states; (5) historical insights into the intent of the local state constitution; (6) economic and social considerations; and whether anything in these approaches demand more strict standard to be applied to the state's action. See **State v. Glenn**, 707 A. 2d 736 (Conn. App. 1998), **State v. Glenn**, 740 A. 2d 856 (Conn. 1999) and **State v. Ross**, 646 A. 2d 856 (Conn. 1994), cert. den. 513 U.S. 1165 (1995).

Idaho was also asked to reject Greenwood on state constitutional grounds in **State v. Donato**, 2001 WL 200149 (Idaho). The court notes that similar phraseology is not enough to deny breaking ranks with the U.S. Supreme Court. There must be some uniqueness of the state constitution and long standing jurisprudence. They felt that garbage is garbage whether it is in New York or Idaho. It is subject to intrusions by neighbors, dogs, children, and strangers and it turned over to some third person to place in an accessible public dump. This represents a sensible approach. Vermont says the burden is on the defendant to explain how and why they should interpret the Vermont constitution as providing greater protection than its federal counterpart. **State v. Hayes**, 752 A. 2d 16 (Vt. 2000) citing **State v. Porter**, 671 A. 2d 1280 (Vt. 1996) and **State v. Brunelle**, 534 A. 2d 198 (Vt. 1987).

CHAPTER TWO
PROBABLE CAUSE

I.   Probable Cause Defined

To obtain a search warrant the officer must present underlying facts and circumstances that show probable cause. To justify a warrantless search probable cause plus some specific exception to the warrant requirement must be shown. For an arrest warrant to issue, probable cause must be established. For a warrantless felony arrest to be valid the officer must have acted upon probable cause. For a warrantless misdemeanor arrest the offense must be committed in the officer's presence unless the misdemeanor has been excepted from the general law applicable to misdemeanor arrests and made subject to the felony arrest law. See the discussion of the misdemeanor law of arrests at Chapter Twelve, section IV and the decision in **Atwater v. City of Lago Vista,** *et al.*, 121 S. Ct. 1536 (2001).

Thus probable cause is pivotal. What is probable cause? Probable cause to arrest for a felony is most often stated to exist where:

1.   At the moment of the arrest or before (but never after),
2.   facts and circumstances,
3.   within the knowledge of the arresting officer,
4.   and of which the officer has reasonably trustworthy information,
5.   would warrant a reasonable and prudent person,
6.   in believing,
7.   that a particular person,
8.   has committed or is committing a crime [*felony or misdemeanor*].

Probable cause to search exists where:

1.   At the moment of the search or issuance of the warrant,
2.   the officer knows facts and circumstances,
3.   with reasonable grounds to believe,
4.   that the search,
5.   of the place, person or thing,
6.   will uncover objects sought,
7.   and that the objects sought will aid in the apprehension or conviction or both of the offender,
8.   and the information within the officer's knowledge is reasonably trustworthy,
9.   and would lead a man of reasonable caution and prudence to believe that,
10. he or she will find the instrumentality of a crime or evidence pertaining to a crime

Neither definition deals in terms of suspicion. This was not always the case. In **Stacey v. Emery**, 97 U.S. 642 (1878), the Court echoed the then popular definition which was: "Such a state of facts as would lead a man of ordinary caution to believe or to entertain an honest and strong suspicion that the person is guilty." Even this definition requires more than mere suspicion and probably more than what is known today as articulable suspicion. The **Stacey** case was a civil action brought by the arrestee for damages arising out of a wrongful seizure of goods. The Court firmly stated that probable cause, which, of course, is less than required to convict, is a defense to an action for a wrongful taking. The Court went on and added that the question of malice or good faith is not an element in the case. It is not a question of motive. If the facts and circumstances before the officer are such as to warrant a person of prudence and caution to believe that the offense has been committed, it is sufficient.

The Court has gone on to further instruct us on probable cause. One of the lynchpin cases is **Brinegar v. United States**, 338 U.S. 160 (1948). Brinegar was convicted of importing intoxicating liquors from Missouri into Oklahoma in violation of 27 U.S.C. §223. Factually, the officer had arrested Brinegar five months earlier for the same type of offense; he had seen Brinegar loading liquor into a car or truck in Joplin on at least two other occasions during the preceding six months; he knew that Brinegar had a reputation for hauling liquor; the officer personally observed the seemingly loaded car; Brinegar accelerated as he passed the officers. When they caught him, he got out of the car and the officers asked him, "How much?" and Brinegar said "Not too much." Did the officers have probable cause to stop Brinegar? The Court reiterated that less evidence is needed for probable cause than is needed to justify condemnation or conviction, but it has to be more than a bare suspicion. It said fair leeway must be given for enforcing the law in the community's protection, and that some room must be allowed for mistakes on the part of the officers. However, these mistakes must be mistakes of reasonable persons, acting on facts leading sensibly to their conclusion of probability. As such, it is the best compromise for these often opposing interests. Yes, there was probable cause. But in terms of risk of error, a certain level of probability which might ordinarily suffice should not be considered adequate when the officer neglects to utilize the means at hand to reduce the risk of error. See **Adams v. Williams** (*infra*). This is the heart of the reasonableness requirement of the Fourth Amendment.

Next, consider **Henry v. U.S.**, 361 U.S. 98 (1959). Henry was convicted of receiving stolen radios. The Court felt compelled to try to define bare suspicion. It said that, (as the early American decisions both before and immediately after the adoption of the Constitution held), common rumor or report, suspicion or even strong reason to suspect was not adequate to support a warrant for arrest. The Court added that the good faith of the officer is not enough, and that an arrest is not justified by what the subsequent search discloses. True, a crime had been committed. Some whiskey had been stolen from a terminal in the neighborhood. The defendant's friend was a suspect but the defendant had not been suspected of criminal activity before. The defendant was riding in the car with the theft suspect. The defendants stopped in a residential alley and picked up packages. They drove away normally. All this activity involved outwardly innocent movements. They wore no masks and showed no behavior of fleeing men or men acting furtively. The packages were picked up in a residential section and not from a terminal or trucking platform. The Court said not every man who carries a package is subject to arrest nor are the packages subject to seizure. The shapes and designs of the packages were not unique nor was the manner in which they were carried. In finding no probable cause, the Court held that, under our system, mere suspicion is not enough for an officer to lay hands on a citizen.

Under the Court's decision in **Jaben v. U.S.**, 381 U.S. 214 (1965), the Court said that in seeking probable cause the judge must ask these questions: What makes you think that the defendant committed the offense charged? Is there enough information to enable the judge to say that the charges are not capricious and that they are sufficiently supported to justify bringing into play the further steps of the criminal process?

The Court has held that two tests must be met for a finding of probable cause. First, there must be information, which, if true, would directly indicate the commission of the crime charged. Second, there must be information which relates the source or sources that directly incriminate the defendant. For example, in **Whiteley v. Warden**, 401 U.S. 560 (1971), Whiteley was convicted of breaking and entering. The complaint consisted of nothing more than conclusions and the individuals' names. The complaint was based on an informer's tip but even that fact was omitted from the complaint. The Court said additional information must be in some sense corroborative of the informer's terms and that additional information must not be extraneous information.

This set the stage for **Illinois v. Gates**, 462 U.S. 213 (1983), wherein the Court said that corroboration of the details of an informant's tip by independent police work is of significant value. It also said that the courts must continue to conscientiously review the sufficiency of affidavits on which warrants are issued but that corroboration, through other sources of information, reduce the chances of its being a reckless or prevaricating tale. Whether the police have done everything necessary to reduce (but not eliminate) reckless, vengeful, prevaricating stories is the key question the judge must answer.

With the adoption of **Gates** and its limitation on the **Aguilar** rule (*infra* at Ch. Three), much more must be understood about corroboration of a tip, whether it comes from an anonymous tipster or from a known informant. The critical problem will center on a concern whether the matters corroborated are mere innocent details or whether the details verified, though innocent, are reasonably indicative of non-innocent activity. Quite frankly, subjective judicial opinion can and will play a significant role in these cases. That is not inherently bad and certainly in the pre-arrest and pre-search warrant issuing area it is the best that can be hoped for. However, in the post-arrest and post-search area where illegality has been uncovered it will put the neutrality and detachment of the judiciary to the test.

The **Gates** opinion resurrects a need to more closely examine two important prior decisions. They are **Draper v. United States**, 358 U.S. 307 (1959) and **Adams v. Williams**, 407 U.S. 143 (1972). Both of these cases involved tips by known informers, and shared the "indicia of reliability" concern and the role of corroboration expressed in **Gates**.

In **Draper**, a regular paid informant came to the officer and told the officer that Draper had recently moved to Denver and was "peddling" narcotics. The informer said Draper had gone to Chicago and he was going to bring back 3 ounces of heroin on either the 8th or 9th of September. The informer gave the officer a description of Draper and the clothing he was wearing and said he would be carrying a tan zipper bag and that Draper habitually "walked real fast." Thus the informer has not seen the drugs in the possession of Draper. There is indication of some detail but the future activity is what was at issue. Sure enough, on September 9th, a man looking like Draper, wearing the exact clothes, carrying the bag and "walking real fast" was seen alighting from the Chicago train. The arrest "went down" and the drugs were discovered. Did the officer have probable cause based on the tip and corroboration of the known details? Yes, said the Court. Everything corroborated all but one piece of information – that Draper would have drugs. If everything corroborated was true could the police reasonably believe the one missing piece would also be true? Yes. The personal verification of every other detail surely could lead to that conclusion, said the Court. Though in **Draper** the details verified were in and of themselves innocent, the past reliability of the informant was critical.

What was known by the officer in **Adams**? A known informant approached the officer at 2:15 a.m. in a high crime area of Bridgeport, Connecticut. The informer told the officer that in a nearby vehicle a man was seated who carried narcotics and had a gun at his waist. The officer called for assistance and approached the vehicle to investigate. The officer tapped on the window, asked the person to get out of the car, but instead Williams rolled down the window. The officer then reached for the waistband and pulled the loaded revolver which could not be seen from outside the car. Was this a tip completely lacking in indicia of reliability? No. Though not a probable cause case but rather a **Terry** reasonable fear case, the tip puts a man in a car early in the morning in a high crime area. Those things being verified, the failure of Williams to get out of the car fortified the "fear of safety" and the reach by the officer, at the exact point where he was told the gun would be. This "grab" was reasonable under these **Terry**-type circumstances. Finding the gun in that precise place, the Court said, tended to corroborate the reliability of the informant's further report of narcotics and did not suggest a lawful explanation for the gun's possession. That gave the officer probable cause to arrest and conduct a search incident to that lawful arrest.

At the time of these cases, one of the keys to corroboration decisions was the fact that in each case the police were dealing with known informants. Both decisions, as an aside, made derogatory remarks about anonymous informers. **Gates,** therefore, was a surprise. First, there was an anonymous tipster in **Gates**. Second, unlike **Draper** and **Adams,** the police sought and obtained a warrant, therefore, there was no possibility of "after-acquired" evidence impacting upon the judicial probable cause finding. Third, in all three cases the courts were examining future events and corroboration. What did the **Gates'** police verify? First, they obtained some financial records and also thereby secured a more up-to-date address. Second, they verified airline reservations. Third, they found the motel in West Palm Beach and the Illinois car used earlier by the wife to drive to Florida that was registered to the Gates. Fourth, they verified that Gates and a woman left the very next day as indicated would happen in the tip. An Illinois judge must have felt that the *modus operandi* was verified because he issued the warrant.

Probable cause is not a "neat set of legal rules" according to the Court. Tips vary in value and reliability. More rigorous scrutiny of honest citizens is always less likely while scrutiny of those with criminal records must be more rigorous. Anonymous tips cannot survive **Spinelli** (*infra*) unless subjected to independent police investigation which then allows the police to move beyond "bare bones" affidavits such as are seen in **Spinelli**. Reasonable corroboration is needed. Certainty of other predictions of the informer's uncorroborated information is not required; the Court applies the "more probably right about other facts" of **Adams** and **Draper**. As long as the chances of reckless or prevaricating tale have been reduced (not eliminated), then a warrant can issue. If an informer gives verified accurate information it is also likely that the informer had access to the other unverified information. This is the key to taking otherwise innocent detail and parlaying it into probable cause.

The tests established by the Court are summarized as follows:

1. The more probably right about other facts test;
2. Independent investigation sufficiency test;
3. Reduction of reckless or prevaricating tale test; and
4. Probability of access to the information by the informer test.

Were these tests satisfied in **Green v. State**, 551 A. 2d 127 (Md. Ct. Spec. App. 1989)? A regular informant specifically described the person and his clothes as one who sold cocaine from the steps of a house on Etting Street. The police went to the street and saw a man who fit the description sitting on some steps. Green ran down those steps and up the steps of the next house. Before he could enter that house he was apprehended. The ensuing search produced the drugs described (cocaine) plus some heroin which was not described. Were the above tests met? Should this case now be tested against **Illinois v. Wardlow** (*infra* at p. 88) as headlong flight?

Did the police in **U.S. v. Johnson**, 862 F. 2d 1135 (C.A. 5th 1988) have probable cause under these four tests? This case involved an unknown female informer who said she had driven two black males (naming them) from California to Fort Worth. She said the two men were en route to the bus station. They were going to lockers 17 and 20 and from those lockers two suitcases would be retrieved. One of the suitcases was described. The suitcases, she said, contained drugs and she said the men were probably armed. The police set up the stake-out. They verified the identity of the men and saw them retrieve the suitcases from lockers 17 and 20. The police watched them buy tickets to Houston and saw them check the bags to Houston. The **Gates** test would seem to show that she was "probably right" about the ultimate conclusion.

Caveat: Probable cause to seize does not necessarily mean that there will be a constitutionally recognized right to search. Facts discovered upon the lawful seizure may demand an immediate release. Suppose an officer "runs" an auto tag and the information received tells the officer that the owner has had his or her driver's license suspended, can the officer stop (seize) the car? Yes. Suppose the "suspended" owner is a female, can the officer require the driver to produce a license? Yes, but only if the driver is the same gender as the suspended owner. This issue surfaced in a Washington case. The driver was a male with a pony tail and the car had tinted windows which made a gender identification difficult. The suspended owner was in the car's passenger seat. Once the officer realized this distinction and having observed no other illegal activity, the officer should have allowed the car to proceed. He did not, and discovered that the male driver was also "suspended." The situation escalated and a large amount of drugs were found strapped under the car. Everything had to be suppressed. **State v. Penfield**, 2001 WL 477645 (Wash. App. Div. 3).

There is one additional probable cause standard applied by judges that has nothing to do with searches and seizures. The judge was called upon to decide in pretrial phase of a case in which no indictment had been returned whether there appears to be sufficient evidence to justify a trial. That, of course, is not the issue in the search and seizure context. It does not matter whether such evidence sought is found or if found will eventually even be admissible. The decision, for example, to issue a warrant based on probable cause as stated in an affidavit that itself is based on hearsay. That hearsay most often would not be admissible at the trial. But as stated, success of a case being proven beyond a reasonable doubt *is not* a warrant issuing concern since the warrant issuing process is not the beginning of the adversarial process. The two standards should never be confused. They are quite separate because they serve separate purposes.

II.   The Role of Flight or Furtive Gestures in Probable Cause Determinations

A.   Decisional Law

In a companion case to **Terry v. Ohio,** the Court decided specifically that merely talking to narcotics addicts for about eight hours did not raise an inference that the defendant was a drug dealer. Therefore, it found no articulable suspicion. **Sibron v. New York**, 392 U.S. 40 (1968). In that same opinion the Court decided **Peters v. New York**, where a police officer heard strange noises at his door leading him to believe his apartment was about to be forcefully entered. The officer investigated and saw two men he had never seen before "tiptoeing furtively" in the hallway. The officer entered the hallway and the men fled down the stairs. The Court called this strong grounds to believe in probable cause and said: "deliberately furtive actions and flight at the approach of strangers or law officers are strong indicia of *mens rea* and when coupled with specific knowledge on the part of the officer relating the suspect to the evidence of crime, they are proper factors to be considered in the decision to make an arrest." The issue is what acts or movements will justify either an arrest or an investigative stop? Under what circumstances will mere suspicion be raised to articulable suspicion when there are furtive movements or flight? Under what circumstances will articulable suspicion be raised to probable cause by furtive gestures or flight?

First, consideration should be given to furtive gestures or flight and their impact on a probable cause determination. As has been seen, it takes a totality of events to add up to probable cause. Without more, flight is not a reliable indicator of guilt. It takes other known circumstances to make its import less ambiguous. Of course, when coupled with specific knowledge on the part of the officer relating the suspect to the evidence of crime, flight or evasion may properly be considered in assessing probable cause. But flight alone is generally insufficient to give police probable cause to arrest. Not all furtive movements and not all flights give probable cause. Even when flight reasonably appears designed to avoid apprehension, there is no probable cause unless combined with other information upon which the officers are entitled to rely. In **State v. Talbert**, 449 So. 2d 446 (La. 1984), all the police had was a surprised look and a retreat into an apartment and no more. The police were not there on a tip nor was there any other information that a crime was being committed in this area.

A significant number of the flight or furtive gesture cases are drug cases. Many of them rely on as one of the "coupling" points the police officer's experience as a narcotics officer. The state must offer more than a mere conclusion on this point. There must be proof of the experience, otherwise there will be no credible evidence that the officer knew he was witnessing a drug transaction. Without such proof, the court has only a mere flight case. **Trusty v. State**, 508 A. 2d 1018 (Md. 1986).

The Supreme Court had "heated up" the flight or furtive gesture battle by one comment in their decision in **California v. Hodari D.**, 499 U.S. 621 (1991). There the Court said: "California conceded below that Officer Pertoso did not have the "reasonable suspicion" required to justify stopping Hodari, see **Terry v. Ohio**, 392 U.S. 1 (1968). That it would be unreasonable to stop, for brief inquiry, young men who scatter in panic upon the mere sighting of the police is not self-evident, and arguably contradicts proverbial common sense. See Proverbs 28:1 ('The wicked flee when no man pursueth'). We do not decide that point here, but rely entirely upon the State's concession."

When this language is coupled with the point strongly made in **Bostick** that the reasonable person test presupposes an innocent person, **Florida v. Bostick**, 501 U.S. 429 (1991), it can be concluded that a new rule was about to be adopted. The only contrary indication given by the Court that not all "flights" are suspect enough for at least a **Terry** stop comes from **Bostick** where the Court said a refusal to cooperate, without more, does not supply grounds to seize. A definition of "without more" was needed and was given in **Wardlow**.

The Court in **Illinois v. Wardlow**, 528 U.S. 119 (2000), decided that articulable suspicion can arise, in the right circumstances, from the act of flight. The Court did not rule that flight "per se" is articulable suspicion. Instead, it continued its common sense driven contextual analysis. The place was a well-documented high-crime area. Wardlow saw the police and ran once eye contact was made. When seized, he was frisked and a gun was felt. Since Wardlow was a convicted felon, he should not have had the gun. The flight was not provoked; the decision to run was Wardlow's alone. An ambiguity was created that needed to be resolved. High crime area is relevant when flight is not provoked. The Court admits that there is no scientific

88

certainty judging suspicious behavior thus we have to fall back on common sense. Headlong flight is not going about one's business. Innocent people may be stopped for the **Terry** minimal intrusion.

A Georgia court found that flight from the officers who only had articulable suspicion to conduct a Terry stop gave the officers probable cause to arrest the defendant who fled into a motel room. Since the officers were investigating a very recent burglary in the area they had exigent circumstances to cross this defendant's threshold of the motel room. The arrest was made and the officers were about to remove him when the defendant asked for his jacket. In checking the pockets for a weapon, evidence of the burglary was found and other items from the drug store were in plain view and were also properly seized. This case clearly illustrates the "seamless web" properties of Fourth Amendment doctrines or indeed the potential that the "web" can be broken. The burden is on the judge to make these calls.

B.   Check List: Flight/Furtive Gestures

I.   The decision to stop or arrest a person: was it:
    A.   conclusion jumping, or
    B.   common-sense dictated?

II.   Supreme Court:
    A.   Rule: **Peters**:
        1.   clear evidence of a crime or its attempt,
        2.   deliberate furtive gestures or flight,
        3.   when strangers or police approach,
        4.   conclusion: probable cause.
    B.   *Dicta*: **Hodari D.**:
        1.   not unreasonable,
        2.   to stop for **Terry** purposes,
        3.   people who scatter in panic,
        4.   upon mere sighting of police.
    C.   Rule: **Bostick**:
        1.   a refusal to cooperate or consent,
        2.   without more,
        3.   does not supply grounds to seize.
    D.   Rule: **Wardlow**
        1.   high crime or crime scene area,
        2.   headlong flight by merely seeing police,
        3.   conclusion: articulable suspicion to stop.

III. Resolving the **AMBIGUITY** of most flight or furtive gesture cases.

    A.   Totality of all the circumstances:

        1.   includes common sense;

        2.   includes credible proof of the training and experience of the officer; and

        3.   includes, in grave danger cases, a balancing test.

    B.   Consider

        1.   prior contact of defendant with police,

        2.   must be more than mere guilt by association,

        3.   lawful police presence or stop,

        4.   was there a plausible innocent explanation:

            a.   under the circumstances,

            b.   offered by the defendant,

            c.   if offered and plausible did it make sense under these circumstances?

        5.   was there a known crime and;

            a.   what was the source?

            b.   was there corroboration?

            c.   did a description of the perpetrator exist and what is the "match?"

            d.   was the defendant critically located in relation to the crime?

            e.   if not mere movement can conduct be labeled as "flight?"

        6.   was there a suspected crime and:

            a.   what was the source:

                i.   informant, or

                ii.   circumstances?

            b.   was articulable stop thus justified?

            c.   did flight occur upon questioning or was it a mere movement/walking away?

        7.   was there a furtive gesture?

            a.   these are the most difficult cases;

            b.   what is normal activity as opposed to abnormal (furtive) activity?

                i.   tearing up or destruction

                ii.   stuffing things in waist or pocket or bag, *etc.*?

III. What is Not Probable Cause: Articulable Suspicion

The purpose here is not to discuss **Terry** and its progeny in substance. Rather it is to look at seven factual scenarios to contrast what does not constitute probable cause from that which is probable cause. Articulable suspicion is that position between probable cause and mere suspicion; it is somewhat akin to the religious tenet of purgatory. In fact, the word articulable was specifically "coined" by the Court so that it could have its own meaning separate from articulated and articulatable.

In **Terry v. Ohio**, 392 U.S. 1 (1968) Officer McFadden, a long-term experienced street cop, saw some men he had never seen before and things did not look right to him. The men individually appeared to be "casing" a store and did so by peering through the window five or six times each. Another man joined them. Fearing that they might have guns, McFadden approached them. The Court carved out from this activity the concept of articulable suspicion that gives a right to detain and investigate. Here there was conduct which led the experienced officer to suspect that criminal activity was afoot by possibly armed and dangerous persons. What would the average prudent citizen have thought about this activity of these men? Were these acts of preparation as opposed to acts of perpetration? Do police have to wait until the crime is attempted to intervene? No.

In **Brown v. Texas**, 443 U.S. 47 (1979) two officers saw two men in an alley who, upon seeing the patrol car, turned and walked away from each other. It was just after noon. The appellant looked suspicious to the officers. The officers, unlike McFadden in **Terry,** did not claim suspicion of any misconduct nor did they have any reason to believe that Brown was armed. This did not even amount to articulable suspicion. This was a mere movement and not a flight case. **Brown** and **Wardlow** are, therefore, the point-counterpoint cases.

Next review **Reid v. Georgia**, 448 U.S. 438 (1980), a *per curiam* decision. A fellow got off a plane in Atlanta. He looked occasionally over his shoulder at a second man. He came in from Fort Lauderdale. The other man also carried the same kind of shoulder bag as Reid. The second man caught up with Reid in the lobby and briefly spoke with Reid before they left the terminal building together. The DEA asked for identification and for ticket stubs. It was a credit card purchase and the men had stayed in Fort Lauderdale for only one day. The men appeared nervous during this encounter. Ultimately they consented to the search of their bags and as they went back into the terminal Reid ran and abandoned his shoulder bag. Cocaine was found in the abandoned bag. The drug courier profile was used to justify and supply the articulable suspicion. The Court disagreed and said this was an inchoate and unparticularized suspicion or hunch.

After discovery, on a number of occasions, that groups of 8 to 20 people had been guided over the border by a person wearing distinctive shoes and that the people were always picked up on clear weekends between 2 a.m. and 6 a.m., the police positioned themselves near the pickup point and only stopped the one truck that had passed them on the way to the pickup point and was now making the return trip within the carefully estimated time of such a round trip. Here the Court found plenty of objective facts and circumstances that justified the investigative stop. **U.S. v. Cortez**, 449 U.S. 411 (1981). But what they observed was not probable cause to arrest and conduct search incidents thereto.

In **Florida v. Royer**, 460 U.S. 491 (1983), a person purchased a one- way ticket to New York City from Miami under an assumed name. He checked luggage also with that assumed name. But, the officers did not know this when they stopped him. They used the American Tourister drug courier profile. He carried American Tourister luggage which appeared to be heavy; he was young; casually dressed, appeared pale and nervous; paid with a large number of bills; and did not fully fill out the luggage I.D. tags. On these facts the only thing the officer could do was to ask to examine the ticket and his license after identifying himself as an officer. There might have been articulable suspicion here (the Court says there was but not with the same authority as in **Terry**). Of course, there was no probable cause.

A clearer case of articulable suspicion was made out in **U.S. v. Place**, 462 U.S. 696 (1983). Place's behavior at Miami's airport aroused suspicion. Officers approached him, identified themselves and requested the ticket and some identification. Place complied and even consented to a search of his luggage. But because his flight was about to leave they did not search the luggage. Place was overheard saying that he "knew they were cops." The police looked on the address tags and noted two discrepancies in the two street addresses and then they found out that both addresses were bogus. The police called the DEA in New York. This certainly was ample articulable suspicion for the New York authorities to use when Mr. Place deplaned.

IV. Criminal Profile

Nothing better illustrates the different functions of the police as investigative adversaries and judges as neutral and detached than the area of criminal profiles. Police are taught to be suspicious and this is good. To protect and serve, the law enforcement officer must keep a wary eye on all that he surveys. The officer must be different from the rest of the population. The average citizen is often unaware of impending criminal danger. That is why the non-victim eyewitness can be so unreliable. The citizen is not trained to recognize subtle perpetration and certainly not to recognize preparation. This task we have assigned to our law enforcement officials.

As part of their initial and in-service training, police are taught a series of criminal profiles much the same way as they are taught the value of clue accumulation in a criminal investigation. If only taken as awareness "arousers" they certainly are helpful. However, what we have seen is a phenomenal growth of the profile as a tool for more than arousal. With Supreme Court indirect sanction, the profile has been parlayed into a device to justify limited seizure to a full-fledged justification for a full-fledged arrest.

In the October 1988 term, the Supreme Court had apparently decided to face head-on the issue of the drug courier profile in a more significant way than they did in **Mendenhall, Royer**, **Reid** and **Rodriguez**. Whether intentionally or not, it has watered down **Terry v. Ohio**, and has provided the growth of the "chameleon" called the profile. It is a "chameleon" because it defies a constant definition and seems to fit whatever case it comes upon just as the chameleon changes colors to fit its background.

Your attention is directed to a significant article on the drug courier profile written by an appellate court judge. The article, Becton, *The Drug Courier Profile: "All Seems Infected that Th' Infected Spy, As All Looks Yellow to the Jaundic'd Eye."* 65 N. C. L. Rev. 417 (1987), clearly points out that there is no uniform profile, that it changes to fit the circumstances of each case and that judges have a tendency to "jump on the band wagon" because the hunch turns up such good results in terms of contraband.

The case the Court had chosen to review was **U.S. v. Sokolow**, 831 F. 2d 1413 (C.A. 9th 1987). It is a case typical of **Mendenhall, Reid, Royer** and **Rodriguez**. As much as that type of case is problematic, the more serious case is the case decided by the old Fifth Circuit in **U.S. v. Ashcroft**, 607 F. 2d 1167 (C.A. 5th 1979), which parlayed association and presence as profile concepts into full-fledged probable cause for arrest. The court did a nice job "dancing" around **U.S. v. Di Re**, 332 U.S. 581 (1947). The **Ashcroft** case clearly shows the extent to which the profile can be taken. Was Ashcroft guilty? He was, but the linking proof was tenuous at best. Are we going to become a police state? This is the critical question.

Compare the cases by starting with **U.S. v. Di Re** as the base case. Di Re was charged with knowingly possessing counterfeit gasoline ration coupons. He was arrested without a warrant. Why? Because he was there – present while a friend of his was arrested for possession of some coupons. Nothing pointed to Di Re's complicity. Of course, when Di Re was searched he also had some coupons that were counterfeit. The officers had no information indicating that Di Re was in the car when Reid obtained coupons from Buttita, the other occupant of the car. The Court then said: "The argument that one who 'accompanies a criminal to a crime rendezvous' cannot be assumed to be a bystander, forceful enough in some circumstances, is farfetched when the meeting is not secretive or in a suspicious hide-out but in broad daylight, in plain sight of passers by, in a public street of a large city, and where the alleged substantive crime is one which does not necessarily involve any act visibly criminal...presumptions of guilt are not lightly to be indulged from mere meetings. "Besides, when asked who was guilty, Reid, the targeted criminal, pointed to Buttita and not to Di Re. The Court then said, "any inference that everyone on the scene of a crime is a party to it must disappear if the government informer singles out the guilty party." This language had been taken to mean by many that mere presence at the scene of a crime is not enough and to mean that innocent people can have guilty friends and there is not guilt by association. The language is not that clear.

In any event, the **Di Re** case set the stage for **Ashcroft**. Ashcroft was convicted of conspiracy to distribute cocaine but says he was arrested without probable cause. Although Ashcroft was present at the place where cocaine was to be sold he did not participate in the negotiations. There were two incidents. At the first he sat on a sofa watching television about two feet away from the negotiating table. He did not talk but heard everything. The second episode took place 13 days later. When the undercover agent entered, Ashcroft and a woman left the living room and went to an adjoining bedroom. They closed the door. The arrest of the others went "down." Ashcroft was discovered in the bedroom sitting on the bed and talking with the woman. Ashcroft was arrested and searched. When Ashcroft was arrested and searched, he said he owned the cocaine.

Because of the "fruits" argument the critical issue became probable cause. The court said there was probable cause. Why? First a reasonable person would think that someone present at two cocaine sales in the same apartment was somehow involved, especially when he does not live in that apartment. Second, the record revealed that the judge and the officers were aware of the practice followed by some drug dealers of hiding in another room until the deal is consummated in case there is an arrest so they can claim "innocent bystander" protection. The court added, "While we realize the question is a close one and should probably be limited to the particular facts of this case, we find probable cause existed...." It distinguished **Di Re, Sibron** and **Chadwick** saying presence was the only factor linking those defendants to criminal conduct. The crime here was behind closed doors and involved conduct suspicious to view. The lone dissenter cited **Di Re** and merely said, "Presence alone is not sufficient to constitute probable cause," and "hearing a conversation about an unlawful act does not implicate the listener." The most salient point had to be the "known use of innocent bystander status ruse" – a part of the drug dealer profile. The court did not feel comfortable with the decision. It had to know they were opening a very large door.

Of course the Fifth Circuit was not the only court apparently to either abandon or water down **U.S. v. Di Re.** Consider the decision of the Ninth Circuit in **U.S. v. Baron**, 860 F. 2d 911 (C.A. 9th 1988). From the opinion it is not clear that the police had any suspects other than the addressee of the package and the brother of the shipper of the package sent from Miami to Hawaii. In any event the package had been intercepted and a beeper was attached. The beeper's trail led to the addressee and he took the package to the brother's apartment. The brother lived there with his girlfriend, defendant Baron. As the three left the apartment they were stopped. Since a "tracing" powder was placed in the package, they took Baron to a darkened room to use a fluorescent lamp. That test proved positive. Taking her to the room converted an investigative stop into an arrest. Was there probable cause? Yes, said the court. Since the beeper changed tones while in the brother's house they felt there was enough. They called it a close question and said, "in finding probable cause based on association with persons engaged in criminal activity, a significant consideration is whether the nature of the criminal activity is such that it could not normally be carried on without the knowledge of all persons present." It appears that the *actus reus* was fully satisfied upon knowledge alone. What *mens rea* was present?

Consider the Ninth Circuit's **Sokolow** case. Although convicted of possessing cocaine with intent to distribute, the Ninth Circuit reversed Sokolow's conviction. What conduct caught the government's attention? He bought two Honolulu to Miami to Honolulu round trip airline tickets with cash ($2100) from a wad of $20.00 bills in the names of Kray and Norian. The ticket agent called the DEA. The DEA called the phone number given by Sokolow. The answering machine was on and the ticket agent said it was Sokolow's voice. But the phone was listed in Karl Herman's name. The DEA did not know that Sokolow and Herman both lived at this address. On July 25, the day of the return to Honolulu, Sokolow had a layover in Los Angeles. The DEA observed Sokolow and he "appeared to be very nervous and was looking all around the waiting area." He was wearing a black jump suit and a large amount of gold jewelry and had carry-on luggage.

He was stopped as he waited for his taxi in Honolulu. A sniffing dog was used. After a false positive on the first bag, the positive on the second bag backed by a second "sniffer" yielded the booty. Unfortunately the police seized Sokolow, thus the DEA moved from mere confrontation to seizure — seizure that must at least be supported by articulable suspicion for **Terry** or probable cause for an arrest. The police suspicion was based solely on the drug courier profile: (1) short trip to a source city; (2) paid cash for ticket; (3) carried luggage; 4) appeared nervous in L.A.; (5) dressed weirdly; (6) answered a phone via an answering machine even though phone was registered to another.

The trouble, the court said, is that a lot of people do the things Sokolow did and they are not guilty of anything. There was no particular conduct here that shouted criminal. In fact as it turned out Sokolow was traveling under his own name. The court closed its opinion by quoting Becton saying, "[C]ourts should consider the profiles as nothing more than an administrative tool of the police." It is hazy in form, susceptible to great adaptations, and almost entirely speculative. It may generate good police work, but absent more, it certainly would generate bad law. **U.S. v. Sokolow**, 831 F. 2d 1413 (C.A. 9th 1987).

Finally, in another case, a drug courier profile composed entirely of factors consistent with innocent activity may not be, in itself, the basis for stopping a motor vehicle on the highway for investigation, said the Virginia Court of Appeals. These two defendants were stopped because they were: (1) young; (2) black; (3) driving northward; (4) interstate highway; (5) rental car; (6) Florida tags; and (7) acted nervous in response to an officer's rolling surveillance. **Taylor v. Commonwealth**, 369 S.E. 2d 423 (Va. Ct. App. 1988).

The hope for final resolution of the use of profiles did not materialize in the Supreme Court's opinion in the **Sokolow** case. No one was more frustrated than Justice Marshall. He said,."..the majority thus ducks serious issues relating to a questionable law enforcement practice, to address the validity of which we granted certiorari in this case," and later said, "The majority's hasty conclusion to the contrary serves only to indicate its willingness, when drug crimes or anti-drug policies are at issue, to give short shrift to constitutional rights."

What did the Court say? Consider first the decision of the majority. It, in essence, totally avoided the profile issue, holding that some of the factors had evidentiary significance regardless of whether they are set forth in a "profile." **U.S. v. Sokolow**, 490 U.S. 1 (1989). The Court concluded that "a court sitting to determine the existence of reasonable suspicion must require the agent to articulate the factors leading to the conclusion, but the fact that these factors may be set forth in a 'profile' does not somehow detract from their evidentiary significance as seen by a trained agent." No mention was therefore made by the majority of the "chameleon-like" nature of profiles and the fact that they seem to be made up after the confrontation. The burden of how to handle them has been squarely thrown into the laps of the trial courts of the United States. This will create significant diversity of opinion and further lack of uniformity. It tangentially treated the custody issue raised by the Ninth Circuit. This will be discussed in Chapter Twelve.

Since Sokolow, courts that accept the use of profiles for articulable suspicion-based stops have been wrestling with which ones to credit. Florida, for example, has back-to-back cases where one profile was found wanting and the other approved. Both cases involved "personal" profiles created by the individual police officers. Both involved Interstate 95; the route of choice for drug couriers. In the first case it was 4:15 A.M.; the driver was alone; the driver was about 35 years old; out of state tags; large car; male driver; casually dressed driver; the driver was obeying all traffic laws; the car was on I-95. For these reasons the car was stopped. On these facts the court could find no "rational inference" between the acts observed and the suspected concealed criminal conduct. **State v. Johnson**, 561 So. 2d 1131 (Fla. 1990).

In the second case the defendant was stopped for following too closely. (Despite the fact that the Florida court had indicated in **Johnson** that they would require no independent criminal conduct or other violation of law to support a profile, it made a big difference in this case.). When stopped the defendant acted nervously; was traveling north on I-95; in a full sized car with a big trunk; with Massachusetts tags but with New York insurance inspection stickers; registered to someone else; trunk items in the back seat; ignition key separate from the other keys; and a CB in the car. By the way, it was 1:55 p.m. Here the court found a "rational inference" to link the profile to the suspicions to permit the detention to await the drug dogs. **Crisswell v. State**, 564 So. 2d 480 (Fla. 1990). Both cases clearly illustrate that the battle over profiles had not ended but that **Sokolow** is now encouraging police to use not only "official" profiles but also to use their own "individual" profiles.

In **U.S. v. Taylor**, 917 F. 2d 1402 (C.A. 6th 1990), the police used the following profile:

1.   arrived from a drug source city (Miami);
2.   walked away from the gate
     a.   nervously,
     b.   hurriedly, and
     c.   faster than other passengers;
3.   constantly looked backwards as he walked;
4.   carried a tote bag that he held tightly to his body; and
5.   left the terminal walking very fast.

The court noted that a "trained" officer might find this suspicious, but the officer in this case had just been assigned to this drug unit and had little training in identifying a drug courier. The officer admitted on the stand that there is "...no true 'drug courier profile'..." The court said the officer cannot have it both ways. Some comments were made by the officer about the defendant's "grungy" clothes and differing from the rest of the passengers. To this the court said, "there is no dress code for passengers...." Another officer said her suspicions were based on "nervousness" and race. The court was not pleased by that racial attack. It concluded that Taylor's behavior was "unsuspicious behavior."

Some very pointed and critical comments regarding profiles comes from Colorado's Supreme Court even though it was not a seizure case. That court ruled that criminal profiles are inadmissible as substantive evidence of a defendant's guilt and, in the case before them, it was not harmless error. The court did not bar the use of criminal profiles in all cases (in this case the state used the drug courier profile). The court noted that in **Reid** (*supra*), the Supreme Court classified the drug courier profile as a "somewhat informal compilation of characteristics believed to be typical of persons unlawfully carrying narcotics." Arizona went further and defined them as "a loose assortment of general, often contradictory, characteristics and behavior used by police to explain reasons for stopping and questioning persons about possible illegal drug activity." **State v. Lilly**, 959 P. 2d 799 at 801 (Ariz. 1998). Some courts call them too **elastic.** They are, as Colorado says, informal, unwritten, and ill-defined and are used subjectively and not intuitively. Colorado further notes that some characteristics are typical of most people, *e.g.*, people do travel in blue jeans who are not drug couriers; they wear crosses, do not wear watches, appear nervous, *etc.* Colorado further notes that using the drug profile had a tendency to include more people than it excludes. When deplaning they suggest that one should not get off first, last nor in the middle of the crowd. It also suggested that one should not buy a one-way or a round-trip ticket, and, above all, do not have a need for money. **Salcedo v. People**, 999 P. 2d 833 (Colo. *en banc* 2000). As substantive evidence the profile is dangerous. As an investigative tool it may have its place and this was all that the U.S. Supreme Court approved in **Sokolow**. However, the profile has such a chameleon-like personality that it often appears to be made up after the fact. Some even make sense, on the surface, if not based on race or ethnicity. For example, take the package from the high-source city or state. Ask the question which states are not high-source states? High source for whom? To be sure all states that border other nations or great bodies of water are high source states. But for many years Tennessee and an area outside of Memphis was a high-source state for Indiana and Chicago.

But let us assume Texas, for example, is a high source state. What packages sent from Texas fit the package profile? Heavily taped – non-drug shippers do not use a lot of tape? Method used to ship – no one but drug shippers use overnight priority services? Shipping charges paid for in cash – no innocent person pays cash for shipping? Use of a hand-written hand bill – no one fills out forms anymore? These were the profile points used to dog-sniff a package in Minnesota. This profile, as weak as it is, did not lead to a search since it was "sniffed" to gain probable cause but it was delayed two or three hours while a warrant was obtained. It did contain marijuana. The motion to suppress was denied and that decision was upheld on appeal. Why? First, it was not seized from the possession of the defendant but it was none-the-less seized. It passed muster under **U.S. v. Van Leeuwen**, 397 U.S. 249 (1970). Since there was "suspicion" even though it may not have been articulable suspicion in the purest terms, but add in the profile and Minnesota found articulable suspicion under the totality of the circumstances citing Sokolow. As an aside, it noted there was no relevance that it was sent to a person with an Hispanic name. **State v. Lopez**, 2000 WL 1468049 (Minn. App.). Note: had this package been intercepted by Fed Ex without police involvement the same result would have prevailed without having to justify the use of the police profile.

Another profile that is worth noting is the "street gang member" profile. Without question, costumes play an important role in the life of street gangs. Whenever an officer sees the "uniform" or colors of a particular gang, he knows much about their modus operandi due to continuous briefings on recent gang activity. To be sure the officer's interest will be piqued and if he sees two or more of the gang members "hanging together" his suspicions should be aroused. The gang's track record, historically, is often not that of community service (unless selling drugs, burning buildings, assaulting the elderly, terrorizing and shaking down business are community service). When two or more are "hanging out" – doing nothing – nothing wrong at the moment, can the officer do more the merely approach them and try to engage them in conversation (a non-**Terry** – mere confrontation)? Without more, that is all the officer can do. A pre-emptive strike based on a gang member's profile is not enough to indulge this form of seizure. The officer can ask them to move on but they do not have to obey that order since **Papichristou v. Jacksonville**, 405 U.S. 156 (1972) a choice to remain in a public place (absent a true emergency) "is as much a part of his liberty as the freedom of movement in side frontiers…." This, however, was strongly contested when Justice Thomas, in his dissent in **Morales,** said several states have dispersal statutes. See the footnote in his dissent in **Morales** at page 109, fn.7, listing the current dispersal statutes from 36 states.

The Morales case referred to is **Chicago v. Morales**, 527 U.S. 41 (1999). In an attempt to retake control of the streets in parts of Chicago and to quell the reasonable fears of its residents (particularly those in the "poorer" neighborhoods) caused by street gangs, Chicago passed an ordinance. The features were (1) a police officer observes a person whom the officer believes is a street gang member loitering in a public place with one or more persons; (2) the officer may order such person to leave; (3) any person who does not promptly leave may be arrested and for failure to obey the dispersal order faces a six month sentence, a fine of up to $500, community service or all three (as well as prosecution for any crime discovered as a result of the search incident). The ordinance appears to have worked well. The Chicago homicide rate dropped 26%. 89,000 dispersal orders were issued in three years and 42,000 arrests were made. Only two of thirteen trial judges found the ordinance constitutional. The rest felt it failed to notify individuals exactly what conduct was prohibited and it encouraged capricious action by the police. After all, some poor innocent person could get swept up in the "policing."

In any event, Illinois felt that the ordinance was unconstitutionally vague because it did not distinguish between innocent conduct and conduct calculated to cause harm. The U.S. Supreme Court agreed by a 6 to 3 vote. Justice Thomas' impassioned dissent notes: "I fear that the Court has unnecessarily sentenced law abiding citizens to lives of terror and misery. The ordinance is not vague." He continues, citing Justice White, that "any fool would know that a particular category of conduct would be within its reach." See White's dissent in **Kolender v. Lawson**, 461 U.S. 352 (1983). Thomas further notes that adults had to be recruited to help children walk safely to school. Indeed, we know that some children join gangs in a hope to survive.

The most insidious form of profiling is racial profiling. Assumptions are made that people of color should not drive expensive cars and should not even rent them, but if they do they must be drug couriers or dealers. Maryland, New York, New Jersey, and California among the many have had several infamous episodes. One prominent executive in Maryland (an African-American) was stopped over 24 times at the same place as he went to and from his professional work-site. Did he exceed the speed limit – yes, by a whopping two or three miles an hour – and he was even stopped because he was the only person observing the posted limit. This offense is called D.W.B. – driving while black.

New Jersey had been attempting to reverse this insidious practice that became an official part of their state police agency to the point that even officers of color were using it (often to avoid re-assignment, discipline, dismissal, *etc.*). A report entitled **"Interim Report of the State Police Review Team Regarding Racial Profiling Allegations"** was released in 1999. The report gave rise to the valid use of the selective enforcement defense that can even be raised for the first time on direct appeal and a guilty plea does not waive this defense. Indeed, New Jersey believes racial profiling and selective enforcement are synonymous and interchangeable. The Attorney General admitted the existence of profiling on race and that African-Americans were treated differently when stopped, how stopped, how they were questioned, how they were searched, how they were asked for consent searches, and even that drug dogs were always brought to the scene of auto stops of blacks and not of whites. If an African-American establishes profiling, that is in itself plain error to let the case go forward because, as New Jersey holds, it is clearly capable alone of producing an unjust result. See **State v. Williamson**, 763 A. 2d 285 (N.J. Super. A.D. 2000) and its companion case, **State v. Ross**, 763 A. 2d 281 (N.J. Super. A.D. 2000). In Ross the defendant traveled in the far left lane in his BMW for a whole three-quarters of a mile but he was not passing other cars (probably because he saw the trooper in his rear view mirror.)

V.   An Analytical Framework Based on Substantive Law

Though not to be overcome by hyper-technical ities, probable cause must still meet a certain amount of form and substance to prevent over-breadth of discretion and unbridled governmental conduct. By analogy, probable cause, as a matter of proof, is like the difference between an attempt and the completed crime. As there is in every completed crime, an attempt, there is in all proof beyond a reasonable doubt cases those things that would satisfy probable cause. As an attempt falls short of a completed crime, that information necessary to establish probable cause (and for strategical and tactical reasons, often does) can fall short of proof beyond a reasonable doubt. Thus courts must not look for perfection.

Like the problems presented by attempt law (before the Model Penal Code) where preparation had not yet ripened into perpetration, thus no conviction could be had, probable cause may still exist even though proof beyond a reasonable doubt is unattainable. In fact, probable cause is often based on hearsay most of which may not be or cannot be used in the trial of the cause. Without the hard proof necessary the case may well fail, but that does not taint the probable cause. In the context of a grand jury finding, probable cause (but not in the case of an issuing magistrate without independent source, attenuation, or inevitable discovery) may be based on illegally obtained evidence. **U.S. v. Calandra**, 414 U.S. 338 (1974).

This whole matter of probable cause raises the point of whether probable cause applies only to felonies and not to misdemeanors. The primary non-warrant arrest power at common law regarding a misdemeanor was very simple. An arrest could be made only if the misdemeanor was committed in the officer's presence. Absent statutory modification, the "in the presence" rule is still the law. This reflected and still reflects the recognition between the more serious threat that felonies present to society. However, see the discussion of **State v. Lester** (*supra* at page 21).

In footnote 2 of **New York v. Belton**, 453 U.S. 454 (1981) the Court noted that the validity of the custodial arrest of Belton had not been questioned. This raises the possibility that the Court is well aware that a problem exists in working with the misdemeanor-felony distinctions. And in footnote 3, they made clear they were only settling the **Chimel** (*infra* at Chapter Twelve) "wingspan" questions in regard to auto passenger compartment searches.

When the law says the offense has to be committed in the officer's presence, it means that the officer had to know an offense was being committed and was not just making a lucky guess. The law has always regarded the use of mere suspicion as a possible source of harassment and oppression. Therefore, the officer was required at common law to announce the purpose of the arrest and what law was broken at the time of the arrest. The officer could not wait until his return to the station to research the law.

The corollary rule is also true. The officer cannot hope that that for which he arrested the defendant will later turn out to be probable cause for a felony which may be unprovable yet justify the arrest. Even for probable cause for a felony the officer must recite facts known at or before the arrest that led him to believe a felony was in progress or had been committed. If he cannot, then mere suspicion alone existed for the arrest. The law prohibits fishing expeditions.

An arrest is not made legal by what it yields. It is good or bad when it starts and does not change character from its success. This was demonstrated when a drug enforcement agent saw a woman in Atlanta whose bail condition was that she stay in Ohio. He arrested her for bail jumping because she told the officer she had not been given permission to leave Ohio when so questioned. The problem was that the Bail Reform Act had only one criminal penalty and that for a failure to appear. Since the officer did not know of any missed required appearances he had neither probable cause to believe a felony had been committed nor a misdemeanor committed in his presence. Therefore, the evidence found on the defendant's person was the fruit of an illegal arrest. **U.S. v. Williams**, 594 F. 2d 86 (C.A. 5th 1979). As it was said in **U.S. v. Di Re**, 332 U.S. 581 (1947), "It is the officer's responsibility to know what he is arresting for, and why, and one in the unhappy plight of being taken into custody is not required to test the legality of the arrest before the officer who is making it."

One further problem involving misdemeanor arrests justifies comment. There are a number of state agencies which have been given enforcement powers. Very often these enforcement powers are limited only to conduct involving the agency's area of interest. For example, in Louisiana, fish and wildlife officers were not given general peace officer status. They were limited to arrests for the enforcement of game laws. In that state an officer of the department suspected a person of violating drug possession laws at the misdemeanor level. The officer made an arrest. The arrest was deemed illegal. The question then arose whether the arrest could be justified as a citizen's arrest. The Louisiana Court had to reject that theory because in Louisiana, a citizen could arrest only for a felony. The arrest and the fruits of the search incident had to be declared void and inadmissible. **State v. Longolus**, 374 So. 2d 1208 (La. 1979).

The modern use of probable cause to arrest for a misdemeanor is upheld despite the common law tradition requiring a warrant or commission in the presence of the officer. Why? Arkansas gives us the best answer through **State v. Lester**, 2001 WL 126176 (Ark.). The misdemeanor involved a defendant who did not pay for his gasoline. These are "gas drive-off" cases. It was reported immediately to the police who very quickly stopped the defendant and arrested him without a warrant and without having seen the incident. A statute authorized an arrest in other circumstances but did not include this type of crime. However, when the Arkansas court reviewed **Gerstein v. Pugh**, 420 U.S. 103 (1975) and **County of Riverside v. McLaughlin**, 500 U.S. 44 (1991), it found that the U.S. Supreme Court only expressed a preference for a warrant but that the Court never has invalidated an arrest in a public place supported by probable cause because a warrant was not first secured. The Supreme Court's primary concern has been the prompt judicial review of the probable cause issue. Arkansas concluded that the Supreme Court does not make such warrantless arrests for misdemeanors a Fourth Amendment issue.

Arrests and searches for felonies must be based on probable cause. The form and substance must have some logical basis, or to put it another way, we should avoid the great logic faults: The non-sequitur; hasty generalizations; and glittering generalities. The focus of this section centers on the two-fold problems of both definitions of the information that the officer: (1) leads him to believe; and (2) would when tested against a person of ordinary caution, that reasonable person would also believe in the purpose to either search or arrest. This two-fold test is to prevent the use of the logic faults. The test is society's attempt to avoid the one-sided adversarial view of one whose whole life is involved in the "war against crime." It is a balancing and moderating mechanism which is an attempt to "de-emotionalize" the crime fighting process.

It is more than a loop-hole. The test should be viewed as a **fail-safe device**. Those who are charged with enforcing laws must spend most of their time with less than the best. It would be easy to parlay what would be innocent looking facts into criminal conduct because officers are trained to be suspicious and conscientious observers of conduct. What society asks is, tell us your story and let us judge whether the conduct would lead the less well-trained eye to the same conclusion; that the inferences point more to a specific criminal involvement than to a general look of evil or even to some possible lawful activity. Therefore, the presented **facts** must point to more than some general evil; it **must point to a specific, describable crime**.

Several tips regarding a methamphetamine center and "chop-shop" operation were received by a federal-state task force. Through aerial photographs, ether odors detected, security lights aimed outward from the buildings, motion sensing lights at the gates and infra-red light sources, the officers concluded the tips were correct and they applied for and received a warrant. The court said "when viewed as a whole.. ." there was a substantial basis for finding probable cause under the totality of the circumstances. **Fouse v. State**, 2001 WL 246427 (Ark.).

Three decisions illustrate whether good or faulty logic was used to arrive at the probable cause decision. In **Bradshaw v. State**, 2001 WL 120054 (Tex. App. San Antonio) the issue whether probable cause existed for a warrant for a house based on what was found during a lawful search of a delivery service box. No additional facts had been developed by the police. Drugs were found in the box. That led the police to apply for a warrant to search the defendant's house. What facts were revealed by the contents of the box that logically point to the house? Does mere control of the box, without more, point to the house? Forty-five thousand dollars of currency was found in the box and the money smelled of marijuana. Do these facts, without more, point to the residence? No. A second logic fault, the glittering generality, was also used for the residential warrant. The affidavit stated that "quantities of currency and other evidence and documents would be constantly maintained at the residence given his long-term involvement in the drug trade."

Perhaps the most perplexing problem in drug cases involves finding drugs in a residence shared by two or more people. Is there sole possession or joint possession? How can logic be employed without reliance on one of the great logic faults? Two decisions from 2001 illustrate the analysis that should be made. The first, **State v. Reese**, 774 So. 2d 948 (Fla. App. 2001) dealt with the defendant's proximity to the contraband. The court notes that mere proximity is not enough when standing alone as a fact. Indeed, that would be conclusion jumping. The state must show facts and circumstances that the defendant (1) had dominion and control, (2) was aware of the contraband and (3) knew of the illicit nature of the contraband. In this case the police had a warrant for the house and the defendant was standing at the front door when the police arrived. She immediately shut the door. She was next seen at the doorway of the bathroom. She was removed from that doorway and the contraband was seen in the toilet bowl . Can it be concluded, logically, that even though she was the only one of the tenants in the house that there was probable cause to arrest and ultimately try her for possession? Here we have, as the court notes, "a joint occupant alone, in close proximity to contraband in plain view   "about to be destroyed and she is blocking the entrance to the room of the attempted destruction. This may not be proof beyond a reasonable doubt but it is good probable cause to arrest and charge.

The second case comes from Maryland and involves contraband and two persons present where one looks more guilty than the other. How can both be arrested? Did the police jump to a conclusion or was the conclusion reasonable? The police had a warrant to search the house and they lawfully entered. Two men were present. One was still smoking a marijuana cigar; the other, the defendant in this case, was not smoking marijuana. There were several burnt cigars strewn about the room and some un-smoked marijuana in plain view. The defendant received his mail at this address. His bedroom was searched and cocaine was found on the dresser and inside the dresser drawers. Cash was found: $500 on top of the bed and $12,000 under the box spring. The defendant says he was not the someone they wanted. The court notes the unlawful possession may be constructive as well as actual and joint as well as exclusive. The factors to use affirming at least joint possession are: (1) Proximity; (2) Knowledge of the presence of contraband; (3) Presence of circumstances from which a reasonable inference could be drawn that the defendant was participating with others in the mutual use and enjoyment of the contraband and (4) Possessory right in the premises. All of the tests were met in this case. **Herbert v. State**, 766 A. 2d 190 (Md. App. 2001).

However, courts will take into account the experience and training of the officer coupled with all other surrounding facts and circumstances when making the judgment. But as already stated, one cannot jump to a conclusion. Experience and expertise are relevant to the probable cause determination. Its relevance in a particular case must be sufficiently conveyed so that it can be understood by the average reasonably prudent person.

Consider the case of **Spinelli v. United States**, 393 U.S. 410 (1969). What did the Court say about this affidavit? Without the informant's tip there would have been no reason to suspect let alone believe a crime was in progress. Going to and from an apartment is not unusual or evil in itself. Having two telephone numbers is not highly unusual. The assertion that Spinelli was known as a gambler and one who associates with gamblers the Court characterized as a "bold and unilluminating assertion of suspicion that is entitled to no weight...." Thus all but the last paragraph had to go. And unless that paragraph met **Aguilar** or **Gates** today, it is no more than a bare conclusion. The **Spinelli** case also illustrates that a "snow job" or encyclopedic recitation of words will not be permitted to take the place of probable cause. **It is not the quantity of words; it is the quality of those words** as facts and whether the inferences they raise run logically to probable evidence of a crime or location of the evidence of a crime.

Therefore, the probable cause rule is akin to the circumstantial evidence rule. In circumstantial evidence we reason from known facts that are proven to establish such ultimate facts as are conjectured to exist. But circumstantial evidence must exclude pure guess work. More than that, the inference sought must logically follow; it must compute. Thus known gamblers can have two phones and not be engaged in using them for illegal purposes. The two proven facts do not necessarily support the ultimate fact that the police believe. In this context let us consider the **Spinelli** affidavit.

Affidavit in Support of Search Warrant

I, Robert L. Bender, being dully sworn, depose and say that I am a Special Agent of the Federal Bureau of Investigation, and as such am authorized to make searches and seizures.

That on August 6, 1985, at approximately 11:44 a.m., William Spinelli was observed by an Agent of the Federal Bureau of Investigation driving a 1964 Ford convertible, Missouri license HC3-649, onto the Eastern approach of the Veterans Bridge leading from East St. Louis, Illinois, to St. Louis, Missouri.

That on August 11, 1965, at approximately 11:16 a.m., William Spinelli was observed by an Agent of the Federal Bureau of Investigation driving a 1964 Ford convertible, Missouri license HC3-649, onto the eastern approach of the Eads Bridge leading from East St. Louis, Illinois, to St. Louis, Missouri. Further, at approximately 11:18 a.m. on August 11, 1965, I observed William Spinelli driving the aforesaid Ford convertible from the Western approach of the Eads Bridge into St. Louis, Missouri. Further, at approximately 4:40 p.m. on August 11, 1965, I observed the aforesaid Ford convertible, bearing Missouri license HC3-649, parked in a parking lot used by residents of The Chieftain Manor Apartments, approximately one block east of 1108 Indian Circle Drive.

On August 12, 1965, at approximately 12:07 William Spinelli was observed by an Agent of the Federal Bureau of Investigation driving the aforesaid 1964 Ford convertible onto the Eastern approach of the Veterans Bridge from East St. Louis, Illinois, in the direction of St. Louis, Missouri.

Further, on August, 12 1965, at approximately 3:46 p.m. I observed William Spinelli driving the aforesaid 1964 Ford convertible onto the parking lot used by the residents of The Chieftain Manor Apartment approximately one block east of 1108 Indian Circle Drive.

Further, on August 12, 1965, at approximately 3:49 p.m., William Spinelli was observed by an Agent of the Federal Bureau of Investigation entering the front entrance of the two-story apartment building located at 1108 Indian Circle Drive, this building being one of The Chieftain Manor Apartments.

On August 13, 1965, at approximately 11:08 a.m., William Spinelli was observed by an Agent of the Federal Bureau of Investigation driving the aforesaid Ford convertible onto the Eastern approach of the Eads Bridge from East St. Louis, Illinois, heading towards St. Louis, Missouri.

Further, on August 13, 1965, at approximately 11:11 a.m., I observed William Spinelli driving the aforesaid Ford convertible from the Western approach of the Eads Bridge into St. Louis, Missouri.

Further, on August 13, 1965, at approximately 3:45 p.m., I observed William Spinelli driving the aforesaid 1964 Ford convertible onto the parking area used the resident of The Chieftain Manor Apartments, said parking area being approximately one block from 1108 Indian Circle Drive.

Further, on August 13, 1965, at approximately 3:55 p.m., William Spinelli was observed by an Agent of the Federal Bureau of Investigation entering the corner apartment located on the second floor in the southwest corner, known as Apartment F. of the two-story apartment building known and numbered as 1108 Indian Circle Drive.

On August 16, 1965, at approximately 3:22 p.m., I observed William Spinelli driving the aforesaid Ford convertible onto the parking lot used by the residents of The Chieftain Manor Apartments approximately one block east of 1108 Indian Circle Drive.

Further, an Agent of the F.B.I. observed William Spinelli alight from the aforesaid Ford convertible and walk toward the apartment building located at 1108 Indian Circle Drive.

The records of the Southwestern Bell Telephone Company reflect that there are two telephones located in the southwest corner apartment on the second floor of the apartment building located at 1108 Indian Circle Drive under the name of Grace P. Hagen. The numbers listed in the Southwestern Bell Telephone Company records for the aforesaid telephones are WYdown 4-0029 and WYdown 4-0136.

William Spinelli is known to this affiant and to federal law enforcement agents and local law enforcement agents as a bookmaker, an associate of bookmakers, a gambler, and an associate of gamblers.

The Federal Bureau of Investigation has been informed by a confidential reliable informant that William Spinelli is operating a handbook and accepting wagers and disseminating wagering information by means of telephones which have been assigned the numbers WYdown 4-0029 and WYdown 4-0136.

/s/ Robert L. Bender
Robert L. Bender
Special Agent, Federal Bureau of Investigation.
Subscribed and sworn to before me this 18th day of August, 1965, at St. Louis, Missouri.
/s/ William R. O'Toole

VI.   Probable Cause for Arrest: Different from Probable Cause for Search of a Place?

If police have probable cause to believe that there is contraband in a place, does it follow that, without linking information, they automatically have probable cause to arrest anyone present in the house? The answer is no. Probable cause for one purpose does not always provide probable cause for the other. We have seen that principle illustrated by the "wingspan" doctrine where the Court curtailed, in **Chimel** (*infra* at Chapter Twelve), broad searches of places where an arrestee was found. The opposite is also true. In **U.S. v. Connally**, 479 F. 2d 930 (C.A. 9th 1973), the police knew that cocaine had been taken from certain premises not long before they arrived. But they did not know who might be inside the house, how long such persons might have been there or what relationship these individuals might have to the prime suspect in the case. All the agents knew was that some contraband probably remained on the premises. The court said that, "Even certain knowledge that contraband is within a dwelling does not constitute probable cause to arrest whoever happens to be inside" and cited the leading case of **Johnson v. United States,** 333 U.S. 10 (1948). The critical issue then is whether the same quantum of evidence is required for a probable cause to arrest as opposed to that required to conduct a search. This is the point made by La Fave in his treatise at section 3.1 (b). All courts, La Fave says, assume the same is required and he says this is understandable. But, he goes on, "while it is true that there is a common ground for discussing the quantum required, it does not follow that probable cause to arrest or to search are in all respects identical." As the **Connally** case shows this is clearly not the case.

Each, La Fave continues, requires a showing of probabilities as to somewhat different facts and circumstances. In the case of arrest the conclusion concerns the guilt of the arrestee, whereas in the case of a search the conclusions go to the connection of the items sought with the crime and to their present location. The right to search is not dependent upon the right to arrest. A warrant to search is not invalid simply because there are no grounds to arrest any particular person. As stated, all the law tries to do is to avoid pitfalls in logic.

VII. Probable Cause: The Warrant and the Doubtful or Marginal Case

In an earlier section it was mentioned that the standard of probable cause is the necessary leeway given law enforcement. The leeway is that officers are not required to arrest or search on the basis of either beyond a reasonable doubt nor by clear and convincing evidentiary standards. Although an argument could be made that they are to meet a preponderance standard, it is my opinion that even that is too high, yet it could be workable as a starting point for the judge viewing suppression issues.

This then raises that point of the leeway in a case in which a warrant was issued but the case for probable cause was doubtful or marginal. Too often the tendency is to jump to the conclusion that since the warrant process was used, all doubt must be resolved in favor of the state. As the **Spinelli** case points out, that is not the conclusion to be drawn. Only after an adequate affidavit is presented and a hearing is held can the leeway be given in the doubtful or marginal case. Consider two leading cases on this point.

The first case is **U.S. v. Ventresca**, 380 U.S. 102 (1965). After conviction, Ventresca persuaded the Court of Appeals to agree with him that the affidavit was insufficient upon the question of probable cause. The affidavit was in no way as conclusory as the **Spinelli** affidavit. The Court began its analysis noting that there is a preference to be accorded searches under a warrant that might not be sustainable had there been no warrant. To do otherwise would in fact keep police from seeking warrants. The commands of the Fourth Amendment are practical and not technical and absolute. In overruling the decision of the Court of Appeals, the Court said, "...where these circumstances are detailed, where reason for crediting the source of information is given, and when a magistrate has found probable cause, the courts should not invalidate the warrant by interpreting the affidavit in a hyper-technical, rather than commonsense manner."

Perhaps one court may have forgotten this last point. To be sure, to win an appeal, the state must argue the right theory. In an Ohio case, the state failed to argue that the purse searched in the house was a container that could and did contain the things sought by the valid warrant. Instead it allowed the defense to frame the issue as a consent search that probably was coerced. The tragedy is that the state missed the real issue and appellate court was in no mood to point out that preference for a warrant would have saved the evidence. The case was not remanded; the judgment suppressing the evidence was affirmed. **State v. Keith**, 2001 WL 173, 203 (Ohio App. 2 Dist.) (unpub. op.).

Oregon has a recent case that reminds suppression judges that close calls go to the state when a warrant is used and that the court is not to focus on isolated short-comings: that the entire document must be read as a whole. **State v. Pelster**, 2001 WL 195161 (Ore. App.) citing **State v. Villagran**, 657 P. 2d 1223 (Ore. 1983) and its admonition to use a commonsense and realistic approach. In accord see **Herbert v. State**, 766 A. 2d 190 (Md. App. 2001) and the fact that the state, when it uses a warrant, is "rewarded by a presumption of validity in favor of its warrant application" and the "burden is on the defendant to rebut it, if he can." See also **State v. Shaw and Shaw**, 775 So. 2d 1067 (La. 2001).

In **Massachusetts v. Upton**, 466 U.S. 727 (1984), the Court held that the two-prong test of **Aguilar** was hyper-technical and replaced it with the "totality" test which they felt was more in keeping with the practical, commonsense decisions demanded of the magistrate. They reemphasized that the reviewing court should not have a grudging or negative attitude toward warrants. They said that through **Gates** they rejected after-the-fact, *de novo* scrutiny. There was, in this case, internal coherence with the informant's story and the surrounding facts. The magistrate in this case did not approve a mere hunch or a bare recital of legal conclusions. Finally, citing **Ventresca**, the Court said: "Although in a particular case it may not be easy to determine when an affidavit demonstrates the existence of probable cause, the resolution of doubtful or marginal cases in this area (warrants) should be largely determined by the preference to be accorded to warrants."

VIII. The Moving Target of Probable Cause

One of the points made in **Schmerber v. California**, 384 U.S. 757 (1966) was that although probable cause may be present for one purpose to search without a warrant this may not *ipso facto* be enough to authorize a bodily intrusion unless a real case for exigency is made out. Such a case was made out in **Schmerber**. The Court also indicated a preference for a warrant for bodily intrusion cases. They summed the case up by saying: "That we today hold that the constitution does not forbid the states minor intrusions into an individual's body under stringently limited conditions in no way indicates that it permits more substantial intrusions, or intrusions under other conditions." Thus, the Court gave some hint that the target could move a little according to the privacy interest sought to be invaded. This is particularly true when a warrantless search is conducted. The probable cause remains the same, in all reality, it is the intervention of the neutral and detached magistrate that becomes all important.

This is well illustrated by the Louisiana Supreme Court in its decision in **State v. Fontenot**, 383 So. 2d 365 (La. 1980). Fontenot had secreted a bottle of Seconal in her vagina. Without securing a warrant, the police had the coroner remove the bottle at the local hospital. Although there was a clear indication that the bottle would be found (her friend told the police where it was), they did not secure a warrant and failed to explain why there was insufficient time to secure a warrant. What would have been probable cause under a warrant was not sufficient in and of itself to overcome the need to demonstrate exigency.

Surgical intrusion was also the subject of **Winston v. Lee**, 470 U.S. 753 (1985). The state had moved to compel surgery to remove a bullet which would have proven or disproved complicity in an armed robbery. A clear case of probable cause was made out but the Court decided that such an intrusion implicates expectations of privacy and security of such magnitude that the intrusion may be unreasonable which can only be decided on a case-by-case basis. Notwithstanding the existence of probable cause, a search for evidence of a crime may be unjustifiable if it endangers the life or health of a suspect. Finally, the Court held that:.".the Fourth Amendment's command that searches be `reasonable' requires that when the state seeks to intrude upon an area in which our society recognizes a significantly heightened privacy interest, a more substantial justification is required to make the search reasonable."

After the surgical removal cases, the most perplexing cases remain the body cavity searches. There is no doubt that these searches are highly intrusive, **Rodrigues v. Furtado**, 950 F. 2d 805 (C.A. 1st 1991). However, as the First Circuit said, if the search is supported by probable cause upon a warrant and the method of conducting the search protects the citizens from hygiene and physical problems, the search, as conducted, will be upheld. In the **Furtado** case a mere visual examination was found to be inadequate thus the police applied for a warrant so that the doctor would be permitted to enter the cavity (in this case a female's vagina). A hygienically conducted manual invasion under approved medical techniques was sanctioned. Balancing society's interest against the individual rights, the individual's rights have to give way the court said.

The Ninth Circuit, in essence, agrees with the First Circuit. The Ninth Circuit's rule appears to be that any body cavity search, including visuals, unless based on exigency or consent, must be conducted upon probable cause pursuant to a warrant because of the interest of human dignity and privacy. **Fuller v. M.G. Jewelry**, 950 F. 2d 1442 (C.A. 9th 1991).

Next is there a higher probable cause standard required for the First Amendment type problem? Some had come to that conclusion, but according to the Court that is not so. **New York v. P.J. Video, Inc.**, 475 U.S. 868 (1986). They held that an application for a warrant authorizing the seizure of materials presumptively protected by the First Amendment were to be tested under the same standard of probable cause used to review warrant applications generally.

It can be said with some confidence that the seriousness of the crime does influence the probable cause determination even when there is not explicit acknowledgment of this fact. But perhaps such cases are better analyzed in an "offense deemed to call for immediate response" type cases – that the exigencies of the situation are such that some diminution of the probable cause is required.

CHAPTER THREE
AN ANNOTATED SEARCH WARRANT

I. Jurisdiction: Venue of the Warrant

STATE OF: _____

COUNTY OF: _____

TO ANY LAWFUL OFFICER OF_____ COUNTY,_____:

Blank spaces are the bane of our courts. The more blanks the more a warrant appears to be a general warrant or the detested writ of assistance, both of which are prohibited by the State and United States constitutions. That a minor revolutionary war was fought to establish personal rights need not be elaborated upon. The appropriate comment comes from the Honorable George H. Ethridge in **Elardo v. State**, 164 Miss. 623, 145 So. 615 (1933) where he penned: "The evils flowing from unrestrained power prior to the founding of our government show that such power is more dangerous to the general welfare than an individual criminal, and that it is best for society as a whole that we have these constitutional rights, and that they apply to and protect every person subject to the jurisdiction of our government."

Because of state rules requiring warrants to be issued for only the county in which it is issued unless other criteria apply, a California search warrant was not valid. The California 1st District Court of Appeal saved it, however, since the statute itself was vague and the officer could have reasonably believed the warrant was good. **People v. Dantzler**, 206 Cal. Rep. 526 (Cal. Dist. Ct. App. 1988). Sometimes a judge of one district will issue a warrant for search in another district. Under local statutes is this permissible? Does it make a difference where the warrant is to be returned?

II.   Affiant(s) name(s) and Oath(s) Clause

> *WHEREAS,*   _____,   _____,   _____,   *AND*
> _____, *KNOWN TO ME TO BE A CREDIBLE PERSON,*
> *HAVE THIS DAY MADE COMPLAINT ON OATH BEFORE*
> *ME AS FOLLOWS*:

That the standard form has more than one blank for names of affiants does not mean several names are required. An affidavit may be made by one person. The critical points involve (1) the oath and (2) personal appearance. Since **Aguilar v. Texas**, 378 U.S. 108 (1964), the issuing judge may be called upon to testify at a suppression hearing to determine whether the oath was administered, and whether the elapsed time was sufficient to establish the detachment and neutrality expected at such hearings. The judge must not serve as a rubber stamp for police. Under Fed. R. Crim. Proc. 41(c)(2) it is alright for a U.S. Attorney to serve as an affiant. **U.S. v. Sequoia**, 800 F. 2d 39 (C.A. 2d 1986). Local statutes should be consulted regarding who may be an affiant for particular crimes.

There was a time when judges, particularly justices of the peace, did not bother with a swearing-in ceremony as was obviously required. Transcripts of testimony taken in cases challenging the validity of the lay justice system revealed such responses as: "No, I don't swear'em in – they wouldn't lie to me." Hopefully, today all judges understand the solemnity of the process and the power that is unleashed by a search warrant. The bottom line is that the warrant must be issued by a neutral, detached, and disinterested magistrate. **Coolidge v. New Hampshire**, 403 U.S. 443 (1971); **Connally v. Georgia**, 429 U.S. 245 (1977); **U.S. v. U.S. District Court**, 407 U.S. 297 (1972); **Lo-Ji Sales, Inc. v. New York**, 442 U.S. 319 (1979); **U.S. v. Leon**, 468 U.S. 897 (1984); and **Steagald v. U.S.**, 451 U.S. 204 (1981). The purpose of the "ceremony" is to hang the sword of perjury over the head of the affiant. Not all judges understand the solemnity of the process, however. One would think that something as basic and specifically required by the Constitution as the oath would never be omitted. Yet one federal magistrate failed to put an officer under oath in the process of issuing a telephonic warrant. This constitutionally infirm warrant and its fruits were suppressed by the federal trial judge.

The critical issue, as the Fifth Circuit viewed it, was whether **Leon** and its "good faith" standard could be used to save this warrant. See the discussion of **Leon**, (*infra*) Section VII, this chapter. The Fifth Circuit classified the omission of the oath, in this case, as inadvertent. There was neither allegation nor proof of a biased judge, nor evidence that the police were using reckless falsehoods. Since an assistant U.S. Attorney applied for the warrant there was no way the executing officers could have acted unreasonably in reliance on this otherwise facially valid warrant. The court felt that their decision to uphold the search would not encourage magistrate shopping. They concluded that suppression in this case would not serve a deterrent purpose. **U.S. v. Richardson**, 943 F. 2d 547 (C.A. 5th 1991).

It is unfortunate that the neutrality of the issuing magistrate or judge keeps coming up, but it does. Judges who issue warrants should not put themselves in a position where their integrity can be called into question. In some cases, the judge creates a question by issuing the warrant not from his or her own office, but from law enforcement offices. Courts will "bail them out," but they should not have to. For example, in **U.S. v. Whitehorn**, 652 F. Supp. 395 (N.D. N.Y.) aff'd 829 F. 2d 1225 (C.A. 2d 1987), the court found that neutrality was not violated merely because the issuing magistrate had been at the F.B.I. office when the warrant was issued. There was no showing that it affected his decision. In **U.S. v. Guarino**, 729 F. 2d 864 (C.A. 1st 1984) the magistrate went to the F.B.I. office to see the pornography taken during the first search and then the magistrate approved the second warrant. The court upheld the warrant. The inconvenience of bringing all of the evidence to the judge may dictate such an accommodation. Sometimes the magistrate appears to be one with law enforcement and yet the warrant is upheld. In **U.S. v. Dorman**, 657 F. Supp. 511 (W.D. N. C. 1987), the magistrate called a detective and ordered him to participate in the investigation. Unfortunately, this looks like the judicial branch had taken over the executive branch, yet the search was upheld. A judge will sometimes make comments that appear to show a personal bias. Such was the case in **U.S. v. Bowers**, 828 F. 2d 1169 (C.A. 6th 1987). Fortunately the expression of bias came after the surveillance order and was probably the result of what the judge learned from the surveillance, thus the warrant was upheld.

One final issue of neutrality concerns the practice of judge shopping. Just how can a warrant be approved by a judge after it has been turned down by another? Theoretically it cannot, but it happens quite often. More often than not, the police know which judges are pro police and which are not. That is why **Leon** is such a dangerous case unless the reviewing courts carefully scrutinize the warrant issuing process. There is one case that approved a form of judge shopping. A judge turned down a warrant and the police, with that judge's permission, went to the second judge who also knew that the first judge had turned the warrant down. The second judge issued the warrant. The reviewing court felt that this conduct meant that the first decision was not a final decision, thus estoppel and *res judicata* did not apply as they otherwise would have. **U.S. v. Savides**, 658 F. Supp. 1399 (N.D. Ill. 1987).

Four Corners or Contemporaneous Record

How many writings are required, by the U. S. Constitution, for a valid warranted search? Only one – the warrant itself. Nowhere in the Fourth Amendment is there a requirement for a written application or affidavit. The Constitution only directs that information, under oath or affirmation, be given to the issuing magistrate for his or her decision. The only written instrument required is the warrant itself. As a result, it can be concluded that the complaining officer need only be sworn and state facts supporting issuance of the warrant. If the magistrate finds probable cause, the magistrate would reduce these facts to the written form of the warrant and the search could proceed.

One possible result of this process would be that the magistrate would not in fact transcribe everything heard. These omissions could merit a challenge to the warrant's sufficiency regarding probable cause. Of course, no warrant can issue without probable cause. Should the defendant prevail on the challenge or should the state be able to prove the pre-search information that was in fact given to the magistrate? Courts use the following procedures to resolve this issue.

Some courts require that all warrants must be supported by a written application or affidavit. Only the information set forth in this application or affidavit may be used to later assess the magistrate's probable cause determination when challenged by the defendant's motion to suppress. Information presented to the magistrate may not be considered. This procedure is known as the "**Four Corners Doctrine.**" When this procedure is used, the magistrate is called to testify at the suppression hearing to verify the use of the oath, the length of time consumed in the process and why he or she found probable cause. Other states permit a combination of testimony and writings (both under oath). But to permit review, the live testimony must be recorded in writing, subscribed under oath and attached to the warrant and incorporated by reference. This point is emphasized in the following case: "It is an anomaly in judicial procedure to attempt to review the judicial act of a magistrate issuing a search warrant upon a record made up wholly or partially by oral testimony taken in the reviewing court long after the search warrant was issued. Judicial action must be reviewed upon the record made at or before the time that the judicial act was performed. The validity of judicial action cannot be made to depend upon the facts recalled by fallible human memory at a time somewhat removed from that when the judicial determination was made. This record of the facts presented to the magistrate need take no particular form. The record may consist of the sworn complaint, of affidavits, or of sworn testimony taken in shorthand and later filed, or of testimony reduced to longhand and filed, or of a combination of all these forms of proof. The form is immaterial. The essential thing is that proof be reduced to permanent form and made a part of the record which may be transmitted to the reviewing court." **Gladowski v. State**, 220 N.W. 227, 230 (Wis. 1928).

Other states allow verbal applications or affidavits supplemented by testimony under oath, as long as a record of the issuing process is made. This record can then be presented for review at the suppression hearing in place of or in addition to the magistrate's testimony. This procedure is known as the **Contemporaneous Record Rule**. A written affidavit may also be used but it is not necessarily required.

What is the concern with respect to the use of the procedures described above? Effective law enforcement often necessitates obtaining search warrants with great haste. The importance of time along with the need to protect the identity of confidential informers frequently results in the use of conclusory statements in the affidavit in support of probable cause. Since conclusory statements may not be the basis for probable cause, the magistrate may question the affiant as to the underlying facts and circumstances. If no record is made of the affiant's oral testimony in support of probable cause, and the affidavit is facially insufficient, the reviewing court has no way to assess the evidence that was before the magistrate at the time the warrant was issued. Inherent in allowing the issuing magistrate to take the stand and to fill in the reliability factor at the suppression hearing is the danger that his memory will be faulty, or that his testimony will consist of knowledge he acquired after the warrant was issued. Usually, affidavits which require supplementation in this way are mere conclusions. Since the search and seizure power unleashed by a warrant is awesome, some system of checks and balances must exist to ensure against Fourth Amendment violations.

As stated in **Aguilar v. Texas**, 378 U.S. 108 (1964) the " mere affirmation of a belief of suspicion is not enough." The Court said there must be facts from which inferences can be drawn by a neutral and detached magistrate, one that does not "serve as a rubber stamp for the police," therefore the issuing authority cannot "accept without question the [complaining] officer's conclusions." When information supplied by a confidential informant is offered in support of the warrant, "the magistrate must be informed of the underlying circumstances from which the informant concluded" the defendant had engaged in criminal activity. In **Spinelli v. United States**, 393 U.S. 410 (1969) the Court concluded that the complaining officer did not offer the magistrate any reason to support the affidavit's conclusions and that the affidavit needed further support because sufficient detail was not presented. The Court noted that there was no way to determine whether the conclusions came from casual rumors, or whether it was based on his general reputation, or whether in fact there was credible evidence of on-going wrongdoing.

Balanced against this search for detail, is the fact that the Court constantly, in **Spinelli** and **Aguilar**, referred to the common sense that was to be used by warrant-reviewing courts. As it held in **U.S. v. Ventresca**, 380 U.S. 102 (1965), there is a strong preference to be accorded searches conducted with a warrant. They reminded reviewing courts not to be hyper-technical and that such processes were not to be viewed as essay writing contests. A significant consideration, no matter which procedure is used, is the balancing of the public and private rights, particularly with regard to disclosure of the identity of the confidential informer who gave information to the magistrate. How can courts determine that a fair, common sense conclusion was reached without destroying the government's ability to guarantee confidentiality to its informants? Which of the procedures best serve both public and private needs? These questions will be addressed below.

Telephonic and Fax Warrants

The federal government and a few states now allow telephonic warrants. Even more important in this context is the oath that must be administered prior to taking any testimony. Not being able to see the affiant bothers some judges, especially if the judge does not know the officer or anything about his or her reputation. This continues to be, as it always has been, a part of the Fourth Amendment. **U.S. v. Shorter**, 600 F. 2d 585 (C.A. 6th 1979). See also LaFave, *Search & Seizure* 2d Ed. Sec. 43 (c) (West 1987). In one telephonic warrant case the misidentification of an affiant as an investigating officer rather than as an assistant U.S. Attorney did not justify suppression, however. **U.S. v. Iparraguire**, 628 F. Supp. 831 (E.D. N.Y. 1986).

The one source of trouble to watch for involves comparing the judge's oral authorization with scope of the duplicate original. In **State v. Martin**, 12 P. 3d 548 (Ore. App. 2000), the scope of the original warrant "deviated substantially" from the oral authorization. When those two do not match, the particularity requirement has not been satisfied. The duty is on the officer to do it right. The judge approved a search of apartment 5 at 524 Spruce Street but the warrant merely said 524 Spruce Street. This was more than a mere statutory violation; this was an improper description. Accord see: **Timmons v. State**, 734 N.E. 2d 1084 (Ind. App. 2000).

As an apparent case of first impression at the appellate level, the Michigan Court of Appeals interpreted their "oath before a judge" provision regarding search warrants to be satisfied by the combined use of the telephone and fax machine. The officer "faxed" his affidavit to the judge, the judge administered the oath over the phone, found probable cause and "faxed" the warrant back to the officer. The key (to this court) in warrant issuing is the independent neutral and detached determination of probable cause by a judicial officer and not physical presence. This determination is what the defendant is entitled to and this is what he got in this case, said the court. A written warrant is required and this too was satisfied. An oath was administered. In any event, it provides a process to be tested in other states. **People v. Snyder**, 449 N.W. 2d 703 (Mich. Ct. App. 1990). Of course, if a state's statute requires a personal appearance before the magistrate then this process cannot be used.

It is clear that states are utilizing telephonic warrants as a control on exigent circumstances searches without warrants. Thus, geographic distance from officer-to-judge is not the only justification for such warrants. See **State v. Ravotto**, 755 A. 2d 602 (N.J. Super. 2000). Telephonic warrants are often used in New Jersey for drunk driving blood tests. As this case points out, sometimes there is not time for even that "fast track" process.

The Supreme Court of Indiana had to answer the question whether police must use the faster warrant issuing processes of the fax or telephonic warrant in order to reduce the time that a detained person spends in a proper investigative detention. Though there was probable cause to search the defendant's car, police also had probable cause to search his hotel room. Therefore, they needed a warrant. The defendant was in custody for one hour and forty minutes while the police sought a warrant by personal appearance before the issuing judge. The defense said the police were required to use one of the speedier processes. The Indiana court did not agree. Common sense has to be used in such situations. Diligent pursuit of investigative means has to be employed and those means have to be reasonable but not perfect. The court cited **U.S. v. Sharpe**, 470 U.S. 675 (1985) and its diligent investigative pursuit rule. The officer in this instance prepared the affidavit immediately, found a magistrate, and presented his facts in a fairly prompt manner. Since the gun and drugs were found in the purse of his companion, the police, with independent probable cause facts, had reason to believe that both the car and the hotel room contained more drugs. Thus the court said this detention of the driver and his car were not unduly long. To have decided otherwise would have put the Indiana court in the position of encouraging "hair-splitting" and that might discourage the use of warrants altogether. Indeed, the faster processes were created to discourage questionable exigent circumstances-based searches. The police, in this case, were also trying to avoid that problem. The driver's detention was not unduly long and it does not appear that the police, by using the longer process, did so to exploit the situation for interrogative purposes. **Mitchell v. State**, 745 N.E. 2d 775 (Ind. 2001).

Good Faith Reliance on a Judge's Decision to Issue a Warrant

One further issue needs to be brought up at this point and that involves the document used and the technicality required in its preparation. No case serves as a better example than **Massachusetts v. Sheppard**, 468 U.S. 981 (1984). Massachusetts, as in a number of other states, has a number of preprinted forms of search warrants; some are general, some specific. On this particular Sunday, the court had only controlled substances warrant forms. What was to be sought included a potpourri of things linked to a homicide. The judge made a valiant effort to edit the form to conform to the needs of the situation. He, in good faith, overlooked one thing that should have been stricken. The Massachusetts court said since there was no good faith exception the warrant was invalid. Since **Leon** had been decided this same day, the Supreme Court examined **Sheppard** and found that the officers reasonably believed that the search they conducted was authorized by a valid warrant. The Court concluded by saying that.".. suppressing evidence because the Judge failed to make all the necessary clerical corrections despite his assurances that such changes would be made will not serve the deterrent function that the exclusionary rule was designed to achieve...." The Court remanded **Sheppard** to the Massachusetts court for a rehearing. The Massachusetts court upheld the validity of the warrant on rehearing, thus accepting the Supreme Court's analysis. **Com. v. Sheppard**, 394 Mass. 381 (1985). In **Com. v. Burt**, 393 Mass. 703 (1985), and before the final decision in **Sheppard**, the court of Massachusetts approved a residential search that was made out on a motor vehicle search form because the place was more than adequately described and the references to motor vehicles thus became trivial creating "little danger of confusion."

Are the police permitted to rely on an otherwise constitutionally sound warrant where the only mistake is that of a magistrate who strikes through or deletes words on the form that should not have been deleted? Deletions that are readily apparent clerical or ministerial errors on the part of the issuing authority should not penalize the police. Such was the holding in **Com. v. Truax**, 397 Mass. 174 (1986). There the court said, "This error in deletion of printed language on the form located adjacent to language that should have been deleted is no more than a clerical error and does not affect the validity of the warrant." The Ninth Circuit also saved a warrant under good faith where the Magistrate did too much editing of the warrant by striking the notice and inventory requirements of the warrant. **U.S. v. Freitas**, 856 F. 2d 1425 (C.A. 9th 1988). Those requirements can only be waived, if at all, by the defendant.

Some states categorically reject **Leon** as repugnant to their own constitutions, traditions, or statutes. For example see decisions from Delaware and Iowa. Delaware cites its own constitution as the reason as does Iowa. **Dorsey v. State**, 2000 WL 1566510 (Del.) and **State v. Clinic**, 617 N.W. 2d 277 (Iowa 2000). Iowa's decision received concurrences from all participating justices. Delaware's decision faced strong indent from two of the five justices on the court. Iowa provided a list of other states rejecting all or part of **Leon,** at footnote 3. That footnote is reproduced here: Iowa is not alone in rejecting the good faith exception under its state constitution. The states of Alaska, see **Blank v. State**, 3 P.3d 359, 370 (Alaska App.2000), Connecticut, see **Marsala**, 579 A. 2d at 68 , Idaho, see **Guzman**, 842 P. 2d at 677, Michigan, see **Sundling**, 395 N.W. 2d at 315, New Hampshire, see **Canelo**, 653 A. 2d at 1105, New Jersey, see **Novembrino**, 519 A. 2d at 857, New Mexico, see **Gutierrez**, 863 P. 2d at 1067-68, New York, see **Bigelow**, 497 N.Y.S.2d 630, 488 N.E. 2d at 458, North Carolina, see **Carter**, 370 S.E. 2d at 562, Pennsylvania, see **Edmunds**, 586 A. 2d at 905-06, and Vermont, see **Oakes**, 598 A. 2d at 126-27, have done likewise. A lesser number of states have followed **Leon**. See **Crayton v. Commonwealth**, 846 S.W. 2d 684, 689 (Ky.1992); **State v. Brown**, 708 S.W. 2d 140, 146 (Mo.1986); **State v. Wilmoth**, 22 Ohio St.3d 251, 490 N.E. 2d 1236, 1238-39 (1986); **State v. Ward**, 231 Wis.2d 723, 604 N.W. 2d 517, 531 (2000). Illinois has rejected the good faith exception only under **Krull**-type circumstances. See **People v. Krueger**, 175 Ill. 2d 60, 221 Ill. Dec. 409, 675 N.E. 2d 604, 612 (Ill.1996).

During 2000 we saw at least four decisions where the court found that no police officers could reasonably have assumed the warrant was valid. Those cases are:

122

Thorp v. State, 2000 WL 1707103 (Fla.), **Simmons v. State**, 734 N.E. 2d 1084 (Ind. App. 2000); **State v. Belmontes**, 615 N.W. 2d 634 (S. D. 2000); and **Colaw v. Com.**, 531 S.E. 2d 31 (Va. App. 2000).

Some of the **Leon** language left the impression that a contrary result might be dictated. This was clarified by the Court's decision in **Malley v. Briggs**, 475 U.S. 335 (1986) where an officer's civil liability or immunity from suit was at issue. **Leon** through **Malley** creates a reasonable officer test when determining whether the officer gets immunity from suit based on a warrant he or she secures. In essence they said: "Defendants [referring to police officers] will not be immune if, on an objective basis, it is obvious that no reasonably competent officer would have concluded that a warrant should issue; but if officers of reasonable competence could disagree on this issue, immunity should be recognized." **Malley** at 341. The California Supreme Court determined that the **Malley** language should apply at a suppression hearing. **People v. Camarella**, 818 P. 2d 63 (Cal. 1991).

There would be fewer problems in this area if police officers were better trained and if prosecutors were required, in all cases, to pre-approve warrants. The affiant is to create an affidavit based only on the facts known. This message is clear. Police officers often feel insecure about their ability to write. Thus the Court said warrant writing and affidavit writing is not an essay contest. Some police have only a hunch and borrow language from prior "good" warrants to get their warrant. This is a risk run but the practice must be condemned. Some officers "borrow" language because of insecurity. This means that some courts are being too restrictive as to form.

It was bad enough when old warrants were used as guides or to help an officer cheat on probable cause. However, a more significant problem has arisen with the use of computers as word processors. Within the police data banks there lurk all the "good" phrases to use. In the name of speed or convenience or perhaps even laziness, let alone evil motives, police are using these devices to come up with the "right" words to get a warrant.

The problems of the computer age and warrant issuing are well illustrated by **State v. Coleman**, 826 S.W. 2d 273 (Ark. 1992). One clause, the clause dealing with permission to search at night, was a focal point. The computer language was as follows: The house is "...so situated that the approach of the officers serving this warrant can be readily detected." This language was used. The court said that was regrettable since the facts known were more specific. The house in this case "... was located on a cul-de-sac with only one way of entering, and the affiant had been informed that the defendant watched for cars approaching his house and that he had a gun." The court said it was good that some other independent language existed in the affidavit because if only the computer generated language existed this search application would have been the same as a check-list warrant, which of course is no good. Arkansas made it clear they would not tolerate "...rote use of the computer generated..." phrases. Police can be their own worst enemy. By using these kinds of phrases judges must now suspect all warrants and thus conduct tedious examinations of computer generated warrants, and for that matter, all warrants.

III. Description of the Place Clause

1. *THAT AFFIANTS HAVE GOOD REASON TO BELIEVE AND DO BELIEVE THAT CERTAIN THINGS HEREAFTER DESCRIBED ARE BEING CONCEALED IN OR ABOUT THE FOLLOWING PLACE IN THIS COUNTY: TOGETHER WITH ALL APPROACHES AND APPURTENANCES THERETO.*

So often, officers and courts fail to adequately and specifically describe the place to be searched. The rules on this are fairly clear. Of course, the law does not require a perfect description.

Does failure to designate district, section, township and range, especially with regard to rural property, render the warrant invalid? There is no need for positive specificity as long as there is a description good enough to enable the officer to find the place with reasonable certainty. **Cole v. State**, 237 So. 2d 443 (Miss. 1970). It has generally been held that a description which enables the officer to readily find the place is sufficient. **Steele v. United States**, 267 U.S. 498 (1925) and **Com. v. Truax**, 397 Mass. 174 (1986).

However, there must not be a material variance between the affidavit and the warrant as to the place to be searched. **Crosby v. State**, 144 Miss. 401, 110 So. 132 (1926); **Stephens v. State**, 183 Miss. 829, 184 So. 327 (1938); and **Morton v. State**, 136 Miss. 284, 101 So. 379 (1924). For an immaterial variance, see **United States ex rel. Hurley v. Delaware**, 365 F. Supp. 282 (D.C. Del. 1973) and **United States v. Rytman**, 475 F. 2d 192 (C.A. 5th 1973). The general rule is that a faulty description of the place as found in the warrant can be cured if the place is properly described in the affidavit and the affidavit is either physically attached to the warrant or incorporated by reference. The Sixth Circuit went one step further in holding that where one of the

124

executing officers is also the affiant then the affidavit need not be attached nor incorporated by reference. **U.S. v. Gahagan**, 865 F. 2d 1490 (C.A. 6th 1989). This latter rule makes good common sense in most cases. Accord: **State v. Pitts**, 2000 WL 1678020 (Ohio App. 4) where a reasonable description was given.

Not only can problems arise as to finding the right place but also as to searching the right places upon the site to be searched. In **Taylor v. State**, 134 Miss. 110, 98 So. 459 (1924), the warrant authorized the search of a building occupied by Joe Taylor as a residence. They also searched the outhouse and yard. The court said the officers had no right to search any place except that described in the warrant. The trailing language of this warrant may take care of the problem, do not rely on it. Spell it out. Local rule may allow the search of the curtilage; if so it would be reasonable to rely on such a rule. **Garrison** (*infra*), however, did not save the search in **State v. Adams**, 5 P.3d 903 (Ariz. App. 1 2000). A warrant was issued to search a theater. The police did not know that within that building an illegal apartment was created. This distinct area was searched and it was in the apartment that incriminating evidence was found. The court found that the theater owner had an objectively reasonable subjective expectation of privacy in this illegal apartment. Failure to describe the apartment was fatal to the state. The court felt that zoning ordinances do not destroy privacy rights.

In a federal case, the warrant authorized the search of the defendant's residential property including "any barns located on the premises." The barn was separated from the house by a fence. This barn was closer to the defendant's house than to his neighbor's. The fence was trampled and a path to and over the trampled fence led to the barn from defendant's house. This was considered a sufficient description. **United States v. Frazier**, 491 F. 2d 243 (C.A. 6th 1974).

In **Steele v. United States**, 267 U.S. 498 (1925) the Court said a description is sufficient if the officer with the warrant can ascertain and identify the place intended. If a place is one business with two street numbers, specifying one is sufficient if the entire building is serviced by one elevator so that the rooms above both numbers have access to it. Accord: **People v. Amador**, 100 Cal. Rep. 2d 617 (Cal. 2000); zip code not needed.

Where police unreasonably believe two adjacent premises are part of the same operation as where nothing outside or inside indicates multiple occupancy, the police exceed the scope of the warrant when the premises they enter are not described in the warrant. **U.S. v. Palmer**, 505 F. Supp. 812 (M.D.N.C. 1981). But it is clear that one warrant will do the job since separate warrants are not necessary. **Williams v.**

State, 240 P. 2d 1132 (Okla. Crim. 1952). Clarity of description is all that is necessary. But see the discussion of **Maryland v. Garrison**, (*infra*).

Indeed it is sometimes difficult to determine whether some areas, buildings, sheds, etc. are part of the described premises. In a case from Maryland, a rape had occurred at a health club. A warrant issued to search the location of "7963 Baltimore-Annapolis Boulevard and seize evidence including: bed sheets or bedding, sex toys, occupancy documents, and pill bottles." Did this include a storage area that was searched and where the evidence was found? The outside door to this area was marked 7959A. The interior doors that would have led the police to this space were sealed off due to a fire code requirement. However, the phone line in that area was registered to 7963 and mail for the defendant was also delivered to 7963. The motion to suppress was denied. The appeals court found that the area remained a part of the whole and under **Maryland v. Garrison**, it also was validly entered because the officer acted reasonably. The old doors on the inside of the building were still in place and when they went in, it looked like a gym equipment storage area. Nothing told them "stay out." **Jackson v. State**, 752 A. 2d 1227 (Md. App. 2000).

In an Oregon case the warrant issued to search the premises at 442 W. Centennial, Springfield, Lane County, which was described as a single-story, wood-framed dwelling, white and black in color, located on the north side of W. Centennial with the numbers 442 being located on the residence. The officers went there, searched and found nothing in 442. An unattached garage with the number 442½ was behind the house. The garage contained an apartment with a separate lockable entrance. The police searched 442½ and found drugs. Was the word premises broad enough to include this garage apartment? No, according to the Oregon Supreme court in **State v. Devins**, 768 P. 2d 913 (Ore. 1989). Their earlier case law said that if only one residence was described only one could be searched. Since the garage was only white and not black and white, the word premises was given a narrow definition. The importance of adding language seeking to search "other buildings, *etc.* threat" becomes of ultimate importance in most if not all of the states.

Mistakes are made. Which ones are to be excused and which are fatal will always be there to torment suppression judges. In **State v. Sterling**, 759 So. 2d 60 (La. 2000), the warrant described the place as a single occupancy structure to wit: "3024 Wall Boulevard, a red brick two story structure with a white front door and trim with the municipal number 3024 visible from the street and located on the front door." The police, upon entry, discovered two numbers, 3022 and 3024. 3022 was the lower apartment and 3024 was the upstairs apartment. The police searched 3022, the target's apartment. The trial court suppressed the evidence. The high court reversed. Why? The police asked the upstairs resident where BAM stayed (the target person). He said downstairs. The police knocked, announced, and gave the warrant to BAM as he opened the door. By carefully limiting their search to the right apartment to which the probable cause pointed, the police satisfied the particularity requirement. This appears to comport with **Maryland v. Garrison** (*infra*).

Good Faith Descriptions of the Place

The Supreme Court has added the description of the place to be searched to the growing list of "good faith" exceptions in the search and seizure area. In **Maryland v. Garrison**, 480 U.S. 79 (1987) the Court was called upon to review a warrant that described the third floor of a building as one apartment when in fact it was two. When police discovered their error they left the undescribed apartment but not before they had discovered contraband drugs. Of course, the defendant who controlled the undescribed apartment was prosecuted. Ultimately, the Maryland Court of Appeals reversed and remanded for a new trial saying that the evidence should have been suppressed. They found the outcome was determined by "elementary search and seizure principles" and they spoke of exceptions only "jealously and carefully drawn." They said the police had no justification for entering these premises, regardless of appearances. In looking at the diagram set out in the state opinion the police had to know there were two apartments. The court labeled the description as imprecise. This seems to be overlooked by the U.S. Supreme Court. Rather than posturing their decision on the Maryland constitution alone, the Maryland court held that this warrant was offensive to both the Maryland and U.S. Constitutions. Therefore, the Supreme Court had jurisdiction.

The Supreme Court upheld the search saying, "While the purpose justifying a police search limits the permissible extent of the search, the Court has also recognized the need for some latitude for honest mistakes that are made by officers in the dangerous and difficult process of making arrests and executing search warrants." Further the Court said, "...the validity of the search...of the entire third floor depends on whether the officer's failure to realize the over-breadth of the warrant was objectively understandable and reasonable." Now that is interesting. In the first part of the opinion they find the warrant valid and here they call it over-broad. How far are judges going to allow this good faith exception to travel? Should they keep in mind the preference for the warrant and give close calls to the police when they use the process?

Consider **Com. v. Carrasco**, 405 Mass.316 (1989) where that court, citing Garrison, upheld a search warrant that described the second floor as having one apartment when, in fact, there were two. The court said, "We conclude that the police were not required to interview the owner or other occupants of the building or to take other steps that might disclose their interest in the premises." They were not required to risk disclosure of their surveillance and thereby jeopardize their investigation by going to the second floor before applying for the warrant. However, sometimes the detail in the description can be so complete, so positive, even **Garrison** will not save the day. In **Com. v. Treadwell**, 402 Mass. 355 (1988), the court noted "... the warrant specified two separate distinguishing factors to designate the apartment to be searched; that apartment was 'over no. 17 and the it had a sticker on its door reading Make MY Day'...." The court held that since no apartment had both characteristics and each of two had one characteristic the broad discretion to choose either one made the warrant invalid.

In **U.S. v. Collins**, 830 F. 2d 145 (C.A. 9th 1987), the police altered the address then found that neither it nor the original one was the right place. The court called this description "remarkably unparticular" and said they got the address wrong twice and the side of the street wrong once. Since the physical description did not bring them to the right place the evidence had to be suppressed. Other decisions have addressed the address problem. In a Seventh Circuit case the number was wrong but the officers could read the affidavit's description to get them to the right place, thus the evidence was admissible in **U.S. v. Bentley**, 825 F. 2d 1104 (C.A. 7th 1987). Thus if the detail in the warrant is sufficient to get the officers to the right place there can be no reasonable possibility that any other premises would be entered despite a wrong number. **U.S. v. Ridinger**, 805 F. 2d 818 (C.A. 8th 1986). Even if there is an inadvertent omission of the address in the warrant it is not fatal if the agent who applied for and would execute the warrant knows precisely which place was described in the application. **U.S. v. Bonner**, 808 F. 2d 864 (C.A. 1st 1986).

All Vehicles Present Clause

The typical search warrant for a residence and its curtilage often includes the phrase "and all vehicles on the property." Such was the situation in **People v. Juarez**, 970 P. 2d 937 (Colo. 1989). A non-resident's van was searched and contraband was found. The non-resident sought suppression but the court felt that the "all-vehicles" clause covered any vehicle present on the property and that probable cause existed to believe the contraband was somewhere on this property including this vehicle. Massachusetts follows the curtilage rule and upheld an auto search as being within the scope of the described premises. **Com. v. Signorine**, 404 Mass. 400 (1989). Accord **U.S. v. Alva**, 885 F. 2d 250 (C.A. 5th 1989).

Most courts generally accept the principle that a warrant covers vehicles within the curtilage as long as the "scope" is reasonable. Some defendants have urged that such a rule should only cover those vehicles actually controlled or owned by the possessor of the premises. This was the defense argument in **U.S. v. Gottschalk**, 915 F. 2d 1459 (C.A. 10th 1990). The Tenth Circuit rejected the argument as had the Fifth Circuit in **U.S. v. Cole**, 628 F. 2d 897 (C.A. 5th 1980). It appears that only the Seventh had agreed to this defense approach, **U.S. v. Percival**, 756 F. 2d 600 (C.A. 7th 1985).

However, the Tenth decided to qualify the general rule to some extent. They held that a warrant covers only those automobiles which appear, based on objectively reasonable indicia, present at the time of the search, to be controlled by the possessor of the premises. This would eliminate those cars driven onto the premises by some third person while the search is being conducted. But it might not include a car of a guest present at the beginning of a search where the keys are found in the guest's room or luggage. In any event there is no perfect answer to this question.

An Iowa decision, in the "all vehicles present" warrant situation, requires that a *nexus* be established between the items sought and the search of vehicles not belonging to the controller(s) of the premises. In this case the car searched was one belonging to a person who arrived after the warrant was issued according to the language in the warrant that said to search "the persons and vehicles of any other subjects at the residence after the signing of the search warrant." This was seen by the Iowa court as a "dragnet search warrant." The court thought that the required *nexus* was not established because this defendant and this automobile were not on the premises when the warrant was issued. For all that was known, this defendant was a "mere arrival" and because no facts linked this defendant to the place otherwise, it could not be concluded that the defendant was a "late arrival." The court did not address the "no innocents possibly present" issue. The court closed by saying that **Leon** and good faith-reliance on the magistrate's approval was not applicable to this case. **State v. Jamison**, 490 N.W. 2d 565 (Iowa 1992). Thus, for Iowa, contrary to other courts, "all vehicles present" warrants seem to be rejected.

It is better to describe outbuildings to avoid the issue of whether the warrant includes garages and the like. In **U.S. v. Franzion**, 780 F. 2d 1461 (C.A. 9th 1986), the term residence included an attached garage. In **U.S. v. Nonner**, 808 F. 2d 864 (C.A. 1st, 1986), a detached garage was found to be part of the residence. A toolshed and the car in the yard were found to be part of the "premises known as defendant's street address." **U.S. v. Griffin**, 827 F. 2d 1108 (C.A. 7th 1987). Accord: **Sowers v. State**, 724 N.E. 2d 588 (Ind. 2000) where an outbuilding was included in the basic description. The use of the words "appurtenances" in this sample warrant includes all outbuildings or structures within the curtilage. See the discussion of the curtilage in the chapter on Open Fields.

Establish the Nexus

Of course probable cause must be established that the place or thing (including persons) contains the evidence of the crime. Usually courts are given direct information on the issues. It is not always that easy. In the "reasonable-to-assume" department consider the case of **U.S. v. Anderson**, 851 F. 2d 727 (C.A. 4th 1988), where a defendant, while away from his home, offered to sell a gun and silencer that had been used in a homicide to certain informers. The police applied for a warrant to search the defendant's home even though no one had ever seen the gun there. Was this fatal to the validity of the warrant? No. Why? Acknowledging a split among the circuits whether probable cause can be inferred from these kinds of circumstances, the Fourth Circuit decided it could be. They joined the Ninth, Eighth, Sixth and old Fifth Circuits in that view and rejected the Eleventh and First Circuit's position that requires more positive proof between the place to be searched and the item to be seized. Thus the Fourth says such *nexus* may be established by the nature of the item and the normal inferences of where one would likely keep such evidence.

The *nexus* issue can arise in a number of contexts. In **Com. v. Burt**, 393 Mass. 703 (1985) the defendants who were charged with stealing from parking meters challenged warrants for the search of their homes and automobiles. Can it be said that the coins and containers used in these thefts would be "expected reasonably to be found in the place searched?" Does such a *nexus* have to be based on direct observation? The coins were reasonably to be expected in their cars and homes and direct observation is not necessary. All that is necessary is to consider the type of crime, the nature of missing items, the extent of the suspect's opportunity for concealment and normal inferences as to where a criminal would likely hide stolen property. The *nexus* in this case was found sufficient.

Unless the *nexus* is established the warrant must fall. Using a profile that drug dealers often deal from their home (after a search of the business address failed to yield evidence) was not enough of a *nexus* in **State v. Mische**, 448 N.W. 2d 415 (N. D. 1989). These officers were truly on a fishing trip. Some facts must point in that direction.

Only a probability of criminal activity, not a *prima facie* showing is needed to establish probable cause to search a place. Reasonable inferences can be drawn concerning where the evidence (in this case the large quantities of methamphetamine-making supplies were kept and used. Just because the selling activity takes place away from the defendant's home does not mean it is unreasonable to believe that the home is the source storage and manufacturing area. Thus, a *nexus* was established in **State v. Miller**, 14 S.W. 3d 135 (Mo. App. 5 2000). This was a case of first impression in Missouri. However, that conclusion must be reasonable. That some guests that have visited a home "might be drug involved" and the fact that garbage has not been "put out" for two weeks was not sufficient inference to create a *nexus*. **State v. Thieling**, 611 N.W. 2d 861 (N. D. 2000).

Nexus should be present when the thing sought was not actually viewed by the affiant, however, *nexus* shown as to one item does not disappear when other evidence is sought for which there is no *nexus*. In a Washington case there was *nexus* for possession of drugs that were sold but none existed to show that the house was the manufactory site. This court said the warrant was valid despite this. Thus, evidence of manufacturing found during the legitimate "possession search" would be admissible under the plain view doctrine since the officers were conducting an otherwise lawful search for possession crimes. **State v. Coutts**, 2001 WL 88244 (Wash. App. Div. 2) (unpub. op.).

Anticipatory Warrants

There is a warrant type called the anticipatory warrant. The police may know that certain drugs are going to be delivered to a certain place but the time of delivery is uncertain. These have been approved in their limited context. However, a warrant for a floating poker game was bad because the location was to be left to the officer's discretion. **Com. v. Baldwin**, 509 N.E. 2d 1202 (Mass. 1987). In **U.S. v. Hendricks**, 743 F. 2d 653 (C.A. 9th 1984), an anticipatory warrant was deemed invalid because there was no probable cause to believe that the contraband would be taken to the defendant's residence after it was picked up. However, **Leon** saved the evidence.

An anticipatory warrant was found invalid in one Florida case because the affiant had no actual knowledge justifying a finding of probable cause. The information was at best a guess because there was some indication that on prior occasions the drug middleman had visited the defendant's home prior to making marijuana deliveries. **Renckley v. State**, 538 So. 2d 1340 (Fla. Dist. Ct. App. 1989).

The best and most often accepted form of the anticipatory warrant is the police controlled delivery cases. This is well illustrated by **Com. v. Soares**, 384 Mass. 149 (1981). The court upheld the anticipatory warrant for two primary reasons. First "...the object of the search was subject to the control of law enforcement...and that delivery would occur immediately upon obtaining the search warrant." Second, the court said that "...the goal of encouraging the use of warrants is hardly fostered by requiring...actual delivery of known contraband to the premises...putting them to a choice between undertaking an immediate unwarranted search or taking time to obtain a warrant and risking the destruction or concealment of potential evidence."

Alabama has rejected the use of the anticipatory warrant since it could find no constitutional provision or statute authorizing the use of these warrants. The package in this case was properly intercepted and searched by U.S. postal authorities. The police in Birmingham were notified and an anticipatory warrant was obtained form a district court judge. Thus a "controlled delivery" was set in motion. The Court of Criminal Appeals approved the search. Alabama does not believe a warrant can be issued until a crime has been committed. Of course, an attempt to possess, *etc.*, had been committed but nonetheless there indeed is no actual possession until acceptance of delivery. This court was not even willing to use "good faith" to save this case because they said there was no reasonable reliance on the judge's decision. **Turner v. State**, 2000 WL 356316 (Ala.).

Pennsylvania now accepts anticipatory warrants. The court said they do not *per se* violate the state constitution. Its case involved a controlled delivery of marijuana. The felt that by approving this procedure, it would encourage police to use the warrant process that ensures "pre-search review by a neutral magistrate...." **Com. v. Glass**, 754 A. 2d 655 (Pa. 2000).

IV.   Naming the Owner/Controller Clause

2.   *THAT THE PLACE DESCRIBED ABOVE IS OCCUPIED AND CONTROLLED BY*:

"What's in a name?" Though it is nice to insert the name of the owner or tenant of the property, it is not essential to the validity of the warrant. Therefore, John Doe search warrants are permissible. The general position that it is proper to name the owner or occupant if known, but, if he is unknown, this fact will not prevent a search of premises when probable cause exists and the property to be searched is described with sufficient clarity. **Dixon v. United States**, 211 F. 2d 547 (C.A. 5th 1954).

However, the New Jersey Supreme Court does point out one exception. It was announced that a search warrant for unnamed persons at a specified place was general therefore void. Among the things to be searched were people. This is an often overlooked distinction. Thus where it is possible that the fruits sought are most likely to be on the individuals at the place specified those persons should be named or specifically described. This is especially true as in the case where the search of the place specified shows no signs of illegality and the only evidence of the gambling paraphernalia sought came through the arrests made of those who were on or walked onto the premises while the search was being conducted. The warrant in this case called specifically for the search of unnamed persons. **State v. Sims**, 382 A. 2d 638 (N.J. 1978). Without separate probable cause a power to search anybody that "happens by" cannot be upheld. **People v. Jackson**, 446 N.W. 2d 891 1175 (Mich. Ct. App. 1989). However, as noted in Chapter Thirteen, there are exceptions if the state follows the "no innocent persons present" rule. Under this rule persons present in a totally illegally private place may at least be frisked.

The Oregon Court of Appeals has decided to follow the "no possible innocents present" rule when assessing a search warrant that says to search "all individuals and occupants found to be frequenting said premises." The question, as the court sees it is "...whether the information supplied the magistrate supports the conclusion that it is probable anyone in the described place when the warrant is executed is involved in the criminal activity in such a way as to have evidence thereof on his person." The court clearly recognized that there are times when individualized descriptions are not always possible. The burden is on the magistrate to give strict scrutiny to an "all persons present" affidavit and why a general and not a specific description is given. **State v. Ingram**, 802 P. 2d 656 (Ore. Ct. App. 1990).

A warrant authorizing the search of a specific address and two residents described only as Mexican male, 20's, 5'7", medium build with black curly hair and Mexican male, 5'6", heavy build with black hair was sufficiently particular to pass Fourth Amendment muster. **State v. Martinez**, 753 P. 2d 1011 (Wash. Ct. App. 1988). Why? Because it described the persons who lived at that address, the court said.

Consider the case in which two visitors arrive at an apartment just as the police are finishing a valid search. The visitors knock on the door and are pulled into the apartment at gunpoint by the police. The police, looking for drugs, notice a bulge in the crotch of the female visitor's pants. She was persuaded to remove the bulge. It proved to be a bag containing heroin. As far as the police knew, these people were mere visitors because the police could not show prior contact or connection with this apartment or its tenants. The bulge did not look like a weapon. The search was declared illegal. **People v. Miller**, 25 Crim. L. Rep. 2377 (Ill. App. Ct. 1979). For a discussion of who can be searched while a warrant is executed see **Ybarra v. Illinois**, 444 U.S. 85 (1979) as discussed in Chapter Twelve.

V.   Description of the Thing(s) Sought Clause

3. *THAT SAID THINGS ARE PARTICULARLY DESCRIBED AS FOLLOWS*:

There are two problems here. One involves the description that is essential to the validity of the warrant. The other is what happens to seized property not described in the warrant. The first problem is relatively easy to handle. The second involves the delicate balancing that all courts must do when individual rights collide with society's rights.

For property other than what is obviously illicit or contraband in plain view, the thing or things to be seized must be described with some particularity. The description "stolen property" is no description. The more detail given the better the warrant. However, technical requirements of elaborate specificity have no proper place in this area. **United States v. Ventresca**, 380 U.S. 102 (1965). What should be avoided are sweeping descriptions that authorize broad, unlimited exploratory searches. The warrant cannot leave what is to be taken to the individual judgment of the officer; the warrant cannot sweep broadly. **Marcus v. Search Warrant**, 367 U.S. 717 (1961).

The second problem, as already stated, is loaded with emotionally charged words. A consideration of United States Supreme Court decisions is essential to the understanding of the relative problems. It is best to begin with **Marron v. United States**, 275 U.S. 192 (1927). The things described in **Marron** were "...intoxicating liquors and articles for their manufacture." Ledgers and bills were taken and the defendant claimed they were not within the above description. The court said that the requirement that warrants shall particularly describe the things to be seized makes general searches under them impossible and prevents the seizure of one thing under a warrant describing another. As to what is to be taken, nothing should be left to the discretion of the officer executing the warrant. It was held that the seizure of the ledger and the bills was not authorized by the warrant. Note that the ledger and the bills were seizable under the then existing search incident law. See the discussion of search incident in Chapter Twelve.

Some Arizona officers had a warrant to search for drugs and firearms. While searching they found a box with a plain-covered, closed, columnar business record book inside. They opened it, read it, and discovered that it had information on drug transactions. As it was not mentioned in the warrant it was not seizable under the warrant. Plain view was not applicable because it was not readily apparent that it was connected with a crime. **State v. Shinault**, 584 P. 2d 1204 (Ariz. Ct. App. 1978); accord see **Arizona v. Hicks**, 480 U.S. 321 (1987) as discussed in Chapter One.

In **Stanford v. Texas**, 379 U.S. 476 (1965), the warrant authorized the seizure of books, paper, records, *etc.*, that tended to show that defendant was a communist. After a five-hour search, several hundred books, periodicals and private papers were seized. Since these were literary ideas, scrupulous adherence to specificity was required, but the Court, in *dicta*, did recognize the "contraband" distinction. Later the court said it cannot tolerate unconfined searches and indiscriminate seizures. The warrant in **Stanley v. Georgia**, 394 U.S. 557 (1969), gave the officers no authority to seize films, only gambling materials. Here again was jealous protection of First Amendment rights. Yet the Court, by innuendo, recognized a "plain view" theory of seizure. As further evidence of zealous protection of First Amendment rights consider the case of **Walter v. U.S.**, 447 U.S. 649 (1980). Some movies depicting homosexual behavior were miss-delivered to a private party. That party opened the boxes, saw suggestive drawings and tried to view the films without a projector by holding them to the light. This revealed nothing. The private party called the F.B.I. and delivered the films to them. The F.B.I. used a projector and viewed the films. The court held this an unauthorized screening and an unreasonable invasion of privacy because no warrant was obtained. The F.B.I. possession was lawful (seizure) but the view (search) was bad. Plain view does not save it because the F.B.I. plain view cannot exceed the scope of the private search. Since the third party could not see anything, the F.B.I. was so limited. The screening was a significant expansion of the private search.

The Missouri Court of Appeals has emphatically made clear that one cannot use an otherwise valid search warrant to get a thing not listed in the warrant that is known to exist and for which ample time existed to obtain a warrant. **State v. Kelsey**, 592 S.W. 2d 509 (Mo. Ct. App. 1979).The facts were as follows: The defendant, Dr. Kelsey, was convicted of second-degree murder in connection with the February 11, 1976, killing of Cynthia Jane Hall. From March 11 to March 30, 1976, DEA Agents Eapman and Connor investigated illegal drug sales allegedly being made by the defendant. The defendant and his wife lived on the second floor of a structure that also housed the doctor's office on the ground floor. On March 24, during the agents' fifth visit to the office-residence, Mrs. Kelsey told them to leave by a round-about route because the house was under surveillance by county authorities who were trying "to pin a murder rap on Dr. Kelsey because an ex-girlfriend was shot and killed" when the doctor was away from home. Upon the doctor's return, she said, he had handed her a .25 caliber gun and said, "hide this because the authorities will be looking for it." Five days later, Mrs. Kelsey showed the agents the gun. Each agent was able to memorize surreptitiously the gun's serial number before Mrs. Kelsey returned it to the rear bedroom. The next day, March 30, the agents asked Dr. Kelsey if they could see the gun. Visibly upset, the doctor refused. The agents then rendezvoused with a waiting group consisting of a federal prosecutor, state prosecutors, and various federal and local law officers. Armed with a federal search warrant authorizing the search of the Kelsey property for Valium, Librium, and marked money, the group went to the Kelsey house where the gun was seized.

The court said the only reason the house was entered when it was was to get the gun. It noted that when the gun was found the search was immediately stopped. The only place they searched was the bedroom where they knew the gun to be. This destroyed the possibility that this was a good faith search for drugs. The police had plenty of time to obtain a warrant. This is a perfect example of a pretextual search.

Saving Some Un-particular Descriptions

Courts will try to uphold warrants that have plenty of probable cause to believe a crime has been committed but fall a little short on description of the things to be seized. Why? To do otherwise, they feel, would discourage police from applying for warrants. The case law that has developed in recent years concerning the particular description of things breaks down into certain categories. Those categories are:

1. Not overly broad;
2. Overly broad;
3. All persons present;
4. Kid porn cases;
5. Catchall phrases,
   a. good description plus catchall;
   b. permeated with fraud etc. businesses; and
6. Severance doctrine cases.

In the not overly broad category, consider **U.S. v. Truglio**, 731 F. 2d 1123 (C.A. 4th 1984). The warrant said to seize records of a prostitution ring. The records were on tape cassettes and they were seized. The court said it would have preferred the word "records" to be modified by the words "written and electronic" but ruled the word "records" took into account all new methodologies. In **U.S. v. Pryor**, 652 F. Supp. 1353 (D. Me. 1987), the court approved the seizure described in the warrant as "twenty and one hundred dollar bills." The case involved a bank robbery. The court said there was no other way to describe the stolen money. Again common sense and not hyper- technicality rules.

said there was no other way to describe the stolen money. Again common sense and not hyper- technicality rules.

A warrant authorizing the seizure of tax and business records for a particular time period was not overbroad. **Watts v. Kroczynski**, 636 F. Supp. 792 (W.D. La. 1986). And files and records identified by patient names were not overbroad in **U.S. v. Word**, 806 F. 2d 658 (C.A. 6th 1986). Files relating to "purchasing, dispensing and prescribing of controlled substances" was held not to be overbroad in **U.S. v. Hayes**, 794 F. 2d 1348 (C.A. 9th 1986). Finally, a warrant authorizing the seizure of "cocaine and controlled dangerous substances" was not overbroad and therefore did not authorize a general search. The search was limited to the seizure of evidence of a single crime. **U.S. v. Sierra**, 585 F. Supp. 1236 (D. N.J. 1984). The **Sierra** case thus suggests a contextual analysis should be applied. Such was the approach taken by the Massachusetts court in **Com. v. Kenneally**, 383 Mass. 269 (1981). The description of the things merely read "all" records and papers of an insurance agency. This overly broad description was cured when the court said that since the business was not licensed by the state and since it had closed its doors, those two facts, coupled with well founded allegations of failure to deliver policies and make payments, was sufficient to take it out of the "too much discretion in the officer category."

In the overly broad category the First Circuit held that the language "a quantity of obscene materials, including books, pamphlets, magazines, films and prints" did not meet constitutional standards. **U.S. v. Guarino**, 729 F. 2d 864 (C.A. 1st 1984). Where a more precise description is available, even **Leon's** "good faith" doctrine will not save a bad description, according to the Ninth Circuit. The use of a list of statutory citations was not enough. **U.S. v. Spiloto**, 800 F. 2d 959 (C.A. 9th 1986). The same court also ruled out "good faith" when the warrant described "unnamed obscene, lewd, lascivious or indecent materials." It found the language overbroad. **U.S. v. Hale**, 784 F. 2d 1465 (C.A. 9th 1986). A warrant that described "several hundred cartons of women's clothing" was too broad. There was no way to distinguish the stolen goods from the "good" goods. Other information was reasonably available that would have allowed the police to make a better description. The police in this case had a "ball" because they took everything in sight. The court said even **Leon** would not save this case. **U.S. v. Fuccillo**, 634 F. Supp. 358 (D. Mass. 1986).

It is important to recognize that in some cases the list of things to be seized that is part of the affidavit is often very specific and several pages long. The judge is not about to rewrite the multi-page list on the face of the warrant. The judge in such cases uses a broad description followed by an "incorporation by reference and attached hereto clause." This is quite acceptable as long as that list is in fact attached, so that it can guide the officers and limit their discretion. But what effect does it have when such a list is not attached nor present at the scene of the search? Should the items taken be suppressed? Such was the question in **Com. v. Taylor**, 383 Mass. 272 (1981). In **Taylor** a six- page list of specifically described jewelry was a part of the affidavit. The warrant referred to the list but it does not appear from the suppression hearing first held in the case that it was attached and there was no evidence at the hearing that the list was present at the search. The court held that once the defendant established that the list was not attached the burden was on the state to prove that the officer had the list with him at the search. Failure of such proof, they felt, required the evidence to be suppressed because the warrant was invalid as being insufficiently specific.

The challenged warrant in **State v. Rose**, 748 A. 2d 1283 (R.I. 2000) contained the following description: "Any and all evidence of breaking and entering of dwellings, and possession of stolen goods, to include, but not limited to jewelry, coins, collector's items, electronic equipment, etc." The defendant said the police knew there was a more specific description. The court felt that there was some urgency regarding the issuance of this warrant. The defendant who had been arrested was about to be released on bail. Thus time was of the essence since he would likely remove or destroy evidence at his house. The court held "the language employed in the warrant was as specific as the circumstances permitted" so particularity was satisfied. This represents a decision that uses common sense. Some courts lose sight of that.

A number of warrants have issued authorizing the search of all persons present. Some have been upheld where there was ample probable cause to believe that no innocents would be present and that all present, therefore, were connected with the criminal activity. **State v. Pecha**, 407 N.W. 2d 760 (Neb. 1987); **U.S. v. Graham**, 563 F. Supp. 149 (W.D. N.Y. 1983); and **U.S. v. Offices Known as 50 State Distributing Co.**, 708 F. 2d 137 (C.A. 9th 1983). However, such warrants are not upheld unless the connection is real. In an "all persons present" warrant the object place was an after hours saloon. Such a place in and of itself does not give rise to probable cause that everyone there was "bad." **State v. Hinkel**, 353 N.W. 2d 617 (Minn. App. 1984). See also **State v. Prior**, 617 N.W. 2d 260 (Iowa 2000).

The "kid porn" cases have received favorable treatment. A warrant issued to seize "materials relating to child pornography" was not overbroad in **U.S. v. Weigand**, 812 F. 2d 1239 (C.A. 9th 1987). A similar result was reached in a case authorizing the seizure of "materials showing prepubescent children." **U.S. v. Diamond**, 820 F. 2d 10 (C.A. 1st 1987). Only one court was willing to acknowledge that kid porn cases are judged by less stringent standards. They felt that "nude children involved in explicit

138

sexual conduct" was not too conclusory. **U.S. v. Smith**, 795 F. 2d 841 (C.A. 9th 1986). Accord see **U.S. v. Peden**, 891 F. 2d 514 (C.A. 5th 1989).

The catchall phrase cases fall into two categories. The first is when a specific description is followed by a catchall or when the description in the affidavit was sufficiently detailed but a catchall-like phrase was used in the warrant. The second type of case involves a broad description but the warrant described a business so permeated with criminality that there was very little chance that innocent things would be present.

First, the "permeated" cases. A "bucket shop" was described through and through as fraudulent as was set out in the affidavit. This authorized the seizure of "all of the firm's business documents." **U.S. v. Bentley**, 825 F. 2d 1104 (C.A. 7th 1987). Along these lines see also **U.S. v. Stelten**, 661 F. Supp. 1092 (D. Minn. 1987); **U.S. v. Sawyer**, 799 F. 2d 1494 (C.A. 11th 1986); **U.S. v. Kail**, 804 F. 2d 441 (C.A. 8th 1986); and **Williams v. Kunze**, 806 F. 2d 594 (C.A. 5th 1986).

The permeated analysis was applied to the "...shadowy world of the narcotics" business in **U.S. v. Johnson**, 643 F. Supp. 1465 (D. Ore. 1986). A lot of generic terms were used, but the court felt that it was very difficult to get good descriptions in these kinds of cases. Another warrant was used to seize "illegally copied video tapes." That affidavit clearly indicated that the stolen tapes dominated the inventory, therefore no suppression was ordered. **U.S. v. Vastola**, 670 F. Supp. 1244 (D. N.J. 1987). Finally, "stolen vehicles" passed muster because the probable cause was convincing that the place was a "chop shop." There were some vehicles named in the affidavit but it was very likely they would have been disposed of and others brought in to take their place. The court did not suppress. **U.S. v. Shoffner**, 826 F. 2d 619 (C.A. 7th 1987). All of these cases indicated a common-sense application of the rules.

Would this constitute a sufficient, particular description? "Bank statements, cash receipt books, option purchase records, sales material distributed to customers, employee compensation records, customer sales account records, sales training material, and customer lists." In essence what was sought were all of the firm's records. In **U.S. v. Brien**, 617 F. 2d 299 (C.A. 1st 1980), the affidavit spelled out, in excellent detail, the finely-spun web of a scheme to defraud and the types of records that were required to be kept in the type of business involved. The description here was not too broad and the search need not have been limited only to the records of those customers who had complained. This clearly pointed out the value of the well

But if there is no permeation, then the catchall phrase will be found to be too broad. In one case the court said there could be a more detailed description and then demonstrated how. **U.S. v. Diaz**, 656 F. Supp. 271 (D.P. Rico 1987). For other non-permeation cases see: **In re Grand Jury Proceedings**, 716 F. 2d 493 (C.A. 8th 1983); **Roberts v. U.S.**, 656 F. Supp. 929 (S.D. N.Y. 1987); and **Rickert v. Special Agents**, 813 F. 2d 907 (C.A. 8th 1987).

In the "good plus" cases we often see a prior detailed description followed by a general language such as"other evidence at this time unknown." As long as there is a good affidavit this will be upheld in most cases. In a Supreme Court case a good description plus a catchall was approved since it limited gathering of evidence solely for the crime of false pretenses and no other crime. This was a complex real estate scheme requiring piecing together many bits of evidence. The complexity of the scheme may not be used as a shield to avoid detection when probable cause has been demonstrated that evidence is in the suspect's possession. **Andressen v. Maryland**, 429 U.S. 463 (1976). **U.S. v. Fannin**, 817 F. 2d 1379 (C.A. 9th 1987). The courts often look to see if the discretion of the officers executing it was sufficiently limited. **U.S. v. Brown**, 832 F. 2d 991 (C.A. 9th 1987). See also **U.S. v. Jones**, 801 F. 2d 304 (C.A. 8th 1986); **U.S. v. Khalil**, 633 F. Supp. 1350 (S.D.N.Y. 1986); **U.S. v. Perdome**, 800 F. 2d 916 (C.A. 9th 1986); and **U.S. v. Lamport**, 787 F. 2d 474 (C.A. 11th 1986). For example in **U.S. v. Frederickson**, 846 F. 2d 517 (C.A. 8th 1988), the warrant in an income tax evasion case had a long particularized list closing with this phrase: "…any other instrumentalities and evidence facts recited in the accompanying affidavit make out." Was this fatal? No. The warrant was specific as possible under the circumstances; common sense and not hyper-technicality must rule. *Caveat*: the suppression judge must not lose sight of the plain view doctrine if argued by the state.

But not all are upheld. The warrant in **U.S. v. Leary**, 846 F. 2d 592 (C.A. 10th 1988), included only two limitations: that the documents had to fall within a long list of business records typical of the documents kept by an export company and they had to relate to the "purchase, sale, and illegal exportation in violation of Federal export laws." In this context, the court held, these limitations provide no limitation at all; a general search was authorized.

If the business cannot be shown to be "permeated," however, mere suspicion that there must be other cases within the records will not justify a broad description. In **Com. v. Grossman**, 555 A. 2d 896 (Pa. Sup. Ct. 1989), the police could only point to three specific cases of fraud, thus the description to seize "all insurance files, payment records, receipt records, copies of insurance applications and policies, and cancelled three specific cases of fraud, thus the description to seize "all insurance files, payment records, receipt records, copies of insurance applications and policies, and cancelled checks" was overbroad when the files contained records for over 2,000 clients. The police were "fishing."

The only question that remains is what happens if some of the things are adequately described and some are not; does that inadequacy cause the whole warrant to fail? Not necessarily. The better rule is to suppress that which was not adequately described (and not subject to plain view) and let the rest be admissible if found while searching for the adequately described items. See the cases collected at LaFave, *Search & Seizure*, 2d Ed. Sec. 46 (F) footnotes 105 and 106 p. 258 (West 1987), and cases discussed below.

One of the ways to save evidence properly seized is to use the severance doctrine. The invalidly described can be severed from the validly described. See **U.S. v. Gomez-Soto**, 723 F. 2d 649; **Worthington v. U.S.**, 726 F. 2d. 1089 (C.A. 6th 1984); **U.S. v. Viers**, 637 F. Supp. 1343 (W.D. Ky. 1986); and **U.S. v. Fitzgerald**, 724 F. 2d 633 (C.A. 8th 1983). Also accepting the proposition that bad portions of a warrant can be severed from the good in the "overly broad description" context was the Michigan Court of Appeals in **People v. Kolniak**, 437 N.W. 2d 280 (Mich. App. 1989). See also **Com. v. Lett**, 470 N.E. 2d 110 (Mass. 1984) where that court accepted the severance doctrine for the first time by relying on the **Fitzgerald** case cited above. Finally, when all else fails the prosecutor should use **Leon**. It can be used at least once. **U.S. v. Buck**, 813 F. 2d 588 (C.A. 2d 1987).

Perhaps the most complex case in this area is **U.S. v. Stelten**, 867 F. 2d 446 (C.A. 8th 1989). The National Commodity Barter Exchange was the object of searches in Colorado and South Dakota. The Tenth Circuit felt that the "things described" was overbroad and suppressed the documents seized. The IRS retained some copies of documents taken in that illegal search and they used these copies to obtain indictments in Minnesota. The defendants were unsuccessful in their efforts to suppress their use in trial and thus, despite the obvious "fruits" argument, they lost. The IRS also obtained search warrants in South Dakota based on the same description that was used in Colorado. The warrants were issued for business offices in a residence. A security sweep of the rest of the house produced most of the documents (a fact which did not concern the Eighth Circuit *et al.*). In any event the defendants cited the Tenth Circuit case as authority for suppression in this case. The Eighth felt bound by the Tenth's decision concerning over breadth despite the fact that they did not agree with the Tenth. They found a way to save the evidence, however. The Tenth had not addressed the **Leon** issue and good faith. The Eighth found good faith should have been applied to the Colorado search. The officers in South Dakota merely copied the Colorado description so the Eighth could not talk about their efforts. If the Eighth had applied **Leon** to the South Dakota effort the warrants would and should have fallen. In any event, since the agents in Colorado worked so hard, the warrants in this South Dakota case were saved.

Under six warrants the government seized five truckloads of documents, artwork and other property. The warrant said seize nearly everything having to do with anything the art gallery sold, said, wrote and had. These warrants were obviously overbroad and did not even specify the crimes suspected. They even failed to incorporate the affidavit by reference and failed to attach it, which can cure over-breadth. There was no indication of "permeated with fraud." Even good faith cannot save such a broad warrant when "...no agent could reasonably rely on them." **Center Art Galleries-Hawaii, Inc. v. U.S.**, 875 F. 2d 747 (C.A. 9th 1989).

One final point should be made that is easy to overlook. It is easy to overlook the fact that even if the thing is properly described the affidavit must spell out why it is believed the thing sought is currently at the place or thing to be searched. Failure of that makes all of the rest of this analysis a nullity. As a matter of fact neither **Gates**, **Leon** nor **Sheppard** can save such a warrant because this is not a matter of hyper-technicality. This matter goes to the heart of probable cause. See **Com. v. Flaherty**, 583 A. 2d 1175 (Pa. Super. Ct. 1990).

Some Thoughts on Computer Search Descriptions

For Fourth Amendment purposes, what constitutes an adequate description when the object to be searched is a computer and its database, *etc.*? There is significant activity at the trial court level, however, appellate decisions are a little sparse and of course, there is not yet a U.S. Supreme Court decision. What activity exists at the state appellate level focuses on computer-generated child pornography and its use in child sexual abuse cases. However, what the courts said in these decisions had applicability to other areas where record keeping, accounting, *etc.*, are part of the criminal scheme.

A unique case involving searches of computers arose in Pennsylvania. A search warrant was used to properly seize a computer with a hard disk drive. The incriminating information did not come by use of the regular memory but required the use of software upon a second search to retrieve deleted information still stored on the hard drive disk. The defendant argued that this second search required an additional search warrant; the retrieval of deleted files from the hard disk not seen when the directory of files in storage search was done. Analogizing this case to the "page

142

indentation" analysis cases and the "code busting" cases which require no second warrant the court refused to accept the defendant's argument. **Com. v. Copenhefer**, 587 A. 2d 1353 (Pa. 1991).

The high court of Maine faced head-on the specificity required to seize and search a computer. The defendant in **State v. Lehman**, 736 A. 2d 256 (Me. 1999) said the description was unconstitutionally overbroad. A digital camera was used to photograph girls ages 13 to 16 while taking off their clothes. Lehman told the girls he was going to create a portfolio after downloading them from the camera to the computer. He, of course, had the girls assume positions that exposed their genitalia. The following description was used: "photographs, photo packages, photographic receipts, slides, negatives, *computer files* or *digital images* of the three girls; writings that included the names of the three girls; "*digital cameras,* and camera equipment," and *"all computer equipment and computer related equipment including but not limited to laptops, monitors, key boards, printers, mice, modems, hard drives, CD ROMS, photo scanners, computer disks, tapes, programs to run computers and access data, manuals on operation of systems and programs,* which Peter Lehman would have been able to access, including but not limited to, copies of the contents thereof." The police went to Lehman's house and seized all hardware and software including over 400 computer disks. Did this warrant leave too much to the discretion of the officer? No! "Scrupulous exactitude" is not required, the Maine court held. They then cite cases often containing even more general descriptions. Those cases upheld those warrants. See: **U.S. v. Upham**, 168 F. 3d 532 (C.A. 1st 1999); **U.S. v. Lacy**, 119 F. 3d 742 (C.A. 9th 1997); **Davis v, Gracey** 111 F. 3d 1472 (C.A. 10th 1997); and **U.S. v. Leary**, 846 F. 2d 592 (C.A. 10th 1988).

Five laptop computers found in a closet were held to be within the scope of the warrant authorizing, in part, the seizure of writings, journals, and other information involving the use of explosives in **People v. Gall**, 2001 WL 209780 (Colo.). The court noted that the computers were not boxed but showed some evidence of having been used and could likely be used to contain the type of information sought. In a similar type of case from New Mexico, the description said the "seize pornographic video cassette tapes, *a computer located in the office with discs on software*, a ledger guide to the video cassettes, and eight-millimeter cassettes." First, the court rejected "blanket" suppression – the well-described being saved and only the inadequately described being suppressible. The real concern focused *not* on the computer description but on description of the "pornographic video cassettes." The officers therefore did not exceed the scope of the warrant when they accessed the computer files. **State v. Poatscheck**, 6 P 3d 498 (N. Mex. App. 2000).

The next case comes from the state of Washington and, once more, child pornography was stored on the home computer and used to desensitize children to sexual acts with adults. The description used to authorize the seizure was as follows: "All computer equipment and accessories; including floppy disc, hard disk and CD ROM, hard drive, tape drive, backup optical disc or any other medium of computer data storage, computer programs and computer games, computer monitors, keyboards, printers, central processing units, computer user manuals." In addition to the decisions cited by Maine, Washington also cited **U.S. v. Harvey**, 2 F. 3d 1318 (C.A. 3rd 1993); **U.S. v. Bateman**, 805 F. Supp. 1041 (D. N. H. 1992) upholding similar descriptions. **State v. Mills**, 1999 WL 105 4768 (Wash. App. Div. 1).

VI.   Why the Thing is Needed Clause

4.   THAT POSSESSION OF THE ABOVE DESCRIBED THINGS IS IN ITSELF UNLAWFUL (OR THE PUBLIC HAS A PRIMARY INTEREST IN, OR PRIMARY RIGHT TO POSSESSION OF, THE ABOVE DESCRIBED THINGS).   IN THAT SAID THINGS ARE:

Under this entry it is essential to spell out the specific statutes involved. It is not enough to merely list "contraband" if the subject matter is contraband. The entry should indicate why it is contraband by citing the code section and giving the essence of the language of the statute. In **U.S. v. Crozier**, 777 F. 2d 1376 (C.A. 9th 1985) the second warrant reviewed, the one for the Stein house, was found to be overbroad. That warrant authorized the seizure of "Material evidence of violation of 21 U.S.C. 841, 846, (Manufacture and possession with intent to distribute amphetamine and conspiracy.)" The affidavit for the warrant specified amphetamine, precursor chemicals, including methylamine, P-2-P, ether, and alcohol, laboratory apparatus, makes, formulas, as well as any indicia of ownership and control of the premises. The agent did not have the affidavit with him when he executed the warrant. Even though good faith was approved in **Leon**, the Ninth Circuit felt this warrant was not facially valid and without the affidavit to guide the discretion of the officer, the officer could not reasonably rely on it. This warrant authorized a general search for evidence of an amphetamine business and did not describe any particular property. The court said that **Sheppard** does not apply because this was no technical error. Evidence of good faith was lacking on the part of the police.

VII. The Underlying Facts and Circumstances Clause

5. THE FACTS TENDING TO ESTABLISH THE FOREGOING GROUNDS FOR ISSUANCE OF A SEARCH WARRANT ARE SHOWN ON A SHEET HEADED "UNDERLYING FACTS AND CIRCUMSTANCES" WHICH IS ATTACHED HERETO, MADE A PART HEREOF AND ADOPTED HEREIN BY REFERENCE.

The affidavit must show probable cause and be based on more than suspicion. The warrant must be based on the affidavit. Thus, if there is an "entire absence of the basic affidavit," then the warrant is no good. **Rugendorf v. United States**, 376 U.S. 528 (1964). If the affidavit used words "suspects" then the warrant issued is illegal. **Nathanson v. United States**, 290 U.S. 41 (1933).

What is probable cause? There is a standard definition which is set out in Chapter Two. Of course, probable cause may be based on less evidence than would justify conviction. **United States v. Ventresca**, 380 U.S. 102 (1965). With this in mind, it is said that probable cause exists where the facts and circumstances within the officer's knowledge, and of which the officers have reasonable trustworthy information, are sufficient in themselves to warrant a belief by a man of reasonable caution that a crime is or has been committed. **Brinegar v. United States**, 338 U.S. 160 (1948). This is a practical, nontechnical concept affording the best compromise that has been found between rash police action and community protection. It is best to think of the warrant as a conclusion and the affidavit as that which justifies the conclusion. Therefore, if the affidavit is merely conclusory, then there is not sufficient information upon which to issue a warrant. One must ask the question: was there sufficient detail of the criminal activity as to its content or way of getting the information that raises it above the level of a casual rumor? **Com. v. Kaufman**, 381 Mass. 301 (1980).

At one time the judicial finding of probable cause was not challengeable. That is not the case today as required by **Aguilar v. Texas**, 378 U.S. 108 (1964). The issuing judicial officer can be called upon to testify and the documents involved are subject to judicial review. Thus the days of the "rubber stamp" are at an end. It is essential that the issuing judicial officer show that sufficient time elapsed between the police officer's arrival and the issuance. It is the better practice to cross-examine the officer on the factual matters. Oral testimony is admissible before the judicial officer who is requested to issue a warrant. However, please read the material dealing with the "four corners doctrine" in Chapter Four as to whether the affidavit must be amended before the warrant is issued or what form of record will satisfy the "contemporary with issuance" rule.

The writing of an affidavit is not an essay contest. **Spinelli, Harris**, and several other decisions so hold. The key question that must be confronted by the issuing judge is that of the reliability of the second-hand information. This was the crux of **Aguilar** cited above.

The preference given the warrant under **Ventresca** does depend upon a reasonable, but not perfect, conclusion that probable cause existed. It also depends on information constitutionally gathered and reasonably and sufficiently described. However, if only one piece of information was unconstitutionally gathered by an illegal prior search or seizure does the Fourth Amendment demand suppression of the evidence? No. Since there may be sufficient properly gathered evidence of probable cause described in the warrant, the U.S. Supreme Court has determined that a new suppression hearing should be conducted without the improperly gathered evidence. This was made abundantly clear by the Court's decision in **Kyllo v. U.S.**, 121 S. Ct. 2038 (U.S.). In **Kyllo**, the illegally seized evidence was gathered by the use of a thermal imager. The Court remanded the case for a new suppression hearing saying that the District Court was "...to determine whether, without the evidence it (the thermal imager) provided, the search warrant issued in this case was supported by probable cause – and if not, whether there is any other basis for supporting admission of the evidence that the search pursuant to the warrant produced."

Good Faith and Probable Cause

The **Gates** "good faith reliance" decision was intended to keep reviewing courts from being hypertechnical when reviewing otherwise valid warrants. In one case the police knew the defendant had purchased hydroponic growing supplies, was a subscriber to a marijuana grower's magazine; and had hung blankets at the windows of his house. Then they learned that electrical usage went way up. They took this information to a judge and received a search warrant. The trial court suppressed. The Missouri Court of Appeals felt that great deference as required by **Gates** was not given by the suppression judge to the issuing magistrate's decision to issue this warrant. They found this affidavit was sufficient under the **Gates** guidelines. **State v. Shuck**, 800 S.W. 2d 49 (Mo. Ct. App. 1990). This case could have also relied on **Leon** (*infra*) for both cases continue the "common sense" view the U.S. Supreme Court has long espoused for this area.

No case better illustrates the status of the law abiding, known informant than **Rutledge v. State**, 745 So. 2d 912 (Ala. Crim. App. 1999). A computer technician was called by Rutledge to repair his computer. It was during these repairs that the technician discovered the down-loaded child pornography. The technician reported this to the police and they, in turn, applied for the warrant. The defendant complained that "past reliability" was not established and, therefore, the warrant was no good. The court properly noted that "where, as here, an *ordinary citizen* informs the police that he has seen evidence of a crime or that someone had admitted involvement in a crime to him, he is *presumed to be reliable* and an officer is not required to supply the magistrate with information explaining why he believes the citizen-informant to be reliable" (emphasis added).

That relayed information from a fellow officer is presumptively reliable, see **United States v. Ventresca**, 380 U.S. 102 (1965), but some cross-examination of the officer is demanded. Of course, information from the normal, non-criminal is generally regarded a presumptively reliable. However, the hearsay cannot be too remote, and the conclusion drawn must have a logical base. **Barber v. State**, 241 So. 2d 355 (Miss. 1970). Here a warrant was issued for the search of an apartment based upon information given by the informant's wife to the informant who gave it to the police who in turn relayed it to the justice of the peace. Fourth hand hearsay was rejected by Missouri in **State v. Hammett**, 784 S.W. 2d 293 (Mo. Ct. App. 1989). In this case there was no personal observation by the informant and no corroboration by the police. The reliability of a tip from a fellow officer was upheld in **People v. Lazanis**, 257 Cal. Rep. 180 (Cal. Dist. Ct. App. 1989).

Not often addressed is the question of children as informants for the purpose of issuing search warrants. In this case a 10-year old and an 8-year old turned over marijuana to police and told them where they got it. The court held the fact that they were children does not undermine either their reliability or their sufficiency of knowledge. Therefore, there was ample probable cause for the warrant to issue. **State v. Carver**, 753 P. 2d 569 (Wash. Ct. App. 1988). See also **State v. Graham**, 780 P. 2d 1103 (Haw. 1989) upholding a warrant based on an 8-year old's information.

Information illegally obtained by the government cannot be the basis of the affidavit to support a warrant. In **Davidson v. State**, 240 So. 2d 463 (Miss. 1970), the game warden trespassed to see the tractor. He then told the sheriff and the sheriff obtained the warrant. The steps that precede the search and seizure must be legal.

However, do not confuse this case with states that allow "open fields" to operate where the officer is permitted to trespass.

A large percentage of information comes from informants who are usually less than law-abiding. The reliability of such an informant must be established to the issuing judge's satisfaction. **Aguilar v. Texas**, 378 U.S. 108 (1964) as modified by **Illinois v. Gates**, 462 U.S. 213 (1983). One way that this reliability can be established is through the affiant's past record with this informant. How many times has he or she used the informant? How reliable was his or her information in the past? How many convictions resulted? It should be borne in mind that once reliability is established, it is still essential that sufficient detail be presented to justify the warrant's issuance. Be careful that the detail is not a "snow job" or a series of otherwise innocent facts made to look sinister. **Spinelli v. United States**, 393 U.S. 410 (1969); **Wong Sun v. United States**, 371 U.S. 471 (1963).

The reliability of the information can be self-verifying and corroborated. Where this is done it is proper to issue a warrant. The basis of knowledge test can be fulfilled without a statement of the circumstances from which the informer derived his information, as where the tip is sufficiently detailed that it may be self-verifying; that one could conclude that the informer is relying on more than mere rumor. **United States v. Harris**, 403 U.S. 573 (1971); **Jones v. United States**, 362 U.S. 257 (1960); and **Illinois v. Gates**, 462 U.S. 213 (1983). But more has to be corroborated than the name and address of a suspect and that he or she owns handguns when the charge is selling guns. **Com. v. Nowells**, 390 Mass. 621 (1983).

Freshness or Staleness of the Probable Cause

Another essential of reliability concerns the freshness of the information relayed to the officer. This helps complete the basis of reliability test of **Aguilar**. The affidavit should state not only the date the officer got the information from the informant but also the date the informant obtained the information. This will help the issuing magistrate assess whether the data is mere rumor or speculation and the likelihood that the evidence is still at the place or thing to be searched. This is well illustrated by the First Circuit's decision in **U.S. v. Salvucci**, 599 F. 2d 1094 (C.A. 1st 1979). The affidavit indicated that the informant overheard a conversation that a check-writer was being used to forge checks and that it was kept at a certain apartment. The affidavit cited no dates for the overheard conversation nor for the date the police received the information. The court held these omissions were fatal to the warrant.

It is also fatal where the warrant does not show the time when the alleged criminal activity took place and it cannot be otherwise discerned from the general context of the affidavit. **Collins v. State,** 658 S.W. 2d 877 (Ark. 1983). Thus, where a reading of the affidavit suggested that the informant had provided fresh information about drugs presently being stored in a location that does not permit long term storage the warrant will be upheld. **Com. v. Atchue**, 393 Mass. 343 (1984). Accord **Com. v. Haggerty**, 564 A. 2d 1269 (Pa. Super. Ct. 1989).

There is always significant activity in the "freshness" area. Courts have begun to use the rules somewhat. In a stolen pistol case information that was 8 months old was approved but the court was critical of the delay. **U.S. v. McCall**, 740 F. 2d 1331 (C.A. 4th 1984). A year delay under the totality was upheld in **U.S. v. Marriott**, 638 F. Supp. 333 (N.D. Ill. 1986). A month delay between receiving the information and the application for the warrant was found to be fresh since stolen weapons are not disposed of easily and a magistrate could reasonably conclude the defendant still had them. **U.S. v. Medlin**, 798 F. 2d 407 (C.A. 10th 1986). A delay of 10 days is not too long since possession of guns is a typical ongoing activity. **U.S. v. Shoms**, 786 F. 2d 981 (C.A. 10th 1986). An eleven-month-old tip was not stale since police corroborated some information before making application. The manufacture of controlled substances is a continuing type of crime. **Cauchon v. U.S.**, 824 F. 2d 908 (C.A. 11th 1987). A narcotics conspiracy is the very model of a continuing enterprise that allows the court to relax temporal requirements of non-staleness. **U.S. v. Feola**, 651 F. Supp. 1068 (S.D.N.Y. 1987). Thus, if the affidavit establishes a continuing and protracted type of crime, information that is several months old will be alright said **State v. Woodcock**, 407 N.W. 2d 603 (Iowa 1987). One of the ways to prove continuance and therefore freshness, is to show other cases where old information upheld the type of things sought. In **U.S. v. Batchelder**, 824 F. 2d 563 (C.A. 7th 1987) the police demonstrated that in 19 out of 21 similar cases that guns and silencers are kept for extended periods.

One of the more important issues in determining whether a warrant should issue concerns the "age" of the information – the staleness/freshness issue. The type of crime, the destructibility of and type of physical evidence sought, the quantity involved, the mass, the potential for deterioration, the number of people with access to the place or thing in which it may be found all contribute to this determination of probable cause. Some information is just too old to allow intrusion into private places. Believe it or not, except for some professional hit-men (or women), people who use guns and silencers rarely throw them away thus it is quite possible that a crime involving a gun may be months or even years old and information that comes to light later may still be fresh enough to believe in probable cause. Some stolen items are either so "hot" or so big that quick disposal *vis-à-vis* the date of the crime is somewhat impossible; *e.g.*, road building equipment, cranes, tons of marijuana or cocaine. The duty is on the affiant to demonstrate that un-fresh information is not stale. The duty on the judge is to raise the issue at issuance if not covered in the affidavit.

The appellate court of Idaho has one of the more recent freshness/staleness decisions. See **State v. Carlson**, 4 P.3d 1122 (Idaho App. 2000). The defendant, at suppression, argued that the information was stale because the observations used to create the affidavit were more than 24 days old when it was presented to the judge. The court first notes that staleness depends upon the nature of the factual scenario. It continues by saying there are no magical number of days – case – by – case is used. Then it says suppression courts are to look to the nature of the crime. Is it protracted or continuous in nature? The court then notes that "certain nefarious activities, such as narcotics trafficking, are continuous in nature and, as a result, are less likely to become stale even over an extended period of time." I would add that running a chop shop enjoys that same status. In either case it is the nature of the illicit business and not the thing or things actually seen that allows the search. In either case the product (drug or car part) seen likely will not be there on the date of the search. The "turnover rate" in such nefarious businesses is generally rapid. The observations of the Idaho informant did not involve a user; it involved a marijuana operation. If the detail in such a case is good and the judge is satisfied that rumor is not being relied upon, then warrant should issue and be upheld on suppression.

One of the best statements regarding the issue of staleness or freshness was repeated by Missouri from a case from Maryland. The Maryland court said: "However, the likelihood that evidence sought is still in place is a function not of a watch or a calendar, but of the character of the crime, of the criminal, of the thing seized or of the place searched." **State v. Pattie**, 2001 WL 205989 (Mo. App. E.D.) Citing **Andressen v. State**, 331 A. 2d 78 at 106 (Md. 1975). The issue in **Pattie** was whether a video tape of minors performing sex acts would still exist that was made 13 months before the issuance of the warrant. It was not destroyed.

Anonymous Tipsters

As we have become more embroiled in the war on drugs it became clear that many tips were coming from anonymous sources. Such sources could in no way be checked out under the two-prong test of **Aguilar**. Something had to give. In its opinion in **Illinois v. Gates**, 462 U.S. 213 (1983) the U.S. Supreme Court abandoned its rigid "two-pronged test" of **Aguilar** and in its place adopted the "totality of the circumstances" approach in its stead. The "totality test" includes, but is not limited to, the **Aguilar** approach which will still work very well as "totality" in the known informant case. But "totality" establishes a "corroboration of information" test that allows a reliability finding when the informer is totally unknown. After all, as the Court notes, all we are trying to do is to prevent the use of reckless or prevaricating tales against our citizens. Among the states to adopt Gates are specifically: North Dakota, New Hampshire, Texas, Maryland, and Washington. Massachusetts and New York have rejected **Gates** as has New Mexico.

However, despite the fact that Massachusetts has said it rejected **Gates** it has found a way to accommodate the **Gates** totality test within the **Aguilar** two-prong test. In **Com. v. Germain**, 396 Mass. 413 (1985), an anonymous tip of great detail was corroborated. The warrant was upheld by using **Draper** and **Aguilar**. A like result was reached in **Com. v. Truax**, 397 Mass. 174 (1986). But where the detail given by the anonymous tipster is scant corroboration is not possible. **Com. v. Rojas**, 403 Mass. 483 (1988).

Does the informer's identity have to be disclosed to the judge at the warrant issuing hearing? The identity of the informant need not be disclosed to the judge unless the judge feels he cannot give credence to the information without such disclosure. The court is under no duty to require disclosure to himself or even later, at a suppression hearing, to the defendant. **McCray v. Illinois**, 386 U.S. 300 (1967).

The so-called informer's privilege or the government's privilege to withhold the name and identity of the informer is not absolute, held the Court in **Roviaro v. U.S.** 353 U.S. 1 (1957). The scope of the privilege is limited by its underlying purpose, held the Court. Fundamental requirements of fairness play a role. In a broad sweeping statement the Court wrote, "Where the disclosure of an informant's identity, or the contents of his communication is relevant or helpful to the defense of an accused, or is essential to a fair determination of a cause, the privilege must give way." Failure to so disclose in these circumstance requires dismissal of the action. The only limit on this sweeping statement is found where the Court said disclosure is required "unless there was sufficient evidence apart from his confidential communication." The Court went on to say that there is no bright line but that each case stands on its own facts using a balancing test. In the case before it, the informer was the sole participant other than the defendant in the crime charged. He was the only witness in a position to amplify or contradict the testimony of government witnesses. The defendant was charged not with mere possession, but with a more complicated intent involved crime. Under these circumstances disclosure was required.

The **Roviaro** case does not turn on guilt/innocence but rather is broader and includes trial preparation, and other evidentiary and sentencing issues. An Illinois court agreed that **Roviaro** is a broad based policy statement and requires disclosure in a case challenging the sufficiency of the probable cause in a search warrant and a **Franks** analysis challenge. **People v. Zymantas**, 547 N.E. 2d 536 (Ill. App. Ct. 1989).

In order for the defendant to unmask the identity of an informant there must be a preliminary, substantial showing of some compelling reason to get to that identity. Absent a demonstration of an independent justification for disclosure, no disclosure order should be entered. To do otherwise would throttle the flow of reliable information to the police. **Com. v. Douzanis**, 384 Mass. 434 (1981).

In Massachusetts, where a relatively sensational case revealed that one police officer had "created" a confidential informant and used that creation in over 50 warrants, how to balance the informer's privilege against **Franks v. Delaware** (discussed in Chapter Five) had taken center stage. The Massachusetts court has decided to tell its trial judges to hold an *in camera* hearing with the informant after the defense has properly raised its allegations of "falsity" and before it holds a full-blown **Franks** hearing in open court. The *in camera* hearing is of course to be held without the presence of counsel. **Com. v. Amral**, 554 N.E. 2d 1189 (Mass. 1990).

Once the defense attorney is given the name of the informant can a court prohibit counsel from revealing that identity to the accused? Though there are no hard and fast rules the problem is well illustrated by two cases. In a D.C. Circuit case a judge's order not to reveal the name to the defendant was held to undermine the purpose of **Roviaro**. In the D.C. case where entrapment was the defense, the role of the informer was pivotal and the defendant did not clearly appear to be "predisposed." Thus the court order denied the defendant the ability to adequately cross-examine the informant because counsel could not consult with his client. **U.S. v. Eniola**, 893 F. 2d 383 (C.A.D.C. 1990).

The Seventh Circuit, on the other hand, upheld such a court order to not reveal the name to the defendant. In this case the prosecutor revealed the name at sidebar during a pretrial hearing. The defense said that constituted a waiver. The court said revelation to an attorney, a court officer, is not revelation to one who has a personal stake in the matter, thus it is not a waiver. It said the due process denial of effective assistance of counsel argument was "ridiculous" since the court said the informant could be called as a defense witness even though the state was not going to use the person due to the fact that the informant was promised anonymity. Since what this informer would say would hurt, not help, the defense, no **Roviaro** violation was present. **U.S. v. Herrero**, 893 F. 2d 1512 (C.A. 7th 1990).

The privilege against disclosure of the informer's identity does not violate the Due Process Clause of the Fourteenth Amendment nor the Sixth Amendment right of confrontation at a preliminary hearing with regard to probable cause. The question here is not guilt or innocence. This is a necessary testimonial privilege so as not to discourage informers and for the purpose of continuing their usefulness in law enforcement.

In **Spinelli** and **Draper**, it was held that where the police do not know the basis of the informer's tip, the police should corroborate the information. What these decisions did not specifically say was whether the fact corroborated could be an innocent detail or whether it had to be an incriminating fact. The New York Court of Appeals held that there should be confirmation of sufficient details suggestive of or directly related to the criminal activity informed about to make reasonable the conclusion that the informer was not passing rumor or seeking revenge. Past reliability is not of itself assurance that the informer is now operating on the truth or from first-hand knowledge. **People v. Elwell**, 406 N.E. 2d 471 (N.Y. 1980).

A final word on reliability concerns the problems of the subsequent disclosure that some of the underlying facts and circumstances are lies. The validity of the information can be tested but it must be properly raised at the suppression hearing or trial or both. **Rugendorf v. United States**, 376 U.S. 528 (1964), **United States v. Carmichael**, 489 F. 2d 983 (C.A. 7th 1973); **State v. Boyd**, 224 N.W. 2d 609 (Iowa 1974). Illegal or otherwise invalid information cannot form the basis of a warrant no matter what the ultimate search reveals. "Where the defendant makes a substantial preliminary showing that a false statement knowingly and intentionally, or with reckless disregard for the truth, was included by the affiant in the warrant's affidavit, and if the allegedly false statement is necessary to the finding of probable cause, the Fourth Amendment requires that a hearing be held at the defendant's request." If a false statement is material to probable cause, then the warrant must be voided and the fruits of the search excluded. **Franks v. Delaware**, 438 U.S. 154 (1978). This is fully discussed in Chapter Five.

VIII. The Probable Cause Finding Clause: Ministerial Concerns

6. *THIS COURT, HAVING EXAMINED AND CONSIDERED SAID AFFIDAVIT, AND ALSO*

HAVING HEARD AND CONSIDERED EVIDENCE IN SUPPORT THEREOF FROM THE AFFIANTS NAMED THEREIN DOES FIND THAT PROBABLE CAUSE FOR THE ISSUANCE OF A SEARCH WARRANT DOES EXIT. THEREFORE YOU ARE HEREBY COMMANDED TO PROCEED AT ANY TIME IN THE DAY OR NIGHT TO THE PLACE DESCRIBED ABOVE AND TO SEARCH FORTHWITH SAID PLACE FOR THINGS SPECIFIED ABOVE, MAKING KNOWN TO THE PERSON OR PERSONS OCCUPYING OR CONTROLLING SAID PLACE, IF ANY, YOUR PURPOSE AND AUTHORITY FOR SO DOING, AND IF THE THINGS SPECIFIED ABOVE BE FOUND THERE TO SEIZE THEM, HAVING A COPY OF THIS WARRANT AND A RECEIPT FOR THE THINGS TAKEN: AND BRING THE THINGS SEIZED BEFORE THIS COURT INSTANTER; AND PREPARE A WRITTEN INVENTORY OF THE ITEMS SEIZED, AND HAVE THEN AND THERE THIS WRIT, WITH THEM.

Most states follow the federal rule that unless exigent circumstances are shown, a warrant may be served during the daytime only. The better practice would be to satisfy the court that a nighttime entry is necessary. The Court of Appeals for the District of Columbia found that a nighttime search that was authorized lacked probable cause to enter during the night, but this was only a technical defect in this case because the search took place during the daytime. **U.S. v. Anderson**, 851 F. 2d 384 (C.A.D.C. 1988). Where two statutes govern this issue and they are in conflict the specific statute governs and not the general statute. **Gooding v. U.S.**, 416 U.S. 430 (1974) upheld a search at night as approved by the contraband controlled substances law.

The Minnesota Supreme Court takes the position that when the police act in good faith, any error committed in this context is attributable to the magistrate who should have required the police to make a clearer showing of need before granting the nighttime search authority. **State v. Lien**, 265 N.W. 2d 833 (Minn. 1978). Twenty three states require daytime execution absent special showing; 14 states authorize searches at anytime and the rest have no pertinent position. In one case officers were permitted to conduct a nighttime search but it had to be completed one hour after the drugs arrived. One- half of the shipment arrived later. Police went in 1½ hours after the final delivery. This was approved in **U.S. v. Sequoia**, 800 F. 2d 39 (C.A. 2d 1986).

The Tenth Circuit has held that the nighttime search of a home was offensive to the Fourth Amendment saying: "Absent legislative authority for day or nighttime service, it is for the issuing magistrate to determine the reasonableness of a nighttime execution." Thus they held that this state warrant was invalidly served and that the Fourth Amendment governs, not the fact that Oklahoma law does not require a nighttime endorsement. The Tenth thereby agrees with the Third Circuit cases of **U.S. v. Merritt**, 293 F. 2d 742 (C.A. 3rd 1961) and **Boyance v. Myers**, 398 F. 2d 896 (C.A. 3rd 1968) which based their decisions on the common law aversion to nighttime searches. **O'Rourke v. City of Norman**, 875 F. 2d 1465 (C.A. 10th 1989). The constitutional concern here is the reasonableness requirement and the historical context in which the Fourth Amendment was adopted.

A question arises in this context as to how many entries can be made on a single warrant. The answer is **one**. This was the practice followed in **Ratliff v. State**, 310 So. 2d 905 (Miss 1975). Repeated searches are not permitted under the same warrant. However, if the officers do not relinquish possession, but continue it for several hours or days, then the search is a continued search. **Johnson v. State**, 146 Miss. 593, 111 So. 595 (1927). All states follow the "one bite" rule and generally follow the "continuing search rule" described above.

What is the normal effect of a returned, un-executed warrant? Most states say that it is dead and of no further use. A 1978 Colorado decision took another position. The facts are as follows: (1) A valid search warrant was issued for a car in police custody. (2) Another department of the police had it, therefore, the warrant was unexecuted and returned. (3) The next day a second warrant was issued without a valid affidavit. (4) This second warrant was executed and the incriminating evidence was found. (5) Defendant argued the invalidity of the warrant as rendering the evidence inadmissible. The Colorado Supreme Court held that the prior, unexecuted warrant had not lost its vitality. They reasoned that since the first affidavit was still on file and subject to judicial scrutiny no harm was done. **People v. Hampton**, 587 P. 2d 275 (Colo. 1978). This is the more reasonable position with staleness being the prime concern.

Most statutes or rules require that the police have the warrant with them and to leave a copy upon completion with an inventory of the things taken. It has been held that service concurrent with execution when mandated by rule is ministerial only, and unless prejudice is shown, there will be no suppression. **U.S. v. Bonner**, 808 F. 2d 364 (C.A. 1st 1986). Other courts see the failure to have the warrant as fatal. Florida takes the position that since having it is to prevent violent confrontations the evidence is suppressible when the officers fail to take the warrant with them. **Riley v. State**, 433 So. 2d 976 (Fla. Dist. Ct. App. 1983). The Seventh Circuit will not suppress when failure to have the warrant was not a deliberate attempt to circumvent the warrant's discretion limiting function. They see it as a ministerial rule and prejudice has to be shown. **U.S. v. Stockheimer**, 807 F. 2d 610 (C.A. 7th 1986). Two cases held that not having a telephonic warrant at the search was a ministerial mistake, but the **Hipperle** case says this should be avoided and that court threatened to suppress if the warrant is not at the scene by the time the officers leave the premises. **U.S. v. Hipperle**, 810 F. 2d 836 (C.A. 8th 1987) and **U.S. v. Pryor**, 652 F. Supp. 1353 (D. Me. 1987).

The next major provision deals with the three-fold problem of who serves it, who gets it, and when it is served. The case of **Adams v. State**, 202 Miss. 68, 30 So. 2d 593 (1974) illustrates improper service. A warrant was issued. The DA and the deputy went to serve it. The defendant saw them coming and ran into the house. The DA burst in behind the defendant and found the incriminating evidence. *Then* the deputy came in with the warrant and laid it on the table, but by this time, the search was over. The DA was without authority under the law to serve a warrant and had not been given any by the court. The moral is serve first, then search. That is what appears to be required. Statutory provisions for search and seizure are construed by Mississippi strictly against the state. It was too late when the deputy arrived to legalize the already finished search. This rule now seems harsh under the "good faith" exceptions being carved out by the Court. Each state will have to determine its own disciplinary rules. Fed. R. Crim. Proc. 41 (c)(1) requires that a federal warrant be served by federal officers. The state police served one. This was found to be ministerial and since no prejudice was shown the search was upheld. **U.S. v. Gatewood**, 786 F. 2d 821 (C.A. 8th 1986).

In **U.S. v. Gilbert**, 942 F. 2d 1537 (C.A. 11th 1991), a valid state warrant was issued but the officers who served it were not designated, as required by Florida law, as being given permission to execute. The warrant could have so authorized their participation since it was a place within their territorial jurisdiction. Like Mississippi, Florida strictly construes these service provisions against the state. The evidence obtained was used by the federal government to convict Gilbert. Gilbert argued that the evidence should have been suppressed. The Eleventh Circuit disagreed and said no federal constitutional provision was violated due to the omission of the authorization required by state statute. Unconstitutional means were not used. This decision is in line with the philosophy of **Gatewood** discussed above.

The reverse type of problem was the subject of a Michigan decision. Evidence gathered under a federal warrant quite properly did not meet state standards. The defense argued that the evidence should be inadmissible. The state law requires that a person whose home is searched be given a copy of the warrant before or during the search. The federal law does not require that step. The Michigan court refused to nullify the use of the evidence in their court. They felt it was not an appropriate remedy. **People v. Sobczak**, 2001 WL 4390409 (Mich.).

In what appeared to be a unique problem (but is not) the Georgia Court of Appeals was faced with a valid warrant that was served by the proper officers with the aid of the judge who issued the warrant. Should the search be held valid? The court said no, stating: "To our minds this so conveys the impression that Judge McKeehan had 'thrown in' with officers of the law as to negate any possibility of a finding of 'severance and disengagement form activities of law enforcement.'" **Thomason v. State**, 251 S.E. 2d 598 (Ga. Ct. App. 1978).

Not long after the Georgia case, the U.S. Supreme Court considered a similar matter. The issuing magistrate accompanied police officers to the scene of the search and aided in the search. **Lo-Ji Sales, Inc. v. New York**, 442 U.S. 319 (1979). The Court said this conduct was reminiscent of the 18th century and the reason why the Fourth Amendment was adopted. First of all, with the exception of the two named films, the things to be seized were not particularly described. Too much discretion was left to the officers making the search. The Fourth Amendment does not permit open-ended warrants; those that are to be completed while the search is being conducted. But the worst part of this case was the blending of the judiciary with the police. The judge allowed himself to become a part of, if not the leader of the search. A judge cannot be neutral and detached if he was "one with the police and prosecutors in the executive search...." In closing the Court said: "Our society is better able to tolerate the admittedly pornographic business of petitioner than a return to the general warrant era...." Lawbreakers must be lawfully pursued within the framework of the Constitution.

Some mistakes are ministerial or technical only. Due to a "typo" the judge issuing the warrant was also named as the person to execute it. The court found this a matter of form not substance as the judge did not participate in the search. **U.S. v. Ofshe**, 817 F. 2d 1508 (C.A. 11th 1987).

As to which person to serve, local statutes or rules govern. It is not necessary for an officer to search the entire premises for the owner or to ascertain first whether the owner is anywhere on the premises before he can properly serve the warrant upon a person in possession of the premises. Knock, announce, wait a reasonable interval, unless exigent circumstances have arisen, enter and serve is the general rule.

Some states by rule or statute have a knock and announce rule. Others do not. Such a rule makes little or no sense in the search warrant area because whether the people say "come on in" or whether anyone is there, the authority of the warrant grants temporary possession to the police. Yes, it serves in some instances a function of keeping peace but it also puts the occupiers on guard. We waive the rule when these exceptions can be established: (1) the destruction of the evidence exception; (2) the danger to the person exception; and (3) the useless gesture exception. Police can apply for these waivers in advance or prove them afterwards. In either case some form of judicial approval is required.

Since all of the above noted exceptions partake of the exigent circumstances rule, prior judicial approval should not be required in all cases. Consider **State v. Pelletier**, 552 A. 2d 805 (Conn. 1989). The police in this case had a warrant for a triple murder, armed-robbery suspect. The police had not yet taken possession of the M-1 carbines that had been used and had reason to believe that this particularly violent defendant still had the guns since it had been only 24 hours since the robbery had taken place. Avoiding the issue whether the use of the "bullhorn" was good "knock and announce," the court found sufficient exigent circumstances for failing to comply with the rule.

Some states do not have such a written policy but base it on their own Constitution. Nowhere is such mentioned in the Fourth Amendment. Such a case is **People v. Marinez**, 513 N.E. 2d 607 (Ill. App. 1987). The defendants claimed that the officers failed to knock on the door and announce their authority. The narcotics agent did not know that the Marinez's lived there but believed the premises to be that of a Mr. Rodriguez, a good friend of the defendants. They also believed that Rodriguez was armed (UZI type) and that a controlled buy of cocaine had taken place at this residence. The police say they yelled "police officers – search warrant" several times. They say that as they began to knock on the door it began to open. Strange that three one-inch indentations were found on the door but there was no damage to the lock mechanism. They entered, searched, found a gun and cocaine. The issue, as the Illinois court saw it, was to determine whether under the facts of this case an announcement coupled with a simultaneous entry circumvented the purpose of the "knock and

158

announce" doctrine. Illinois does not have a written rule and that failure to do so does not *per se* violate the constitution. But they follow decisional law and allow violation only under exigent circumstances. Their decisions say that mere presence of either a gun or narcotics is not enough. The Illinois Court held: "As we have stated previously, one of the purposes of 'knock and announce' is to give the defendant time to respond to the presence of the police. If the entry into the dwelling is simultaneous with the 'knock and announce', that purpose is thwarted. Therefore, if the necessary exigent circumstances are absent and the police 'knock and announce' their presence, they must, in form, give the occupants of the dwelling time to respond. To hold otherwise would effectively eliminate the need to ever consider the 'knock and announce' rule."

The only prior knock and announce decision by the Supreme Court came in **Sabbath v. U.S.**, 391 U.S. 585 (1968) interpreting 18 U.S.C. Sec. 3109. The police opened a closed but unlocked door. This did not comply with the statute. Removal of an object to entry and not the destruction of the door is the evil aimed at. No exigencies were shown in that case. This was not a constitutional level decision.

First, in the federal system, courts disagreed whether not securing a waiver and then not knocking and announcing is a ministerial or a constitutional concern. The Third Circuit said suppression is not mandated by 18 U.S.C. Sec. 3109 (1982) for its violation. Besides, in this case the defendant was known to be a fugitive and, therefore, escape was a great possibility. **U.S. v. Nolan**, 718 F. 2d 589 (C.A. 3rd 1983). The District Court for the District of Columbia said that suppression is required when there is no exigency. **U.S. v. Rodriguez**, 663 F. Supp. 585 (D. D.C. 1987); see also **U.S. v. Stewart**, 867 F. 2d 581 (C.A. 10th 1989).

As noted above not much in the way of Fourth Amendment analysis came forth from the Supreme Court. However, that was going to change as this Court began its focus on the issue of reasonableness and searches rather than individually labeled processes. In **Wilson v. Arkansas**, 514 U.S. 927 (1995) the Court held: "that the Fourth Amendment incorporates the common-law requirement that police knock on a dwelling's door and announce their identity and purpose before attempting forcible entry," and "recognized that the flexible reasonableness requirement should not be read to mandate a rigid announcement rule that ignores countervailing law enforcement interests." Id at 934. The Court left it to "the lower courts to determine the circumstances under which an announced entry is reasonable." Id at 936.

This decision aggravated several members of a usually quiet state high court—the Wisconsin court. In **State v. Richards**, 549 N.W. 2d 218 (Wis. 1996) that court held that police are never required to adhere to the rule of announcement when executing a search warrant involving felonious drug delivery. The Wisconsin court upheld the Appeals Court decision to uphold the trial court's decision to admit the evidence. One justice concurred disagreeing with the idea of a blanket exception but agreeing there were sufficient circumstances in this case to justify a waiver of knock and announce. The majority decision flew in the face of a U.S. Supreme Court who rarely draws bright lines and, indeed, is married to a totality jurisprudential view. There was no doubt this case would get the Supreme Court's attention. It was accepted and the decision came down as **Richards v. Wisconsin**, 520 U.S. 385 (1997). Of course the blanket rule was rejected as not being permitted under the Fourth Amendment. Over-generalizations were feared and creeping exceptions were forecast. Knocking and announcing should only be waived when to knock and announce would be dangerous, futile or inhibit the effective investigation of the crime. Despite the fact that the issuing magistrate had originally refused to issue a "no-knock" warrant the court held the decision to enter without knocking should be evaluated by the suppression judge at the time of the entry even when insufficient facts existed at the time of the issuance. Thus, the court is saying entry time is more important than issuing time whether rejected or approved. The court sided with the concurring Wisconsin justice who said there were sufficient facts to justify a no-knock entry.

The Illinois reaction to **Richards** was favorable. An Illinois statute that gave a blanket exception for "no-knock" based on prior gun possession was ruled unconstitutional. See **People v. Krueger**, 675 N.E. 2d 604 (Ill. 1997). However, evidence gathered under good faith reliance on this statute was deemed inadmissible as the **Krueger** court rejected **Illinois v. Krull**, 480 U.S. 340 (1987) and its good faith exception to the exclusionary rule – just another example of the new federalism discussed in Chapter One.

For cases citing using properly **Wilson** or **Richards** see: **People v. Zabelle**, 58 Cal. Rep. 2d 105 (Cal. App. 1996); **State v. George**, 687 A. 2d 958 (Me. 1997); **Com. v. Garner**, 672 N.E. 2d 510 (Mass. 1996); **State v. Knight**, 459 S.E. 2d 481 (N.Car. 1995); **State v. Herrick**, 567 N.W. 2d 336 (N. D. 1997) (mere allegation that drugs are present not enough to waive); **State v. Mastracchio**, 672 A. 2d 438 (R.I. 1996) (trial or suppression judges should do a better job of articulating their findings in knock and announce case); **Wynn v. State**, 699 A. 2d 512 (Md. App. 1997) (use exigent circumstances approach); and **State v. Stevens**, 570 N.W. 2d 593 (Wis. 1997).

Telling bystanders outside the house that as police they have a warrant to enter the target house does not satisfy "knock and announce." **People v. Gifford**, 782 P. 2d 795 (Colo. 1989).

160

Wilson and Richards would cause state courts to take a closer look at this whole area now that it has become a true suppression issue rather than a ministerial concern. Knock, announce that first "we are the police" and second "we have a search warrant" all have to be proven to the suppression court's satisfaction. In addition to the Colorado case (*supra*) more modern cases now exist. In **Com. v. Carlton**, 701 A. 2d 143 (Pa. 1997) the police forgot to announce their purpose though they knocked and announced who they were. There were no exigent circumstances that excused this omission. Likewise, Nebraska found that the mere failure to announce purpose was fatal to the search. **State v. Moore**, 535 N.W. 2d 417 (Neb. App. 1995).

Even more recent cases further illustrate the struggle to apply **Wilson** and **Richards** (*supra*). For example in **State v. Wasson**, 615 N.W. 2d 316 (Minn. 2000) the officers obtained a "no-knock" warrant. One of the questions was whether "boiler plate" language as in **Richards** or case specific facts were used to get judicial approval for the no-knock warrant. Judges were told to watch out for "often persons involved in...or those involved in...." or other generic phrases without case specific factual support when the judge considers a no-knock application. In this case there were specific facts indicating that several weapons had been seized from this place. This was enough to justify this no-knock warrant. It further added that the trial judge made the "reappraisal required for an unannounced entry into a dwelling...." Thus in Minnesota there can and must be two checks on a "warranted" no-knock.

A very practical decision comes from Louisiana. The police entered the defendant's home without knocking or announcing. That was improper. However, no one was at home. Fully recognizing the authority granted by the warrant, the Court noted that even if they knocked and announced there would have been no response. They would have entered anyway in those circumstances. No harm-no foul? **State v. Taylor**, 757 So. 2d 63 (La. App. 5th 2000).

The first warrant that was issued in a Kansas case violated "knock and announce" but no evidence was seized. A second warrant was issued but did not use any information gathered from the first entry. The court held the evidence derived was not "fruits" of the first no-knock entry under the independent source case of **Murray v. U.S.**, 487 U.S. 533 (1988). **State v. Shirley**, 999 P. 2d 259 (Kan. 2000).

To use "no-knock" at the scene, the police must be presented with circumstances that demand such an entry. The police in **Lee v. State**, 2001 WL 431249 (Md. App.) did not face such a situation. At the time they arrived they did nothing to assess the situation and did not even pause to consider a no-knock entry. The evidence had to be suppressed. But where the officer's affidavit supports a no-knock entry, the defendant cannot challenge such an entry. The application for the warrant in this case made out the case that the defendant knew he had been identified and that the police would soon be coming for him. **State v. Peters**, 622 N.W. 2d 918 (Neb. 2001).

How long do officers have to wait? The Ninth says a 15 to 30 second delay justified a forcible entry after the knock and announce. **U.S. v. Ciamnitti**, 720 F. 2d 927 (C.A. 9th 1983). The Tenth Circuit says 5 to 10 seconds is the maximum time that the police have to wait. **U.S. v. Ruminer**, 786 F. 2d 381 (C.A. 10th 1986). The D.C. Circuit felt that waiting 12 seconds without an answer was tantamount to a refusal justifying the breaking to enter to execute a drug search warrant. **U.S. v. Bonner**, 874 F. 2d 822 (C.A. D.C. 1989).

The **Moore** case from Nebraska case (*supra*) also addressed the time question. How long does the officer have to wait? Citing **U.S. v. Mendonsa**, 989 F. 2d 366 (C.A. 9th 1993) Nebraska agrees that without exigent circumstances or an explicit refusal a significant amount of time must pass before force is used – a totality driven analysis. The evidence was inadmissible in **Mendonsa** where only 3 to 5 seconds elapsed. Nebraska also cited **People v. Jennings**, 562 N.E. 2d 1239 (Ill. App. 1990), that held exigency was the key and **U.S. v. Lucht**, 18 F. 3d (C.A. 8th 1994) focusing on "urgent need" and a 3 to 5 second delay that was held not to be sufficient under the circumstances. Nebraska felt that **Wilson** demands this kind of analysis.

A four second wait was sufficient and reasonable, however, under both federal and state constitutions according to **State v. Ordonez-Villanueva**, 908 P. 2d 333 (Ore. App. 1996) Why? Yes this is a **Wilson** driven area, Oregon said. However, readily destructible drugs were being sought in this case. To this court this was enough of an exigency.

Is there a constitutional difference between NOT WAITING for a response and waiting ONLY A FEW SECONDS. Nowhere has the U.S. Supreme Court had made that distinction nor have they provided any specific waiting period. Perhaps a California court has come up with the most reasonable answer to date. That case is **People v. Hoag**, 100 Cal. Rep. 2d 556 (Cal. App. 3rd 2000). In **Hoag** the police only waited 15 or 20 seconds before entering. The California statute on the subject requires "substantial compliance" thus each case will turn on its own facts. In this case the owner was not home and like the court in Louisiana, *supra*, this court said there was standing to move to suppress. On this subject they cite three other states' decisions. They are: **Mazepink v. State**, 987 S.W. 2d 648 (Ark. 1999); **Com v. Carlton**, 701 A. 2d 143 (Pa. 1997); and **Righter v. State**, 704 A. 2d 263 (Del. 1997). In the **Righter** case, a son who had "no property interest" because he did not pay rent to his mother nor did he help in maintaining the apartment was denied the standing to complain. As to the merits, the issue is whether, under the circumstances, the policies underlying the knock, *etc.* requirements were served. They said that the size of the place (big or small) might dictate the waiting time. Certainly the ease or difficulty of destroying the thing sought would also have to be factored in. In other words this is the place to use the totality of the circumstances.

The "need to comply" issues must be addressed. There are a number of cases in this area. In one, a defendant coincidentally opened the door as the police arrived; thus knock and announce was not required. **U.S. v. Johnson,** 573 F. Supp. 998 (D. Kan.. 1983). In another an undercover officer signaled from inside the premises for the police to enter; thus knock and announce was not required. **State v. Cantrell**, 426 So. 2d 1035 (Fla. Dist. Ct. App. 1983). In another case the identity of the police as police was given but they did not announce their purpose. The court found this to be substantial compliance. **U.S. v. Brown**, 663 F. Supp. 164 (D. D.C. 1987). In another case the police did not knock on the porch door but did knock on the main door and this was held to be substantial compliance. **Com. v. McDonnell**, 516 A. 2d 329 (Pa. 1986). Where occupants of a building are aware of the officer's presence the risk of flight and destruction increases. In such a case only a mild exigency is needed to allow immediate entry. **U.S. v. Kovac**, 795 F. 2d 1509 (C.A. 9th 1986). But without an exigency arising at the scene, prior knowledge of dangerous propensities requires the seeking of the waiver. Without such a waiver the evidence must be suppressed. **Com. v. Manni**, 398 Mass. 741 (1986).

The ordinary waiver cases receive approval such as **U.S. v. Manfredi**, 722 F. 2d 519 (C.A. 9th 1983) (defendant known to be armed and violent); **U.S. v. McConnery**, 728 F. 2d 1195 (C.A. 9th 1984) (officer personally knew defendant convicted of violent crimes); **U.S. v. Garcia**, 741 F. 2d 363 (C.A. 11th 1984) (exigency of drug destruction officers reasonably believed); **U.S. v. DeParias**, 805 F. 2d 1447 (C.A. 11th 1986) (good reason to believe murder and kidnapping suspects armed and dangerous); and **U.S. v. Johnson**, 643 F. Supp. 1465 (D. Ore. 1986) (seeing locks *etc.* to prevent forcible entries justified waiver because knock and announce would have been a useless gesture); **Com. v. Scalise**, 387 Mass. 413 (1982) (a constantly moving drug dealer selling small, thus readily disposable packages corroborated by police observation made it alright to waive requirement).

The *how* of the entry is gaining more attention each year. Officers have become more inventive. In a recent Pennsylvania case the officers had the building superintendent knock on the door and announced that he was there to do some maintenance. When the defendant opened the door, the officers stepped forward. Placing his hand on the door and his foot in the opening, the officer announced their purpose to which there was no resistance. The court held that police use of a ruse to initiate execution of a search warrant is permissible where it is followed by an announcement of authority and purpose and by peaceful entry. **Commonwealth v. Regan**, 386 A. 2d 89 (Pa. Super. Ct.); See also **U.S. v. Salter**, 815 F. 2d 1150 (C.A. 7th 1987) and **U.S. v. Alvarez**, 812 F. 2d 668 (C.A. 11th 1987). The most common use is front door – back door. Police out front "knock and announce" and police in the back yell-out "come in." This has not received judicial approval.

Instanter return does not mean instanter as long as returned within the 10 days provided by statute. So said **Meyer v. State**, 309 So. 2d 161 (Miss. 1975) dealing with Mississippi Code § 41-29-157 (a) (3) (1972). This warrant was returned two days after being served. The court said there was no unreasonable delay here. The requirement of a return inheres in the Fourth Amendment and the lack of return was one of the oppressive features of the general warrants which were intended to be prohibited by adoption of the amendment. And in **Berger v. N.Y.** (*infra* at Chapter Fourteen) one of the reasons given by the Court for striking down N.Y.'s eavesdropping statute was that it did not provide for a return on the warrant thereby leaving full discretion in the officer as to the use of the seized conversations of innocent and guilty parties. It is common for rules or statutes to require a receipt to be given for things seized. This is ministerial if not done and thus not fatal. What the defendant can compel is an inventory from the court.

The need for giving the owner or occupier a receipt for things seized needs no explanation as common sense dictates such practice. But local rules should be consulted. They are all somewhat different. Rules or statutes that police must exhibit or deliver a copy of the warrant are deemed by some states to be ministerial only and not constitutionally required. Absent a showing of prejudice, failure to comply does not void an otherwise valid search. A complete failure to make a return is serious and New Mexico and New York say exclusion is the remedy.

How soon after a warrant is issued does it have to be served? Local rule, of course, governs. In most states a warrant has a specific life span stated in days. Ten to fifteen days is the normal life span of a warrant. A few states have no specific time limit but require, as did the common law, that the warrant be served forthwith. The "forthwith" states, when faced with a motion to suppress because of a delay in execution can follow one of two rules. Some say the time is measured by whether the delay was reasonable or not under the circumstances. In other states having the forthwith provision as the time period, the inquiry is whether the probable cause upon which it relied still existed at the time of execution.

Why would any law enforcement officer delay the execution of a warrant obtained? Assuming good faith in obtaining the warrant, there is always the hope that more "fish" will be caught and that by waiting the *cache* of things to be seized will be bigger or that an informer needs protection or because everyone is on vacation, or on and on. All of this is illustrated by the case of **Donaldson v. State**, 420 A. 2d 281 (Md. Ct. Spec. App. 1980). The Maryland court was faced by a hybrid time problem. The statute provided a 15 day life for search warrants while the warrant itself directed that it be served forthwith. In this case the warrant was served 11 days after issuance. Noting that the federal courts have a similar dilemma with their 10 day limit and the forthwith requirement of Rule 41 (c) Fed. Rules Crim. Proc., the Maryland court adopted the federal conclusion. If the warrant is served within the stated time limit the evidence will not be suppressed unless the defendant can show that he was prejudiced by the delay.

Thus where there was not sufficient personnel to execute on the day of issuance, execution nine days later was upheld. **U.S. v. Rael**, 467 F. 2d 333 (C.A. 9th 1972). An nine-day delay was tolerated where the police knew that the heroin would not be at the place unless the defendant was also there because he only used the place to repackage the heroin. **U.S. v. Dunnings**, 425 F. 2d 836 (C.A. 2d 1969). The **Dunnings** court went on to say that even if the delay was for the purpose of effectuating the arrest the delay would not be unreasonable. All federal courts do not agree with that position, however. For a "tougher" interpretation see **U.S. v. Bradley**, 428 F. 2d 1013 (C.A. 5th 1970) and **U.S. v. McClard**, 462 F. 2d 488 (C.A. 6th 1971). An 8-day delay was not unreasonable as long as the probable cause continued. **U.S. v. Shegog**, 787 F. 2d 420 (C.A. 8th 1986). A delay in execution is constitutionally permissible only where the probable cause recited in the affidavit continues up to the time of the execution. That the time will vary between arrest warrants and search warrants is obvious. We are not concerned with staleness in the arrest context, only the statute of limitations.

The issuing magistrate has inherent power to vacate a warrant when he knows it is no longer supported by probable cause. It is the officer's duty to keep the magistrate informed of new facts known. Good faith saved the warrant in **U.S. v. Morales**, 568 F. Supp. 646 (E.D.N.Y. 1983) this one time. The Second Circuit agrees that new information should be presented to the magistrate before execution to determine if probable cause still exists. Such information was found but its lack was not fatal in **U.S. v. Marina-Buitrago**, 734 F. 2d 889 (C.A. 2d 1984).The Sixth Circuit fully agrees that it is the duty of the police to bring new facts to the attention of the issuing judge before a warrant is executed. In this case, after the warrant was issued, police learned that a consent search had been conducted by other police and nothing was found. Executing this warrant was not done in good faith, the Sixth Circuit held. **U.S. v. Bowling**, 900 F. 2d 926 (C.A. 6th 1990).

Until the warrant is served, as already noted, there is a duty on the police to keep the issuing authority apprised of any changes. In **Query v. State**, 745 N.E. 2d 769 (Ind. 2001), the police obtained a warrant to search for drugs based on a confidential informant's controlled buy. However, before the execution of the warrant the lab results revealed that the drugs purchased were not illegal drugs. Instead, the seller sold the informant a look-alike substance. Was this fatal to the validity of the search warrant when it was executed since the police failed to inform the magistrate? No, not in this case. Selling a "look-alike" substance is also a felony in Indiana. Had the warrant been executed before the test results were available the same substance would have been found and seized. Since "meth" always requires chemical testing to prove its identity the court found that no harm occurred. The court did caution police and prosecutors of the state not to over-read this opinion because it was the identical look-alike nature of this substance that "saved the day." No material change occurred here.

A search begun too soon was not invalidated by the Second Circuit. Police had applied for a warrant, heard a radio report that they thought said the warrant had been issued and began to search. During the search they learned the warrant had not been signed. They stopped searching and waited for the warrant. The court found that under the unusual facts of this case suppression would not serve the exclusionary rule's deterrent effect. **U.S. v. Alvarez-Porras**, 643 F. 2d 54 (C.A. 2d 1981). This case would appear to comply with the **Garrison** case.

IX. The Scope of the Search Clause

7. DO NOT INTERPRET THIS WRIT AS LIMITING YOUR AUTHORITY TO SEIZE ALL CONTRABAND AND THINGS THE POSSESSION OF WHICH IN ITSELF IS UNLAWFUL WHICH YOU FIND INCIDENT TO YOUR SEARCH, OR AS LIMITING YOUR AUTHORITY TO MAKE OTHERWISE VALID

ARRESTS AT THE PLACE DESCRIBED ABOVE.

An officer, at all times, is required to seize contraband of whatever nature and whatever it may be discovered so long as the officer is not trespassing or violating the constitutional rights of the possessor at the time the discovery is made. See **Salisbury v. State**, 3 93 So. 2d 434 (Miss. 1974); burglarious tools discovered when searching for murder weapon.

When executing a warrant, officers must limit their activity to that which is needed to find those things described in the warrant. Once they find what they are looking for they should leave (absent some new probable cause with a proper exception to the warrant requirement arising). "The agents, in their search for papers indicating ownership and control might seize irrelevant items such as personal letters and bank statements addressed to the occupant. We do not condone the seizure of items not described in the warrant, but we hold that the agent's violation of the warrant's terms was not flagrant and did not invalidate the seizure of relevant items." **U.S. v. Crozier**, 777 F. 2d 1376 (C.A. 9th 1985).

Other than suppression of illegally seized items, what remedy does the search victim have when non-plain view goods are taken that are clearly outside the scope of an otherwise valid warrant? The D.C. Court of Appeals has provided one answer. While executing a "drug paraphernalia" warrant the police gathered 14 items of personal property such as cameras, TV's, a stereo, and the like. None of these items were described in the warrant and no case for plain view was made, since computer checks did not indicate that these items were stolen. Despite this the goods were turned over to the police property department and held by them through decision in this case. This case was brought by the search victim against the two officers who seized the goods upon a conversion theory. The victim prevailed and was awarded $600.00 compensatory damages and $2200.00 punitive damages. On appeal the award was upheld by the D.C. Court of Appeals. **Smith v. Whitehead**, 436 A. 2d 339 (D.C. Ct. App. 1981).

The permissible intensity of the search within the described premises is determined by the description of the things to be seized. The search should really begin in the areas of the premises known to have the most association with the individual connected with the criminal conduct under investigation – this would be reasonable. The officer should begin the search by looking in place which common sense suggests are the most likely locations of the items specified in the search warrant. Bypassing the obvious can have damaging effect on the reasonableness of the search and lead one to conclude that the warrant was pretextual and thus plain view was not inadvertent. (Wheels in garage and the police are so told but they decide to conduct search of house first).

Would the destruction of a concrete slab found in a back yard be within the scope of an otherwise lawful, warranted search? This was the question presented to the Ninth Circuit in **U.S. v. Becker**, 929 F. 2d 442 (C.A. 9th 1991). This was a newly poured slab within the described premises. Destruction of property is not favored, they noted, but it was clear this slab was poured not long after this defendant's neighbor's and associate's house had been searched. The slab was next to the shop that was suspected to be the drug laboratory. The court felt there was reason, therefore, to believe that this slab was used to hide evidence (which, in fact, it did). The only way to get this evidence, said the court, was to use a jackhammer.

The officers may remain on the premises only so long as is reasonably necessary to conduct the search and only to avoid unnecessary damage to the premises. When the purpose of the warrant has been carried out, the authority to search is at an end. The prior discovery of other things does not expand the authority of the police under the search warrant. In any event, once the authorized search has been completed the police must promptly depart the premises.

Looking for something in a place where it could not be contained destroyed the finding of contraband and could not have satisfied the plain view standards said the Mississippi Supreme Court in **Carney v. State**, 525 So. 2d 776 (Miss. 1988). But anything within the premises is fair game if it can contain the item. The Michigan Court of Appeals upheld the search of two purses of employees in non-public areas as part of a warranted search. These woman had a special connection with the premises – one was the wife of the owner. The purses were not on the persons of the owners. Since purses could have concealed the items sought the warrant covered them the court held. **People v. Stewart**, 420 N. W. 2d 180 (Mich. Ct. App. 1988).

Arizona, for instance, had a "murder scene" exception to the warrant requirements which was struck down. **Mincey v. Arizona**, 437 U.S. 385 (1978). The Court reminded everyone that a warrantless search must be strictly circumscribed by the exigencies which justify its initiation. The other people in Mincey's apartment were located and removed from the scene before the homicide officers arrived and began their search, thus the emergency nature of the scene had vanished. The mere fact that law enforcement may be made more efficient can never by itself justify disregard of the Fourth Amendment. The court would not hold that the seriousness of the offense under investigation creates in and of itself an exigent circumstance. Discretion is not to be left to the police officer. It rests in the *neutral* and *detached* magistrate.

A similar problem arose in **Arizona v. Hicks**, 480 U.S. 321 (1987). The Court has underlined the fact that search and seizure are two acts not one. They felt compelled to define the word *search* in the **Hicks** case and stressed the importance of what is "obvious evidence of a crime or contraband" as defined first in **Coolidge**. As **Coolidge** taught us under branch one of the *plain view* doctrine, when police officers, under a right to be present, inadvertently come across obvious evidence of a crime or contraband unrelated to the purposes of the search they may seize it. But to search something not so obvious and seize something not so obvious is outside the doctrine's scope. This was the problem in the **Hicks** case. While searching for guns the police noticed two expensive stereo components which they suspected were stolen. They turned the units around and wrote down the serial numbers. The numbers were phoned in and, yes, they were stolen. The police seized the items. Although the recording of the numbers was not a seizure, the moving of the stereo equipment was a search separate and apart from the lawful search. The Court held that *plain view* did not render this search reasonable. The Court wanted us to understand that **Mincey** did not overrule plain view. The police in **Hicks** did not have probable cause to believe the stereos were stolen; they only had suspicion. The Court was unwilling to create a "cursory inspection" exception. This was a wise choice since such a term could apply to all intrusions if broadly interpreted and a narrow interpretation would jam the trial dockets with retrials. The only "cursory" they tolerate is looking without disturbing.

A visitor to a house would hope that if his host's house were searched his personal property would be exempt. Well, his hopes are dashed, says the Pennsylvania Supreme Court in **Com. v. Reese**, 549 A. 2d 909 (Pa. 1988). As long as the item is part of the general contents of the house and a place where the thing sought could be stored, it is subject to the warranted intrusion.

Consider **Michigan v. Tyler**, 436 U.S. 499 (1978). There had been a fire and the Fire Chief, as required by law, entered the burned premises some hours after the fire when it was first safe to determine the cause of the fire. Evidence of a fuse, thus arson was discovered. Was a warrant needed? Yes and No. The entry to fight a fire requires no warrant and that once in the building, officials may remain there for a reasonable time to investigate the cause of the blaze. Thereafter, additional entries to investigate the cause must be made pursuant to warrant procedures governing administrative searches. Missouri held that a limited search of a house for evidence following the discovery of bodies was OK saying that it was within the purview of **Michigan v. Tyler**. **State v. Epperson**, 571 S.W. 2d 260 (Mo. 1978). But the facts seem to indicate that Missouri is reading too much into **Michigan v. Tyler**. The officers entered when they smelled the odor of decomposing bodies. Since the defendant had left them there for several days even when pressed for the whereabouts of his family by his relatives it is hard to believe an emergency existed. That information could have been radioed in and a warrant obtained very quickly. In **Tyler**, however, the only reason that the fire officials were allowed to go in was for a continuing administrative search. The only reason they were allowed to reenter 5 hours later was that the smoke was initially too thick for further investigation. The administrative search cases, like border search cases, should not be read as equal to normal search and seizure cases. See also **Michigan v. Clifford**, 464 U.S. 287 (1984) limiting, by distinction, **Tyler**.

Taking an insurance adjuster along to help determine whether other art objects were stolen was condemned in **U.S. v. Waxman**, 572 F. Supp. 1136 (E.D. Pa. 1983). Seizing an entire file cabinet to keep records intact was criticized but since the other records were not used by the government the search was upheld. **U.S. v. Shilling**, 826 F. 2d 1365 (C.A. 4th 1987). Searching the backpack of a visitor as the visitor was leaving was found not to be within the scope of the warrant. **U.S. v. Stepprow**, 833 F. 2d 777 (C.A. 9th 1987). The police exceeded the scope when men's clothing was taken since the warrant specified women's clothing. **U.S. v. Fuccillo**, 634 F. Supp. 358 (D. Mass. 1986). The police went beyond the scope when they searched an attorney's office and went through all his files. Concerned with attorney client privilege the court struck down this search. **Klitzman, Klitzman and Gallagher v. Krut**, 591 F. Supp. 258 (D.N.J. 1984).

What about looking at documents not named? As long as the police were within the scope they are allowed to open them to see if they are the ones described. Once they know it is not the right document the police must stop reading it. **U.S. v. Slocum**, 708 F. 2d 587 (C.A. 11th 1983).

The police may search any container on the premises if the thing sought may be contained therein. **U.S. v. Giwa**, 831 F. 2d 538 (C.A. 5th 1987) (approving the search of a visitor's flight bag); **U.S. v. Gray**, 635 F. Supp. 572 (D. Me. 1986) (jacket could be searched); **U.S. v. Gray**, 814 F. 2d 49 (C.A. 1st 1987) (pockets of windbreaker belonging to visitor draped over a chair as a possible repository); **U.S. v. Reyes**, 798 F. 2d 380 (C.A. 10th 1986) (cassette recording seizable under business records warrant); and **U.S. v. Gomez-Soto**, 723 F. 2d 649 (C.A. 9th 1984) (briefcase and micro cassette – officers have authority to examine and search personal effects if such might contain items described).

In one of the more unusual scope cases the Tenth Circuit lost perspective and suppressed all evidence taken by the federal officers while executing a valid federal search warrant because they took a state officer along to search without a warrant for state evidence of other crimes. **U.S. v. Medlin,** 842 F. 2d 1194 (C.A. 10th 1988).

X. The Authorization Provision

WITNESS MY HAND THIS, THE _____ DAY OF _____ 19___.

_____
(OFFICIAL TITLE)

The problem of blank dates or improper dates has much perplexed courts. There appear to be two lines of cases; the one not mentioning the other. The strict constructionist line does not forgive blank or improper dates thus invalidating the search and its fruits.

Consider, for example, **Johnson v. State**, 202 Miss. 233, 31 So. 2d 127 (1947). The court said if undated search warrants were allowed to be placed in the hands of officers with no date fixed therein for the reasonably early execution and return thereof, and after execution the court was allowed to insert the essential date or dates by amendment, the door to the equivalent of the odious general warrant or writ of assistance would be open. The date appeared on the warrant as 12th Day of Johnson, 194 _____. This had to be read as no more than the 12th day of blank, 194 blank. Again in **Nobles v. State**, 222 Miss. 827, 77 So. 2d 288 (1955), the court strictly construed the date. The affidavit and warrant were dated May 9, 1953, a past date. The constable changed the May 9 date to May 15, 1953. This past date was impossible, the court opined, thus making the warrant equivalent to making it returnable to a blank date; thus it was void.

The other line of cases could be called the incorporation by reference cases. The first, **Hendricks v. State**, 144 Miss. 87, 109 So. 263 (1926) recognized the problem of "mere oversight." The warrant bore a date earlier than the affidavit. The court then stated, "it was recited in the search warrant involved that the affidavit upon which it was based was made on the day the search warrant was issued." Following **Hendricks** the court overlooked a blank date by saying, "Here the warrant incorporated by reference the affidavit which had a complete date." Thus it was clear to the court that both were executed on the same date. **Meyer v. State**, 309 So. 2d 161 (Miss. 1975).

The place for the judge's signature raises the issue of who may issue a warrant as to office, person and venue. Rubber stamps are taboo. The stories of judges leaving pads of warrants pre-signed or pre-stamped are legion. That this is an obvious constitutional violation needs no more mention.

This duty to sign is non-delegable. It is a judicial function, not a ministerial function. It cannot be performed by a prosecutor. **Coolidge v. New Hampshire**, 403 U.S. 443 (1971). The question whether a court clerk could issue one was settled in **Shadwick v. City of Tampa**, 407 U.S. 345 (1972). It was held that as long as the clerk worked only for the court under close judicial supervision the clerk could sign a warrant.

The authority to issue came to the fore in a case from Washington. The issue was framed in three parts, **first**, whether a warrant may issue only under "authority of law;" **second**, whether the clerk acted under the authority of law; **third**, whether suppression is the appropriate remedy. The statutes demand authority of law. Next, no statute could be found authorizing a clerk, as opposed to a judge, to order issuance of a warrant and there was no city ordinance to that effect. But courts can, of course, issue, but the word "court" does not mean the entire institution including employees who are not judges. Until there is such a statute or ordinance no clerk may issue a warrant. But should the exclusionary rule apply? Yes, because Washington's high court does not accept **Leon** so that evidence incident to the arrest was suppressed. **State v. Walker**, 999 P. 2d 1296 (Wash. App. 2d 2000).

A warrant was saved in Arkansas even though it was signed by the court clerk instead of the magistrate as required by state law. The signing took place before the change in the law thus it was saved. **Starr v. State**, 759 S.W. 2d 535 (Ark. 1988). However, "good faith" should not save a warrant issued beyond one's jurisdictional power because such is not a technical deficiency; it involves the power to act and a lack of power is a nullity. **Com. v. Shelton**, 766 S.W. 2d 628 (Ky. 1989).

And the Ninth Circuit saved a warrant obtained by an export officer rather than a U.S. Attorney or federal law enforcement officer as required by F.R.C.Pro. 41(a). The good faith-reliance exception was applied. There was no evidence of intentional and deliberate disregard of the rule. It certainly did not change the underlying probable cause.

There are times when a joint federal-state warrant is issued. The warrant must meet federal requirements for federal purposes. The federal government requires a warrant to be issued by a court of record judge. A Justice of the Peace issued this warrant. The rest of the Constitutional requirements were met. The warrant was upheld even through the J.P. court was not a court of record. **U.S. v. Comstock**, 805 F. 2d 1194 (C.A. 5th 1986).

But what is the status of a warrant that a judge fails to sign? Is such an omission constitutional requiring suppression *per se* or is it ministerial thus requiring a showing of actual prejudice before there can be suppression. One court, relying on decisions from the Second Circuit, Arizona, California and Kansas held that the lack of signature on an otherwise valid warrant is a ministerial defect which does not invalidate the warrant. They thus rejected decisions from Connecticut, Kentucky, Michigan and Ohio that hold that such a warrant is a nullity. The rationale for upholding a warrant is that as long as a judge in fact performs the substantive task of determining probable cause and the authorization of the issuance, the Fourth is satisfied. Unless the warrant statute absolutely requires a signature, unsigned but validly issued warrants are good. **Com. v. Pellegrini**, 405 Mass. 86 (1989). As noted, Connecticut has held that failure to sign a warrant, even though an oversight, renders the document invalid. The signature is essential to its issuance. **State v. Surowiecki**, 184 Conn. 95, 97 (Conn. 1981).

XI. Search Warrant Checklist

I. Are all necessary blanks filled in and consistent with affidavit when necessary?
- A. state_____
- B. county_____
- C. date on warrant and affidavit consistent ___yes ___no
- D. signatures affixed ___yes ___no
- E. signature on warrant by one authorized to issue:
  - ___ judicial officer
  - ___ clerk working under direction of and only for judicial officer (check local rule/statute)
- F. name(s) of affiant(s) filled in ___ yes ___ no
- G. Are affiants within class of those permitted by rule or statute ___ yes ___ no

II. Time elapsed during issuance process
- A. time begun__:_____ /___/___
  -      hr min   mo date yr
- B. time ended__:_____ /___/___

hr min   mo date yr

III.   Is description of place sufficient?
- A.   Dwelling place
  - 1.   single dwelling ___ yes ___ no
    - a.   rural___yes ___no
      - 1.   curtilage included ___yes ___no
      - 2.   other buildings beyond curtilage___yes ___no
      - 3.   other land controlled by owner/occupier beyond curtilage ___yes ___no
    - b.   urban/suburban
      - 1.   single residence type ___yes ___no
      - 2.   single residence in converted/former single house ___yes ___no
        - a)   indicia # of
          - (i) mailboxes _____
          - (ii) utility meters ____
          - (iii) other describe ___
        - b)   who observed_____
      - 3.   single residence in apartment building
        - a)   floor___Apt#_____
        - b)   storage area to be searched ___yes ___no
        - c)   garage area to be searched ___yes ___no
  - 2.   Single dwelling plus business ___yes ___no
    - a.   for residence only ___yes ___no
    - b.   for business place only ___yes ___no
    - c.   Business place ___yes ___no
      - i.   business place all under one address with all buildings contiguous with one entrance ___yes ___no
      - ii.   business place under two or more addresses with more than one entrance ___yes ___no
  - 3.   business places, more than one address, not contiguous – does detail exist to permit the entry of all addresses listed ___yes ___no

IV. Control/Ownership
    A.   is/are name(s) of person(s) who control(s) necessary because they are also to be searched ___yes ___no
    B.   if person(s) is/are to be searched and names are known is/are detail(s) of physical description sufficient ___yes ___no
    C.   are separate arrest warrant(s) necessary ___yes ___no

V. Are things to be seized adequately described ___yes ___no

VI. Are laws offended properly described
    A.   cited by number ___yes ___no
    B.   essence of statute spelled out ___yes ___no

VII. Is search for
    A.   daytime use ___yes ___no
    B.   nighttime use ___yes ___no
    C.   If nighttime is there sufficient exigency to permit/is local rule satisfied ___yes ___no

XII. INFORMANT CHECK LIST

I. Reliability of Person
    A.   Fellow Police Officer
        1.   Overt – Name _____
        2.   Covert (undercover)
               (If yes proceed to point II) ___yes ___no
    B.   Average Citizen
        1.   Name_____
               (if citizen permit)
        2.   Description of Citizen to protect anonymity
            a.   age range_____
            b.   occupation_____
            c.   prior criminal record_____
               (there had better be *none*)
    C.   Informant With Criminal Record

1. Name_____
(if not given go, to next sub-point)
2. Description of past reliability
   a. how many times used before_____
   b. how many times reliable_____
   c. detail of prior information
     (1)_____
     _____
     _____
     _____
     (2)_____
     _____
     _____
     _____
     (3)_____
     _____
     _____
     _____
     (4)_____
     _____
     _____
     _____
     (if not satisfied, ask for name again – if
     refused, deny application for warrant)
   d. Anonymous Tipster ___yes ____no

II. Freshness Tests
   A. Type of crime _____
   B. Date of incident reported_____
   C. Date info given to police_____
   D. Date of warrant application_____
   [*Caveat*: the more "fluid" the crime, the closer the dates
   must be]

III. How Information Obtained by Informant
   A. If Average Citizen or Informant With Criminal Record
     1. Personally observed ___yes ___no
       (if *no*, then there is double hearsay – if so and
       informant is average citizen not directly involved
       in crime, deny.)

2.   Personally involved in crime ___yes _____no (a person who implicated himself in the crime raises his/her reliability factor)

3.   If not involved in crime, is there sufficient detail to show that target crime is based on more than casual rumor ___yes ___no (if no – deny)

4.   If answer to 3 is yes, are details more than a series of innocent details made to look sinister ___yes ___no
(if no – *deny*)

IV.   Corroboration/Anonymous Tipster

     A.   Does tip itself give basis for writer's predictions ___yes ___no

     B.   Was there independent police investigation ___yes ___no

     C.   Did investigation corroborate details of the tip * ___yes ___no

     D.   Are the details given self-verifiable ___yes ___no

     E.   Chances of a reckless or prevaricating tale substantially reduced ___yes ___no

     F.   Can it be said there was a fair probability that tipster got information from

         1. suspect himself ___yes ___no

         2. someone suspect trusted ___yes ___no

     G.   Substantial basis to believe probable cause exists ___yes ___no

*Note: check local decisional law. Some states accept **Gates** only if detail corroborated directly links to non-innocent detail or yields only non-innocent inferences.

CHAPTER FOUR

THE VERACITY CHALLENGE TO THE SEARCH WARRANT

I.   An Introduction to Franks

Most of the discussion in Chapter Three, The Annotated Search Warrant, is concerned with *sufficiency* challenges. Brief mention is made of *veracity* challenges by citation to **Franks v. Delaware,** 438 U.S. 154 (1978). The function of this chapter is to discuss, in some detail, veracity challenges that were constitutionally mandated by **Franks**. With sufficiency challenges, the defense challenges the conclusion reached by the issuing authority, saying that there were not sufficient facts to rely upon, or that the affidavit and other information presented were merely conclusory. With veracity challenges, the information presented is generally sufficient and not conclusory. Rather, the argument is that the facts presented by the affiant are untrue.

The issue presented in **Franks** was stated as follows: "This case presents an important and longstanding issue of Fourth Amendment law. Does a defendant in a criminal proceeding ever have the right, under the Fourth and Fourteenth Amendments, subsequent to the *ex parte* issuance of a search warrant, to challenge the truthfulness of factual statements made in an affidavit supporting the warrant?" Delaware said the answer was no. The United States Supreme Court said the answer was yes. How and why did the Supreme Court come to its conclusion? The Court called this a longstanding issue. It noted that at one time a majority of states prohibited veracity challenges. By the date of this decision, the Court, in footnote 3, indicated that only 11 states had an absolute prohibition against veracity challenges. In footnote 4 the Court said only two federal circuits prohibited such challenges. Those that approved veracity challenges did so on a constitutional basis. Whether these courts were correct was not important. The important conclusion to be drawn was that there was a significant split of authority that thus created this longstanding issue.

On page 164 and 165 of the opinion the Court cites language from an opinion of Judge Frankel and further states: "[W]hen the Fourth Amendment demands a factual showing sufficient to comprise 'probable cause', the obvious assumption is that there will be a *truthful* showing (emphasis in original). This does not mean 'truthful' in the sense that every fact recited in the warrant affidavit is necessarily correct, for probable cause may be founded upon hearsay and upon information received from informants, as well as upon information within the affiant's own knowledge that sometimes must be garnered hastily. But surely it is to be 'truthful' in the sense that the information put forth is believed or appropriately accepted by the affiant as true." With that said, the Court then met the six arguments raised by the State of Delaware regarding veracity challenges and came to six conclusions.

First, it said that "a flat ban on impeachment of veracity could denude the probable-cause requirement of all real meaning." **Second**, it said that the hearing required for the issuance of warrant would not stop or "discourage lawless or reckless misconduct." **Third**, sanctions or threats of prosecution, *etc.*, were not likely to keep lawless or reckless misconduct from happening. **Fourth**, it held, "allowing an evidentiary hearing, after a suitable preliminary proffer of material falsity, would not diminish the importance and solemnity of the warrant issuing process." **Fifth**, it said "the claim that a post-search hearing will confuse the issue of the defendant's guilt with the issue of the State's possible misbehavior is footless." **Finally**, the Court held it was not creating a new process. The Court stated, "We see no principled basis for distinguishing between the question of the sufficiency of an affidavit, which also is subject to a post-search re-examination, and the question of its integrity."

Having met the state's argument, it was then the task of the Court to give direction regarding the burden upon the defendant and when that burden shifted to the state. Procedurally, this is the heart of **Franks**. The Court held: "There is, of course, a presumption of validity with respect to the affidavit supporting the search warrant. To mandate an evidentiary hearing, the challenger's attack must be more than conclusory and must be supported by more than a mere desire to cross examine. There must be allegations of deliberate falsehood or of reckless disregard for the truth, and those allegations must be accompanied by an offer of proof. They should point out specifically the portion of the warrant affidavit that is claimed to be false; and they should be accompanied by a statement of supporting reasons. Affidavits or sworn or otherwise reliable statements of witnesses should be furnished, or their absence satisfactorily explained. Allegations of negligence or innocent mistake are insufficient. The deliberate falsity or reckless disregard whose impeachment is permitted today is only that of the affiant, not of any non-governmental informant. Finally, if these requirements are met, and if, when material that is the subject of the alleged falsity or reckless disregard is set to one side, there remains sufficient content in the warrant affidavit to support a finding of probable cause, no hearing is required. On the other hand, if the remaining content is insufficient, the defendant is entitled, under the Fourth and Fourteenth Amendments, to his hearing. Whether he will prevail at that hearing is, of course, another issue." At 171 and 172.

What then are the criteria that must be met to compel a hearing where witnesses are produced? **First**, there must be an allegation that the affiant lied. An allegation that informers lied to the affiant is insufficient. **Second**, the affiant's falsehoods must go to the heart of the probable cause issue. If there is sufficient information for probable cause, absent these falsehoods, the affidavit is sufficient. **Third**, the affiant's false statements must be deliberate or made in reckless disregard of the truth. Mere negligence or innocent mistakes do not count. **Fourth**, it is not enough to allege the falsehood goes to the heart of probable cause, the defendant must offer proof. The proof must point to the particular lie or lies and be supported by affidavits or "sworn or otherwise" reliable statements of witnesses. If such evidence is not furnished, the defendant must provide a good explanation why such evidence·is not offered.

If these criteria are met, then a hearing is required. These criteria are required to give real meaning to the presumption of the validity of the warrant and the affidavit or contemporaneous record upon which it was based. To do otherwise would in fact drive police officers away from the warrant process, and the Court has been ever mindful of avoiding rules that result in more, rather than fewer, warrantless searches.

II.   The States' Reaction to Franks

How then have the states reacted to **Franks**? A consideration of state cases follows. They, of course, cannot "shrink" a defendant's rights but have any of them made the hurdle easier for the defendant? Have the states willingly or begrudgingly accepted **Franks**? The first point of debate among the states is whether failure to include information in the affidavit, or failure to present known information for the contemporaneous record, constitutes a lie or reckless falsity. A number of states take the position that such omissions are not within the purview of **Franks**. These states could be labeled the "strict constructionist" states.

New Hampshire appears to strictly construe **Franks**. **State v. Carroll**, 552 A. 2d 69 (N.H. 1988). It held that the New Hampshire constitution did not require a different result than mandated by **Franks**. North Dakota adopted **Franks** in **State v. Padgett**, 393 N.W. 2d 754 (N. D. 1986). To this court, recklessness or falsity must be

180

shown by more than allegation of some innocent mistake or negligence. It held there must be an intent to deceive. **State v. Morrison**, 447 N.W. 2d 272 (N. D. 1989). See **State v. Saiz**, 427 N.W. 2d 825 (S. D. 1988); and **U.S. v. Edelsen**, 529 A. 2d 774 (D.C. App. 1987) (in accord).

Two of Montana's more recent "veracity challenge" cases clearly recognize the "redact the bad and see if what is left constitutes probable cause" rule. In **State v. Kuneff**, 970 P. 2d 556 (Mont. 1998), the Montana Supreme Court noted that the portions remaining are to be reviewed *de novo* rather than deferentially, to determine whether probable cause exists to justify issuance. In this case, some marijuana had been unlawfully seized and was used as part of the probable cause. However, the remaining marijuana that was used to secure the warrant was lawfully seized and the "tip" relied upon was a good tip. This was sufficient to uphold the evidence seized.

In **State v. Worrall**, 976 P. 2d 968 (Mont. 1999), the issue was whether false statements were indeed included in the warrant application. **Franks** had been adopted by Montana in 1983 and they fully agreed that mere negligence or innocent mistake do not constitute "false information." The **Worrall** case serves as blueprint for warrant reviewing judges. This court says that: (1) the defendant is required to make a substantial preliminary showing of the false information included; (2) a hearing then must be held wherein the defendant must prove by a preponderance that the information is false; (3) the court must excise the false and judge the balance (*de novo*) to see if adequate probable cause exists; if probable cause exists, admit the evidence or uphold the verdict, *etc.* Montana adds, as do some other states, that the defendant does not have to prove that the person providing the information for the warrant application did so knowingly, intentionally, or with reckless disregard for the truth. This is a departure from the **Frank's** rule.

Kentucky can be said to require fairly strict adherence to **Franks**. In its case there was an expressed unwillingness to include negligence or innocent mistakes within the **Franks** coverage. **Com. v. Walker**, 729 S.W. 2d 440 (Ky. 1987). See also **State v. Cannon**, 634 S.W. 2d 648 (Tenn. Crim. App. 1982); **Lanier v. Com**, 394 S.E. 2d 495 (Va. App. 1990); **State v. Stebner**, 546 N.E. 2d 428 (Ohio App.1988); and **Morgan v. State**, 738 P. 2d 1373 (Okla. Crim. 1987) (in accord).

The theory of most of these courts is that "reckless disregard for the truth" had a definite meaning. These courts distinguish between negligent and reckless misrepresentations. See **Com. v. Nine Hundred and Ninety-Two Dollars**, 402 Mass. 65 (1988) and **Com. v. Caldez**, 402 Mass. 65 (1988). A more recent decision from Massachusetts emphatically reconfirms these points. The challenged warrant involved a search warrant for cocaine. The defense said that at a **Franks** hearing it is the duty of the state to prove that the informant made the challenged statements to the affiant-officer. The court succinctly reminded the defense that it was a defense motion and that they were required to show that the detective made the false statements either intentionally or with a reckless disregard for the truth. The court went on to note that mere negligence is not enough in any case but especially here where the defense did not even show that a false statement was made. The appellate court, as an aside, also said it was proper to exclude the defendant from the hearing while the informant testified. It noted that "informers' privilege" is not absolute, but it should be respected "as far as reasonably possible consistent with fairness to a defendant." The defendant received, through counsel, a right to air the issue of whether such an informant actually existed and whether the officer falsely represented the informant's words. **Com. v. Ramirez**, 729 N.E. 2d 295 (Mass. App. 2000).

Connecticut has accepted **Franks** as written rather than giving it a local twist under their own constitution. It was satisfied with the **Franks** standards. **State v. Glenn**, 707 A. 2d 736 (Conn. App. 1998) aff'd without opinion, 740 A. 2d 856 (Conn. 1999).

A number of courts have concluded that omissions are as much of a lie as the direct lie or reckless use of the truth. For example, the California Supreme Court said the failure to reveal the criminal past of the informer was as fatal as an out-and-out-lie; that a bad faith omission is the same as a lie. **People v. Kurland**, 618 P. 2d 213 (Cal. 1980). See **State v. Bowen**, 999 P. 2d 286 (Kan.. App. 2000) (This court uses the term "deliberate omissions.").

Thus, there can be fatal omissions; but all courts accepting this theory define them as probable cause conclusion-changing fatal omissions. These courts say that even if the omitted information is included, if it can still be fairly determined that there was probable cause, then there is no **Franks** violation. In Wisconsin a **Franks** hearing is not required if, after the judge adds the omitted language, there is still probable cause, **State v. Buckner**, 447 N.W. 2d 376 (Wis. App. 1989). In another Wisconsin case the defendant alleged that the magistrate would not have found the informant to be credible had the police informed him that the informant had told two stories regarding the source of the marijuana. Was this a fatal omission? The appeals court noted that the officer made personal observations of the defendant's place noting the drug activity and also gained knowledge of the drug activity from the Lake Winnebago drug enforcement unit's records. To be sure some facts were omitted that would have been important. But is "important" the same as "deliberate falsehood or reckless disregard?" Not necessarily, but the court decided to include the omissions to see if the warrant could have been issued as required by **Franks** at 438 U.S. 171-172. As a result the court saw no reason to grant the defense relief. **State v. Pluim**, 2000 WL 36276 (Wis. App.) (unpub. op.) This case is highly recommended as a blueprint for these types of issues.

In yet another decision from Wisconsin, the defense said reliance on "stale, irrelevant and deceptive information" was fatal. The deception issue for this illegal junk dealer was that he sold parts when, in fact, he bartered. The court was not impressed, since the defendant received value as a result of his illegal junkyard. The defendant also alleged the use of exaggeration; that he did not sell 65 vehicles to a recycler as the affidavit alleges, only 35. This was labeled an inaccuracy since one sale would have been enough. There was no **Franks** issue here. **State v. Scheidegger**, 2000 WL 489749 (Wis. App) (unpub. op.). See also **People v. Grady,** 755 P. 2d 1211 (Colo. 1988).

Delaware would agree with Wisconsin. It has not fully decided the omission issue, but did say in **Blount v. State**, 511 A. 2d 1030 (Del. 1986), that omissions must be omitted by the affiant with an intent to distort the truth, but that where omitted facts do not diminish the probable cause the **Franks** threshold has not been met. Utah also said only omissions made falsely are taken into account. **Youd v. Johnson**, 788 P. 2d 529 (Utah App. 1990). See also **State v. Doyle**, 336 N.W. 2d 247 (Minn. 1983). In a more recent Minnesota decision the appellate court noted the "great deference" to be given to the issuing judge's determination of probable cause required by **Illinois v. Gates**, 462 U.S. 213 (1983). The omission in this case was a lack of a section in the affidavit regarding the informant's reliability or the basis of the informant's knowledge. However, the information, as noted in the affidavit, was independently confirmed and consistent with the informant's story. Next, the "fatal" omission, as viewed by the defense, was that the wheels on the defendant's car were not 5 star aluminum wheels. That can hardly be a fatal misrepresentation since the rest of the detail about the car was accurate. The defense also attacked the police use of training, experience, and inference drawing as a falsehood. This, too, was rejected as a ground to overturn the warrant. **State v. Voeung**, 2000 WL 31772 (Minn. app.) (unpub. op.).

South Carolina has adopted the theory that an omission is the same as a positive false statement. The omission in **State v. Missouri**, 524 S.E. 2d 394 (S. C. 1999) was simple. The confidential informer told the police that the defendant would sell him crack but it was not there now. This last clause was omitted from the affidavit. This omission was classified as exculpatory information. If you put this exculpatory information in the application would an issuing magistrate find probable cause? No.

When something is recklessly included the judge is to remove it and *de novo* determine if probable cause remains. When something of consequence is omitted the judge inserts the omitted item(s) and determines, *de novo*, if the addition destroys probable cause. In a Washington case the fact that the neighbor's house was also suspected of housing a marijuana growing operation was omitted. When inserted, in this case, it still did not destroy the probable cause that pointed in the defendant's direction, **State v. Neuroth**, 1999 WL 730500 (Wash. App. Div. 1) (unpub. op.). In a Nebraska case, the police failed to tell the issuing court that they had asked for and had been given consent to search the same premises described in the warrant and that search, which lasted a mere 15 minutes, turned up nothing. This omission was not fatal. The court said that it could not see how a "15 minute consent search performed several hours earlier would have dissipated the probable cause otherwise shown." The court added that the defendant's affidavit did not support the dissipation theory. It could have also said a consent to search does not have to be supported by probable cause, thus if the police had probable cause at the time of the consent, it was not "used up." The police probably used the consent to help make their subsequent search more efficient – sort of a legal "sneak-a-peek" search. **State v. Quesada**, 1999 WL 1111594 (Neb. App.) (unpub. op.).

Arizona says the trial court is not only to redraft the affidavit by deleting falsehoods but must redraft by it "adding the materially omitted facts." **State v. Carter**, 700 P. 2d 488 (Ariz. 1985) cited in **State v. Buccini**, 796 P. 2d 910 (Ariz. App. 1990). Florida says the warrant should be read as if the omissions were present. If the omission thus added destroys probable cause, the warrant is fatally flawed. **Sotolongo v. State**, 530 So. 2d 514 (Fla. Dist. Ct. App. 1988). See also **State v. Jardine**, 46 Crim. L. Rep. 1317 (Idaho App. 1989); **Redding v. State**, 383 S.E. 2d 640 (Ga. App. 1989); and **State v. Wing**, 559 A. 2d 783 (Me. 1989) in accord.

In Florida's latest **Franks** decision, the issue was whether false statements were used and material omissions occurred in a warrant for the blood sample taken from the defendant. The defense contended there was a misstatement about a witness' description of events in the park that night and an omission about the medical examiner's conclusion that the victim had not bled profusely. The suppression judge had ruled that indeed there were some problems of misstatement but the misstatement was not willful and, if removed, the rest of the affidavit still yielded probable cause. The Florida Supreme Court disagreed. They felt the police knew of the false statements. The description of a big, tall man did not fit the original tall and thin man; bald, not long hair; white, not dark complexion, *etc.* A moan became a muffled scream; no baseball cap to a baseball cap wearer. These problems coupled with other unrelated evidentiary problems caused the court to overturn the conviction. **Thorp v. Florida**, 2000 WL 1707103 (Fla.).

The Kansas Supreme Court indicated that it might consider whether omitted information met the **Franks** test, but did not have to in the case before it, since the defendant withdrew his **Franks** allegations before the suppression hearing. **State v. Toler**, 787 P. 2d 711 (Kan.. 1990).

New Mexico said that: "The issue of whether facts intentionally omitted or misstated in an affidavit are of such materiality that their non-disclosure or misstatement may lead to invalidating the search warrant, turns on whether these facts, because of their inherent probative force, give rise to a substantial probability that, had the information been set out correctly or correctly stated in the affidavit it would have altered a reasonable magistrate's decision of probable cause." The omission in the New Mexico case was that, although the affidavit stated that the informant had not been arrested before August, 1981, in fact he had been arrested before September 1, 1981. The officer explained that to give the post-August, 1981 arrest would have destroyed confidentiality. The affiant-officer also called the defendant's car "expensive and expensive to insure." It was a Porsche, but it was old and only worth $1,500.00 at the time of the affidavit. The New Mexico court felt that neither omission went to the heart of probable cause. **State v. Donaldson**, 666 P. 2d 1264 (N.Mex. 1983). See also **Connelly v. State**, 571 A. 2d 881 (Md. Ct. Spec. App. 1990).

An excellent case dealing with an omission comes from Ohio and demonstrates the need for the reviewing court to avoid getting "caught up" in the omission and always allowing that to influence the issue of independent probable cause. The police in the Ohio case were concerned about a fugitive that might get away if they merely approached his safe house by car. They engaged a helicopter to fly over the farm at the same time. As they approached, the officer in the helicopter saw eight large marijuana plants. The ground officers arrested the fugitive. The helicopter officer reported the marijuana and the ground officers did a "protective sweep" which they did not have grounds to do. They saw more evidence. When they applied for the warrant they omitted the sweep information. The appellate court noted that the probable cause that came from the fly-over was sufficient in itself to validate the issuance of the warrant. **State v. Clary**, 1996 WL 560522 (Ohio App. 4th Dist.) (unpub. op.).

Though there is the debate over the issue of omissions equating with lies, there appears to be no debate concerning the general difficulty a defendant faces in overcoming the warrant's presumed validity. An Arkansas court, for example, had to remind defendants that it is their burden to show invalidity with supporting documents even in a "close-call" **Leon** "good faith" type case. The **Franks** standards are not reduced in any type of case where the warrant's validity is presumed. **Hicks v. State**, 773 S.W. 2d 113 (Ark. App. 1989). Merely alleging that the affidavit contained false information is not sufficient. **State v. Hedge**, 772 S.W. 2d 683 (Mo. App. 1989). However, when it is shown that the officer did lie about past reliability, for instance, then **Leon** cannot be used to thwart **Franks**. Why? **Leon** is confined to the objectively ascertainable questions whether a reasonably well-trained police officer would have known that the search was illegal despite the magistrate's authorization. **State v. Duskey,** 358 S.E. 2d 819 (W.Va. 1987). And any reasonably well-trained officer knows about **Franks** and perjury and the critical issues created by either **Aguilar** or **Gates**.

A sufficiency challenge is not a **Franks** veracity challenge despite allegations of the use of tainted information. **People v. Dunn,** 553 N.Y.S. 2d 257 (N.Y. App. 1990) citing their lead case of **People v. Glen**, 331 N.Y.S. 2d 656 (N.Y. 1972). So too, a vague assertion that disclosure might be helpful or that it might lead to exculpatory evidence does not meet the burden. **Com. v. Bonasorte**, 486 A. 2d 1361 (Pa. 1984). Likewise a mere denial of the existence of a confidential informant fails to rebut the presumed validity of a search warrant. North Carolina says that in such a case a judge can and should summarily deny suppression. **State v. Locklear,** 353 S.E. 2d 666 (N.Car. 1987).

The issue of how to treat merely negligent omissions was at the center of **Wilson v. State**, 752 A. 2d 1250 (Md. App. 2000). The defense really *never* argued **Franks** but Judge Moylan of the appeals court said the defense introduced it as "The Shadow Presence of **Franks v. Delaware**." The defense mentioned a "**Franks** hearing" in his brief but one was never formally held by the trial court. But the trial court went outside the "four corners" and allowed the detective to be examined by the defense. Thus the defense has had the full benefit of **Franks**. What was shown during that hearing were mere negligent omissions of "arguably" exculpatory material or at most rumor discrepancies. Judge Moylan was unhappy that the trial judge did not push the defense to declare itself before going outside the four corners as required. But this procedural omission was not fatal.

In an Arkansas case the inclusion of "false" priors did not render the rest of the warrant invalid. **Stephenson v. State,** 2000 WL 1586313 (Ark. app.). In yet another case, the affidavit omits the time of any drug activity in the home. However, the time could be inferred from the information as given. **Yancy v. State**, 2000 WL 1586327 (Ark. App.).

No court appears to disagree with this approach. An Alaska court found unacceptable a motion memorandum that did not have supporting affidavits nor satisfactory explanations for their absence. **Davis v. State**, 766 P. 2d 41 (Alaska App. 1988). See also **State v. Toler**, 787 P. 2d 711 (Kan.. 1990). In fact one court had to chastise their judges for "jumping to conclusions" in the **Franks** context. A Michigan court said it is judicial error to order production of the informant on the basis of the defendant's affidavits alone. The court said this will not do. The trial court immediately dismissed the case because of failure to produce. The appellate court said if the affidavits support the idea of a **Franks** hearing then a hearing must be held. They also said the trial court is to determine the credibility of the witnesses who would support both sides before it can even consider dismissing the case. Courts are not to jump to conclusions. **People v. Thomas**, 436 N.W. 2d 687 (Mich. App. 1989).

All courts appear to be in harmony on the issue of how to treat most properly raised **Franks** challenges. They all appear to agree that taking the well-pleaded and supported allegations to be true, the warrant may still provide sufficient probable cause to uphold the warrant.

In a Colorado case, the trial court found that a detective failed to disclose that the informer had actively participated in major drug transactions. He also failed to disclose that the informant was a paid informant and was not particularly good at being an informant. A **Franks** violation was found. The problem, as the Colorado court saw it, was that even if these portions were struck from this warrant there was still adequate information remaining to support probable cause. It also found that the detective did not understate or overstate his relationship with and knowledge of this informant. Thus, since the missing facts did not render the affidavit inadequate, the warrant should not have been invalidated. **People v. Grady**, 755 P. 2d 1211 (Colo. 1988). See also **Bevill v. State**, 556 So. 2d 699 (Miss. 1990). As Montana held, the inaccuracies must defeat the application, and they do not if they are mere inaccuracies. If the facts concluded by the affiant are not true but not totally inaccurate, the warrant should not be set aside. **State v. Hembold,** 767 P. 2d 864 (Mont. 1989).

One Texas defendant said one statement was a lie, e.g., "I wish you had more money because I've got 50 more pounds of marijuana to sell" and the personal knowledge of the officer statement was a lie because it was information given him by other officers. Neither of these allegations were exactly true. The warrant indicated that the affiant was working with other officers. The defendant admitted at the hearing that he might have mentioned the additional marijuana, but argued these were not his exact words. The court found the words used were an "accurate characterization" of the defendant's statement. **Martinez v. State**, 2000 WL 12703 (Tex. App. Dallas).

A Connecticut court held, and rightly so, that alleging omissions is not enough. The defense must show how the omission is material to the determination of probable cause. Who owned the property in this case was not important; who used it was important. **State v. Salvatore**, 749 A. 2d 71 (Conn. App. 2000). Accord: **State v. Anderson**, 2000 WL 557850 (Wash. App. 1) (unpub. op).

However, an allegation that the informant is a fellow officer is most critical because a judge analyzes the truthfulness required by federal and state court decisions. As the court says, it is like not having an affidavit at all. **State v. Jones**, 2000 WL 1195412 (So. Car. 2000).

Language that is surplusage, even if false, is not what **Franks** "targets." Surplusage is not necessary to finding probable cause. **State v. Campbell**, 538 A. 2d 321 (R.I. 1987). Certainly innocent mistakes do not count. **Com. v. Walker**, 729 S.W. 2d 440 (Ky. 1987). It is only material falsehoods (or material omissions) that count. **State v. Carter**, 700 P. 2d 488 (Ariz. 1985); **State v. Buccini**, 796 P. 2d 910 (Ariz. App. 1990); and **Lyons v. State**, 796 P. 2d 210 (Nev. 1990) and **Doyle v. State**, 995 P. 2d 465 (Nev. 2000).

What then is critical? It depends upon a totality analysis and not upon a decision to chastise police or supervise their work. But when will exaggerations be material? The following two cases from Montana and Indiana are illustrative.

During the investigation, the police officer misread a term in a contract for deed and, as a result of this mistake, the officer wrongfully apprised the court of the defendant's financial condition. The court found this to be a mistake which "significantly exaggerated the amount of money spent by the defendant" and required these references to be excised from the affidavit. Whether there was still enough left for probable cause had to be determined after the excision. **State v. Baldwin**, 789 P. 2d 1215 (Mont. 1990).

The issue before the Indiana court was whether the use of the adjective "numerous" when applied to an informer was a **Franks** lie or reckless disregard of the truth when in fact the informant had only been used in two other cases. No, said the court, this did not violate **Franks**. It said, "we do not perceive the word 'numerous' to be such an exaggeration as to have misled the judge...." **Williams v. State**, 528 N.E. 2d 496 (Ind. App. 1988).

What about mislabeling the informer as confidential? Florida had a "mislabeling" case. The undercover police officer was denominated a confidential informant when in fact he was a presumptively reliable fellow police officer informant. This was found not to be fatal. The court noted that the affiant was trying to protect the undercover officer and was trying not to uncover a valuable "plant." Thus it found the representation was not false in that sense. **State v. Stokes**, 550 So. 2d 519 (Fla. App. 1989) and **State v. DeLeon**, 2000 WL 646502 (Ohio App. 2) (unpub. op).

Can the misstatement of a date be critical? It depends. In a Nebraska case the only inaccuracy in one sentence of the affidavit was the exact date of a photo identification session. The defendant failed to show that this was deliberate, reckless or, in reality, how it even went to materiality of the issuance. **State v. Wakeman**, 434 N.W. 2d 549 (Neb. 1989).

On the other hand consider this case from Maryland. The defendant said he has a right to make a **Franks** challenge but that he was thwarted because the state would not supply the dates of the relied-upon surveillance. The court agreed that the dates were critical and said: "the accused's right to show a material omission in an affidavit was made intentionally or with reckless disregard for the truth... 'cannot be upheld'...without specific dates of the identity relied upon for the affidavit." In this case there was the possibility of misidentification thus raising an alibi defense. The court said the failure to provide the surveillance dates effectively prohibited the **Franks** issue. **Connelly v. State**, 571 A. 2d 881 (Md. Ct. Spec. App. 1990).

As to the issue of alibi and whether a "sufficient showing" has been made to invoke a **Franks** hearing, some common sense must be applied by the trial court. In an Illinois case the defendant presented an alibi affidavit and supported his affidavit with that of his wife. Both affidavits said he was not home at the alleged targeted time. Could a judge permissibly conclude that a hearing was not required because the affidavits came from interested parties? Yes, said Illinois in **People v. Tovar**, 523 N.E. 2d 1178 (Ill. App. 1988).

Suppose two affidavits are used to obtain a warrant. What if they are inconsistent, does that fact automatically require excision of both, thus requiring suppression? Not necessarily, especially where the inconsistency only goes to the amount of detail. Where one is more detailed than the other, the required **Franks** threshold has not been met. See **Rodriguez v. State**, 781 S.W. 2d 946 (Tex. App. 1989). Other inconsistencies could, of course, demonstrate that the affiant was lying or reckless.

What lies are material will vary from state to state and even from judge to judge in the same state. It is up to the appellate courts of each state to provide some guidance to suppression judges.

In an Alabama case, the affiant said he got the information directly from the informant. In fact the affiant got the information from a fellow police officer who got the information directly from the informer. The court found this was intentional or at least reckless under **Franks** and when this lie was struck (which included the informer's information) there was no probable cause left. They felt this failure to inform the issuing court of the proper identification of the source was at least reckless if not intentional. The search warrant was found to be invalid when the statement was excised. The court concluded by saying: "[T]he fact that probable cause existed and could have been readily shown by a truthful affidavit... does not change the result, since it is the truth of the affiant's statement, not the confidential informant's statement that is material to the magistrate's decision to issue the search warrant." It is clear to Alabama judges what types of lies or recklessness will not be tolerated. **Villemez v. State**, 555 So. 2d 342 (Ala. Ct. Crim. App. 1989).

Perhaps the most difficult problem of **Franks** *qua* **Franks** is trying to determine what is recklessness. Several courts are trying to give their suppression judges some guidance. The police in **State v. Jensen**, 915 P. 2d 109 (Kan.. 1996), gave their facts to the judge and then presented their informant personally to the judge so that he could relate his additional and critical facts. The informant was sworn but he did not reveal that he was working for the police and judge failed to ask him. Was this a fatal omission? No, said the court. It was the judge's duty to determine this and his failure cannot be charged to the police. Probable cause was stated, thus the police could reasonably rely on the issued warrant. Note: **Leon** was not cited but it is obvious they were relying on that theory.

The contested statement in an Ohio case was "there is no air conditioning and yet the owner's house has a much higher electric bill than the adjacent houses for non-drug related reasons." But there was an air conditioner but it would have been seen only if the officer trespassed on the defendant's curtilage. The court held this was not an intentionally-made false statement even though it was an erroneous statement. Thus, the warrant was good. **State v. Gantz**, 665 N.E. 2d 239 (Ohio App. 1995), rev. denied 74 Ohio St. 3d (1996).

The **Franks** inquiry is based solely on what was or was not included in the affidavit which was based only on known facts that preexisted the issuance of the warrant. "Bootstrapping" is not allowed to be used by the judge before whom the **Franks** motion is heard. This was ably pointed out by **State v. Manuel,** 570 N.W. 2d 601 (Wis. App. 1997). When announcing why he was denying the **Franks** motion, the judge noted that Mr. Manuel's admissions corroborated his involvement in the crime. However, these admissions did not exist prior to the issuance of the arrest warrant. That never justifies denying a **Franks** motion. Indeed, the whole theory of the exclusionary rule is to mandate that only pre-warrant facts be judged at a suppression hearing and this rule also applies to **Franks** hearings.

Sometimes it is not possible for the informant-police officer to personally apply for the warrant for any number of legitimate purposes. Such was the case in **State v. Rufus,** 993 S.W. 2d 490 (Ark. 1999). The affiant officer was not the officer who observed the drug transaction. Was this omission a fatal defect? No, said the court. Why? If you add in the "who," the facts do not change – probable cause still exists.

Iowa accepted **Franks** in **State v. Goff,** 323 N.W. 2d 204 (Iowa 1982). That court in 1990 had to determine whether the police failure to check out the informer's tip was "reckless disregard." First, the court said it is entirely possible that the defendant can show that the officers actually entertained doubts about the veracity of the informer's statements. In such a case failure to check would constitute recklessness. Second, inferences from the circumstances can be shown to create what should have been an obvious reason for the officers to doubt veracity. Thus failure to investigate was reckless. Failing these tests, however, mere negligence in accepting the story is not enough. **State v. Niehaus,** 452 N.W. 2d 184 (Iowa 1990). In yet another case, the defendant contended that the officer could not rely on the informant's story because it was against the reality of the facts. The informant said her little lost dog went upon the defendant's property and when she went upon the property to get her little dog she saw drugs through a window. Defendant said that could not have happened because his fierce large dogs would have eaten her little dog. The officers testified there were no dogs around on the day the warrant was served. The officer was found not to be reckless in accepting the story as true. **State v. Prestwick,** 783 P. 2d 298 (Idaho 1989). What both of these courts were in essence saying is that corroboration is only required in **Gates** -like situations or where there is not enough detail to properly credit the story. Thus the general corroboration requirement cases should be a guide in this area.

What all of the appellate courts are saying in a broader sense is that only in the rare case will the lower court's judgment be overturned. What they try to balance is the tough preliminary burden the defendant shoulders under **Franks** so as to keep it rigorous without automatically precluding or requiring an automatic hearing in each case. The burden should not be too onerous to make the **Franks** hearing un-achievable in the appropriate case. **People v. Lucente**, 506 N.E. 2d 1269 (Ill. 1987).

Even where a hearing is requested and granted, the decision not to suppress will be given great credence and will not be overturned lightly, as long as the court did not jump to a conclusion. Reviewing courts are in apparent agreement that such decisions will not be reversed unless "clearly erroneous" which requires a review of the whole record to see if there was an adequate basis for the findings. The deference given to such conclusions is not boundless. See **State v. Speers**, 554 A. 2d 769 (Conn. App. 1989); **State v. Smith**, 448 N.W. 2d 550 (Minn. App. 1989); and **Hyde v. State**, 769 P. 2d 376 (Wyo. 1989).

There are other issues that were not specifically addressed in **Franks** that should be mentioned. For example, are the general discovery rules in each state linked to **Franks**? In a California case the state argued that general discovery (**non Brady-non Jencks**) could not be used to supply a defendant information that would allow him to do a **Franks** veracity challenge. The California court held that general discovery and **Franks** are not so linked. They said that if a defendant had independent grounds to get discovery and that as a result **Franks** information is uncovered, then so be it. The state cannot disobey such an order. Such discovery (not the types constitutionally mandated) is within the sound discretion of the court. The defendant who has no independent grounds, but uses discovery to mount a **Franks** attack, however, can be stopped under the exercise of discretion until the defendant makes the required **Franks** threshold showing. **People v. Broome**, 247 Cal. Rep. 854 (Cal. App. 1988).

More important, however, is the clash of **Roviaro** (*supra* at Ch. Three) and its confidential informant exception and **Franks**. This issue was not addressed in **Franks**. What is the suppression court to do when the defendant makes what appears to be an adequate showing under **Franks** when the state refuses to produce the informer due to the confidentiality promise? Is an otherwise good case to be thrown out or is there another way to approach the problem? There is another way. In a Massachusetts case the defendant appeared to the trial judge to have met the **Franks** hearing threshold. The defendant's affidavits identified the person whom he believed to be the informant and he said that person had never been a reliable police informant in the past, particularly with regard to drug-related criminal activity. A hearing on the motion for disclosure was held. The state refused to reveal the informant and the trial judge suppressed the evidence. That ruling gave the state the right to take an interlocutory appeal. The Massachusetts court then addressed the issue of balancing the public interest in protecting informants and the public interest in deterring illegal police conduct. The Court well noted that **Franks** does not provide an answer to this problem. Because of Franks, the court said this was more than a mere demand to reveal the informant. If the defense is right, that this was not a reliable informant, then his information was not worthy of the issuing authority's attention.

The trial court's method was found to be too drastic to resolve the **Roviaro-Franks** dilemma. Instead, the Massachusetts high court said the trial court should have held an *in camera* hearing to first interrogate the warrant's affiant and, if necessary, the informant himself to see if there is a substantial preliminary showing that the affiant had made reckless or intentionally false statements. If the answer is yes that probable improper material statements were used, then a full **Franks** hearing is to be held with required disclosure. Then, if the state refuses to disclose the informant, the evidence must be suppressed. This *in camera* hearing, according to the court, may be done without counsel being present, or with counsel present under a proper "not-to-reveal" order. **Com v. Amral**, 407 Mass. 511 (Mass. 1990).

Pennsylvania appears to agree with this approach. In **Com. v. Bonasorte**, 486 A. 2d 1361 (Pa. 1984), the Pennsylvania Supreme Court held that a failure to produce an informant for an *in camera* interview was sufficient to justify suppression, especially where the informant's information was central to the probable cause finding and not mere surplusage.

Choice of law (conflicts) can sometimes be critical to a **Franks** issue as illustrated by **State v. Fleming**, 755 P. 2d 725 (Ore. App. 1988). In this case the defendant had apparently committed a homicide in Oregon. However, the convicting evidence was gathered in the state of Washington. The alleged **Franks** violation was the failure to inform the Washington magistrate that the affiant knew that the informer had failed two polygraph tests. He said if the magistrate had known this the warrant would not have been issued. The Oregon court said, "Because the warrant was issued in Washington by a Washington magistrate, we analyze this assignment under Washington law." The Oregon court went on to find that Washington will only consider fatal omissions and that this would not have been a fatal omission in Washington.

One question remains that had not been specifically answered by a direct opinion of the U.S. Supreme Court. Suppose the affiant is a private citizen and not a police officer. Do the **Franks v. Delaware** rules apply to such an affidavit? Twice in the history of Illinois jurisprudence has this question arisen. In **People v. Born**, 447 N.E. 2d 426 (Ill. App. 1983), the sole affiant was a private individual and the defense urged a lack of veracity. The trial court denied a **Franks** hearing saying it only applied to government affiants. The appeals court said they could find nothing in **Franks** distinguishing informants. In fact in **People v. Hall**, 359 N.E. 2d 1191 (1971), the Supreme Court vacated and remanded such a case to Illinois for reconsideration, citing **Franks.** See 438, U.S. 912 (1978). The issue arose again in 2000 and the appeals court affirmed a trial court's **Franks** hearing on a non-governmental affidavit in **People v. Hoye**, 726 N.E. 2d 180 (Ill App. 2d 2000).

III.   Conclusion

The fact is that some unscrupulous police officers will lie to obtain convictions. Some device had to be created to deter this kind of activity. Balanced against this very real problem is the need to encourage all police to use the warrant process and to uphold the validity of warrants. For these reasons the very tough standard of **Franks** was developed putting a significant burden on the defense to secure a hearing on the veracity issue. Except for the "omissions can be lies" debate, the state courts have not sought to expand defendant's rights and, therefore, strictly follow **Frank's** teachings.

Again the reasoning of the Connecticut Supreme Court in **Glenn** (*supra*) bears noting. That court said it could "...see little logic of benefit that would result from rejecting..." the Franks rule. Why? They felt that the "deterrent effect of the basic exclusionary rule is not served..." by allowing such a challenge when the false statements are made by informants and not the police. "Accuracy by hindsight" is not, nor never has been, required. Truthfulness is a great ideal but does that mean that every fact is necessarily correct? Hearsay, tolerated in the warrant issuing process, will be ferreted out in the determination whether the case is "worth trying" hearing, or if tried, at the trial itself where the trier of fact will not even hear it.

The court goes on to say that insisting on complete factual truthfulness would create a "Catch-22 situation" forcing the police to do an exhaustive investigation which would be all but impossible without a search warrant and, I might add, that not many defendants would give a consent and even if they did they would not consent to a search as thorough as the one that the warrant allows. Inaccurate and unreasonable are two very different concepts as very ably noted by Kipperman in his article "Inaccurate Search Warrants as a Ground for Suppressing Evidence," 84 Harv. L.Rev. 825 (1971). The court then quotes from a Seventh Circuit decision where that court said: "[G]ood faith errors cannot be deferred...[and] do not negate probable cause. If an agent reasonably believes facts which on their face indicate that a crime has probably been committed, then even if mistaken, he has probable cause to believe that a crime has been committed." **U.S. v. Carmichael**, 489 F. 2d 983 at 988-989 (C.A. 7th 1973). Finally, the Connecticut court notes that "it makes little sense to increase the workload and delay in an already busy system by allowing challenges to errors that are beyond the state's control and do not address the case's ultimate merits." **Glenn** at 740 A. 2d 863 (Conn. 1999).

What the trial court has to avoid is jumping to conclusions. Remember, veracity can be impeached. Just make sure that a judge has a reason to go beyond the four corners of the warrant, affidavit, and the warrant issuing hearing.

CHAPTER FIVE

CONSENT SEARCHES

I.   CONSENT: General Principles

Not all searches require a search warrant. A citizen may consent to a search. As long as that consent is freely and voluntarily given, the search will be upheld. The consent must not be the "fruit" of a "poisonous tree." It will be upheld if all these tests are met. As will be demonstrated by the following materials, probable cause to seek a consent to search is never the issue. The consent area of search and seizure law is one of the few areas where the police can act upon no suspicion at all. Practically speaking, police often, but not always, seek consent when a mere suspicion or hunch arises. The critical concerns in consent searches center on the voluntariness of the consent, the power of the person to give consent, the scope of the consent given and the duration of the consent. Therefore, due process, standing and reasonableness are the primary concerns. The lack of probable cause or mere presence of only a bare or mere suspicion does not factor in the decision regarding the validity of a consent.

No case better illustrates the lack of a need for probable cause than **Florida v. Bostick**, 501 U.S. 429 (1991). The issue there was whether Mr. Bostick was seized when approached by officers while Mr. Bostick sat on a bus. The Court found no seizure. Thus, the consent given was not a product of an illegal seizure. The Court stated at the beginning of Part II of the opinion, that "the officers lacked the reasonable suspicion required to justify a seizure...." **Bostick** at 2386. Since no seizure had taken place, the consent given was not affected by the fruits of the poisonous tree doctrine. If Mr. Bostick's consent was invalid, it had to be found illegal upon some other ground. The case was remanded to see if his will was overcome in some other way or whether he limited the scope of his consent. But the fact that the police did not have probable cause or even articulable suspicion plays no role in the process. If Bostick "chose to permit the search of his luggage...." at 2388, the evidence was lawfully found. To hold otherwise would require overruling too many decisions, according to the majority in their response to the dissent on this issue. **Bostick** at 2388.

Although several states have fully accepted the "no suspicion or probable cause needed" position of Bostick, two courts' decisions are noted to reflect that acceptance. The first case comes from Arkansas. In **Howe v. State**, 2001 WL 167801 (Ark. App.), the court saw a justifiable reason for the initial auto stop. The officer admitted that he did not fear that Howe was armed or dangerous. Nonetheless, the officer asked for consent to pat down Howe. Howe said yes. Of course, the court said, neither probable cause nor articulable suspicion is needed to seek a consent. The Supreme Court of Colorado agreed as evidenced by its decision in **People v. Brazzel**, 2001 WL 237521 (Colo. *en banc*). The court said, yes it "would have been easy for the officer to have secured a warrant   " in this case. But it ruled that was not necessary since the defendant voluntarily consented. The trial judge erred in granting the motion to suppress without first determining voluntariness since that was the only issue of consequence.

In its head-long flight to distance itself from the U.S. Supreme Court and to give its citizens more rights under the New Federalism, the New Jersey Superior Court has decided that an officer needs articulable suspicion to seek a consent upon an automobile stop by its decision in **State v. Carty**, 332 N.J. Super 200 (App. Div. 2000). In **State v. Yanovsky**, 2001 WL 410337 (N.J. Super. A.D.), they were asked not to apply that rule retroactively. The court declined that invitation for all cases pending at the time of its decision in **Carty**. It noted that **Carty** had been accepted for a certified hearing at the New Jersey Supreme Court but felt comfortable in creating the articulable suspicion standard and in rejecting the basic philosophy that no suspicion is required under **Bostick** to seek a consent. It also failed to realize that the criminal world thinks that if they say yes there will be no search or that they think they have found the perfect way to stash illicit drugs.

II.   The Voluntariness Issue

The burden of proving that the consent was freely and voluntarily given is on the prosecution. The leading case on this point is **Bumper v. North Carolina**, 391 U.S. 543 (1968). This duty, the Court said, cannot be discharged by showing no more than mere acquiescence to a claim of lawful authority. The issue in **Bumper** was whether a search can be justified as lawful on the basis of consent when that consent has been given after the official conducting the search has asserted that he possessed a warrant when in fact he did not have a valid warrant. When an officer announces he has a warrant in effect he is saying that the occupant has no right to resist the search. This is a form of coercion; colorably lawful coercion when the officer does not have a warrant. Thus, the Court held Bumper's consent to be invalid.

Would this constitute a valid consent under **Bumper**? The police lawfully arrested a defendant and sought a consent to search his house. The arrestee gave a consent that was limited in scope, allowing the search of only certain rooms. The police then threatened to seek a search warrant at which point the arrestee consented to a whole house search. The Eleventh Circuit did not see this as an attempt to harass or intimidate. Rather the court saw it only as "informing him of his alternatives." **U.S. v. Garcia**, 890 F. 2d 355 (C.A. 11th 1989). Of course, the threat to get a warrant in this case was based on the fact that the police had sufficient probable cause to get a warrant. It also acknowledged the power of the police to secure the house awaiting the issuance of a warrant. See **Illinois v. McArthur**, 121 S. Ct. 946 (2001).

A fairly recent case from Ohio further illustrates the point made by the Eleventh Circuit. The defendant, Turner, had tried to purchase a money order with three counterfeit twenty-dollar bills. An officer was sent to the scene. Turner told the officer he got the bills from a friend as rent money. Turner was told several times he was not under arrest. The officer asked if he could search Turner's car and Turner said no and "Don't know why you need to search my car." Turner was taken to the station house and shown a consent form. He was told that the officer would try to get a warrant but there was no guarantee a judge would approve one. Turner blurted out, "I've got a nine in the car and I didn't want to be arrested for CCW." He signed a consent form. The Ohio court said the consent was not coerced. **State v. Turner**, 2000 WL 125966 (Ohio App. 2) (Unpub. op.).

Some tricks are "dirtier" than others said the Alaska Supreme Court in one of their consent cases. The issue, as this court saw it, "is really whether that conduct falls below an accepted standard for the fair and honorable administration of justice." **Nix v. State**, 621 P. 2d 1347 (Alaska 1981). Such a decision recognizes the supervisory power of courts over police activity. A standard like this, however, does not provide much guidance except that certain conduct may be outrageous enough to warrant its application. A court must be able to distinguish between strategic deception and outrageous conduct. In **Nix**, the police suspected that the defendant and others were involved in a burglary. In order to gain information for a search warrant a police officer went with a person who was the sister of defendant Miller to Miller's apartment. They knocked on the door and were admitted by a friend who was staying there. The police officer was in plain clothes and was never introduced as a police officer nor did the officer misrepresent who he was. The sister said she was there to get money. Five minutes later they left. Through the plain view of the stolen property a warrant was issued. This conduct was not "outrageous" according to Alaska because there was no affirmative misrepresentation and the officer did not exceed the scope of the consent; he did not "rummage" around but merely stood and observed. This conduct did not shock the universal sense of justice; it was strategic deception.

Many states have long recognized the invalidity of such a ruse as practiced in **Bumper**. Mere acquiescence after an illegal search has begun is not a waiver or consent. The officer of the law is supposed to know that the private citizen is always silently objecting to an unlawful invasion of his premises. Consent must be freely given and not given because of official authority or under color or process issued by an officer claiming to have authority.

The use of a ruse is not always bad, however. In **Lewis v. U.S.**, 385 U.S. 206 (1966) the defendant converted his home into a drug sales center and invited people there to buy drugs. His mistake was the invitation he issued to an undercover narcotics agent. The consent to enter was not rendered invalid in this case, under these facts, because the agent was invited and he was willingly admitted. The court held that the pretense resulted in no breach of privacy because this home became a commercial center, thus the bags of marijuana that were purchased were admissible. No other "search" activity took place in the house. This, also, was a strategic deception case.

In one case the defendant was in lawful custody and the officer, who had probable cause, told the defendant that he had the right to refuse to give consent but the officer also said if he refused a warrant would be sought. The defendant asked the officer if the officer had probable cause and whether the consent scope could be limited. The officer said yes to both questions. The defendant consented. The arrest was valid and the court felt that the threat to get the warrant was nullified (or at least neutralized the threat), thus, the consent given was valid as there was no taint to remove or attenuate. **State v. Johnson**, 16 P.3d 680 (Wash. App. 2001).

Sometimes courts must focus on the consent issue and the use of a ruse or some deception as vitiating the consent, but arrive at the right result in a warrantless entry case by distinguishing the use of undercover agents who pose as drug buyers as in **Lewis v. U.S.**, 385 U.S. 206 (1966) from other deceptive practices. In a federal case from New York, the officers seeking drug information posed as gas company employees who said they were looking for gas leaks. In **Lewis** the officers posed as fellow-bad guys posing as drug buyers. That was upheld but **Lewis** was never intended to undo cases like **Bumper**. The court in **Giraldo** finally concluded that "The original entry was illegal. 'Consent' was obtained by falsely inducing fear of an imminent life-threatening danger." That was all that really needed to be said. **U.S. v. Giraldo**, 743 F. Supp. 152 (E.D.N.Y. 1990). This was more than strategic deception.

When a defendant withholds his or her consent to search, the prosecution cannot, according to California, comment on that fact and cannot urge the jury to consider this as evidence. **People v. Redmond**, 633 P. 2d 976 (Cal. Dist. Ct. App. 1980). This makes sense with regard to its use in the case-in-chief and is consistent with other decisions in other areas.

Further illustrating the point that the defendant's refusal to consent and thereby to insist upon his or her constitutional rights is not to be exploited is **Com. v. Welch**, 584 A. 2d 517 (Pa. Super. Ct. 1991). In **Welch** the officer was permitted, over objection, to testify about the refusal to consent. The Pennsylvania court said this error required a new trial. It also felt that the Fifth Amendment assertion case law should apply by analogy to this area. The court indicated that no one should be put in this "no win" situation. To allow such testimony says to the jury that the defendant has something to hide. Thus, this is one of those cases where the prejudicial effect outweighs the probative value. The court noted that anyone "with a sense of privacy would likely object...." Therefore, one cannot assume such a refusal is an attempt "to prevent the discovery of incriminating evidence...." It concluded by saying that if people assume that the assertion of the Fifth is a "badge of guilt...the same effect would follow from one's refusal to allow a search of one's residence or possessions." This decision makes sense when the defense does not invite the question. This was the basic issue in **Welch**. During the case-in-chief an officer was allowed to testify over objection to the fact of the refusal to consent. Such, of course, tells the jury that the defendant had something criminal to hide; indication of a guilty conscience. The court felt that one asserting such a right may as likely have a sense of privacy as well as expressing the preference for the police to have a warrant. The court held the evidence inadmissible saying: "The integrity of a constitutional protection simply cannot be preserved if the invocation or assertion of the right can be used as evidence suggesting guilt." The **Bumper** case must be the guide for this area.

The question that then arises is whether the defendant has to object to the search when it is conducted. Most courts have answered the question negatively as seen in **Boyd v. State**, 164 Miss. 610, 145 So. 618 (1933). There was an effort made by the state to show that the appellant did not object to the search. This does not constitute a waiver by the citizen to an illegal search. A citizen is not required to resist the officer. A waiver of protection is not created by the defendant by failing to object to the search. This makes sense in light of **Bumper's** "mere acquiescence" language. Trying to determine which gestures are "mere acquiescence" and which gestures are permission is a factual determination to be made by the suppression judge.

Therefore, the dividing line between tacit consent and mere acquiescence is not an easy one to draw. Consider for example, **State v. Brady**, 585 So. 2d 524 (La. 1991). The object found in the closet that was searched was a dead body. The defendant had called the police to her house to report a stabbing. She answered the door and let the police enter. The trial court suppressed the search of the closet saying it was without consent. Without discussing the trail of blood as creating an exigency, the Louisiana Court addressed the consent issue. The court found, specifically citing **Bumper**, that this was not mere acquiescence. It also felt that " the immediate opening of the particular place on which probable cause focused was within the scope of the tacit consent of the person who had yielded her expectation of privacy to the objective of finding the killer."

A related problem concerns permission given to search something after an illegal search has already begun. This is best illustrated by **Taylor v. State**, 337 So. 2d 773 (Fla. Dist. Ct. App. 1978). A boat pulled into port. An officer boarded, firmly stating that he was looking for undersized lobsters. No consent is then given. He looks about on deck. Then the officer asked if he could look in the hold of the boat. The boat owner said "yes" assuming that the officer had authority to search anyway. Thus came the discovery of the contraband. Without proof by the state of freely given, voluntary consent the acquiescence to a further search growing out of an illegal search yields illegal evidence. The "fruits of the poisonous tree" doctrine does apply to this area. Of course, one would have to determine whether attenuation took place in such circumstances. The unlawful search and its impact were not attenuated in the case.

Therefore, a common dilemma faced by courts is whether a consent can ever be voluntary when it is given following an illegal entry. In a Maryland case an illegal entry was made into a private club suspected of being a place of drug distribution. Once inside, the police explained the situation to the person in charge and asked for and obtained a signed consent to search. There was no extreme pressure applied so that it can be said to be a voluntary consent *but for* the illegal entry. The entry did not reveal any incriminating evidence. By seeking a voluntary consent something in the nature of an attenuation took place. Not all courts would agree with this conclusion. The Maryland court said it is incongruous to find the consent voluntary but tainted by the illegal entry. It said that if there was a real choice to consent or not then the illegality had attenuated. The court thus rejected the LaFave suggestion that such a consent though voluntary could never be any good. See LaFave, *Search and Seizure*, §8.2(d). Their decision does make good "attenuation" sense. The totality of the circumstances doctrine requires an analysis of all the factors that operate on the consent decision and that includes prior illegality and whether in fact the effects of the illegality were still impacting the consent decision. **McMillian v. State**, 584 A. 2d 88 (Md. Ct. Spec. App. 1991).

The Court of Appeals of Wisconsin also had to use the attenuation doctrine in **State v. Vorburger**, 2001 WL 59398 (Wis. App.). The court determined that the two defendants were unlawfully arrested and the effects of that arrest were not attenuated when the consents were sought and given. Though this court confuses an overpowering **Terry** seizure with an arrest, there is no doubt there was only mere suspicion and not articulable suspicion nor probable cause. In the face of a three-to-one police to defendant ratio, and by denying the female suspect the right to use the restroom unless accompanied by an officer, it was clear that the illegality of the seizure was still operating and not attenuated when their consents were given. See also **State v. Grace**, 17 P.3d 951 (Kan.. App. 2001) when the consent to the pat-down came on the "heels" of the unattenuated invalid **Terry**-stop; and **State v. Sakezeles**, 2001 WL 98661 (Fla. App. 3d Dist.) where two consents to search an apartment were invalidated. The first consent was given by the defendant and the second consent was given by the owner of the apartment who walked into the apartment only to find it being searched. The taint was not dissipated.

Along the lines of the area to which the consent extends consider **Commonwealth v. Shaw**, 383 A. 2d 496 (Pa. 1978). The police were allowed into the house by the defendant's sister. They told her they were investigating a murder and asked to speak to her brother. She said he was home and called upstairs for him. No response. She called again. No response. Shuffling noises were heard. Without the sister's permission the officer ran upstairs. The brother and some others were found and arrested. An expended shotgun shell was taken from another sibling of the defendant's brother. There was, by the way, no pre-existing evidence that the defendant was linked to the killing. It was known that he was an associate of those suspected. However, a private residence is not a public thoroughfare. The consent only went to the entryway and no more. The "shuffling" in this case did not amount to exigent circumstances because the defendant was not considered an actor in the prior crime. For a case discussing the scope of a consent search where other incriminating evidence was found before the thing sought and found in a place where the police had a right to be searching see **People v. Torand**, 622 P. 2d 562 (Colo. 1981), and plain view materials generally in Chapter Six.

"No" does not always mean "No" to a police officer and, when sensing this, the citizen often "caves in." Is this consent? No. Officers armed with a bad check arrest warrant heard from an unproven informant that the person might be at a certain apartment. The fully uniformed officers knocked, asked and were told that the woman they wanted was not there. The police insisted on seeing the defendant's female companion. The defendant ultimately said "O.K." While inside, marijuana was discovered causing this defendant's ultimate conviction. Saying that the state has the burden of proving a valid consent, the Louisiana Supreme Court, held this was a coerced consent. **State v. Wolfe**, 398 So. 2d 1117 (La. 1981). Although there is no "scrupulously honored" rule akin to the interrogation area, courts would do well to recognize such an analysis, since this area also requires an analysis of overbearance of the consenter's will as a due process concern.

Obtaining consent through a veiled threat will throw a doubt on the voluntariness of the consent. A former postal employee would not give consent. The postal inspectors applied for a warrant. One of the inspectors explained that a warrant would allow them to "tear the walls down" and that a consent search would not be as thorough. Defendant then consented. This consent was given because of the threat and invalid said the trial court. The Eighth Circuit, saying it was a close question, upheld the trial court. **U.S. v. Kampbell**, 574 F. 2d 962 (C.A. 8th 1978). This case, of course, recognizes that any authorized search is coequally extensive in scope and "destructive" potential, thus there is no difference between a court authorized search and consent searches as to scope. Any material misrepresentation of law should cause a consent to be found invalid.

In one case an appellate court found no illegal detention when a debarking train passenger was stopped, but it remanded the case to the trial court for a determination of voluntariness of the consent. The trial court found that the consent was not voluntary due to the fact that the defendant was surrounded by two officers with another plainly nearby at the exit to the station. One officer held the defendant's arm when the consent was sought and the other was holding the bag to be searched as the defendant also grasped it. The defendant let go of the bag which was taken as a nonverbal consent or acquiescence. Finding the circumstances intimidating and a failure to advise of a right to withhold consent as "instructive," but not dispositive, the court held the consent was involuntary in what the judge labeled as subtle coercion. **U.S. v. Maragh**, 894 F. 2d 415 (D. D.C. 1991).

However, the police do not get a "bad" consent because of the unexpressed fears in the mind of the consenter. In **Reid v. Com.**, 2001 WL 242259 (Va. App.), the defendant said she consented to the search of her purse because she feared the police would tow her friend's truck and leave her stranded on Interstate 64. This was not even a possibility *and* it was not threatened.

The use of a ruse or trick to gain access to a room was brought into focus by the Pennsylvania Superior Court. There had been some furniture burglaries that remained unsolved. The state police had been to the defendant's house on another totally unrelated matter. After the officers returned to their quarters and while reviewing the inventories of these burglaries one officer thought he recognized some items on the list that he had seen at defendant's house. The officer decided to go back to the defendant's house to get a better look at the furniture. When met at the door, the officer told the defendant he wanted to talk about a car that the defendant had reported as stolen. The officer was invited in, he asked a few questions about the car theft, and upon visually confirming his suspicions regarding the furniture, he told the defendant he was a suspect in the furniture burglaries. He gave the defendant his **Miranda** warnings and asked to view the furniture more closely. The court felt that the consent was no good. The misrepresentation vitiated the consent. The defendant was deceived. The officer exploited the trust. The court went on to say that denying the police use of such deception does not add any extra burden to their criminal investigation tasks. Finally, the court held, the use of illegally obtained information cannot form the basis of the probable cause for a search warrant. **Com. v. Poteete**, 418 A. 2d 513 (Pa. Super. Ct. 1980). Here there was a misrepresentation of fact. Not all courts would agree with the foregoing case because they would see this as mere strategic deception and not as egregious conduct.

Unlike other "well-defined exceptions to the warrant requirement" this exception is not based on any need to show either probable cause to search or articulable suspicion to conduct a limited intrusion. In fact it appears that the police officer need not in fact have any but the barest of suspicions to ask for the right to search (if any suspicion is needed). The crux of the consent law area centers on the officer identifying himself or herself as an officer of the law and non-coercive request for a search.

Does the officer have to identify the reason for the request to search? Common sense dictates a positive answer only because it helps in the analysis of whether the consent was voluntary, knowing and intelligent. It is hard to imagine an officer walking up to a person an asking for a right to search "just because I want to." The officer could, it appears, do just that and if everything else is "clean" a consent thus given could be found to be voluntary, knowing and intelligent. Thus what do the cases say about "purpose announcements?" Are they mandated or merely mentioned as a factor to be taken into account when determining validity of the consent? In **Bumper** (*supra*) the police did not appear to tell the owner of the house why they wanted to search, only that they had a warrant. The lie was the reason for the downfall of the search in this case and not the failure to explain why they wanted to search. In **Frazier v. Cupp** (*infra*) it appeared that the consenter knew why the police wanted to search the duffel bag. Likewise in the **Matlock** case (*infra* at page 9) the police did announce why they wanted to search; they said they were looking for the gun and the money. The key to **Matlock** was not the "why" but the "who" of the consent and whether the woman had authority to consent. In the **Watson** case (*infra*), Watson was under arrest and of course knew what the officers were looking for when he persisted in his consent. The defendant in **Florida v. Royer**, (*infra*) was told by the police that they were in fact police and they asked **Royer**, without saying why, to produce his airline ticket and his driver's license. He gave both without saying O.K. This first "consent" was not thought to be unconstitutional; in fact it was labeled as a "consensual inquiry" at that point. **Royer** at 503. It was the second consent based on the failure to return the ticket and the license that were found to be impermissible.

As a Massachusetts court points out, the police in seeking a consent need not "disclose everything that they might have in mind when seeking…" a consent. In this case the defendant was in the father's house and police asked the father for the right to enter the house to talk to his son about a person's death. The defendant said this was a pretext because their intent was to make an arrest. The court rejected the argument.

The arrest that did occur did not exceed the scope of the consent because the police did not make such a promise in their request nor did the father qualify his permission to enter the home. **Com. v. Sanna**, 1997 WL 1441 (Mass. App. Ct.) (By the justices of the Supreme Judicial Court).

The answer to the problem here presented, if there is an answer, is implied from **Schneckloth v. Bustamonte**, 412 U.S. 218 (1973). In **Schneckloth** the defendants were stopped because one headlight and the license plate light were not working. It appears that the police merely asked for a right to search. It does not appear that the police stated why they wanted to search. The Court noted there was no probable cause to search. **Schneckloth** at 227. They also said that under these circumstances there were no "...inherently coercive tactics..." used in this case. **Schneckloth** at 247. Thus it can be said that failure to tell the defendant "why" is not fatal. It also appears that when asked "why" the police should not lie. In any event the "totality" test is to be applied in these cases. Finally, we now clearly know, through **Bostick** (*supra*), that probable cause is not needed to ask for a consent and the wise defendant would ask why.

III. Who Can Give Consent?

A. Standing to Give or Object to Consent: In General.

The next major problem is that of who can give consent; the **standing** issue. Very often the consent to search is given by some third party and evidence is found that is to be used against the other co-owner, user or tenant of the property searched. There are several United States Supreme Court cases that are basic to any discussion of this issue.

The problem of the joint use of a duffel bag came up in **Frazier v. Cupp**, 394 U.S. 731 (1969). This duffel bag was being used jointly by the defendant and his cousin, Rawls. It had been left in Rawls' home. The police, while arresting Rawls, asked him if they could have his clothes. They were directed to the duffel bag and both Rawls and his mother consented to its search. Since Rawls was a joint user of the bag, he clearly had authority to consent to its search. Defendant, the Court went on, in allowing Rawls to use the bag and leaving it in his house, must be taken to have assumed the risk that Rawls would allow someone else to look inside.

The issue in **United States v. Matlock**, 415 U.S. 164 (1974) was whether Mrs. Graff's relationship to the east bedroom was sufficient to make her consent to search valid against Matlock. The officers told her what they were looking for and asked if they could search the house. She and Matlock occupied the same bedroom; Mrs. Graff indicating she was the wife of Matlock even though this was not true. Four thousand nine hundred and ninety-five dollars in cash were found in a diaper bag in the only closet in the room. The Court held that proof of consent will include that consent given by a third party who possesses common authority over or other sufficient relationship with the premises or effect sought to be inspected. Such consent is binding on the absent cotenant. Accord see: **State v. Bartlett**, 2000 WL 235303 (Kan.. App.); **State v. Cadena**, 2000 WL 254331 (Minn. App.).

A rather unique case of a person acquiring a right to consent was decided by the Tenth Circuit in **U.S. v. McAlpine**, 919 F. 2d 1461 (C.A. 10th 1990). The consenter had been forcefully held at the trailer for six months. One day she called the police, told them the story and consented to a police search of the trailer. When the police arrived they were let in by the kidnapped victim. Police saw guns and other items. They sent for a warrant and subsequently, under the warrant, gathered the condemning evidence. The question was whether under **Matlock** and **Rodriguez** (*infra*) the kidnapped victim had a sufficient relationship to give a valid consent. The court said there was enough. Why? She was of that "class of victims who actually cohabit with their abusers and who are not free to leave for fear for their physical or psychological well-being." This, the court felt, gave her a right to consent because the residence was also hers, thus a right of mutual access had arisen, destroying in the perpetrator any expectation of privacy in the shared property. Finally, they said the police had a reasonably based belief in her ability, under these circumstances to consent.

A wife's consent to a visual inspection of her husband's garage by police, which gave sufficient information to obtain a warrant was at the center of **Logan v. State**, 2000 WL 676210 (Miss.). The defense said this search was unconstitutional because the owner himself did not consent. However, they did not contest the wife's authority but argued that she was intimidated. The trial judge who observed her as witness did not agree with that. Some doubt existed that she was told she could refuse to consent but, of course, that is not a Fourth Amendment requirement. All courts appear to agree that if a person has standing in the property, that person can give a valid consent. Other persons with standing assume that risk. See, e.g., **State v. Wagner**, 1997 WL 7205 (Ohio App. 3d Dist.) and **U.S. v. Kim**, 1997 WL 47745 (C.A. 9th Cal.).

Does a hotel clerk have the sufficient privacy relationship with a rented room that his consent to a search is valid (without more) against the defendant? No, the

Court said in **Stoner v. California**, 376 U.S. 483 (1964). There was nothing in the record to indicate that the police had any basis whatsoever to believe that the night clerk had been authorized by the defendant to permit the police to search his room. It is true that a person who rents a motel room undoubtedly gives "implied or express permission" to maids, janitors, *etc.*, to perform their duties. However, the night clerk and the police were not here performing those duties. The court concluded by saying that a guest in a hotel room is entitled to constitutional protection against unreasonable searches and seizures.

Stoner issues still arise. Consider this Illinois case. The cocaine in the case was discovered by the maid when she opened a suitcase she thought had been left behind by the one whom she thought was a former occupant. She told her boss who in turn called the police. The hotel manager opened the room also thinking the defendant had abandoned the room. The defendant returned but denied ownership of the suitcase. The police opened the bag. Focusing only on the police entry, the court said the police could not take advantage of the manager's good faith belief in his right to enter. Then they said since the police took the bag from the defendant Vought and not from the maid or manager, the case of **U.S. v. Jacobson** and footnote 17 of that opinion applied and this case was thus distinguishable from the prime facts of **Jacobson**. **People v. Vought**, 528 N.E. 2d 1095 (Ill. App. Ct. 1988); accord on similar facts **Farmer v. State**, 759 P. 2d 1031 (Okla. Ct. Crim. App. 1988).

Just as a hotel guest gives only a limited consent to repair and clean a room, renters and owners often give limited consents to repair or inspect devices within the home or apartment. Such was the case in **Com. v. Gutierrez**, 2000 WL 380539 (Pa. Super). The defendant leased a unit in an apartment building which had a contract with a fire alarm company to inspect, repair etc. the alarm system. To this the defendant had to accede. The alarm company had a set of master keys to access the apartments. The defendant's apartment alarm gave a "trouble signal call" (not a fire) and the inspector entered, opened the alarm box, saw a shoestring, pulled the shoestring and got a bag of white powder. The agent went to the police, relayed his information to them and took the police into the apartment and the powder tested positive as cocaine. Other items were seized relevant to drug dealing. The court found, as it had to, that the company's consent was limited to very specific functions and taking police into an apartment to search and seize (where no life was in danger) was not within the scope of the prior consent of the tenant. If the alarm company employee had removed the powder from the apartment and had given it to the police then the private action doctrine would have caused a different result and the evidence would have been admissible.

If a hotel room is secure against unreasonable searches and seizures, is a dormitory room also given that protection? In **Piazzola v. Watkins**, 442 F. 2d 284 (C.A. 5th 1971) a student's room was searched by police under a university regulation reserving the right to inspect rooms. The court said that this regulation cannot be construed or applied so as to give consent to a search for evidence for the primary purpose of criminal prosecution. The university had no authority to consent to or join in a police search for evidence of a crime. This ruling comports with the landlord-tenant rules as set out in **Chapman v. United States**, 365 U.S. 610 (1961). A landlord has no right to consent to a search of the tenant's premises. This would not be true, however, for the public areas of the rental complex where there is common usage.

When a landlord rents or leases property to a person the landlord gives up the right of possession and retains only a reasonable right of inspection that is usually regulated by statute as to time and frequency of such inspections. The inspection right does not give rise to a general criminal investigation search right and **Chapman** so holds. However, when the lease or rental period is up the possession right is said to return to the landlord. If the tenant unlawfully holds over does the tenant retain an expectation of privacy or can the landlord treat the tenant like a trespasser thus allowing police to enter and make a search? The answer is not easy because of the protection given tenants under the landlord-tenant statutes concerning eviction, and the fact that the landlord could accept a rental payment thereby making the tenant a tenant-at-will. In such a case the police are well advised to treat the case as one of possession in the tenant and to take whatever information the landlord has gathered independent of police influence (avoiding the state action doctrine) and to test it before a magistrate by seeking a warrant.

In **State v. Chuey**, 2000 WL 487738 (Ohio App. 9) (unpub. op.). Mr. Chuey was a boarder in Mrs. Yergin's home and paid $250 a month for a private room and board. He was free to use the common area. He, of course, stored his personal belongings in his room. Mrs. Yergin consented to a search of her home because her son, subject to home arrest, tested positive for cocaine on a random drug screen. She did tell police about her two boarders. All persons present, including Chuey, were frisked and then seated in the living room. Chuey could not see the officers enter his room. Thus, he made no objection to this entry. But he learned of it when they asked for a key to his safe. He said it was not locked and opened it. Cocaine, by dog sniff, was found. Chuey was arrested. The police, once they knew of the boarders, should have conducted the required **Illinois v. Rodriguez**, 497 U.S. 177 (1990) common authority inquiry. The burden was not on the landlady nor on Chuey. The canine sniff was non-consensual. The safe opening was tainted by the illegal entry.

Most courts have made clear that the failure of a tenant to make rental payments in and of itself does not give the landlord possession, but at most only a right to seek possession or at least to bring an action for breach of contract. As was pointed out in **People v. Kramer**, 562 N.E. 2d 654 (Ill. App. 2 Dist. 1990), the lease is still in force thus the possession and right to consent still lies with the tenant. The Illinois Court correctly pointed out that **Chapman** did not address this issue. They also noted the fact that a landlord has a right to bring eviction or other actions is not the same as having the possessory power to consent. Citing **Chapman** as controlling and **Rodriguez** as not applicable, an Illinois appellate court held that a landlord could not consent to the search of a tenant's apartment just because the tenant was three months behind in rent. The fact that a landlord has a right to an action for distraint or eviction does not give the landlord the right to consent to a search. **People v. Kramer**, 562 N.E. 2d 654 (Ill. App. 2 Dist. 1990) also held that **Rodriguez** (*infra*) only covered mutual use cases and not those based on landlord-tenant property interests. As a footnote to this case, it is sad that the police could have taken the landlord's information concerning the marijuana and could have secured a warrant that would have led to the conviction of this defendant.

A work-release prisoner was living at the YMCA. Earlier in the day in question, the prisoner's counselor gave permission to search the prisoner's room. The police did not seize the credit card then but waited until a second search. The court held that whether the counselor could give permission or not was not at issue. It held that consents to searches are not continuing consents. The failure to meet the issue of who can give consent is not critical if it is assumed that as a prisoner certain rights are withheld until release. A work release program still involves incarceration. Administrative searches of inmates have been upheld. **People v. Jackson**, 373 N.E. 2d 729 (Ill. App. Ct. 1978). But was this an administrative prison related search? Or was it a search for general criminality? It did not matter to this court. However, not all courts would agree with this rationale. The Pennsylvania Superior Court has held that a work release prisoner did have a reasonable expectation of privacy in a work site locker. They noted that the search did not take place on prison property. The court did say, however, that it may make a difference if the search of lockers, *etc.*, were part of the conditions for work release. Then, they indicated, the prisoner would have had notice of such an intrusion. **Commonwealth v. Gabrielle**, 409 A. 2d 1173 (Pa. Super. Ct. 1979), and would have been given the option of accepting the conditions or staying in prison.

Mississippi was faced with a third-party consent case in **Barton v. State**, 165 Miss. 355, 143 So. 861 (1932). The house was rented by a woman and a man named Carter. Police asked if they could come in. She did not object, but invited them in. The defendant was in the house. When asked about him, the woman said he was a visitor. Defendant heard this and acquiesced in this statement. The court said even if he had any right or title to the premises, which he did not have, he heard it, acquiesced in it, therefore, he cannot be heard to complain. (Too much should not be read into this statement!) In another case the police knew the defendant was in charge of the hotel room to which they gained access. When they were let in by his female companion, the defendant came out of the bathroom and said nothing. The court said his silence was not consent. Failing proof of the woman's shared control, the evidence was illegally seized. **Robinson v. State**, 578 P. 2d 141 (Alaska 1978). Cases such as this would require some direction by the U.S. Supreme Court. That direction would ultimately come in the **Illinois v. Rodriguez** decision discussed at the end of this section. But obviously if the defendant who has standing objects to the search a different result would be reached. A direct objection would suffice, of course. The problem is many trial courts, once a consent is found, often stop the inquiry and admit the evidence. Many of the cases involve coequals. What of the inferior giving a consent in the presence of the superior? Washington had such a case. Here the police knew that the defendant was the real party with ultimate control. He was on the premises and the police handcuffed him. They bypassed him and received permission from an underling with sufficient control to consent. The trial judge failed to gather evidence on whether the defendant by words or conduct objected to the search. The case was remanded. They therefore joined the Ninth Circuit in this type of analysis. **State v. Leach**, 761 P. 2d 83 (Wash. Ct. App. 1988) citing **U.S. v. Impink**, 728 F. 2d 1228 (C.A. 9th 1988).

Such cases as these assume that failure to object is a duty and that somehow one vote is all that is needed. This is not an "unknown unsuspected person with standing being present" type of situation. Such cases do away with ability of the defendant to stand silent and the rule that a silent defendant is always thought to object to an unlawful search. See **People v. Cosme** (*infra)*. Delaware addressed the issue and found that despite the fact that the owner of the car was also present the driver's consent to search was valid. The consent was given out in the presence of the owner. The owner remained in the car and the driver gave the consent while seated in the patrol car. The owner's consent was not sought and the owner did not object to the search. Using the "control-of-the-automobile" test and **U.S. v. Matlock**, the court found sufficient authority in the driver to consent. It then emphasized the fact that the owner impliedly consented by failing to object. **Matlock,** of course, involved an absent person with equal or greater authority. The court addressed this by saying, "While the validity of a third party consent is less certain when one with a superior privacy interest is present, the presence of such a person is not wholly determinative of whether or not the consent search was valid." **Ledda v. State**, 564 A. 2d 1125 (Del.

Sup. Ct. 1989). Why is this not mere acquiescence? Does the assumption of the risk rule of **Frazier v. Cupp** negate both objection and "mere acquiescence?"

The Washington Supreme Court could have faced the issue of acquiescence head on. They felt that without the consent of those with equal or greater authority such third party consent could not be upheld. Unfortunately they did not address acquiescence. Rather they focused on strictly construing **Matlock** saying it only applies to absent, **non-consenting** persons. **State v. Leach**, 782 P. 2d 1035 (Wash. Sup. Ct. 1989). In any event they reversed the earlier **Leach** decision of the Court of Appeals.

As indicated there remains some question whether a consent search is binding on other co-occupants who have expressly denied such consent. In a unanimous decision the New York Court of Appeals, using an "assumption of the risk" theory, held that an individual who has unrestricted access to control over shared premises is vested in his own right with power to consent to a search even over the objections of others. **People v. Cosme**, 507 N.E. 2d 1096 (N.Y. 1979). It did make one reservation on the scope of this rule where the court said, "We express no opinion as to the outcome in cases where several individuals share common authority over the premises as a whole, but one of their number has carved out a specific area for his exclusive use...." It also declined at this point to apply the rule where the consent is given by one who enjoys less than unrestricted access to and control over the searched premises.

The concept that shared control allows others to consent to a search evidently does not necessarily require constant or daily shared use. Consider the case of the renowned professor who allowed another faculty member and graduate students to have access to his laboratory and equipment therein located. The defendant-professor provided keys. The facilities were not often used by the invitees. During the period of time between 1973 and late 1979, a lab assistant to the defendant became suspicious that illegal drugs were being synthesized. This was reported to the fellow faculty member who was permitted to use the lab. This faculty member required the lab assistant to keep a diary and began his own investigation. Their findings were reported to the government. At the request of the government, the lab assistant and the fellow faculty member agreed to assist in a search of the lab. The search took place. The necessary condemning evidence was found which led to the ultimate conviction of the defendant. The Second Circuit held that consent to search by one with access to the area searched and with either: (1) common authority over the place; or (2) a substantial interest in it; or (3) permission to exercise that access, express or implied, alone validate the search. The government may scrutinize even the most private enclosure if the third party has the authority to permit the intrusion. Granting permission to use enclosed areas forfeits any reasonable expectation of privacy. **U.S. v. Buettner-Janush**, 649 F. 2d 759 (C.A. 2d 1981).

B.   Apparent Authority To Give Consent

When consent is given by a third person, that third person must have the right to give the consent. What happens when a person with apparent authority to consent turns out later, when all "cools," not to have such authority? This brings to light the issue whether police have the right to reasonably rely on the facts and circumstances as they appeared to them at the time.

Such was the issue in **People v. Adams**, 422 N.E. 2d 537 (N.Y. 1981). An officer saw the defendant with a gun pressed to a woman's head. As the officer approached, the woman was released but gunfire between the officer and the defendant was exchanged before the defendant made good his escape. A woman who identified herself as the defendant's girlfriend told police where the defendant lived and that guns were kept at the nearby apartment. Upon arrival at the apartment she opened the door with a key and led the police straight to the arms-filled closet. The guns were seized. After they left the apartment building, the girlfriend informed the police that she did not live in the apartment. Did the police act reasonably? The court indicated that reasonableness was the key, based upon an objective view of the circumstances and not merely the subjective good faith of the searching officers. Ordinarily, the police should make an inquiry to determine whether the consenting person possesses the proper authority. The outcome is analogous to the public safety exception for **Miranda** purposes announced in **New York v. Quarles**. Here the defendant posed an immediate threat by his wild firing of shots and escaping into the same nearby area. Time was of the essence. The tension and drama of the moment brought to bear the reasonable man test of **Brinegar v. United States**, 338 U.S. 160 (1948).

Would the Supreme Court limit apparent authority cases to exigent circumstances, or would they adopt a "good faith" reliance approach in **Illinois v. Rodriguez**, 497 U.S. 177 (1990). A woman complained to police that she had been "beaten up" in what she termed "our" apartment. She had a key and took the officers to the apartment where the warrantless activity took place. Drugs were found and the defendant was arrested. As it was later discovered the woman no longer lived in the apartment. The key to the **Rodriguez** opinion turned on the definition of reasonableness. Did the police have any basis whatsoever to believe that the consenter had authority to permit the entry, became the test. For this point the Court cited **Stoner**. The invitation nor the possession of the key justified the police entry. A totality test must be applied and the police must have probable cause to believe there is authority in the consenter to consent. The trial judge must make this "totality" finding. Factually, the Court emphasized the facts that she told police she had the key, called it "our apartment" several times, and talked about her furniture and clothes that were there, but she never clearly indicated that she currently lived there. The case was remanded to have a "totality" hearing. Clearly the Court has continued to extend their "good faith reliance" posture as opposed to a "good faith motive" posture.

In one early decision that first interpreted **Rodriguez**, the court found that the defendant lived with his mother. He was suspected of being involved in a theft. Police went to the mother's home and she told them he was not there at the time. She admitted that the son (defendant) did live in her house. The police asked the mother if defendant paid rent and she responded by saying that he "is unemployed." Taking that as a no, police then sought and received a consent to search his room. Money was found in a jacket pocket that was hanging in a closed but unlocked closet. At trial the mother said the son paid rent when he was working and the court found a landlord-tenant relationship. However, using **Illinois v. Rodriguez**, the court found that the police reasonably relied on the consent given by the mother. The only troubling point is that it is not clear that the police can make such an assumption (non-tenancy) under **Rodriguez**, because that case would at least require them to ask whether her response meant "no, he does not pay rent." **U.S. v. Whitfield**, 747 F. Supp. 807 (D. D.C. 1990).

In Montana, the consenter was the grandfather of the defendant. The grandson was living in an apartment owned by his grandfather in a building next door to the grandfather's residence. The grandfather did not have a key so the grandfather and the deputy had to use a shop stairway entrance. Some drug paraphernalia was found. The trial judge found common authority. The Montana Supreme Court disagreed and held there was no proof of common authority. Even though there was no rental agreement, this did not mean there was common authority. **State v. McLess**, 994 P. 2d 683 (Mont. 2000).

In **Krise v. State**, 2001 WL 493444 (Ind.), the defendant's house-mate lacked authority to consent to a warrantless search of the defendant's purse found in the house-mate's bathroom. No evidence of mutual use was shown and no apparent authority was shown. Gaining access by a lawful consent is not enough. That consent would not extend to "personal closed containers" like a purse. There was no proof of mutual use of the purse, nor joint access, nor apparent authority.

Indiana faced a **Rodriguez** apparent authority problem in **State v. Foreman**, 1996 WL 116206 (Ind.). A gambling operation was uncovered after a consent was given by a person who said he was the bingo center operator and leaseholder of the premises. The voluntariness of the consent was not an issue. The evidence was suppressed because the consenter had leased the room to the defendant Foreman; a fact not known until after the search. The "fly in the ointment" in this case was that the police did not go far enough to test the consenter's common authority. Rather than asking for a key to unlock the door, the police tore the door off its hinges. This inconsistent behavior, as the court called it, was irreconcilable and inconsistent with the reasonable reliance required by **Rodriguez**. The consent was found to be invalid.

To merely acquiesce to a search when consent is sought, that is to stand silent, fail to object or fail to physically resist, rather than to just say no, implicates more than the Fourth Amendment right to insist upon a warrant. It also implicates the Fifth Amendment right to remain silent which exists separate and apart from custodial interrogations. Clearly when the officer asks the defendant for permission to search, the Constitution demands no duty to even respond to such a request. Just as clear is the fact that the absent co-possessor, user or owner runs the risk that a present co-possessor,-user or-owner will consent to a search. In this type of case the issue of acquiescence is not applicable. This, of course, the "heart" of **Bumper**.

However, where all those with authority are present and one or some consent and one or some stand silent, is it fair to say that a duty exists to speak or resist? Can a person be said to have waived his or her standing or expectation of privacy by exercising Fifth Amendment rights by refusing to acknowledge the request? Where is it written that "assumption of the risk" outweighs the right to remain silent? The decisions often fail to recognize this. Or if they recognize it, they still fail to rule that though the evidence is admissible against the consenter, it is not admissible against the acquiescer. On the contrary they rule it admissible under assumption of the risk. This latter position may make some sense when the person with the greater authority consents (though not much when postured against a fundamental right) in the presence of the person with the lesser interest. It makes no sense when the person with equal or lesser authority consents in the presence of the greater authority. All of this assumes, however, that the police know of the shared control and know of the rankings of authority. In some cases it may be known or obvious. In most cases it will not be known. Should the rule be that when it is obvious that the police do not know or could not be reasonably expected to know of the shared control or who outranks whom that an exception to the right to remain silent should be carved out?

Factually, in **Illinois v. Rodriguez**, 497 U.S. 177 (1990), the defendant was present but asleep when the search was conducted under the "good faith" consent. So Rodriguez was never even given the opportunity to "merely acquiesce." The focus of the case was on the authority to consent issue and not on the "presence of" or ranking of others with authority. The case does say that police have to determine authority but it does not specifically address ranking or presence and "mere acquiescence."

Clearly **Rodriguez** is a Fourth Amendment case and not a Fifth Amendment case. But consider this language from the opinion: "But as we have discussed, what is at issue when a claim of apparent consent is raised is not whether the right to be free of searches has been waived, but whether the right to be free of unreasonable searches has been violated. Even if one does not think the **Stoner** opinion had this subtlety in mind, the supposed clarity of its foregoing statement is immediately compromised...." Is this language saying to trial courts not to make an acquiescence analysis? Perhaps not, but it does not settle the issue. Sooner or later the Court must give more than implied direction.

The "flip" side of the problem involves a consent given by an absent person with authority. In one California case the co-tenant of a dwelling consented to a search of the dwelling. When the police arrived at the dwelling the present co-tenant neither consented nor objected. Reserving the objection issue for a later time, the court held the search good due to the absence of objection. **People v. Veiga**, 262 Cal. Rep. 919 (Cal. Dist. Ct. App. 1989). Again the mere acquiescence issue was resolved against the non-objector.

In **Gordon v. State**, 160 So. 2d 73 (Miss. 1974) the question was whether the stepson, defendant, could complain about search of the stepfather's house when the stepfather gave permission to the officers to enter. The stepfather came out of the house as the officers approached. He "beckoned" them to come up to the house. He told the officers that Gordon was in the house and he wanted them to go in and get Gordon. There were no facts indicating if Gordon regularly lived there or whether he shared in the payments. Since the owner of the place, the court ruled, invited the officers to come in, no search warrant was necessary. It was not indicated where the "fruits" were found. This case presents another unanswered problem. Is permission to enter for the purpose of arrest permission to search, or are officers limited to incidental search and the immediate surroundings rule? The answer to this will be influenced by a standing argument plus a plain view analysis. See **Rakas v. Illinois** as discussed in the Standing to Object materials in Chapter One. The "regularly lived there" language is now suspect due to the standing case of **Minnesota v. Olson** also discussed in Chapter One.

One of the points made by **Minnesota v. Olson** was that an overnight guest could lose privacy rights due to the consent to enter given by the owner-occupant or full-time tenant of rented or leased premises. The Supreme Court of Delaware agrees.

In its case a tenant consented to a search over the silent objection of the overnight guest. Her consent was in writing and was freely and voluntarily given so even though the defendant had overnight standing he could not complain about the validity of the consent. However, this court does say there is a duty upon one who has equal privacy rights, when present, to object to such a search. They assumed, *arguendo*, that the silent defendant had equal authority at most. The innuendo of the case is that someone with lesser authority, of course, cannot escape the penalty of the consent of one with greater authority. They did not have to address this issue since the defendant stood silent in the face of this consent. **Scott v. State**, 672 A. 2d 550 (Del. 1996). Iowa does rank greater and lesser privacy rights. In their case the owner consented and the "part-time occupant" tried to revoke that consent. Iowa says that a person with lesser rights cannot overrule the voluntary consent of the one with greater rights. **State v. Cadotte**, 542 N.W. 2d 834 (Iowa 1996).

North Dakota's case provides a "but for" rule. The consenter in this case was a wife who abandoned the home searched because of continuing abuse by the husband-defendant. Such a spouse does not lose privacy rights when leaving the premises under such circumstances. **State v. Huffman**, 542 N.W. 2d 718 (N. D. 1996). This is a common sense approach.

C.   Consents By and Against Children

Perhaps the most perplexing problem of the consent area is whether children may consent to the search of their parents' or guardians' home. Second, since children have the rights under the Constitution guaranteed to adults (save the jury trial right), can children successfully challenge consents given by their parents of guardians? These issues are the subject of this section.

In one case the issue was whether a 15-year-old son could consent to the search of his father's home. **May v. State**, 199 So. 635 (Miss. 1967). The 15-year-old son went with the officer to the defendant's home and unlocked the front door. The scene was examined. The son found the pistol being sought under the mattress and showed it to the officers. The court ruled that a son could not waive the rights of the father to object to an illegal entry and search of this home. The court did not answer, because it did not have to, the question regarding the action of an adult son who lives with the father. The **Matlock** decision should be a guide in this area. The question always turns on the proof of shared control and, of course, "good faith reliance" as announced in **Rodriguez**, (*infra*). But much has happened since 1967 which throws doubt on this case. Indeed **Gault** and **Winship** had not yet seen the light of day.

States continue to wrestle with the child-authorized entry questions and particularly so when the child is between eleven years and the mid-teens. Alaska had a situation where the police trailed a man who left the scene of an auto accident in violation of law. The trail led to the defendant's house. After the police knocked on the door, they were greeted by the defendant's eleven to fourteen year old son. The police told the boy they wanted to speak to his father concerning a minor traffic accident which had just occurred. The boy admitted the police and sent them into the living room where defendant sat apparently intoxicated. Upon this the defendant was arrested for appropriate driving while under the influence statutes for which the defendant was convicted. Should the evidence of his intoxicated condition be suppressed upon the theory that the entry was not valid since consent was given by a resident minor? The court noted that as long as the state can show, by clear and convincing evidence, that a valid, unequivocal, voluntary, specific and intelligent consent was given then the consent will stand. In this case the boy was old enough to be expected to exercise at least minimal discretion, the court held. Consent was given for the specific purpose of finding the father in an area of the house to which the child would ordinarily have free and open access. Taking the totality of the circumstances into account, this was a good consent. **Doyle v. Alaska**, 633 P. 2d 306 (C.A. 9th 1981).

A twelve-year-old boy's consent to the search of his mother's private bathroom was invalidated in **Reynolds v. State**, 781 S.W. 2d 351 (Tex. Ct. App. 1989). The court said nothing is more private than one's private bathroom but they also muddied the issue by stating that a "child of twelve is generally incapable of waiving his own rights. He is even less fit to surrender those of his mother."

One court held that where a parent routinely leaves 12-and 14-year old sons alone and in control of a house and where the marijuana is left about the house in great quantities that its "odor pervaded the house," those two boys could consent not only to the public areas but also can consent to the search of the parent's bedroom. The Sixth Circuit so held and said the parent "assumed that risk." **U.S. v. Clutter**, 914 F. 2d 775 (C.A. 6th 1990). As can be seen there is definite conflict among the courts on this issue.

Another question that comes up is whether the parents can consent to the search of the child's room, particularly when that child is an adult. The Minnesota court met this question head-on in **State v. Schotl**, 182 N.W. 2d 878 (Minn. 1971). The 22-year-old made a payment to his mother to let him live there. This payment did not cover any particular length of time. Nowhere did it appear that the son had an exclusive right to possession of the room or that he used it regularly. He shared it with his brothers and sisters. This court follows the rule that a parent in control of premises in which the child resides may consent to a search thereof even though it may produce incriminating evidence.

One case proves it does not pay to live with one's parents after marriage. Two officers went to defendant's home where he lived with his mother. The police asked the mother for permission to search his room. Present at the request was the defendant's wife who stood silently. The Louisiana court said absent unusual circumstances, a parent has at least common authority over the residence. The son did not pay rent and nothing changed from the time before his marriage regarding everyone's relationship to all areas of the house. That his mother would consent to search was a risk the defendant assumed by not securing an expectation of privacy. Besides, the court said, she acted as if she believed she had such authority. **State v. Packard**, 389 So. 2d 56 (La. 1980).

California does not fully follow that rule, however. Police sought marijuana that they believed a 17-year-old boy had. The police went to the boy's home where he lived with his parents. The father consented to the search of a locked toolbox owned by the boy. The consent came over the boy's objection. The California Supreme Court held this search illegal. **In re Scott K.**, 595 P. 2d 105 (Cal. 1979). The court reasoned that since minors are persons they must have search and seizure rights. Enforcement of search and seizure rights helps ensure that the fact-finding process meets due process standards. They noted that New Jersey, New York, Ohio, Pennsylvania and Texas extend such rights to children. It would be incongruous, it said, to conclude that parents for any reason could summarily waive children's rights. Looking at the third party consent area, the court was willing to concede the father's control over the house as a valid consent to get to the room. However, the toolbox was not shown to be in the shared control of the father and son. Since children can own property, the search here was found to be unreasonable.

The courts of the U.S. are still struggling to find the right answers to the parental consent to search a child's room and each seems to find a different way of looking at the problem. In **State v. Summers**, 764 P. 2d 250 (Wash. Ct. App. 1988) the court said a parent normally has authority over all the rooms of the house regardless of the pattern of actual entry into a particular room. Even if a child has exercised exclusive control over the room, they say that is not dispositive. Instead, the court said to look at the broader relationship between the parent and the child. Dependency or emancipation can alter the outcome. The emancipated child has greater rights, much like that of a tenant, if he pays rent and otherwise manifests independence. Each case stands on its own, it concluded. Courts are less concerned with parental consents and in fact are very concerned with children's consents. This does make sense.

Another case discussing the factors to consider when assessing a person's ability to consent see **U.S. v. Czeck**, 1997 WL 33489 (C.A. 8th Minn.). They say age, sobriety and experience with the justice system are key factors along with the atmosphere of the place where the consent was given. Would this court recognize a child's right to consent to the public areas of the parent's home? The case raises some doubts.

Florida's latest parental consent case adds yet another twist. The parent who gave the consent, the father, did not live in the home occupied by the son and his mother, former wife of the consenter. The defense argued that the father could not consent because he was not a resident. However, the father owned the house. Two stolen guns were found in the teenager's room. The father had a key. For the court, parental authority and ownership combined for enough to uphold the consent, **State v. S.B.**, 758 So. 2d 1253 (Fla. App. 4th 2000).

When an adult child lives in a parent's home the chances are that the adult child pays rent and exercises some significant control over the private room used for sleeping (assuming the rest of the home is "common area" territory). But do police have to ask about the rent issue? What would indicate a carving-out of superior privacy? Can the police assume apparent common authority when no special locks appear on the door of the adult child's room? An Illinois court held that, absent privacy locks on the door, police do not have to ask about rent and can presume common authority as in **Matlock** plus **Rodriguez** and its "apparent authority" rule. **People v. Brooks**, 660 N.E. 2d 270 (Ill. App. 1996). See also **Colbert v. Com.**, 2001 WL 174809 (Ky.) where the Kentucky Court fully agrees with this reasoning.

D. Electronics and Consents

One final consent issue has to be addressed concerning the acquisition of information. Can one party consent to "interception" by some electronic form that can be used against the other participant? Yes, Title III of The Electronic Surveillance Act permits consent to being overheard. The consent must meet all voluntary and knowing standards. **U.S. v. Koloqziej**, 706 F. 2d 590 (C.A. 5th 1983); **U.S. v. Yonn**, 702 F. 2d 1341 (C.A. 11th 1983); and must not be done for a criminal or tortuous purpose (on the part of the consenter and, of course, by implication, the police). **U.S. v. Vest**, 813 F. 2d 477 (C.A. 1st 1987); and **U.S. v. Underhill**, 813 F. 2d 105 (C.A. 6th 1987). Finally, the Second Circuit held that where a sign tells a prisoner that conversations are monitored and the defendant has signed a form noting this, the prisoner had consented to the taping. **U.S. v. Willoughby**, 860 F. 2d 15 (C.A. 2d 1988).

The only strange cases in the consent area are represented by **U.S. v. Passarella**, 788 F. 2d 372 (C.A. 6th 1986) and **U.S. v. Ordonez**, 722 F. 2d 530 (C.A. 9th 1983). While lawfully executing search warrants, the phone rings and the officers answer and, without identifying themselves, carry on defendant-incriminating conversations. Both courts held since the officers were each a party to the conversations Title III consent applied. In the Ninth Circuit case the owner of the apartment did not want the police to answer the phone. It did not matter. See also **U.S. v. Sangineto-Miranda**, 859 F. 2d 1501 (C.A. 6th 1988).

Not all states agree with the foregoing cases in all respects. Consider, for example, **Com. v. Fini,** 531 N.E. 2d 570 (Mass. 1988). The Massachusetts Court noted that the U.S. Constitution was not violated by such practices through **U.S. v. White**, 401 U.S. 745 (1971) but found that such surveillance requires permission of both parties (where a warrant was not used) under the Massachusetts Constitution. Thus, when the state wants to use the tapes they are inadmissible for any purpose. Of course, the consenter could testify directly. Such a decision requires the informant-consenter to come forward and give live testimony at the trial since the court focused only on the inanimate product of the illegal activity.

IV. Consent and Its Relationship to Other Doctrinal Areas

Since the advent of **Miranda**, where the defendant must be told of his right to remain silent, *etc.*, defense counsel have been urging that where consent is involved in a search, the state should be required to prove that defendants know of the right to refuse consent. How has the argument fared? Consider the case of **Schneckloth v. Bustamonte**, 412 U.S. 218 (1973). While knowledge of the right to consent is one factor to be taken into account, the government need not establish such knowledge as the *sine qua non* of an effective consent. It is only by analyzing all the circumstances of an individual consent that it can be ascertained whether in fact it was voluntary or coerced. The traditional definition of voluntariness has always taken into account evidence of minimal schooling, low intelligence, the lack of any effective warnings to a person of his rights, and the voluntariness of any statement taken under those conditions have to be carefully scrutinized to determine whether it was in fact voluntarily given. Courts have held that when a subject of a search is in custody and the state attempts to justify a search on consent, the Constitution requires that the state demonstrate that the consent was voluntarily given and not the result of duress or coercion, express or implied. Voluntariness is a question of fact to be determined from all of the circumstances. While the subject's knowledge of a right to refuse is a factor to be taken into account, the prosecution is not required to demonstrate such knowledge as a prerequisite to establishing a voluntary consent. Unfortunately, the court gave no direction for consent obtained while in custody. Perhaps the **Miranda** decision can give guidance. See also **U.S. v. Allison**, 619 F. 2d 1254 (C.A. 8th 1980) (where no warnings were given, a subpoena for records was presented, and the defendant said: "Fine. We don't have anything to hide.") The consent was upheld. Another attempt to require "**Miranda**"-like warnings in the consent search area was rejected by a California court on the authority of **Schneckloth v. Bustamonte. People v. Phillips**, 168 Cal. Rep. 863 (Cal. Dist. Ct. App. 1980). South Carolina has accepted **Schneckloth** by its decision in **State v. Forrester**, 2001 WL 114662 (So.Car.). The court saw no reason to hold that its constitution granted its people more rights than the U.S. Constitution.

States have attempted to create protection for juveniles who are lawfully in custody and are asked to give consent to a search of their house and their effects. Colorado, for instance, takes an "interested adult" approach to such custodial consents. However, Colorado will only apply such a statute narrowly to custodial consents. By rejecting the *per se* approach the court did say that the presence or absence of an adult is but one of the things to be considered in a "totality" analysis. **In re S.J.**, 778 P. 2d 1384 (Colo. 1989).

Can the police use a consent to search obtained after the defendant has requested counsel? New York says no, that such a consent is "unavailing." Twice after arrest the defendant made it clear that he would not make a statement until he consulted with his attorney. Further questioning was stopped but he was asked whether he would let police look around. Defendant was told he did not have to consent. He was offered a consent search form which he signed. In rejecting the validity of this consent, the court said that a request for an attorney was no different for obtaining a consent to search or getting a further statement. It went on, saying, "The defendant's rights are no less at stake and the advice of counsel no less important if the police seek a relinquishment of defendant's constitutional right...." The court found no "scrupulous honoring" of his request for counsel. **People v. Johnson**, 399 N.E. 2d 936 (N.Y. 1979). This rule is the strictest rule applied today.

The New York decision makes a lot of sense especially when the defendant requests a lawyer before a consent is given. The Supreme Court has since the beginning of the **Miranda** era called the requests for counsel a "cry for help" meaning that the defendant is saying he in incapable of dealing with the police by himself. In the Sixth Amendment context the court also would not permit any post-invocation waiver of counsel unless a lawyer is present or unless the defendant initiated the interrogation or discussion of the crime.

But courts have and should be careful not to confuse the confession-**Miranda** type cases with consent search issues when it comes to the mere attachment of the right to counsel under the Sixth Amendment. The merely attached but not invoked right to counsel is subject to waiver. Therefore the police should be able to obtain a voluntary and knowing consent after a mere attachment of the right to counsel under the Sixth Amendment. In one Second Circuit case the police obtained a consent to search even though the police knew the defendant had been indicted and his Sixth Amendment rights had attached. The police failed to inform the defendant of the indictment. The court held that the Sixth Amendment simply does not apply when the police request a consent to search. Under these facts the holding is totally consistent with **Schneckloth** (*supra*). **U.S. v. Kon Yu-Leung**, 910 F. 2d 33 (C.A. 2d 1990).

The Court appears to have answered the custody-consent problem in **United States v. Watson**, 423 U.S. 411 (1976). There was no overt act or threat of force against Watson proved or claimed. No promises or other forms of subtle coercion were used. He was arrested and in custody. His consent was given while on a public street; not at the police station. Custody alone is not of itself enough to demonstrate coercion. There was no indication that he was a newcomer to the law, mentally deficient or otherwise unable to consent freely. He was given the **Miranda** warning and told that anything found in the car could be used against him. He persisted in his consent. The Court said to hold that illegal coercion is made out from the fact of arrest and the failure to inform the arrestee that he could withhold consent would not be consistent with **Schneckloth** and would distort the voluntariness standard in that case.

In **Brown v. State**, 281 So. 2d 924 (Miss. 1973), the defendant was told why the police wanted to check the number on the rear axle and he voluntarily consented. The defendant had been given his **Miranda** warnings. Defendant paid his fine and then agreed to allow the inspection. He followed the police to the garage. It was found to be a stolen car. The court ruled that where no force or intimidation is brought to bear on a defendant, and after the original custody ends, the voluntary consent to an inspection for an ID number is legitimate.

The investigative stop cases decided by the Supreme Court, and in particular **Florida v. Royer**, 460 U.S. 491 (1983), point out that the consent cannot be the "fruits of the poisonous tree." Royer's stop was without probable cause and the police kept

Royer's ticket and other property. The Court found an illegal seizure and, therefore, his consent to search his luggage was invalid.

The drug problem has accelerated the consent search cases. In a number of cases police are boarding buses and at random are requesting the right to search luggage. Such was the procedure in **State v. Avery**, 531 So. 2d 182 (Fla. Dist. Ct. App. 1988). The plain- clothed police boarded the bus and displayed their badges. Mr. Avery was one of those foolish enough to say yes both to drugs and to the search. They asked him because he looked nervous and pushed his tote bag under his seat with his feet. Cocaine was found. Was this a coerced consent? Merely approaching a person and asking questions is not violative of the Fourth Amendment. This encounter was not so intimidating that a reasonable person would feel he was not free to leave or say no. The police are allowed on buses. The court said this demonstrated lawful presence. So, there was no misconduct or improper communications by the officers. In fact these officers told Avery that he could refuse. The short concurring opinion said that there might be a difference between feeling free to leave a bus terminal as opposed to leaving a bus seat. Could there be?

The **Avery** court relied heavily on **I.N.S. v. Delgado**, 466 U.S. 210 (1984). With the employer's permission the Immigration Service set up at exits and roamed the premises of the factory. Questions about citizenship were asked of the employees. People were free to work and walk around the factory. The Court held this was not a seizure of the work force. Citing **Royer,** the Court, without specifically addressing the consent issue approved encounters where workers were asked to produce "papers" and they produced them. North Carolina came to the same conclusion in their bus case. See **State v. Christie**, 385 S.E. 2d 181 (N.Car. Ct. App. 1989), relying on **Avery**.

However, the Florida Supreme Court declared the bus consents unconstitutional in **Bostick v. State**, 554 So. 2d 1153 (Fla. 1989) The blocking of the aisle was found to be very intimidating and tantamount to a seizure. The court thus had to reverse **Avery**. **Avery v. State**, 555 So. 2d 351 (Fla. 1989). The U.S. Supreme Court decided to address the bus consent issue by accepting **Bostick** for decision.

Before **Bostick** was decided, the D.C. Circuit took a novel approach to the bus consent search cases. They said that by taking the bus, the defendant chose the cramped quarters and that cannot be attributed to the police. They also discounted the "missed bus" dilemma in that as long as a person feels free to break off the encounter by leaving the bus, that and that alone is determinative. This, by the way, does not necessarily follow from the **Place** and **Royer** cases which this court did not cite. **U.S. v. Lewis**, 921 F. 2d 1294 (C.A.D.C. 1990).

Bostick was decided by the U.S. Supreme Court in June of 1991. The Court found that no seizure had taken place as was discussed in Chapter 1. What they did not decide, however, was "whether Bostick chose to permit the search of his luggage." Although a seizure did not take place the Court said, "The cramped confines of a bus is one relevant factor that should be considered in evaluating whether a passenger's consent is voluntary." But they also said this one factor is not dispositive and thereby reemphasized the totality approach that must be taken and the focus on the police conduct.

To follow or not to follow **Bostick** has thus become the question. For example, a New York court went out of its way factually to announce they would follow **Bostick**. The court said, "There was no detention of the juvenile and not even a hint of harassment or intimidation. The decision to hand over the bag containing the contraband was not the result of coercion." This court did have independent valid grounds to find a seizure (suspected truancy and runaway and a duty placed on the officer by statute) but the opinion was used to announce its **Bostick** position. **In re Gissette Angela P.**, 577 N.Y.S. 2d 774 (N.Y. Sup. Ct. App. Div. 1991).

The District of Columbia Court of Appeals was more cautious in its approach to **Bostick** consents in **Re J.M.**, 596 A. 2d 961 (D.C. Ct. App. 1991). The defendant was on the bus when approached by officers. The 14-year old defendant was asked about his destination and whether he was carrying a gun or narcotics and the defendant said no. The police asked for consent to search a bag and the defendant consented but no drugs were found. The police then asked for the "pat-down" right. The defendant again consented. It was upon this frisk that the cocaine was found. The court then addressed the true problem in such cases where they said: "The freedom to ignore the police requests and the freedom not to consent to a search are surely very similar, if not absolutely identical." It called this a "near-merger," and said the context of the activity and whether "the entire encounter was genuinely consensual" for Fourth Amendment purposes is critical. This court then went on to hold the consent was not voluntarily given. The D.C. court stressed the age of the defendant. It said "[m]inority [age] is in itself a badge of incompetency to handle one's own affairs." Adolescent consent search cases cannot be compared to adult cases in this court's view. However, it did not want to find all juvenile consents invalid and discussed the truly criminally experienced juvenile and his or her ability to consent. Taking the "totality" into account this juvenile did not voluntarily consent. **Bostick** was therefore cautiously accepted.

As already explained, **Bostick** makes clear that the officer requesting consent need have no suspicion, articulable suspicion, nor probable cause to seek a consent to search. How far can this concept be taken? One need look no further than **U.S. v. Liss**, 103 F. 2d 617 (C.A. 9th 1997) for the answer. Police had a person in custody who said the stolen motorcycle was in another person's barn; the barn of Lloyd Liss. The police called Liss and got permission to enter the barn to retrieve the motorcycle. Once in the barn the police conducted a thorough search that revealed drugs. This search took four hours. The police obviously did not have consent to conduct a search for anything other than the plainly obvious motorcycle. Police were told by supervisors to get a consent from Liss. The police went to Liss, told him what they found and Liss said it must be the other man's drugs. The police then asked Liss for permission to search the home. They showed him a written consent form and told him he did not have to consent. They read the consent form to him. Liss signed the consent form. The police asked Liss if he wanted to accompany them and he said yes. Drugs were found and Liss said that he did not "like how he felt." The police stopped searching, called a D.A. who said to arrest Liss and apply for a warrant which was issued. The warrant listed the things found, where found, how found, including the drugs found in the barn. Liss moved to suppress all of it saying the second consented-to search was tainted by the first warrantless, non-plain view search of the barn. The government said they would not introduce the barn evidence but would seek to introduce the home-search evidence. The trial court suppressed only the barn evidence.

Should **Wong Sun's** "fruits" law have been applied? As the Seventh Circuit correctly noted, **Wong Sun** rejected the "but for" rule of suppression and opted instead for the "exploitation of the primary illegality" rule. Thus taint removers like independent source, inevitable discovery and attenuation doctrines may be applied and in fact must be applied before making a ruling. In this case the Seventh Circuit used attenuation to find the evidence found in the house was not tainted by the evidence found in the barn. The court then turned to the thornier issue of the voluntariness of the consent. The defense stressed the motivation of the officers since they had already illegally found evidence of a crime. The court, in essence, held it did not matter in this case and said that when the subject is not in custody, the officer's motivation is irrelevant. Citing **Bostick**, the court reminds us that no grounds for seeking a consent is required. Thus without more, the court said, "The fact that an officer had actual suspicion, however obtained, cannot render invalid a consent for which the officer did not need any suspicion at all to request." Accord see: **Com. v. Ortiz**, 661 N.E. 2d 925 (Mass. 1996).

Therefore, if the police do not exploit the illegality by using it to overbear the will of the owner/possessor, then there is no objective cause and effect. In this case the consent was physically obtained an appreciable distance from the site of the illegal search. Clearly the tone of the meeting at the Liss home was calm and the police showed Liss the consent form. Thus the warrant was not tainted by the illegal search. Finally, the fact that the warrant contained references to illegally found evidence is of no great concern in this case because there was sufficient independent evidence found during the legally consented-to search to support the issuance of the warrant. See also **State v. Avila-Avina**, 991 P. 2d 720 (Wash. App. 2000) and **State v. Richter**, 612 N.W. 2d 29 (Wis. 2000).

The mere confrontation cases where a consent is obtained, like **Bostick**, are always going to be tested by the defense because the line dividing a consensual encounter from a **Terry**-type stop is indeed thin. The basic defense argument will always be intimidation-based; did not feel free to leave argument. "This, of course, was rejected by the Court in both **Hodari D.** (*supra* at Chapter One) and more specifically **Bostick**. For example, consider **People v. Cascio**, 1997 WL 74088 (Colo.) where police observed an illegally parked van. The van was parked was near an area closed due to falling boulders. The police approached and told the Cascios that they were illegally parked. Some nervousness was observed but no guns were drawn by the police and no stand-still orders were issued. The brothers were asked if they had guns. The police were told no and no frisks were conducted. One of the brothers was asked for a consent to search the van and that brother said go ahead. Drugs were found, arrests occurred, *etc*.

The Colorado high court said this was simply begun as a "consensual, everyday contact." It then went on to stress there are "subtle distinctions between a consensual encounter and an investigatory stop." Since this vehicle was already stopped this case was started as an approach case. The police car was not parked as to block the exit of the van (ten to twenty foot separation). The "blinding" lights were not used, only a single spotlight. Only one officer directly approached the van and guns were not drawn nor touched; nor in any other way did the police act in a threatening manner. Indeed the tone was "informative" and as the court notes "mild mannered." The police were acting under a directive to investigate illegally parked vehicles in this area of natural danger. The questioning was "non-coercive." Thus there was no seizure and the court agreed with **Bostick** that no level of suspicion is required to request a voluntary consent. Accord see **U.S. v. Wright**, 1997 WL 28463 (4th Cir. (Va)). The **Wright** case, like **Bostick** involved a bus; in fact a bus station that is a much more public place than the bus itself. The tone of the conversation was stressed as being calm and casual. The personal ability of Mr. Wright to give a voluntary consent was assessed and he was found fully capable of consenting. The only unique feature of the case was that Wright argued that as a convicted felon, such a person would never give a voluntary consent to the search of his bag. The court tersely said "Wright consented to the search of the bag thinking that the police would not look inside the peanut butter jar where the drugs were found." See also **State v. Loveday**, 1997 WL 10301 (Wis. App.) where internalized unexpressed subjective fears if he said no did not overcome a calm "mere encounter." In all these cases, the police demeanor played a very important role.

It is clear that a consent cannot be the direct product of an illegal seizure. It is also clear that during a legal seizure a consent can be sought and obtained if otherwise voluntary. It is also clear that an officer does not have to have probable cause to seek a consent. But as clear as these principles are, certain facts can cause awkward results. Take **Com. v. Parker**, 619 A. 2d 735 (Pa. Super. Ct. 1993), a case involving a consent sought and given during a routine traffic stop. The court appears to say that to ask for a consent unrelated to the traffic stop brings the lawful stop to an end and causes the beginning of an illegal stop. If the officer has not been stretching out the routine traffic stop, the split second "end/beginning" point suggested by the court means that they were truly concerned with pretextuality of the stop. If that was their concern they should have said so. They instead said that such a consent could only be sought upon articulable suspicion. So far the Supreme Court of the U.S. has not made that a constitutional requirement. In fact there are now no pretextual auto stops since the decision in **Whren v. U.S.**, 517 U.S. 806 (1996).

Twice before their **Robinette** decision, the U.S. Supreme Court said no bright line exists requiring police to tell a person that they have the right to refuse to consent to a search or that they had a right to leave the police presence. In **Robinette** their broader concept was reaffirmed. The narrower issue involved whether at the end of a routine traffic stop the police had to tell the person they have the right to leave before the officer can ask for a consent to search the car. Ohio said the Fourth Amendment required this. The Supreme Court disagreed and remanded the case to Ohio reminding Ohio of **Schneckloth v. Bustamonte** and **Florida v. Bostick**. In **State v. Robinette**, 685 N.E. 2d 762 (Ohio, 1997) the Court felt that under the "totality" the consent was not voluntary since he had been illegally detained immediately following the end of the valid traffic stop.

How have other states reacted to **Robinette**? Arizona indicates that it might follow it but their first chance presented a case where the initial traffic stop was totally illegal and it does not appear the consent search was attenuated from the illegal stop. **State v. Richcreek**, 930 P. 2d 1304 (Ariz. *en banc.* 1997). Accord: **People v. Ruffin**, 734 N.E. 2d 507 (Ill. App. 2000). Colorado gave **Robinette** an approving nod but its case, a consensual encounter case, was more like a **Mendenhall** case. **People v.**

228

Cascio, 932 P. 2d 1381 (Colo. *en banc.* 1997). Massachusetts has merely acknowledged it exists. **Com. v. Hidalgo**, 674 N.E. 2d 638 (Mass. 1997). Pennsylvania, like Colorado, mentions it, but its case was more a **Mendenhall** case than a **Robinette** case. **Com. v. Hoak**, 700 A. 2d 1263 (Pa. Super. 1997). Nebraska, through **State v. Scheibelhut**, 673 N.E. 2d 821 (Ind. App. 1997) and Georgia through **Semelis v. State**, 493 S.E. 2d 17 (Ga. App. 1997) have used **Robinette** with approval. See also **State v. Kremer**, 754 A. 2d 964 (Me. 2000).

New Mexico takes the "new federalism" approach. In its case, however, the issue was not a consent but rather an auto and exigent circumstances type-case. Interestingly, this court used **Robinette** as evidence of the Supreme Court's perceived inconsistency regarding the "blanket" auto exception and its "reasonableness" jurisprudence/totality jurisprudence. See also **State v. Carty**, 753 A. 2d 149 (N.J. Super, 2000).

For a case demonstrating an unattenuated illegality and a consent to search see **State v. George**, 557 N.W. 2d 575 (Minn, 1997). This case addresses the same concerns raised in **Whren** and the hidden agenda of the officer. As **Whren** holds, if there is an objectively legal basis for a traffic stop, the fact that the officer has a hidden agenda is of no importance in and of itself. In the **George** case a legally operated motorcycle was stopped because the officer thought the lights were wrongly configured. However, there was nothing wrong with the lights. Once stopped the officer urged and prodded the cyclist into a consent search which yielded evidence of drugs and a gun. George, the defendant, argued pretext in his motion to suppress. At best the officer had only a hunch as to both the headlight configuration and the drugs. The first is fatal; the second is of no moment. But was the illegality of the initial stop, under the totality of the circumstances, attenuated by the time the consent was sought? No, it was not. As this court said, "Short of rejecting the concept of consent to search in the context of routine traffic stops, courts can and should demand sufficient proof in an individual case that the consent to search was truly express, clear and voluntary." In this case failure to tell Mr. George that he had a right to refuse consent plus the presence of two, (not one) officers, equivocal responses disregarded, repetitive consent seeking yielded, at most, "mere acquiescence" which was prohibited by **Bumper v. North Carolina**. In closing, this case is not inconsistent with the analysis required by **Robinette** which itself stressed the function of totality as opposed to a single factor when assessing consents obtained during a traffic stop to seek evidence unrelated to the reason for the stop. Accord: **Allah v. Com.**, 1997 WL 30840 (Va. App.).

Would moving the driver at the beginning of the traffic stop from the vehicle to the officer's cruiser create an inherently coercive atmosphere that would make any consent involuntary? According to the Seventh Circuit the answer is "not necessarily" under the totality analysis required by **Robinette**. Upon completion of the speeding violation paperwork, the defendant was moved to the cruiser and the officer asked the defendant if he could ask him a few more questions. The defendant told the officer to go ahead. The officer asked her about guns and she promptly said there were none. The officer then asked her about drugs. She paused, looked away, and then said there were none. The officer handed her a consent form and she signed it. Drugs were found. A calm officer explained what he was doing and why he was doing it. The fact the questioning occurred in the confines of a cruiser was not determinative. **U.S. v. Thompson**, 1997 WL 55363 (7th Cir. (Ill)).

A consent may be very voluntary under the totality required by **Robinette** but the evidence may be inadmissible on other grounds. In **U.S. v. Elliott**, 1997 WL 74627 (10th Cir. (Wyo.), the encounter was consensual. However, **Jimeno** and not **Robinette** was the key case that needed to be applied. This case points out that the scope of the consent sought and the consent given are equally important. When asking to "look through" the trunk, the officer qualified the request by stating "I don't want to look through each item," and that he wanted to see how things were "packed" or "packaged." The defendant opened the trunk. The officer then pushed and felt the outside of a black nylon bag and thought it was rigid. The officer then unzipped the bag and saw tell-tale signs of drug packaging. Did the officer exceed the scope of the consent? Yes, he did. The additional statements by the officer took him from a broad-in-scope consent to a restricted-in-scope consent. Any reasonable person would come to the same conclusion, the court opined. The officer sought a visual inspection by the added words. Since he "expressly and narrowly limited the scope of his request" the officer exceeded the scope and the evidence should have been suppressed. Accord see: **State v. Forrester**, 2001 WL 114662 (So.Car.), and **Howe v. State**, 2001 WL 167801 (Ark. App.). However, in the face of a specific request to grant a consent, the response will be measured by its own words and nothing fancy is required. Thus, "Sure, why not!" was a good consent in **State v. Seymour**, 1996 WL 128180 (NH).

Before **Robinette** can be used, local statutes should be consulted. In Oregon there is a statute that prohibits asking questions and seeking consents unrelated to the reason for a traffic stop during the stop. Thus, in Oregon, an officer would have to tell the driver that he or she is free to leave before the officer can attempt a **Mendenhall/Bostick** mere encounter. See **State v. Hadley**, 146 Ore. App. 166 (1997).

V.   Scope of the Consent

The scope of the consent is the next topic. How long does the consent last?

How many times can one's consent be used? Is there a spatial limit to a consent? The following cases address these issues.

In **Cobb v. State**, 226 Miss. 181, 83 So. 2d 833 (1955) the question arose whether the comment, "Go ahead and look for it anywhere you want to for it" was an adequate consent as given by the defendant at an "on-the-scene" interrogation and investigation. The defendant said he threw the weapon somewhere. The court found a valid consent. The only question not raised nor answered involves the question of how long is a consent good? It took the sheriff two days by making three or four trips to find the weapon. There is no problem with the continuous search, but how many times can the property be entered after an initial search is ended? Other states have dealt with this issue. The Michigan court found, in **People v. Nawrocki**, 148 N.W. 2d 211, 6 Mich. App. 46 (1967), that according to the testimony, Nawrocki freely and intelligently gave permission to the officer to impound the car and to search it at any time. The car was searched twice and the damaging evidence came from the second search. No testimony was given by defendant to rebut the idea of allowing a search at any time or any number of times. They upheld the search. Such a decision makes sense as long as the car remains in the continuous possession of the police.

The Maine court struggled with the issue twice. The first case was **State v. Brochu**, 243 A. 2d 418 (Me. 1967). On Dec. 5, while the case was still under investigation and before defendant was arrested, the police obtained defendant's permission to search his home. They found nothing. They went back on Dec. 6. One of the bases for justifying this search was that of continuing consent. The court said that the consent on Dec. 5 should be measured by the status of the defendant on the 6th as an arrested accused. There was no evidence that his Dec. 5 consent was discussed or that the police were going back on Dec. 6 on the strength of a continuing consent. The Court concluded the consent had ended by Dec. 6. A better way to approach this is once they left the premises they had used up the consent and it did not depend on his status on Dec. 6.

The second case to come before Maine on this issue was **State v. Chapman**, 250 A. 2d 203 (Me. 1969). This case distinguished **Brochu**. The court said two controlling facts emerge. The first entry was a lawful entry by the express consent and invitation of the defendant. The major distinction was that the police in this case never abandoned their possession and control of the premises. The time limits of continuous consent searches are to be controlled by the general search warrant time limits. This makes good sense.

However, Alaska gives more than "one bite" under a consent where the first consent was specific and voluntary and the later entries on the same day within five hours of the first were found to be closely related, and that court found the later entries were inferentially consented to by the defendant's failure to object. **Phillips v. State**, 625 P. 2d 816 (Alaska. 1980). This case, however, truly disregards " abandonment of the search" law. The "failure to object" point also appears to be taken too far.

Saying that the length of time a valid consent to search lasts depends upon the facts and circumstances of each case, the Delaware Supreme Court upheld a search that took place nearly 20 hours after the original consent. In this case a valid written consent was given. The police did not go beyond the limited scope of the search and only one search was conducted. The police did not conduct the search immediately because the watch, the item to be searched, was in Philadelphia Detention Center personnel hands and more urgent investigative items concerning the case that required immediate attention. Taking all this into account, the court held the consent was still in effect when the search was conducted. **Gray v. State**, 441 A. 2d 209 (Del. 1981). Unlike warrants there is no clear time limit as to when a consent search should begin. This case makes good sense.

Very often a question arises whether the words spoken by the defendant can be taken for consent. For example, does permission to water livestock given to the officers also give them the right to conduct a search? In **Pollard v. State**, 205 So. 2d 286 (Miss. 1967) the defendant was unable to make cash bond. The sheriff promised that the livestock would not suffer. The defendant asked the sheriff to take care of the calves. The court said there is no inherent or implied power to search when officers are given permission to enter land and take care of animals. Only plain view went with these officers and only in places where they had a right to be.

One further problem involving consent to searches concerns the probationer and his acceptance of a search waiver provision. There is not much choice, accept the search provision or go to prison (at worst) or more severe probation conditions (at best). The Supreme Court, although recognizing the probationers have Fourth Amendment rights, was not faced with consent to search as a condition of probation case when they decided **Griffin v. Wisconsin**, 483 U.S. 868 (1987). In states that do not have the statutory scheme that Wisconsin had (reduced probable cause to reasonable cause) it is usually standard for probationers to agree to search terms and conditions. The scope of these consents vary, with some states agreeing with Montana to limited ones. The Wisconsin statutory scheme is the better way. Accord: **Nixon v. State**, 18 P. 2d 631 (Wyo.).

The breadth of the effect of a probationer's consent condition is best illustrated by **In Re Marcellus L.**, 275 Cal. Rep. 649 (Dist. Ct. App. 1990). As a condition of his probation Marcellus had agreed to submit to warrantless searches by any peace officer. He was searched by an officer who did not know of this "prior consent." There was no articulable suspicion nor probable cause for the search. The California court felt the defendant had given up his rights to privacy even though this officer was totally unaware of the "prior consent." It felt the defendant, through the **Griffin** case, had agreed to submit to warrantless, unexpected searches. The court did say that there was a limit to police intrusions. The police must at least cite a "legitimate law enforcement purpose." In this case the defendant, an obvious minor, was not in school during school hours and was near a known "crack house." This saved the conduct from being pure harassment.

Parolees also face similar restriction in their limited freedom. Most of them do sign agreements allowing parole officers to make unannounced searches of their residences. This is required by statute in Colorado and several other states. This type of provision was upheld in **People v. McCullough**, 6 P.3d 774 (Colo. *en banc* 2000). **Griffin** and **Morrissey v. Brewer**, 408 U.S. 471 (1972) that approved a number of restrictive conditions, were used to help them uphold their statute. It noted that the U.S. Supreme Court had not retreated from its position by its decision in **Pennsylvania BD. of Probation and Parole v. Scott**, 524 U.S. 357 (1998). There the Court re-announced that individual suspicion is not needed for "reasonableness" when a convicted but probated or paroled person is the focus.

Once again the Ninth Circuit has captured the attention of the U.S. Supreme Court. This time it involves a person on unsupervised probation who stole some explosive materials, likely made one bomb and used it near his house, was seen escaping from the scene of the burglary by a law enforcement officer. The federal agent discovered that Knights had agreed to a consent search provision in his unsupervised probation that allowed and probation officer or law enforcement officer to conduct such searches. The agent conferred with his supervisor and was permitted to conduct the search. The explosives were found. Calling this a subterfuge and denying that Whren applied, the Ninth Circuit upheld the motion to suppress the evidence. It said this search was not conducted for probation purposes and it violated the Fourth Amendment. The court forgot that he violated his probation by stealing and exploding bombs. The court is obviously upset with the U.S. Supreme Court, and the Ninth Circuit's language, a bit snippy, reveals that attitude. The Supreme Court granted certiorari in this case. **U.S. v. Knights**, 219 F. 3d 1138 (C.A. 9th 2000). In U.S v. Knight, 534 U.S. 112 (2001) the Court held that the warrantless search of this probationer's apartment ws supported by reasonable suspicion and authorized by a condition of his probation even though the evidence of explosive devices and not drugs were being sought.

If one is in the midst of a busy airline terminal does the consent to the search of one's *person* include the right to feel the genital areas? The Eleventh Circuit agreed with the suppression judge and held that in the context of where the search was conducted, the judge was not clearly wrong that the word *person* does not necessarily include genital touching, though if they had been the fact finders, they might not have so limited the scope of the consent. **U.S. v. Blake**, 888 F. 2d 795 (C.A. 11th 1989).

Massachusetts, on the other hand, says, "What, if any, limitations on the consent are implied by the language or conduct of the consenting party is a question in the first instance for the judgment of the police officers to whom the consent is given. The ultimate question is whether, in light of all the circumstances, a man of reasonable caution would be warranted in the belief that some limitation was intended by the consent giver." In this case the defendant opened his jacket and said "search me." The police found the drugs in his shoes. The defendant said that by opening his jacket he only authorized an upper body search. The court did not accept that and they stressed he did not object to any part of the search including his shoes. **Com. v. Cantalupo**, 380 Mass. 173 (1980). Accord: **Pinkney v. State**, 742 N.E. 2d 956 (Ind. App. 2001), noting that the search of the back pockets of the pants did not exceed the scope of the pat-down consent.

When one consents to a "complete search" of his apartment does that mean that police can use the keys provided to enter a storage bin that is not within the apartment but is located next door to the apartment? The Eighth Circuit keying on the keys and the proximity of the storage bin felt the police had not exceeded the scope of the consent. **U.S. v. Ware**, 890 F. 2d 1008 (C.A. 8th 1989).

Scope of consent cases are not always clear-cut. In one case police were asked to enter a home thought to be burglarized because the owner felt the burglars were still there. While in the house, police opened a jewelry box that was obviously too small to contain a human being. Cocaine was found in that box. Citing Lafave, the court held that this was an appropriate step in the investigation of a burglary. Why? The most common burglary involves the theft of personal property. **State v. Bond**, 572 A. 2d 1182 (N.J. Super. Ct., App. Div. 1990).

In this context do the police have to obtain a second consent to search a container within the container? No, says the District of Columbia Court of Appeals. Their statement is to the point and they held: "Valid consent, un-withdrawn, to search a container, extends to a search of other containers found there in, at least where the inner container is such that it could contain the object of the search." **U.S. v. Smith**, 901 F. 2d 1116 (C.A. D.C. 1990). However, viewing videos found during a search was not within the consent nor plain view because this was a sexual abuse case without any report that videos were used during the assaults. **State v. Johnson**, 17 P. 3 (Wash. App. 2001).

Cases like **Smith** have caused several courts some concern. For example, Florida had held that consent to search a car was not consent to search closed containers within the car. **State v. Jimeno**, 564 So. 2d 1083 (Fla. 1990). This decision by the Florida Supreme Court affirmed the holding by the Third District Court of Appeals that found that the consent to search the car did not include the right to open a rolled-up bag on the car's floor. Both opinions were short and to the point and both relied upon a case affirmed by the U.S. Supreme Court which affirmation only addressed the inventory of automobile issues, **State v. Wells**, 539 So. 2d 464 (Fla. 1989) aff'd **Florida v. Wells**, 495 U.S. 1 (1990). Two things are clear. They misread **Wells** and failed to see the severability of the consent and inventory issues. The U.S. Supreme Court thus granted certiorari in **Jimeno**. Subsequent to the Florida decisions in **Jimeno** and prior to the granting of certiorari, the Fifth District decided a case where the defendant signed a consent form granting a right to search the car and its contents thus having a truly distinguishable case. **State v. Walton**, 565 So. 2d 381, 383 n.1 (Fla. Dist. Ct. App. 1990).

The **Jimeno** case was decided in May of 1991 with Rehnquist writing for the seven member majority. **Florida v. Jimeno**, 500 U.S. 248 (1991). A police officer suspected Jimeno was carrying drugs so the officer followed Jimeno as he drove. Jimeno made a right turn at a red light without stopping and the officer lawfully stopped Jimeno. The officer then told Jimeno of the officer's suspicions and asked for consent to search the car. The officer also told Jimeno that he did not have to consent. Jimeno gave the standard "nothing-to-hide-go-ahead-and-search" response. The officer found a brown paper bag on the floor board, opened it and discovered a kilo of cocaine. Florida held a consent to search "the car" was not consent to search containers in the car. The Supreme Court disagreed and reversed the Florida court's holding. The Court said the standard measuring device for scope in such a case is "objective" reasonableness. As they put it "...what would the typical reasonable person have understood by the exchange between the officer and the suspect?" It went on to say that the scope of a search is generally defined by its expressed object. The consenter, if he or she wants to limit the consent should expressly delimit. Drugs are carried in containers and not allowed merely to be in unconfined piles in the car and reasonable people would know that, the Court said. Thus the authorization in this case was not limited to the surfaces of the car's interior. The Court said the result might be different if the container were a locked briefcase; that reasonable people might think that a search of a car might not include such a locked container but a closed paper bag is not a locked briefcase, the Court said. But even that determination calls for the reasonable person approach.

Although **Jimeno** clearly puts the burden on the defendant to limit the scope of the area to be searched when he or she consents, some police activity under unlimited consents is still a matter of concern. In **U.S. v. Ibarra**, 948 F. 2d 903 (C.A. 5th 1991), police secured an unlimited consent to search the defendant's house. The entrance to the attic was boarded over. Police took a sledge hammer and removed the boards, went into the attic and found the incriminating evidence of "money laundering." The Fifth Circuit felt that since the structural integrity of the house was not destroyed or damaged and the mere removal of such a barrier was reasonable and that a reasonable person would understand his consent extended to the barricaded area.

Likewise the Eleventh Circuit, in a post-**Jimeno** case, addressed the issue of the scope of a consent and forced entries. The defendant gave an unlimited consent to search a storage unit. In the storage unit there was a car with a locked trunk. The officers pried the trunk open and found four kilos of cocaine. Having placed no written or oral limitations on the scope of the consented-to search the evidence was found admissible. A general consent to search an area includes the right to open all containers in the same manner as would be permitted under a warrant, the court ruled. If the container could be said to contain the thing sought, that conclusion, if reasonable, allows forced openings. **U.S. v. Martinez**, 949 F. 2d 1117 (C.A. 11th 1992).

The **Jimeno** decision leaves significant maneuvering room for courts to interpret the breadth of the scope of the consent even within broadly-based words of consent. For example, in **State v. Hyland**, 50 Crim. L. Rep. 1103 (Mo. App. 1991) the thing to be searched was a suitcase that was sealed with duct tape. The officer asked if he could "look inside the suitcase" and the defendant said "yes." After opening the suitcase the officer felt inside and found the packaged substance under some clothes. The Missouri court characterized this problem as "devilishly difficult," and distinguished **Jimeno** and because the officer did not tell the defendant what the officer suspected, the words "look in the suitcase" could not be interpreted to mean "look and feel."

Some courts, however, are too restrictive as to scope and the plain meaning of words. In a New Mexico decision the police asked for and got a consent to "inspect" the defendant's car trunk. A dog was stationed downwind to get plain smell and the dog alerted, when the trunk was opened, giving the police probable cause for a full search. The appeals court felt this exceeded the consent given. A sniff is not a search but it is one of the plain senses. Clearly this court has seriously destroyed the right of the police to do their job lawfully. Thus, **State v. Cleave**, 8 P.3d 157 (N.M. App. 2000), will totally undo the plain view doctrine in its entirety. However, there might be hope since certiorari was granted by the New Mexico Supreme Court as No. 20,036 on August 8, 2000.

Probationers are often given the choice to serve hard time or take probation with prior consent to search clause. The defendant in **People v. Spence**, 93 Cal. Rptr.2d 607 (Cal. App.3 2000) gave prior consent to search his place for stolen goods. However, the probation search in this case was specifically for narcotics but the officer did not know of the limitation because the computer print-out did not give any limits. The court had to use the computer foul-up case of **Arizona v. Evans**, 514 U.S. 1 (1995). Unfortunately this system was designed to give incomplete information thus there was no accidental omission or mistake. The search was faulty.

A more usual search limit case is found in **Hughes v. Com.**, 524 S.E. 2d 155 (Va. App. 2000). This defendant said O.K. to a pat-down, and visual inspection inside his underwear but he did not consent to a body cavity search. The court found that the consent was exceeded.

One of the more interesting consent search cases focusing on whether the officers exceeded the scope of the consent given comes from Indiana. In **Smith v. State**, 713 N.E. 2d 338 (Ind. App. 1999) the police made a lawful stop of a vehicle. The police asked for a consent to search the car for guns, drugs, money or illegal contraband. Smith consented. A cellular phone was found and Smith was asked whether it was his but he said that it belonged to his girlfriend. The phone was taken to the patrol car where the battery was removed and a short-out technique was performed which revealed that the internal ESNs did not match the external ESNs meaning the phone had been illegally cloned (reprogrammed) so that use charges would be billed to someone else's number. This was the felony Smith faced at trial where he was convicted. Did this "short-out" search exceed the scope of the consent? Yes, said the appeals court. To be sure, seizing the phone was valid but searching it for its electronic contents exceeded the consent given. The court felt that: "No objective person would believe that by performing a short-out technique on cellular phones to retrieve its electronic contents, the troopers might find the expressed object of their search." The police named the items they were going to look for, thus they went outside the scope of the consent. The fact that the defendant did not object at the moment did not have any effect on the result. The police did not seek an additional consent. But is the Indiana court correct? For example, does a consent to search a car include a jacket left in the car and without an "except my jacket" limitation attached to the consent. If the consent is unlimited the search right includes all containers in the car. The consent search right is coextensive with the right granted under a warrant. See **State v. Matejka**, 621 N.W. 2d 891 (Wis. 2001).

VI.   CONSENT: Summary

Silence in the face of a request to search and failure to object to a search are generally held not to be consent. Consent to an invalid search after it has begun is not a valid consent. A consent can be as broad or as limited as the consenter chooses. Consent for one purpose or consent to be in a specific area is not necessarily a consent to search the entire thing or area. An unlimited consent search is only circumscribed by the general rules governing the scope of searches generally. The use of threats, indirect threats, or force to gain a consent to search are prohibited.

Any person with some control (standing) may give consent to search even though all others with standing have not given consent. However, this is now being questioned. The courts seek common authority or control in the individual consenting and if that is found then the consent is good. Landlords, hotel managers, and dormitory officials generally do not have authority to consent to the search of houses or rooms currently occupied by someone else. If police are reasonably misled to believe another person has common authority to give a consent, such consent will be upheld. Persons with common authority appear to be able to consent even over the objection of others who are present and even where the others fail to object. The status of this last point has not been fully settled by Supreme Court decisions, but it seems to be a proper natural extension of the common authority rule and its assumption of the risk rationale. Parents of minor children and even of adult children who live in the parents' home can consent to the search of the child's room in a number of states. They may even consent to the search items of personalty in most states. Children in some states are given the right to consent to search areas where the family had equal access. Many of the cases in this area are being decided on a case-by-case basis.

Consents, like warranted searches, have a life-span. There is no clear-cut rule on how long a consent lasts. Most courts generally agree, however, that once the search is conducted and the police leave the place or thing, the consent ends with the abandonment of the search. Consents must be freely, voluntarily, and intelligently given. There are no *Miranda*-like warnings required in this area. Consent is tested under the "totality" rule. If a consent is given after an illegal arrest and while that custody continues, the attenuation doctrine must be applied to determine whether the consent was the product of the arrest or whether it was free of that taint. Thus consents can be the "fruit of the poisonous tree."

VII. CONSENT - Check List

A. **How Gained**:
   1. after illegal search already begun ___
   2. ruse or colorable announcement of authority ___
   3. invited ruse ___
   4. silence (when can failure to object be taken as consent)
   _____
   If none of the above, proceed to B.

B. **Why**:
   1. true emergency ___
   2. suspect not in custody but suspected of crime ___
   3. suspect in custody (no warnings required)
      a. lawful custody ___
      b. unlawful custody (fruits issue) ___
   4. place believed to contain criminal evidence ___

C. **Where Gained**:
   1. street or other public area ___
   2. home/office/hotel/etc. ___
   3. police station or other government area ___

D. **Who Gave Consent**:
   1. owner/possessor ___
   2. third party (issue of shared possession or control):
      a. shared possessor ___
      b. hotel manager ___
      c. dorm supervisor ___
      d. principal of school, etc. ___
      e. driver of car ___
      f. wife ___
      g. parent ___
      h. child ___
      i. multiple possessors and present and one says yes and others say no ___
      j. good faith reliance on one with apparent authority in true emergency ___ or after proper inquiry regarding authority ___

E. **When Given**:
　　1.　　pre-custody (pure VKI [voluntary, knowing and intelligent] analysis) ___
　　2.　　post-custody (totality used) ___
　　　　a.　　lawful custody (VKI only) ___
　　　　b.　　unlawful (attenuation and then to VKI) ___
F. **What Consent Given (Scope Issues):**
　　1.　　limited consent ___
　　2.　　thoroughness of search (bound by warrant scope cases) ___
　　3.　　length of time consent lasts
　　　　a.　　as to when to begin ___
　　　　b.　　as to when to end ___
　　　　c.　　more than (1) one bite? ___
　　　　　　(continuous or abandoned search)

VIII. CONSENT: Basic Rules

Rule 1:　Probable cause is not needed; nor is articulable suspicion or any suspicion for that matter.

Rule 2:　Consent must be voluntary.

Rule 3:　No **Miranda**-like warnings are required.

Rule 4:　Most ruses to enter are not tolerated; *but* failure to inform the consenter of all the reasons for a search *etc. not* a ruse.

Rule 5:　Attenuation doctrine fully applicable.

Rule 6:　Assumption of risk doctrine prevails in "absent other" cases.

Rule 7:　Person who consents must have authority, *but;*

Rule 8:　Police can in "good faith" rely on one with apparent authority.

Rule 9:　Juveniles *may be able* to consent to search of public areas of parents' home.

Rule 10:　Juveniles have some limited privacy rights.

Rule 11:　Scope and length of consent generally governed by search warrant rules.

Rule 12:　Consent may be revoked.

Rule 13:　Parolees/Probationers can consent in advance to parole, *etc.*, connected searches.

Rule 14:　Defendants can limit scope of search.

Rule 15:　Police can limit scope of search.

Problem Area: multiple people with standing – all are present – one consents – others deny consent – search conducted – admissible fruits against whom?

240

IX. AN OVERVIEW OF CONSENT SEARCHES

A. CONSENT: THE KEY CASES FROM THE UNITED STATES SUPREME COURT

Florida v. Bostick, 501 U.S. 429 (1991)

Consent does not require probable cause, articulable suspicion or even mere suspicion. It only requires proof of:

1)   A police request for permission to search, **and**
2)   A verbal or physical response to the request either a:
     a.   yes;
     b.   no;
     c.   or scope limited yes.

Bumper v. North Carolina, 391 U.S. 543 (1968)

1)   Silence (without a "yes" gesture) is treated as a resounding NO!
2)   The consent must be voluntary in the same sense as a confession must be voluntary.
3)   Lies by officer vitiate any consent
     a.   Officer says I *have* a warrant—but does not
     b.   Officer says I can and will get a warrant—but cannot make that guarantee
     c.   Officer says a consent search will be less destructive – NOT SO!

Lewis v. U.S., 385 U.S. 206 (1966)

Some ruses used to get a consent are indeed the same as a lie – but posing as drug buyers gaining entry to a house that has become a commercial drug center and the willingness to accept the decoys was sufficient to uphold the consented-to entry and the plain view evidence, *etc.*, gathered therein.

Schneckloth v. Bustamonte, 412 U.S. 218 (1973)

Unless there "are inherently coercive tactics" used, failure to tell a defendant:

1)   Why they seek consent—not fatal;

<u>OR</u>

2)   That the defendant can refuse the search—not fatal.

Frazier v. Cupp, 394 U.S. 731 (1969)

1)   Anyone with shared control of the item can consent to a search – must have personal standing (see **Rakas** and **Salvucci**).

2)   Non-presence of other owner or person with standing—a fact but *not* necessarily required. But certainly that is the risk run by the other person.

United States v. Matlock, 415 U.S. 164 (1974)

1)   First case in which Court approved the fact that police verified consenter's standing.

2)   Common authority of consenter rules—but the primary possessor was *not* present.

Stoner v. California, 376 U.S. 483 (1964)

1)   Recognizes that a person's hotel room is the "home" away from home

2)   Hotel clerk does not have general authority to authorize search of a room despite hotel's right to clean room and fix things.

Chapman v. United States, 365 U.S. 610 (1961)

A landlord has no right to consent to a search of the tenant's realm of privacy.

Illinois v. Rodriguez, 497 U.S. 177 (1990)

1)   Solidifies rule that consenter must have standing.

2)   Announces reasonable reliance rule: that police must verify standing *and* can reasonably rely on that consent if, under the totality, a reasonable person would also have relied on the representations of shared control—the apparent authority rule.

3)   Consent was given outside presence of "true" possessor. But "true" possessor was present during search. But this case did not clarify:

      a.)   ranking of others; nor

      b.)   presence; nor

    c.) "mere acquiescence."

U.S. v. Watson, 423 U.S. 411 (1976)

  1) Custody—consent case

  2) Custody (seizure) and custody (**Miranda**) are not enough to demonstrate coercion.

  3) Custody consent may be valid even if police do not tell consenter the he/she has the right to withhold consent.

  4) Continues **Schneckloth** rule.

Florida v. Royer, 460 U.S. 491 (1983)

Consent arising from and a part of an unattenuated illegal seizure is *no* consent.

Ohio v. Robinette, 519 U.S. 33 (1996)

  1) Repeats theory that "no bright line" exists requiring police to tell a person that they:

    a) Have a right to leave after receiving a traffic ticket; and

    b) Have the right to refuse to consent.

Griffin v. Wisconsin, 483 U.S. 868 (1987)

Suggests that search consent conditions for probationers and parolees are okay.

Florida v. Jimeno, 500 U.S. 248 (1991)

  1) First case to address and define "scope of consent search" issue.

  2) Unless consenter limits "scope" consented to search can be as broad or as narrow as the request suggests.

  3) Treat it like a contract-offer and acceptance.

CHAPTER SIX
PLAIN VIEW

I.   Foundation of the Plain View Doctrine

Though plain view was not created by the U.S. Supreme Court in **Coolidge v. New Hampshire**, 403 U.S. 443 (1971), it was in **Coolidge** that the Court gave a rather full exposition of the limits of the doctrine's applicability. Its purpose was to identify the circumstances in which plain view has legal significance. The unfortunate problem was that much of **Coolidge** was a plurality opinion, which required resolution of the unresolved doctrines announced in the case. However, most if not all of the *obiter dictum* of **Coolidge** has now been resolved.

Under what circumstances may police seize obvious evidence of a crime that inadvertently comes to their attention while they are where they have a right to be? The Court wanted to make clear that plain view *alone* (Court emphasis) is never enough to justify the warrantless seizure of evidence. Plain view while an otherwise lawful search is being conducted justifies the seizure of inadvertently discovered, obvious criminally - related evidence.

Therefore, there are two branches to the plain view rule announced in **Coolidge** as illustrated by the following chart:

PLAIN VIEW

BRANCH ONE	**BRANCH TWO**
1.) **While conducting an otherwise valid search (warrant, consent, exception, or exigency)**	1.) **While constitutionally at a place (including open fields)**
2.) **Inadvertently (Surprise? No Non-pretextual Yes)**	2.) **Inadvertently (Surprise? No Non-pretextual Yes)**
3.) **See an object while within the lawful scope of the search that is either:**	3.) **See an object that is either:**
A. Contraband	**A. Contraband**
or	or
B. Obvious evidence of a crime (Probable Cause)	**B. Obvious evidence of a crime (Probable Cause**
4.) **Officer may seize**	4.) **Officer obtains fullest measure of probable cause**
	5.) **Must secure a warrant**
	or
	Prove exigent circumstances or get consent.

Why are the police allowed the right of seizure of other evidence while conducting a proper in scope, otherwise lawful search? "It would often be a needless inconvenience and sometimes dangerous – to the evidence or to the police themselves– to require them to ignore it until they have obtained a warrant particularly describing it." **Coolidge** at 468. Historically, the search warrants used in the states before 1900 all had a provision instructing police to seize other evidence of criminality known to be such while conducting the warranted search. Such a provision can be found in the annotated search warrant reproduced in Chapter Three.

The second limitation noted by the Court was that of inadvertence. The Court said that where the discovery is anticipated, and where the police know in advance the location of the evidence and intend to seize it, the situation is altogether different. Getting a warrant would pose no inconvenience and the Court restated its preference for warrants. The Court in footnote 26 condemned the practice of a planned warrantless seizure by the police officer's action of maneuvering themselves within the plain view of the object they want. This, however, was a plurality holding which had to be resolved at a later date.

The third limitation is that the evidence must be an article of an incriminating character. The "obvious evidence of a crime" requirement comports with the "particularly described" requirement of the Fourth Amendment. By stressing this requirement, the Court is saying that it is hewing the line "by preventing general exploratory searches." The only unanswered question was whether obviousness required absolute knowledge or probable cause; no standard was announced in Coolidge. Though labeled plain view, the Court clearly pointed out that it was not limiting the discovery only to the sense of sight. "Incontrovertible testimony of the senses that an incriminating object is on premises belonging to a criminal suspect may establish the fullest possible measure of probable cause," **Coolidge** at 468. The Court, therefore, created a textbook to be followed and set as examples some 20 prior court decisions as guides.

How would the doctrine be received and would it be strictly or broadly interpreted for the rights of defendants? Some indication in the decision also created the issue of "unaided" senses. Would that also be required? Were all senses, including the tactile senses, within the scope of the doctrine? Much remained to be decided.

II. The Supreme Court and Its Subsequent Plain View Cases

A. Obvious Evidence of a Crime – Texas v. Brown and Arizona v. Hicks – is it a requirement?

Is an opaque green balloon tied at the top containing something other than air, obvious or immediately apparent evidence of a crime? That was one of the issues raised in **Texas v. Brown**, 460 U.S. 730 (1983). Rehnquist, writing for the plurality in **Brown,** reminds everyone that the polestar case of **Coolidge** was only a plurality opinion. Plain view, he says, is simply an extension of whatever the prior justification for an officer's "access to an object" may be. Then he says, "immediately apparent" was very likely an unhappy choice of words, since it can be taken to imply that an unduly high degree of certainty as to the incriminatory character of evidence is necessary for an application of the "plain view doctrine." Citing **Payton** (*infra*), he says:"[T]he seizure of property in plain view involves no invasion of privacy and *is presumptively reasonable, assuming that there is probable cause to associate the property with criminal activity*" (emphasis by Rehnquist). Thus, *know* is not the standard; probable cause to believe is the standard to use for immediately apparent. In **Brown,** a trained officer was aware of the use of balloons to secure drugs and conceal them from sight. The officer, therefore, had probable cause.

This decision undid years of a stricter standard as represented by the following Texas case. In this case, officers came across an unlabeled bottle of pills. These pills were seized and determined to be a controlled substance. As the state chemist admitted on the stand, it would have been impossible to determine the contents with any degree of certainty by merely looking at them. The court said a seizure is allowable only when it is immediately apparent to the police that the thing is incriminating. It meant absolute knowledge as opposed to probable cause. **Howard v. State**, 599 S.W. 2d 597 (Tex. Ct. Crim. App. 1979).

Would the Court be willing to relax the standard further by allowing "plain view" to operate at the articulable suspicion level? No. The majority opinion in **Arizona v. Hicks**, 480 U.S. 321 (1987) did two things. First, it put to rest the plurality disputes of **Coolidge** and **Brown**. The Court through Scalia said: "We now hold that probable cause is required." By this simple, direct statement the decision accomplished its second goal. Reasonable or articulable suspicion would not satisfy the obvious or immediately apparent standard. By finally settling this area, states now have a standard which they are accustomed to applying; the probable cause standard. States like Texas would have to re-examine their early decisions. Rehnquist spoke in terms of having probable cause and not absolute knowledge in order to search a container under the plain view doctrine. The probable cause can come from training or experience, *i.e.*, the uniqueness of the package may announce its contents in a probable cause context. The theory is limited by the logic fault doctrine of "conclusion jumping." Credible proof is required on the issue of training or experience. Lucky guesses are not allowed.

In one case the government tried to convince the Tenth Circuit that an innocuous container located next to an object of usual criminality meant that the container was also "crime involved" and thus could be opened under the plain view doctrine. The Tenth Circuit did not accept the argument because the container used was a lens case and even though it was found next to a syringe, that did not necessarily mean that, in a probable cause context, the lens case was criminally involved. The government was unable to demonstrate "distinctiveness as a drug container." **U. S. v. Donnes**, 947 F. 2d 1430 (C.A. 10th 1991). Mere location of an otherwise innocent item does not, in its view, create probable cause to believe the item is connected to a crime. Some *nexus* must be established to avoid the application of a logic fault. Factually, however, the syringe and the lens case were found in a glove – a strange place to store such disparate items. Equally strange is that the court said a warrant should have been used to open it. Why? The government considered it was neither a usual drug container nor a container that announced its contents. Therefore, probable cause to seize an item is not probable cause to open it. The Tenth Circuit made this point clear and thus adhered to the Branch Two Theory of **Coolidge**: that a warrant was needed.

B. Inadvertence – Texas v. Brown, Arizona v. Hicks, and Horton v. California.

Rehnquist, in Brown, characterized inadvertence as not knowing in advance the location of certain evidence and therefore not intending to seize it. He went on to say that "Whatever may be the final disposition of the inadvertence element of plain view, it clearly was no bar to the seizure here." The defendant, Brown, was stopped at a lawful road block for driver's license checks. Rehnquist said the police probably had a general expectancy that narcotics might be present in some of the cars they halted. The record did not indicate more than this general expectation. There was no indication that Brown was a target. Summing up inadvertence, Rehnquist wrote: "The inadvertence requirement of plain view, properly understood, was no bar to the seizure here…." Though absolute surprise is not required, generalized expectations do not destroy inadvertence. But Brown was a plurality opinion.

In the **Hicks** case the police wanted reasonable suspicion to allow them not to seize the item, rather they wanted the reasonable suspicion to allow them to have a "cursory inspection" exception that would allow them to move the object or open it or explore what could not be readily seen. So they would use this to gain inadvertently an immediately apparent view. The Court said no to that. Scalia wrote, "We are unwilling to send police and judges into a new thicket of Fourth Amendment law, to seek a creature of uncertain description that is neither a plain view inspection nor yet a full-blown search." To be sure, the confusion on the Court would lead to a number of inconsistent decisions.

Other courts were not satisfied by the inadvertence requirement in its application. North Carolina felt compelled to clarify the point for its judges and police. The decision is **State v. White**, 370 S.E. 2d 390 (N. C. 1988) and involved a county search for stolen goods taken from county areas. While executing the warrant, the police found only one target item, but they seized other items listed on incident reports and several items taken from city jurisdictional points that were under investigation by city police. The defendant contended there was no plain view. The Court of Appeals held that inadvertent means "unanticipated" or "unexpected" – "wow" instead of "bingo" – thus found that the police were working within the proper parameters of the plain view doctrine. The North Carolina court was correct in that **Coolidge** did not define inadvertence. The surprise standard applied by the Court of Appeals was the one generally favored until Rehnquist spoke of generalized expectations in **Brown**. **Hicks** really did not shed great light on the subject. The North Carolina court then turned to the Sixth Circuit for guidance on the subject and that court's opinion in **U.S. v. Hare**, 589 F. 2d 1291 (C.A. 6th 1979). The **Hare** court set out a two step inquiry. (1) did police prior to the search have probable cause to secure a search warrant for the items subsequently seized, but not listed in the warrant, at the location to be searched? If so, the seizure is illegal. (2) if not, then did the police have probable cause to believe that the seized items were evidence of criminal conduct where the seizure took place? So how would one apply this test? The police in this case suspected they would find more. But suspicion is not probable cause. Taking the incident reports of other break-ins made the suspicion articulable or reasonable. Since there was no proof that the police withheld information to circumvent the warrant requirement, their conduct was not violative of the Fourth Amendment as to the items on the incident reports, but as to the items not on the warrant and not on the incident reports, they lacked probable cause, and thus these items were suppressible. The dissent said simply that this decision would encourage exploratory rummaging around.

The Second Circuit used the "prior knowledge that an item will be found" and "suspicion that such item might possibly be found" distinction. **U.S. v. $10,000**, 780 F. 2d 213 (C.A. 2d 1986). This comported with the Rehnquist view in **Brown**.

Would this be a proper application of the "suspicion not knowledge" rule of the Sixth and Second Circuits? A warrant sought two items. One item was supported by probable cause; the other was not. While searching both are found. Can the non-supported item be seized under plain view? The Massachusetts Supreme Judicial Court held that the seizure of the non-supported item – the heroin – in places where the ring could have been found could be justified under plain view. That certainly gave a new definition to inadvertent. **Com. v. Lett**, 470 N.E. 2d 110 (Mass. 1984), which is inconsistent with **Com. v. Accaputo**, 380 Mass. 435 (1980) which said drugs seized under an invalid administrative warrant could not be called inadvertent since they were mentioned in the warrant. But the **Lett** decision presaged what was to come.

Since **Texas v. Brown**, like **Coolidge** was a plurality opinion and since **Hicks** mainly dealt with the issue of the nature of a search, the Court needed to face inadvertence head-on and did so in **Horton v. California**, 496 U.S. 128 (1990). This 7 to 2 decision says this part of **Coolidge** is not binding on the court, thus it need not be overruled. First, it held, that "even though inadvertence is a characteristic of most legitimate 'plain view' searches, it is not a necessary condition." Second, they emphasized the "immediately apparent" or "certain probative value" aspect of the evidence. Third, suspicion that an item might be found should not immunize it from seizure. With this, it elevated **Texas v. Brown** to majority status. Fourth, the scope of the search (rightfully there) was emphasized as a proper restriction on possible general searches. Thus 47 states and 12 circuits must reevaluate their inadvertence decisions. What the decision did not deal with are pretextual searches because in **Horton** the things seized (guns) were directly related to the crime for which the other evidence was sought (robbery).

The issue of pretextual searches was not directly addressed by the majority but was addressed by the dissenters. The majority view implies that "scope" violations will tell lower courts when a search is pretextual and thus, a general search. **Horton** (*supra*). The pretextual search issue may have been resolved by the **Whren** decision discussed in Chapter Twelve at Sec. III.

C.   The Police Are Lawfully There – New York v. Class, 475 U.S. 106 (1986)

Sometimes the police not only have a right to be there, but there is at least one occasion when they have a right to a view and the citizen who blocks or obstructs that view can expect an intrusion to clear the view. Such was the case in **New York v. Class**, 475 U.S. 106 (1986). Vehicle identification numbers (VIN) are mandated by law to help in the control of the stolen car industry. That VIN, for the past several years, has been located on the forward facing edge of the dashboard so it is viewable from the windshield. Mr. Class obstructed his VIN and the officer who had lawfully stopped the car entered the car to move the obstruction. In so doing, the officer saw a gun protruding from underneath the driver's seat. This plain view to exercise statutory plain view was lawful.

In a *per curiam* decision of **Recznik v. City of Lorain**, 393 U.S. 166 (1968), the Court held that a private home remains such and does not become a public place open to the public because of the congregation of a large number of persons. Several people stopped police and told the police that gambling was going on at a certain address. Police drove to the immediate area and noticed an "unusually large number of cars parked in the vicinity." They confronted the defendant outside the building and warned him that there better not be anything illegal going on and told the defendant they would return in an hour. They returned 20 minutes later, tried to look through the windows, could not, and therefore simply entered the premises. The dice game was seen. The police seized evidence and arrested nearly everyone. A continued search located more gambling paraphernalia. The trial court determined that this residence was a commercial establishment, thus the officer's entry was a risk assumed by the defendant. Unfortunately, there was nothing in the record to support that finding. The Supreme Court rejected the bare assertion that the mere congregation of a lot of people made the place a public place destroying its residential character. Thus "open invitation consent" was missing in this case.

Now that the U.S. Supreme Court has officially approved sobriety check-points in **Michigan v. Sitz**, 496 U.S. 444 (1990) (but not 100% roadblocks for all other reasons) police will be where they have a right to be in such instances. Thus plain view and smell rights will arise. Since the U.S. Supreme Court approved the use of drug sniffing dogs as a reasonable extension of the officer's senses, **U.S. v. Place**, (*infra*), can drug-sniffing dogs be present at these otherwise valid stops and would their use violate the Fourth Amendment?

The Tenth Circuit said such dogs could be used. It concluded that since the brief detention was reasonable (in this case a license and insurance check) and since the dog alerted before the "check" was complete, no Fourth Amendment violation occurred. **U.S. v. Morales-Zamora**, 914 F. 2d 200 (C.A. 10th 1990). The court in **Morales-Zamora** tangentially addressed pretextuality for setting up the road block by focusing only on the **Place** decision that a canine sniff is *sui generis,* thus not a search. Unfortunately the defense did not attack the scope issue involved in the pretextual analysis. A better explanation of why the dogs were present was needed, but obviously not required.

During a routine automobile stop a passenger may give the officers some concern for their safety. One response is to ask for identification. In **State v. Cook**, 15

P.3d 677 (Wash. App. Div. 3 2001), the passenger complied, but when pulling his driver's license a "knotted piece of plastic fell out of a cigarette pack in plain view of the officers. The officer was able to testify that he recognized this as a form of packaging typically used for narcotics. This plain view was upheld.

III. Plain Senses: With a Little Help From My Friends

A. Plain View

The unaided eye, ear, and nose cannot trespass. The law controls the aided ear somewhat through electronic surveillance statutes under Title III. Soon after **Coolidge** was decided, courts were under the impression that eye-enhancing devices (such as binoculars) were forbidden. In **Dow Chemical Co. v. U.S.**, 476 U.S. 227 (1986), the court approved photographs being taken and said, "the mere fact that human vision is enhanced somewhat, as least to the degree here, does not give rise to constitutional problems." The same day the Court approved "naked-eye" flyover observations at 1,000 feet in **California v. Ciraolo**, 476 U.S. 207 (1986). The court said in its first beeper case that "we have never equated police efficiency with unconstitutionality, and we decline to do so now." **U.S. v. Knotts**, 460 U.S. 276 (1983). The beeper aided the visual surveillance of the moving car upon public roads. In 1989 the Court approved the use of a hovering helicopter at 400 feet to aid the eye. **Florida v. Riley**, 488 U.S. 445 (1989). What have these messages said to other courts?

Unaided plain view, save for ordinary eyeglasses, had been the rule not the exception. However, police agencies still try to enhance their view by the use of telescopes and other view aiding devices. Just as often courts have rendered such things seen with view enhancers as inadmissible. Consider the case of **U.S. v. Taborda**, 635 F. 2d 131 (C.A. 2d 1980). The surveillance in **Taborda** had been conducted by means of a high-powered telescope. The government failed to demonstrate what could have been seen with the naked eye and what was viewable only with telescopic assistance. The court said the vice of telescopic viewing allows observation not only of what the householder should realize might be seen by unenhanced viewing, but also of intimate details which he or she legitimately expects will not be observed either by the naked eye or enhanced viewing. Thus the warrantless, enhanced invasion was held to be improper.

In a like vein consider the case of the officer who had to lean off a fire escape to see in a window. Whether the police have a right to be on a fire escape was to be

252

decided on a case-by-case basis, the court held. Assuming, however, that this officer was lawfully present, could he lean over to look in a window not directly visible from a normal position on the fire escape: No, said the court in **State v. Alexander**, 406 A. 2d 313 (N.J. Super. Ct. 1979).

The problem of plain view and the "naked eye" is clearly illustrated in this decision. The court held that the use of binoculars was unconstitutional. The dissent said the drapes should have been drawn. But the majority said that if it had been an activity that involved a substantial risk to life rather than pornography distribution as this was, a different result may have been forthcoming. **People v. Arno**, 153 Cal. Rep. 624 (Cal. Dist. Ct. App. 1979).

However, when binoculars are not used to peer inside buildings or vehicles, use of such vision enhancing devices does not vitiate the search, the Ninth Circuit held. The court relied on the fact that over flights along the west coast were reasonably expected and use of binoculars by government agents were commonplace in this area. **U.S. v. Allen**, 644 F. 2d 749 (C.A. 9th 1980). Also holding that plain view by aerial observation does not violate the Fourth Amendment see **State v. Davis**, 627 P. 2d 492 (Ore. Ct. App. 1981). In any event, one can see that the issue was far from settled. For example, one state has approved the use of the zoom lens and said it is not a sophisticated device, nor is it special equipment not generally in use. **State v. Vogel**, 428 N.W. 2d 272 (S. D. 1988).

That plain view can come from sense enhancing devices that are generally available to the public was unanimously approved in the **Kyllo** case from the Ninth Circuit. However, five members of the Court ruled that thermal imaging devices are not generally available to the public. Therefore, it held that a warrant must be secured to use Thermal "imagers." The concern of the five justices was directed at devices available to the military and the CIA. Thermal imagers were acknowledged to be unsophisticated, but the real concern was for the use of other technology such as laser technology that can monitor conversations in a house through a beam of invisible light and other more sophisticated technology. It was Justice Scalia who led the Majority in this decision. His concern for the sanctity of the home of the owner or renter has been strong despite his lack of concern for guests. He is a true believer in the "Castle Doctrine." His position in this case, therefore, is no surprise. **U.S. v. Kyllo**, 121 S. Ct. 2038 (U.S.). Justice Stevens wrote for the dissent and was critical of a failure to define what is "general use" since these thermal image devices may be purchased or rented by anyone who can dial one of six 800 numbers and since over 11,000 of this type of scanner is already in circulation.

B.   Plain Smell

If the eye can be aided somehow, can the nose be enhanced? Can the police use trained dogs to sniff out controlled substances and explosives? The controversy surrounding the use of sniffing dogs abounded. The Ninth Circuit at one time rejected their use without there being present some reasonable suspicion. The California Supreme Court has approved their use in all cases. In **People v. Mayberry**, 644 P. 2d 810 (Cal. 1982) the court held that the "limited and nonintrusive olfactory investigation performed in this case did not constitute a search thereby invoking..." the Fourth Amendment. All luggage from Florida flights was "sniff-tested" because of the Florida connection. The dog alerted the officer to the Mayberry suitcase. The luggage was not then searched. The defendant was confronted when he picked up his luggage. He consented to a search of the suitcase; marijuana was found. Agreeing with the Fifth Circuit, the California Supreme Court held that there was no reasonable expectation of privacy in odors emanating from luggage. The court noted that two cautions must be observed. First the "expertise" of the dog must be established and second, that a warrant, consent or exigency must be present to search the container.

Hopefully, the issue was finally settled in **U.S. v. Place**, 462 U.S. 696 (1983). The court said a canine sniff by a well-trained narcotics detection dog that does not require opening of the luggage is constitutionally proper. The sniff discloses only the presence or absence of narcotics, a contraband item. The information obtained is thus limited. The canine sniff is *sui generis* and exposure of luggage to the sniff is not a search within the meaning of the Fourth Amendment. Accord: **State v. Scheetz**, 950 P. 2d 722 (Mont. 1997).

What of the tactile senses of touch and taste? The Supreme Court had not, before 1993, specifically passed on these senses. Other courts had. Hawaii approved plain feel in **State v. Ortiz**, 662 P. 2d 517 (Haw. 1983); as did the D.C. Circuit in **U.S. v. Williams**, 822 F. 2d 1174 (C.A. D.C. 1987). For an article on the subject see Note, *The Case Against a Plain Feel Exception to the Warrant Requirement*, 54 Chi. L. Rev. 683 (1987).

Finally, though the eye cannot trespass and the sense of smell cannot, can an aided sense of smell through the use of a dog that trespasses destroy the admissibility of the evidence seized? That was the question presented in **U.S. v. Stone**, 866 F. 2d 359 (C.A. 10th 1989). The police had stopped the defendant lawfully upon a speeding violation. The officer smelled a drug odor while writing the ticket. Stone would not consent to a search but did agree to follow the officer to a nearby police station. The DEA was called and the officer was told Stone was a suspect. A magistrate refused to issue a warrant. Stone was released. Another officer stopped Stone a little later at the request of the DEA. Stone said he was not speeding and that he had already been stopped and given a ticket. The officer asked to see the ticket and Stone said it was in the back of the hatchback. He opened the hatchback. At that point, the DEA arrived with the dog and the dog circled the car and jumped in the back and "keyed" a duffle bag. The rest of the car was searched. The court labeled the dog's act as instinctive. Such instinctive actions did not violate the Fourth Amendment. There was no evidence that the handler encouraged the dog to jump into the car. The articulable suspicion to stop turned into probable cause and brought into action the mobility exception.

C. Plain Feel

"Plain feel" has a legitimate place in the gathering of evidence. Most often these cases will and almost always do arise out of the fear-based **Terry** pat-down. This is well-illustrated by **U.S. v. Salazar**, 945 F. 2d 47 (C.A. 2d 1991). The DEA agents were found to have a legitimate **Terry** frisk right. While frisking the defendant one of the officers felt "the crackling plastic that betrayed the presence of crack vials." The police were informed that he was a drug dealer. If the police, while doing a legitimate pat-down for weapons "feel something that their experience tells them is drugs, the pat-down gives them probable cause to search the suspects for drugs."

There may be other instances in which touching is required. For example, a police officer giving aid to a fallen citizen in an attempt to perform some reasonable first-aid may likewise, due to the exigency, legitimately touch such a person. When testing these cases, the trial court should rule on pretext first. If there is no pretext the next hurdle to surmount is the training and experience factor. Most courts are already able to make this analysis in the ordinary **Terry**-type case and need only apply that analysis to a probable cause inquiry.

The defendant, in a Minnesota case, left a "known crack house" at 8:15 p.m. and two officers, observing this behavior, decided to confront the defendant and to check him for contraband and weapons. The officer ordered the defendant to submit to a pat-down and the defendant complied. A small lump the size of a pea was felt. By pinching his fingers on the lump the officer determined it was "crack" in cellophane. On removal, the lump was indeed "crack" – 0.20 grams. The trial court recognized plain feel and refused to suppress the evidence. The Minnesota Supreme Court said the **Terry** stop in this case was justified but, because the Supreme Court has never recognized plain feel, they determined that plain feel was not a recognized exception to the warrant requirement when the officer had to manipulate the object to determine its criminality. The lack of immediate determination of probable cause doomed this search. This court also felt, despite finding the stop justified, that the officers were attempting to "flout the limitations of **Terry**." The police continued poking around and the lack of immediate independent probable cause concerning the nature of the items was critical. The Minnesota court also indicated that touch is less reliable than sight as a sense and, of course, is more intrusive. Touching is a search; sight is not a search. Once the officer knew no weapon was present the frisk right was over. The decision left room for seizing something immediately apparent but this was not such a case. **State v. Dickerson**, 481 N.W. 2d 840 (Minn. 1992). This case was accepted for certiorari.

Florida, on the other hand, had a clearer case of probable cause arising from plain feel thus they recognized the constitutionality of the arrest that followed the touching. In **Doctor v. State**, 51 Crim. L. Rep. 1066 (Fla. 1992), the police conducted a lawful frisk of the groin area. Immediately the officer said it felt like "peanut brittle" which, because of his training and experience, led him to believe it was a large quantity of crack cocaine. This was enough probable cause to seize the package and to remove it. The court was convinced that the size, shape and texture "severely limited the possibility that the package contained a substance other than crack cocaine." Thus what works for crack may not, without more, apply to leafy or powdery substances.

The Supreme Court, as noted, chose the Minnesota case to resolve the issue of the proper limits of plain feel as plain touch. The Court felt it had already established its constitutionality in **Terry** and all it needed to do in this case was to set parameters for police officers. The Court assumed, as it must, the factual picture painted by the appellate courts of Minnesota. It held that the offending nature of the item touched must be immediately apparent and that the officer is not permitted to "squeeze, slide and manipulate" the item in order to identify it. **Minnesota v. Dickerson**, 508 U.S. 366 (1993).

Within weeks of the **Dickerson** decision, courts in Pennsylvania and North Carolina approvingly cited **Dickerson,** thus indicating a willingness to accept it. The officer in the Pennsylvania case felt a crunchy granular object in the crotch area of the suspect. The officer felt he had probable cause, arrested the defendant and searched him at the police station. This officer testified to 50 prior touching experiences, thus he was able to satisfy the "immediately apparent" prong of **Dickerson. Com. v. Johnson**, 631 A. 2d 1335 (Pa. Super. 1993). The North Carolina court said the continued questioning of the suspect about the bulge the officer felt meant that the bulge did not give immediate probable cause to their officer. **State v. Wilson**, 437 S.E. 2d 387 (N.Car. App. 1993).

256

Six months after **Dickerson**, Illinois, through one of its appellate courts, accepted **Dickerson** in **People v. Mitchell**, 630 N.E. 2d 451 (Ill. App. 1993). It coupled the facts that the police had just observed the suspect with crack-smoking items in his car with the sensate impression that arose upon the frisk to believe that the "immediately apparent" prong had been satisfied.

The one unanswered question concerned the "plain feel" without probable cause or articulable suspicion of luggage, *etc.*, not personally in the physical possession of the owner. People who travel have a tendency to allow others to touch their baggage, *e.g.*, airline employees, taxi drivers, bellhops and so forth. They even can expect other passengers to touch things in overhead bins, under seats and at baggage pick up areas. Do these contexts also allow law enforcement to manipulate such containers to get plain feel or are the rules of **Dickerson** applicable?

The Supreme Court chose **Bond v. U.S.**, 529 U.S. 334 (2000) to settle this issue. The passenger put his bag in a rack directly above his bus seat. A border agent at a check point boarded the bus (not at the border or its functional equivalent) to check immigration status. Having completed this he walked toward the front of the bus. Along the way he squeezed soft luggage in the overhead rack. A brick-like object was felt in Mr. Bond's bag, and Bond consented to an opening of the bag. The brick was methamphetamine. The agent was "fishing" because he had neither articulable suspicion nor probable cause to touch any bag nor did he have anyone's consent. This touching was not protected by the border search exception discussed in Chapter Nine. *First*, the Court recognized luggage as "effects" for Fourth Amendment purposes. *Second*, did the defendant lose a reasonable expectation of privacy by placing his bag in the rack? No, he did not because "flyover" cases involved no physical invasion, so those cases, **Ciarolo** and **Riley**, could not be used. *Third*, could the passenger expect a certain amount of touching by transportation employees or other passengers? Yes, but he would not expect those people to "feel the bag in an exploratory manner." Thus, the defendant's Fourth Amendment rights were violated. Only Justices Breyer and Scalia disagreed. Does this case answer the question whether suitcase puffing to stir odors would also violate a person's Fourth Amendment rights? It should. The manipulation to aid a dog sniff would seem to be prohibited by this decision. Time will tell.

D. Plain Hearing

As previously indicated, Title III, the electronic eavesdropping law, takes care of hearing when unconsented to by either party, by allowing "searches" upon probable cause by judicial warrant. Sometimes, whether by consent or warrant, information is overheard outside the "cause." We call this plain hearing "windfall evidence." When addressing the issue of scope under wiretaps, we refer to the fact that the warrant says seek evidence of Crime A only. While listening the agents get information involving unknown and unsought crimes. What should happen with this "windfall" evidence? Is there a "plain hearing" exception like the "plain view" rule of **Coolidge v. New Hampshire**? Sec. 2517(5) requires prior judicial approval before the government can use "windfall" evidence. If a judge approves progress reports and extends the warrant, is that tantamount to judicial approval? Yes. **U.S. v. Van Horn**, 789 F. 2d 1492 (C.A. 11th 1986). Courts can also interpret whether the evidence is windfall or just part of the genre of crimes already approved to be sought. **U.S. v. Young**, 822 F. 2d 1234 (C.A. 2d 1987). Sometimes police think what they are hearing is more about the same crime and only later upon close analysis is it discovered that a windfall has occurred. If believed, a late filing of the amendment to the application will be excused. **U.S. v. Southard**, 700 F. 2d 1 (C.A. 1st 1983).

Windfall evidence shares what was thought to be the inadvertence requirement of plain view. The issue is whether the police concealed from the judge a high likelihood that evidence of other crimes would be revealed. If so, that would be bad faith. However, mere belief in other crimes and a failure to reveal them does not justify a conclusion of bad faith. **U.S. v. Levine**, 690 F. Supp. 1165 (E.D.N.Y. 1988). Since this inadvertence requirement is statutorily mandated it was not changed by the Court's decision in **Horton v. California** (*supra*).

There are other scope issues as well. For example, in **U.S. v. Borch**, 695 F. Supp. 898 (E.D. Mich. 1988), the defendant did not place the phone properly on its cradle. The police overheard the conversation that took place in the room and said it was covered by the wiretap that had been authorized. The court held this was not a wire communication that had been authorized, thus it suppressed the conversation. Not all courts would agree with this position, however.

The Sixth Circuit has joined other courts by applying plain hearing to evidence gathered during a lawful wiretap when the phone was left off the hook by the defendants, allowing officers to overhear a conversation in the room where the telephone was located. The court analogized such conduct to the plain view doctrine and called it a "lucky break." **U.S. v. Baranek**, 903 F. 2d 1068 (C.A. 6th 1990). In **Baranek**, the phone was "off-the-hook" for two hours and fifteen minutes. Fifty minutes of conversation were recorded during this time period. The **Borch** case was cited by the Sixth Circuit but it would not direct this court's inquiry. First, the court saw the conversation in the room heard over the phone as a wiretap turned into a bugging device. This, of course, was not authorized nor anticipated by the issuing judicial officer. Thus, there is no way that this "risk" could be "squeezed in" under this authorization. **Baranek** at 1071. Second, they approached the problem from the plain view doctrine perspective. The court focused on the inadvertency issue. The court found a lawful intrusion, thus the police were where they had a right to be. The inadvertent act of failing to properly replace the telephone was not anticipated, therefore, it was truly an inadvertent act. Next, what was heard was immediately apparent evidence of a crime. The court said the government got a "lucky break of sorts" and "stumbled across the evidence." Since nothing in the statute prevents this police behavior there appeared to them to be no reason to exclude the evidence. Although they did not address the issue, there also appears to have been no time to go out and secure a bugging permit.

Well-trained drug officers and most reasonable general police officers know that drug dealers have gone "high-tech" and use telephone paging devices to aid them in their drug deals. When a dealer's paging device is properly confiscated by police, may they press the button and secure the names of the dealer's customers and suppliers? That was the issue in **U.S. v. Meriwether**, 917 F. 2d 955 (C.A. 6th 1990). The Sixth Circuit did a **Katz** analysis under **Smith v. Maryland** (the pen register case) and found no basic Fourth Amendment expectations of privacy. It also found no violation of the Electronic Surveillance Act. Under a "pure" plain view analysis the result is correct because the defendant in this case had no standing in the message that he delivered to the paging device. Had the evidence gathered been used to upgrade the charge of the owners of the pager a different plain view analysis would have been required. With lawful presence and immediately apparent being satisfied the critical question would be centered on the exigency or need to forego a warrant. Without a satisfactory explanation of the exigency there is a reasonable case to be made for suppression under the warrant preference doctrine.

One of the common practices followed by police during a raid of a drug dealer's apartment or house is to answer the phone. Those that seek to buy drugs are told to come on over. As the customers arrive they are arrested for their attempt to buy. Nothing in the Electronic Surveillance Act appears to prohibit this practice. As long as the police are not violating a reasonable expectation of privacy by answering the phone, the risk for the defendant without standing in the house or apartment is one that a citizen takes when making phone calls. This plain hearing is usually viewed as a consent issue and not under plain view. See **U.S. v. Passarella**, 788 F. 2d 372 (C.A. 6th 1986), **U.S. v. Ordonez**, 722 F. 2d 530 (C.A. 9th 1983), and **U.S. v. Sangineto-Miranda**, 859 F. 2d 1501 (C.A. 6th 1988).

IV.   Being Lawfully There

The entire plain view doctrine is based on the concepts of lawful police presence coupled with lawful activity on the property. The **Coolidge** opinion listed activities which if otherwise properly based could serve to give the officer his plain view. It listed: (1) Searching with a warrant; (2) Hot pursuit; (3) Search incident; (4) Exigent circumstances; and (5) Non-search activity in an area where police have access. There are, of course, others that have been inferentially approved since then. In **Texas v. Brown**, the plain view came as a result of the proper investigative stop; in **Florida v. Riley**, open fields and plain view were recognized. When the court indicated "on any lawful" search they meant any lawful search (with all scope limitations).

The lawful police presence is to be judged from a Fourth Amendment perspective. The U.S. Supreme Court recognizes no legitimate expectation of privacy in the "open fields." **Hester, Oliver** and **Dunn** (discussed in Chapter 8). Those cases assume an otherwise illegal act; trespassing. But since there is no societally protected privacy right, the police are lawfully present for Fourth Amendment purposes. Thus, in states that follow **Hester,** *et al.,* there is no problem. In states that reject **Hester** and "open fields" the trespass would negate any finding of plain view rights. Local constitutions, statutes, and decisions should be consulted.

It is often easy to look at this as a one-step inquiry and limit it to only a finding of lawful presence. Courts are careful to require a second step and that is a finding of a lawfully performed search. Any search that exceeds the scope of reasonableness as to the places investigated will cause plain view to fail.

One issue to be considered from a plain view perspective concerns the placement of video cameras for law enforcement purposes in public restrooms. If the camera scans an area that would be viewable by any member of the public, how have the police unreasonably intruded into privacy at a constitutional level? People have a reasonable expectation of privacy in stalls with doors that can block the casual look of passing members of society. The Washington Court of Appeals joins most other states saying that a closed bathroom stall is an area of privacy in **City of Tukwila v. Nalder**, 770 P. 2d 670 (Wash. Ct. App. 1989). Some courts are unwilling to apply such Fourth Amendment analysis. The court overlooks the number of assaults and kidnappings that have taken place in such restrooms and, in particular, as such criminal conduct impacts on children. Instead they approach the problem from a Due Process analysis under the guise of the Fourth Amendment.

Of course, "being lawfully there" means as it relates to searches in the privacy areas of that defendant where he has standing. The officer can gain his plain view advantage quite illegally as is pointed out in the Open Fields materials of Chapter Nine. The police can even get a neighbor to let them set up a look-out point in the neighbor's home or from the neighbor's yard. **State v. Vogel**, 428 N.W. 2d 272 (S. D. 1988).

How far can the police and the neighbor go in aiding the officer beyond allowing them to use a vantage point? This was the primary issue in **West v. State**, 588 So. 2d 248 (Fla. App. 1991). The police received a tip regarding marijuana in the defendant's yard. The police sought consent to search but were denied. They then got the neighbor's permission to take a view from the neighbor's yard. The solid fence surrounding the defendant's backyard was too high. A step ladder was borrowed from the neighbor and the plants were seen. Was this evidence admissible? Were the police where they had a right to be? Yes. Did the police trespass on the curtilage? No, and remember, the eye cannot trespass. Could the police have done a fly-over? Yes. Did the defendant have a reasonable expectation of privacy? Yes. Why did this court rule the evidence inadmissible? The court held that securing the ladder to do the non-trespassory peering was prohibited by dicta in **Ciarola**, 476 U.S. 222 in which the ladder example was given; this is what LaFave calls "extraordinary efforts," citing LaFave and Israel, *Criminal Procedure* §3.2 (c) at 172 (1984 and Supp. 1990). This court was in the position in which it felt compelled to follow the *dicta* of the U.S. Supreme Court. Did the Supreme Court, however, prohibit the use of all ladders or only those that leaned against the defendant's fence? The *dicta* does not clarify this point. There would be a world of difference in using the defendant's fence to aid the view and not touching it at all. What is the difference between looking out of the neighbor's second story window and using a ladder whose only support is the neighbor's yard? None, in reality. Too much should not be read into Supreme Court *dicta*, especially when measured against subsequent case law.

But for the most part, many of the plain view cases do not arise from open fields. Consider the Maine case of **State v. Cloutier**, 544 A 2d 1277 (Me. 1988). A police officer while on patrol was fully aware of recent burglaries of homes in the area. He saw a darkened house at 8:00 p.m. but a light was shining from the basement. Saying the officer had the status of an invitee, Maine held that his peering through the basement window after trying to rouse the occupants was valid thus the warrant secured to further search and seize the marijuana plants he saw growing in the basement was properly issued.

In a number of cases plain view comes through consent. Sometimes that consent is through the open-invitation-to-the-public type of case. Sometimes the consent is to a limited access area as in the next case. A member of the Fraternal Order of Eagles, turned informer, told police of gambling at the local club house. The police decided they wanted to take a look and had one agent accompany the informant. The informant showed her credentials which the door keeper did not view, let alone question. The officer was introduced as a guest. The officer used the plain view acquired to secure a search warrant. The defendant argued that consent would not have been given for the officer to enter had they known his true identity. Defendant lost. Although Ohio would suppress if the officer affirmatively misrepresented himself or herself, it was unwilling to suppress in this context. **State v. Posey**, 534 N.E. 2d 61 (Ohio 1989). Massachusetts in a similar kind of case held that the officer's misrepresentation of his identity is not dispositive of the issue since police are permitted to use "decoys and to conceal the identity of its agents." For them, for a misrepresentation to rise to a violation of an expectation of privacy there must be evidence "to show reasonable enforcement of a policy to exclude persons other than members and their guests." **Com. v. D' Onofrio**, 396 Mass. 711 (1986).

V. Exigent Circumstances and Plain View

The plain view doctrine – branch two does not allow seizure unless exigency is shown. In these cases, the officer is not conducting an otherwise lawful search but the officer is where he or she has a right to be. Without consent or warrant no seizure can take place unless an exigency can be demonstrated. The determination of what constitutes an exigency is always difficult. Would a reasonable fear that the evidence would be destroyed by a codefendant seeing another being arrested be sufficient exigency to secure the apartment until a warrant arrived? Would drugs seized in plain view during a search for other people in the apartment be admissible? These were the questions confronting the Fourth Circuit in **U.S. v. Turner**, 650 F. 2d 526 (C.A. 4th 1981).

The factors to use for determining whether exigency exists are: (1) Degree of urgency involved and the amount of time necessary to obtain a warrant; (in this case 2 hours); (2) Reasonableness of belief that contraband is about to be removed or destroyed; (police were present because they heard it was about to be moved); (3) Possibility of danger to police guarding the site; (4) Information indicating the possessors of the contraband are aware that the police are on their trail; (probably saw arrest in parking lot of apartment building); and (5) The ready destructibility of the contraband – (cocaine easily flushable). Against these tests, the officers were acting reasonably in **Turner** case. But waiting four and one-half hours to seize something discovered by plain view shows a lack of exigency. See **Com. v. Sergienko**, 399 Mass. 291 (1987). The foregoing case illustrates the kind of analysis required by courts in determining whether the officers acted reasonably in seizing the incriminating evidence.

In **State v. Foxhoven**, 2001 WL 195082 (Iowa App.) the police arrested the defendant outside his home. While questioning him, he admitted that there were drugs in the house. The police entered without his consent and found the drugs. However, there was no reason to believe that there was anyone in the house who could have seized the drugs and destroyed them. Without a showing of an objectively reasonable belief that occupants inside a house are aware of the officer's presence and might destroy the drugs, these officers "jumped the gun" and should have secured the premises and applied for a warrant.

Twice the Court has had an opportunity to create a "murder scene" exception and twice the court has rejected the concept. Its latest rejection came in **Thompson v. Louisiana**, 469 U.S. 17 (1984), a *per curiam* decision. The homicide team arrived 35 minutes after the murder-suicide attempter had been taken to the hospital. They entered and searched. This violated the Fourth Amendment. Such a search was not justified because a homicide recently occurred there. The Court said there is no "murder scene" exception but only, perhaps, a right to go quickly through the house to see if there are any other victims. The warrantless search was not permissible in **Mincey v. Arizona**, 437 U.S. 385 (1978) and it was not permissible in this case. But allowing them to go quickly through the house would carry plain view rights with it. This was confirmed in **Maryland v. Buie**, 494 U.S. 325 (1990) and is discussed in Chapter 12. The **Buie** case approved the use of protective sweeps and the apparent ability to seize the evidence found in plain view.

Views from public roads were approved in **State v. Lorenz**, 622 N.W. 2d 243 (S. D. 2001). The views were obtained by the estranged wife of the defendant on her visits to her husband's home. She reported them to the police. The police went to the address and from the road verified her sightings and observed several plants. They took photographs and obtained a warrant. The court ruled that the marital privilege does not cover observations; only communications. Besides, the officers had the plain view alternative and what they observed on their own was in itself sufficient to establish probable cause for the warrant.

VI. Conclusion

This chapter started with a chart derived from **Coolidge**. Because of the plurality status of many of the sections of **Coolidge**, several decisions have been required to arrive at a majority position on the contested points of "inadvertence" and "immediately apparent." The inadvertence requirement is only germane to a pretextual search inquiry. Having a hope of finding incriminating evidence or even pre-existing probable cause to believe the evidence is there does not raise pre-textuality by themselves. Exceeding the scope of the lawful search or leaving after finding quickly an unrelated item can raise the pretextuality defense.

The immediately apparent, or obvious evidence of a crime, is not limited to things that announce their illegality. However, mere suspicion of illegality and articulable suspicion of illegality are not enough. The police must demonstrate probable cause to believe in the illegality. Other than these changes, the Court has maintained the lawful presence rule and still continue to distinguish the two branches of plain view though there are very few police activities left that are not a lawful search.

VII.   Plain View Checklist

If plain view is used to justify admissibility:

I.   **Determine which branch applies**:
A.   Branch One - already conducting lawful search ___

B.   Branch Two - merely lawfully at a place ___
(if B, then use V after II-IV are satisfied)

II.   **Inadvertence**
A.   Pretextual-bingo ___ search or seizure invalid
B.   Hunch or hope-or probable cause ___
search or seizure or both may be valid as
long as not pretextual
C.   Scope reasonable ___

III.   **Obvious evidence of a crime (immediately apparent) –
(use probable cause standard)**
A.   Thing speaks for itself ___
B.   Thing gives probable cause to believe that it is
evidence of a crime ___
C.   Thing is only articulably suspicious or merely

suspicious ___
(if C, it may not be seized or searched)

IV. Helping the senses
A. Object or method used to help senses not unique ___

B. Object or method used to help senses unique ___
(if B, search or seizure invalid)

V. Exigency (applies to Branch Two only)
Spell out why no time to secure warrant
A. Danger to or destruction of evidence ___
B. Danger to police or others ___
C. True emergency ___
D. Scope reasonable ___

CHAPTER SEVEN
OPEN FIELDS

I. Open Fields Exception to the Warrant Requirement Phase One – Pre-Curtilage

Before the courts began complicating the area, the rule was very simple. The right of privacy in a house, as a Fourth Amendment concern, stopped at the outside surface of the outside walls. Anything illegal that was done outside that sphere was considered done in the open fields. The rule developed in a rural America in an age of ample space. Basically, the Fourth Amendment protects "persons, houses, papers and effects." Does the protection exist as to the "back 40?" How far away from the house does the protection exist? Can the officer trespass upon land, observe some illegality, and seize the evidence of that illegality? Does the posting of no-trespassing signs have any effect? What role does a fence play?

It is acknowledged that **Hester v. United States**, 265 U.S. 57 (1924), set out the "open fields" doctrine. It was held that a visual search by police who were trespassing was not within the Fourth Amendment's protection. The theory was that open areas are not covered by the Constitution, therefore, it would be futile to secure a warrant since none was required. The case was decided long before the Court adopted the privacy analysis now required by **Katz**.

Hester was charged with concealing distilled spirits. Officers concealed themselves some 50 to 100 yards from the house. They saw Hester hand another man a quart bottle. The police called out. The men bolted and the officers fired a shot. Hester dropped a jug which he had obtained from a nearby car. It broke, but some moonshine was left in the bottom half. The other man threw his bottle away. The Court said: "The only shadow of a ground for bringing up the case is drawn from the hypothesis that the examination of the vessels took place upon Hester's father's land. As to that, it is enough to say that, apart from the justification, the special protection accorded by the Fourth Amendment to the people in their 'persons, houses, papers, and effects', is not extended to the open fields. The distinction between the latter and the house is as old as the common law." The officers were trespassing on Hester's father's land, upon which Hester lived and in which he had his own right or standing. The Court knew of this and it was therefore no oversight as to that issue. The "apart from the justification" language cited above was a tangential reference to exigent circumstances as an exception.

The next pronouncement of "open fields" came in the 1974 decision of **Air Pollution Variance Board of Colorado v. Western Alfalfa Corp.**, 416 U.S. 861 (1974). The state inspector went on the outdoor premises of the defendant without his knowledge or consent. The inspector was there to make a pollution test. It was daytime. No warrant was required by state law. At no time did the inspector enter the defendant's buildings. The Court said that the inspector sighted what anyone in the city could see – the plumes of smoke from the chimneys. The inspector was on defendant's property but "we are not advised that he was on premises from which he was excluded." Even though he could have operated within or without the premises "...he is well within the 'open fields' exception to the Fourth Amendment approved in **Hester**." The "within or without" language refers to the fact that this was an administrative search case and all that that implies.

What neither of these cases satisfactorily answered was the question regarding the function of fences, walls and "no trespassing" signs on open fields. This complication comes from **Air Pollution** in which the Court says "we are not advised that he was on premises from which he was excluded." A trespass is a trespass. Whether there is a fence to climb, a sign to pass, a wall to scale, or the mere act of stepping over an imagined boundary line makes no difference. The Court said that the invasion of privacy, if it can be said to exist, is abstract and theoretical. Thus the Court apparently was not willing to concede a right of privacy to anything but the inside of the house or business building. But a change was coming.

II. Open Fields – Phase II – Lower Court Limits on Hester

Some federal courts had limited the open field area to those areas outside the "curtilage." Curtilage, at common law, meant the building or buildings attached to or adjacent to the dwelling house, used in support of the dwelling house. Thus, the land immediately surrounding the curtilage would not be "open fields." These cases totally disregard **Hester**, because all that took place was not far from the Hester house.

The trouble with the curtilage principle is that the courts, the police and the citizen must engage in a "how long is the leash" or "how high the moon" argument. Consider the Georgia decision of **Norman v. State**, 216 S.E. 2d 645 (Ga. App. 1975). In this case, the court said a search made within the curtilage without a warrant is unconstitutional and void. The court cited a federal case where an area within 70 to 80 yards of the house was within the curtilage and an Oklahoma decision in which the curtilage extended 100 yards from the house. It concluded by saying: "The truck here which was within 200 feet of the house and within 100 feet from the barn must also be assumed to be within the curtilage." This evidence might have been excluded; not on "open fields" but upon the fact that a closed truck was broken open, and thus that an expectation of privacy was violated. There is nothing inherently illegal for a truck to be sitting on one's property. However, the mobility exception could be applied.

North Carolina got involved in the trespass dispute in one decision. An officer was standing on high school property and observed a lean-to shed. There was no residence attached to this 19.9 acres of property and no "No Trespassing" signs. The officer knew of a stolen tractor meeting the description of the tractor in the lean-to shed. He walked upon the property, checked the serial number, and found it to be the stolen tractor. The North Carolina Court of Appeals said there was no reasonable expectation of privacy as this was an open field and, in checking the serial number, the officer was acting reasonably. The court made the point that it was visible to the naked eye by an officer who was in a place where he had a right to be. **State v. Boone**, 225 S.E. 2d 740 (N.C. Ct. App. 1977). Since curtilage is a doctrine requiring the presence of a dwelling, the decision was quite reasonable. The defendant then appealed to the North Carolina Supreme Court. Although appearing to accept a curtilage limit to open fields, the court approvingly cited the trespass theory of **Hester**. They said the principle had been applied "by the Court on prior occasions." Thus in affirming the Court of Appeals they evidently rejected the "where they had a right to be" rationale of the Court of Appeals and focused on the trespass. **State v. Boone**, 230 S.E. 2d 459 (N.C. 1977). This court apparently forgot about the requirement of a dwelling.

It was not clear whether the North Carolina and Georgia courts based their decisions on their state constitutions or upon the U.S. Constitution. But in a Wisconsin case, that court clearly based its decision on the U.S. Constitution under the improper assumption that it could give greater rights to the defendant than the U.S. Supreme Court does under the U.S. Constitution. Wisconsin adopted a version of the curtilage rule. **Conrad v. State**, 218 N.W. 2d 252 (Wis. 1974).

The Illinois Court wrestled with the "open fields" doctrine and whether to adopt the privacy or curtilage tests that had been adopted by various federal circuit courts. Though Illinois seems to have adopted the "pure" rule of **Hester**, the court mentions that a police officer in a plane at a reasonable altitude had a right to be where he was. They also classified the trespassory investigation as alright because the buildings were more than 100 yards from the site of the stolen property. Yet, it approvingly cited **Hester** and said of **Air Pollution**, "...it is notable that in **Air Pollution** the smoke in question was plainly visible from off the defendant's property but the government agent had to go on the property to take the incriminating test of the smoke." **People v. Lashmett**, 389 N.E. 2d 888 (Ill. App. Ct. 1979).

A California Court re-examined the "open fields" issue. Calling the **Hester** rule a product of another era, it held that the rule as announced in **Hester** was no longer viable. The court would rather rely on an "expectation of privacy" theory and whether that expectation was violated by an unreasonable (trespassory) intrusion by the government. The court said that if the normal indicia of privacy (hedges, fence, etc.) are present, then the police must secure a warrant to enter the premises. **Burkholder v. Superior Court**, 158 Cal. Rep. 86 (Cal. Dist. Ct. App. 1979). See also **Chilton v. State**, 611 P. 2d 53 (Alaska 1980), (which case did not cite **Hester** and found the trespass offensive thus negating the "plain view" discovery of evidence).

The problem of curtilage and open fields, as has been noted, created much uncertainty which was neither required nor desired by the **Hester** rule. The Seventh Circuit had created certainty by using curtilage, but coupled it with a *per se* 75-foot rule as being that area of expected privacy. The Fourth Circuit was asked to adopt that standard. It refused to do so, continued its "many factors" test. **U.S. v. Van Dyke**, 643 F. 2d 992 (C.A. 4th 1981).

It almost appeared that "open fields" was becoming a lost doctrine, having become confused with the "plain view" doctrine and the broader and more general "expectation of privacy" principle. This is illustrated by the split Ninth Circuit and its decision in **U.S. v. Wheeler**, 641 F. 2d 1321 (C.A. 9th 1981). The key fact involved an officer climbing upon a pile of tires to see over a six foot fence, ostensibly to get the defendant's attention on an unrelated matter and the officer's viewing, as a result, of contraband in the defendant's yard. This view was used as the basis for obtaining a search warrant. The defendant sought suppression of the evidence. In the majority opinion, the court characterized the problem as one of plain view, and found the officer was where he had a right to be. No allusion to "open fields" was made. The concurrence based its approval on the fact that the defendant invited the problem by stacking tires next to the fence so that any person passing by could stand and look into the yard. The author of the concurring opinion also agreed that the officer was where he had a right to be and noted that, but for the tires, there could have been an expectation of privacy.

Certainly with time to secure a warrant, the police in another case learned that stolen dynamite was located in a car on the farm owned by the defendant's father. The father was not home so the officers proceeded to the farm where, in an open field, the car was sighted. It appeared to have been abandoned since it had expired plates, open doors and the lock removed from the trunk. The car had been registered in the father's name but had been purchased for the use of the son. The dynamite was found upon opening the trunk. Assuming, as the court had to, that **Hester** was still the law, the question of the search of the trunk as an area of reasonably expected privacy became the core issue. Considering the fact that a highly dangerous cache was being sought, the court may well have been justified in finding a valid exigency but the court did not use that theory. Instead it found that a trunk without any lock or indicia of security did not constitute an area of privacy. The court did not address the issue whether there was time to secure a warrant nor the police ability to seize the car until a warrant could have been obtained. Only the dissent noted the lack of exigency, however, in that context, the dissenter was wrong. The case had none of the exigencies of escape or destruction of evidence as was present in the **Hester** case, but it did have a danger to society possibility. Confusing signals from courts would only create future problems for law enforcement. **U.S. v. Ramapuram**, 632 F. 2d 1149 (C.A. 4th 1980). The case also illustrates that most Fourth Amendment problems cannot be resolved upon one doctrine but that it often takes several to make a proper analysis.

The attack on the "open fields" doctrine continued. On May 5, 1982, the Sixth Circuit in **U.S. v. Oliver**, 686 F. 2d 356 (C.A. 6th 1982), decided an "open fields" case. The Sixth Circuit held that **Hester** was still good Fourth Amendment law. Oliver was a farmer whom the police had reason to believe was growing marijuana on his farm. They walked around a gate on a path adjacent to it. "No Trespassing" signs were posted. Two open fields of marijuana were discovered. Only from defendant's land could the marijuana be seen. Clearly, there was an intentional trespass no worse in form than in **Hester**. The Sixth started their opinion with a discussion of **Katz**. They found nothing in **Katz** that in any way overruled **Hester**. In fact, it held, "any expectation of privacy that an owner might have with respect to his open field is not, *as a matter of law*, (emphasis by the court) an expectation that society is prepared to recognize as reasonable." They also noted that the placement of the "No Trespass" signs had no effect. This, of course, is the analysis required by **Katz** and **Greenwood**.

II.   Phase III – Open Fields – Revisited

Noting all of the foregoing activity in the area the Supreme Court decided to use the **Oliver** case as the vehicle to announce a new "Open Fields" exception to the warrant requirement. The Court decided that the **Katz** expectation of privacy had to be brought into the picture as had so many of the other courts in the country. Thus in **Oliver v. U.S.**, 466 U.S. 170 (1984), the court would begin to carve out a new rule. They were quick to point out that **Katz** is the "touchstone" of modern Fourth Amendment analysis. Equally important was the fact that courts were not to lose sight of the fact that we protect only those expectations that society is prepared to recognize as reasonable. Then they said: "In this light, the rule of **Hester v. U.S.**....that we reaffirm today, may be understood as providing that an individual may not legitimately demand privacy for activities conducted out of doors in fields, except in the area immediately surrounding the home." Certain enclaves, they noted, should be free from arbitrary government interference. As for fences and no trespassing signs the Court said: "It is not generally true...that such things...effectively bar the public from viewing open fields in rural areas."

Saying that Holmes recognized the curtilage as a protected area (which is difficult factually), the Court said curtilage is not open fields. The Court used only the broadest definition of curtilage thus giving no specific guidance to the courts below. Somehow, in this opinion, one gets the impression that there are "bright lines" which everyone would recognize. The guide provided was: "the area to which extends the intimate activity associated with the `sanctity of a man's home and the privacies of life....". This was a clear departure from **Hester** in that there was no direct mention of curtilage in **Hester**. The common law definition developed in an era when the house primarily served three functions only: (1) Eating place; (2) Sleeping place; and (3) Gathering place.

The bodily excretory and urination functions took place in an "outhouse." Before refrigeration, things that required such storage were kept in spring houses or fruit cellars often also outside the house building. In some instances (Jefferson's Monticello), the kitchen was located in an unattached building. How could such a definition cover the modern era? In a number of cases the common law recognized carriage houses as within the curtilage while other decisions said no to that concept. The doctrine developed in a rural setting and was a rural doctrine. How does it operate in the suburban setting and should it apply to the urban setting at all? The **Oliver** case did not satisfactorily settle these issues.

The Court thought it was avoiding a case-by-case analysis with its definition in **Oliver**. That was not the case. In 1987, the Court made its first (if not last) attempt to provide better guidance in **U.S. v. Dunn**, 480 U.S. 294 (1988). Dunn had a 198-acre ranch in Texas, which was completely encircled by a perimeter fence. There were several interior fences made mainly of posts and barbed wire. The house was one-half mile from a public road. A fence encircled the house and a nearby greenhouse. Two barns were located approximately 50 yards from this fence. The front of the larger of the two barns was enclosed by a wooden fence and had an open overhang. Locked, waist-high gates barred entry into the barn and netting material stretched from the ceiling to the top of the wooden gates. The officers, without a warrant, went upon the property, crossed two fences, and stood halfway between the barn and house. They received "plain smell" from the barns and went over the last fence and to the windows. They did this at least twice more and the next day, the police secured a warrant.

Was the barn within the curtilage of the residence? The Court said that can only be "resolved with reference to four factors": (1) The proximity of the area claimed to be curtilage to the home; (2) Whether the area is included within an enclosure surrounding the home; (3) The nature of the uses to which the area is put; and (4) The steps taken by the resident to protect the area from observation by people passing by. It said these are not always going to yield a correct answer. How did Mr. Dunn do? Not well. The Court applied these factors to the barn as follows: (1) Distance – 50 to 60 yards – substantial distance – no inference that barn is an adjunct of the house; (2) Privacy of house – was not included in that fence – stands out as a distinct portion of ranch – quite separate from the residence; (3) Nature of use – though nobody could tell until the officer's trespass, a drug manufacturing laboratory did not sound "homey;" and (4) Steps taken to carve out privacy – livestock fences are not privacy fences. The fact that one would have to drive or walk one half mile from a public road to be a passerby should not concern us. Trespassers are a fact of life (especially during hunting season). These officers stood outside the curtilage of the house and observed all that they could observe – they were in the open field.

One of the possible unanswered questions of **Oliver** and **Dunn** is whether curtilage is a "residence only" exception, or is there a curtilage rule for business property as well? The Supreme Court has held that the Fourth Amendment protects a person's reasonable expectation of privacy in the office setting (**Mancusi** and **Ortega**, see Chapter 1). Nothing in **Oliver** and **Dunn** seems to address that issue. **Western Alfalfa** may provide the answer, even though it was an administrative search case rather than a general crime search case. In **Western Alfalfa** (*supra*) the Court said: "Depending upon the lay-out of the plant, the inspector may operate within or without the premises but in either case he is well within the 'open fields' exception...approved in **Hester**." The Court also said it was "not advised that he was on premises from which the public was excluded" but that is when they went on to lay out the "open fields" applicability. **Dow Chemical** (*infra*) cannot be used to any great degree in this context since it was a fly-over case. Besides, the above cited cases were all administrative search cases.

In any event, the Illinois Supreme Court met the "business curtilage" issue head-on and flatly denied the concept saying that **Hester, Oliver** and **Dunn** were not to be extended to businesses. In this case police went to a gravel storage area behind a plumbing supply business and found a stolen car. To gain access to the gravel area they walked up a private driveway. The court held that a privacy analysis and not a curtilage analysis should be applied. **People v. Janis**, 565 N.E. 2d 633 (Ill. 1990). The present tendency of the Supreme Court to rely on the common law and not to expand it makes the Illinois decision a proper analytical tool.

Virginia faced the issue of business premises and whether "open fields" applied. Specifically the property was on the water and the entry was upon a warehouse and its adjacent dock. The police vantage point in this case was not one where a regular business invitee would be found. Virginia concluded that through **Dow Chemical**, the Supreme Court has indeed said there are business premises "open fields" despite the fact that it was a fly-over case. The observation of the untagged fish from private property heavily "posted" violated an expectation of privacy and was an invasion of business curtilage. **Johnson v. Com.**, 1998 WL 72865 (Va. App.).

As indicated, the urban setting and the curtilage would cause some difficulty. The defendant in an Illinois case was raising marijuana in her back yard in an area separate from her family's use of the yard. The patch was located in a well-weeded corner of the yard which was partially bordered by a hedge but not otherwise fenced. The tops of the plants were seen by officers standing in a yard two houses away. She urged that the police could not seize since her plants were within the curtilage. The court used **Katz** instead, saying that since she took no steps to shield the plants from view, her expectation of privacy was not reasonable. The court accepted the entry as violating neither **Katz** nor **Dunn**. The "plain view-probable cause only" branch possibility was not discussed – (**People v. Schmidt**, 522 N.E. 2d 1317 (Ill. App. Ct.

1988)), nor was exigency. The police had the "fullest measure of probable cause" under **Coolidge,** but there was no record made on exigency and whether there was time to secure a warrant.

Illinois approached the problem as a privacy matter, but impliedly held no curtilage because no privacy fence existed. It probably would have made no difference because the plants could be seen two houses away. The Maryland Special Court of Appeals, however, dismissed a view from next door and emphasized the warrantless entry upon curtilage in a suburban-urban town house setting. That is the proper way to handle the matter, of course. The officer in **Brown v. State**, 540 A. 2d 143 (Md. App. 1988) knocked on the front door several times. No one answered so the officer went around back through an open gate in the six- foot high wooden fence. As he arrived at the back door, defendant was throwing tin foil packets out the window into the back yard. Drugs were found by the officer. The Maryland Court declared this fenced area curtilage in which the defendant enjoyed a reasonable expectation of privacy. It should have treated this case under the exigent circumstances doctrine or as a pure plain view case. The result would be the same but the analysis would have been less suspect. Curtilage is really a rural property doctrine.

The District of Columbia Court of Appeals has also wrestled with curtilage and the **Dunn** tests in the urban setting. The "proximity to the home test" of **Dunn** in an urban setting where lots are often small is probably irrelevant. In such cases, the Court pointed out, because of the way homes are placed, it would almost be impossible to show a limit to one's privacy interest. Thus a fence may not establish privacy in and of itself. Finally, they said that the uses of one's property may be more important in showing an intimate tie to the house. At any rate curtilage in the city does not automatically come with a fence. **Horton v. U.S.**, 541 A. 2d 604 (D.C. Ct. App. 1988). This makes good common sense especially if the court is willing to conduct a plain view analysis.

That "open fields" and the curtilage doctrines do not work in an urban context does not mean that police are without means of obtaining evidence. The urban cases are better handled by using a "reasonable expectation of privacy" analysis coupled with a "plain view" analysis. In a Colorado case police peeked through cracks in a six-foot high privacy fence while standing on a two-foot, unmaintained strip of land owned by the defendant that abutted an alleyway. Given the visible spaces in this fence along this public alley, the court felt there was no reasonable expectation of privacy in the fenced yard. Signs were not posted on the unimproved, unmaintained strip of land and the cracks in the fence were not filled. The court applied the **Dunn** tests to the case and also found it "wanting," but it need not have taken that approach. **People v.**

Wimer, 700 P. 2d 436 (Colo. App. 1990). The more important question is what did the police do after getting plain view; seize or secure a warrant? Was there an exigency?

One court in Louisiana recognized the open fields doctrine in an urban setting. This case involved a vacant lot next to the defendant's home and the cocaine found in plastic bottles under an old tire in that vacant lot. **State v. Green**, 683 So. 2d 1292 (La. App. 1996).

A Florida case held that a warrantless search of a fenced lot in a well populated urban area was an "open field" search and thus did not violate the Fourth Amendment. A small warehouse was in the middle and rear of the lot. The area was mainly residential, but no one lived on this lot and it was not an "advertised" commercial piece of property. **O'Neal v. State**, 689 So. 2d 1135 (Fla. App. 1997).

Cases such as the foregoing point up the wisdom of Holmes in **Hester**. Privacy rights end at the outside wall's surface of the house said Holmes. Sometimes the simplicity of a rule protects more rights than a complex rule about which courts disagree. Bright lines can be better in some instances than hazy ones. At what point do we become too technical in an effort to avoid a police state?

Assuming that the police were lawfully present in a common hallway of an apartment building, a New York court correctly found that a canine sniff alerting to drugs within the apartment, coupled with other information, yielded probable cause for the issuance of a search warrant. This court rejected a decision of the Second Circuit that held that "sniffs" of homes were somehow different than "sniffs" of personal property and, thus, an invalid search – **U.S. v. Thomas**, 757 F. 2d 1359 (C.A. 2d 1985) – **People v. Dunn**, 553 N.Y.S. 2d 257 (N.Y. Sup. Ct., App. Div. 1990). This decision comports with **Johnson v. United States**, 333 U.S. 10 (1948) and also clearly illustrates that a "curtilage" rule would frustrate law enforcement in the urban apartment building context. It may also illustrate why Holmes did not create a curtilage rule for "open fields" in **Hester**. Trying to force a case like this within **Hester** *et al.* makes no sense whatsoever. Common areas of large or small apartment complexes are better suited to a plain view analysis.

How have **Oliver** and **Dunn** fared as decisions otherwise? It does not appear that Mississippi has changed its rule that prohibits open field searches on private property. New York, which at one time gave greater protection on private land than the Supreme Court had announced that it will accept **Oliver**. **People v. Reynolds**, 528 N.Y. Supp. 2d 5 (N.Y. 1988). Oregon has partially retreated from the recognition of the open fields doctrine. If the occupant of the property has posted "No Trespassing" signs or has done something else just as effective as fencing, then police have no right to enter even non-curtilage property in that state. **State v. Dixson**, 766 P. 2d 1015 (Ore. 1988).

New York now believes that the posting of "no trespassing" signs does make a difference with regard to the physical trespass of areas that would otherwise be open fields. The New York court was critical of the U.S. Supreme Court's apparent partial abandonment of **Katz** in the **Oliver** decision. New York found that its own use of **Katz** required them, under their own constitution, to reject some of the philosophy of **Oliver**. Thus a landowner who posts "no trespassing" signs or uses some other means to prohibit entry to his property outside the curtilage gains for property owner or controller a reasonable, societally protected expectation of privacy. **People v. Scott**, 593 N.E. 2d 1328 (N.Y. 1992). Thus **Reynolds** and **Scott** must be read together.

When looking at gates, fences, and no trespassing signs, New Jersey gives us an interesting method of analyzing them for privacy/non-privacy impact. This court said: "The efforts made here by the owner to keep people off the property were feeble and not reasonably calculated to provide the expectation of privacy now claimed by the defendants. **State v. Gates**, 703 A. 2d 696 (N.J. Super. 1997).

A baited private field was at the center of the controversy in **Quintrell v. State**, 499 S.E. 2d 117 (Ga.App. 1998). Two DNR officers went upon this private land and video-taped the man-made tree stands used to lure game for easy kills. People were also caught on the tape. The main culprit had the owner's permission to enter the land; the officers did not have that permission. Private land, the court noted, does not for that reason alone constitute a zone of privacy that is protected by the Fourth Amendment. They agreed with **Oliver** that an open field need not be "open" nor a "field." The filming and arrests were constitutional.

The defendant in a Louisiana case argued that because the area invaded was a thickly wooded area, it could not be classified as an open filed. This defendant also lost under **Oliver.** The Louisiana court hints that if a "few affirmative steps to prevent others from observing the site" had been taken it might have found an expectation of privacy. It also noted, however, that there are "relatively rare instances where a warrant would be needed to search an open field." Because nothing was done to prevent anyone from walking down the path, the officers did not need a warrant to search this area. **State v. Taylor**, 714 So. 2d 143 (La. App. 1998).

North Carolina accepted **Dunn** and **Dunn's** guidelines in **State v. Tarantino**, 368 S.E. 2d 588 (N. C. 1988) aff'ing 358 S.E. 2d 131 (N. C. App. 1987). It found that going upon a porch of a boarded-up building and looking through 1/4" cracks of the building with the aid of a flashlight violated **Dunn**. Massachusetts, on the other hand, says that it has not yet adopted "open fields" under its own constitution. It is not clear from its opinion whether it will accept the principle but the court said even if it did no proper record was made in this case and it also concluded that land developed for commercial uses does not fall into the category. **Com. v. John G. Grant & Sons, Co.**, 403 Mass. 151 (1988).

Private business premises were the subject of **Johnson v. Com.**, 496 S.E. 2d 143 (Va. App. 1998). A fish warehouse building plus a dock that were adjacent to the creek were the subject of an entry in this case. An officer entered the property without a warrant. No trespassing signs were posted, but a sidewalk did lead to the front of the premises that was only open during regular business hours and chained-off when the business was closed. The officer saw 30 or more untagged striped bass below the gunnel on the deck of the defendant's boat, and more were seen on the scales about to be packed for shipping. This was illegal and the defendant was charged with fish and game violations. The state lost. The business curtilage rule was used.

One of Florida's latest decisions dealing with business curtilage is **Ratcliff v. State**, 2001 WL 227387 (Fla. App. 5 Dist. 2001). A stolen "semi" was discovered by the police at a truck stop. A tow truck was called. The tow driver recognized the truck as one he had pulled out of a lake just a week earlier. The police were given the address as the Bargain Box, a business establishment. The business was closed, but from the highway the trailer could be seen that went with the Ryder truck found earlier. The police entered the gravel driveway and parked behind the building to make an absolute identification. The state argued that business curtilage is given less protection. In this case there were no barricades or the like. The court noted a lack of a definitive case from the U.S. Supreme Court for this area. It felt that the issue was whether the defendant demonstrated a subjective manifestation of privacy in the area behind the business. The court held that this business owner "made no effort to exclude access by the public or others to the area behind his store." It held that there was "simply no objective or subjective manifestation that Ratcliff asserted a right to privacy in the area behind his store and thus a warrantless search did not violate his Fourth Amendment rights."

The crux of the open fields doctrine is that a trespass for the purpose of securing evidence of a crime against the person with standing is permitted in the open fields. To enter the home or land curtilage to the home to search for evidence requires probable cause plus a warrant or exigency. Of course a person could consent to such an entry even without the police having probable cause.

In **State v. Mogen**, 993 P. 2d 699 (Mont.2000), the police received an anonymous tip that Mogen was growing marijuana in a garden near the Yellowstone river along which his property lay. Three officers approached by river and photographed the marijuana while they stood below the ordinary high water mark. That area is "open fields" in Montana. One of the officers, a game warden, was asked to go along in order that curtilage not be trespassed. The trial court denied the suppression and the Montana high court upheld the trial judge's ruling that these officers went to great pains to stay away from the curtilage-protected area.

A Georgia defendant lost his case because the sodomy he performed on his victim was done in a wooded area not within the curtilage of his home. The court noted that "open fields" need not be fields or even open in common speech terms. **Mauk v. State**, 2000 WL 122162 (Ga. App.)

A California officer received a tip that marijuana was being grown at a place called Bowen Ranch; a remote mountainous area. The officer parked his car on a dirt road and by foot went some 200 to 300 feet onto the defendant's property and some 20 to 30 feet away from the trailers when he spotted a green tarp under which marijuana was growing. The officer returned to his car, drove to the trailer and met the defendant and told him marijuana was growing there. The defendant said that was his constitutional right. The officer asked if he could go back and get a better look and the owner said yes. Other plants were spotted. The officer left, secured a warrant, seized the evidence and on suppression the defense won. Why the reversal? The initial view was outside the land curtilage to the trailer. The court says, in essence, that open fields presupposes a trespass otherwise it would be a "public place" exception. That this man did a bad job of hiding his plants is not the officer's fault. As a postscript, the court noted that all pre- Proposition 8 decisions are no longer the law if they give defendants more rights than the U.S. Constitution. **People v. Channing**, 97 Cal Rep 2d 405 (Ct. App. Div. 2 2000).

Idaho takes a somewhat complex approach for determining what are open fields and what is curtilage. First, the court must apply curtilage boundaries in the context of the setting or locality of the residence itself. Then, the judge must consider the differences in custom and terrain when contemplating what is private and what is not. In some places lot sizes are large and in other areas they are quite small; rural areas should be judged separately from semi-rural and so on. In this case the marijuana meditation garden was 230 feet from the house and not within the curtilage of the house-trailer. **State v. Webb**, 943 P 2d 52 (Idaho 1997).

An Illinois defendant lived in a trailer. He killed his wife and incinerated her body in a burn pile some 150 feet from his trailer. This burn pile was not curtilage to the trailer. **People v. Nielson,** 718 N.E. 2d 131 (Ill. 1999).

What if the police enter curtilage for a lawful purpose having no intent to gather criminal evidence against the person with standing as to the home? Can a court use common sense and admit the evidence that came within plain view? Consider the decision of a federal judge in **U.S. v. Daoust,** 728 F. Supp. 41 (D. Me. 1989). The object of the police investigation in **Daoust** was Mr. Whittmore. Daoust was known to be only an acquaintance of Whittmore. State police officers went to Daoust's home to ask him questions about Whittmore. No one answered the door. The police went around the house to see if there were other entrances. They looked into an unobstructed window and saw a semi-automatic weapon fastened to the ceiling of the kitchen. The police left. An inquiry turned up the fact that Daoust was a convicted felon who was never pardoned thus the possession of the gun was illegal. A warrant was issued. The defendant said the police could only come to his front door and that they were not permitted to otherwise intrude upon his curtilage. The court said the initial encroachment to seek out other doors to the house was reasonable and part of a lawful purpose which had not ended when they got plain view of the gun, thus no reasonable expectation of privacy was violated. The standard open fields case envisions an unlawful trespassing entrance to seek evidence of a crime. Police efforts to gain evidence against the controller of the place is the key. Where that is not the goal common sense dictates the result in **Daoust.** Such a decision also points out the wisdom of the "totality" jurisprudence demanded by the Supreme Court. Accord: **State v. Deary,** 2000 WL 101213 (La.) and **Burdy Shaw v. State,** 10 S.W. 3d 918 (Ark. App. 2000).

Most states appear to follow the Maine federal court's lead and philosophy. Idaho in **State v. Rigoulot,** 846 P. 2d 918 (Idaho 1992) and **State v. Clark,** 859 P. 2d 344 (Idaho App. 1993), both recognized the "legitimate purpose [of those] who restrict their movements to places where ordinary visitors would be expected to go..." and any observation along the way would come within the plain view doctrine. This was repeated in **State v. Cada,** 923 P. 2d 469 (Idaho 1996), in which the police failed to satisfy the "legitimate purpose" prong.

The state of Washington also recognizes the legitimate business/plain view exception in **State v. Williams,** 1997 WL 208066 (Wash. App. Div. 2) (unpub. op.). The police went to the defendant's home to serve some papers. No one answered the door so they walked a "path in the grass" to the back of the house where they heard a motor noise like those used to operate halide light transformers. They smelled marijuana, and observed cardboard-covered windows on the back building. They left, got a warrant, searched, and discovered a marijuana growing operation. Was the use of this path a "substantial departure from an impliedly open access area?" Since their business was legitimate there was no violation of the Fourth Amendment. The Washington court provides the following list of factors to consider: (1) How private was the observation point; (2) How normal was the route chosen; (3) Was the agent secretive; (4) Was the discovery accidental; (5) Did the agent create the vantage point; and (6) Was it the most direct route to accomplish the legitimate goal?

In urban and most suburban areas there are no open fields but there is curtilage to the house. We often call curtilage a yard in this context. Residential curtilage incursions by the police run the gambit from lawful business having nothing to do with physical evidence gathering. When lawfully on such premises their greatest asset is plain view, plain smell and plain hearing. However when police enter a yard through a gate without a warrant, consent or exigency they will, most often, lose their evidence. One exception could be going to a house to interview a witness, being unable to raise anyone out front, then walking around the back, and getting plain view. There are several cases of this ilk, some of which are cited in these materials.

In an Oregon case the police received an anonymous tip that "speed" was being produced at a garage behind a certain house. The officers entered the alley behind the house but could not see anything. They opened the gate in the chain link fence and through an open side door saw evidence of beakers, flames, *etc.*, in other words, a "meth" lab. The officers knocked and asked if they could come in and were told no. The defendant came out and closed the door. They told the officer they were heating up varnish for antlers. The defendant excused himself to go to the bathroom in the house. Surprisingly he did not return. A bad consent to search the garage was taken from the wife – the defendant went in the back door and out the front. The trial judge refused to suppress the evidence. The defendant, however, won on appeal. There was no implied consent to leave the public alleyway, open a gate and enter the back yard. The fence itself, the court says, corroborates the presumption of non-consent. The court goes to some length to explain the function of sidewalks, drive ways and visible door bells as an implied consent to enter. None of that was present in this backyard. **State v. Somfleth**, 8 P.3d 221 (Ore.App.200).

As one Illinois case puts it, there has to be a privacy interest to protect for one to be violated and in an apartment context of a multi-unit building there is no privacy in a back porch for the second story tenant. Curtilage of the owner was entered but tenants have no interest to protect in the publicly accessible areas. **People v. Hunley**, 728 N.E. 2d 1183 (Ill.App. 1st 2000).

In **State v. Holmes**, 1996 WL 585158 (Wash. App. Div. 3) (unpub. op.), a marijuana growing operation was involved. Two officers went through woods and saw some 50 root balls piled on the property (not uncommon on marijuana farms) and they could smell marijuana growing. They left and secured a warrant. The defense said the police had to trespass to actually see the root balls and get the plain smell. The trial court suppressed the evidence and the Washington Supreme Court affirmed believing that the officers went through a barbed wire fence to get their view and smell. Washington rarely finds open fields. See **State v. Thorson**, 990 P. 2d 446 (Wash. App. Div. 1 1999) and **State v. Ross**, 959 P. 2d 1188 (Wash. App. Div. 2 1998). They do recognize the doctrine, however. They were quite correct in their decision in **State v. Dyerson**, 17 P.3d 668 (Wash. App. Div. 3 2001) where the court said that "open view," as they call it, does not apply to a police officer's warrantless entry into and search of a defendant' garage. They rightly said that an open garage is not an invitation to come onto the curtilage to search. It is not clear that the officer had plain view of the drugs from outside the curtilage. In fact it appears he could not have had that view because the driveway was hidden from public view. Even assuming that the officer was there on lawful business "no respectful citizen" would have entered this area of privacy without an emergency.

For a case in which the curtilage was entered to secure evidence against the controller of the place, see **U.S. v. Certain Real Property**, 719 F. Supp. 1396 (E.D. Mich. 1989). The police were given a tip by neighbors that drug sales might be going on at the house in their neighborhood. To confirm their suspicions the police decided to dress up as city garbage collectors. Since the city picks up the garbage inside the curtilage the police felt this ruse was necessary. The police went upon the curtilage and collected the trash and garbage from the backyard of the defendants. Their suspicions were confirmed and a warrant issued. This was found to be a violation of the curtilage principle. This was not inadvertent activity as was seen in **Daoust**; rather, it was intentional and for the express purpose of gathering condemning evidence against these controllers of this property. Could the inevitable discovery doctrine be used in such a case? Probably not, because police were operating under suspicion and not probable cause.

In one Florida case, officers received an anonymous tip about marijuana in the defendant's back yard. Police walked between the lawn of the residence and a wooded section of the defendant's property so they could see the rear of the house. With binoculars they spotted six or seven marijuana plants on a picnic table on the lanai of the residence. Without securing a consent or warrant the officers seized the plants. The "seeing" or plain view was done in open fields, but without consent, exigency, or warrant, the lanai was within the curtilage. The evidence should have been suppressed. **Abel v. State**, 668 So. 2d 1121 (Fla. App. 1996).

Some police do not "jump the gun" as illustrated by **State v. Costin**, 720 A. 2d 866 (Vt. 1998). The police had suspicions that the defendant was growing marijuana in his garden. They set up a video surveillance unit outside his curtilage. Once they gathered enough evidence they sought and obtained a search warrant. The court upheld this surveillance under both the federal and state constitutions.

Suppose police have a warrant to search a house. Suppose one officer goes some 250-300 yards from the house and sees a thermos. Can the officer, without violating the scope of the warrant seize this thermos? Yes. These woods, 250 to 300 yards from the house, constituted open fields thus the limiting language of the warrant did not control activity in the open fields. **State v. Pelletier**, 673 A. 2d 1327 (Me. 1996).

An Idaho case makes a point that if curtilage includes out buildings it also includes the land between the house and the outbuilding in question. This, of course, should have been obvious. Police believed the 110' from the house to the garage and the driveway that led to the garage upon which they stood was somehow open fields. They were wrong. **State v. Cada**, 923 P. 2d 469 (Idaho 1996). See **State v. Pinkham**, 679 A. 2d 589 (N. H. 1996) [in accord as to driveways].

Obviously, the open fields exception does not apply to an open garage right next to the house when the garage is not a part of an access route to the house and is hidden from the street. Thus, there is no implied invitation to enter the open garage. The evidence seen cannot be used for a warrant. **State v. Dyerson**, 2001 WL 96085 (Wash. App. Div. 3).

In another Idaho case the defendant's 20 acres and the garden on that property (with marijuana) was some 230 feet from his house trailer. The garden was hidden from the home by trees. Defendant lost. **State v. Webb**, 943 P 2d 52 (Idaho 1997).

Five marijuana plants were found between the defendant's house and the ginseng shed. Were these plants outside the curtilage? Yes, said the Wisconsin high court in **State v. Martwick**, 604 N.W. 2d 552 (Wis. 2000). The property of the defendant was approximately 1.52 acres, the plants were 50-75 feet from the house. It was not farm property. There was no fence around the property or other enclosure. The plants were in a dense area of trees and not within the low cut area surrounding the house. The dense area was not groomed; it looked like woods. Weeds and wild flowers surrounded the house in the low cut area. The trial judge was not clearly wrong in refusing to suppress. There were no fences and no "No Trespassing" signs. The court analyzed the distances in relation to the size of the property and concluded that just because a piece of property is small that does not mean all property is curtilage. The defendant announced his limits on curtilage by the low cut areas and their contrast with the untended area. He did not plant or cultivate trees in the wooded area where the marijuana plants were found.

A Colorado court fully and rightfully understands the intrusive nature of a search and that activity that does not intrude physically into a protected area is not a search. This, of course, is the heart of "open fields." In **People v. Oynes**, 920 P. 2d 880 (Colo. App. 1996) police stood in an open field and viewed the interior of the defendant's house with binoculars. Since the eye cannot trespass, no search occurred, and the warrant issued in this case was valid.

A Vermont police officer made two trips to the woods behind the defendant's house. He did not see what he was told he would see on the first trip. The second time he took the informer with him and this time he saw the marijuana plants. The wooded area behind the house belonged to the defendant but there were no signs posted nor was there any fence save an ornamental fence. Thus, no expectation of privacy existed as to the back woods approach to the house. The court reaffirmed its position that a natural boundary such as woods does not create a reasonable expectation of privacy. The one minor issue was whether evidence that the trees were trimmed to make it easier to walk in the wooded area automatically turned this wooded area into curtilage. The court said the absence of picnic tables, barbeque grills "or other privacies of life" negated such a finding. **State v. Hall**, 719 A. 2d 435 (Vt. 1998).

However, Montana held that capturing thermal escape from a house by the use of thermal imaging devices is the "taking" of evidence form the home. It was done without a warrant. How close was the officer? 25 to 30 feet. Was this search within or without the curtilage? It was found to be search within a protected area. **State v. Siegal**, 934 P. 2d 176 (Mont. 1997).

Thermal imaging was also the subject of a decision from Tennessee. Probable cause for the warrant came in larger part from a thermal escape reading of the defendant's home. The court was not persuaded that privacy was invaded by the use of this "non-invasive, non-intrusive method of defecting elevated outside surface temperature." Nothing inside the house can be seen; no intimate details of the defendant's life are revealed. But Tennessee agrees these cases to the contrary. However, without more concrete detail, the reliance on thermal imaging to issue a warrant means conclusory level statements were relied upon without stating why the conclusions were valid. Thus the warrant did not state probable cause. **State v. Norris** 2000 WL 710506 (Tenn. Crim. App.) (unpub. op.).

Siegal might lead defense attorneys to assume that Montana would not use a curtilage analysis or, if it did, it would always find a driveway and front yard of a house within the curtilage. This conclusion was well-founded, since Montana has consistently held that its constitution gives a defendant greater privacy rights. However, in **State v. Hubbel**, 951 P. 2d 971 (Mont. 1998) a driveway and an unfenced front yard were not found to be curtilage but under **Dunn** and the Montana Constitution. The lack of fence, shrubbery, and screening on the porch meant this front area was not within the curtilage. This, of course, would meet **Hester** standards, but does it truly meet **Dunn**'s proximity standard? The front yard was not put to any special use as would also be required by **Dunn**. Police saw what any casual passerby would see in plain view. The **Hubbel** case points out the difficulty of using a rural doctrine in an urban or suburban setting. The trail of blood and bullet holes that they followed to the front door was seen in plain view and gave them at least probable cause and perhaps exigency to enter. But as an open fields case it leaves much to be desired. Several other states have also addressed the thermal imaging issue. For example, California's First District Court of Appeal held that the warrantless use of a thermal imager violated the Fourth Amendment but that the police had sufficient independent probable cause to sustain the warrant issued for the search in **People v. Deutsh**, 52 Cal. Rep. 366 (Ct. App. 1996). The court admits that a majority of courts accept thermal imaging as not unreasonable but that the minority decisions are better reasoned. It found that **Karo** (the beeper in the carton case – taken into the house and "tracked") governs these cases and not **Knotts** (which only revealed what could be seen by the general public). It agrees that a thermal scan is not intrusive but they fail to realize that in **Karo** there was a surreptitious intrusion of the beeper as opposed to naturally escaping light, sound, or heat. Intrusiveness and invasion have thus far been the key to U.S. Supreme Court analysis. The court uses a spatial analysis or "was the protected space invaded' approach as it has done since **Katz**.

Kentucky, however, used a different approach in upholding a thermal scan. Using **Katz** and the open fields case of **Oliver**, it concluded society would not be willing to find a reasonable expectation of privacy in escaping heat. Penetration or non-penetration was the key for this court. It found that the scan did not reveal any intimate details of life in the house. The court also cited the fly-over cases of **Ciarolo** and **Riley**.

The Third Court of Appeal of Louisiana agrees with Kentucky by its decision in **State v. Niel**, 617 So. 2d 1111 (La. App. 1996). It primarily relied on **Place**, the dog sniffing case. Florida, through the Fifth District, approved the use of an imager. It was a case of first impression for Florida. **State v. Siegel**, 679 So. 2d 1201 (Fla. App. 5th 1996). Minnesota faced the issue in **State v. Duwenhoegger**, 2000 WL 821483 (Minn. App.) (unpub. op.), in which both thermal imaging and surveillance tapes were used in this investigation of a conspiracy to murder case. Without much discussion, the thermal imaging which was used to prove that the defendant had removed a window to help gain access to the house of the target victim was approved.

In a Nevada case, the defendant attacked thermal imaging as unreliable, thus the warrant issued using the surveillance results could not support the search warrant used in this case. An expert testified on behalf of the state about the reliability of imaging, therefore, the court was thus justified in considering this and all other evidence presented for the issuance of the warrant. **Garrettson v. State**, 967 P. 2d 428 (Nev. 1998).

North Dakota disagreed with Nevada and said a thermal warrant was not good and that the police could not rely on the warrant under the good faith doctrine of **Leon.** It held that growing something in the house, without more, provided no *nexus* that marijuana was the crop. **State v. Lewis**, 527 N. W.2d 658 (N. D. 1998). A *nexus* was shown in an Ohio case where garbage bags with marijuana trash lawfully discovered was used along with the imaging. This was enough to uphold the warrant. **Gates, Greenwood** and **Leon** were combined to save the warrant. **State v. LeMay**, 1999 WL 437021 (Ohio App. 5th) (unpub. op.).

Pennsylvania says that warrantless thermal imaging is a violation of the Fourth Amendment. **Com. v. Gindlesperger**, 706 A. 2d 216 (Pa. Super.), aff'd. 743 A. 2d 898 (Pa. 1999). It held that intimate details are revealed and cited **Payton** (the threshold crossing case). The court saw a big difference between garbage put out for collection and escaping heat. It contrasted the reliability of drug sniffing dogs and mere heat readings – the lack of the ability of thermal imaging to distinguish between legal and illegal heat. The court held that **Karo** governed.

Finally, another Tennessee defendant said the warrant issued was based on thermal imaging, thus it was valid. The court found there was no **Katz** expectation of privacy in escaping heat and agreed with the decision of the Ninth Circuit that no intimate details were revealed. That Ninth Circuit decision was accepted for decision by the U.S. Supreme Court. Thus, we will have the answer through **U.S. v. Kyllo**, 190 F. 32 1041 (C.A. 9th 1999). This was a drug task force case. Local Oregon police provided the federal agent with information that Kyllo was growing and distributing marijuana from his house. The federal agent verified the prior arrest records of the defendant and then subpoenaed his electrical usage records and found an abnormally high use strengthening suspicion of a "grow" operation. The federal agent, from his car parked across the street, used a thermal imager and "passively recorded heat emanations" from the house; a higher amount of heat loss than from the other two units in the triplex. The federal magistrate issued a warrant for the search. The indoor "grow " operation was indeed discovered. The motion to suppress was denied. **Kyllo** argued that a warrant was needed to use the thermal imager. The Ninth Circuit used **Oliver, Katz, Smith v. Maryland** (the pen register case) and **Ciarolo** and **Dow Chemical** (the camera plain view case) to analyze the problem. First, it found no intrusion – no literal or figurative intrusion. Here the court cited **Place** (the dog sniff case). Second, it said this means there was no expectation of privacy. Third, the court addressed whether there was an objective reasonable expectation of privacy and relied heavily on **Dow, Ciarolo** and **Riley** and found no revelation of "intimate details." Therefore, the use of the imager without a warrant was upheld.

The **Kyllo** case was decided by a five to four margin. The Court determined that, although the officer was outside the curtilage of the home, his capturing of heat emissions was a surveillance of the interior thus a search of the interior. This was, in part, a reaffirmation of the **Karo** decision, (see Chapter Fifteen). The majority, led by Justice Scalia, was more concerned about even more sophisticated devices than thermal imagers. Indeed, the fact that most companies that sell replacement windows, insulation, and siding often use such devices to sell their products received little attention by the majority. The real concern centers on electronic devices that use laser beams to listen to conversations inside a home or other buildings and other yet-to-be invented monitoring devices.

This potential perplexed Justice Stevens who wrote for the dissenters. Passive measurement of heat does not reveal details of the home's interior; only information that likely could have been detected by neighbors or passers-by was revealed, according to Stevens. Stevens went on to say that "For the first time the Court assumes that an inference can amount to a Fourth Amendment violation." The dissent went on to note that the majority failed to describe "how much use is general public use...?" These devices can be rented by calling one of a half dozen 800 numbers and more than 11,000 of this newer model and its competitors are already in use. In any event, the place from which the reading was taken caused no concern. The officer was where he had a right to be. **Kyllo v. U.S.**, 121 S.Ct 2038 (2001).

IV.   Phase IV – The Fly-Over Cases

At common law the property owner was said to own not just the surface of his property but he or she owned from heaven to the center of the earth. No one in modern times would seriously doubt the right of government to cut that down some. Zoning, land use regulation, planes, and other modern innovations have seriously restricted the extent of ownership. The more serious question is to what extent is there a societal right of privacy that cannot be invaded by police flying over one's property. By 1986, there were conflicting decisions from all levels of courts.

The Court in **California v. Ciraolo**, 476 U.S. 207 (1986), would announce their first fly-over decision. The facts are quite simple. The police got anonymous tips regarding a marijuana farm. They tried "open fields" but two fences blocked their view. One officer secured a private plane and at 1,000 feet saw the plants and photographed them with an ordinary 35mm camera. They secured a warrant and made the productive search. The California Supreme Court held that this focused, non-routine flight was invalid in the Fourth Amendment context, and ruled that the evidence should have been suppressed under the Fourth Amendment. The Supreme Court of the United States disagreed and reversed.

Everyone agreed that this area was within the curtilage, giving the defendant standing thus also eliminating the possible use of open fields. Even so, did the flyover by police at 1,000 feet violate an expectation of privacy that is reasonable? Curtilage does not always defeat plain view as illustrated by the "view from neighborhood property cases." The police were in navigable airspace for fixed wing aircraft. From this physically non-intrusive vantage point, they could see the plants with the naked eye. That they meant to be there is not relevant. Anyone in this airspace could have seen what the police saw. One who grows illicit drugs in his back yard cannot be entitled to assume his unlawful conduct will not be observed by passing aircraft "…or by a power company repair mechanic on a pole overlooking the yard." Private and commercial flights are routine. No warrant was required for the fly-over. That same day, the Court approved the use of a camera in a fly-over for the plain view doctrine in **Dow Chemical Co. v. U.S.**, 476 U.S. 227 (1986).

So the fixed wing aircraft in navigable airspace issue was settled. One more problem remained. How about the hovering helicopter at a lower altitude? The answer came in **Florida v. Riley,** 488 U.S. 445 (1989). The Court set out the issue as, "Whether surveillance of the interior of a partially covered greenhouse in a residential backyard from the vantage point of a helicopter located 400 feet above the greenhouse constitutes a search...." Unlike the 5-4 opinion of **Ciraolo**, this decision was a 4-1-4 plurality opinion. White wrote for Rehnquist, Scalia and Kennedy with O'Connor concurring separately. O'Connor had been with Burger, White, Stevens and Rehnquist in the **Ciraolo** majority.

The plurality said Riley could not reasonably have expected that his greenhouse was protected from public or official observation from a helicopter had it been flying within the navigable (500') minimum. Helicopters at 400' are not proven to be a rare occurrence. His use of the greenhouse was not interfered with by the flight. There was no undue noise, wind, dust, or threat of injury shown. In fact, there are no minimum height regulations for helicopters because of their hovering ability.

O'Connor's concurrence is even a stronger statement of why there could be no expectation of privacy. She said that F.A.A. safety regulations should play no part in the decision. But she said the question is whether members of the public expect that helicopters fly that low regularly. Her difficulty was that the fact had not been proven – a burden to be carried by the defendant. One of the dissenters agreed with O'Connor, but said that the burden is on the state to demonstrate such regularity of low level flights such as this one. Such a plurality opinion means there will be more activity in this area. But it also says that six justices agree that such activity can be viewed as a lawful search.

The Oregon Court of Appeals, though somewhat willing to accept fixed wing fly-overs at normal speed were unwilling to accept hovering helicopter's surveillance. It thus rejected **Florida v. Riley** by citing its own constitution. **State v. Ainsworth**, 770 P. 2d 58 (Ore. Ct. App. 1989). **Ainsworth** reached the Oregon Supreme Court and that court reversed the Court of Appeals by saying that the officers had a right to be where they were when the observations were made and, therefore, the purposeful police conduct did not constitute an unreasonable invasion of privacy. **State v. Ainsworth**, 801 P. 2d 749 (Ore. 1990).

Picking up on the altitude and disturbance issues in **Riley,** the Colorado Court of Appeals ruled that a helicopter surveillance at 200 feet was an invasion of privacy. They felt that a warrant was required. It also found that 200 feet was not a routine altitude in this area of Colorado. It also noted that there was a lot of noise and physical disruption at this altitude. **People v. Pollock**, 796 P. 2d 63 (Colo. Ct. App. 1990). Potentially defense attorneys stand a good chance of winning helicopter search cases.

The Alabama Court of Criminal Appeals fully accepted the use of helicopters. The twist in its case was that National Guard personnel and helicopters were used. The defense said this had to violate some law. The court turned to a Tenth Circuit case for the answer. The hybrid nature of the National Guard as both a state and federal unit was emphasized in that it is subject both to gubernatorial and presidential call. Their enlistment, of course, is first to the state guard and until they receive a federal call they are state servicemen and women. See **U.S. v. Hutchings**, 127 F. 3d 1255 (C.A. 10th 1997). The Alabama court then noted that Alabama law specifically provides that the guard may be called to aid law enforcement. Ala. Code §31-2-28. The legitimacy of such a statute was approved in another federal case. See **U.S. v. Benish**, 5 F. 3d 20 (C.A. 3rd 1993). Their service also did not violate the Posse Comitatus Act which provides an exception for the National Guard. See **Gilbert v. U.S.**, 165 F. 3d 470 (C.A. 6th 1999). That act does not apply until the guard is called into federal service. But even if the guard were federalized it is still uncertain that suppression should be the result. The court cites four federal cases that so held. See **Doggett v. State**, 2000 WL 869509 (Ala. Crim. App.).

In an Illinois case the police flew over the defendant's property and saw the marijuana. This, of course, gave them probable cause. But rather than securing a warrant they decided to search and seize without a warrant. The defense argued that the plants were not in the open fields but were within the curtilage of the home. The Illinois court noted that plain view alone was not enough to justify a warrantless seizure for use as evidence even if it is contraband. Since there were no exigent circumstances, the seizure was unlawful. However, the issue of a valid consent was not determined in the trial court, so the case was remanded for that determination. **People v. Accardi**, 671 N.E. 2d 373 (Ill. App. 1996). The court is quite correct in concluding that fly-overs when properly conducted under **Ciarolo** and **Riley** only may yield probable cause and a warrant, consent, exigency or true exception must be present to allow seizure of the goods as evidence.

A Tennessee defendant argued that a helicopter flight by police at 300 feet violated his constitutional rights. Both **Riley** and **Ciarolo** were cited in support of the fly-over. There was no proof by the defense that he could reasonably claim that his property would not be subject to observation from that altitude. The defense offered no proof, as suggested in **Riley**, that the fly-over interfered with this defendant's use of the greenhouse or other part of the curtilage. In fact flying helicopters, because of a nearby paper plant, were a regular occurrence in this area of Tennessee. **State v. Ware**, 1999 WL 378341 (Tenn. Crim. App.) (unpub. op.).

A Washington appellate court had to determine what rule to follow when assessing an allowable altitude. Looking at various state standards, the court decided to use FAA standards stating that "they are the most consistent." Thus the 500 foot vantage point "is no more intrusive than police standing on a public street corner or other legal vantage point." **State v. Wilson**, 988 P. 2d 463 (Wash. App. Div. 3 1999).

V.   Conclusion

In summation, the open fields exception to the warrant requirement operates today on two separate levels. First, by allowing the trespass, police may seize items of personalty and other elusive evidence not contained in a building in addition to the seizure of individuals who, by probable cause, are connected to the criminal evidence and are roaming about the open fields.

For example, in **Hester** the remains of the distilled spirits and the persons of Hester and his friend were seized. In **Air Pollution**, analysis of the smoke was seized. Dynamite was seized in the **Ramapuram**, and marijuana growing in the open was taken in the **Schmidt** case.

The open fields exception may also operate to waive the warrant requirement to search at the plain view level, but not to seize unless some exigency, consent or other exception exists when the ultimate evidence is in a building. These appear to be the directives of the **Wheeler**, **Dunn**, **Ciraolo**, **Dow Chemical**, and **Riley** decisions.

The vehicle in the open fields cases can be searched and seized from the viewpoint of an item that is the evidence of the crime itself as in the **Boone** case. In **Boone** the tractor was no different than the distilled spirits in **Hester**. Otherwise, if the vehicle is a suspected container, open fields allows the plain view, and the mobility exception should allow the search of the vehicle. Of course, as **Hester** showed, abandoned property may be seized by anyone, thus **Ramapuram** could well have been justified on that basis alone.

The more critical problems of what constitutes open fields in any context and whether open fields should be a rural doctrine only are not easily resolved. Legitimate argument exists for defense counsel, therefore, in all police trespass cases. Effective advocacy would require pursuing suppression in all such cases.

OPEN FIELDS REMINDERS

I.   FOURTH AMENDMENT PROTECTION IS NOT EXTENDED TO OPEN FIELDS.

II.   PROPERTY OUTSIDE THE CURTILAGE OF THE HOME IS OPEN

FIELDS.

III.   OPEN FIELDS DO NOT HAVE TO BE "OPEN" OR "FIELDS."

IV.   CURTILAGE:
An area and buildings that serve and support the intimate activities associated with the sanctity of a home as:

      a) an eating place,
      b) a sleeping place, and
      c) a gathering place.

V.   CURTILAGE
Resolved by using four factors:

      a) proximity of area to the home,
      b) whether area is enclosed within an enclosure surrounding the home,
      c) how the area is used; is it "home support" centered, and
      d) steps taken to prevent observation.

VI.   A RURAL DOCTRINE *difficult* to apply in urban areas – use standard privacy analysis under the PLAIN VIEW doctrine.

VII.   No definitive rule from U.S. SUPREME COURT re: "no trespassing" signs; LOCAL LAW prevails.

VIII.   ONLY OWNER OR LAWFUL OCCUPIER HAVE STANDING TO COMPLAIN.

IX.   NO fully definitive case from U.S. SUPREME COURT REGARDING BUSINESS PROPERTY CURTILAGE – but see **Western Alfalfa** (*supra*).

X.   Curtilage may be invaded lawfully under the legitimate business/plain view route taken rule developed in several states – includes also standard exigent circumstances exception.

FLY-OVER CASES REMINDERS

I.   FIXED-WING AIRCRAFT AND VIEWS FROM THEM CONSTITUTIONAL WHEN DONE FROM NAVIGABLE AIR

SPACE.

II. NON-DESTRUCTIVE HOVERING HELICOPTER PLAIN VIEW IS PERMISSIBLE: CHECK LOCAL LAW.

III. USE OF CAMERA PERMISSIBLE DURING "LAWFUL" FLY-OVERS.

IV. LOCAL LIMITS, IF ANY, MUST BE CONSULTED.

CHAPTER EIGHT
ABANDONED PROPERTY EXCEPTION

I.   Introduction

Abandoned property may be seized by police and used against the defendant at trial. There is no reasonable expectation of privacy in abandoned property. Why not? It has long been a principle of the common law that there is no title or possession in anyone in abandoned property until the first captor seizes the property and takes possession. In other words, it is "up for grabs." Determining whether property is abandoned or merely lost or mislaid when it is subject to capture is generally determined by all the facts and surrounding circumstances.

The pure personal property analysis is not often, nor need it be, applied in most of the cases considered in these materials. One case, however, rightly applied property law and wrongly applied inventory search principles. In **State v. Ching**, 678 P. 2d. 1088 (Haw. 1984), a lost article was turned over to the police who in turn inventoried the contents of the pouch discovering evidence of a crime. The police urged that it was abandoned when, in fact it, was a lost item. Of course, only abandoned property is subject to the abandoned property exception. But the court severely limited the scope of the inventory or community care-taking function. To protect themselves against claims of misappropriation of property or loss and to protect against the possibility of explosives, police can reasonably inventory property and try to determine if it holds clues to ownership so that it can be returned. These are things that any citizen could, and in fact, must do, because appropriation of lost goods can either be larceny or other crimes if the intent and act converge at the appropriate time under larceny or statutory offenses that govern the area.

Oregon on the other hand recognized that the police have a statutory duty to return lost goods and to do so they have a duty to search the container to determine if there are indications of ownership. Plain view of contraband thus discovered then allows the warrantless seizure of the drugs so discovered. **State v. Pidcock**, 759 P. 2d 1092 (Ore. 1988).

One of the earliest recognitions of the abandoned property rule is found in **Hester v. United States**, 265 U.S. 57 (1924) which is also cited as the first open fields exception case. Police saw an exchange of a quart bottle. An alarm sounded, and Hester went to his car, grabbed a gallon jug and ran. The officers pursued. Hester dropped the jug, breaking it. Henderson, the other man, threw the quart bottle away. The officers picked up these bottles which still contained some illicit whiskey. Making a distinction between the house and the grounds around it, the Court disregarded the trespass issue and found that abandoned property in open fields is subject to warrantless seizure. More important is the fact that property purposely abandoned even while any form of police pursuit is in progress is subject to seizure. This was reaffirmed in **Hodari D.** (*infra*).

The balance of these materials will deal with property that has been abandoned in three contexts:

1. Truly abandoned property;
2. Police conduct that causes abandonment; and
3. Trash and garbage as abandoned property.

II.   True Abandonment

There are any number of circumstances when an abandonment occurs that is not inspired by police conduct. The cases are quite simple. Anyone who abandons property is subject to the whims of the captor and the use the captor wishes to make of such property. Consider the following cases.

Michigan's high court has made one of the best statements regarding the analysis required in an abandoned property case. In **People v. Darcy**. 549 N.W. 2d 536 (Mich. 1996), it said: "Although many courts discuss the issue, borrowing heavily from the law of property, at least one has made the reasonable observation that the inquiries are not precisely the same. In the context of a search, the ultimate question is whether Darcy retained a reasonable expectation of privacy in the property to be searched, an inquiry that is *"illuminated, but not controlled, by the question of ownership."* **Darcy** at p. 536-537 citing **U.S. v. Cella**, 568 F. 2d 1266, 1283 (C.A. 9th 1997).

The loss of privacy by a smuggler abandoning his ship during a storm was recognized by the Fifth Circuit in **U.S. v. Edwards**, 644 F. 2d 1 (C.A. 5th 1981). The smuggler was rescued from his vessel during a raging storm. By calling for and accepting help, the defendant voluntarily abandoned his ship. Thus, the 30,000 pounds of marijuana were admissible. Here the court called upon general principles of maritime law to determine the property's status.

In **U.S. v. Oswald**, 783 F. 2d 763 (C.A. 6th 1986) the defendant's car caught fire. Instead of staying near the scene, he fled the immediate area. He tried to make some discreet inquiries seeking the car's location and to find out if he could get the cocaine laden suitcase. The court held this subjective desire to recover his property was insufficient to overcome the objective inferences that could be drawn from his initial flight; thus, he was held to have abandoned his car.

The old "container-left-by-the-roadside" gambit was the subject of **U.S. v. Walker**, 624 F. Supp. 99 (D. Md. 1985). The defendant's contact was supposed to pick up the grocery bag at a certain roadside location. The court found that this defendant relinquished his interest in the property by leaving the bag out in an open area along a roadside in a rural setting. These are truly indicia of abandonment and not lost or mislaid property. By doing this, subjecting his property to caption by any passerby, he was found to no longer have any reasonable expectation of privacy. Therefore, the location of the item factors in when making the abandoned property analysis.

When the defendant removes considerable property from the location of his essentially fraudulent operation and leaves other indications of a hasty but permanent departure, the things left behind can be found to be abandoned. **U.S. v. Binder**, 794 F. 2d 1195 (C.A. 7th 1986). Hence, the condition of the place can be a factor.

A discarded satchel was the object in **U.S. v. Jones**, 707 F. 2d 1169 (C.A. 10th 1983). When the police later asked Jones about the satchel, he disclaimed any ownership. The court said spoken words and acts done by the defendant indicated a manifest intent to relinquish any expectation of privacy, and he had abandoned the satchel. Denial of ownership can be found to be a positive and voluntary act.

Normally, police may act, if at all, only upon facts and circumstances known at the time of the search or seizure. The Second Circuit has extended this principle somewhat for the abandonment area. It said that the police are not necessarily confined to those facts and circumstances known by the officers at the time of the search. Subsequently discovered events may support the inference that the defendants chose and manifested their decision not to return. The police discovered that the defendants had settled in another state within a few days after leaving the premises where the foot locker had been discovered. **U.S. v. Levasseur**, 816 F. 2d 57 (C.A. 2d 1987). The quality of the property as abandoned was such when taken, thus, the police were fortunate not to have invaded something protected by privacy.

The police do not win all abandoned property claims. In **U.S. v. Mulder**, 808 F. 2d 1346 (C.A. 9th 1987), a hotel guest was found not to have abandoned the property he left in his room past check-out time. He returned within 48 hours and inquired about his property. He had been billed for an extra night's lodging despite his absence. All of this, the court felt, militated against a finding of abandonment. But if the facts justify a finding of the abandonment of a hotel room, it will be upheld. **Com. v. Paszko**, 391 Mass. 164 (1984). Each case stands on its own and must be judged by the totality of the circumstances.

A more recent hotel/motel case illustrates the foregoing principles. In **State v. Williams**, 2000 WL 139569 (Fla. App. 2) a pair of officers went to a motel clerk regarding the activities of a known prostitute who exited Room 2. The clerk was happy to see the police and said he wanted the occupant out of the room. The police went to the room, knocked and gave the occupant the clerk's message. Williams, the occupant said OK but that he needed to pack. The officer and Williams chatted while Williams packed. When finished Williams left the room. As the officer asked if he got everything, Williams said yes. Williams returned his key and left in his truck. The officer then searched the room and found the contraband. The trial court suppressed the evidence. The appellate court reversed. Why? First, the motel owner's request was within the rights created by a Florida statute. Second, the ultimate entry by the officer came after Mr. Williams left the premises. Thus there was no expectation of privacy when the officer discovered the contraband. There was no "forced" abandonment.

A South Dakota defendant was involved in an auto accident. Before the police arrived, he left the scene on foot and left his keys in the car. Did he retain an expectation of privacy in the glove compartment where the drugs were found? No, said the court in **State v. Anderson**, 548 N.W. 2d 40 (S. D. 1996). Accord see **Walker v. State**, 493 S.E. 2d 193 (Ga. App. 1997). Walker stopped his car voluntarily and not upon police command. As police approached, however, he fled. This act was a voluntary relinquishment of an expectation of privacy at the time the car was searched. Accord see **Thompson v. State**, 680 So. 2d 1014 (Ala. Crim. 1996) where at the approach of police the defendant threw down his keys, disclaimed ownership and even any acknowledgment of the vehicle. Why was he stopped? Articulable suspicion.

More recently, two other courts have had to take a close look at defendant who walked away from their respective cars and whether the cars were abandoned. One defendant won and the other lost his argument.. The cases are **Thompson v. Com.**, 2000 WL 108444 (Va. App.) (unpub. op.) and **State v. Tweedt**, 2000 WL 1587514 (Iowa App.). In the Virginia case the defendant saw the officer tailing him. He sped up, went one block, properly parked his car, locked it and ran into an adjacent house. The officer knocked on the door of the house and called the tags in. It was not reported stolen. The male suspect refused to come outside. The police decided to impound the car for investigation and called a tow truck. The car was opened with a "Slim Jim" and ultimately seventy hits of cocaine were found. The state argued that the car was abandoned. The appellate court used the objective standard and viewed, properly, that the acts of proper parking and locking could not be seen as an act of abandonment. The defendant's conduct was labeled as an act "...consistent with the continuing assertion of an established possessory right" and that his refusal to meet the police "did not manifest abandonment."

The Iowa police came upon an accident scene and a car in the eastbound lane facing westbound and no one around it. A tire was flat and had front end damage but not signs of blood. A search was conducted with evidence confirming drunk driving was found. The court found that under these facts the car was abandoned and the police did not act in bad faith in seizing and searching this car. After all the police did try to locate the owner and when found, he refused to go with them to the car.

The Hawaii Supreme Court held that silence does not constitute abandonment. The bag in question in this case was two feet from the defendant. There were three other men with the defendant in the sauna. The court said to find abandonment here "would be to twist both logic and experience into a most uncomfortable knot." **State v. Joyner**, 669 P. 2d 152 (Haw. 1983). Silence, unlike a disclaimer, would be treated much the same way as it is in the consent area. After all police may ask but the citizen is not required to answer. Here there was a lack of a positive act. Accord: See **Stanberry v. State**, 684 A. 2d 823 (Md. 1996).

Virginia also says that the **"totality"** doctrine applies to abandonment cases. The most important **"totality"** aspects to look for are denial of ownership and physical relinquishment. By way of *dicta*, it said that verbal disclaimers in the face of an illegal arrest cannot be considered as evidence of abandonment. In this case, there was mere silence when the police asked who owned the bag. People have a right to remain silent when questioned by the police, they held. Further, the fact that no one else in the vicinity claimed ownership is not evidence that this owner abandoned nor that any owner abandoned. Without saying so, the court truly showed that it understood, therefore, the difference between lost, misplaced and abandoned property and nothing in these facts eliminated lost or misplaced goods possibilities. **Com. v. Holloway**, 384 S.E. 2d 99 (Va. Ct. App. 1989).

The final case is **U.S. v. Saunders**, 719 F. 2d 882 (C.A. 6th 1983). The defendant left her unclaimed bag at the carousel. She was asked about it and she neither claimed it nor disclaimed it. She said she had not claimed it because she was not going straight home. The court said this was not a clear disclaimer and, thus, it was not abandoned. Doubt should be resolved in favor of the owner of the property.

III. Police Caused Abandonment

Perhaps the greatest judicial activity regarding abandonment cases concerns "drop" cases where the defendant throws or drops the incriminating evidence because of police conduct. Until 1988, there was no real guidance except **Hester** which involved arguably lawful police conduct. Much of the abandonment law that would develop came from illegal police conduct. Before considering the 1988 decision of the Supreme Court, one should understand the law that preceded it that involved both legal and illegal police conduct.

A New York case dealt with the issue of completed abandonment. The police officer testified that the defendant "dropped a tin box" just prior to the police officer making contact with the defendant's hand. The court felt this was not enough to prove abandonment. It was impossible to determine if the defendant was merely clumsy or whether in fact he was throwing the box away since the officer picked the box up immediately after the drop. **People v. Anderson**, 24 N.Y. 2d 12 (1969).

A more recent Florida case illustrates a clear police caused abandonment in a public area. The police, on a hunch, tried to stop a young man. Rather than stop, the young man rode off on his bicycle and as he did he threw something to the ground. The police picked up the marijuana and then found the young man, arresting him. Despite the illegality of the attempted seizure of the defendant, his act in abandoning the property did not save him. It is not a search for the police to pick up abandoned property where there is no reasonable expectation of privacy. A person's otherwise voluntary abandonment of property cannot be tainted or made involuntary by a prior attempted illegal stop, the court said. But, the court went on, only when the police begin to conduct an illegal search can the subsequent abandonment of property be held to involuntary as being tainted by the prior illegal search. In closing, the court said to watch out for spurious abandonment claims especially where a particular officer or department always seems to come up with abandoned property. **State v. Oliver**, 368 So. 2d 1331 (Fla. App. 1979). This theory was approved in **Hodari D.** (*infra*).

How far can the abandonment doctrine be taken where the initial stop and detention are illegal? Quite far, according to the New York Court of Appeals. The police were investigating a homicide. A suspect, doing nothing illegal, was standing on a street corner. The police pulled up and asked him to get in the car. The subject complied. The police drove off with the suspect. The police asked if he was "clean" and the suspect indicated that he did not have a weapon. A few minutes later the police saw the suspect throw something out of the car. The police stopped the car and retrieved the gun. The court labeled the seizure of the defendant as clearly unlawful, but held that the act of throwing the gun away was an act independent of the prior (and continuing) illegal seizure. The New York court distinguished between spontaneous action and deliberated action. The court would not necessarily agree with the Florida court's analysis. As New York saw the instant case, the suspect's action was not a direct response to the police conduct. If it were, the evidence would have been inadmissible. It found the suspect had sufficient (though short) time to reflect, formulate a strategy, and rid himself of the gun. **People v. Boodle**, 418 N.Y. Supp. 2d 352 (N.Y. 1979). New York thus brought the attenuation doctrine to bear on the police caused abandonment area.

Can the abandonment be the result of a trick where the police likely have probable cause but do not want to bother with a warrant? The police received a tip from a reliable informant that the defendant had drugs in his apartment. The police made a phone call to the defendant saying a search warrant had been issued for his apartment and that he had better get the drugs out. It worked because the defendant came running out of his apartment with a tool box full of drugs which the defendant threw away when the police tried to stop him. Reluctantly, the court upheld the admission of this evidence. **People v. Porras**, 160 Cal. Rep. 627 (Cal. App. 1979). This appears to be a case of strategic deception and not one involving egregious, society offending conduct

Does abandonment remove the taint of an attempted illegal arrest?. According to the Fifth Circuit, abandonment, like consent, must be freely done in order to be effective. Thus where the abandonment is a product of police misconduct, that relinquishment cannot be said to be voluntary. It apparently disagrees with the

Florida's holding. **U.S. v. Morin**, 665 F. 2d 765 (C.A. 5th 1982); accord **In Re Hodari D.**, 265 Cal. Rep. 79 (Cal. App. 1 Dist. 1989) The **Hodari D.** case was accepted by the U.S. Supreme Court for decision and is discussed below.

An Oregon court applied the abandoned property exception to an automobile. The defendants were trying to elude the police chase and fled into a dead-end alley. They got out of the car and ran away from it. The police took custody of the car and thoroughly searched it and all its contents. In the trunk was a closed sack which the police opened discovering a gun. Since this car was abandoned the police did not need a warrant. The court felt there was not legitimate expectation of privacy in the car since it was abandoned. **State v. Green**, 605 P. 2d 746 (Or. App. 1980).

Further illustrating that abandoned property cases are always close calls., consider the Indiana Court's decision in **Jones v. State**, 409 N.E. 2d 1254 (Ind. App. 1980). While some police knocked on the door seeking entry without a warrant, taking with them a hotel maid with a pass-key, other officers observed the room's window and they saw a tin foil packet thrown out of that window. After the toss, the defendant invited the officers in. Acknowledging a lack of probable cause to go into the room, the court noted that the presence outside the window was not unlawful. Since no unlawful conduct had taken place at the time of the abandonment the act was voluntary thus the evidence was admissible.

In **U.S. v. DeParias**, 805 F. 2d 1447 (C.A. 11th 1986), the defendant fled to avoid apprehension. Clothing that was left behind at his girlfriend's apartment was found to be abandoned. Here there was a lawful police investigation and that is not, by itself, such coercion that the abandonment should be considered involuntary. The innuendo, of course, is that any attempted illegal conduct makes such an abandonment illegal; **Hodari D.** changes this conclusion.

A Maine case involved both premises and objects in those premises. Police conducted a search of an apartment that the landlord said had been vacated. However, another person who was living there had not yet moved out. Once the defendant found this out he "felt unsafe" and decided to move out and told the landlord he had taken everything he wanted., and that he would not return. Nearly a month later the police again, with the landlord's permission, entered and searched and gathered incriminating evidence. The defendant said his abandonment was not a product of "his free will." The issue, in Maine's view, was whether leaving the place and things in it was an act of free will that purged the taint of the first clearly illegal entry. The answer was that his act of leaving involved no direct police coercion, thus, the evidence was admissible. **State v. Hunt**, 682 A. 2d 690 (Me. 1996).

A defendant was asked to leave the plane with the officers. He left his bag behind. He denied that he had any luggage. The court felt this bag was abandoned even though the defendant later, at the interrogation session, admitted owning the bag. The court said this was not enough to reassert his interest in the property. **U.S. v. Nordling**, 804 F. 2d 1446 (C.A. 9th 1986). In a like manner the defendant's repeated disavowals of ownership of a bag under his train seat constituted an abandonment. **U.S. v. Carransquillo**, 670 F. Supp. 40 (D. D.C. 1987). At most, because of its location, the property was lost or misplaced unless the police knew the defendant was the true owner. Even so, disavowal trumps the defendant's gambit.

A police officer was unlawfully in the backyard of the defendant's urban home when he observed the defendant throwing tin foil packets out of a window into the yard. Were these packets of drugs abandoned? A Maryland court took the position that throwing drugs into one's own backyard where one had a right of privacy is a bizarre act, but it is not abandonment. **Brown v. State**, 540 A. 2d 143 (Md. App. 1988). They are right because the place a person chooses to store his own property on or in his own property is no way an act of abandonment.

The Texas Court of Criminal Appeals adopted a new rule for the Texas courts. Abandonment, it holds, consists of two components: (1) the defendant must intend to abandon the property; and (2) the defendant must freely decide to abandon the property; and (3) the decision to abandon must not be the product of police misconduct. Texas looks for a voluntary act independent of any police misconduct. **Comer v. State**, 754 S.W. 2d 656 (Tex. Cr. App. 1986). The Texas court adopted a due process view by this decision.

These case thus serve as background for **Michigan v. Chesternut**, 486 U.S. 567 (1988). On this rare occasion all nine justices agreed on the outcome. The facts are simple. Four officers were in a marked cruiser when they observed a man standing on a corner being approached by a man alighting from a car. When the man on the corner saw the police he turned and began to run. The police decided to follow him to see where he would go. They caught up with him and tailed him. No words, no sirens, no blue lights – just a tail. The defendant emptied his pockets as he walked. The police stopped and picked up the packet of codeine. At this point the police discovered the man waling back toward them. He was arrested. Was this an investigatory pursuit a seizure? No, it was not a seizure. A reasonable person would believed he was free to leave. The police conduct here would not have communicated to a reasonable person that an attempt to capture or otherwise intrude upon the defendant's movement had taken place. The car was not operated aggressively nor used to block his course or control his direction or speed. The Court did acknowledge that having a police cruiser paralleling your strides could be intimidating, however, that alone is only a police presence and not a seizure. The evidence should have been admissible.

What did the court **not** decide? This was not a foot chase nor a case where the object was apprehension, cases which Michigan relied on to hold the evidence inadmissible. The Court said in footnote 8: "We, of course, intimate no view as to the federal constitutional correctness of either of those Michigan state-court cases...." and in footnote 9 it said: "We therefore leave to another day the determination of the circumstance in which police pursuit could amount to a seizure under the Fourth Amendment." That would hopefully be resolved by the **Hodari** case and it was.

Justices Kennedy and Scalia wrote a concurring opinion in **Chesternut** labeling the decision as "no bold step" because defendant's flight gave police ample cause to stop him. The Court, they noted, found no more than an absence of improper conduct. They felt that neither the chase nor investigative pursuit need be included in the lexicon of the Fourth Amendment. There was no control by the law enforcement officials. The felt they missed a chance to decide the "unmistakable show of authority" issue. That still must be decided, they noted.

Perhaps that would be decided in **Brower v. County of Inyo**, 817 F. 2d 540 (C.A. 9th 1987) which was argued January 11, 1989. The police believed Brower was driving a stolen car and they gave chase. The chase lasted 20 miles achieving high speeds and ended with Brower killing himself when he tried to run a roadblock that had been set up to stop him. The "1983" action said a seizure occurred when the chase started. Though not all issues will be decided by this case, Scalia asked one telling question. He wondered why the Court should not adopt a rule that encourages people to obey police officers and then have them litigate the legality of the stop later. (Florida?). Counsel thought that rule too harsh. The case as decided is discussed in Chapter One.

It was still too early to know the impact of **Chesternut**. One of the first cases to deal with **Chesternut** was **Hawkins v. State**, 758 S.W. 2d 255 (Tex. Ct. Crim. App. 1988). Distinguishing **Chesternut**, the Texas Court found police illegality and said that abandonment caused by police misconduct cannot stand. They applied the **Chesternut** totality standard. This case, they felt, was more than a mere approach by law enforcement officers and the decision to abandon was a *direct result* (court emphasis) of the misconduct. Texas clung to its due process view which of course was shared by the Fifth Circuit.

In yet another police approach case, the Court of Appeals for the District of Columbia said it could distinguish between the act of merely setting an item down and the act of abandonment. These are factual questions. They found abandonment here because the defendant "tossed it" or left it with no expectation of privacy. His expressed intent to retrieve it later was irrelevant because his ability to do so would depend on the fortuity that another person with access to the hallway would leave it alone. No mention was made of **Chesternut. U.S. v. Thomas**, 864 F. 2d 843 (C.A. D.C. 1989).

In summary the Texas Court of Criminal Appeals said it best when it said that abandonment is made up of two elements. First, there must be an intent to abandon and, second, the decision must be arrived at freely and not be the mere product of police misconduct. The defendant in this case was illegally stopped and his act of kicking the syringe under the car was not independent of the unlawful stop. **Comer v. State**, 754 S.W. 2d 656 (Tex. Cr. App. 1986). Accord: **State v. Grant**, 614 N.W. 2d 848 (Iowa App. 2000) and **State v. Silva**, 2000 WL 533065 (Ore. App.) (unpub. op.). **Hodari D**. would not change this result.

The indication given by the unanimous Court opinion in which Scalia and Kennedy only concurred, was that any attempt at an illegal seizure might constitute grounds to rule inadmissible any abandoned evidence. The **Terry** "show of authority" language was cited. The Court said "the police conduct involved here would not have communicated to the reasonable person an attempt to capture or otherwise intrude upon respondent's freedom of movement." The Court then talked about sirens, flashers, and commands to halt as well as the display of weapons and the fact that none of these were used in **Chesternut**. It, therefore, held there was no seizure.

When looking at these police conduct cases a closer examination of **Hester** is required. The presence of the police on Hester's father's land, though a trespass, was found to be outside the Fourth Amendment's zone of protection because it was in the "open fields." A number of the cases cited in these materials represent police activity in unprotected zones; they took place on the streets. Thus it is not the place that concerns us.

Whether a seizure of the individual took place is the critical question. Strictly speaking, and without **Chesternut**, if no seizure was in effect, then the act of abandonment was not the product of a seizure even if the attempt at the seizure was illegal; that is, without probable cause. It should go without saying that an abandonment caused by a legal seizure or a legal attempt at a seizure is of no concern due to the search incident doctrine.

Thus the focus must be on the attempt at illegal seizures. **Hester** is not much help here. All we learn from **Hester** was that an "alarm was given." By whom, we do not know. Assuming the worst, that the revenue agents, without guns pulled, yelled out for the men to stop, we have only an attempted seizure. It fell short because Hester and his friend ran and abandoned the jugs of moonshine. Assuming the alarm was give by an ally of Hester let us assume that the officers had no probable cause to be where they were but had only at best articulable suspicion. If they had no probable cause then the attempted seizure was illegal. What result?

The Court in discussing **Hester** in **Brower v. County of Inyo**, 489 U.S. 593 (1989) said of the conduct of the officers in **Hester**: "Thus, even though the incriminating containers were unquestionably taken into possession as a result (in the broad sense) of action by the police, the court held no seizure had taken place." The use of the parenthetical was not without meaning "in the broad sense" then the Florida case was the proper approach to police caused abandonment. The New York case is also correct. In the Florida case there was no seizure of the individual; only an attempt at a seizure. In the New York case there was a seizure thus abandonment could only yield usable evidence if there was attenuation.

The Court in **Brower** went to a great deal of trouble to distinguish a mere announcement of authority and a show of authority that leads to a seizure. All announcements of authority are not seizures but all seizures involve the announcement plus an intentional acquisition of physical control. Thus in **Tennessee v. Garner**, 471 U.S. 1 (1985), the pointing of the gun constituted the physical control and in **Brower** the placing of the "semi" to block the road was the physical control. In **Hester** there was no physical control thus the abandoned evidence was admissible.

All such cases would have to be analyzed against **Brower** and not **Chesternut**. If **Brower** meant what it apparently said, then the "reasonable person" test for seizure is no longer the standard to be applied. (See discussion of **Brower** in the materials discussing the Fourth Amendment and the Exclusionary Rule). The dispute in **Brower** set the stage for **Hodari D.**. Decided by the Supreme Court on April 23, 1991, the Court in **California v. Hodari D.**, 499 U.S. 621 (1991), clearly decided to agree with the Florida position and to disagree with the Fifth Circuit's decision. Hodari was seen by police fleeing a group as the officers approached. During the chase and before he was tackled, Hodari threw a rock of crack-cocaine away. Assuming, as the Court, did that there was not probable cause for an arrest nor articulable suspicion for the stop, the attempted illegal seizure did not taint the evidence. They said: "The cocaine abandoned while he was running was in this case not the fruit of a seizure, and his motion to exclude the evidence of it was properly denied..." by the trial court.

Hodari D. would dictate the results of **Oliver**, the Florida case, **Boodle**, the New York case and **Porras**, the California case. There was no seizure in **Oliver** when the abandonment took place; there was a seizure in **Boodle** and the court properly had to apply attenuation; and no seizure had taken place in **Porras** when the drugs were thrown away. A discussion of what constitutes a seizure can be found in Chapter One.

A Texas police officer approached a man to ask if he had been in a recent fight in the area. The officer did not command him to stop nor did the officer touch the man. In response, the defendant spit out cocaine. Was this a violation of **Hodari D.** or was it **Hodari D.** in action. It was voluntary abandonment; the type approved by **Hodari D.** There was no police misconduct here under both **Hodari D.** and **Mendenhall**. **Hollingsworth v. State**, 15 S.W. 3d 586 (Tex. App. 2000).

An Indiana defendant ran from police officers as they approached him. The officer asked him to stop. He responded by saying "I didn't do anything." The officer opened his car door and again asked the defendant to stop, but the defendant took off running. As one can see there was no submission to command and no one had touched him. Two objects fell from the defendant's jacket pockets when he ran; a hand gun and an ammunition magazine had fallen. No stop had yet occurred when the gun and magazine were seized and found to be abandoned. **State v. Belcher**, 2000 WL 202524 (Ind. App.).

A companion case to **Terry v. Ohio**, **Sibron v. New York**, 392 U.S. 40 (1968), became the focus of another case from Indiana. In **Swanson v. State**, 730 N. E. 2d 205 (Ind. App. 2000), the defendant was detained for a possible alcohol violation. He had his hands in his pockets. Police told him to take his hands out of his pockets cocaine fell to the ground. Unlike **Terry** and very much like **Sibron** the crime suspected was not an inherently dangerous felony. His hands were in his pockets before police stopped him and no furtive movements were observed. He did not, according to police testimony, appear to be intoxicated. This defendant had not, like **Sibron**, spent any time with known drug addicts. Therefore, like **Sibron**, there was no fear to dispel and the cocaine was not abandoned.

A defendant in a Washington case abandoned his jacket. He says that his stop was based on a pretextual stop. Washington has rejected the **Whren** case and does allow their courts to determine if an automobile stop was a pretext even if there is a lawful basis for the stop. The Washington driver was stopped because his car's windshield was cracked, a violation of statutes. It was on the driver's side running diagonally to the bottom of the passenger side. A license check determined her license was suspended, she was ordered out of the car, frisked and put back in the car. A jacket was on the floor board, the officer went back to his car and then returned, had her get out so he could search the interior. The jacket was no longer there. He circled the car and saw it on the ground stuffed under the passenger side of the car where her husband sat.

Was this jacket abandoned or was it a product of police illegal conduct? First this was not a pretextual stop. The pocket belonged to the passenger and he was never touched by the officer although he was ordered to stay in the car (the officer was alone and this was seen as O.K.). Did the passenger abandon the jacket? The defendant passenger denied it was his. He also said he did not put it under the car. Believing that the officer saw the coat in the car the Washington court found a voluntary abandonment because there was "no unlawful police conduct..." and held "the subsequent abandonment does not eliminate the illegality of the initial possession." **State v. Reynolds**, 2000 WL 1208353 (Wash. App.2) (unpub. op). The point being made by the Washington court is that even if there is an illegal act by the police, the abandonment, to be "bad", the defendant must show a nexus between the alleged illegal detention and the act of abandonment. This is illustrated by **Hunter v. State**, 244 Ga. App. 488 (2000). In **Hunter** the police were about to execute a no-knock warrant. The defendant and others were outside that apartment standing near a car with its hood up. One officer ordered these men to the ground while holding a shot gun and telling them what was about to happen. The warrant was executed and the men were allowed to stand up and guns were not pointed at anyone (the shot gun; pistols were holstered). A second officer saw a match box on the ground, picked it up, opened it and found it contained 5 or 6 rocks of cocaine. At this point the men were seized. Ultimately Lee admitted it was his.

The court held that the officer who found the match box was exiting the house where he had a right to be. The finding of the match box was unconnected with the earlier detention. There was no evidence by Lee that he abandoned the box because of the initial detention. It is not clear when that abandonment occurred; it may have happened as the police were approaching the apartment. Since Lee was not seen jettisoning anything as he was seized or during the seizure, and the fact that it was discovered by a totally different officer means that it was not a product of the order to lie down.

IV. Garbage and Trash – One Man's Trash is Another Man's Evidence of Criminal Conduct.

It is not a pretty sight. Police officers going through garbage bags and trash cans. Police climbing into and out of "dumpsters." But we learn a great deal about people from their garbage and trash. Should police be able to go through a person's trash without a warrant? If so, what limits should be placed on the right? Here again the Court had not provided direction and would not until 1988. The following cases represent the state of the law before May of 1988.

In a California case the question was whether garbage in cans placed near the street was abandoned property thus subject to warrantless seizure. The fact that the cans were on public property played an important role in the case. Thus the "right to be where the police were" concept of plain view was brought into this area. The street was not a constitutionally protected area. But more important, the California court said, was whether there was a reasonable expectation of privacy. That is where the cans come in. The court went into the fact that many municipalities hire private firms under heavy regulation to collect garbage which they felt refuted the idea of garbage becoming public property. Thus, the court held that the defendant had not given up their reasonable expectation of privacy until the garbage was mixed and lost its identity in the garbage truck. Here the officers picked over the garbage after it was dumped into the truck but before it was mixed and lost its identity. Thus they held the evidence inadmissible. **People v. Krivda**, 486 P. 2d 1262 (Cal. 1971). However, the Federal circuits have held that one does not have a reasonable expectation of privacy in trash placed for collection. **U.S. v. Reicherter**, 647 F. 2d 397 (C.A. 3rd 1981). **U.S. v. Michaels**, 726 F. 2d 1307 (C.A. 8th 1984), held that when one places the garbage out for collection in a public area or in close proximity to a public way or in a communal trash bin there is no reasonable expectation of privacy. The Ninth Circuit agrees with the general rule and held that trash placed in trash bags and left for removal is deemed abandoned. The fact that the police collected it instead of the garbage men made no difference. **U.S. v. Kramer**, 711 F. 2d 789 (C.A. 9th 1983). The Second Circuit even upheld a six month search of garbage in **U.S. v. Terry**, 702 F. 2d 299 (C.A. 2d 1983). The Fifth Circuit sees it as a standing issue and they said when the defendant puts his trash in a trash pile he loses standing. **U.S. v. Compton**, 704 F. 2d 739 (C.A. 5th 1983).

In **U.S. v. Gregg**, 629 F. Supp. 958 (W.D. Mo. 1986) a trash collector agreed to put the defendant's "stuff" in special bags supplied by customs agents. The trial court said this was alright. On appeal, the Eighth Circuit said the search of the trash by the customs agents was alright also. **U.S. v. Gregg**, 829 F. 2d 143 (C.A. 8th 1987). Subsequent cases from the Second and Ninth Circuits confirmed their earlier views. **U.S. v. Caputo**, 808 F. 2d 963 (C.A. 2d 1987) and **U.S. v. Dela Espriella**, 781 F. 2d 1432 (C.A. 9th 1986). Thus for them California represents the most defendant oriented position. How did other states treat trash? Most of them decided as the circuits had decided.

One of the better reasoned cases came from Alaska. In **Smith v. State**, 510 P. 2d 793 (Alaska 1973). The police staked out the defendant's apartment for twelve days. During the stake-out, a garbage dumpster was also kept under surveillance. As the defendant dumped garbage, police were instructed to remove it and search it. Two garbage bags were removed in which was found evidence that linked the defendant to unlawful drugs. On this information, a warrant was issued for the defendant's apartment. The court first noted that the Fourth Amendment does not apply to abandoned property. Second it said that items of garbage placed in a receptacle outside the dwelling are abandoned. It reached this conclusion on the basis of Mascolo's comments in his law review article at **20 Buffalo Law Rev. 399 (1970)** as noted by the court on page 795 of the opinion. Mascolo said the intentional throwing away of something is a relinquishment of all title, possession or claim. He also noted that the throwing away is not presumed but requires supportive proof. Once proof of abandonment is adduced the expectation of privacy disappears. Certain factors must be taken into account, the court said. These factors are:

1. where the trash is located;
2. whether the dwelling is multiple or single unit;
3. who removed the trash; and
4. where the search of the trash takes place.

The court then turned to the "privacy" analysis in this case. The points made were:

1. this dumpster accommodated several apartments;
2. many people from the apartment would certainly look into it;
3. all municipal pickups were made from this dumpster;
4. any tenant must be aware that scavenging could take place;
5. dumpster was located outside the building in a parking area; and
6. trash could be removed by
   a. children,
   b. stray dogs, and
   c. visitors.

The court said, "taking these various factors together, we are unable to conclude that appellant could have harbored an objective reasonable expectation of privacy in the dumpster." **Smith** at 798.

Michigan adopted the rationale of the Alaska case. **People v. Whotte,** 317 N.W. 2d 266 (Mich. Ct. App. 1982) wherein that court held there was no reasonable expectation of privacy where the defendant places garbage in an open backyard where dogs and others regularly tore open the trash containers. The Minnesota Court said it was alright to go in the backyard a few feet to retrieve trash. This was also approved by the Ninth Circuit in **U.S. v. Kramer,** (supra). The Minnesota Court held that the backyard enjoyed a lesser expectation of privacy and, in any event, the defendant's use of the property as a place for commercial drug dealing eliminated any residual expectation of privacy that he might have had with regard to the area entered by the officers. **State v. Krech,** 403 N.W. 2d 634 (Minn. 1987).

Well, it was time for the Supreme Court to rule and it chose a case from California where the **Krivda** rule was still operating. The case is **California v. Greenwood,** 486 U.S. 35 (1988). The issue, as the Court saw it, was "whether the Fourth Amendment prohibits the warrantless search and seizure of garbage left for collection outside the curtilage of a home." It said: "it does not." This was not one of those expectations of privacy that society is prepared to accept as objectively reasonable. Garbage at the streets is readily accessible to animals, children, scavengers, snoops and other members of the public, the Court noted. Since the garbage man could have gone through it, so could the police. It cited the **Reicherter** case (supra), and talked about unanimous rejection of privacy rights as exhibited by the circuit courts and provided a long list of those cases plus the state cases in accord. The Court dismissed a Due Process Clause argument as without merit. This was a 6-2 decision with Kennedy taking no part. Only Brennan and Marshall dissented. Their dissent was based on the container law of **U.S. v. Jacobsen**, **Chadwick** and **Sanders**. They disagreed that people would support the proposition of garbage clawing.

As can be seen there is no answer here except a negative implication regarding picking up trash from the back yard. The curtilage part of the issue will have to be settled, but as the Court is presently constituted, the worst possible vote would be 5-4 in favor of entering, by a few feet, the back yard to pick up trash exposed to the same people that can go through the garbage at the curb. Time will tell. For a case denying the police this privilege to enter see **U.S. v. Certain Real Property**, 719 F. Supp. 1396 (E.D. Mich. 1989), a post-**Greenwood** decision.

Saying that the state constitution provides broader protection than the U.S. Constitution when it comes to garbage, a New Jersey Court held that police may go through garbage only if they have information which, though less than probable cause, reasonably may have induced a conscientious and experienced police officer to believe that their exploration would uncover evidence of a crime. **State v. Pasanen**, 552 A. 2d 212 (N.J. Super. Ct. 1989). The court added that the answer does not necessarily turn on whether the garbage is located on or off private property. Such property is not abandoned but the privacy right can be overcome by a showing of articulable suspicion.

Another New Jersey court, using its own constitution, refused to follow **Greenwood** by holding that the accessibility of garbage to outsiders is not dispositive because there is a difference between a scavenger and a police officer searching for evidence of a crime. Thus, they held the police need the consent of the owner, or probable cause plus a warrant, or exigent circumstances and probable cause to conduct the search. They did say the police could seize the garbage while awaiting the issuance of a warrant. **State v. Hempele**, 552 A. 2d 212 (N.J. Super. A.D. 1989). It is difficult to figure out how one has a lack of privacy against a scavenger but has one against police. This is not at all like the hotel maid cases. In any event, the New Jersey Supreme court affirmed the two decisions at 576 A. 2d 793 (1990)

Connecticut has decided to accept **Greenwood** by its decision in **State v. DeFusco**, 606 A. 2d 1 (Conn. App. 1992). This court saw no reason to reject **Greenwood** since their citizens had never been accustomed to a more protective rule concerning garbage. Idaho was asked to take a "new federalism" approach and give its citizens more rights, but the Idaho Supreme Court refused the invitation. **State v. Donato**, 2001 WL 200149 (Idaho).

On the other hand two of Indiana's intermediate appellate courts split over whether Indiana's constitution provides more protection than the U.S. Constitution. One court said a warrant is needed to search trash bags and the other accepted **Greenwood** as not offending the state constitution. Obviously the Indiana Supreme Court must resolve this irreconcilable conflict. See **Moran v. State**, 625 N.E. 2d 1231 (Ind. App. 1993); aff'd 644 N.E. 2d 536 (Ind. 1994) and **Bell v. State**, 626 N.E. 2d 570 (Ind. App. 1993).

Greenwood has not settled all garbage cases. Some courts read the Supreme Court's "outside the curtilage" language in Greenwood as meaning that garbage within the curtilage is protected by the Fourth Amendment. This strict interpretation cast doubts on decisions like those from Alaska and Michigan cited above. Some, however, read the same language as only creating an "open question" not yet settled. The "open question" position was the interpretation preferred by the Seventh Circuit. That court held that garbage placed within the curtilage for regular collection was not protected by a reasonable expectation of privacy. They did not attempt an answer regarding garbage cans regularly kept at the residence but in an otherwise accessible area. That was to be left for another day. **U.S. v. Hedrick**, 922 F. 2d 396 (C.A. 7th 1991). Suffice it to say not all questions have yet been answered. The answers may come from the **Sampson** cases from Maryland discussed below.

Two garbage cases from the year 2000 are worth noting. The first is from Rhode Island. It was a case of first impression for them and they had the benefit of 12 years of **Greenwood** development. The Rhode Island police had a murder on their hands. A note at the scene indicated that the last person who had contact with victim may have been a New Hampshire man. They go to New Hampshire where Briggs lived but a tenant of his said he was not home. They, accompanied by a New Hampshire state police officer, got back in their car and saw the tenant drive away in Briggs' pickup truck. They followed the tenant and saw him take a white garbage bag out of the back of the truck and put it in a dumpster also owned by the defendant. This was outside a set of apartments that the defendant also owned. The police seized the bag and returned to the original site to await Briggs. Briggs arrived at 7:00 PM. The police met Briggs, expressed their condolences, and asked if he could help them. Briggs invited them into his apartment. He said he was there but left and she was alright. He said she called him the next morning and volunteered to let them look at the caller 'ID box. Next he volunteered a gun and allowed then to inspect it. He was then invited to go to the local police station for questioning. They left in separate cars. At the police station he was told that he was a suspect. He consented to talk, waiving Miranda rights. However, the major argument of the defense centered on the garbage bag. They said New Hampshire law applies and that the bag was still his even after it was put in the dumpster and not subject to a warrantless search. Rhode Island D.A.'s argued that their law applied.

An "interest weighing" approach was taken. Rhode Island's law was found to govern because it had the most significant interest. The court then turned to the search of the garbage bag itself. The trial judge suppressed the evidence. The state argued it was abandoned and if not that it was left in a place of "no reasonable expectation of privacy in the bag or its contents," since many persons had access to the dumpster. Public accessibility came to the forefront of this battle. The court said the defendant did not have an objectively reasonable expectation of privacy in the bag or its contents. Why? It was put in a communal dumpster in a parking lot of a multi dwelling tenement about fifteen miles from defendant's residence. Thus the trial judge's decision to not admit the evidence was in error. **State v. Briggs**, 756 A. 2d 731 (R.I. 2000).

The second case comes from Maryland and its Court of Special Appeals. **Sampson v. State**, 744 A. 2nd 588 (Md. App. 2000). This court said the motion to suppress should have been granted because the evidence was seized by the police by trespassing onto the defendants' properly to search through trash bags. The garbage bags were not at the curb but were close enough to the street that the officer did not have to walk on her property to seize the bags. Several "corner cut" baggies with cocaine residue were found in the bags. The court noted that Lafave says **Greenwood** is not an abandoned property case. Funny, that is also what the U.S. Supreme Court said. In any event these bags were on the lawn thus still within the curtilage. The next issue was centered on her admission that they were placed for collection that day but she insists her consent went only to the trash collectors and not to anyone else; not even the police. The "high road" was taken and the Maryland Court addressed the issue of "subject to rummaging" by persons. It "borrowed" from New Jersey and the high court decision in **State v. Hempele**, 576 A. 2d 793 (N.J. 1990). Maryland said that court "...expressly recognized the significant difference between a homeless person scavenging...and an officer...scrutinizing the contents of a garbage bag for incriminating materials." Indeed there is a difference but does that make any difference with regard to a general expectation of privacy and whether it is reasonable? These are indeed great words but not supportable under **Greenwood** and can be justified only under the local laws and the state constitution. The court ends by suggesting to police that they wait until the trash collectors pick it up. The same officers will be scrutinizing, won't they?

However, the Sampson case went to the high court of Maryland and they reversed the Special Court of Appeals. Why? They noted that most states had not fully agreed with the curtilage limitation and felt that the unreasonable expectation of privacy of a person who puts garbage out for collection was the only true measure. In their case the front yard was very shallow. They noted that the curtilage discussion in **Greenwood** was almost an afterthought. They also cite several cases that either overlooked curtilage or used it but not as a controlling factor. They went on to say: "The law that has emerged since **Greenwood** is essentially the same as it was before that case was decided, although it is based less on the property concept of abandonment than on the conclusion that, by depositing the trash in a place accessible to the public for collection, the depositor has relinquished any reasonable expectation of privacy." In fact Maryland noted that Kansas felt that the "curtilage concept was not part of the Court's rationale in deciding the issue." They then cited **State v. Kimberlin**, 984 P. 2d 141 (Kan. 1999). The court then said: "To suggest that the concept of curtilage has any meaning to people in the context of placing their trash for collection is absurd." The said people put them where they have to put them to get the collectors to collect it. This case challenges the Supreme Court to" put up or shut up." **State v. Sampson**, 765 A. 2d 629 (Md. 2001). The wisdom of the Alaska and Michigan cases still shines.

One of the unanswered questions involves the modern device, the paper shredder. Does a person who shreds his paper create an expectation of privacy even though he bags and places the shreds at curbside? A federal district court judge took the position that shredding was not covered by **Greenwood**. The defendant said and the trial judge agreed that shredding was an act of privacy. The court pinned its decision on the "ready accessibility" language of **Greenwood** and the painstaking reconstruction required to "un-shred" means that the material was not readily accessible. The judge then ruled that society would think the expectation of privacy subjectively taken was objectively reasonable and, therefore, protected. **U.S. v. Scott**, 776 F. Supp. 629 (D. Mass. 1991). However, was the Supreme Court really concerned with more than location? The judge's decision sounds nice but no empirical data exists to support his decision as to the use of the materials.

The judge's decision also appears to assume that only law enforcement would do the "painstaking" work on shredded papers. That assumption may be false. The garbage of famous persons, including a former President, has been taken by interested passers-by and in one instance the things gleaned from the garbage were used to construct a personal story about the personality of the subject not otherwise known or revealed. In fact, it has been said that we can learn a lot about a person from his or her garbage.

V.   Conclusion

Once the government claims that the lack of a warrant was due to the status of the property as abandoned, the court must use a totality of the circumstances analysis. At first, the court must determine whether the property could in fact be classified as abandoned, lost, mislaid or in possession of someone. Abandonment requires proof of some positive act or proof of factors that would lead one to reasonably believe that the property is abandoned. Location, condition of the place where found, and denial of ownership all have to be taken into account. Next, the court must determine whether the act of abandonment was voluntary or police induced. If police induced, was the police activity lawful? If the police activity was not lawful can some "taint remover" such as attenuation save the evidence? With regard to garbage and trash we know that the U.S. Supreme Court has declared that garbage, etc., outside the curtilage of the home is not covered by a societally protected right of privacy. As for garbage, *etc.*, within the curtilage, some conflict exists as to how strictly to read **Greenwood.**

VI. ABANDONED PROPERTY CHECKLIST

1. Determine the status of the personal property as it came into police possession. Was it:
    a.   lost,
    b.   misplaced, or
    c.   abandoned?

2. If lost or misplaced there arises in the police a community care-taking function. Determine whether the police activity regarding to personal property exceeded the scope of their authority as care takers by assessing these factors:
    a.   to find the true owner;
    b.   to protect themselves from civil claims (bailee duty); and
    c.   to protect themselves and the public from dangerous instrumentalities.

    If the scope exceeded an inventory, a search for crime has taken place. Do a standard warrantless search analysis to determine admissibility.

3. If abandoned property was the abandonment caused by illegal police conduct? If not admit. Key: police chase alone is not a seizure. Test abandonment during a seizure by **Chesternut/Hodari D.**

4. True Abandonment—no police cause—test by local law definition but remember:
    a.   disclaimer of ownership can constitute abandonment—look for a positive and voluntary (**Hodari D.**) act—Silence is not like a disclaimer; and
    b.   look for indicia of abandonment—"totality" rule applies

5. Garbage and Trash Cases:
    a.   was there state action;

314

b. was there a reasonable expectation of privacy:
    1) outside curtilage – no; or
    2) inside curtilage – yes (we think)

c. was there a reasonable expectation of privacy:
    1) manner of protecting garbage or trash – no steps taken - no expectation; or
    2) manner of protecting garbage or trash – extensive steps taken – perhaps an expectation- if found do a standard abandonment analysis.

d. **Greenwood**: caution: an expectation of privacy case and not an abandoned property case.

CHAPTER NINE

ADMINISTRATIVE SEARCHES: THE FOURTH AMENDMENT AND HEALTH, SAFETY AND WELFARE CLAUSES OF THE CONSTITUTION

I.   Regulation of Life and Business: The Government Need to Intrude

With the Franklin Roosevelt Administration came the growth of regulatory schemes, the likes of which the Populists never envisioned. Noble goals mushroomed that protected the people from the robber barons of industry, the people from their own foolhardiness, and everyone from illicitly run enterprises. Building codes, safety codes, fire codes, and housing codes developed on the local scene. Businesses never before licensed now had to be licensed and inspected and re-inspected. Federal programs involving welfare, safe working conditions, trade in dangerous instrumentalities, and tax programs all required regulation and, therefore, intrusion into the premises of the business proprietor. To what extent does the Fourth Amendment apply to all of these areas of regulation of peoples' lives? Does it apply at all?

The administrative exception to the standard criminal warrant requirement is perhaps the most confusing because it does not have a singularly based exception theme. In fact, it is multi-thematic in that it shares or borrows from many of the other exceptions. It is a bit of exigency, a bit of consent, and a doctrine that requires a different analysis of the privacy expectation. It covers business activities of all kinds; it covers all major health and safety concerns; welfare matters fall within its coverage.

Sometimes a warrant is required but the probable cause standard is held at a lower standard than required for general criminal investigative conduct. Sometimes a warrant is not required despite the fact that the state action will uncover evidence of criminality in both the administrative and standard context.

Sometimes a warrant is not required because of the exigencies of the conduct involved (the fire and accident cases). Sometimes a warrant is not required because of a form of prior and continuing consent (the closely regulated industries and sensitive position – drug testing cases). In fact, in these latter contexts, it is often both exigency and consent mixed together. As an exception to the standard criminal warrant requirement the well-defined circumscription of the investigating officer's discretion is the key. Most often this is spelled out in the statute or ordinance which governs the conduct or is necessarily implied therefrom. Private and public interests are balanced and when the public need outweighs the private right, the warrant requirement is reduced or eliminated.

Consider, for example, **O'Connor v. Ortega**, 480 U.S. 709 (1987). In this case Dr. Ortega, a public employee of a state hospital, brought a 1983 action complaining of the search of his desk and files. The search took place because Ortega was absent and the hospital needed certain files and because he was suspected of needing "discipline." Does such an employee have a reasonable expectation of privacy in his desk and files at his place of work? The answer to that question is yes under **Mancusi v. De Forte**, 392 U.S. 364 (1968), and public employees do not lose that right simply because they work for the government.

The second question is whether that reasonable expectation can be overcome for administrative reasons, without a warrant, and on less than probable cause. The answer to this question is also yes, it can be overcome because a warrant requirement would be unworkable. There are any number of legitimate reasons that a public employer might need to invade the privacy areas of the employees. These work related needs can include a need to safeguard or identify state property or records in an office, even in connection with a pending investigation into suspected employee misfeasance. Work-related searches are merely an incident of the primary business of the agency. One cannot make every government office function a constitutional matter. As long as the intrusion was reasonable and, for these purposes only, there is no warrant requirement. If employees want to avoid exposing personal belongings at work all they have to do is simply leave them at home, the Court said. But they added: "The scope and inception of the intrusion must be reasonable and not excessively intrusive."

In **Embury v. State**, 15 S.W. 3d 367 (Mo. App.2000), the police received a call regarding a possible fire at housing authority property. When the officer arrived he saw some smoke coming from a storage/tool shed. He entered and realized the smoke was fog-like and strongly smelled of ether. Other items of a "speed" lab plus legitimate tools were also present. This led to Embury's arrest. Embury argued "workplace" privacy under **Mancusi** and **O'Conner**. This court rejected that in this case and found no Fourth Amendment protection for Embury. The defendant did not own the shed, and he did not have the right to bar others from it. He was only a part-time employee and there was at least one other key to the shed. Anyone else that entered this building (on public land) could see what the officer saw. It was not an office – there was no desk or phone to even hint of a private work place. It was mainly used for storage. The court noted that the defendant probably did not want anyone to see this "lab," but that expectation was not reasonable.

Before reviewing other leading cases in the area recall the Fourth Amendment:

> "The right of the people to be secure in their persons, houses, papers, and effects, against unreasonable searches and seizures, shall not be violated, and no Warrants shall issue, but upon probable cause supported by Oath or Affirmation, and particularly describing the place to be searched, and the persons or things to be seized."

Unlike Amendments Five and Six, nowhere in the Fourth Amendment is the word *crime* or any form of the word *crime* used. The right to be secure against unreasonable searches and seizures shall not be violated. Warrants require probable cause, upon oath or affirmation, and the place to be searched must be spelled out, and the things sought must be particularly described. Several of the problems faced by the Court involved criminal sanctions for refusing entry to allow an inspection. Others also provided fines for violations found as a result of the inspections. Yet in other instances the law did not provide criminal sanctions for refusal but the inspection could certainly yield evidence of a crime.

This latter possibility was the situation in **Wyman v. James**, 400 U.S. 309 (1971). The defendant was a welfare recipient who refused admission to her home when requested by the case worker. The New York law said that such a refusal could work a cut-off of rights to receive future welfare payments. Is that reasonable? Yes, said the Court. The Court upheld the inspection right on the grounds that it served a valid and proper purpose. They said it was not an unwarranted invasion of personal privacy and violated no right guaranteed by the Fourth Amendment. **Camera** and **See** (see cases noted below) were distinguished because those cases involved criminal sanctions for refusal to allow inspection. The reasonableness of the search (inspection) was based on the fact that the New York statute had several safeguards. A notice, in writing, was sent several days before the proposed visit and no forced entry was allowed. The termination of benefits (the seizure?) was upheld because of the reasonableness of the inspection method thus provided. Some concern was expressed over such devices as mass raids conducted during early morning hours. The Court said these types of raids would be constitutionally challengeable.

Since nowhere in the Fourth Amendment does it say that criminal sanctions to refuse consent must apply, was the Court correct in its rationalization by distinguishing **Wyman** from other administrative search cases? There is no doubt that the word *unreasonable* in the amendment would allow for sensible legislative schemes. An abstraction like "reasonable" is indeed entitled to a workable interpretation expressed in terms of public versus private needs.

II. When is a Warrant Required?: Closely Regulated versus Merely Regulated Activities

What is "reasonable" in any context is important. Could it depend on the type of business in which one engages? Certainly the Court so recognized this all-important distinction when a refusal to enter is interposed. Consider Mr. Biswell's business. Biswell sold guns and was licensed by the Federal Government. To do business under the federal license, Biswell knew that he had to keep records and allow his business to be inspected. It was inspected and several sawed-off rifles were discovered. He cried "foul" and "unreasonable search and seizure." The federal law allowed the inspection of the records and firearms stored on the premises. The officer came during regular business hours and entered without force. The officer gave Biswell a copy of the law and told Biswell he must comply. Biswell complied rather than face a criminal charge for refusing.

The Court said that in the context of a regulatory inspection system of business premises which is carefully limited in time, place and scope, the legality depends on the statute and not on the consent. Thus, Biswell's compelled consent was brushed aside and the word *unreasonable* was about to be interpreted. The problem of guns and the danger of having them in the wrong hands was emphasized. The Court deemed the agent's conduct, as prescribed by the statute, as reasonable. They went on to say that in this business, if inspection is to be of any value as a deterrent to illegal practices, it must be unannounced and frequent. In closing, the Court as much as said that when a man goes into this business, he knows what is expected of him. It acknowledged, approvingly, that the government kept all fire-arms dealers well informed of legislative and regulatory changes. **U.S. v. Biswell**, 406 U.S. 311 (1972).

Of course the statute must be closely followed. The A.T.F. statute involved in **Biswell** allows inspections without notice only during regular business hours. Conducting an inspection of the books one hour before regular business hours while in the business place for other purposes under a valid warrant that did not describe the books and records could not be upheld under the authority of the A.T.F. statute. **U.S. v. Limatoc**, 807 F. 2d 792 (C.A. 9th 1987). But if followed properly there is no need for a warrant even to seize the records. **U.S. v. Trevino**, 679 F. Supp. 910 (S.D. Tex. 1989).

In a like manner states began the fight against high insurance rates and the stolen car and parts businesses. Statutory authorization for the warrantless inspection of the books and records of auto junkyards was held to be constitutional by Michigan. The basis of their opinion was the closely regulated industry theory of **Biswell** and the implied consent that one gives when going into this business. **People v. Barnes**, 370 N.W. 2d 464 (Mich. App. 1986); accord; and with regard to a pawnbroker case; see **Howell v. Roberts**, 656 F. Supp. 1150 (N.D. Ga. 1987).

Does the fact that the insurance industry is heavily regulated automatically make it a "closely" regulated industry dispensing with the administrative warrant requirement. The answer from a California court was no! This court could find no case that the threat of fraud and sharp practices justified a warrantless, surprise inspection approach. Public health and safety are not at issue here, the court found. Thus it held that a warrantless administrative inspection scheme is not necessary for the insurance industry. **De La Cruz v. Quackenbush**, 96 Cal. Rep. 2d 92 (Cal. App. 2d 2000).

The next closely regulated case dealt with by the Supreme Court would be the junkyard regulation scheme of New York which New York determined to be unconstitutional. The case is **New York v. Burger**, 484 U.S. 691 (1987). The Court said that like general junkyards and secondhand shops, auto junkyards, relatively new in the historical sense, are a closely regulated industry, and therefore may be exempted from the warrant requirement. The state has a substantial interest in regulating this industry. A regulatory scheme designed to eradicate auto theft is a legitimate goal. This statute informs the operator that regular inspections will be made, it sets forth the scope of the inspection, tells the operator how to comply, and who is authorized to conduct the inspection. Moreover, the Court said, the time, place, and scope of the inspection is limited to impose appropriate restraints upon the inspecting officer's discretion. Finally, the fact that police officers (rather than a bureaucrat) conducted the inspection was not fatal. It was not rendered illegal by the fact that the inspecting officer also has the power to arrest individuals for violations other than those created by the scheme itself–*e.g.*, receiving and concealing stolen property. Accord: **Com. v. Tremblay**, 722 N.E. 2d 34 (Mass. App. 2000).

New York believed that the Supreme Court has made it too easy for the state to label and qualify an industry as "closely regulated" by the **Burger** decision. Thus, in **People v. Keta**, 593 N.E. 2d 1328 (N.Y. 1992) the New York court, reviewing the statute upheld by the Supreme Court in **Burger**, rejected **Burger** and its holding. They said the closely regulated exception was supposed to be narrow but that it now tends to "swallow the rule" by permitting police an "expedient means of enforcing penal sanctions." They were most concerned that the statute did not create an administrative program that was truly unrelated to criminal law enforcement.

Random stops of trucks on highways not "controlled" by regular truck inspection stations were upheld under an administrative provision that provided adequate notice. **New York v. Burger** (*supra*) was cited as controlling. The Kansas court said this was a pervasively regulated industry with a "substantial governmental interest" and the requirement of notice was fully observed, since all truckers were kept notified of any changes in the law. Necessity was established by statistics showing that those who traveled highways with fixed inspection stations had a violation rate of 0.0% to 0.3%,whereas those stopped on non-inspection-station highways had a violation rate of 1.8% overweight and 15.4% safety violation rate. **State v. Crum**, 19 P.3d 172 (Kan.. 2001).

California, through one of its appellate courts, has determined that its warrantless inspection statute governing retail alcoholic beverage establishments creates a highly or closely regulated industry that justifies frequent and unannounced inspections. They said the legislation met all of the **New York v. Burger** requirements as to substantial governmental interest, advance notice, with discretion properly limited. **People v. Paulson**, 265 Cal. Rep. 579 (Cal. Ct. App. 1990).

New York v. Burger, though an eminently wise decision, opens the door to possible unjustified harassment by over – inspection. Such was the issue presented to the Fourth Circuit in the case of **Turner v. Dammann**, 848 F. 2d 440 (C.A. 4th 1988). A civil rights suit was brought against the police for allegedly making too many "bar checks" at a topless bar. The Fourth Circuit approved trial on the issue and said the police were not entitled to the cloak of qualified immunity. The court emphasized that it was not the program but its execution that was challengeable. There appeared to be no objective reason for the repeated checks and, therefore, a triable issue existed. They noted that the basic standards governing administrative searches condemns the baseless isolation of a single establishment for grossly disproportionate intrusions.

One year after **New York v. Burger**, the Ohio Supreme Court struck down its warrantless administrative search scheme for those holding liquor licenses because it failed to provide time, place, and scope limitations on such searches as were present in the New York scheme approved in **Burger**. Quite frankly, one of Ohio's main concerns was the pretextual administrative search problem. The court said a warrantless administrative search may not be used to obtain evidence of general criminality. The state should not be able to do under the state liquor laws what it is prohibited from doing otherwise. They may have gone too far, however, for they closed their opinion by saying that "evidence obtained as a result of a warrantless administrative search may not be used in a criminal prosecution under a statute of general criminality." **State v. V.F.W. Post 3562**, 525 N.E. 2d 773 (Ohio 1988). Hopefully this rule does not apply to proper administrative schemes.

Ohio also has a statute that allows the random stop of commercial vehicles for safety inspections. Though the goal is laudable, the decision to stop must be based on the **Burger** requirements regarding "time, place and scope" of the inspection. The statute in this case did not restrain the officers in this context, rather, complete discretion was left to each individual inspecting officer. Just as important, however, is Ohio's recognition that trucking is a closely regulated industry. **State v. Landrum**, 2000 WL 283064 (Ohio. App. 4 2000). Therefore, a proper statute can be crafted by the legislature. In any event, when a statute does not involve a closely regulated industry and fails to establish "a predictable and guided" regulatory presence, then the attempt must fail. **Allinder v. State of Ohio**, 808 F. 2d 1180 (C.A. 6th 1987); and **Hansen v. Ill. Racing Board**, 534 N.E. 2d 658 (Ill. Ct. App. 1989) where discretion was not limited.

The **Biswell** and **Burger** cases demonstrate both a proper legislative-administrative set of standards as well as an industry clothed with an aspect of real danger or threat to public well-being. Thus, if a balancing test of private versus public need is used, the public need wins out. But it also demonstrated the licensed industry problem which will be discussed below. Pennsylvania, for example, has found that environmental protection pertaining to solid waste is in the nature of a "heavily regulated" industry thus allowing surprise warrantless inspections. **Pa. Dept. Env. Serv. v. Blosenski Disp. Service**, 566 A. 2d 845 (Pa. 1989). More important to this court was the fact that as in **Biswell** and **Burger**, the legislature had created a well-defined statutory scheme.

This was not so in the caterer's case. A party was held one night at the caterer's place. A federal agent was at the party and he suspected that some bottles used at the party were refilled liquor bottles in violation of the federal tax laws. The agent did nothing that night. A few nights later, another party was being held. This time the agent, with others, attended and proceeded to the basement where the liquor was stored. This was done without consent. The liquor was stored in a room in the basement. The door was locked. The agents asked that it be opened, the boss was called, he arrived and refused. The officers broke the lock and seized several bottles of liquor suspected of being evidence of the liquor law violation. The statute provided for inspection but only provided for a fine upon a refusal to inspect. The statute did not provide for a seizure nor was there the nicely drawn regulatory scheme that Mr. Biswell faced. The Court said that without such detailed provisions the Fourth Amendment applied. The seizure here was illegal. There was plenty of time to get a warrant.

It should be remembered that there is nearly as much danger in getting "bad" whiskey as there is of being shot with an illicit weapon. Untaxed whiskey can have a legitimate source, but, as often, it has a questionable source health - wise. But does the statute require the tax for health reasons or merely for revenue reasons? In any event, the lack of a good set of standards was the factor that distinguished between this case and Mr. Biswell's problem. **Colonnade Catering Corp. v. U.S.**, 397 U.S. 72 (1970). Accord: **Com. v. Waltz**, 749 A. 2d 1058 (Com. Ct. Pa. 2000).

Some goals of legislative activity are absolutely necessary because of an unwillingness of private industry to take the needed steps to cure certain ills which affect the health and safety of employees. These goals, legislatively expressed, provide moral or ethical responsibility. Such is the intent of the Occupational Safety and Health Act (OSHA). To enforce its ends, inspections are needed. Such inspections are a result of a complaint or are a part of departmental industry – by – industry inspection policy. Thus Mr. Barlow's problem came to the fore. An inspector showed up at Barlow's Inc. one day and asked Mr. Barlow if he could inspect the premises. Barlow asked if anyone had made any complaints. The OSHA man said no. Barlow asked if the agent had a warrant. The agent said no, your name was picked by the computer (or some other random method).

Noting that this was not the type of regulated industry that was the subject in the **Biswell** case, the Court would look to **Camara** and **See** (discussed below) as their guides. The Court held that the warrant requirement would impose no large burden on the government. Most businessmen will consent, they observed. The Secretary of Labor provided regulations for seeking compulsory process if entry was refused. It puzzled the Court why such a regulation was adopted if to get such process was so damaging. Besides, the Court said, the types of things they were looking for would not be lost as a result of a lack of surprise.

So a warrant is required when entry is refused, but by what standard should the warrant be issued? Of course, if there was specific evidence of a violation the standard of criminal law probable cause would be met. However, that standard is not required for this type of administrative inspection. There has to be the type of showing that was required in **Camara**. That is reasonable, specific legislative or administrative standards for conducting such inspections. **Marshal v. Barlows' Inc.**, 436 U.S. 307 (1978).

Interpreting **Barlow's** broadly, the government, in a subsequent matter, applied for a "wall-to-wall" warrant upon a complaint by an employee regarding OSHA violations. The lower court denied it and the government appealed. The court looked at the law and such warrants were no *per se* limited. They looked at the facts of the employee complaint and decided that a "wall – to – wall" warrant was proper as other courts had so held. **In Re Inspection of the Workplace**, 741 F. 2d 172 (C.A. 8th 1984).

Relying on **Barlow's,** a district court struck down as unconstitutional the Federal Mine Safety and Health Act's warrantless search provisions. The Supreme Court disagreed. **Donovan v. Dewey**, 452 U.S. 594 (1981). The warrantless inspections were found reasonable. Mine owners were fully aware of this sufficiently comprehensive and defined scheme. This is an industry with a very poor record in the safety and health area and Congress so found. Congress could therefore determine that a system of warrantless inspections was necessary to make the law effective. The statute provided a program that was certain and regular in its application unlike that found in **Barlow's**. Besides, the government, through Congress, had removed this from the general OSHA coverage, singling it out for special "closely regulated" treatment.

Since **Camara** and **See** are the polestar cases for **Barlow's**, a consideration of them is essential. Both cases dealt with local governments and their attempts to inspect premises. One involved the entry into a private dwelling and the other an entry into a commercial building. These cases were decided by the Court on the same day.

In **Camara v. Municipal Court**, 387 U.S. 555 (1967), there was a complaint that Camara was using his apartment in violation of the city housing code. Inspectors went there and Camara would not consent to their entry. The essence of the Court's opinion follows. *First*, a citizen is entitled to know the authority and limits of the inspector's right to inspect. As the reader will recall, Mr. Biswell, the firearms dealer, was well informed. *Second*, the burden of obtaining a warrant is not likely to frustrate the governmental purpose. If a true emergency exists, the search could then be conducted without a warrant. Thus, the Court brought to this area the exigent circumstances doctrine of the criminal area. Note that there was no real emergency in Mr. Barlow's case with OSHA. It was a routine inspection and lacked any compelling urgency which the Court in **Camara** said constituted an emergency. The Court acknowledged the need for and the goals of such inspection programs. But these can be achieved within the confines of a reasonable search warrant requirement.

Next, the Court said the same standards of probable cause need not be applied to inspection warrants as are applied to criminal investigations. The issuing magistrate or judge must weigh the need for the inspection in terms of the reasonable goals of the code's enforcement. However, there have to be reasonable legislative or administrative standards for conducting such inspections. Of course, no two programs will be alike. But such factors as a passage of time since the last inspection, the nature of the building as a single or multiple dwelling unit, or the conditions of the entire area can be taken into account. As can be seen, information on the particular building may be lacking. If, however, a valid public interest exists as tested against the code's standards, then there is justification for an intrusion with a suitably restrictive search warrant. The reasonableness standard of the Fourth Amendment has been met. If the tests outlined above are met the routine inspection can be sanctioned.

Although the Court said warrants should be sought after entry is refused, unless there is an emergency, they soon clarified that statement in the **Biswell** and **See** cases. The companion case to **Camara** was **See v. City of Seattle**, 387 U.S. 541 (1967). **See** dealt with a commercial establishment; a warehouse. The basic principles of **Camara** were made applicable except that a refusal was not necessary before a warrant could be issued in a commercial building inspection case. Recognizing a need for surprise, the Court thus approved advance warrants. Yet they still insisted upon a proper legislative or administrative standard as guides for the issuing magistrate or judge which in turn would necessarily restrict the discretion of the inspecting officials. More important, they did recognize certain accepted regulatory techniques as licensing programs which require inspection prior to operating a business or marketing a product. This point was re – emphasized in **Biswell**. The warrant is mentioned as an evidence gathering device. Would some other device meet the test of satisfying the Fourth Amendment in the administrative context? Consider **Donovan v. Lone Steer, Inc.**, 464 U.S. 408 (1984).Under the Fair Labor Standards Act the Secretary of Labor is given the power to issue subpoenas relating to any matter under investigation. A subpoena was served on an employee of the motel in question. The motel said that the subpoena constituted an unlawful search and seizure because a judicial warrant had not been issued which it said was required by **Barlow's**. The District Court agreed with the defendant motel owner saying that **Barlow's** held that the government could not enter upon the premises without having first obtained a warrant. The Supreme Court said the district court read **Barlow's** too broadly. The entry of a public lobby of a motel for the purpose of serving an administrative subpoena is scarcely the sort of act which is forbidden by the Fourth Amendment. The subpoena in question did not authorize entry or inspection of the motel premises. It merely said produce relevant records. Non-consensual entries of private areas were not sought or approved by subpoena. Subpoenas of this kind were first approved in **Oklahoma Press Publishing Co. v. Walling**, 327 U.S. 186 (1946) and reconfirmed in **See v. City of Seattle** (supra) in 1967.

In a New York case the police impounded a car involved in an accident to conduct a safety inspection. No warrant was used. Instead the police relied on a specific statute that told them to make such a determination. However, the act said nothing about seizures without warrants. Did the police have the authority to impound absent a specific directive or warrant? New York approached this problem as a "pervasive regulation" type area. The closely regulated industries cases were analyzed. Since the scope of the intrusion (safety defects inspection) was strictly tailored to its purpose, the warrantless seizure was upheld. **People v. Quackenbush**, 670 N.E. 2d 434 (N.Y. 1996).

An Ohio court found that the liquor dispensing industry is "closely regulated." Agents, acting as customers, "bought their way into the Eagles club." However, they did not tell the door keeper who they really were and in fact used the "out-of-towners" ploy leading the doorkeeper to believe they were Eagles from another town. This "misleading statement" violated the consent more so than a mere denial of membership would have. The administrative statute does allow surprise inspections during regular hours but it does not say anything about how the officers gain entry (announced or ruse). However, the court here notes that U.S. Supreme Court cases generally only approved announced entries and Ohio likes "knock and announce" closely regulated industries inspections except in exigent circumstances. No evidence of exigency was developed in the lower court. **F.O.E. Aerie 0582 Twin City v. Liquor Cont. Comm.,** 1997 WL 559475 (Ohio App. 10 Dist.). Another Ohio court had to determine whether a "vacant property license ordinance" created a closely regulated industry that did away with the administrative warrant requirement. It held that it did not. **State v. Finnell,** 685 N.E. 2d 1267 (Ohio. 1996).

Since parents have the right to educate their children at home can the state create administrative regulations that treat home education as a closely regulated industry that would allow surprise inspections? This issue came up in **Brunells v. Lynn Public Schools,** 1997 WL 785595 (Mass. Super). The judge's answer was that: "Thus, on balance, the limited, pre-announced periodic inspections of the plaintiff's home are reasonable searches which do not require a warrant under the Massachusetts constitution." Yes, home education is, to this judge, a closely regulated industry. Expect more on this.

If one is involved in garbage, trash, *etc.*, one can anticipate they may well be in a closely regulated industry due to the toxicity issues involved. In Illinois, sewage and electroplating were at issue. The warrantless search scheme was upheld. **People v. Electric Plating Co.,** 683 N.E. 2d 465 (Ill. 1997). Trash haulers are closely regulated in Pennsylvania. **Township v. Britt,** 695 A. 2d 958 (Com. Ct. Pa. 1997). Asbestos abatement is closely regulated. **Abateco Serv. Inc. v. Bell,** 477 S.E. 2d 795 (Va. App. 1996).

Are massage parlors closely regulated? Certainly they are subject to reasonable regulation. But according to Michigan, they are not closely regulated nor are they likely to approve such a statute if passed and brought before them. **Gopra v. City of Ferndale,** 551 N.W. 2d 454 (Mich. App. 1996).

III.   Pretextual Search Possibilities

The next problem in this area concerns the inspection upon a valid, warrantless entry that turns into a criminal investigation. How does the Court deal with that? Though not all possible answers have been provided, the basic point came up in **Michigan v. Tyler,** 436 U.S. 499 (1978). Tyler and another ran a furniture store. A fire broke out causing extensive damage. After the fire was out, but before the smoke cleared and the embers cooled, the fire chief and another entered the burned-out building where a couple of containers of a flammable liquid were discovered. An hour and a half later a police detective, called by the fire chief, went in and took some pictures but left because of the smoke and steam. One half hour later the fire chief and the detective took the containers to the fire station. The next morning, the fire chief, whose duty it was to determine the origins of all fires, went back in and made a cursory exam. An hour after that, the police entered, conducting a further warrantless investigation.

It is interesting to note that the Court says that there is no shrinking of a person's reasonable expectation of privacy because the person wears a firefighter's uniform and not a police uniform. Here they were applying the state action doctrine. The Court went on to say that searches for administrative purposes are encompassed by the Fourth Amendment. Expectedly, the Court said that, except for certain well-defined classes of cases, searches without a warrant are unreasonable. The probable cause showing may vary with the object, but the necessity of the warrant continues.

Generally, a warrant is needed to investigate a fire. However, the Court held there is room for an exigency. But the Court felt the Michigan interpretation of exigency was too narrow because it began with the dousing of the last flame. Of course, prompt action is necessary to prevent further fires; to preserve evidence from intentional or accidental destruction. Noting that the sooner the fire department finished their work the sooner private parties could begin their recovery efforts, the Court held the officials needed no warrant to remain in a building for a reasonable time to investigate the cause of a blaze after it had been put out. If this entry was legal, the gathering of evidence while inspecting for the cause of the fire was also legal; the plain view doctrine was therefore recognized in this context. The Court found that the entries made at 8:00 a.m. and 9:00 a.m., just a few hours after the fire was out were merely a continuation of the efforts begun when the smoke and steam were too heavy for safe continuance of the inspection. However, the entries made after those earlier entries were too remote in time and required warrants.

What the Court did not discuss was the authority of the police officer to enter with the chief and then on his own the next morning. The Court seems to be saying that the police officer accompanying one who validly has a right to enter get the protection of those rights. If that is so, they have undone some other strong principles and have in fact opened what could be the flood gates of a possibly harmful oppressive technique. No doubt there are already cooperative efforts between local agencies where the police need an entry but do not have probable cause. All the police would need is a building or housing inspection warrant to be issued to the appropriate agency and then the police could tag along "to help serve the warrant to preserve the peace." Would plain view come into play? Yes, but it would be limited to gaining probable cause only, unless an exigency truly appeared giving rise to a right of seizure. If the police did not wish to go along, all they would need to do is have the inspector primed for observation so that upon his return the inspector could be the reliable informant for the warrant that would give the police their legal access. A case such as **Michigan v. Tyler** had the potential of undoing 200 years of Fourth Amendment protection.

Upon what evidence is the dire consequence forecast? The reader is reminded of **Piazzola v. Watkins**, 442 F. 2d 284 (C.A. 5th 1971), where the police convinced university officials to let them tag along upon a university inspection under a written consent to inspect for waste. The prediction is not so far – fetched.

The concern for bootstrapping, subterfuge and pretextual administrative searches was well recognized by the Ninth Circuit in **U.S. v. $124,570 U.S. Currency**, 873 F. 2d 1240 (C.A. 9th 1989). Viewing airport security screenings as an administrative search policy, they became concerned about the regular use of private security people encouraged to go beyond (with regularity and for reward) the scope of such safety screenings. These people, even after determination that explosives and weapons were not present, often had people open bags so they could get a view. The court, citing **Camara,** expressed great concern that what they were seeing was the use of administrative searches turning them into a tool for general law enforcement criminal investigatory purposes. Plain view, tainted by hope for reward, could not be tolerated – too many zealots seem to have been fostered. Thus, the court suppressed the money and vacated the forfeiture. Clearly such private security people had become agents for the government.

And the police will play games, as illustrated by a New Jersey decision. The police were very involved in an investigation trying to discover evidence of general criminality. They went upon the premises suspected of being involved in stolen goods fencing. The premises was a tavern. The police entered under the guise of enforcing the liquor laws and searched in the non – public areas. The Court held this was not a regulatory search as contemplated by the statute, but was a search for criminal evidence in disguise. **State v. Williams**, 403 A. 2d 31 (N.J. App. Div. 1979), aff'd 417 A. 2d 1046 (N.J. 1980). Such clear pretextual search conduct must be prohibited.

Read broadly, **Michigan v. Tyler** contained language that promoted unwarranted entries after a fire by arson investigators. Subsequently, the **Clifford** case presented a question as to the authority of arson investigators, in the absence of exigent circumstances or consent, to enter a private residence without a warrant to investigate the cause of a recent fire. The Court refused to exempt from the warrant requirement all administrative investigations into the cause and origin of a fire and affirmed that administrative searches generally require warrants. If reasonable privacy interests remain in fire – damaged property, the warrant requirement applies unless consent has been given or exigent circumstances exist. Here the fire was out, police and firemen had left the scene, and private securing efforts had begun before the arson team returned to search. The investigators determined what caused the fire by their intrusion into the basement. The further search of the upstairs areas was beyond seeking cause (administrative) and became a search for evidence of a crime. Even an administrative search does not give fire officials license to roam freely through the victim's private residence. **Michigan v. Clifford**, 464 U.S. 287 (1984).

On the issue of exigent circumstances see **State v. Hoffman**, 567 A. 2d 1134 (R.I. 1990). An explosion had occurred; the fire was out and not likely to reignite, but because of the possibility of collapse that would destroy the boiler, *etc.*, as the suspected cause, the inspector went on the premises. Evidence of arson was found. The court upheld the search under **Clifford** since the object was not crime search but fire – cause – search based. The fact that fire – cause search evidence could have been destroyed while seeking an administrative warrant meant sufficient exigency was demonstrated. The timing of the entry was also found to be reasonable since there was no great delay.

The Eleventh Circuit recognized a limit to the scope and discretion of a firefighter when conducting an administrative search. The fireman went back into the house looking for spot fires and to secure valuables from being taken by vandals. He found and seized phony money. The court held that these bills had been unlawfully seized and his actions were within neither administrative search, exigent circumstances nor inventory exceptions to the warrant requirement. Standardized procedures which narrowly channeled his discretion were not followed. **U.S. v. Parr,** 716 F. 2d 796 (C.A. 11th 1983). But all courts would not agree with this, especially as to the exigent circumstances and plain view issues.

If limited to seizing only what a fire marshal properly saw when investigating the cause of a just extinguished fire, then the Pennsylvania Superior Court came to a sensible conclusion when it allowed the police officer to seize the evidence when told about it by the fire marshal. The court said since the fire marshal could have seized the drugs and since the police officer only seized that which was described the evidence was admissible. The court indicated it would not have tolerated the police officer going beyond the scope of the plain view gathered by the fire marshal. **Com. v. Person**, 560 A. 2d 761 (Pa. Super. Ct. 1989).

Montana came to the right conclusion in a post-fire seizure for all the wrong reasons, even though they suppressed the evidence. The firefighters had seen an extensive marijuana growing operation and reported that to the police. The police entered after the firemen had left. They did so without a warrant even though they had sufficient time to get one. They did not seize the house awaiting a warrant. The evidence was not seen during a lawful search (Branch One of Plain View) but during a lawful presence by the firefighters (Branch Two of Plain View). That plain view gave the police probable cause but without consent, warrant, or exigency they could not enter and seize under **Coolidge v. New Hampshire**. There appeared to be no exigency in this case and there was no consent. Thus a warrant would have been needed. Therefore, Montana's constitution is really no different. The problem is that Montana does not seem to understand the seamless web of all the U.S. Supreme Court decisions regarding the Fourth Amendment. **State v. Bassett**, 982 P. 2d 410 (Mont. 1999).

Leaving a fire scene briefly to interview the injured residents at the hospital and then returning to the scene did not violate **Tyler** and **Clifford**, said the Pennsylvania Superior Court in **Com. v. Ellis**, 549 A. 2d 1323 (Pa. Super. Ct. 1988). Though the administrative search could be said to have been abandoned, the decision looks more like a common sense approach.

There are a significant number of instances when the government may intrude upon privacy without probable cause. Consider the actions in the following cases. For example, under federal law, agricultural inspectors may inspect packages being sent from Hawaii to the mainland to make sure there are no plants with pests or diseases. The package opened in this case contained hashish. The Court said the opening was reasonable even without probable cause. **State v. Kelly**, 661 P. 26 2d (Mont. 1983). In yet another case, the fruitfly quarantine by California came up in **People v. Guardado**, 194 Cal. Rep. 598 (Cal. Dist. Ct. App. 1983). The state citrus industry was in danger. The Medfly check points were reasonable even though highway patrolmen conducted the inspection rather than agricultural department inspectors. This is consistent with the **Burger** decision.

There are some police searches that are in fact unrelated to general criminal investigations but are directly related to a duty created by statute. For example, the police are required to investigate auto accidents and fill out reports that require names, licenses, and proof of insurance. This is an administrative duty; a non-crime related duty. When and under what circumstances can an officer "enter" the purse or wallet of an injured driver to obtain the information to satisfy the non – crime related duty. This was the issue in **People v. Wright**, 804 P. 2d 866 (Colo. 1991). In **Wright** the officer searched the purse of a conscious, generally available accident victim and found cocaine, marijuana and paraphernalia. Finding that there were reasonable alternatives to the warrantless entry, the Colorado court held there was no administrative justification for the entry in this case.

In **U.S. v. Transon**, 572 F. Supp. 295 (M.D. Tenn. 1983), the court upheld a search of the defendant's personal effects by a V.A. hospital administrator because the public interest was served by prohibiting the introduction of prohibited materials into the hospital. The caretaking function is also implicated in these kinds of cases. As such, the rules governing booking and jailing inventories would govern. See Chapter Thirteen Sec. IX (*infra*).

To be kept in mind is the fact that the search scheme cannot exceed the scope of the authority of the statute. Race track inspectors were given the authority to inspect race track dorm rooms. The Court felt this went beyond the statutory authority and extended to the inspectors excessive discretion. **Serpas v. Schmidt**, 808 F. 2d 601 (C.A. 7th 1986). The regulations were patched up and once again it was struck down. The Court indicated the rooms were private in character even though they were assigned to racetrack employees by their employers. **Serpas. v. Schmidt**, 827 F. 2d 23 (C.A. 7th 1987).

Courts are reasonably concerned about the problem of pretextual searches. They should not occur. Where the purpose is to search for evidence for a criminal prosecution, there has been a pretextual administrative search. Unless a search is a routine administrative search the administrative search doctrine cannot be applied. **People v. Pace**, 475 N.Y. S. 2d 443 (N.Y. Sup. Ct. App. Div. 1984).

However, not all law enforcement inspired administrative searches are bad. The defendant in one case said that the bank regulators were the "stalking horses" for the F.B.I. and said that the documents taken should have been suppressed. The Eighth Circuit said this agency inspection was not improper merely because the things it sought could also have been, and in fact were relevant to a criminal as well as civil proceeding. They held that the agents were acting lawfully and fulfilling their administrative duties. The fact that they inspected because of information provided by the F.B.I was not critical in this case. **U.S. v. Copple**, 827 F. 2d 1182 (C.A. 8th 1987); accord, see **U.S. v Nechy**, 827 F. 2d 1161 (C.A. 7th 1987) where a pharmacist was suspected of drug dealings in an illicit manner.

How to treat public school students regarding searches for contraband and weapons had become a grave concern and continues to be a real and significant problem. Even the issue of athletes and drug use had to be dealt with. Desks, lockers, purses, back packs, baggy clothing, and even lunch boxes can and often do hide all forms of contraband and weapons as recent history teaches us. Even the cars brought to school can be repositories for such items. Yet children are people and as such they are entitled to the U.S. Constitution's protection. The full panoply of the people's right "to be secure in their persons, papers, houses and effects" also apply to them. What exigencies and circumstances allow warrantless search instructions? The U.S. Supreme Court would deal with these issues regarding the schools and children in two cases. The first is **New Jersey v. T.L.O.**, 469 U.S. 325 (1985), the search case; and the second is **Vernonia School District v. Acton**, 515 U. S. 646 (1995), the drug testing of athletes case. The discussion of these decisions follows.

The Court apparently has settled one issue concerning the search of public school students by public school officials. The narrow issue in **New Jersey v. T.L.O.**, 469 U.S. 325 (1985) was whether a search by a school official, without police involvement or pressure, and for the sole purpose of enforcing school rules requires probable cause. The Court made clear that the unreasonable search prohibition applied to public school officials. This, of course, had to be said to preserve the state action theory. The Court also recognized that children have a legitimate expectation of privacy. To say otherwise would have undone **Gault** and its progeny.

The crux of the case then turned solely on whether probable cause would be required. The Court requires not probable cause, but reasonableness. Reasonableness is to be determined by whether the search was justified at its inception and, as conducted, whether it was reasonably related in scope to the circumstances which justified it. The measure adopted must be reasonably related to the objectives of the search and not excessively intrusive in the light of the student's age and sex and the nature of the infraction. Cited within the case for support that the school can enforce its rules by seeking (reasonably) offensive materials (cigarettes) are the **Camara** and **Barlow** cases, two of the leading administrative search cases.

In **Vernonia** the U.S. Supreme Court addressed the issue of random drug testing in the public school. It upheld the school's policy requiring student athletes to submit to random drug tests. Other efforts to eradicate a drug problem in the school had failed; thus this policy was adopted. Why? Evidence was convincing that student athletes were the center of the drug problem. The Court balanced the nature of the privacy interest, the character of the intrusion, the nature and immediacy of the governmental concern against the efficacy of the means chosen (testing) for meeting the problem.

Justice Scalia continued by saying that children do not shed their rights at the "school house gate" *but* students and student athletes especially have a diminished privacy interest as compared with members of the general public. When the student offers himself for the team, the physical exam, insurance waivers, and obedience to the rules of conduct, *etc.*, are all part of the package. Thus, if a drug problem is caused by athletes it makes sense to make sure athletes are drug free. Further, the Court also noted that the intrusion was not severe because the urine samples were collected in a setting similar to that of public restroom. Only drugs were tested for and the results went only to school personnel and ***not*** to law enforcement. The Court further felt the need was compelling and immediate. Only three justices dissented, disagreeing with the "special needs" analysis. They preferred an individualized suspicion requirement to justify such testing.

Let us examine some decisions that have addressed **T.L.O** and **Vernonia**. Before taking on **T.L.O** concerns let us examine one well written case addressing the **Vernonia** drug testing issue That case comes from the Court of Appeals of Indiana. It is well written and addresses some of the **Vernonia** history and whether Indiana's constitution agrees with the U.S. Constitution. That decision and opinion is **Linke v. Northwestern School Corp**. 734 N.E. 2d 252 (Ind. App. 2000). The students and parents brought the action to challenge the school system's drug testing policy. That policy covered all students participating in any extracurricular and curricular activity. This included, in addition to sports, participation in Honor Society, S.A.D.D., prom committee, and more. The policy was instituted after two students died of drug overdoses and one was killed in a car accident resulting from use of inhalants.

The hallmark of the ability to use drug testing rests on the "special needs analysis" jurisprudence. The major criticism of this approach, the Indiana court notes, has been that the policies were adopted without proof that "suspicion based testing" is ineffective. Despite that, the court acknowledged "an explosion of drug testing policies…" adoption in their own state including the expansion of testing to no-athletic areas and had been the subject of numerous cases in the Seventh Circuit from Indiana litigants. The court said that **Todd v. Rush County School**, 133 F. 3d 984 (C.A. 7th 1998) upheld this expansion, but that in **Willis v. Anderson Comm. Sch. Corp.** 158 F. 3d 415 (C.A.7nd 1998), the same court refused to uphold the policy section that applied to students suspended for fighting. In fact that same court expressed reluctance to uphold the **Vernonia** policy. They felt compelled to adhere to their own **Todd** decision. See **Joy v. Penn-Harris-Madison Sch. Corp.**212 F. 3d 1052 (C.A. 7th 2000) where the Seventh Circuit refused to include nicotine in the drugs tested for.

In this posture, the Indiana court felt compelled to test its own constitution to see if it provided a different result. The language of the Indiana Constitution is exactly the same as the Fourth Amendment. Was there anything, however, in the history of its drafting and ratification that would demand a different result? The more important question to ask is whether before the U.S. Supreme Court determined that the Fourth

Amendment was the base rule, were the decisions of the local high court more or less protective of search and seizure rights. Did state provisions by constitution or statute give greater protection? The court then noted the Indiana preference for individualized suspicion as expressed in **Moran v. State**, 644 N.E. 2d 536 (Ind. 1994). It then agreed with Justice O'Connor's dissent in **Vernonia**. The court saw no reason to "depart" from the **Moran** preference, but also noted Scalia's case-by-case suggestion in **Vernonia's** majority opinion.

The **T.L.O.** cases, linked as they are to conduct giving school discipline suspicion, do not suffer from the same attacks as **Vernonia**. Let us examine a few more recent **T.L.O.** type cases. Once a decision like **T.L.O.** is released it is likely that conduct not anticipated in the opinion will occur and evidence seized will be offered or used. The competing sides will seek either expansion of or strict limits on the official conduct sanctioned in that opinion. The following decisions demonstrate that struggle. **T.L.O.** was a possessory violation case. The vice principal was looking for the cigarettes that **T.L.O.** must have had in her possession when she was caught smoking in the girls' bathroom. That he found drugs was an inadvertent discovery.

Should **T.L.O.** apply to non-possessory type school violations? Personally, I do not think so. Why search a person who was merely disturbing the peace in the cafeteria by yelling obscenities, for example? Suppose a student violates the school's closed campus policy. A reasonable principal might suspect the reason for the absence was to get drugs, bombs, or guns, but is that sufficient without more to search the returning student? That was the question in **State v. B.A.S.**, 2000 WL 1737837 (Wash. App.1). When the student was searched, 40 grams of marijuana was found by the school attendance officer. The court noted that **T.L.O.** requires that the search be "justified at its inception." This student did not show signs of intoxication by drugs, *etc.*, when he returned to the school and did not even smell like a marijuana user. The school admitted that it searches all students seen in the parking lot area. This was labeled as a "blanket supposition." Concerns alone are not enough, the court noted – there must be a *nexus* that connects the concerns with the particular student. However, do the recent shootings at schools across the country now dictate such a policy?

In a vaguely similar case to **B.A.S.**, a student reported a missing ring. The school then strip- searched two students. The New Mexico court, in the civil damages case, noted there was no probable cause nor articulable suspicion. The damage award was upheld. There was no individualized suspicion as required by **T.L.O.** for these strip searches. There was no qualified immunity from damages suit.

Just because a person is a student does not mean that **T.L.O.** follows the student home. The state thus improperly relied on **T.L.O.** for this warrantless search. See **In re A.C.C. v. State**, 2 P. 3d 464 (Utah. App. 2000).

School lockers were not the subject of **T.L.O.** But **T.L.O.** would encourage searches of lockers both with and without probable cause or even articulable suspicion. The lockers are school property to be sure and most public schools provide the locks or require the student to register the combination or key to their privately owned locks. A case from Maryland's high court puts the issue of locker searches in perspective. **In re Patrick Y.**, 746 A. 2d 405 (Md. 2000). The statutes of Maryland and the State Board of Education by law provide that school lockers are always treated as school property. These provisions specifically provide that the lockers are subject to search by the appropriate designated official as is all school property. The provisions also prohibit local schools from establishing any other policy. The local school system in this case violated the state policy by establishing a probable cause standard for a search. When Patrick's locker was searched a gun and a pager were found. He fought the delinquency proceeding on the grounds of no probable cause to search under the county policy. The local judge followed the law and found him guilty as a delinquent. The Court of Special Appeals affirmed and the case went to the Appeals Court on certiorari. Again his conviction as a delinquent was affirmed.

The court cited school locker cases upholding warrantless, *etc.* searches: **In re Isaiah B.**, 500 N.W. 2d 637 (1993); **Shoemaker v. State**, 971 S.W. 2d 178 (Tex. App. 1998); **People v. Overton**, 229 N.E. 2d 596 (N.Y. 1967); and **S.A. v. State**, 654 N.E. 2d 791 (Ind. App. 1995). The court also cited cases upholding a reasonable expectation of privacy in lockers: **Com. v. Cass**, 709 A. 2d 350 (Pa.1998); **State v. Joseph T**, 336 S.E. 2d 728 (W.Va. 1985); they also cited cases where the school has to prove absolute necessity: **State v. Michael G.**, 748 P. 2d 17 (N. Mex. 1987); and **S.C. V. State**, 583 So. 2d 188 (Miss. 1991). The Maryland court then demonstrated that the attempt by the local school system to undermine the law held out no hope for this juvenile.

We are seeing more police officers working in schools. How does that affect the **T.L.O.** analysis? Indiana says such an officer gets the benefit of **T.L.O.** This is as much as saying that the officer is a school official. Georgia says the officer is not a school official and standard search and seizure law applies. **In re C.S. v. Indiana**, 2000 WL 1342137 (Ind. App.) and **Patman v. State**, 2000 WL 898081 (Ga. App.). See also **D.B. v. State**, 728 N.E. 2d 179 (Ind. App.2000).

T.L.O. does not address the **Miranda** issue of custodial interrogation. Should that requirement also be reduced or even dispensed with? In a Washington case one student "snitches" on another. That student was brought to the vice principal's office and was questioned about the marijuana and made incriminating admissions. This court looked to a California case that dispensed with the **Miranda** requirement and cited **In re Corey L.**, 250 Cal. Rep. 359 (1988). They also cited a Pennsylvania case that reached a similar result. **In re D.E.M.**, 727 A. 2d 570 (Pa. Super. 1999). See also **State v. McKinnon**, 558 P. 2d 781(1977). Thus Washington declined to apply **Miranda** to the questioning of a student by a vice principal.

The final two cases in this section are fairly standard **T.L.O.** search cases where reasonable grounds existed for the searches. In, **In re Murray** 525 S.E. 2d 496 (N. C. App. 2000), the principal received an unsolicited tip that Murray was carrying a gun. This gave the principal reasonable grounds to search the book bag. In **Convington County v. G.N.** 767 So. 2d 187 (Miss. 2000), the court held that school officials did not need a warrant to search the defendant's pick-up truck. The tip came from a teacher who was told by another student of the drinking that had been going on.

IV.   Drug Testing Cases

The major administrative intrusion problem of the 1980s centered on the drug testing of public employees and of employees who work for a heavily regulated industry. Two cases were selected to resolve the issues. Those cases are **Burnley v. Rwy Labor Exec.'s Assoc.** 839 F. 2d 575 (C.A. 9th 1988) and **Nat'l Treasury Employees' Union v. Von Raab**, 816 F. 2d 170 (C.A. 5th 1986). Before a discussion of these cases let us consider some prior drug testing cases.

The Third Circuit upheld random urinalysis and urinalysis as part of the annual medical exam for police officers of a New Jersey municipality as a lawful administrative search policy. The court found that the policy covers a closely regulated industry (policing), thus subject to the administrative search exception to the Fourth Amendment. **P.B.A. of New Jersey v. Washington Township**, 850 F. 2d 133 (C.A. 3rd 1988). Mandatory drug testing of fire fighters was deemed unconstitutional because the danger of drug impaired officers, though significant, is not catastrophic. Without adequate justification, it cannot be upheld according to the Sixth Circuit in **Lovvorn v. Chattanooga**, 846 F. 2d 1539 (C.A. 6th 1988). Random drug testing of police officers of Boston, Massachusetts was ruled unconstitutional. The court said a positive urinalysis does not necessarily indicate present impairment. Reasonable suspicion would be the better way, the court said. But the court declined to uphold the search under the administrative search rationale. **Guiney v. Roach**, 686 F. Supp. 956 (D.C. Ma. 1988); accord **Wrightsell v. City of Chicago**, 678 F. Supp. 727 (N.D. ILL. 1988) and **Penny v. Kennedy**, 846 F. 2d 1563 (C.A. 6th 1988).The Federal Bureau of

Prisons instituted a mandatory drug testing program. It was struck down by a California based district court judge. The Court preferred the individualized suspicion bases for drug testing also. **Amer. Fed. of Gov't Employees v. Meese**, 43 Crim. L. Rep. 2262 (N.D. Cal. 1988). Random urinalysis for Justice Department Employees was enjoined because not justified at its inception and because it would not measure fitness for duty nor deter drug use. **Harmon v. Meese**, 690 F. Supp. 65 (D. D.C. 1988). The elite drug investigation unit of the New York City Police Department was subject to random drug testing and that plan was upheld by the New York Court of Appeals. The Court balanced the reduced privacy expectations against the need of the government to ensure that those on the front line of the war on drugs remain drug free. The constant exposure to the drug culture and the temptations it offers gives the department a very serious interest in ensuring that these police refrain from using drugs. **Caruso v. Ward**, 534 N.Y.S. 2d 142 (N.Y. 1988). With the foregoing cases serving as background, let us examine the two cases on drug testing accepted and decided by the Supreme Court during the October 1988 Term.

The first case is **Burnley** (*supra*). This case involved the industry's mandatory post-accident testing as suggested by federal regulation. The first issue involved state action. Since the employers conducted the tests the "no-state-action" argument was raised. The Ninth Circuit felt that there was significant involvement by the government by developing these rules and in the regulation of their implementation. Since the government played a dominant role, the Fourth Amendment was implicated. The second set of issues involved justification and scope. The court said the tests were not justified at the inception because accidents, by themselves, do not create reasonable grounds, therefore particularized suspicion should be required. As to the scope, the court said that tests cannot measure current drug intoxication nor degree of impairment but can only discover post-use residue. It also found there was no implied consent. Finally, the court addressed the administrative search issue, saying that although railroading is a closely regulated industry, those regulations now and down through the years were aimed at the owners and not the employees. Unless employees are the principal concern of industry regulation, administrative search principles cannot be applied.

National Treasury involved union challenges to the urinalysis program for Customs Service employees seeking transfer to certain sensitive jobs. The Fifth Circuit upheld that process as a constitutional search because drug officers should not be drug users or "you don't send a rabbit to guard a lettuce patch." The function of the Fourth Amendment is to protect personal privacy and dignity against unwarranted intrusion by the government. They said there are few activities in our society more personal or private than the passing of urine. Even the individual who willingly urinates in the presence of another does not reasonably expect to discharge urine under circumstances that facilitates the discovery of personal physiological secrets. Unlike one's hair or handwriting, one's urine is not routinely exposed to public gaze. Thus the Fourth Amendment is implicated.

The court had to use the balancing interest tests and looked at scope and justification. As to the scope and manner, the sample taker does not watch. Advance notice is given. The test is not performed until after a transfer decision has been tentatively approved. Dignity is maintained. The discretion is limited in that the test is either positive or negative. If positive there can be no prosecution and the employee cannot lose his or her other job. As for justification, the court recognized the serious impact that drugs are having on our society. This agency enforces drug laws. They felt there can be no doubt about the employee's honesty. These people are firearms carriers and as such could be dangerous when high on drugs. The most practical private place was used for the testing. The test is voluntary since it applies only to those seeking the job and they were not penalized for refusing or for testing positive. Thus, to some extent, it can be said to be consensual. The process, therefore, was seen to be a reasonable condition of employment. Finally, it was found to be a suitable administrative search. The court analogized the job to a closely regulated industry and, therefore, it does not violate the "less – intrusive – measures" rule.

Calling compulsory urinalysis appropriate and necessary to maintain the effectiveness of the military establishment, the Court of Military Appeals upheld the process even though the service member may be denied privacy while producing the sample. The Navy program requires direct observation unlike the process in **Treasury Employees**. The justification accepted by the court was based on Lawrence Taylor's admissions that he secreted urine in his body to beat the National Football League's drug testing program. The process was found not unreasonable *per se*. **Unger v. Ziemnial**, 27 M.J. 349 (U.S. Ct. Mil. App. 1989).

The urinalysis cases were released on March 21, 1989. The railroad case re-titled **Skinner v. Rwy Labor Exec. Assoc.**, 489 U.S. 602 (1989) upheld the tests by a vote of 6 for, 1 concurring, and 2 dissents. Justice Kennedy delivered the Court's opinion. After detailing a history of alcohol problems and the railroad, statistics were cited noting the impact of both alcohol and drugs on accidents in the industry. This, of course, led to a discussion of the proposed regulations that were ultimately adopted and their scope. The first issue addressed was whether the regulations constituted state action. The answer was yes because "…[t]hese are clear indices of the Government's encouragement, endorsement, and participation, and suffice to implicate the Fourth Amendment." Next the Court held that the collection and testing of urine intruded upon expectations of privacy that "society has long recognized as reasonable..." and "that these intrusions must be deemed searches under the Fourth Amendment." The Court then had to address whether this kind of search was reasonable by balancing the intrusion against legitimate governmental interests by waiving the warrant requirement. The Court stressed that the covered employees were involved in "safety-sensitive" tasks. As for the warrant issue they said: "Indeed in light of the standardized nature of the tests and the minimal discretion vested in those charged with administering the program, there are virtually no facts for a neutral magistrate to evaluate." It also felt that the burden of obtaining the warrant would likely frustrate the governmental purpose behind the search in that the delay could result in the destruction of valuable evidence.

The individualized suspicion standard of **New Jersey v. T.L.O.** was mentioned to make sure railroad supervisors were not bound by the probable cause standard. The Court also said that the intrusions were no more risky, health-wise, than what was approved in **Schmerber**. The only issue that concerned them was the possible observation issue in taking urine samples. The regulations here did not provide for that but they felt that such observation might be desirable to ensure integrity of the sample. It felt the medical environment was about as dignified as one could get. Though **T.L.O.** was cited, they did indicate that it was not the "floor" for allowable evidence gathering in all searches. In fact the Court said that in this type of case, particularized suspicion would seriously impede an employer's ability to obtain the information despite its obvious importance. They felt that the standards of **Clifford** and **Tyler** should apply and not **T.L.O.** Thus they held that the government's interests would "be significantly hindered if railroads were required to point to specific facts giving rise to a reasonable suspicion of impairment before testing a given employee."

In the wake of **Skinner** courts are having to decide whether mandatory drug and alcohol testing statutes are valid when not related to an industry. Pennsylvania had a statute requiring blood-alcohol testing whenever an auto mishap involved personal injury or death. The statute did not require probable cause for the test only "reasonable grounds to believe." Rather than hold that the statute required probable cause, the Pennsylvania court felt the triggering device for the test was the mere fact of injury or death. This violates the Fourth Amendment, according to this court. The court was unwilling to recognize "driving" as a highly regulated industry for administrative search purposes though they did acknowledge the state's vital interest in getting drunk drivers off the road. **Com. v. Danforth**, 576 A. 2d 1013 (Pa. Super. Ct. 1990). See also **Com. v. Kohl**, 576 A. 2d 1049 (Pa. Super. Ct. 1990), which reinforced the **Danforth** decision.

One of the more important drug testing cases would come by way of a case decided by the Fourth Circuit. In **Ferguson v. City of Charleston**, 186 F. 3d 469 (C.A. 4th 1999) in which the Fourth Circuit upheld a testing policy used by a South Carolina public hospital that tested pregnant women without probable cause or warrant. The hospital was looking for cocaine use and addiction. Positive results were given to the police and prosecutor. Women were arrested and threatened with prosecution if they did not enter and complete drug treatment. **Vernonia**, **National Treasury** and **Skinner** were used to justify the policy. None of the pregnant women consented to the tests but the Fourth Circuit upheld the tests under the "special needs searches" announced in **National Treasury,** *et. al.* The government interest was found to be great and court found the searches (test) effective and the only way to accomplish the goal of persuading women to stop using cocaine. The intrusion (the test and not the arrests) was found to be minimal. The lone dissenter said the intent of the intrusion was for law enforcement purposes thus **National Treasury**, *et al.*, could not be used as support for the policy.

The decision in **Ferguson** was released March 21, 2001, and the process used in this case was found to violate the Fourth Amendment. The pre-arranged delivery of positive drug use results to the prosecutor was found unreasonable despite the fact that such results also had a "course of treatment" medical purpose. This was no surprise. But it does "cloud", but not overrule, the risk run that such evidence gathered might be surrendered to the police voluntarily by the hospital, the doctor or the staff. As Justice Scalia points out, in his dissent, that risk is always present when one confides in or leaves with someone evidence of a crime or evidence that can be used to charge a crime. His concern is, perhaps, that the Court has opened an attack on the "trust your friends with care" rule (as I call it).Indeed would it not be possible for the state actor to seek such information from a doctor or others by way of the subpoena?

Information currently held by power companies, bank, telephone companies, and the like, may share their information on individual customers with the law enforcement community. This was the conclusion reached in **California Banker's Assoc. v. Schultz**, 416 U.S. 21 (1974). For the most part, however, record-keepers prefer that the police, *etc.*, use the subpoena process perhaps because of the result ultimately reached in **Ferguson** and also their concern over potential lawsuits by the person whose record were revealed. The language of the majority in **Ferguson** does throw a "cloud" on **California Bankers**, but the majority position cannot be seen as overruling that case since the Court does not overrule by implication. The majority does recognize the use of a warrant to get the urine test results and, of course, consent for the test with the knowledge it will be given to the police would also be upheld.

Justice Kennedy concurred in the result because this was a policy that was driven by law enforcement and not the goals approved in **Skinner**, **Treasury Employees**, and **Vernonia School District** where "special needs" were recognized as an exception to the warrant requirement. The need here was legitimate but the connection to law enforcement doomed it for him. He wants to make sure the limits of **Ferguson** are clearly understood. He says, "If prosecuting authorities then adopt legitimate procedures to discover this information and prosecution follows, that ought not to invalidate the testing." It is my personal view that Kennedy's suggestion might satisfy the three dissenters (Scalia, Rehnquist, and Thomas) and attract at least Justice O'Connor. But this is just a guess based on past performance of these justices. In any event **Ferguson et al. v. City of Charleston et al.**, 121 S. Ct. 1281 (2001) is now on the books.

The second case decided March 21, 1989, was **Nat'l Treas. Emp. Union v. Von Raab**, 489 U.S. 656 (1989). This was a 5 to 4 decision with two separate dissents; namely one by Marshall which Brennan joined and a dissent by Scalia which Stevens joined. The "interdiction employees testing program" was upheld as reasonable. The "classified-information-handling-employees" issue was not decided because they felt there was not enough information to determine if such regulations were reasonable. The purposes of the program are to deter drug use among those eligible for promotion to sensitive positions and to prevent promotion of drug users to those position. This the Court felt was a substantial governmental interest. The discretion of the service is limited. The drug crisis was noted. The need for unimpeachable integrity and judgment was acknowledged as an operational reality. Such employees, in fact, should expect close scrutiny. The Court said, "The mere circumstance that all but a few of the employees tested are entirely innocent of wrongdoing does not impugn the program's validity."

Scalia felt that doing away with even the individualized suspicion standards with no statistical proof of a problem, as had been noted in **Skinner**, was wrong. Scalia also felt this was one of those "ends justifies the means" cases that Brandeis complained of in **Olmstead**. And Scalia further cited Brandeis where he said; "...the greatest dangers to liberty lurk in insidious encroachment by men of zeal, well-meaning but without understanding."

Citing **National Treasury Employees Union v. Von Raab**, New York held that random drug testing of New York City corrections officers was constitutionally permissible. The court said choosing to work in this "paramilitary milieu" meant that the officers gave up some of their cherished rights and did so voluntarily. **Serlig v. Koehler**, 556 N.E. 2d 125 (N.Y. 1990).

The **Guiney v. Roach** (*supra*) decision was appealed to the First Circuit. During the pendency of that appeal the Supreme Court decided the **Skinner** and **National Treasury** cases. The First Circuit remanded the case to the district court for a new decision in light of these decisions. The First Circuit did note that the police drug testing program was aimed at gun carrying police officers and to those who participate in drug interdiction. They also noted that the program covered other employees as well with no justification in the record indicating why they were covered. Their concern was more for the non-gun carriers and non-interdiction personnel because they felt the others were covered by **National Treasury**. The First Circuit offered no advice to the district court as to how it should decide the balance of the case other than to read **National Treasury. Guiney v. Roache**, 873 F. 2d 1557 (C.A. 1st 1989).

The appellate court of New Jersey has determined that random unannounced suspicionless urine tests of transit police officers is proper. The risks inherent in the job of gun toting law enforcement coupled with split second decision- making the job requires makes these tests necessary and reasonable. **New Jersey Transit PBA Local v. New Jersey Trans. Corp.**, 675 A. 2d 1180 (N.J. Super. 1996).

V.   Conclusion

Employees and employers, landlords, property owners and school children, of course, have personal Fourth Amendment rights. But in the administrative context those **rights are balanced** against the **government's needs** to uphold some **compelling state interest**. Whether a full probable caused based warrant, administrative warrant based on administrative probable cause, or no warrant is needed at all, depends upon context. The context often comes from the legislative scheme. Suffice it to say, if the sole purpose of the search is to find items of general criminality unrelated to the administrative scheme, then full Fourth Amendment rights apply.

The Court has consistently held that a refusal to allow an entry can have one of two effects if the scheme is deemed reasonable. Benefits or licenses can be suspended or withheld. Refusal can supply the necessary administrative probable cause. A third effect, in the closely regulated industry area, would be to allow a forced entry. Which result then is determined by whether the legislation properly classifies the industry or activity as closely regulated or not. If closely regulated, warrantless search schemes will be upheld if there is a proper set of discretion limiting provisions with proper prior notice of such terms given to the individual. The statute must be carefully scrutinized to determine if a closely regulated industry was legislatively determined. Regulations that indicate otherwise will be determinative. However, regulators cannot create a closely regulated industry without such enabling legislation. Even though a statute may label an industry as closely regulated, a court may disagree with that label especially where non - health and non - safety matters are concerned. The key would be the result of balancing private versus public need.

In the non - closely regulated industries warrantless, non-consensual searches are not permitted. There is, therefore, a warrant requirement. However, the criminal standards of probable cause are not required. The administrative warrant standard is set out in **Camara** (*supra*).

The fire cases are governed by the exigent circumstances doctrine. Where the statute or ordinances create a duty to investigate the cause of all fires no warrant is needed to make a first and safe entry on the property for such an investigation. Like other exigency cases, one can stay too long, look in the wrong places, and make too many entries.

The disciplinary cases, whether of employees or school children, allow some warrantless activity as long as it is not pretextual. There is always state action when the searcher is a government employee. Whether there is state action when the searcher is a private person will depend on either police involvement or the presence of government regulations which drive or compel the search. (**T.L.O**. and **Skinner**).

Drug testing programs have as yet only been officially sanctioned for gun-carrying public employees. The court factually only had before it those who sought employment in or transfer to the interdiction branch of the government agency. Broad dicta in **Von Raab** has led several courts to approve random drug testing of already hired gun - toters. These people are treated more like a closely regulated industry.

However, prearranged delivery of incriminating evidence at the behest of the government without the full consent of the person, **Ferguson**, is prohibited but the same information sought by subpoena or warrant can be accessed by the government. The **Fourth** and **California Banker's**.

VI.   Administrative Search Reminders

A.   Was this apparent administrative search pretextual criminal search:

Clifford   1.   conducted by police; or

2.   conducted by administrative official under direction or control or police?

B. Was an administrative warrant required (non-closely regulated industries?)

Colonnade

and   If a warrant was required and one was not used, was there:

Barlow's   1.   consent; or
and
Wyman   2.   exigency?

and

Tyler
and
Camara   If a warrant was required and
               used was there administrative
and   probable cause for its issuance?

See   If a warrant was required and used was the scope of the search reasonable:
and   1.   as dictated by the statute; or
Lone Steer 2.   as dictated by the nature of the public
and   concerns of the statute or ordinance; and
               3.   as not exceeding the allowable
Oklahoma Press discretion of the official?

C. Is this an area where no warrant is required
Biswell   (closely regulated industries.

and   How does the court determine if an industry is closely regulated?
Burger   The court must read the statute and determine the:
and   1.   "historical" perspective;
Dewey   2.   nature of the threat to public concerns and the need for surprise inspections;
               3.   notice given to anyone in such a business;

4.   control of the scope of such inspections (discretion control);
5.   persons authorized to conduct; and
6.   times when such inspections may occur.

If a well-defined scheme coupled with a legitimate goal is found, no warrant is required.

D.   What invasions of the person or person's personal property are allowable in the employer-employee context?

O'Connor   Was there state action because either:
                        1.   government employer conducts
and   intrusion or;
Skinner 2.   government regulation compels intrusion?

                        If state action is found is the purpose
and   of the intrusion legitimate because:
                        1.   the business of the government
National   requires the records contained
Treasury   in containers at the work site; or
                        2.   the government supervisor has legitimate disciplinary concerns;
and   3.   the government regulation involves a significant safety, *etc.*, concern?

Vernonia
                        If state action is found and the purpose is legitimate was scope and discretion properly limited?

and

CHAPTER TEN
THE BORDER SEARCH EXCEPTION

I.   Basic Principles

As was stated in **U.S. v. Ramsey**, 431 U.S. 606 (1977), the border search is a true exception to the warrant requirement. Unlike other exceptions, however, it is not based on exigent circumstances. Where, then, are the roots of the border exception? First, there is what the Court calls the longstanding right of the sovereign to protect itself by stopping and examining persons and property crossing into the country as a necessity. These searches and stops are deemed reasonable since they occur at the border. **Ramsey** at 616. Second, the same Congress that penned the Fourth Amendment recognized this plenary power and passed the first Customs statute granting the power to search when a reason to suspect concealed goods existed. The **Ramsey** Court cited **Boyd v. U.S.**, 116 U.S. 616 (1886), wherein it was stated, "it is clear that the members of that body did not regard search and seizures of this kind as 'unreasonable' and are not embraced within the prohibition of the amendment." It should be noted that the Court used the word "suspect" and not the phrase "reason to believe." More significant is the argument that the power to regulate international commerce is broad. It is necessary to prevent smuggling, undesirable aliens, and prohibited articles from entering the country. **Ramsey** at 619.

Thus, border searches may be based on a standard less than probable cause. It is usually stated as a reasonable suspicion which is roughly equivalent to articulable suspicion but which is really even less than that. Border suspicion allows an intrusion much broader than is allowed by articulable suspicion; it allows a search. **Ramsey** at 613. That search is called a "routine border search." Suffice to say that the word "routine" connotes intensity or scope. What is routine when applied to things is different when applied to persons.

The **Ramsey** Court borrowed this language from **U.S. v. 37 Photographs**, 402 U.S. 363, 376 (1971): "But a port of entry is not a traveler's home. His right to be let alone neither prevents the search of his luggage not the seizure of unprotected, but illegal, materials when his possession of them is discovered during a search…." The Court determined that border searches are reasonable by the single fact that the person or item in question entered the country from the outside. **Ramsey** at 619. If all of this is so apparent, what was unique about the **Ramsey** case? It involved international mail coming into the country unaccompanied by a person. Thus, both the customs and postal inspection laws were involved.

Envelopes under the postal inspection laws are only to be opened when the customs officers have reason to believe they contain other than correspondence. Any messages inside are not to be read. In **Ramsey**, the customs inspector noticed eight envelopes from Thailand, a known source of illicit drugs. The envelopes were bulky. They were all from the same address but were being sent to eight different addresses in the Washington, D.C. area. This was held to be reasonable grounds to open the envelopes. The Court emphasized that these envelopes could have been opened had they been physically carried into the country. The Court was not willing to grant a greater right to mailed-in envelopes. **Ramsey** at 623. The Court could find no statute creating any expectation of privacy at the border for mail. **Ramsey** at 723, note 17.

The dissenters chose to characterize the case as one involving the First Amendment, freedom of expression, and the right to send private communications. They feared the wholesale secret examination of all incoming international mail. Obviously, they did not believe that an envelope containing papers feels unlike an envelope containing other matter. **Ramsey** at 632.

In **U.S. v. Safari**, 849 F. 2d 891 (C.A. 4th 1988), a customs agent, assigned to examine incoming mail, noticed a package sent to Virginia Beach from Pakistan. The agent squeezed the package and noted that it had a powdery texture to its contents. He cut the package with a blade and white powder was extracted which, when field tested, proved to be heroin. The package was then fully opened, and it revealed a book with heroin concealed in its covers. This package was sent to a postal inspector who then delivered it to the DEA who ordered the package sent on to the defendant's postal box. Safari called for the package, left the post office, and was stopped. He was charged with possession with intent to distribute in both state and federal courts. Virginia dropped the charges because Safari's motion to suppress was granted. The federal court did not believe it was bound by that decision since the federal government was not a party to that action, therefore, there was no collateral estoppel (nor a silver platter violation). Safari then argued the Fourth Amendment was violated when the customs agent opened the package. Citing **Ramsey**, the court found plenty of articulable suspicion in that it came from a known source country, was heavier than normal, and felt powdery.

Noting that the **Ramsey** decision reserved the question of when a border search might become unreasonable, the Second Circuit set certain criteria in a case in which the customs officers removed and searched the artificial limb of the defendant who was returning from Venezuela. The Second Circuit rule derives from their philosophy that "reasonableness is determined by weighing the warranted suspicion of the border official against the offensiveness of the intrusion." Guided then by **Schmerber**-like considerations, the court balanced humane behavior against the substantiality of the suspicion, to arrive at a totality of the circumstances. **U.S. v. Sanders**, 663 F. 2d 1 (C.A. 2d 1981). The evidence was admissible. But as **Montoya** (*infra*) teaches, this position cannot be taken too far.

Because we no longer recognize the "silver platter" doctrine, and because of the dual sovereignty doctrine, and the possibility that a border search may yield evidence of a crime that offends both state and federal law, it is essential that the border search be, in fact a border search and that applicable federal statutes are properly applied yielding "non-poisonous fruits." If the search is conducted properly by the federal government the state, if it recognizes "reverse silver platter," can admit the evidence at its trial even though its own officers would not have been permitted to conduct such a search.

The issue in **U.S. v. Sandoval-Vargas**, 854 F. 2d 1132 (C.A.9th 1988) required the court to interpret 19 U.S.C. Sec. 482 and its "suspicion" requirement. Upholding the right of customs agents to search without a warrant, probable cause, or even articulable suspicion, the court held that "suspicion" under this statute is satisfied when a car or person being searched has just entered the U.S. from outside. No particularized or individualized suspicion is required. The fact of entry is enough. But some *dicta* in the case noted that more is required for mail coming into the country.

A district court judge in Hawaii felt bound by that *dicta*. The judge held that U.S. Customs officials may search incoming international package mail only upon reasonable suspicion that it contains contraband. **U.S. v. Nguyen** 701 F. Supp. 747 (D. Haw. 1988). Quite frankly, why mail would be given more protection than a human being is a bit of a mystery.

Can customs detain a traveler whom they suspect to be a "balloon swallower" for 16 hours? This was basically the question the Supreme Court had to answer in **U.S. v. Montoya de Hernandez**, 473 U.S. 531 (1985). The defendant was held incommunicado for 16 hours. At her border search it was determined that her abdomen was very firm and full. She said she was pregnant. The agents asked her to take a pregnancy test. She agreed to an X-ray until she found out that she was to be taken away in handcuffs. She was then given the option of returning to Colombia, submitting to an X-ray, or staying in detention until she had a monitored bowel movement. She said she would go back home. She refused all water and food and refused to use the toilet facilities. A federal magistrate issued a court order authorizing an X-ray and rectal exam plus the pregnancy test. She was not pregnant and the rectal exam produced 88 balloons containing 528 grams of 80 per cent pure cocaine.

The Court, reciting the history of border searches, concluded that section by saying that the Fourth Amendment balance between the interests of the government and the privacy right of the individual is struck much more favorably to the government at the border. With this in mind, they held."..that the detention of a traveler at the border, beyond the scope of a routine customs search and inspection is justified at its inception if customs agents, considering all of the facts surrounding the traveler and her trip, reasonably suspect that the traveler is smuggling contraband in her 'alimentary canal." "This, therefore, created a "particularized and objective basis for suspecting the particular person of the alimentary canal smuggling...." standard. This standard focuses on common sense and ordinary human experience and not some rigid criteria. In this case the defendant's detention for the period of time necessary to either verify or dispel the suspicion was not unreasonable.

Thus, when the defendant "crosses" the border, the custom's agents can pat a lump on the back of the defendant and lift the defendant's shirt to see what is causing the bulge even without reasonable suspicion. **U.S. v. Charleus**, 871 F. 2d 265 (C.A. 2d 1989). This would be a proper routine border search as applied to a person.

The New York Court of Appeals was unwilling to accept the principle, suggested by **Ramsey,** that merely crossing the border creates the necessary suspicion for a pat-down of the individual as had other courts. Instead, they held that there must be some suspicion, less than a **Terry**-type suspicion, to justify a pat-down. The court based their reasoning on **Montoya** and the fact that the Supreme Court did not address the validity of the pat-down in that case. Its concern centered on the possibility of harassment or other arbitrary action based on race or gender. The pat-down in this case was justified the court said. Why? The defendant arrived alone, carrying a single suitcase from a distant country believed to be a major source of drugs. The defendant also appeared agitated and nervous. All of this, the court concluded, was sufficient to suspect criminal activity. By so holding, they deny the language in **Ramsey** about the right to stop and examine persons and property and that such acts are reasonable "…simply by virtue of the fact that they occur at the border...." The U.S. Supreme Court said this should "require no extended demonstration...." This was the position taken by the concurring opinion in the New York case. **People v. Luna**, 538 N.Y. S. 2d 765 (N.Y. 1989).

The **Montoya** case decided that the search was proper in the case before the Court but it does not help sort out routine from non-routine searches. For the most part the federal circuits are delineating the distinction between the two. For example, consider this language from a district court's opinion in **U.S. v. Lamela-Vazquez,** 719 F. Supp. 68 (D. P. Rico 1989): "The First Circuit had held that searches of in-transit passengers at San Juan's airport are border searches. **United States v. McKenzie**, 818 F. 2d 115, 119-20 (1st Cir. 1987); **United States v. Mejia-Lozano**, 829 F. 2d 268, 271 (1st Cir. 1987); **United States v. Franchi-Forlando**, 838 F. 2d 585, 587-88 (1st Cir. 1988). In-transit passengers (those who are not deboarding) have no more protection against routine suspicionless border searches than do arriving passengers. **United States v. Mateos-Sanchez**, 864 F. 2d 232, 239 (1st Cir. 1988). A border search can be made by customs agents with no suspicion whatsoever, **United States v. Montoya de Hernandez**, 473 U.S. 531, 538, 105 S. Ct. 3304, 3309, 87 L. Ed. 2d 381 (1985), and the basis for selecting subjects to search is not questioned; it can even be based on ethnicity. **United States v. Martinez-Fuerte**, 428 U.S. 543, 562-63, 96 S. Ct. 3074, 3085, 49 L. Ed. 2d 1116 (1976); **Montoya**, 473 U.S. at 538, 105 S. Ct. at 3309 . "More intrusive border searches of the person such as body cavity searches or strip searches, however, require at a minimum reasonable suspicion of criminal activity." **United States v. Charleus**, 871 F. 2d 265, 267 (2d Cir. 1989). The dilemma, as the district court saw it and in fact as the New York court saw it, is where do pat-down searches fit? Are they routine or non-routine? Both courts view pat-downs perhaps as not being routine [a view not shared by the Eighth Circuit in **U.S. v. Oyskan**, 786 F. 2d 832 (C.A. 8th 1986) but both courts found suspicion enough to conduct the pat down. In

Lamela the search occurred in San Juan while the U.S. bound Colombian awaited his next flight.

The Tenth Circuit had to decide whether the drilling of a compartment of a truck was a routine search or whether reasonable suspicion was required. The nervous defendant in this case got more so when the customs officer discovered an apparent secret compartment of this truck. That was enough suspicion, the court held, to detain the defendant in a holding cell while the compartment was drilled wherein 101 pounds of marijuana were discovered. **U.S. v. Carreou**, 872 F. 2d 1436 (C.A. 10th 1989).

Georgia, unlike New York, accepts the routine border search definition. In fact, it approved the use of evidence derived from a pat-down that required that outer garments and shoes be removed and that wallets and purses be emptied. The court said this required no justification other than the person's decision to cross our national boundary. It also noted that a strip search is considered non-routine and that requires "real" or reasonable suspicion. In the case before them the customs officer felt a lump around the defendant's thigh and this justified the partial strip search used in this case. **Safford v. State**, 522 S.E. 2d 565 (Ga. App. 1999).

II. Routine Border Searches

Why the issue of "routine" versus "non-routine" searches? If a search is labeled routine, the majority of the circuits use what is called the "no suspicion" standard whereas they require "reasonable suspicion" in the "non-routine" search cases.

A case from the First Circuit illustrates this distinction. The defendant tried to come into the country with heroin on her person. Customs agents became suspicious and searched her. She was arriving from Beirut (a source city), and she gave a questionable story about her reasons for coming. She had a thin face, but she was rather bulky around the mid-section. This was a matter of proportionality. She brought clothing for a two- or three-day stay, but told the officers she was going to be in the country for ten days. When told she was going to be searched, she misinterpreted some hand signals and lifted her skirt revealing the bulge. She then admitted she was carrying heroin. Was this a routine search?

The court said most circuits label as "not routine" strip and body cavity searches. It said this search was neither of those. The court felt the standard for searches should be based on a single criteria. Were there enough facts as related to allow this degree of intrusion? The more intrusive the search, the more facts are needed. Finally, it concluded that reasonable suspicion is only needed for "non-routine" searches thus agreeing with the Fifth Circuit and its decision in **U.S. v. Afanador**, 567 F. 2d 1325 (C.A.5th 1978) case. Thus, for "routine" searches, a "no suspicion" standard should prevail. **U.S. v. Braks**, 842 F. 2d 509 (C.A.1st 1988); see also **U.S. v. Santiago**, 837 F. 2d 1545 (C.A.11th 1988).

The **Braks** decision was thus consistent with this court's decision in **U.S. v. Franchi-Forlando**, 838 F. 2d 585 (C.A. 1st 1988). In this case a plane was traveling from Colombia to Spain when it made a scheduled stop in Puerto Rico. The defendant had boarded in Colombia and was bound for Spain, thus his luggage had been "checked through" and was in the baggage area of the plane. Customs officers opened the baggage area and searched his luggage, finding cocaine. Defendant was charged with importation. Customs regulations provide that there may be no search of luggage unless the owner opens or refuses to open the bags. Defendant argues that regulation was applicable to his case. The First Circuit did not agree with him. It held that the regulations only applied to those accompanying their bags and does not apply to baggage in an aircraft. Therefore, customs could search the defendant during the stop.

III.   What is a Border?

The question, What is a border? must be dealt with. Is a border a line or a zone? If it is a zone, how far does it extend? These were the questions presented in **Almeida-Sanchez v. U.S.**, 413 U.S. 266 (1973). The Immigration and Nationality Act allows searches of automobiles within a reasonable distance of the border. A federal regulation established the reasonable distance as 100 air miles from any U.S. boundary. The search in the instant case took place 25 miles from the border on a road that did not directly connect with Mexico. The Court recognized the border was not a line but it did not establish a zone theory either. Rather the Court recognized that searches may be made at the border or its functional equivalent. **Almeida** at 272. As examples of functional equivalents, the Court cited a station near the border where two or more roads extending from the border met or the instance where a non-stop flight from Mexico City landed in St. Louis. These are functional equivalents. If a search takes place outside the functional equivalent, it must meet normal Fourth Amendment standards.

The state of Washington has had occasion to deal with the "functional equivalent" border problem. A search was made of two passengers aboard a British Columbia-to-Washington ferry, not at its first stop in U.S. territory, but at its second stop. Was this warrantless border suspicion search made at the functional equivalent of the border? The Washington Court of Appeals said no because more than 51 cars and

78 passengers got on board at the first stop in the U.S.. It held there was no way that officials could conclude that these two came all the way from Canada with this many people and cars boarding. **State v. Quick**, 796 P. 2d 764 (Wash. Ct. App. 1990).

Sometimes the functional equivalent can be preempted by statute. This was the case in **U.S. v. Bareno-Burgas**, 739 F. Supp. 772 (E.D.N.Y. 1990). Two duffel bags were bound for Colombia. The plane was to stop in Miami before going on to Colombia. A search was conducted at La Guardia. Note that the bags would have been taken off the plane in Miami and X-rayed before being sent on to Colombia. Was La Guardia the border or its functional equivalent? Yes, said the district judge because control was surrendered. But because this case came under the currency reporting statute, La Guardia was not a "port of departure" as required by that statute. Therefore the defendant had not yet failed to file a currency report and as a result the law, had not yet been violated when the legal border search took place.

Since **Almeida,** the circuit courts have developed a new category of search area called the "extended border." An "extended border" is an area that is beyond the "functional equivalent," but is not clearly a fully protected area. Consideration of two cases is germane.

In **U.S. v. Santiago**, 837 F. 2d 1545 (C.A.11th 1988), the court was faced with the issue whether an area was "functional equivalent" or "extended border." "Functional equivalent" requires the use of the "no suspicion" standard, whereas "extended border" requires a "reasonable suspicion" standard. The court then set the criteria to show functional equivalent. It is a three part test and has these elements which the government must show: (1) reasonable certainty that the border was crossed; (2) lack of time or opportunity for the object to have changed materially since the time of the crossing; and (3) performance of the search at the earliest practical point after the border is crossed. If these tests are met then "functional equivalent" is established. In this case the passengers were traveling on a plane from the Bahamas, landing in the U.S. first at Atlanta. The agents kept the defendants under surveillance immediately and constantly after landing. They conducted the search as soon as the defendants claimed their luggage. Here, therefore, was "functional equivalent" thus the "no suspicion" standard could be applied.

An "extended border" search can be justified as long as it qualifies under the following three criteria also. They are: (1) reasonable certainty that the border was crossed; (2) lack of time or opportunity for the object to have changed materially since the time of the crossing; and (3) there must be reasonable suspicion that criminal activity is occurring. As noted, both "functional" and "extended" have the first two elements in common and that only the third element changes. **U.S. v. Espinoza-Seanez**, 862 F. 2d 526 (C.A.5th 1988).

IV.   Vehicles and the Border Issue

In 1975, the Court was faced with the Border Patrol's use of roving patrols near the Mexican border, which was supposedly forbidden in **Almeida**. Because of bad weather, a standard checkpoint was closed. Two patrol cars, with lights on to illuminate passing cars, saw Brignoni-Ponce's car and pulled it over. Illegal aliens were discovered. The Court of Appeals said this was a roving patrol, thus prohibited. The issue in **U.S. v. Brignoni-Ponce**, 422 U.S. 873 (1975) was whether a roving patrol could stop a vehicle in an area near the border and question its occupants when the only ground for suspicion was that the occupants appeared to be of Mexican ancestry? **Brignoni** at 876. Since roving patrols must operate within the Constitution, the patrol must have at least reasonable (articulable?) suspicion to make the stop. Thus, such random stops on mere suspicion are prohibited. Standing alone, looking like a Mexican, is not reasonable suspicion.

In **U.S. v. Molina**, 700 F. Supp. 13 (S.D. Tex. 1988), no reasonable suspicion was established in this roving patrol case. Why? The defendant was driving a large car with tinted windows. The court rejected the "profile" that this was a smuggler's car. The stop was made at 6:00 p.m. and 80 miles from the border. The car had a Texas license plate. This road was not an unusual place to be for a person from Mission, Texas. This man's driving was not erratic for this small, two-lane road.

On the same day that the Court announced **Brignoni-Ponce,** the Court rendered its opinion in **U.S. v. Ortiz**, 422 U.S. 891 (1975). The issue was whether the government could set up a check-point some 62 miles from the border and say it was a functional equivalent. The Court said no. At traffic check-points removed from the border and its functional equivalents, officers may not search private vehicles without consent or probable cause. **Ortiz** at 897.

Would that end the check-point questions? No. The following year, the Court decided **U.S. v. Martinez-Fuertes**, 428 U.S. 543 (1976). In fact, it was the very same check-point that was involved in **Ortiz**. **Ortiz** prohibited searches, but that case reserved the question whether check-points were permissible for a limited stop and question procedure. Arbitrary and oppressive interference cannot be allowed. What is arbitrary must, however, be weighed against the public interest. **Martinez** at 554. The inquiry into residence status is a modest interference, said the Court. No doubt, these stops are seizures within the Fourth Amendment. The flow of traffic at these points is too heavy to require reasonable suspicion for a limited stop to answer one or two basic residence questions. In such a stop, there is no search and the visual inspection is limited to what can be seen without a search. **Martinez** at 558. Finally, the Court said, a warrant is not required to set up such checkpoints for the limited purpose of stop and question as here authorized. **Martinez** at 567.

As the distance from the border increases, so must the strength of the facts underlying the suspicion. Thus, when a car has a Mexican "Turista" sticker on it and the occupants of the car act furtive when watched, in the middle of Atlanta, nearly a thousand miles from the Mexican border with hundreds of towns and roads between Atlanta and Mexico, such facts do not yield a sufficient reason to believe an illegal border crossing had occurred, or, that in this case, that Atlanta was the functional equivalent of the border. **U.S. v. Gonzales-Vargas**, 496 F. Supp. 1296 (N.D. Ga. 1980).

Border searches at the border, or its functional equivalent, do not require probable cause and that stop and question techniques at places beyond the border are permitted. However, any intrusion beyond stop and question requires at least reasonable suspicion for a limited intrusion and probable cause for a full-scale search. Finally, the mode of entry, hand carried, shipped or mailed is of no truly significant importance at the border or its functional equivalent.

That **Brignoni** is not to govern boats in waters leading to the sea was decided by the Supreme Court in **U.S. v. Villamonte-Marquez**, 462 U.S. 579 (1983). A customs officer, accompanied by a Louisiana State Police Officer, boarded a sailboat to check registration papers under 19 U.S.C. Sec. 1581. While on board, the odor of burning marijuana was detected and the state policeman looked down an open hatch and saw burlap wrapped bales which proved to be marijuana. The Court held the boarding to be reasonable. Boats that can take to the open sea present a very different problem than autos. The outward markings (by licenses) on autos also present a major difference. No check-points can be established on water-highways are different – there are no identifiable roads on the water. Thus the search was upheld.

V.   Contemporaneousness of the Border Search

How soon after a proper border seizure does a search of a container have to be conducted? Is a three day wait too long? No, said the Supreme Court in **U.S. v. Johns**, 469 U.S. 478 (1985). Nothing in **U.S. v. Ross**, 456 U.S. 798 (1982)) requires that such a search be performed immediately or even soon thereafter. They closed by saying that although officers may not indefinitely postpone such complete searches, this three-day delay was not unreasonable.

VI.   Terry and the Border

To what extent does the stop and frisk doctrine of **Terry** apply in the border search area? This was the issue presented to the Court in **U.S. v. Cortez**, 449 U.S. 411 (1981), in which the focus was on the stop issue. The facts are simple and based on well-drawn conclusions to reasonable inferences. The smuggling of illegal aliens over a constant route at a pick-up point by a person who wore distinctive shoes and who drove a vehicle that could hold eight to ten people, gave rise to a stake-out. The suspect vehicle had to travel west and return east lest they drive right back into Mexico. The pickup always occurred between 2 a.m. and 6 a.m. on clear weekend evenings. Such were the conditions on the weekend in question. Between 1 a.m. and 6 a.m. only 15 vehicles proceeded west and only two of those were pick-up trucks with camper shells. Licenses were recorded and one of those pickup trucks made the round trip in the designated time. Was this the articulable suspicion necessary to make an investigative stop? Yes, it was, said the Court. Taking the totality of the circumstances into account, a trained officer drew inferences and deductions that might well elude an untrained person. This yielded a particularized suspicion that those in this pickup truck were engaged in wrongdoing. The intrusion upon privacy associated with this stop was limited and was reasonable in scope, as justified.

VII.   Which Direction?

For cases holding that items to be exported are subject to same broad powers as imports read: **U.S. v. Swarovski**, 592 F. 2d 131 (C.A. 2d 1979); **U.S. v. Stanley**, 545 F. 2d 661 (C.A.9th 1976); and **U.S. v. Ajlouny**, 476 F. Supp. 995 (E.D. N.Y. 1979).

Some things are exported by mail. Are those items, such as letter and sealed packages subject to letter-postage, free from inspection, or are they subject to the broad powers of the border search exception? The Court noted that first-class mail inspections must meet Fourth Amendment standards but held that first-class mail is not beyond the reach of all inspection. In the case at hand, the Court was faced with a 29 hour delay of a first-class package. The person who mailed the package used a fictitious return address and drove a car that had Canadian tags. The post office was in the state of Washington. This man was already under investigation for coin smuggling activities. The nature and weight of the package fit the *modus operandi* of the smuggling crime. The Court held that all of this information justified the detention of the package without a warrant while an investigation was made. The detention was equated with a **Terry**-type intrusion. The search warrant, after this investigation, was obtained as promptly as possible under the circumstances, since certain information had to come from Tennessee. The Court held that, "Detention for this limited time was, indeed, the prudent act rather than letting the packages enter the mails and then, in case the initial suspicions were confirmed, trying to locate them en route and enlisting the help of distant federal officers in serving the warrant." **U.S. v. Leeuwen**, 397 U.S. 249 (1970).

The previous case did not settle all of the issues in this area. The question of whether things and person leaving the country also enjoy no protection needed a definitive answer. The Court did, however, give a hint of what might be the answer in **California Banker's Assoc. v. Schultz**, 416 U.S. 21 (1974). **California Banker's** involved the interpretation of the Bank Secrecy Act of 1970 enacted to cure the unavailability of records of those possibly engaged in illegal activities using domestic banks to transfer funds to foreign financial institutions. Deep into the opinion, citing import cases, the Court made the following comments: "and if those entering and leaving the country may be examined as to their belongings and effects, all without violating the Fourth Amendment, we see no reason to invalidate the Secretary's regulations here."

Relying on the above quoted language, the Second Circuit upheld the warrantless search of a carton being sent to the Mideast from the U.S.. The carton supposedly held air conditioner parts. Instead it contained recently stolen sophisticated communications equipment destined for the PLO. Admitting the statement from **California Banker's** was *obiter dictum*, they noted that both this court and Ninth Circuit had come to the conclusion that both directions of border flow were covered and cited **Swarovski** (*supra*) and **U.S. v. Stanley**, 545 F. 2d 661 (C.A.9th 1976). See also **U.S. v. Franchi-Forlando**, 838 F. 2d 585 (C.A. 1st 1988). The court went on to say that even if reasonable suspicion is lacking (which was present in this case), this type of search does not violate the Fourth Amendment. Nothing was found in the federal statutes requiring probable cause for such searches. **U.S. v. Ajlouny**, 629 F. 2d 830 (C.A. 2d 1980).

VIII. Beyond Our Borders: Any Rights?

Since the border exception exists to prevent wrongful crossings in either direction. it obviously cannot be employed when the search is conducted totally outside the borders of the United States. However, if a warrantless search is conducted on foreign soil, does the Constitution's protection extend to such searches? Does the Fourth Amendment protect anyone beyond the borders?

These were the questions present to the Court in **U.S. v. Verdugo-Urquidez**, 494 U.S. 259 (1990). In **Verdugo**, the warrantless search took place in Mexico. Verdugo was not a citizen or alien resident of the United States, but he argued that the evidence should be suppressed in his case in the U.S. court. A 1957 decision had determined that the Fifth and Sixth Amendments applied extraterritorially to U.S. citizens abroad. **Reid v. Covert**, 354 U.S. 1 (1957). In **I.N.S. v. Lopez-Mendoza**, 468 U.S. 1032 (1984), the Court held that illegal aliens had Fourth Amendment rights. However, in **Johnson v. Eisentrager**, 339 U.S. 763 (1950), enemy aliens arrested on foreign soil and in German based prisons were not entitled to habeas corpus relief. Resident aliens were, on the other hand, found to be persons for Fifth Amendment purposes in **Kwong-Hai Chew v. Colding**, 344 U.S. 590 (1953), and the resident aliens have the protection of the Fourteenth Amendment in **Yick Wo v. Hopkins**, 118 U.S. 356 (1886).

With this history in mind, the Supreme Court held in **Verdugo** that Mr. Verdugo was not protected by the Fourth Amendment because he was not a citizen, resident alien, or person with a "voluntary attachment to the U.S.," and because the place searched was located in Mexico. Stevens concurred only on the basis that "…searches of noncitizen's homes in foreign jurisdictions…." are not covered by the Fourth because "American magistrates have no power to authorize such searches." Kennedy concurred, believing no due process rights were violated in this context. Brennan, Marshall and Blackmun dissented.

IX.   Sample State Court Border Decisions

1.   **Saunders v. State**, 758 So. 2d 724 (Fla. App. 2d Dist.2000).

A Coast Guard officer with a marine unit of the Fort Myers Police Department was in U.S. jurisdiction waters in a Coast Guard vessel when he saw a 21-foot boat – a pleasure craft operated solely by Saunders. He boarded the boat accompanied by a single Fort Myers police officer. The Coast Guard officer conducted a routine administrative boarding to check and make sure that the vessel was in compliance with *all* laws. There were no personal flotation devices. Saunders appeared under the influence and Saunders subsequently failed the field sobriety tests. The Coast Guard officer turned Saunders over to the local police, and that gave rise to this case. The stop was lawful under **U.S. v. Villamonte Marquez.** The Florida Court noted that these suspicionless boardings have been a practice for a very long time.

The court then noted that the Fort Myers police unit did not direct this investigation, nor for that matter did the Fort Myers police unit take any active part in the investigation except to take custody of appellant once he was arrested. The boarding with the Coast Guard officer did not change the "essential character of the boarding."

2.   **Davis v. State**, 754 A. 2d 1111 (Md. App. 2000).

The defendant (and another) arrived at BWI on a non-stop flight from Jamaica. Thus the Baltimore Airport was *the* border. The two were separated from others and taken to a secondary inspection area. Ms. Davis appeared nervous, sweated and shifted her weight from one foot to another. The customs inspector had a female officer pat Ms. Davis down. That officer felt a padded area around Davis' waist and thighs. When Davis lowered her slacks, a white powdery substance was discovered, wrapped in clear plastic and held in place with thick electrical tape. A similar experience occurred after the patting down of her male companion. Of course, this pair was carrying cocaine. The court said pat-downs are routine when conducted at the border or its functional equivalent. The court was unwilling to find that partial disrobement went beyond a routine border search, but even if it did, they said there was ample cause to support this action. The baggy clothing that alerted the customs people was properly considered with other factors, as the court says in Footnote 5, but they refused to say that fact, standing alone, would be sufficient.

3.   **State v. Cleave**, 8 P.3d 157 (N.M. App. 2000).

Disregarding U.S. Supreme Court law that a dog sniff from outside a privacy area is not a search, this court, after a lawful stop and consent to inspect a trunk based on ample articulable suspicion, found the alerted-to evidence inadmissible. Clearly New Mexico is out of "sync" with the U.S. Supreme Court.

4.   **People v. Disnoyers**, 2000 WL 311025 (N.Y.).

A hospital employee was stealing drugs, sutures and other items on a regular basis. He then would, after accumulating enough, ship them to Haiti. This case fully recognizes the right of customs to inspect items that go in or out of the country. The border search in this case was a routine search. It also notes that the higher degree of intrusion goes with each increment in the degree of suspicion. It also stated that "old" New York case, decided before the development of the current law would not govern them. In fact, the old **Esposito** case was aimed at deterring local agents from using federal agents to conduct a search for them. The federal agents in this case declined prosecution because the amount was too small.

5.   **Gutierrez v. State**, 22 S.W. 3d 75 (Tex. App. Corpus Christi 2000)

The stop was conducted at a border control checkpoint that was permanent. Thus, the initial stop of defendant's vehicle was lawful. A dog alerted to drugs and this gave probable cause to search. Therefore, the border agents could turn the defendant and the evidence over to the state for prosecution.

6.   **Romero v. State**, 2000 WL 177456 (Tex. App. San Antonio) (un pub. op.)

Some 68 miles from the Mexican border a border patrol agent sees the defendant driving north. What caught the agent's attention? First, he was going 35 mph in a 70 mph zone and tried to "hide" himself when the agent drove alongside. He had done some weaving in his lane when the agent was behind him. It was also obvious that the rear seat had been removed from the crew-cab truck, thus it was possible that illegal aliens or narcotics were stored in the space (as experience dictated.). So the agent pulled the vehicle over to check license and citizenship status. A very strong odor of carpet freshener wafted from the cab and the officer saw freshener sprinkled on the floor. The agent asked for and received permission to look in the tool box in the back of the truck. Six bundles, or 169 pounds of marijuana, were discovered. This was turned over to the state for prosecution. Was this stop reasonable? Yes. Under **State v. Luera**, 561 S.W. 2d 497 (Tex. Crim. 1978) and **Renteria v. State**, 989 S.W. 2d 114 (Tex. App. 1999) this stop was proper.

7.   **State v. Pena**, 2000 WL 1700 135 (Wash. App. 3)

The state in this case won continued use of the extended border (articulable suspicion standard) for stopping people and vehicles. Thus, the evidence gathered by a border patrol officer was lawfully found. A well-detailed case such as this is worth reading.

CHAPTER ELEVEN
EXIGENT CIRCUMSTANCES

I.   Introduction

There are times when the delay necessary to secure a warrant would endanger the lives of the officers or others. The delay may also seriously and realistically impair or destroy the ability to secure the evidence of a crime. There are times when true emergencies affecting the lives or safety of others call for prompt, almost unthinking action. In such situations, the emergency or exigency of the situation allows the officer to bypass the warrant requirement and gives the officer the right to enter a Fourth Amendment protected area. This is called the exigent circumstances exception.

As will be seen, this doctrine cannot be used without a probable cause base, at least in the evidence destruction, escape or danger to an officer cases. Thus probable cause plus exigency is what is needed to justify warrantless intrusions. The exigency is usually said to require more than a mere hypothecated case of destruction of evidence, possibility of escape, or danger to officers or others. Generally, proof of the reasonable belief in the necessity of entry without a warrant must be demonstrated by the facts known to the officer at the time of the entry. Without such proof the police will be unable to take advantage of "plain view" in the escape and danger cases because they will not be lawfully present – a place where they have a right to be. Of course, probable cause is an absolute must in the evidence destruction cases. The balance of this chapter will deal with representative views of the federal and state courts on the issue. No two cases are alike and each case stands on its own. Thus, the cases should be read in that limited context.

II. A View From the Top – A Few United States Supreme Court Cases

Though not the first case ever on the subject, **McDonald v. U.S.**, 335 U.S. 451 (1948), amply demonstrates a lack of exigency. Even the probable cause in this case appears to have been garnered illegally as noted by Justices Frankfurter and Jackson. In any event, through a transom above the door, police saw illegal gambling operations. Rather than secure a warrant, the police immediately broke in and seized the evidence and arrested everyone present. The issue was simple. What were the compelling reasons for bypassing the warrant requirement? The Court found there were no compelling reasons. Why? The police in this case had the premises under surveillance for two months. Once probable cause finally arose, (according to Justice Douglas) the police could not point to evidence of escape or that the property was in the process of destruction. The only reason for the action was to avoid the inconvenience of securing a warrant and that is no justification for avoiding a warrant.

In **Warden v. Hayden**, 387 U.S. 294 (1967), however, the Court found sufficient exigency to enter the defendant's home without a warrant. It said, "The Fourth Amendment does not require officers to delay in the course of an investigation if to do so would gravely endanger their lives or the lives of others." The police had ample probable cause that the gun toting Hayden was the robbery suspect who had been, within a few minutes of the robbery, traced to his house. The Court held, "Speed here was essential...." The police knew he was armed and knew that he was a risk, both of danger *and* escape. Coupling the fresh pursuit with the facts of a fleeing and armed man, a sufficient exigency existed to cross the threshold of the house.

Next is **Vale v. Louisiana**, 399 U.S. 30 (1970), where exigent circumstances were not found for the search of Vale's home. Upon a valid arrest warrant, Vale was captured outside his house thereby denying any possible plain view and search incident of surroundings under **Chimel** (*infra* at Chapter 13) and the wing-span doctrine. The police entered the house anyway and found narcotics. No one else was present in the house. Vale's mother and brother arrived while the search was in progress. The Court said no exceptional situation existed to allow the warrantless search. Louisiana had taken the position that the easy destructibility of narcotics gave rise to exigency in and of itself. The Court disagreed. The officers were not responding to an emergency. They were not in hot pursuit. The goods seized were not in the process of destruction nor were they about to be removed from the jurisdiction. They knew Vale lived there and knew he was in the narcotics business for some time. The Court held that the arrest of Vale on the street could not provide its own "exigent circumstance" so as to justify the warrantless search of the arrestee's house.

Even the IRS must observe Fourth Amendment requirements under the "levy" provisions of the tax code and may not enter corporate offices without a warrant unless there are exigent circumstances. **G. M. Leasing Corp. v. U.S.**, 429 U.S. 338 (1977). The agents delayed for two days (after an initial view) before they made the warrantless entry during which they made the seizure. This, the Court held, proved there were no exigent circumstances. Obviously, there was plenty of time to secure a warrant.

In **Mincey v. Arizona**, 437 U.S. 385 (1978), the police wanted a murder scene exigency exception simply because a homicide had occurred at the place. The Court did recognize that police may enter when they reasonably believe that a person within a place may need immediate aid and also that when they come upon the scene they may make a sweep to see if other victims are present or to see if the killer is still there. But in **Mincey** the questioned search took place after the victim and others were removed. The search, in fact, lasted four days and, in that context, no emergency or exigency could have existed. The fact that murder was the root crime created no reason to presume exigency. Efficiency of law enforcement, in this context, cannot be tolerated. Thus compelling need was not found.

The Court has taken the position that the mere fact of probable cause to arrest an individual does not give the police the right to cross the defendant's threshold unless there is consent, warrant or exigency. **Payton v. New York**, 445 U.S. 573 (1980). See the discussion of **Payton,** *et.al.*, in Chapter Thirteen.

When it comes to automobiles, the court has consistently allowed warrantless searches and seizures based upon the car's ready mobility creating therefore the exigency needed to bypass the warrant requirement in most though not all cases. For a full discussion of the mobility exception see the materials that deal with that subject in Chapter Thirteen. In the beeper installation and tracking case of **U.S. v. Karo**, 468 U.S. 705 (1984) the Court was unwilling to allow tracking of the beeper within the privacy area of a building unless a warrant was first procured because tracking the object's movements within a building is a search. The Court said: "Those suspected of drug offenses are no less entitled to that protection (the warrant) than those suspected of non-drug offenses." Without truly exigent circumstances, it noted, a warrant was required even if it meant the number of warrants to be sought was large. See further discussion of this point at Chapter Eleven.

Indicating that the Court has not yet changed its mind about the probable cause base for exigent entries, consider this language from **Minnesota v. Olson**, 495 U.S. 91 (1990): "In **Payton v. New York**, the Court has no occasion to 'consider the sort of emergency or dangerous situation, described in our cases as 'exigent circumstances,' that would justify a warrantless entry into a home for the purpose of either arrest of search.' This case requires us to determine whether the Minnesota Supreme Court was correct in holding that there were no exigent circumstances that justifies the warrantless entry into the house to make the arrest. The Minnesota Supreme Court applied essentially the correct standard in determining whether exigent circumstances existed. The court observed that "a warrantless intrusion may be justified by hot pursuit of a fleeing felon, or imminent destruction of evidence, or the need to prevent a suspect's escape, or the risk of danger to the police or to other persons inside or outside the dwelling." The court also apparently thought that in the absence of hot pursuit there must be at least probable cause to believe that one or more of the other factors justifying the entry were present and that in assessing the risk of danger, the gravity of the crime and likelihood that the suspect is armed should be considered. Applying this standard, the state court determined that exigent circumstances did not exist. We are not inclined to disagree with this fact-specific application of the proper legal standard. The court pointed out that although a grave crime was involved, respondent "was known not to be the murderer but thought to be the driver of the getaway car," ibid., and that the police had already recovered the murder weapon, ibid. "The police knew that Louanne and Julie were with the suspect in the upstairs duplex with no suggestion of danger to them. Three or four Minneapolis police squads surrounded the house. The time was 3 p.m., Sunday... It was evident the suspect was going nowhere. If he came out of the house he would have been promptly apprehended." Ibid. We do not disturb the state court's judgment that these facts do not add up to exigent circumstance." Citations omitted.

Finally, an exigency that exists for one purpose does not, beyond plain view, justify the search for an unrelated purpose. Once the officers go outside the scope of the original exigency search, new probable cause, exigency, consent, warrant or other exception to the warrant requirement must exist to justify the unrelated search. **Arizona v. Hicks**, 480 U.S. 321 (1987). In **Hicks**, the police had completed the warranted murder scene search when they decided to touch a turntable to get to its serial number because they suspected it was stolen property. An exigency did not exist on this mere suspicion. Thus the Supreme Court said the Fourth Amendment requires a combination of probable cause plus compelling need to justify an exigent based warrantless search. An examination of some federal and state cases involving exigency follows. These cases will be divided into three broad categories: evidence destruction, danger to officers or others, and true emergencies demanding official response. A discussion of protective sweeps will conclude the chapter.

III.   Evidence Destruction or Escape

In the evidence destruction cases or the probable escape cases, the police have probable cause to believe the evidence or felon sought is within the premises. That is a mandatory requirement that must be met before there can be any discussion of the exigency that existed to cross the threshold without a warrant. Once police convince the court of the probable cause regarding the presence of the person or evidence, they then must establish the facts relied upon to believe that if they delayed to get a warrant the evidence or person would disappear. The police should be required to prove more than a hypothecated (profile based?) case. They must also demonstrate that the situation "exploded" in the sense that the probable cause for both points arose rather quickly. The more planning time the police had, the less likely it is that they can show exigency. Consider these cases to see how faithful the courts have been to these precepts.

The "no planning time" case has finally come to us by way of **Illinois v. McArthur**, 121 S. Ct. 946 (2001). Police went to the defendant's house with the defendant's wife who needed their protection to remove her things. They waited outside with the husband. After she came out she took the officers aside and whispered that her husband had "drugs in there" and that they were " under the couch." The police confronted McArthur and asked for a consent to search for the drugs and he said no. The police said that was okay but he could not re-enter his home, without a police escort, while the wife and the other officer went to see if they could get a warrant. The defendant acquiesced and did not object when the officer twice followed him into the house (once for cigarettes and once to make a call). The officer did not conduct a search either time. The warrant arrived and a misdemeanor amount of marijuana was found under the couch.

The Court acknowledged that on these facts no exigency arose to allow a warrantless search. The securing of the house and denial of entry were seen as minimal intrusions. The claim of the police was plausibly a "specially pressing or urgent law enforcement need, i.e., 'Exigent circumstances'... which may permit temporary seizure without a warrant." The Court then cited **Warden v. Hayden**, 387 U.S. 294 (1967). It went on to say that a *per se* rule of unreasonableness is not used but that "...privacy-related and law enforcement - related concerns to determine whether the intrusion was reasonable." This decision drew eight votes with a special concurrence and only one dissent. Souter's concurrence was perhaps a little more direct in its support because he thought a pure exigency existed; a "...present risk of destruction." All Stevens had to say was that all the judges in Illinois did a balancing approach and got it right and their decisions should not be disturbed since the crime was so minor. Which means he might otherwise agree.

In **U.S. v. Pantojo-Soto**, 739 F. 2d 1520 (C.A. 11th 1984) the defendant saw the government's agent and ran from the office into the service bays of the gas station. This, the court felt, raised a real exigency that the drugs would have been destroyed if the police had taken the time to get a warrant. The court stressed the fact that the probable cause as to the presence of the drugs had arisen just a few minutes before the defendant's retreat. That probable cause came from the field testing of the capsules just a few minutes before the arrests were attempted. It was not until then that police knew the drugs were indeed present at the gas station. This appears to meet the **McArthur** standards.

In **U.S. v. Kunkler**, 679 F. 2d 187 (C.A. 9th 1982) probable cause existed and the drug dealer was acting very wary and extremely curious. This demonstrated that the dealer was suspicious that something had gone wrong and created exigent circumstances to enter the premises due to a real fear that the evidence would be destroyed. Note also that it did not appear from the facts that there was sufficient probable cause in this case prior to the attempted undercover deal to get an anticipatory warrant for this place. This should always be considered in those jurisdictions which allow anticipatory warrants. However, it should also be noted that the officers in this case merely secured these premises. They sent for a search warrant and when it arrived they conducted the search. This demonstrated a reasonable approach when manpower is available. This also would have been approved in **McArthur**.

As these cases indicate, the trial court is to look for a lack of sufficient time to prepare the affidavit, locate a magistrate and obtain the warrant after probable cause arises coupled with or because of the imminent destruction of evidence or possibility of escape. When a short time has elapsed between a crime and complaint, exigent circumstances sometimes make immediate police action imperative. In **State v. Welch**, 449 So. 2d 468 (La. 1984), the police were able to show facts indicating why flight was believed and not merely hypothecated. In this rape/assault case a bath could eliminate evanescent linking-evidence, thus destruction was probable. However, the court failed to take into account a semen comparison that could have been done at any time.

Any number of factors should be considered. In one case, the ease with which the officer purchased the drug made it likely that there were more drugs present, thus probable cause arose. The persons present in the house were both unmarried and unrelated – no family. An arrest of a friend in their presence for a serious offense meant a high likelihood that the evidence would be destroyed. **State v. Camp**, 333 So. 2d 896 (Ga. App. 1985). The Georgia Court went on to say that they would not require the premises to be sealed up tight and watchmen put at the doors to stop further sales and then have the officer try to find a magistrate at 3:30 a.m. to issue a warrant. Unfortunately this last comment makes this sound like a convenience decision – where's the exigency? Perhaps Georgia will take a second look at this type of case now that **McArthur** has been decided.

The Minnesota Court, on the other hand, might have required the house in the Georgia case to be cleared. In **State v. Hatton**, 389 N.W. 2d 229 (Minn. App. 1986), the court said where the occupants of the room are locked up and unable to destroy the evidence and where more officers could have been available to guard the motel room and prevent entry by anyone else, then there is no exigency. I am not sure **McArthur** demands this, but it would satisfy **McArthur**.

Also consider **State v. Heumiller**, 317 N.W. 2d 126(S. D. 1982). The police had the only two people who could have possibly gone into the house to destroy the evidence. They said it is hard to find an exigency here. There was no hot pursuit in this case. Although the officer said he went in to find others, the officer came right out after finding guns in the first room he searched. If the police can truly show, however, that even with assistance they could not effectively secure the premises due to such factors as size of building, number of exits and time of the night, then a court can find an exigency. **State v. Moulton**, 481 A. 2d 155 (Me. 1984).

The **Stackhouse** case from Maryland presents a court hewing a tough line on exigency by rejecting hypothecated destruction and requiring specific indicia of destruction. Here, after an arrest of the defendant, the police searched the attic of the house and found the evidence. The Maryland Court said police must show a specific threat to known evidence. No strong likelihood of evidence destruction was shown in this case. But unlike the few jurisdictions that require "destruction in progress", their position represents the middle road between "in progress" and "hypothecated" — probable cause based threat. The court went on to say that the mere presence of some third person who could destroy evidence was not enough unless *imminence* was shown. If police can show that a particular person had attempted to conceal evidence or otherwise acted furtively and then that person being present and not under arrest could spell out exigency. In this case the third person present was the defendant's sister. But she did not act furtively. She was holding her baby, acted like she did not care and she left the house when asked. **Stackhouse v. State**, 468 A. 2d 333 (Md. 1983). This would have been an excellent case for the application of **McArthur's** rule.

Exigent circumstances search cases are narrowly circumscribed and can only be judged on facts known before the entry. The burden of proof is on the prosecution to show the necessity and failure to substantiate the officer's conclusion renders the search illegal. If doubt exists as to whether the officer reasonably concluded that the search was justified, such doubt must be resolved in favor of the defendant whose property was searched. **People v. Jansen**, 713 P. 2d 907 (Colo. 1986). And as California notes in rejecting the hypothecated case, the officer may not rely on unparticularized suspicions or hunches. **People v. Duncan**, 720 P. 2d 2 (Cal. 1986). Thus, the mere showing of ready destructibility will not be enough. The government must show a good reason to believe that destruction is imminent. **Ingram v. State**, 703 P. 2d 415 (Alaska App. 1985). **Ingram** was known to have already tipped off his wife and another about the police presence. They felt this presented a "clear and immediate likelihood of destruction." This was at least articulable suspicion if not probable cause to believe that an exigency existed.

Following the principle of **Schmerber v. California**, 384 U.S. 757 (1966), New Jersey held that the evanescent nature of some evidence (blood alcohol level) may create an exigency of its own. Such cases stress the combination of probable cause with the issue of the time required to secure a warrant in the face of such rapidly deteriorating evidence. **State v. Dyal**, 478 A. 2d 390 (N.J. 1984); see also **Ortega v. State**, 669 P. 2d 935 (Wyo. 1983) where the first entry was based on emergency and reentry was due to the discovery of evanescent evidence which thus justified the warrantless second entry.

Police can be the cause of their own undoing when attempting to demonstrate exigency. As Rhode Island has held, time to secure the warrant is not the only factor to be considered. But it is a very relevant factor especially in evidence destruction or escape cases. The police in this case prepared for this arrest for three hours, thus there was plenty of time to secure a warrant. **State v. Beaumier**, 480 A. 2d 1367 (R.I. 1984); accord **U.S. v. Thomas**, 893 F. 2d 482 (C.A. 2d 1990). When police have complete control over the timing of events it is hard to say an exigency exists. Police in one case knew that two buyers of drugs were registered at a hotel awaiting the arrival of their seller. The police knew the identity of the seller and intercepted him when he arrived in town. The police convinced the seller to cooperate and controlled the delivery time. They also knew the buyers were waiting "patiently." Instead of using the hour necessary to obtain a controlled delivery anticipatory warrant, the police sent the seller in, and on his heels, they entered, making the arrest of the buyers and searches incident to those arrests. The Sixth Circuit said the evidence should have been suppressed. **U.S. v. Ogbuh**, 982 F. 2 1000 (C.A. 6th 1993). Clearly this was a case of police creating their own exigency which, of course, is prohibited. The Sixth Circuit was very harsh on the police and prosecutor's motives. The concurring-dissenter saw the case in the proper, non-emotional context. However, if the jurisdiction does not recognize anticipatory warrants (see Chapter Three) would the police action in this case have been reasonable? What impact would telephonic warrants (see Chapter Three) have on a case like this?

That the police should not be able to create their own exigency is one of those rules that makes good sense. For example, in **State v. De La Paz**, 766 A. 2d 820 (N.J. Super. 2001), a drug packaging distribution center was the target. It was 2:40 A.M. and four cruisers pull up to the dark side of the house where the suspected drug operation was taking place. They did call in for a warrant but they did not get a response so the officers tried to sneak into the house but their attempt alerted the suspects. The officers broke in. Had they not tried to get in through the window the packaging would have continued. The court said careless and foolish police acts (real or pretended) do not create exigency. Yes, the officers had probable cause but nothing occurred that required their immediate response. Their lack of experience with the warrant process was also not an exigency. No evidence existed that the suspects were posing an immediate danger, in fact there was no mention of any weapons revealed in this case. The only exigency in this case was of the officers' creation.

However, Georgia has one of the few genuine police caused exigency cases that upheld the admission of the incriminating evidence found during the entry of a home. In **State v. Peterson**, 2001 WL 208365 (Ga. 2001), the police arrested all the adults from a house in which several children resided. Two uniformed officers went into the house to make sure the children were taken care of. The two children were in a bedroom on the second floor. A detective arrived and told the uniformed officers to contact the relatives. The detective went upstairs to check the children. Evidence linking the defendants to the murder of a child, which the remaining children confirmed, were "tools" in the murder. The defense argued non-exigent police-caused plain view. The court stated that the need to take care of the children exigency was caused by the police arrests but a second exigency arose that justified the entry to care for the remaining children. The evidence of the murder was thus admissible.

For a case illustrating that the mere presence of drugs at a place without more does not create an exigency that does away with the warrant requirement, see **People v. Guerin**, 769 P. 2d 1068 (Colo. 1989). In **Guerin** there was a pattern of ongoing activity which corroborated the anonymous tip. In fact there was no indication that the operation would stop its sales at that location since it was a legitimate business by day. Failure to show destruction or removal of the illicit business doomed the warrantless entry. A case of hypothecated destruction is not enough. In a like vein, when police have in custody the only person who could possibly "sound an alarm" it is very difficult for the government to urge exigent circumstances. **U.S. v. Veillette**, 778 F. 2d 899 (C.A. 1st 1985).

Indiana was faced with a case involving drugs, rape and other crimes in a motel room. Without specifically saying so, the court probably looked at the nature of the motel room as a transient abode and coupled that with the fact that a victim was known, by the defendants, to be at freedom. Thus the court held there was sufficient exigency for the entry without a warrant. **Bergfeld v. State**, 531 N.E. 2d 486 (Ind. 1988). This type of reasoning had been "fleshed out" in **Myers v. State**, 454 N.E. 2d 861 (Ind. 1983) where a motel room occupied by a Kansas citizen, driving a Kansas truck was seen as a person with little or no Indiana ties who had a record in several other states, thus leading to a conclusion of imminent escape. But, as Missouri has held, where a man was in a building for several hours prior to the search and where the entire area was staked out so that there was little likelihood of escape, then the police had ample time to get a warrant. **State v. Varvil**, 686 S.W. 2d 507 (Mo. App. 1985); see also **State v. Kao**, 697 P. 2d 903 (Mont. 1985). The **McArthur** approach would have worked well in this cases.

The telephonic warrant states are faced with one additional factor to be considered. Many states feel that since telephonic warrants were permitted to cut down the number of warrantless entries, the failure to use the process must be factored in, especially in the evidence destruction or escape cases. **State v. Ringer**, 674 P. 2d 1240

(Wash. 1983) citing Marek, *Telephonic Search Warrants: A New Equation for Exigent Circumstances*, 27 CLEV. ST. L. REV. 35 (1987).

More courts are beginning to recognize the dilemma faced by police when they know destructible evidence is in a house but cannot show "destruction in progress" as apparently required by **MacDonald**. In fact most police will honestly admit they can show no more than a possibility of destruction. One answer to this dilemma is to permit a seizure of the house or other property pending the arrival of a warrant. Michigan says, "...where the police can show an objectively reasonable basis to believe the risk of destruction or removal of evidence is imminent – that immediate action is necessary before they can obtain a warrant – they may enter a residence for the limited purpose of securing the premises pending issuance of a search warrant." Because of the **MacDonald** rule they held that searches for the evidence under exigency are limited to those situations where police can show "actual observation of removal or destruction or such an attempt." This resolution of the problem is most reasonable. **People v. Blasius**, 459 N.W. 2d 906. (Mich. 1990). And it is clear that the Supreme Court agrees by its decision in **McArthur** that allows seizure of the house while waiting for the warrant decision.

The one problem courts should be alert to in such cases is whether the police in such circumstances have created their own exigency. This is well-illustrated by **U.S. v. Duchi**, 906 F. 2d 1278 (C.A. 8th 1990). In this case the police arranged for a controlled delivery and knew the defendant had destroyed evidence quickly in the past. Upon the delivery the police went in without a warrant and arrested the defendant. Finding plenty of time to secure a warrant, plus the fact that a book had been substituted for the drugs, the court in **Duchi** found there was no exigency to justify the entry. The court said if there was exigency created by the alteration of the package it was due to the police conduct and investigative strategy and that conduct cannot justify a warrantless entry. What the police should have done was to secure an anticipatory warrant. However, not all states allow the use of the anticipatory warrant.

IV. Danger to Officers or Others

In addition to its destruction of the evidence aspect, the **Pantojo-Soto** case, cited in section III, also demonstrates a "danger to officers or others" case. The police had probable cause to believe that **Pantojo-Soto** and others were methaqualone sellers although they did not at an earlier time have probable cause as to the location of the drugs. As the agent approached, the suspect ran into the service bays of the gas station. Other officers (undercover agents) were on the premises. With the timing of the sale and the discovery of the agent outside, the police were reasonable in believing that there was danger to the officers on the premises. **U.S. v. Pantojo-Soto**, 739 F. 2d 1520 (C.A. 11th 1984).

The mere presence of a gun in a place alone may not be enough to raise the danger exigency. (Consider **U.S. v. Satterfield**, 743 F. 2d 827 (C.A. 11th 1984)). No one was in Satterfield's house after the arrest, but the police had reason to believe the shotgun was in the house. The police also believed that a friend of Satterfield, who was still at large, could return at any moment and get the shotgun. Was this an exigency? The court said the exigent circumstances doctrine applies only when inevitable delay incident to obtaining a warrant must give way to an urgent need for immediate action. It felt that since police knew no one else was in the place there was no exigency – no immediate threat existed – only potential danger. More officers could have been summoned to the scene to prevent others from entering. All they had to do was radio. Again, **McArthur** could be used in these instances.

But knowing that a gun is inside a house in which children live creates enough exigency for the police to enter without a warrant. **U.S. v. Antwine**, 873 F. 2d 1144 (C.A. 8th 1989). The defendant, Antwine, had brandished a gun at officers of the F.B.I. who went to his house posing as other than officers. Antwine got suspicious, pointed the gun, causing the officers to withdraw. Local police were summoned and Antwine finally gave up, surrendering himself in his front yard where he was arrested. A "sweep" seeking others was then conducted of the house and two children were found. Since the F.B.I. decided to leave the children at the house, they sought and found the gun for the children's safety. Without fully justifying the need for the sweep, the court saw this case as being "akin" to the **Quarles** "public safety" exception to **Miranda's** requirements. They also said this was a close case, but they did not view the trial court's refusal to suppress the gun as clearly erroneous. Sometimes the law can have a "heart."

The known propensities of a person to be violent can establish exigency to enter a place to make an arrest. In **Verez v. Com.**, 337 S.E. 2d 749 (Va. 1985), the defendant was known to be a particularly violent drug dealer. Coupling that fact with the fact that there is an informant inside can lead the police to the reasonable conclusion that there is a high probability of violence likely when an announced arrest is attempted.

No more pressing exigency exists than the need to enter a room in which a sniper who has just shot and killed an officer is "holed up." A delay in such a case would not be the wisest thing to do. Here there is always a potential for more death. Police action will then be required to prevent additional harm. The police in the cited case had probable cause to believe that defendant was in this apartment. **Jones v. State**, 440 So. 2d 570 (Fla. 1983).

One case illustrates that exigency can have an ending point as well as a beginning point. Police are told upon arrival at a domestic dispute scene that the defendant had a gun hidden in a guitar case. The police did not open the guitar case on arrival but waited until they had subdued the defendant and had completely removed him from the room where the guitar case was located. The Maryland Court said there were no exigent circumstances at that point to justify the warrantless opening of the guitar case. Why even discuss exigency? The court noted that the defendant, though seized, was not under arrest, thus no search incident rights arose. Second, there was no consent to the search given by the defendant. Thus, it said that only the exigency doctrine could be applied but no exigency existed here. **Shuman v. State**, 574 A. 2d 345 (Md. Ct. Spec. App. 1990). **Shuman** is a strict application of exigency. In fairness there does not appear to be evidence of prior gun-using violence in this case and people can lawfully own guns. If a court follows the "mere presence of a gun without more" rule then the result is fully understandable.

Minnesota adds to the context of exigency by focusing on the totality of the circumstances as creating a compelling need to cross the defendant's threshold. The court says to look at these factors: "(a) whether a grave or violent offense is involved; (b) whether the suspect is reasonably believed to be armed; (c) whether there is strong probable cause connecting the suspect to the offense; (d) whether the police have a strong reason to believe the suspect is on the premises; (e) whether it is likely the suspect will escape if not swiftly apprehended; (f) whether peaceable entry was made. The offense in the case before them was grave because the 9-1-1 call from the defendant's daughter said he was threatening to burn the house down and when the police got there the defendant was seen standing in a pool of liquid with a lighter in his hand and yelling was heard by the neighbors and they told the police this when they arrived. There were exigent circumstances in this case. **State v. Miranda**, 622 N.W. 2d 353 (Minn. App. 2001).

Finally, in the officer-in-danger exigency cases, consider **Com. v. Davidson**, 556 A. 2d 897 (Pa. Super. Ct. 1989). A man and his female companion were lawfully stopped and the man was arrested for drug trafficking. Nothing but a pen knife was found on him. The police decided to drive his car to the station house and to take his female companion in that car. Knowing that drug dealers are often armed, the female's attempt to get at her heavily-laden purse prompted the officer to fear the presence of a gun. He seized the purse and found a gun and considerable drugs and money. The

Pennsylvania court found that this was a valid protective search. This is a common sense decision.

V.   To Knock Or Not To Knock and Exigency

From 1789 until 1995, the decision to knock and announce or execute a warrant without knocking and announcing was not seen as a constitutional issue but was seen only as an administrative concern. With its decision in **Wilson v. Arkansas**, 514 U.S. 927 (1995) the "no knock" issue was made a matter of constitutional concern with further detail provided in **Richards v. Wisconsin**, 520 U.S. 385 (1997) and **U.S. v. Ramirez**, 523 U.S. 65 (1998). What does the Court say? No better source exists than the **Ramirez** decision, of a unanimous Court, where chief Justice Rehnquist explains their prior holdings. From page 70 of Ramirez we find these words: "In two recent cases we have considered whether and to what extent "no-knock" entries implicate the protections of the Fourth Amendment. In **Wilson v. Arkansas**, 514 U.S. 927, 115 S. Ct. 1914, 131 L. Ed. 2d 976 (1995), we reviewed the Arkansas Supreme Court's holding that the common-law requirement that police officers knock and announce their presence before entering played no role in Fourth Amendment analysis. We rejected that conclusion, and held instead that "in some circumstances an officer's unannounced entry into a home might be unreasonable under the Fourth Amendment." Id. at 934, 115 S. Ct. at 1918. We were careful to note, however, that there was no rigid rule requiring announcement in all instances, and left "to the lower courts the task of determining the circumstances under which an unannounced entry is reasonable under the Fourth Amendment." Id. at 934, 936, 115 S. Ct., at 1918, 1919.

In **Richards v. Wisconsin**, 520 U.S. 385, 117 S. Ct. 1416, 137 L. Ed.2d 615 (1997), the Wisconsin Supreme Court held that police officers executing search warrants in felony drug investigations were never required to knock and announce their presence. The Court concluded that this blanket rule was overly broad and held instead that "[i]n order to justify a 'no-knock' entry, the police must have a reasonable suspicion that knocking and announcing their presence, under the particular circumstances, would be dangerous or futile, or that it would inhibit the effective investigation of the crime by, for example, allowing the destruction of evidence." Id., at 1421.

Destruction was the key issue in **Ramirez**. The officers in this latest "no knock" case were told about weapons that were likely to be found in the garage. To neutralize that threat an officer broke the garage window and pointed a gun through that open window. The defendant thought a burglar was breaking in and he pulled a gun and fired it into the garage ceiling. A shout of "police" caused the owner to throw the gun and to lie prone on the floor. He admitted he fired the gun and that he was a convicted felon. He moved for suppression and the trial court suppressed and the Ninth Circuit affirmed.

The issue of damage was addressed. *First*, the Court notes that neither **Wilson** nor **Richards** address the damage issue. *Second*, they note some damage can indeed be expected. *Third*, the critical issue in damage cases turns on the "touchstone" of reasonableness. *Fourth*, "Excessive or unnecessary destruction of property in the course of a search may violate the Fourth Amendment, even though the entry itself is lawful and the fruits of the search not subject to suppression" (at page 70). In this case the police had probable cause to believe that an escaped felon named Shelby was believed to be in Ramirez's home. Shelby had a violent past and vowed to do no federal time. Dangerousness abounded in this case. The conduct of the police in this case was labeled by the Court as "clearly reasonable." The court tells us to re-read **Pennsylvania v. Mimms**, 434 U.S. 106 (1977). At this point they "uncork" the one unanswered question. Does excessive or unnecessary destruction of property during a search violate the Fourth and require suppression? Put another way as they did in footnote 3, was there a "sufficient causal relationship between the breaking of the window and the discovery of the gun to warrant suppression of the evidence"? In this case the breaking was reasonable so they did not have to address that issue. They closed by noting that 18 U.S.C. §3109 merely codified the common law and the reasonableness standard of **Richards** is the beacon to follow.

As an aside since Wisconsin's "blanket rule" was overruled, the Wisconsin court had to figure out what to do with defendants who lost suppression motions while Richards was the law. The answer was simple. The rule was at the time the "rule of the land" and as such, as held in **State v. Ward**, 604 N.W. 2d 517 (Wisc, 2000), the evidence was admissible and remains admissible. This is a good faith-reliance on appellate decision case. (See the discussion of the "good faith" taint remover in Chapter One).

The District of Columbia, under the D.C. Code §23-524(a)(1995) and their own case, **Poole v. U.S.**, 630 A. 2d 1109 (D.C. App. 1993) require (1) "concrete particularized evidence" that they reasonably believe weapons were on the premises and (2) there was a realistic possibility that the occupant or occupants would use the weapons against them. Thus in **Moore v. U.S.**, 2000 WL 177590 (D.C.) the question was whether such a reasonable fear existed. The police were told they would confront three men with guns in their waistbands. These facts were included in the affidavit; information that came from a reliable informant who observed the men and the guns in the apartment to be searched. But did police have gun-using propensity evidence? Yes, these men said they would use the guns to protect their drug business. This was sufficient to waive knock and announce, especially since the warrant was issued to gather those weapons.

Kansas was faced with a somewhat unusual set of circumstances in **State v. Shirley**, 2000 WL 262914 (Kan..). Two search warrants were involved in Mr. Shirley's case. The first was a violation of no-knock waiver standards. The execution of that warrant caused the death of a police officer. Because of the shooting the police arrested Shirley and did not execute the first warrant. A second warrant was issued at 10 a.m. (seven hours after the first attempt). That affidavit also included the first affidavit. The second warrant was executed and the defendant claims the evidence as gathered were fruits of the poisonous tree (the aborted -no-knock attempt). The court here agreed with the appeals court that the no-knock portion of the first warrant was "bad." Citing **Segura v. U.S.**, 468 U.S. 796 (1984), the Court said since the first warrant was not executed, as a search and the second warrant used no information gathered in the first, aborted attempt, there was an independent source for the evidence seized. (See the discussion in Chapter One).

VI.   True Emergency

"Because the emergency exception... requires that the entering officer subjectively believe that the an emergency exists, the officer's motivation is the linchpin...." In **Frazier v. Cast**, 771 F. 2d 259 (C.A. 7th 1985), the testimony indicated there was no real concern for Mr. Frazier's health – only the hypothecated possibility. The real reason for the entry was the desire, an impatient desire, to arrest Frazier. The exigency argument was an afterthought. Most courts, therefore, require a showing of an immediate need for police assistance in the protection of human life to bring this exception to bear. The police must be motivated by the emergency and not by the intent to arrest or secure evidence. There must be a reasonable connection between the emergency and the area entered. **State v. Cecil**, 311 S.E. 2d 144 (W.Va. 1983) In this case police entered a trailer looking for a missing child. The police were required to promptly assess ambiguous information concerning life threatening consequences thus their actions were found to be proper.

In **State v. Ohlinger**, 475 N.W. 2d 54 (Mich. 1991), the police entered the defendant's home without a warrant and ultimately arrested the defendant for drunk driving and other traffic charges. Why was this arrest upheld? The police arrived at the scene of an automobile accident and were told that one of the drivers who had been injured left the scene. Concerned that he might need medical attention they followed his trail to his home. They knocked; no response. They had another officer call the home; no response. Fearing the worst, they entered and finally found the defendant in his bedroom. He was not seriously injured though his head was bleeding. What Ohlinger was, however, was drunk. The primary motivation for entry was to provide medical help. If the motivation is legitimate the officer does not have to avoid making an otherwise lawful arrest when lawfully in a residence.

In **U.S. v. Good**, 780 F. 2d 773 (C.A. 9th 1986) the police were contacted immediately about a person being pistol-whipped, stabbed and thus in need of help. Police then learned that Good had taken one of the stabbing victims with him. They went to his house looking for the victim. Good had apparently gone home rather than take his victim to a hospital. This, the court held, gave rise to a reasonable belief in the police that someone with Good had been seriously injured and that entry was necessary to assist the injured person. His conviction for unlawful possession of a firearm by a felon was upheld. The court also indicated there was not even time to get a telephonic warrant. Being on the premises lawfully, police were allowed to seize the gun seen in plain view in the defendant's truck.

Conduct prompted by the motive of preserving life has been upheld by courts in a wide variety of circumstances as long as the search is not motivated by intent to arrest or seize evidence. In **Smith v. State**, 419 So. 2d 563 (Miss. 1982), strong probable cause existed to believe that Mrs. Roberts was in trouble because when defendant was arrested he had bloody hands. When police receive a call for help after a shooting they have a right to enter. The plain view of the gun in one case gave rise to probable cause that it was the weapon used. **State v. Jolley**, 321 S.E. 2d 883 (N. C. 1984). This was, of course, justified under branch one of the plain view doctrine – a legal exigent search was underway and the gun was immediately known, due to probable cause, to be crime involved. Likewise, where the police have been involved in a gun battle and are told by someone that a woman and child might be in the apartment, the police have the right to enter at the end of the gun battle to see if anyone needs aid. **Bolden v. State**, 634 S.W. 2d 710 (Tex. Crim. App. 1982).

In yet another case, police observed an abused child at a hospital and learned that there were other children at home. The police went to the apartment to see if these children were alright even though the abusive parents told the police that a neighbor was taking care of them. While standing in the hall, police had the neighbor coax the children to come to the open door so that the police could check on their condition. While waiting, the police saw a paddle and asked the neighbor about it. The neighbor told them she had seen the parents use it on the deceased child. The police then seized the paddle. The court said the seizure was justified on plain view through exigency. **People v. Bruen**, 500 N.Y.S. 2d 806 (N.Y. App. Div. 1986).

Suppose an emergency situation arises which calls for police action but when police arrive at the scene the injured owner of a place says, "Don't come in." Can the police cross the threshold to search for the assailant even though they are told he is gone? The police, when they arrived soon after the report of the assault, saw spent bullet casings, blood on the porch, broken glass and blood on the protesting owner. How were they to act? Was it probable that the assailant was still there? Was it probable that she had been told to tell police the assailant was gone to allow a later escape? Was it probable that others were injured in the house needing treatment? If the answer to all of these is yes then the threshold may be crossed for a limited search for the assailant or others injured. Thus the case came within the exigency doctrine under the totality of these circumstances. So finding, the court in **People v. Thompson**, 770 P. 2d 1282 (Colo. 1989) admitted the marijuana that was hanging in plain view.

The justification for the emergency branch of the exigency doctrine is that the preservation of human life is paramount to the right of privacy. **State v. Fisher**, 686 P. 2d 750 (Ariz. 1984). But the state must be able to point to specific and articulable facts from which it may be determined that the action was necessary thus calling for immediate police response. **State v. Paahana**, 666 P. 2d 592 (Haw. 1983) and **Koza v. State**, 681 P. 2d 44 (Nev. 1984). The specific and articulable facts are not always easy to determine. Suppose police go to an apartment building in response to a brutal attempted rape of an elderly woman. Suppose there are no blood trails, moans or other indication of further victims in the building, but the police hear loud music blaring from a brightly lit next door apartment. Is it reasonable for the police to believe that there might be other victims needing aid and thus to enter the apartment? A California court answered in the affirmative and, held the police were acting with a benevolent purpose and in light of the brutal attack, found that a delay may have resulted in the unnecessary loss of life. **People v. Cain**, 264 Cal. Rep. 339 (Cal. Ct. App. 1989).

There can be little doubt that an emergency exists when fire officials receive a report that the cellar of a building is covered with oil and cans of an incendiary nature are scattered about and near a working oil furnace. **Com. v. Marchione**, 422 N.E. 2d 1362 (Mass. 1981). But no emergency exists where the victim of a sleeping pill overdose is in the hospital and the nature of the prescription is known to the physician. Thus in **State v. Williams**, 367 N.W. 2d 314 (Iowa App. 1985) the entry of the house was held invalid.

At least one court has found that the emergency doctrine applies to animals as well as people. **State v. Bauer**, 379 N.W. 2d 895 (Wis. App. 1985). The police found a dead, two-year-old, emaciated horse. The humane officers were called. They knew of prior problems with this place. The court found a compelling need to stop ongoing suffering of other animals and said the entry was motivated by a desire to render aid.

Whether an emergency exists and whether aid can be rendered are generally the key questions. It is always a close call in the death cases. In a Pennsylvania case a man had been reported missing and someone else had used his credit card since that report. The police were called by the daughter who told them that there was a large, unfamiliar garbage bag in the basement. Since this sounds like a dead body case, true emergency principles do not seem to be present. But sometimes courts sense the possibility that there might still be life and let a search stand as justified under the emergency doctrine. Fortunately, in this case, consent was given for the search but the court felt bound to talk about an emergency justification. **Com. v. Maxwell**, 477 A. 2d 1309 (Pa. 1984). An Illinois court appears to have dispensed with the "need for aid" criteria and found an emergency to exist by the presence of a known dead body. The court did try to talk logically about the "apparently dead often are saved by swift response" but the odor of rotting flesh in this case seemed to indicate a person beyond help. **People v. McGee**, 489 N.E. 2d 409 (Ill. App. 1986).

The emergency aid exigency is not without its limits and merely speculative entries based on very sketchy information may be deemed unreasonable. In a Michigan case police heard a radio report of a possible shooting from an anonymous source who did not know the location of the motel, the room involved, or even the correct name of the motel. Two adjoining rooms were mentioned in the report. The report did not indicate whether anyone was even injured. Without attempting any corroboration, the police went to the two named rooms and forced themselves into the room, seized a gun and narcotics in the twenty to thirty minutes in the room. The Michigan Supreme Court was unwilling to protect this search and seizure because of the high speculation and low reasonable belief that a person needed aid. **People v. Davis**, 497 N.W. 2d 910 (Mich. 1993).

Finally, a New York court reminds everyone that even exigency has a scope limit and once the emergency is resolved the right of continued search stops. In this case a 20-minute search was found to be properly limited. **People v. Taper**, 481 N.Y. S. 2d 745 (N.Y. App. Div. 1984). Once the police determined that no one else needed help they stopped this search and subsequently secured a warrant for a further search.

VII.   Protective Sweeps

As discussed in the search incident materials in Chapter Twelve, the protective sweep cannot be justified under the wingspan doctrine of **Chimel**. If they are to be upheld at all, they must be sustainable on an exigency base. Are courts to use a probable cause base or are they to allow the hypothecated case based on profile allowing the police to "plain view" themselves through the premises? These are the issues that had to be addressed. There had been an exponential growth of the "protective sweep" approach to searches incident to arrests. How had they fared? Several courts expressed concern that general searches prohibited by **Chimel** may be undertaken upon the pretext of a protective sweep. The general justification in these cases (most often) was that drug dealers and their friends are dangerous and may be hidden in other areas of the house. Several courts had approved them. **U.S. v. Jackson**, 700 F. 2d 181 (C.A. 5th 1983); **U.S. v. Whitten**, 706 F. 2d 1000 (C.A. 9th 1983); **U.S. v. Riccio**, 726 F. 2d 638 (C.A. 10th 1984); **U.S. v. Hill**, 730 F. 2d 1163 (C.A. 8th 1984); **U.S. v. Palumbo**, 742 F. 2d 656 (C.A. 1st 1984) (but too broad in this case); **U.S. v. Escobar**, 805 F. 2d 68 (C.A. 2d 1986); **State v. Bakke**, 723 P. 2d 534 (Wash. App. 1986); **Tamborino v. Superior Court**, 226 Cal. Rep. 868, 719 P. 2d 242 (1986); **U.S. v. Standridge**, 810 F. 2d 1034 (C.A. 11th 1987); and **U.S. v. Whitehorn**, 813 F. 2d 646 (C.A. 4th 1987) (not well motivated in this case, however).

A number of these cases met the **Chimel** problem head on and were prone to take an "exigency-not-anticipated-by-**Chimel**" approach. Others used **Segura,** the "seizure-awaiting-warrant" case as having justified protective sweeps. Most of these cases dealt with incidents of arrest and not "awaiting-warrants" type factual situations. The First Circuit declared a protective sweep illegal in **U.S. v. Curzi**, 867 F. 2d 36 (C.A. 1st 1989). The F.B.I. had tailed a terrorist (suspected) to a house in Cleveland. No search warrant was secured. The house was surrounded by a SWAT team. By phone the occupants were ordered out. First three children and then three adults came out of the house. Without pausing, the officers entered the house and a security check or protective sweep was made. Guns and explosives in plain view were found. A warrant was obtained and executed. The First Circuit saw the ploy here as a sophisticated bootstrapping operation. The police knew they would enter the home no matter who exited. The First Circuit would approve a protective sweep only if there is probable cause and either consent, exigency or other acceptable reason for forgoing a warrant. In this case the house was staked out for nearly a day and they isolated it for over 2 hours. They had all the information they needed, therefore, for up to a day. The court said time was ample, manpower abounded, the premises were surrounded and secured, the neighbors had been led to safety and the whole thing went down during the daylight hours – a situation well in control. There was no exigency. On the other hand, the Eighth Circuit noted, by not looking for the stolen money but only for the gun they had seen in the defendant's hand before his arrest, the police had sufficient exigency to make a sweep of the defendant's house to protect the children who were to be left alone at the house. **U.S. v. Antwine**, 873 F. 2d 1144 (C.A. 8th 1989).

In **Hunter v. Com**, 378 S.E. 2d 634 (Va. Ct. App, 1989), the wounded owner of the house claimed that there were other armed persons in the house. The SWAT team entered and within a few minutes other police entered to secure what had been "swept." The second entry group was approved by the Virginia court as a continuation of the sweep begun earlier under a proper exigency. The court noted that the only evidence seized was that in plain view. How could the Virginia court justify this? Consider this language from the opinion:

> "Here, Hunter had summoned the police to his home and then told Commander Bennett at the scene that there were three armed people inside the house. This information provided a valid legal basis, conceded by the accused, for the SWAT team to enter the home and search for victims and armed persons. The SWAT team had to proceed carefully in their search and were not in the position to seize any items seen in plain view. Seizing evidence found in plain view during a search for armed suspects could have made a dangerous situation even more dangerous. Following the initial sweep, additional police officers went into the secure areas to make sure no suspects could leave the house or tamper with the scene. We conclude that the procedure did not violate the defendant's rights because the time lapse between the initial sweep and the subsequent entry was minimal and because there was no extension of the search during the second entry but merely a search of items found in plain view. The subsequent entry by Detective Kennedy was not a re-entry but a continuation of the first lawful entry by the SWAT team."

Virginia borrowed the rationale from an earlier Wisconsin decision, **La Fournier v. State**, 280 N.W. 2d 746 (Wis. 1979) which approved immediate entry by other officers for the purpose of securing plain view evidence that could not be secured by the officer who was then rendering assistance. Though neither **Hunter** nor **La Fournier** is totally unreasonable, they are the kinds of decisions that encourage police officers to test the time and entry limits of exigency. Courts should be aware of that when tempted to expand the exigent circumstances doctrine.

In a Maryland case the police entered a building to arrest a defendant on a valid warrant. The defendant emerged from the basement and was arrested. Police had no reason to believe (in the sense of probable cause) that anyone else was there or that any danger existed, but they "swept" the basement anyway and came up with the plain view evidence. The Maryland court said, "But when the privacy expectation is high, only the most exigent circumstances will justify a warrantless intrusion; when the sanctity of the home is involved, there are few exceptions to the warrant requirement." Urgency, immediacy and compelling need must be demonstrated. A mere possibility that others might be present without more, they held, is not enough. **Buie v. State**, 531 A. 2d 1290 (Md. 1988). The **Buie** case was accepted by the Supreme Court and arguments were held in December of 1989. **Buie** was decided February 28, 1990. As the Supreme Court saw the issue, the focus was whether "protective sweeps" required probable cause or articulable suspicion and not whether such sweeps were ever permissible. A majority of the Court held that articulable suspicion is all that is needed to justify a sweep during a proper in-home arrest. They also noted that such a sweep will only allow plain view of areas and things that can contain the body of a person. The court made clear this is an exigency driven matter and not a part of the **Chimel** "wingspan" doctrine. **Maryland v. Buie**, 494 U.S. 325 (1990).

The **Buie** case did not significantly change basic exigency law that requires an ending point to the exigency. Once the purpose for the sweep is over the police who have not run upon another exigency, or do not have a valid consent or warrant must vacate the house or other property. As one court held, the exigency that permits a protective sweep does not justify a three-hour warrantless search for evidence. The court said that once the cursory inspection permitted under **Mincey**, **Hicks** and, now **Buie**, is over, the exigency ends. In this case they were seeking perpetrators and victims. As the court noted, the authorization for a warrantless search must be limited lest it becomes a means for avoiding the warrant requirement altogether. This was a particularly troublesome case due to the fact that a police officer was shot to death at this scene. **Com. v. Lewin**, 555 N.E. 2d 551 (Mass. 1990).

However, **Buie** will invite "pro-police" courts to expand warrantless searches. Illustrative of that potential is a decision from a New York appellate court. A defendant had just come out of an apartment when he was arrested. Looking in the slightly opened door the police decided to open it fully to see if other drug dealers were present. They did see others whom they arrested upon entering because of what was seen in plain view. Viewing drug enforcement as inherently dangerous, this court felt the officers were justified in their actions. **People v. Febus**, 556 N.Y.S. 2d 1000 (N.Y. Sup. Ct., App. Div. 1990). The inherently dangerous language in **Febus** makes it sound like they were accepting the hypothecated case of danger rather than requiring proof that either because of warnings shouted by the arrester, or because the arrest was particularly noisy, the police had at least the articulable suspicion required in **Buie** to make a sweep.

Buie also failed to address by way of *dicta* whether "outside-the-house" arrests ever justify a sweep of the home. The Court's rule only permitted sweeps when an "in-home" arrest was made even though the defendant was outside the home but still at the arrest scene. The **Buie** case casts some doubt on cases like **Antwine** (*supra*). The Court will have to address this issue soon. The "in-home" limitation appears to be just that; otherwise they would not have modified the word arrest.

I was sure that the entry issue would arise despite the tight facts of the **Buie** decision. Indeed the issue arose in a case from Texas. **Reasor v. State**, 12 S.W. 3d 813 (Tex. Crim. 2000). Reasor had just returned to his home after selling and delivering cocaine to his customers. As he drove in his driveway the police blocked his car and drew their guns. Evidence with white powder was seized and **Miranda** warnings were given. It was "at this point," the court noted that three officers entered the house to do a protective sweep. After the sweep was completed, the officers took the defendant inside his home. No evidence of crime was found in their sweep. A consent to search was given by the defendant that was found to attenuate any search problems. However, since this court had not addressed the "protective sweep" doctrine, it decided to lay out some instruction on the issue. They found the sweep illegal. No officer expressed any concern that some third person was in that home and posed a danger to their safety. So no necessity was shown as required by **Buie**. There may indeed be a threat to the police from inside a house when the initial arrest takes place outside the house. However, there must be testimony regarding the facts of more than a hypothetical threat. In this case the officers had no suspicion of a threat to their safety, let alone an articulable one. In fact they had just arrested one of the most peaceful drug dealers in America. The neighborhood appears to be a simple middle class area of tract houses and not the "mean" streets of a major city. Police must not think that the protective sweep is automatically good in all cases.

VIII. Conclusion

The exigent circumstances doctrine requires a determination that the time needed to secure a warrant will truly jeopardize the ability to seize the evidence, capture the felon or protect the life of another.

The evidence destruction cases require first a probable cause showing of the evidence's presence and second, a probable cause showing of the realistic risk of destruction, not merely an hypothecated risk. The older "evidence in the process of destruction" standard no longer seems applicable. Courts, however, have shown a strong reluctance to accept mere ready destructibility as sufficient justification to enter the premises without a warrant. Practically speaking, the more sizable the cache – the larger it is, the heavier it is – all courts seem to require stronger probable cause of destruction. The more evanescent the evidence the more willing the courts have been to ease the probable cause requirement. On the other hand, the more that police have probable cause as to the location of the person or evidence, the less likely the police cry of exigency will be heeded. Most courts still are resisting hypothecated escape or destruction justifications offered. Courts should be careful in the drug raid cases that they are not being lured into profile-based hypothecated warrantless entry approvals.

Though the probable cause standard is clearly enunciated in escape, destruction or danger to officer cases, such is not the case in true emergency cases. Courts often speak in terms of reasonable and articulable facts and also note the existence of self-verifying details that called for prompt, reflexive action. The more corroborative details of bloodshed that exist the more prone are courts to allow entries even over the objection of an owner or possessor of the property. Life is more dear than the privacy right.

As was discussed in the search warrant chapter, close calls on probable cause when a warrant is used will be resolved in favor of the government. The opposite rule is true, however, in the exigency cases. Close calls are resolved in favor of privacy. This is certainly true in the escape, destruction and danger to other officers cases but is not applied so strictly in the true emergency cases due to the "life is dear" preference. The true measure is the entry motive: if to search, then even in the face of an emergency, the exigency played no part in the entry except to be used as a ruse. In such a case the evidence gathered is inadmissible.

One final *caveat*. The exigency doctrine does not exist for the convenience of the government. It is not countenanced as a method of enhancing police efficiency. The best way to judge a case of exigency is to view the situation as either a "flashflood" or seepage. The closer the police are to a flashflood of information the more likely one can legitimately find an exigency. If the information was always here the less likely such seepage yields exigent circumstance.

VIII. Exigency Check List

A.   Identify type of exigency
   1.   Destruction _____
   2.   Escape _____
   3.   Danger to officer or other _____
   4.   True Emergency _____
   5.   Protective Sweep _____

B.   If Destruction:
1.   Probable cause to believe evidence present?
       ___yes ___no (if no rule inadmissible on this ground)
2.   How long did probable cause exist before entry?
       _____
       (note: length of time key at this point)
3.   At what time did probable cause arise
       daytime _____ evening _____
       past midnight but before 9:00 A.M. _____
4.   Is evidence easily destructible because evanescent
       _____yes _____no
5.   Did police use mere possibility or profile based
       destructibility theory ___yes ___no
       (if yes rule evidence inadmissible)
6.   List facts of probability persons present but not under
       arrest   and   why   believed   they   would
       destroy:_____
       _____
       _____
7.   List reason why other personnel not available to secure
       premises:_____
       _____
8.   If exigent circumstances present was evidence seized:
       a.   that for which there was probable cause
              yes ___ no ___
       b.   plain view evidence
              yes ___ no ___
       c.   seized within proper scope
              yes ___ no ___
       d.   seized before target evidence
              yes ___ no ___
9.   Telephonic warrant jurisdiction – why was this process by-
       passed:_____
       _____

C.   If Escape
1.   Hot pursuit case? yes ___ no ___
       (this is the time factor)
2.   Defendant armed? yes ___ no ___
       What facts indicate further flight probable manpower
       issue:_____

   size of building issue:_____

   type of crime_____

   connection of suspect w/community:_____

D. If Danger to Officer or Other

(arises from arrest of prime felon cases)

1. How would defendant know that person present inside is undercover agent:_____

2. Is there a mere presence of gun

  yes ___ no ___

3. Is there a presence of gun plus persons with propensity to use it:

  yes ___ no ___

4. Is there a presence of a gun plus persons who could inadvertently be injured by it

  yes ___ no ___

E. If True Emergency

1. How information gained

 a. 911 or other call

  yes ___ no ___

   i. caller identified

   yes ___ no ___

   ii. caller person present at place

   yes ___ no ___

   iii. caller anonymous

   yes ___ no ___

   iv. facts corroborated

    yes ___ no ___

 b. Police observe or hear circumstances

  yes ___ no ___

   i. immediate need response reasonable

   yes ___ no ___

   ii. police motivated by the emergency

   yes ___ no ___

   (no pretextual entries allowed)

2. List specific and articulable facts known before entry:

_____

_____

_____

3. Dead body case reasonable belief that life may still be saved: yes ___ no ___

(note: presence of odors of decaying body may deny this entry)

F.   If Protective Sweep
1.   Be most careful to observe articulable suspicion here (profile based-hypothecated case not a valid sweep)
2.   Does it appear police were going to enter anyway

yes ___ no ___

3.   Look for planned arrest scenario
4.   Did police truly limit scope

yes ___ no ___

5.   Spell out facts of immediacy and compelling need

_____

_____

_____

G.   Identifying Police Created Exigency
1.   Was the exigency foreseeable/unforeseeable?
    a.   was the operation planned

        yes___no___

    b.   was a forced entry planned

        yes___no___

2.   Was a warrant prepared?

yes___no___

3.   Was a warrant in the process of preparation?

yes___no___

4.   If answer to either 2 or 3 is *yes* why was it not secured before the operation took place
    a.   did the exigency intercede while an attempt to secure the warrant was underway?

        yes___no___(If yes, then likely an exigency)

5.   If conclusion is that there was before the operation:
    a.   ample probable cause and
    b.   time to obtain a warrant and
    c.   a plan that will create an emergency entrance then there is *no* exigency

IX.   Exigency Reminders

A.   The words exigent or exigency are defined in terms of:
- urgent need

- emergency
- pressing or compelling need

B. What major interests would be affected by delay (the one to three hour warrant issuing time):
  - escape
  - evidence destruction
  - danger to others
  - life threatening emergencies

C. Warrant securing processes not to be overlooked:
  - affidavit and application preparation
  - finding a judicial officer
  - solemn warrant issuing process
  - hearing - four corners doctrine?
  - questions by court
  - query? does telephonic warrant process shorten issuance time?

D. **REMEMBER**
  - if exigent both the search and seizure functions can be performed

E. **Question**
  - are we moving closer to the hypothetical case of destruction and away from probable cause?

F. What is the dilemma in Knock and Announce exigency – are we too suspicious of police motives?

G. How do police create their own exigency thus losing exigent circumstances rights?

H. Can the use of anticipatory warrants resolve some cases?

Exigency and Contraband: Five non-exclusive relevant factors determining exigency. Taken from **State v. Ellison**, 1998 WL 731584 (Del. Super.).

1. The degree of urgency involved in the situation and the amount of time necessary to obtain a warrant;

2. The reasonable belief that the contraband is about to be removed from a particular location;

3. The possibility of danger to the police officers guarding the sight of the contraband while a warrant is sought;

4. Information indicating that the possessors of the contraband are aware that the police are on their trail; and

5. The ready destructibility of the contraband and the knowledge that efforts to dispose of narcotics and to escape are characteristic behaviors of persons engaged in narcotic traffic.

CHAPTER TWELVE
INCIDENTS OF ARREST AND DETENTION

I.   Introduction

    This chapter focuses on the issues of arrest or detention of a person and the legal incidents that flow from a legal stop. The consequences of illegal police conduct and its effects on a court's jurisdiction are also considered. The topics specifically covered are: (1) Entries to make arrests in dwellings and other apartments; (2) Pretextual stops/arrests; (3) Searches incident to arrests; (4) Searches incident to searches; (5) Stop and frisk; (6) Hot pursuit; and (7) Jurisdiction and the illegal arrest. Other related topics are covered elsewhere. Probable cause to arrest, the felony/misdemeanor distinction, and criminal profiles are discussed in the Chapter Two. Issues of standing, state action, attenuation, inevitable discovery, independent source and good faith are discussed in the Chapter One on the exclusionary rule.

II. Entries to Make Arrests

A. Decisional Law

The U.S. Supreme Court has held that a probable cause based warrantless and nonconsensual entry into a suspect's home in order to make an arrest prohibits the use of evidence discovered in the house. **Payton v. New York**, 445 U.S. 573 (1980). The Fourth Amendment was created to protect both people and property. Warrantless searches and seizures of property conducted without a warrant are condemned by the plain language of the Fourth Amendment. The warrantless arrest of a person is a species of seizure required to be reasonable. Physical entry of the home, done unlawfully, was the chief evil the Amendment sought to prohibit. Absent exigent circumstances, the threshold of the house may not be crossed without a warrant or consent, and any evidence gathered therein is inadmissible. But is the arrest otherwise lawful? Does the attenuation doctrine apply to searches and interrogations conducted outside the house?

In the final paragraph of the majority opinion, the **Payton** Court considered the question whether an entry would be permitted when the officer has an arrest warrant for the individual but not a search warrant for his home. The Court held: "If there is sufficient evidence of a citizen's participation in a felony to persuade a judicial officer that his arrest is justified, it is constitutionally reasonable to require him to open his doors to the officers of the law." Thus, the Court found that an arrest warrant impliedly gives a limited authority "to enter a dwelling in which the suspect lives when there is reason to believe the suspect is within." With the foregoing the Court raised the problem of "knock and announce" or "no knock entries" to execute the arrest warrant. The safer practice would be to secure both an arrest warrant for the person and a search warrant for his residence making him the object to be sought therein as evidence of a crime. Then the "knock" or "no knock" issues can be resolved under traditional decisional law the general guidelines for which are set out in three leading cases discussed in Chapter Three.

There is a limit to **Payton,** as announced by the Court in **New York v. Harris**, 495 U.S. 14 (1990). **Payton** only requires suppression if the evidence is taken while *within the protected area*. Harris was arrested without a warrant, consent, or exigency, but upon probable cause. A statement, after a proper **Miranda** warning and waiver, was taken from the defendant at the police station and not while they were in the house. The Court said this was not the fruit of the illegal entry but was the fruit of a probable cause based custody (legal arrest). The "evidence gathered therein" language was not inadvertent language in **Payton. People v. Segoviano**, 725 N.E. 2d 1275 (Ill. 2000) (in accord).

Payton tells us that probable cause alone does not justify the breaking of a building to effect an arrest and gather evidence. The roots of that part of **Payton** are found in **Miller v. U.S.**, 357 U.S. 301 (1958). There were no warrants in **Miller**. The police did not expressly demand admission and did not state their purpose. They broke in and arrested the defendant. **Payton** now limits **Miller's** holding by ruling there is no right to expect an open door after knocking and announcing but it did establish "knock and announce" requirements for federal arrest warrant law which should continue after **Payton**. However, this decision did not establish knock and announce as a constitutional requirement since the principle is based on tradition or statute and is not found in the Fourth Amendment. That issue would be raised and decided in **Wilson v. Arkansas** and **Richards v. Wisconsin** discussed in Chapter Three.

What **Miller** did not answer and **Payton** did not define is the issue of what constitutes exigent circumstances for bypassing either the warrant or knock, or both, when required. For direction in that area, the Court's plurality opinion in **Ker v. California**, 374 U.S. 23 (1963) must be considered. The officers in **Ker** entered quietly and without announcement in order to prevent the destruction of contraband. They had obtained a passkey from the manager of the building. The justices pointed out that this case was "loaded" with probable cause. Additionally, Ker's furtive conduct in eluding the officers shortly before the arrest was grounds for the belief that Ker might well have been expecting the police. Therefore, the Court found a satisfactory exigent circumstance to bypass the warrant and knock and announce. To seek a consent in this instance would have been both foolish and dangerous, the Court reasoned.

A more explicit recognition of the exigent circumstance exception came in **Sabbath v. U.S.**, 391 U.S. 585 (1968). By a radio strapped to an informer who gained entry to the defendant's apartment, the agents knew that the defendant was in the apartment. The agents had neither arrest nor search warrant. The agents went to the door, knocked, waited a few seconds, turned the knob on the door, and entered the apartment. The Court said this was a breaking. No semantic games will be employed to require the destruction of the door. Rights will not be given up that easily. The amount of force used to open the door is unimportant. Turning to the issue of exigent circumstances, the Court rejected the government's theories. The government wanted an exception that an announcement might have endangered the informant or the officers. The Court noted that there was no factual foundation for such an exigency. There was no basis to assume that the defendant was armed or that the informant was in any danger. Besides, there was no showing by an independent investigation that the defendant had narcotics in his possession, so that the agents were unable to take advantage of the "destruction of evidence" exception. This is fully discussed in the search warrant materials at Chapter Three. This decision is a rejection of the hypothecated case of exigency.

Once police have a warrant for the defendant's arrest there is one more substantial issue beyond "entry," "knock and announce," or "exigent circumstances" concerns. The Court in **Payton** did not address the issue of an entry into some third party's dwelling to serve a warrant of arrest. Resolution of the third party's dwelling issue came in **Steagald v. U.S.**, 451 U.S. 204 (1981). The Court said: "The issue in this case is whether, under the Fourth Amendment, a law enforcement officer may legally search for the subject of an arrest warrant in the home of a third party without first obtaining a search warrant. *Concluding that a search warrant must be obtained absent exigent circumstances or consent, we reverse....*" (emphasis added). As they launched into the rationale of the opinion, the Court noted that they assumed, without deciding, that the information about the whereabouts of the defendant was sufficient to establish probable cause for a search warrant. In any event, the conclusion by the officers was never subjected to detached scrutiny. Without exigency or consent, untested conclusions would create a significant potential for abuse.

While searching for the man named in the arrest warrant the officer came across cocaine. A search warrant was then sent for while a second warrantless search was conducted, which produced more incriminating evidence. Under the later-obtained search warrant 43 pounds of cocaine were uncovered. Despite all this, the Court reminds us of the presumption of innocence: "The right protected – that of presumptively innocent people to be secure in their homes from unjustified, forcible intrusions by the government-is weighty." It also noted that to the extent that searches for persons pose special problems, they believed that the exigent circumstances doctrine was adequate to accommodate legitimate law enforcement needs. However, no exigency existed here.

Only Justices White and Rehnquist dissented. The most telling point of their dissent concerned when the dwelling of another may become the dwelling also of the arrestee. They say that could happen in a few days and even when the arrestee maintains a separate residence elsewhere. The uncertainties thus created and the imponderable variety of questions created concerned them most. The White-Rehnquist dissent issue was faced in **Minnesota v. Olson**, 495 U.S. 91 (1990). Olson was an overnight guest in another's home when the police entered to make the warrantless arrest. The Court said a person gains an expectation of privacy in such a situation, therefore, the warrantless entry without consent or exigency violated the guest's rights. Why? It so held because guests expect that their host will respect the guest's privacy interests even without the guest having a legal interest in the place or the ability to legally authorize who may enter the premises.

However, the overnight guest runs the risk that the owner will consent to the police entry and that consent trumps the acquired privacy right according to the majority in **Olson**. That is what happened in **State v. Grant**, 614 N.W. 2d 848 (Iowa App. 2000). That court recognized the right of the possessor to consent to the search of the guest's bedroom, but not the jacket of the guest found in the room. Stupidly, the guest denied owning the jacket; thus, it was deemed abandoned. See also **State v. Brown**, 612 N.W. 2d 104 (Iowa App.2000).

Minnesota subsequently says that the protection of **Olson** can be overcome by plain view independent evidence of a crime if the officer gets the view from an unprotected or non-Fourth Amendment area. The gun was seen in plain view. **State v. Talley**, 2000 WL 136082 (Minn. App.) (unpub. op.). An independent crime seen by the officers institutes a new reason for a search incident with "Wingspan" attached.

Other warrantless entries have been before the Court. The next case concerned a warrantless entry of the defendant's home to arrest a D.U.I. suspect. **Welsh v. Wisconsin**, 466 U.S. 740 (1984). A first offense in Wisconsin for D.U.I. is a non-jailable offense. Of course, even for this offense the defendant has to submit to or refuse a breath test. In any event, the defendant in this case walked away from the scene before police arrived. Police trailed him rather promptly to his house. They knocked on the door and were admitted by the defendant's daughter. The police went to the defendant's bedroom and arrested him. Would this constitute exigent circumstances? No. "Our hesitation in finding exigent circumstances where house arrests are involved is especially appropriate when the underlying offense is relatively minor." In the minor offense category presumably unreasonable (warrantless) searches are most difficult to rebut and the burden on the state is very heavy. It is a matter of proportionality and the gravity of the offense is important. Notice that the Court is not stifling all such searches, but they are saying that it would be difficult to justify such a search. The fact that this was evanescent evidence did not persuade them. (See Chapter Eleven.) Note also that the consent given by the daughter to enter the public areas of the house obviously did not extend to the private bedroom. The Wisconsin Supreme Court had decided the case on the basis that there were exigent circumstances. It was this finding that compelled the Court to take the case. Repeating that warrantless entries of homes are presumptively unreasonable, and stressing the sanctity of the home, the Court, when looking at this legislatively classified minor offense, said in such cases the presumption of unreasonableness is difficult to rebut. Had Wisconsin classified DUI as a serious crime rather than a mere civil offense the Court would have been presented with a closer question. Thus, "...the gravity of the underlying offense..." is an important factor when making an exigency analysis. **Welsh** at 753. The public safety threat was over, and no issue existed concerning the defendant's need for medical attention.

The destruction of evidence issue – dissipation of the blood alcohol level – was next addressed. Wisconsin made the offense non-criminal with no imprisonment possible. By so classifying the activity, Wisconsin said it is not important and in that posture a warrantless entry could not be made on this state of the law and "on these facts...." **Welsh** at 754. Thus, there is a possibility that evanescent evidence could allow an entry in a misdemeanor case. However, was there a consent to enter in this case? Yes, there was. The Court was unable to address that issue since it was not decided at the trial level because the trial court said there were exigent circumstances. Thus, from the facts used by the Court, there is only an indication that the stepdaughter answered the door and the police entered. The Court, because of the record, assumed no valid consent. However, this should not be taken to mean that a youth could not give such a consent. That is yet to be decided by the Court.

The South Dakota court dealt with a non-jailable offense and a hot pursuit into the home of the defendant in **State v. Flegel**, 485 N.W. 2d 210 (S.Dak.1992). This court focused on an exigency. It examined the evanescent evidence rule since blood-alcohol level was at issue. However, it felt that balancing privacy, non-), jailability, and dissipation meant no exigency existed to cross the threshold. The case was remanded to resolve the validity of the consent to enter that was given by the father to enter the son's (defendant's) home.

The next "entry" case is **Washington v. Chrisman**, 455 U.S. 1 (1982). A young university student was observed on campus carrying a gin bottle. State law prohibited people under 21 from having alcoholic beverages. This young man, Overdahl, was stopped by an officer and was asked to produce his identification.

Overdahl said it was in his dorm room. Rather than let his quarry get away, the officer accompanied Overdahl to his room. Overdahl went in and left the door open so that the officer who remained outside, could "plainly" see the entire room where the ultimate defendant, Chrisman, sat surrounded by his drugs and paraphernalia. The officer entered and confirmed the nature of the evidence, arrested Chrisman, and gave **Miranda** warnings. Chrisman argued that the officer had no right to enter the room and seize contraband without a warrant. Since no one has a right to contraband, the only issue would be whether the plain view was fairly obtained. Monitoring the movements of an arrested person is reasonable. Once he arrested Overdahl, the officer could accompany him to his room for the purpose of obtaining identification. The officer thus had a right to stay at Overdahl's elbow at all times, so exigent circumstances as outlined in **Payton** are not needed. In the final analysis, police are going to continue crossing the threshold as in the **Payton** case. The Court will not nail down any one exigency leaving that to the lower courts to analyze on a case-by-case basis.

In **State v. Wren**, 768 P. 2d 1351 (Idaho 1989), the court decided the following issues: "May police officers, in whose presence a nonviolent misdemeanor has occurred, pursue the alleged offender into his home and seize him there without an arrest warrant?" It held that they *may not* unless: (1) The pursuit is triggered by flight from a lawful arrest outside the home; and (2) Exigent Circumstances, other than the pursuit itself, make it necessary to enter the home without a warrant. Here, the defendant had been making noise in his backyard. The police answered a complaint and told Wren to "quiet down." Wren walked into his home, but came back out and directed some expletives at the police. As he began to re-enter his home, the police followed him into the house and chased him into the living room. They subdued him and perhaps for the first time told him he was under arrest. There is some dispute whether they told him to stop or announced an arrest outside the house. In any event, the search incident produced marijuana. Since exigency is based on necessity, the risk of danger, destruction or loss of evidence or escape must be especially clear if the underlying offense is relatively minor. Hot pursuit, the court said, is not an exigency in and of itself. Hot pursuit plus exigency justify the entry into one's home to make a warrantless arrest.

In a like manner, the Washington Court of Appeals held that a traffic offender's home could not be entered without a warrant despite the fact of hot pursuit in **City of Seattle v. Altschuler**, 766 P. 2d 518 (Wash. Ct. App. 1989). The defendant ran a red light and he was pursued to his home some 12 blocks away in a 30 m.p.h. chase with siren wailing, lights flashing, and loud speaker blaring. As the garage door was descending, an officer entered the garage and arrested the defendant. Here, the court noted, there was no grave offense, nor a person believed to be armed. What evidence was there to destroy? His escape had been stopped and he was cornered. Accepting the precept of the **Welsh v. Wisconsin** case, the court agreed that hot pursuit is not an exigency in and of itself. The court said the home could have been watched while a warrant was secured. Since the police had blocked his driveway, his ability to leave by car was seriously curtailed. Since the arrest, therefore, was unlawful, the conviction for resisting arrest was unlawful.

There have been some interesting developments with regard to **Steagald** since it was issued. **Steagald** involved an arrest target in Steagald's home and the evidence suppressed belonged to Steagald. Should search incident rights have been extended to the arrest target because no warrant was secured for the owner's home? Two courts have said the arrest target should also get **Steagald's** protection. **Com. v. DeRosia**, 522 N.E. 2d 408 (Mass. Sup. Jud. Ct. 1988) and **U.S. v. McIntosh**, 857 F. 2d 466 (C.A. 8th 1988). These interpretations fit the Court's analysis in **Minnesota v. Olson**, (*supra*).

The case of **State v. Meyer**, 1998 WL 876800 (S. D.), is a fairly pure **Steagald**-like case. The police went to Meyer's home with an arrest warrant to seek a suspect in a crime. The granted motion to suppress was upheld. The court said: "**Steagald** creates a distinction between the interests protected by an arrest warrant and a search warrant. An arrest warrant may open the door of the suspect but it does not, without consent or exigency, open the door of a third person." It closed by suggesting that the officers, acting prudently, should have secured a search warrant to find the subject of the arrest since they knew where he was.

One of the questions left unanswered in **Olson** was whether a mere guest or social guest had any reasonable expectation of privacy or standing in the home of another. In a 5-1-3 decision the Supreme Court seems to say no. **Minnesota v. Carter,** 525 U.S. 83 (1998). Before discussing the majority opinion, let us examine the historical concurrence written by Justice Scalia. He is no lover of the general right to privacy some believed was announced in **Katz**. He is a strong believer in the "that society is willing to protect" theory and the new federalism that has grown in the last three decades. He says further expansion of what gets protected is left to "the good judgment, not of this Court, but of the people through their representatives in the legislature." Once again he takes us back to our roots and scolds the attorney general of Minnesota for not reading and citing the search provisions of the first 13 states as the "parents" of the Fourth Amendment to the Bill of Rights.

He notes that Pennsylvania and Vermont used the term "their houses" but that many of the others used "his," the singular possessive pronoun. But he notes that "their houses" truly meant "their respective houses" and said that interpretation was the outgrowth of the "castle doctrine." In fact he cites the seminal case of **Semayne v. Gresham**, 5 Co. Rep. 91a, 93a, 77 Eng. Rep. 194, 198 (K.B. 1604) and that they "proclaimed that the house of anyone is not a castle or privilege but for himself and shall not extend to protect any person who flies to his house." " He further notes that **Johnson v. Leigh**, 128 Eng. Rep. 1029, 1030 (C.P. 1815) held that "in many cases the door of a third person may be broken where that of the Defendant himself cannot; for though every man's house is his own castle, it is not the castle of another man." He then goes on to cite a Massachusetts case that gave protection to a boarder of a house and cited this limiting language, "when speaking of the boarder... the occupiers or any of his family... who have their domicile or ordinary residence there... including a boarder or a servant... who have made the house their home" as getting the protection but, he says, they added, "the house shall not be made a sanctuary for one such as a stranger or perhaps a visitor who upon pursuit takes refuge in the house of another for the house is not his castle and the officer may break open the doors or windows in order to execute his process." He then sums up his conclusions by stating (critically), "We went to the absolute limit of what text and tradition permits..." (in **Olson**) "when we protected a mere overnight guest against an unreasonable search of his host's apartment..." and then added "it is entirely impossible to give that characterization to an apartment that he uses to package cocaine." He closes by saying that to give a 31-year-old decision like **Katz** more credence than the clear text of the Fourth Amendment and its 400-year-old supporting tradition is to destroy the people's right to direct their elected representatives as to what they really want.

That being said, what exactly did the Court hold in **Minnesota v. Carter**, 525 U.S. 83 (1998)? The Court did not address the legality of the officer's "plain view" and solely addressed Carter's expectation of privacy or standing. They did not, as I read it, address the "social guest but not an overnight guest" issue. What they did decide is summed up, in their words:

1. Respondents here were obviously not overnight guests, but were essentially present for a business transaction and were only in the home a matter of hours.
2. While the apartment was a dwelling place for Thompson, it was for these respondents simply a place to do business.
3. Property used for commercial purposes is treated differently.
4. While it was a "home" in which the respondents were present It was not their home.

5.   The purely commercial nature of the transaction engaged in here... and... the relatively short period of time on the premises and the lack of any previous connection between the respondents and householder.
6.   These were people who were simply permitted on the premises.
7.   There was no legitimate expectation of privacy and we do not have to decide, in this case, whether the officer's observations constituted a "search."

Justice Breyer concurred primarily on the ground that no search took place because the officer had not entered curtilage to the specific apartment and he had seen what any passerby could have seen. If the case were to come back on that issue, I believe that the vote, at best, would be 6-3.

The very first court to use **Carter** was the Eighth Circuit, but it did not involve a house entry; rather it involved an automobile search (pick-up truck). The primary issue was seen as one involving standing and the failure to prove that the driver had his uncle's permission to use the truck. The driver appealed and the Eighth Circuit said of **Carter,** "We note that recently the Supreme Court has observed that in determining whether a defendant is able to show the violation of his (and not someone else's) Fourth Amendment rights, the definition of those rights is more properly placed within the purview of substantive Fourth Amendment law than within that of standing." Thus, the core issue of **Carter** was not faced in **U.S. v. Lyton**, 161 F. 3d 1168 (8th C.A. 1998).

B.   Threshold Crossing: Warrantless Arrests: Evidence Gathering

I.   Misdemeanors: Lawful:
   A.   consent to enter given by one with standing.
   B.   *major* exigency exists [by implication]. **Welsh v. Wisconsin**, 466 U.S. 740 (1984) and **Payton v. New York**, 445 U.S. 573 (1980).
II.   Felonies: Lawful:
   A.   consent to enter given by one with standing.
   B.   exigent circumstances – standard application.
   C.   third person's home – no standing in Defendant. [police carry no rights to plain view or search incident/wingspan]. **Payton**
III.   Unlawful Entries: Consequences:

A.   Defendant's Home
1.   arrest – lawful for jurisdictional purposes
2.   plain view--not lawful – "fruits" of privacy invasion
3.   search incident: in the home
    a.   of person – unclear – unlawful "fruits" – police may be limited to frisk – better to wait until booking inventory at jail
    b.   of wingspan – unlawful "fruits"
4.   interrogation incident in the home – unattenuated "fruits" in most cases. **Payton/Harris**

B.   Third Party's Home-Defendant *Mere* Guest:
1.   arrest – lawful for all purposes--no standing
2.   search incident – in home:
    a.   of defendant – o.k.
    b.   of wingspan – not permitted due to unlawful entry--no help from "sweep" or "plain view" exceptions **Steagald v. U.S.,** 451 U.S. 204 (1981).

C.   Third Party's Home – Defendant *Overnight* Guest:
1.   same result as Defendant's home
2.   standing exists in Defendant **Minnesota v. Olson**, 495 U.S. 91 (1990).

D.   Third Party's Home – Defendant-Business invitee
1.   no standing in commercial/business guests
2.   **Minnesota v. Carter,** 525 U.S. 83 (1998)

E.   Attenuation Doctrine/Fruits/Unlawful Entries:
1.   applies only to evidence taken within the privacy area.
2.   does *not* apply to evidence taken outside the privacy area--no need to--search outside the privacy area is otherwise lawful. **New York v. Harris**, 110 S. Ct. 1640 (1990) [note: **Harris** is a **Miranda**

case and not a search case – search conclusion by implication].

IV.   Escorted Views: Lawful: Any Crime:
   A.   police with justifiable reason may accompany freshly arrested Defendant to his home.
   B.   police not required to give up their "quarry."
   C.   plain view applicable. **Washington v. Chrisman**, 455 U.S. 1 (1982).

THRESHOLD CROSSINGS

First: Determine Nature of Crime:
   a.   misdemeanor--in presence/art. susp.?
   b.   felony--probable cause/art. susp.?

Second: Determine whether warrant for arrest exists:
   a.   misdemeanor
   b.   felony

Third: 1.   If warrant for *misdemeanor* exists:
   a.   if no state rule--follow **Welsh v. Wisconsin** *dicta* and **Payton** *dicta*
   b.   *but* check state rule whether arrest warrant without search warrant gets officer across threshold.

   2.   If warrant for felony exists:
   a.   be sure *no* state rule exists that also requires search warrant for defendant's home.
   b.   follow **Payton** *dicta*

Fourth: If *NO* warrant for arrest exists:
   1.   Determine if defendant has standing in place entered:
   a.   do **Payton/Olson/Carter** analysis – D's own home – or – overnight guest – or--business invitee – mere social guest

   2.   If D has standing was there:
   a.   exigency – higher standard for misdemeanor entries – see **Welsh v. Wisconsin** *and*
   b.   make sure it is *not* routine felony arrest *per* **Payton** in felony case
   c.   consent – consult consent cases to make sure consenters had *apparent* authority to grant

consent and that scope of consent not exceeded

3.   If D has *no* standing follow **Steagald,** *but* remember scope of search incident limited to person of arrestee *and* no plain view *or* search incident rights in *home* of third person as against the third person but may have plain view as against the visitor if a joint possession type case

<u>Fifth:</u>   Remember:

1.   The arrest for a felony without warrant, consent, or exigency *but* based on probable cause *is* otherwise lawful and *only* the search incident wingspan (and perhaps in-house inculpatory statement gathering) are proscribed, thus, search incident of the arrestee in the place and other evidence gathering outside the protected area *are* lawful not requiring a fruits analysis under **WongSun** – see **Harris**

2.   Though a police officer may not compel an arrestee (absent a search warrant – see **Summers**) to take police into the arrestee's home, an officer may accompany an arrestee into his or her home if arrestee requests the entry – see **Washington v. Chrisman**

C. Warrantless Felony Arrests Based on Probable Cause

Standing Issue – Targeted Defendant

- no standing in third person's home if targeted defendant is a mere guest – arrest of targeted person lawful, of course – search incident of defendant and things he controls should then also be lawful

- standing exists in third person's home when targeted defendant is an overnight guest – entry without consent or exigency is unlawful cutting off search incident rights within that home *but* frisk should be alright since arrest is otherwise lawful – later search incident may not be attenuated from illegal entry and may not be contemporary *but* booking and jailing inventory for this otherwise lawful arrest would appear to be proper – plain view of police not lawful as to third person *or* targeted defendant – exigency or consent of third person to enter cures warrantless entry

- no standing when targeted defendant is arrested in public areas of an apartment building in which defendant has his home or in which he is an overnight guest in third person's home

- standing of course exists when in his own home – entry by police lawful only when they have exigent circumstances, consent or, at a minimum, an arrest warrant – *however* – arrest itself is lawful *but* no plain view/no search incident/presumptive coercion for **Miranda** purposes – attenuation doctrine applicable.

III. Pretextual Stops and Arrests

A. The Background for Whren

After **Gustafson** and **Robinson** (discussed in the next section) a custodial arrest based on valid cause arising from a minor traffic violation has been held sufficient to justify a full search of the arrestee. Police now have an incentive to use custodial arrests for minor crimes pretextually to avoid probable cause and warrant requirements of the Fourth Amendment when the officer only suspects the arrestee of further and more serious criminal activity. Should anything be done? Are pretextual arrests legal? How can one measure police motivation when "intent" as an element of crimes is so poorly defined? Should further limits be placed on police discretion to make arrests? The U.S. Supreme Court in **U.S. v. Lefkowitz**, 285 U.S. 452 (1932), held that, "an arrest may not be used as a pretext to search for evidence." In **Robinson,** the Court merely cited **Lefkowitz** but did not expressly overrule it. It did say, "It is the fact of the lawful arrest which establishes the authority to search" and "that intrusion being lawful, a search incident requires no additional justification."

Before going further, a good argument can be made to allow pretextual arrests. First, as **Stacey v. Emery** (*supra*) taught, probable cause is probable cause. The good faith or malice of the officer plays no role in that fact. So motive should not be a factor. Second, if we do not allow good motive to legitimate an illegal arrest then why should we allow bad motives to destroy a perfectly good arrest? Is not that the teaching of **Giordenello** (*supra*) and its progeny? For example, in **U.S. v. Van Ness**, 868 F. 2d 1167 (D.C. Ct. App. 1990), the defense attorney wanted to challenge the officer's motive for the arrest to try to show that with more arrests his chances of promotion were greater. The trial judge denied this line of cross-examination. The

D.C. appellate court agreed with the trial judge. Some few questions were allowed on this "bias issue" before the judge denied further questions. It found no reversible error.

What occurred in **Lefkowitz**? The significant concern in the case was that an arrest warrant based on a proper complaint sufficiently charging a crime was used as a pretext to conduct a search incident to that arrest because the officers were not able to know the papers sought were there and could not meet particularity standards when it came to describing those papers. The Court clearly noted that no fresh offense took place in the officer's presence nor did they have probable cause to believe in a fresh felony.

Therefore, what appears now to be prohibited after **Chimel**, **Gustafson**, and **Robinson** was very unclear. To use probable cause on a prior committed offense to produce a person for questioning on an unrelated offense appears suspect, but to produce him for questioning on the charge is not. However, through **Colorado v. Springs**, we learn that, as long as **Miranda** advisements are observed, a defendant is not entitled to know the subject matters to be covered when he waives his **Miranda** rights. Thus pretextuality in that context is not taboo.

To use probable cause or an arrest warrant on an unrelated charge to get physical (or mere) evidence on the unconnected newer charge does sound suspicious in terms of **Lefkowitz**. **Go-Bart Importing**, cited in **Lefkowitz**, dealt with a two-year- old conspiracy, an illegal entry, forced consents all in the hope."..that evidence of a crime might be found...." The **Go-Bart** concerns are now dealt with by other cases and chief among them is **Bumper v. North Carolina** and its coercive consent decision. The "wingspan" doctrine of **Chimel** is really the true limiting device chosen by the Court and its reference to pretextuality in **Gustafson** and **Robinson** has to mean conduct outside **Chimel** and **Colorado v. Springs**.

Does pretextual mean "mere hopes" or even "high hopes" of finding something else? It does not if we take the words of Chief Justice Rehnquist seriously. As he indicated in the plain view cases, leading to the elimination of the inadvertence requirement, the hope of finding something else while properly looking for other evidence is not inherently evil. That same rationale can be applied to an objectively proper arrest with all the incidents attendant thereto. See **Texas v. Brown**, 460 U.S. 730 (1983) and **Horton v. California**, 496 U.S. 128 (1990). Only the dissent discussed pretextuality *vis-à-vis* inadvertence in the 7-2 decision in **Horton**. The only significant fact that can be gleaned from the U.S. Supreme Court's earlier pretextual search and arrest decisions is all of them were based on a pure Fourteenth Amendment due process analysis that predated the application of the Fourth Amendment to the states through the Fourteenth as announced in **Mapp v. Ohio** (*supra* at Chapter One). A very valid argument can be made that pretextuality is an anachronism when police activity otherwise satisfies Fourth Amendment pronouncements.

In any event, pretextuality was still a matter of concern. A district court in Illinois rejected the "objective standard" of two federal circuit decisions which said look not at the officer's presumed motives. **U.S. v. McCambridge,** 551 F. 2d 865 (C.A. 1st 1977) and **U.S. v. Hallman,** 541 F. 2d 196 (C.A. 8th 1976). In rejecting the rationale of these cases, the court said if you did that then you would never find a pretextual arrest. Yes, the court agreed, proving subjective motives is a problem, however, the objective standard ignores rather than solves the problem. The objective standard does away with the "jealous regard" of individual rights dictated by **Mapp.** The court went on to say, "We cannot reward the officer for subterfuge." **U.S. v. Keller,** 499 F. Supp. 415 (N. D. Ill. 1980). Though the **Keller** case is one of the best reasoned cases against the objective standard, it still "flies in the face" of the clear command of **Gustafson** and **Robinson** (*infra*).

The attack on **Robinson** and **Gustafson** is grounded on local constitutional requirements as required by **Oregon v. Haas.** Michigan rejected **Gustafson** and **Robinson** as did Washington. Oregon took the more practical route in **State v. Tucker,** 595 P. 2d 1364 (Ore. 1979). Some of this reaction is based on the acknowledged fact that some officers are using the valid misdemeanor arrest as a pretext to otherwise "get at" the person stopped. Oregon recognized this as a fact of life and did not find such a practice objectionable enough to prohibit such police conduct. The defendant had run a stop sign while on his bicycle. The officers admitted that he was a suspicious looking character and that they really were not concerned about his violating the traffic law. The defendant was taken to the police station where it was subsequently discovered that the bicycle and the T.V. in the bike's basket were stolen. Citing **U.S. v. Robinson,** the court said they saw no reason to get into a pretextual arrest definition. They could find no reason to turn an otherwise valid stop into an invalid stop because the officer's primary purpose was other than enforcing the traffic law. The Constitution, they said, does not require such a strained approach. Objectively valid stops will not be tainted by subjective intent. **State v. Tucker,** 595 P. 2d 1364 (Ore. 1979).

The most scathing attacks upon **Gustafson** and **Robinson** can be found in a law review article cited as Folk, T.R., *The Case for Constitutional Constraints Upon the Power to Make a Full Custody Arrest*, 48 Cinn. L. Rev. 321 (1979). Folk indicates that the failure "to define 'reasonableness' of custody beyond the requirement of probable cause actually has become anomalous." Since anomalous means irregular or abnormal it is difficult to understand his position. When a person commits an act declared "criminal" by society the right of custodial arrest arises in society. That we have not always put such people in full custody is due to custom and usage, not law. Of course, that was the exact point made in **Gustafson** and **Robinson**. He, like others, most fear the pretextual arrest as the way to partake of **Schmerber**, **Chimel** and other search incident cases. The U.S. Supreme Court could have limited custodial arrests or forbidden them when pretextual. They were aware of such conduct and did not so limit the rule announced in **Gustafson** and **Robinson**.

Alaska has found a middle-of-the-road method of partially accepting **Gustafson** and **Robinson**. They would allow a search, but would not permit the opening of closed containers especially where the justification is pre-incarceration inventory. Insofar as such an inventory is not an incident of arrest, they do reject **Gustafson**. But is the court correct to assume that the ultimate jailing is not an incident of arrest. Their reasoning would not square with **Schmerber**, **Cupp**, **Rochin**, **Irvine**; all discussed below and certainly throws grave doubts on the use of booking and jailing inventories discussed below at section IX. **Reeves v. State**, 599 P. 2d 727 (Alaska 1979).

Joining the list of states offended by the practice of full field strip searches for minor offenses is Illinois through one of their district appellate courts. The court found that strip searches are "humiliating, degrading, and embarrassing." Thus, in their decision, a person arrested for a misdemeanor for which there is a present bail cannot be subjected to a "fishing expedition." The police tried to justify this search on grounds of police safety, maintenance of order in the jails and to disclose the fruits of the crime. Since this person would not have been incarcerated such a search was not justified. **People v. Seymour**, 398 N.E. 2d 1191 (Ill. App. Ct. 1979). The court did not address the issue of a "pat-down" which would be legitimate for safety purposes when the "stranger" is taken to the station house to post bond. On appeal the Illinois Supreme Court took a different approach and upheld the search. Since the police did not know whether his record would move the charge from a misdemeanor to a felony, the police had a right to protect themselves from danger, to lock him up, and conduct this search. The Court, however, did express concern whether full-field strip searches were appropriate in all custodial arrests. **People v. Seymour**, 416 N.E. 2d 1070 (Ill. 1981). Interestingly, the same Illinois intermediate appellate court upheld a traffic violation seizure that was used intentionally and pretextually to get to a man the police suspected to be a murderer. **People v. Anderson**, 531 N.E. 2d 116 (Ill. App. 2 Dist. 1988).

Kansas takes a hard line saying that an officer who observes speeding has not only the authority but the duty to stop that vehicle even though the primary motivation for doing so is the investigation of a different crime. **State v. Guy**, 752 P. 2d 119 (Kan. 1988). This, like the Oregon case, is the epitome of the pure objective analysis.

The Eleventh Circuit adopted a modified objective test to be applied. **U.S. v. Smith**, 799 F. 2d 703 (C.A. 11th 1986) and **U.S. v. Bates**, 840 F. 2d 858 (C.A. 11th 1988). Florida in **Kehoe v. State**, 521 So. 2d 1094 (Fla. Sup. Ct. 1988) and the Tenth Circuit in **U.S. v. Guzman**, 864 F. 2d 1512 (C.A. 10th 1988) all have adopted the Eleventh Circuit's pretextual traffic stop analysis. The standard is whether a reasonable police officer would have stopped the vehicle absent an additional invalid purpose. **U.S. v. Kikumura**, 698 F. Supp. 546 (D. N.J. 1988). It appears that Utah has also taken this position. **State v. Sierra**, 754 P. 2d 972 (Utah Ct. App. 1988) and **U.S. v. D'Antoni**, 856 F. 2d 975 (C.A. 7th 1988).

In any event, courts were still wrestling with the **Gustafson/Robinson** decisions. Colorado, which at one time rejected **Gustafson**, had to uphold custodial arrests for driving without a license since such powers were conferred on police by statute. **People v. Meredith**, 547 A. 2d 10 (Colo. 1988). Connecticut finally adopted **Robinson** to some extent. Upon a custodial traffic arrest, under their constitution, a search which is to be limited to a search for weapons may be conducted and the search must be limited to what appeared reasonable to the officer at the time. **State v. Dukes**, 547 A. 2d 10 (Conn. 1988).

States were still having some difficulty trying to decide the scope of arrest law in their states. The 1988 decision of the Texas Court of Criminal Appeals illustrates this. The defendant was arrested for a cracked taillight. Would that justify the stop of the car even though it was possibly a crime (not visible from 100')? No, the court said, this arrest is bad and the "fruits" of the search incident are inadmissible. No real mention of pretextual arrest was made but the concern could be read between the lines. **Vicknair v. State**, 751 S.W. 2d 180 (Tex. Ct. Crim. App. 1988). The awesome power given police when an automobile is involved definitely flavored their decision. After a few years Texas has decided to abandon its subjective pretextual stop rule and has adopted the purely objective stop rule in its place. Therefore, if an officer has any objectively justifiable reason to stop a defendant, it does not matter that the motive was to stop the defendant for a totally unrelated purpose. They also made clear that they would not accept the "modified objective test" which asks the question whether a reasonable police officer would have made this stop if the subjective intent was not present. **Garcia v. State**, 827 S.W. 2d 937 (Tex. Crim. *en banc* 1992). The Texas position is, in essence, the position taken by Oregon in the **Tucker** case (*supra*).

States like Alaska which either rejected **Gustafson-Robinson** or allowed only searches for weapons upon minor crimes arrest have found they have had to expand their exception of **Gustafson-Robinson**. Alaska now allows the search of containers on the person of the arrestee even if the container is too small to hold a conventional weapon as long as the officer reasonably believes that an unusually small weapon is concealed therein. **Jackson v. State**, 791 P. 2d 1023 (Alaska Ct. App. 1990). All police in Alaska have to do now is learn how to testify – and they will. It would have been simpler to have recognized **Gustafson** rather than challenge the imagination of the police.

B. Pretextuality: The End of the Fourth Amendment Concern?

It appears that the Supreme Court has finally put the issue of pretextual auto stops to rest for Fourth Amendment purposes through their decision in **Whren v. U.S.**, 517 U.S. 806 (1996). A car sat at an intersection at a stop sign for 20 seconds or more – an unusual observance of the sign. The driver was staring into the lap of the passenger. As the officers "u-turned" to take another look, the car made a quick right turn and sped off. The car stopped, however, at the next traffic signal. The police pulled up next to the car and one officer got out, approached the car, identified himself, and told the driver to put it in park. All of this took place in a "high drug incident" area of Washington, D.C. Plainview revealed large plastic bags of what appeared to be crack cocaine in Whren's hands. The occupants were arrested and several types of drugs were discovered by the incident search. The stop to warn about traffic violations was a pretext, argued the defense, but the trial court denied suppression and the defendants were convicted. The D.C. Court of Appeals upheld the convictions saying the officer's subjective motives were not relevant if a reasonable police officer would also have made this stop. The defense argued that probable cause is not enough. They argued the only motive for the stop must be traffic without consideration that other criminal evidence might be seen. Can ulterior motives invalidate a police stop that is otherwise lawful? No, said the U.S. Supreme Court, and it suggested that **Gustafson** and **Robinson** be studied more carefully. The bottom line is simple. The Court says: "For the run-of-the-mine case, which this surely is, we think there is no realistic alternative to the traditional common-law rule that probable cause justifies a search and seizure."

C. Post – Whren Decisions

Since **Whren** was decided several courts have reacted to it. Let us examine those cases and see if state courts are willing to accept **Whren**.

The defendant in a Connecticut case was seen "aggressively hitchhiking" by standing in the road. Coupling this with a radio report of a burglary and robbery in the vicinity, the officer decided to do a **Terry** stop so he get an explanation for this "aberrant" behavior. When the officer got a closer look at the person, he felt the man fit the description of one of the burglars and evasive answers to questions caused the officer to have the defendant empty his pockets while awaiting the burglary-robbery investigator. The defendant said that the initial seizure was pretextual, thus illegal. In citing **Whren**, the court noted that: "We emphasize that the standard for determining whether reasonable suspicion or probable cause existed in a given scenario is an objective rather than a subjective one... and that the ultimate questions of reasonable suspicion to stop and probable cause are subject to *de novo* review on appeal." So Connecticut appears willing to accept **Whren. State v. Rodriguez**, 684 A. 2d 1165 (Conn. 1996).

One Florida appellate court said the test is "could have" stopped not "would have" stopped when assessing the reasonableness of a seizure. Thus, it is fully in line with **Whren. Pretrel v. State**, 675 So. 2d 1049 (Fla. App. 1996).

The Appeals Court of Massachusetts reads **Whren** approvingly *but* tightly. In their case a stop was made not to enforce a law but because the officer thought the driver was "lost and needed help." This court requires a law enforcement motive and will not accept the "good Samaritan" motive. **Com. v. Canavan**, 667 N.E. 2d 264 (Mass. App. 1996).

Nevada follows **Whren** as noted in **Gama v. State**, 920 P. 2d 1010 (Nev. 1996). Speeding was the issue. Why? On most Nevada highways the speed limit is 65 and that is not often enforced as confirmed by the stopping officer. On a first observation the speed was 73 m.p.h. In the interim, a car like Gama's was described to the trooper as one that might be carrying drugs. So the officer again caught up to Gama, called the narcotics unit and clocked Gama going 56 m.p.h. in a 45 m.p.h. construction zone. The stop was made. Narcotics officers arrived with their drug-sniffing dog. The dog "alerted," and the search ensued. The drugs were found. The issue was simple, was this evidence the fruits of a pretextual stop? Under their prior case law it would have been illegal fruits. However, this court agrees with the Supreme Court and they overruled their "would have" rule and adopted **Whren's** "could have" rule. Likewise, see **State v. McCall**, 929 S.W. 2d 601 (Tex. App. 1996), where they held that the officer's motive is not the issue as recognized in earlier Texas Court of

Criminal Appeals cases. Also in accord, see **State v. Trudeau**, 683 A. 2d 725 (Vt. 1996). The Vermont court carefully noted that such a stop only invoked certain immediate police rights such as plain view, *etc*. The stop right does not create greater search rights.

As West Virginia wisely notes, there must be actual lawful cause underpinning the stop. A mere hunch is not enough. The officer in **State v. Andrew**, 474 S.E. 2d 545 (W.Va. 1996), had only a hunch that a juvenile petition had been filed and assumed Andrew had not paid his traffic citation. A forceful stop without justifiable cause cannot qualify as a consensual encounter.

The reason for the stop must be based on legitimate objective facts leading to a conclusion that an illegality is occurring or has occurred for **Whren** to be invoked. If those facts cannot be articulated then the stop is indeed pretextual. Such was the conclusion of the Minnesota Supreme Court in **State v. George**, 1997 WL 13232 (Minn.). However, we do not know this court's position on **Whren** because only the concurring justice cited **Whren**. However, nothing in the majority opinion indicates a rejection of **Whren**. The concurring justice was centered on the validity of the consents sought upon traffic stop.

Arizona's case discussing **Whren** distinguished between a sufficient reason for a stop and a mere instinctive, intuition driven motive to stop. In the latter instance **Whren** cannot be used since no lawful basis for a seizure existed independent of the "real" reason for the stop. But they do indicate a willingness to accept **Whren** in the proper case. **State v. Gonzalez-Gutierrez**, 927 P. 2d 776 (Ariz. *en banc.* 1996). Operating on a "hunch" therefore is not **Whren** protected. The Supreme Court would agree with this.

Arkansas fully accepts **Whren** upon a probable cause based stop. In fact they say that: "In assessing the existence of probable cause, *our view is liberal rather than strict* "(emphasis added). **Burris v. State**, 954 S.W. 2d 209 (Ark. 1997). However, Arkansas some three years later has put some qualifications in the use of **Whren** by their decision in **State v. Sullivan**, 16 S.W.3d 551 (Ark. 2000), if not overruling **Burris** by implication, which, of course, no court can do because it is a gutless move. We may come to know the case as the "roofing hatchet" case since the U.S. Supreme Court has been asked by the state to take certiorari. Anyway, one justice says **Whren** is mostly *dicta* and felt that pretextuality must be dealt with on a case-by-case basis which, of course, was the standard before **Whren** – the standard the U.S. Supreme Court jettisoned. The Arkansas court says they are giving some but not total authority to make pretextual arrests. The U.S. Supreme Court said courts were not to judge that;

the courts were only to judge whether there was a lawful basis for the stop. If the stop was lawful, the nature of the stop determined what followed immediately. **Whren** cannot be read more broadly than that.

A California defendant argued that the normal test for probable cause should not apply to traffic stops and thus argued the "reasonable police officer" standard rejected by **Whren**. This court stressed that **Whren** requires the application of the traditional common law probable cause rule. **People v. Rodriquez**, 62 Cal. Rep. 2d 345 (Cal. App. 1997). The District of Columbia case says that a D.C. officer who observes a Virginia car without a valid Virginia inspection sticker has probable cause under **Whren** to make a stop. **Russell v. U.S.,** 687 A. 2d 213 (D.C. App. 1997).

Subsequent to the **Petrel** case (*supra*), Florida's high court weighed in on the **Whren** debate through its opinion in **Holland v. State**, 696 So. 2d 757 (Fla. 1997). Per **Holland,** the Florida court accepts **Whren** and thus overruled the "reasonable officer" test first announced in **State v. Daniel**, 665 So. 2d 1040 (Fla. 1995). The **Holland** case dealt with the issue of exceptions to **Whren** raised in **Whren** itself. **Whren** noted exceptions would be very rare. In **Holland** a "dangerousness" exception was urged in that a stop at night by an unmarked police car would be "dangerous." Indeed, the officer in this case so testified. However, the Florida court said one officer's subjective opinion was not enough to create a rare exception. To go down that path would tend to allow the exceptions to **Whren** "to take over the rule of **Whren.**"

In a Georgia case a loud exhaust system provided probable cause for a stop. The officer did admit the exhaust noise was not the primary reason for the stop. **Buffington v. State**, 492 S.E. 2d 762 (Ga. App. 1997). An Illinois case involved a faulty brake light even though "it" masked other reasons for the stop. **People v. Thompson**, 670 N.E. 2d 1129 (Ill. App. 1996). Accord see **State v. Hollins**, 672 N.E. 2d 427 (Ind. App. 1996) where a failure to use a turn signal justified a stop, and **State v. Ready**, 565 N.W. 2d 728 (Neb. 1997) where the defendant used the wrong turn signal.

Iowa, agreeing with **Whren,** says that: "For Fourth Amendment purposes, the constitutional reasonableness of traffic stops does not depend on the actual motivation of the individual officers involved." **State v. Predka**, 555 N.W. 2d 202 (Iowa 1996). Accord see **State v. McBreairty**, 697 A. 2d 495 (N. H. 1997) where speeding observed trumped any issue of pretext. A corroborated anonymous tip justified a stop in **State v. Bjerke**, 697 A. 2d 1069 (R.I. 1997). Rhode Island had (two years before **Whren**) adopted a "pretext is no issue" rule in **State v. Scurry**, 636 A. 2d 719 (R.I. 1994). So far, only one Washington appeals court has adopted **Whren. State v.**

Ladson, 939 P. 2d 223 (Wash. App. 1997). One opinion still exists from another pre-**Whren** decision. See **State v. Chapin**, 879 P. 2d 300 (Wash. App. 1994).

Despite the fact that the Arkansas Supreme Court approved the use of **Whren** in a floppy license plate case, they appear to have two rules regarding pretextual stops. Without citation to their 1997 decision in **Burris** (*supra* at the preceding page) they found that police stopping a person going 40 m.p.h. in a 35 m.p.h. zone was merely a pretext to arrest and conduct a search incident. It relied on previous local cases from 1986 to 1993 and **U.S. v. Lefkowitz**, 285 U.S. 452 (1932). This indeed will cause consternation among trial judges; joy among defense attorneys, sorrow to prosecutors and total disbelief if an average citizen ever finds out. Sometimes, consistency is *not* the hobgoblin of small minds. **Arkansas v. Sullivan**, 16 S.W. 2d 551 (Ark. 2000). For some reason the Arkansas Supreme Court thought that **Whren** did not mean what it said. They felt it was mostly *dicta*. Therefore, they found that an officer who stopped a car knowing it belonged to a non-law abiding citizen did so unconstitutionally under the U.S. Constitution. That person, Sullivan, was stopped for speeding and an improperly tinted windshield. The officer, upon receiving Sullivan's license said it was at that point that he knew of Sullivan's reputation regarding narcotics. A rusting roofer's hatchet was seen on the floor of the car. The formal arrest took place and the car was searched and drugs were found. He successfully moved for suppression alleging the arrest was a pretext and a sham. The Arkansas high court affirmed the suppression. A rehearing was requested and the Arkansas court said, "we do not believe that **Whren** disallows...." such a suppression.

However, Arkansas was wrong. In a *per curiam* opinion, the Court reversed the Arkansas decision as "flatly contrary to this Court's controlling precedent." The opinion goes on to cite **Atwater v. Lago-Vista** (the seat belt arrest case; **U.S. v. Robinson** (the full field search on a misdemeanor arrest case); and, of course, **Whren**. The Court also soundly criticized the Arkansas court for saying that they could interpret the U.S. Constitution more liberally than the U.S. Supreme Court had interpreted it. The concurring justices noted the Arkansas concerns and felt there could be an exponential growth "like an epidemic of unnecessary minor-offense arrests." They hoped that would not happen, but if it did, they also hoped "the Court will reconsider its recent precedent." **Arkansas v. Sullivan**, 2001 WL 567705 (U.S.). The legitimacy of any arrest, therefore, must be analyzed by reference to the combined rules of **Gustafson**, **Robinson**, **Whren**, **Atwater**, and **Sullivan**.

D. The Historic Postscript to Whren

A final thought on pretextuality. In 1878 the Supreme Court said we were not to look at the motive of the officer in conducting an arrest or a search. The good or bad faith of the officer is not relevant: if the officer has the requisite cause for a seizure or search that is all that is important. See **Stacey v. Emery**, 97 U.S. 642 (1878) where the Court said: "If the facts and circumstances before the officer are such as to warrant a man of prudence and caution in believing that the offense has been committed, it is sufficient." The **Whren** case is merely a faithful following of **Stacey v. Emery.**

CHECKLIST: Pretextual Arrests – Are There Any?

History   Pretextual arrest doctrine was developed:

1.   early on after adoption of exclusionary rule while remnants of due process analysis of arrests still existed;

2.   before 4th Amendment was applied to the states;

3.   during the continuing debate over what constituted a search incident--scope doctrine; and

4.   before the plain view doctrine was fully developed.

Remember: Probable cause to arrest for a felony is dependent upon an objective analysis of the police conduct and *not* upon their subjective intent.

Important: The search incident doctrine as we know it today attaches to all arrests for any conduct labeled a crime *unless* the state chooses under their own constitution to distinguish minor crimes from major crimes.

Recent Development: Courts concerned about the use of arrest powers on minor crimes to gather evidence of a greater crime have been developing a modified objective test – "was stop and arrest reasonable despite the pretextual purpose?" test.

| Key Supreme Court Cases: | **U.S. v. Lefkowitz; Stacey v. Emery; Franks v. Delaware; Gustafson** and **Robinson; Chimel.; Payton et al. Horton v. California; Scott v. U.S.;** and **Whren.** |

True Pretextuality:

1. corruption of administrative search law
2. "piggy-back" searches when *no* need exists for "in aid thereof" and done solely to avoid warrant process of state or federal government.
3. corruption of consent search law:
   a. landlord entries;
   b. hotel personnel entries; or
   c. "good guy" entries is into "non-business" premises.

Final Thought:

Are pretextuality and egregiousness synonymous when viewed in light of the Court's 14th Amendment cases? Is society truly outraged and offended? Certainly the defendant is, but if all other 4th Amendment rules are observed, what is there to complain about?

IV.   Search Incident to Arrest: General Theory

When a person is lawfully arrested there arises in the police the right to conduct a search of the person. If the defendant commits a misdemeanor or a felony in the presence of an officer or if the officer has probable cause to believe that a felony has been committed, then the officer can arrest and search the defendant as an incident to a lawful arrest. This is true even if the information on the felony is hearsay as to the officer as long as all other tests of reliability are met. **Draper v. United States**, 358 U.S. 307 (1959).

A custodial arrest of a suspect based on probable cause is a reasonable intrusion under the Fourth Amendment. Since that intrusion is lawful, a search of the person incident to the arrest requires no additional justification. It is the fact of lawful arrest that allows the search. A search of a person after a lawful arrest is reasonable under the Fourth Amendment. This is true even if the person is taken into custody based on a failure to have a valid driver's license. The police officer does not have to be in fear of his or her life. **United States v. Robinson**, 414 U.S. 218 (1973). The fact that the defendant has never had a police encounter before; that the offense for which he or she is arrested is trivial; that no police regulation or statute requires custody for minor offenses does not matter. **Gustafson v. Florida**, 414 U.S. 260 (1973); a crime is a crime and allows a search incident and there are no pretextual stops for conduct labeled as a crime. **Whren v. U.S.**, 517 U.S. 806 (1996).

There had been some negative reaction to **Robinson** and **Gustafson**. Some states, by interpreting their own constitution, have rejected both decisions. The Michigan court cites its own interim bail statute as preventing such searches for minimum traffic violations. That statute merely allows a pat down for weapons. **People v. Garcia**, 214 N.W. 2d 544 (Mich. Ct. App. 1978). Other states have decriminalized their minor traffic offenses. Likewise, the Washington Supreme Court held that a minor traffic offense alone does not justify an arrested motorist's search. In fact it said a violator should only be arrested on such a charge when the motorist refuses to sign a written promise to appear on a charge. **State v. Hehman**, 578 P. 2d 527 (Wash. 1978). Then and only then would the search incident doctrine arise absent consent, exigency, or plain senses.

Berkemer (*infra*) backfired on the police in a 1988 Ninth Circuit decision. The defendant was stopped for suspected driving without a valid license. They put the defendant in the cruiser while awaiting information on his license. The police went into the defendant's car and searched two zippered bags because he had made some furtive movements when they had originally approached him. The court found no arrest had taken place thus it was only a **Berkemer** traffic stop with no right search incident. The only troubling point of the case is that the Ninth Circuit assumes the probable cause requirement applies to misdemeanor arrests. That kind of fuzzy tinkering with historical exposition does away with three centuries or more of felony/misdemeanor distinction arrest law. **U.S. Parr**, 843 F. 2d 1228 (C.A. 9th 1988) . However, that distinction is more historical than constitutional.

Like the Ninth Circuit, Wisconsin, by following **Berkemer**, found that a defendant stopped on articulable suspicion of drunk driving and asked to perform a field sobriety test was not under arrest, therefore, no search incident rights existed. **State v. Swanson**, 475 N.W. 2d 148 (Wis. 1991). Clearly, both decisions told police that they cannot have their "cake and eat it too." **Berkemer** addressed seizures less than arrests and *then* related it to the **Miranda** issue. Clearly, articulable suspicion only gives at most the "frisk" right.

Although some states rejected **Gustafson** and **Robinson**, a few like Arkansas and Iowa tried to take **Gustafson** and **Robinson** a step further to provide options to the officer regarding a search right. In Iowa, for example, the police could treat a traffic infraction as a civil offense and issue a citation but the officer was still given the search incident right. The U.S. Supreme Court refused to allow the search incident right for mere non-criminal violation. See **Knowles v. Iowa**, 525 U.S. 113 (1998).

Defense attorneys continued their assault on **Gustafson** and **Robinson**, and taking heart in the **Knowles** decision, they thought they had the case that would cause the Court to overrule those cases. The arrest of a mother in Texas for failure to wear her seat belt and for her failure to have her children seat-belted was the case the defense bar felt would cause the Court to "soften its stance." Texas made her conduct a crime; a very low level misdemeanor to be sure. The officer personally observed her conduct. He stopped her, arrested and handcuffed her. He took her to the jail where she was fully "booked," jailed for an hour and then taken before a magistrate who released her on a bond. She was charged. She entered a no contest plea and paid a $50 fine which was the only penalty she faced since this crime carried no jail time. Despite a lack of proof, the attorneys argued that at common law only arrests for breach of the peace misdemeanors were permitted to be warrantless – crimes tending to violence and not crimes such as this seat belt crime. The Court said this position is not correct nor "even necessarily the better reading of the common-law history." The Court pointed out that before America was founded "negligent carriage driving" was an arrestable offense created by Parliament. The Court felt that the worst thing they could do would be to create a rule that requires "line drawing" by the officer at the scene for a "compelling need to arrest." That would, in this author's view, embroil courts in hours of argument on suppression of evidence motions not to mention the endless appeals processes that would follow.

At the end of the opinion the Court lists the states that permit warrantless arrests for public or criminal offenses at the misdemeanor level. The 50 states and the District of Columbia have one common requirement. The offense must be committed in the officer's presence or view. However, the Court does not discourage the states, through their legislatures, to regulate by statute rather than asking the Court to regulate by Constitution. Without question this decision protects **Gustafson** and **Robinson, Whren**, *et al.*, **Atwater v. City of Lago Vista**, *et al.*, 121 S. Ct. 479 (2001).

V. Search Incident: The Mere Evidence Rule

If one can search the defendant and examine his or her clothing, what more can be done? As long as the person is lawfully under arrest, the officer can take fingerprints, have him or her give a handwriting exemplar, submit to a lineup, or give a voice exemplar. Even blood can be taken as long as the tests of **Schmerber v. California**, 384 U.S. 757 (1966) are met with regard to humane and medical techniques. Local rules should also be consulted. Fingernail scrapings were allowed in **Cupp v. Murphy**, 412 U.S. 291 (1973).

Indeed, because of the increased concern regarding the problem of drunk driving (or drugged driving) there has been increased activity in the blood drawing area. Why? Simply, there is no better evidence of intoxication. It is the best evidence. The problem, however, is that blood-alcohol levels reach a peak and begin to dissipate after the last drink or drug is consumed. Wait too long and the evidence at trial will generate a debate over dissipation and extrapolation. Whether the average jury will understand or accept expert testimony on extrapolation is the problem. To this end, either the police will have to have a warrant or exigent circumstances. Indeed, some states demand a warrant but many of those states, like New Jersey, encourage but do not demand the use of telephonic warrants. But even that process takes some time and with the new.08 standard juries may not accept extrapolation. Several states do not permit telephonic warrants and those with a strong "four-corners" rule may never allow telephonic warrants. Those states are most in need of good rules governing search incident and the evanescent evidence exigency exception to allow warrant - less blood drawing in a scientifically proper and humane manner. (See the discussion of the "Four-Corners" rule in Chapter Three).

Whenever blood is drawn there is force used. **Schmerber** and its progeny require that humane techniques be employed. One of the most recent "force" cases comes from Arizona through **State v. Clary,** 2 P.3d 1255 (Ariz. App. 2000). The court reminds us that the force used is to be judged by the reasonable person standard and not a reasonable police officer standard. A telephonic warrant was obtained, but the defendant still refused to submit after service of the warrant. Several officers restrained the defendant on the floor so that a phlebotomist could draw the blood. The test showed a.19 alcohol level. The trial court admitted the blood alcohol evidence. The issue on appeal was whether the state statute authorizing the taking of blood by warrant for criminal prosecution purposes allowed the force used in this case. The statute was silent on the force issue. The majority notes that if force is not allowed the statute is superfluous. Using the entire legislative activity on toughening drunk driving laws, the court held that the use of reasonable force was intended. No one can thwart a warrant, they noted, in any context. In fact, another statute makes it a crime to resist execution of a warrant. The court went on to note the long history of reasonable force in Arizona decisional law citing **State v. Lewis**, 566 P. 2d 678 (Ariz. 1977). Part of the rule of such cases as **Lewis** is, of course, the rule that the force should be no more than is reasonably necessary; force that does not "shock the conscience." **Schmerber** was cited and discussed. They also noted blood drawing is quite different from surgery which requires an adversarial hearing under **Winston v. Lee**, (*infra*.). The court continued by discussing the "degree of force" issue as set out in **Graham v. Connor**, 490 U.S. 386 (1989), where the Court, in a non-blood case, set out criteria to use when excessive force is alleged in a civil rights action. There the Court gave us another one of its "balancing tests." What are judges to look at in a use of force case:

1) the nature and degree of the intrusion are balanced against the governmental interest in securing the evidence;
2) the severity of the crime at issue;
3) the safety of officers and others;
4) amount of resistance;
5) without hindsight was the police conduct reasonable under the circumstances?

The Arizona court then found that "the trial court did not err in finding these officers properly employed force to overcome physical resistance" of the defendant in trying to avoid being convicted of a felony. There was "no alternative but to overcome his resistance with reasonable force." As can be seen, this case applies with equal force to non-warranted resisters.

Another issue swirls around blood tests and refusals. Two cases from Wisconsin consider police action by passing breath tests to get blood tests. Those decisions are: **State v. Drews**, 2000 WL 1124237 (Wis. App.) (unpub. op.) and **County.... v. Bridwell**, 2000 WL 1678261 (Wis. App.).

In **Drews**, the defendant wanted a breath test but the police insisted on a blood test. In **Bridwell**, the defendant said he was not even given a chance to decline a breath test; that the officer went straight to blood test. Drews took the position that **Winston v. Lee** (the surgery case) governs and then cited a Ninth Circuit case that says it is unreasonable to give a blood test when the driver asks for a breath test. **Nelson v. City of Irvine**, 143 F. 3d 1196 (C.A. 9th 1998). But **Drews** lost because of **City of Madison v. Bardwell**, 266 N.W. 2d 618 (Wis. 1978) in which the Wisconsin Supreme Court said which test to use is for the law enforcement agency – there is no right of refusal just because the legislature authorized three different types of tests. Exactly three months later the issue was revisited in **Bridwell** with only the slight twist that no choices were given. He too argued the Ninth Circuit decision; that because the U.S. Supreme Court denied certiorari that **Nelson** must be the law of the land. Of course, denial of certiorari means no such thing. **Bridwell** also said that the "no knock" case of **Richards v. Wisconsin** also demands a reversal. That argument was properly rejected under **Schmerber** rules.

That humane techniques are required was emphasized by **Rochin v. California**, 342 U.S. 165 (1952). Rochin had swallowed something. The officer took Rochin to a doctor and told the doctor to pump his stomach. The tube was forced down Rochin's throat and he was forced to vomit. Two morphine capsules were found. This violated the Fourteenth Amendment. Two years later the court limited the **Rochin** case to intrusions that were violent, brutal, or unreasonably coercive. **Irvine v. California**, 347 U.S. 128 (1954).

Would threatening an arrested person with the use of a catheter to get a urine specimen be the type of offensive police practice prohibited by **Rochin**? The Tenth Circuit held that the threat is not quite the same as the invasion, thus the coerced sample was admissible. **Yanez v. Romero**, 619 F. 2d 581 (C.A. 10th 1980). Why? A court order could be sought and likely granted since surgery would not be required.

The California court was faced with evidence of diseased semen ejaculated from an incest defendant by means of massaging his prostate gland. Acknowledging that the body is not a sanctuary for concealed evidence, the court said when such an intrusion is permitted the character of the intrusion must be found to be appropriate. The more intense, unusual, prolonged, uncomfortable, unsafe, or undignified the procedure, or the more it intrudes upon essential standards of privacy, the greater must be the showing for the procedure's necessity. The court held this procedure illegal. **People v. Scott**, 546 P. 2d 327 (Cal. 1978). The most reasonable explanation of the California decision is not in its "humaneness rationale" but in clearly understanding **Schmerber** as illustrated by a 1980 Louisiana Supreme Court opinion. As the Louisiana court correctly stated, such bodily intrusions are prohibited unless: (1) there is a clear indication such evidence will be found; (2) the search is authorized by: (a) a neutral and detached magistrate; or (b) an emergency which threatened destruction of the evidence during the delay necessary to obtain a warrant; and (3) the search or intrusion is performed in a reasonable manner.

In the Louisiana case the female defendant had given the police reason to believe that she had inserted a plastic bottle of seconal in her vagina. Instead of getting a warrant the police "searched" her at a nearby hospital. The court pointed out that there was no emergency because a female officer was present to prevent her from destroying the evidence and because her vaginal secretion would not be able to dissolve the plastic bottle. Thus, there was time for a warrant. **State v. Fontenot**, 383 So. 2d 365 (La. 1980). In comparison, the hour or two delay to get a warrant in the California case did not threaten the destruction of the diseased semen since it was not the type of problem that would disappear that quickly.

Beyond the surgical removal cases, the most perplexing cases remain the body cavity searches. There is no doubt that these searches are highly intrusive, **Rodriques v. Furtado**, 950 F. 2d 805 (C.A. 1st 1991). However, as the First Circuit said, if the search, supported by probable cause upon a warrant that protects the citizen from hygiene and physical problems, is conducted it will be upheld. In the **Furtado** case a mere visual examination was found to be inadequate thus the police applied for a warrant so that the doctor would be permitted to enter the cavity (in this case a female's vagina). A hygienically conducted manual invasion under approved medical techniques was sanctioned. Balancing society's interest against the individual rights, the individual's rights have to give way the court held. The Ninth Circuit, in essence, agrees with the First Circuit. The Ninth Circuit's rule appears to be that any body cavity search, including visuals, unless based on exigency or consent, must be conducted upon probable cause pursuant to a warrant because of the interest of human dignity and privacy. **Fuller v. M.G. Jewelry**, 950 F. 2d 1442 (C.A. 9th 1991).

Of course, in order to get fingerprint or other similar evidence from the body of the defendant, the arrest has to be valid. This was the critical point in **Davis v. Mississippi**, 394 U.S. 721 (1969). In **Davis**, the crime for which the manhunt originated, was rape. The victim was unable to describe her assailant in detail. All she could say was that he was a Negro youth. The local police began dragnet procedures. The only hard evidence left at the scene of the crime were finger and palm prints at a window sill. Twenty-four black youths were picked up without warrants. They were taken to police headquarters, questioned, fingerprinted, and released. Forty or fifty others were questioned on the streets. Davis was one of those taken to headquarters. The prints of the twenty-four were sent to the F.B.I. The report positively connected Davis and the prints. Indicted, tried, and convicted, Davis sought to overturn his conviction on grounds of illegal seizure. The state tried to urge an exception to the illegally seized evidence rule. It was their position that because fingerprint evidence is so reliable it should not be excluded. The Court did not agree because the exclusionary rule is not concerned about the trustworthiness of the evidence but the manner in which it was obtained. The state said that investigatory detentions should be permitted much the same as in **Terry**-type confrontations. The Court said detentions for the sole purpose of obtaining fingerprints are subject to the constraints of the Fourth Amendment. They agreed that this type of detention might be a lesser intrusion than full-scale searches. However, they were unwilling to approve evidence gathering investigatory detentions. Of course they continued this prohibition in **Dunaway v. New York**, 442 U.S. 200 (1979) discussed elsewhere.

The Court once again had to address this type of issue in **Hayes v. Florida**, 470 U.S. 811 (1985). The police met Hayes at his house and they asked him to consent to being fingerprinted. He said no. Then they said we will arrest you and he said he would rather go with them than be arrested. So Hayes was taken to the station house and fingerprinted. The prints matched and a formal arrest followed. The Court said **Davis v. Mississippi** governs. Why? There was no probable cause, no consent, and no prior approval by a judicial officer.

The Court in **Hayes, Davis** and **Dunway** did not say there could never be an investigative seizure, it merely said there can be no seizure without probable cause, or judicial approval or consent. Some states reacted and passed "judicially approved seizure for fingerprinting purposes" statutes. Some states accepted them; some rejected through appellate court interpretations. Ohio adopted such a procedure for juveniles. The Ohio Supreme Court said such an order was valid even though there was no probable cause. The court said the rule required no more than articulable suspicion, a justified intrusion required for law enforcement purposes, and a limited intrusion as to scope, purpose and duration. **In re Order Requiring Fingerprinting of a Juvenile**, 537 N.E. 2d 1286 (Ohio 1989).

Not all courts can agree with **Schmerber**. In a break with the holdings of **Schmerber-Cupp**, the Utah Supreme Court held that under their own constitution, handwriting exemplars could not be compelled. The Utah Constitution provides that the accused, "shall not be compelled to give evidence against himself." The U.S. Constitution provides that no one could be compelled to be a "witness against himself." Upon that distinction in language rested the Court's decision. Massachusetts, on the other hand, has the same provision as Utah, but they accept **Schmerber** on a distinction created early in the history of Massachusetts. In Part II of the **Schmerber** opinion, the U.S. Supreme Court held that the Fifth Amendment privilege protects an accused only from being compelled to testify against himself; it is a privilege guaranteed by the right to remain silent unless the defendant chooses to speak in the unfettered exercise of his own will. The privilege is a bar against compelling communications or testimony, but that compulsion which makes a suspect or accused the source of "real or physical evidence" does not violate it. Against this background the Utah Supreme Court found the word evidence in their constitution to be much broader than the term witness in the U.S. Constitution and included exemplars as well as testimonial evidence. When terms are clearly different, it ruled that those differences should be recognized and given their separate, commonly understood meaning. **Hansen v. Owens**, 619 P. 2d 315 (Utah 1980).

If a bullet can be removed by a minor surgical procedure, using local anesthetic and posing no threat to a defendant's health, should a court order for its removal be upheld? Yes, said the Louisiana Supreme Court in **State v. Martin**, 404 So. 2d 960 (La. 1981). Why? The evidence was: (1) Relevant and not obtainable in any other way; (2) Obtainable by minor surgery through a skilled surgeon minimizing risks; (3) Questioned at a full adversary hearing; and (4) Subject to full appellate review before the operation.

Ultimately, the U.S. Supreme Court would have to address the Fourth Amendment issues inherent in the surgical procedures cases. That opportunity came in **Winston v. Lee**, 470 U.S. 753 (1985). Noting that in **Schmerber** it had reserved the "more substantial" intrusion rule, the Court held that "...the procedure sought here is an example of the 'more substantial intrusion' cautioned against..." and held "that to permit the procedure would violate respondent's right to be secure in his person guaranteed by the Fourth Amendment." The bullet sought in this case, at first, had been thought to have moved more to the surface and would require only a one and one-half centimeter incision plus local anesthesia. Just before the authorized procedure, a new x-ray showed that the bullet was two and one-half to three centimeters deep in the muscle tissue and now would require a general anesthetic. A new hearing was held but the procedure stood approved until the Federal District Court enjoined it. Can the state consistently with the Fourth Amendment compel a suspect to undergo surgery of this kind in a search for evidence of a crime? No. Here there is an expectation of privacy of a magnitude that such an intrusion may be unreasonable. The Fourth Amendment constrains against intrusions which are either not justified or done in an improper manner. Surgical intrusions of all kinds are not prohibited so the courts are saddled with a case-by-case rule. The bottom line is: does the procedure endanger the life or health of the suspect? Both were implicated here but not severely. However, that very uncertainty caused the proposed procedure to be defined as "unreasonable."

What are the consequences of a failure to comply with a court order for a handwriting exemplar, or other "mere evidence" order? This was the issue faced by the Seventh Circuit in **U.S. v. Jackson**, 901 F. 2d 83 (C.A. 7th 1989). The court said such evidence directly related to guilt or innocence on the underlying crime. It felt refusal to furnish such evidence is probative of consciousness of guilt. The evidence was, of course, relevant. As **Huddleston v. U.S.**, 485 U.S. 681 (1988) teaches, such relevant evidence should only be excluded if its probative value is substantially outweighed by the concerns listed in Rule 403, F.R. Evid. Thus they held that a defendant cannot escape a lawful order to produce evidence and may not take advantage of that refusal. Therefore, the trial judge abused his discretion when he ruled, *in limine,* that the government could not introduce evidence of Jackson's refusal to provide the handwriting exemplars.

Can the search incident occur before the official "You are under arrest" announcement? The most recent case on this issue comes from Alabama through **Hopper v. City of Prattville**, 2000 WL 127221 (Ala. Crim. App.). In this case articulable suspicion existed for a drunk driving stop. After the stop, sufficient evidence at the scene required field sobriety tests. The defendant did not pass. The officer then searched Hopper's pants and a marijuana pipe was found. Hopper was then put under arrest formally. This result was suggested by *dicta* in **Rawlings v. Kentucky** as noted in the next paragraph.

Does a person have to be formally arrested before the police can conduct the search incident thereto? Can the police officer who has probable cause to arrest conduct the search first? What were the chances this officer was going to allow this person to drive away in his car? Citing a long list of prior Alabama cases the court said "it is well settled that... a search conducted immediately prior to an arrest *may* be justified as incident to arrest *IF* the police had probable cause to arrest the suspect before conducting the search." (emphasis added.) The court found support in LaFave, *Search and Seizure*, §5.4(a) (2d ed. 1987) and of course **Rawlings v. Kentucky**, 448 U.S. 98 (1980) where the Court said: "where the arrest quickly followed on the heels of the challenged search... we do not believe it particularly important that the search preceded the arrest rather than *vice versa, so long as the fruits of the search were not necessary to support probable cause to arrest.*" (emphasis added). Accord see: **State v. Menzies**, 2000 WL 424277 (Tenn. Crim. App.) (unpub. op.).

VI.   Search Incident: Scope: Wingspan

The second branch of search incident deals with the surroundings. This was brought into focus by **Chimel v. California**, 395 U.S. 752 (1969). It was in **Chimel** that the term "wingspan" had its birth. Prior to **Chimel** the standard search incident rule was broadly stated, allowing a search of the place over which the defendant had control as long as the underlying arrest was valid. But even that rule found some tough going in **Go-Bart Importing Co. v. U.S.**, 282 U.S. 344 (1931) and **U.S. v. Lefkowitz**, 285 U.S. 452 (1932). The limiting language of these cases was disregarded in **Harris v. U.S.**, 331 U.S. 145 (1947). However, like a ping-pong match, the Court reintroduced limiting language in **Trupiano v. U.S.**, 334 U.S. 145 (1948), when the Court said that something more was needed than a lawful arrest. Again the Court reversed field in the subsequently decided **U.S. v. Rabinowitz,** 339 U.S. 56 (1950), which allowed a fairly wide search of desks, safe, and file cabinets. This was the rule that California relied on in justifying the **Chimel** search. In its holding in **Chimel**, the Court said: "The search here went far beyond the petitioner's person and the area within which he might have obtained either a weapon or something that could have been used as evidence against him." By holding the scope of the search unreasonable, the "wingspan" doctrine was born. Thus a warrant is required for a search of the area beyond the immediate control of the arrestee.

The immediate control language makes the test subjective and not objective. The condition of the defendant as a wheelchair-bound person or an athlete may well shrink or expand (reasonably) the area of immediate opportunity to seize a weapon or destroy evidence. If the officers remove the defendant from the room of arrest, they cannot return to that room under **Chimel** and conduct a search. **City of Centerville v. Smith**, 332 N.E. 2d 69 (Ohio App. 1973). However, as will be noted, not all courts agree with this latter conclusion in all circumstances.

The opportunity to seize can reappear in some instances. In **People v. Long**, 288 N.W. 2d 629 (Mich. Ct. App. 1980), defendant was stopped for speeding. He got out of the car as the police approached. His car's front door remained open. He was asked to produce his auto registration. As he and the officer approached the open car the officer saw a large, open folding knife on the front floor. Telling the defendant to wait, the officer secured the knife and lifted the arm rest fearing the presence of another weapon. The lifted arm rest revealed a bag of marijuana. The court held, and rightly so, that the police under these facts did not have to allow this defendant unrestrained access to his car where he might have reached a weapon. The U.S. Supreme Court would ultimately agree: see the discussion of **Michigan v. Long** in Chapter Thirteen.

Would the search of an entire motel room be permissible? Although it would not seem so, see **Johnson v. State**, 252 So. 2d 371 (Fla. App. 1971). The Illinois Court would require the showing of the size and dimensions of the room. In **People v. Jackson**, 373 N.E. 2d 729 (Ill. App. Ct. 1978), the court said they were aware of the **Chimel** doctrine and could not automatically uphold the search of the room where the arrest took place. Virginia allowed the search of a motel room where it was believed that an accomplice existed. But that case would better fit as an exigent circumstances situation. **Kirkpatrick v. Commonwealth**, 176 S.E. 2d 802 (Va. 1970). In fact there are as many cases from state courts that allowed more extensive and less contemporaneous searches than **Chimel** would allow as there are cases that disallowed such searches. The U.S. Supreme Court has not been very vigilant in its supervision of this area. See the cases collected at 19 ALR 3d 727 (1968) and pocket supplement.

One of the frequently overlooked points of the "wingspan" doctrine of **Chimel** is that the arrestee is often in handcuffs and truly unable to reach for weapons or destroy evidence. Some courts have acknowledged this problem and failed to see how the fact of handcuffing would limit the wingspan branch of the search incident exception. **People v. Johnson**, 449 N.Y.S. 2d 41 (N.Y. Sup. Ct. App. Div. 1982). These courts drew their support from the D.C. Circuit's decision in **U.S. v. Mason**, 523 F. 2d 1122 (C.A. D.C. 1975). In **Mason**, the defendant was arrested in his apartment and handcuffed with his hands behind his back. He was not wearing shoes at this time. The police put his shoes on for him. He asked to go to the bathroom, the handcuffs were replaced but this time in front of him. Mason said he wanted his leather jacket from the closet. He pointed out the coat as best he could and started to go for it. At this point, a sawed-off shotgun was seen in a partially opened suitcase on the floor of the closet. Though still handcuffed, the gun was seized under the "wingspan" theory. **Chimel** was quoted extensively. The seizure was found to be lawful. The court noted that the handcuffs "necessarily restricted the area within his reach but did not reduce it sufficiently so as to exclude the closet." This, of course, might have not been true if the handcuffs had been replaced with his hands behind him. The court added, for obvious reasons, that the police would not have been permitted to lead him from place to place just to create "wingspan" rights. Mason was the one who led them to this closet. Thus the shot-gun was found to have been seized reasonably within the spirit, if not the letter, of **Chimel's** law. It also points out the wisdom of viewing **Chimel** as a search limiting doctrine and not as a search granting doctrine.

The Seventh and Second Circuits have also addressed the handcuffing issue. In **U.S. v. Queen**, 847 F. 2d 346 (C.A. 7th 1988), the defendant failed to surrender himself on the date set and a bench warrant issued for his arrest. They found him in his home in a closet under a blanket. He was arrested, handcuffed and taken three feet from the closet when an agent returned to the closet and saw, in plain view, (without moving the blanket) a .357 Magnum. The gun was seized. The court found the search to be contemporary. It also held that the police had reason to suspect a weapon since it took defendant so long to surrender once discovered. The court accepted the principle that even being handcuffed (hands at back) he could have seized the weapon. Therefore, accessibility was present. The court said it was not going to "second guess" the officers where safety was reasonably implicated and saw this not as a police right but a duty to search and seize incident to this arrest. See also **U.S. v. Bennett**, 908 F. 2d 189 (C.A. 7th 1990) which expands upon this principle.

But the Second Circuit said the handcuffing denies to the police the search of a bag in the defendant's possession. It said there was not the slightest danger that the bag or its contents would have been removed. **U.S. v. Gorski**, 852 F. 2d 692 (C.A. 2d

1988). Not all courts accept the "possible" reach theory of the foregoing cases. Indiana felt that it could not accept the state's justification that four people in custody by several officers could, in fact, leap six to eight feet, open a drawer, take out a satchel, open it, and then recover a weapon or destroy drugs. This represents a very strict interpretation of **Chimel's** wing span doctrine and it totally disregards the search history behind the ultimate result reached in **Chimel. Ceroni v. State**, 559 N.E. 2d 372 (Ind. Ct. App. 1990).

Courts often have to reaffirm or reannounce the scope of a doctrine. This was the posture in which the New Jersey Supreme Court found itself. The issue was whether the police could search the car of an arrestee solely on the basis of search incident to arrest. The court said no and that the scope of search incident was limited to the person of the arrestee and the area within his immediate control. The problem with the case, however, was that they were going to allow the defendant to drive his own car to the police station because he had his three-year-old son with him. Normally courts would allow a search of the area of control to at least make sure that he had no reachable weapons. **Chimel**, which the court cites, also mentioned the evidence destruction motive. See the Mobility chapter (*infra* Chapter Thirteen), for a full discussion of this issue. In this case, the police reached under the dashboard and felt envelopes hidden among the maze of wires. Defendant had been arrested for gambling and the envelopes could reasonably be believed, because of their location, to contain betting slips and proceeds. In fact, that is what they contained. Here we have the very type of evidence which could be destroyed. Instead, the court misapplied the random search evil of **Delaware v. Prouse**. In answer to the protection theory, the court used the fact that after the envelopes' discovery the police quickly abandoned the thought of allowing defendant to drive his car. It is not clear, but it does not appear that the officers continued the auto search. Rather it appears that the car was towed. This indicates a recognition by the police of the limited scope of **Chimel** and not the contrary. The unstated feeling of this case is that it really represents, in the view of the court, a pretextual search case. If that is so, then that is the way it should have been decided. That appears to be the point made by the dissenters. **State v. Welsh**, 419 A. 2d 1123 (N.J. 1980). Due to cases like this one the Supreme Court would have to address the issue of search incident of the automobile.

Although **Belton** is fully discussed in the "mobility exception" materials in Chapter Thirteen, it is clear that adding the auto passenger compartment to "wingspan" would officially signal to police that this Court would be willing to expand either "wingspan" or exigent searches, as **Chimel** searches should be called, to include more physical territory. Despite the fact that in **Belton** the search incident of the passenger compartment was upheld even though the defendant could not possibly fly through the air and penetrate a closed door to get at the leather jacket with the zipped pocket to destroy the evidence, some Courts in the federal system have limited the search incident doctrine of **Belton** once the arrestee has been removed from the car. Such was the position taken by the Ninth Circuit in **U.S. v. Vasey**, 834 F. 2d 782 (C.A. 9th 1987). The Sixth Circuit, on the other hand, seems to follow **Belton** to the letter by allowing the search incident even though the arrestee is no longer in the car and in fact is unable to get back into the car. **U.S. v. White**, 871 F. 2d 415 (C.A. 6th 1989).

California, on the other hand, disregards the footnote in **Belton** regarding the vehicular nature of the case and expands **Chimel** by using **Belton** to say that search incident was intentionally expanded by **Belton** in all cases. The California court upheld the search of unlocked baggage even after the suspect has been handcuffed as long as the search is contemporaneous. The **Chimel** case was fully applicable and the court need not have brought **Belton** to bear because of the mere act of handcuffing. The California case only adds unnecessary confusion to the area. **People v. Brooks**, 257 Cal. Rep. 504 (Cal. Dist. Ct. App. 1989).

The key dispute, as already indicated, is what constitutes immediate physical control? Are we truly "winking" at the facts in most cases? Such searches are conducted after physical control of the defendant has been accomplished. The fact that **Chimel** put an end to the practice of whole-house searches when a person was arrested certainly is a legitimate goal and the fact of handcuffing should not factor in if we view **Chimel** as a search limiting doctrine rather than a search granting doctrine. The Alaska court had become embroiled in the control argument. In their case the coat was several feet from the defendant when he was arrested and secured. The jacket searched was now several feet from the defendant. Rather than find this a search incident the court used the exigency doctrine to save the evidence. Since the drugs sold to the informer came from the jacket, to leave it unattended created a risk that they felt would override the warrant requirement. Most courts would have used search incident without question. **Ricks v. State**, 771 P. 2d 1364 (Alaska Ct. App. 1989).

Consider, for example, **U.S. v. Johnson**, 846 F. 2d 279 (C.A. 5th 1988). Defendant was caught with the "goods" on him when he consented to empty his pockets. He was arrested for mail embezzlement. A briefcase which he had been carrying was on the floor of the postal manager's office where the pocket-emptying had taken place. It was not clear when the arrest took place but the court felt that one had taken place by force of facts when the briefcase was searched. Defendant did not consent to this search. The inspector opened it anyway. Was the search of the briefcase incident to arrest? Finding that there was still immediacy of control in Mr. Johnson, it was subject to the search incident doctrine under **Belton**. Clearly, the Fifth Circuit does not agree with the decision in the **Gorsky** case from the Second Circuit (*supra* this chapter).

Until the Supreme Court reverses its automobile context language, other courts should keep the "**Chimel**-non-automobile-actual-grabbing-area" cases separate from the "**Belton-Chimel** – automobile-hypothetical-grabbing-area" cases. As a California court noted, the Supreme Court was only attempting to draw a "bright line" in **Belton** and only for automobile situations. **People v. Stoffle**, 3 Cal. Rptr. 2d 257 (Cal. App. 3 Dist. 1991). Indeed, footnote 3 of **Belton** tells us this.

VII. Search Incident: Contemporaneousness of Things Immediately Associated with the Defendant.

If the Court were totally honest with us, **Chimel** would be seen as a scope limiting doctrine with a time limit only imposed on a search of the surroundings where the defendant is arrested. Other than that, no time limit should be imposed on search incidents in connection with items of personal property carried by or driven by the defendant. If a time limit was imposed to prevent "dropsy," that is the planting of evidence by police, the rule fails because that act can occur contemporaneously with the arrest.

Chimel imposes a contemporaneous requirement. How long does the right of search incident last? In one case, the clothing of the defendant (while defendant was still locked up) was searched ten hours after the initial arrest and incarceration. The Court said, once in custody, the clothing and personal effects were subject to search even though a substantial time period had expired. **U.S. v. Edwards**, 415 U.S. 800 (1974). But then the Court decided **U.S. v. Chadwick**, 433 U.S. 1 (1977), that invalidated a search of a double-locked foot locker an hour and a half after an unchallenged arrest. The Court said, "However, warrantless searches of luggage or other property seized at the time of an arrest cannot be justified as incident to that arrest if the 'search is remote in time or place from the arrest.' " The Court appeared to strengthen the **Chadwick** holding in **Arkansas v. Sanders**, 442 U.S. 753 (1979), where they held that a warrantless search of personal luggage being conveyed by a defendant at the time of his arrest was not allowable where the luggage had been seized and no longer "openable" by the defendant. Under **Chimel** and its danger/destruction rule this makes sense. But what of **Belton**? **Belton** necessarily, while it expanded the search incident scope, also expanded the time period during which the police can conduct the search incident. Thus as the "wingspan" got broader the time to widen the span had to grow also. This was the conclusion reached by the Seventh Circuit in **U.S. v. Fleming**, 677 F. 2d 602 (C.A. 7th 1982). In the **Fleming** case, the defendant dropped a bag while being arrested inside his house. Fleming was removed from the house in much the same way as was Belton when he was removed from the car. The bag that Fleming's partner dropped was not searched until both were secured and outside the house; some five minutes had elapsed. Upon re-entry to the house the bag was searched and the drugs were found. The court completely bypassed, as did the Supreme Court, the issue of weapon-grabbing or evidence-destroying. Instead, they said what could have been done immediately was reasonable when done so quickly after the handcuffing. The court said it would impose no "absolutely contemporaneous" rule in such situations. It did not recognize that some time periods could be too long; some spans are too great. To overcome the fact that the officer in **Belton** was greatly outnumbered, which in itself justified the **Belton** decision, the Court said, "But we do not consider that the presence of more officers than suspects invalidated the search...." The court wanted to make sure that exigency played no part in their opinion. However, **Belton** should not be used in cases like **Fleming**.

Quite frankly, courts have now created quite a bit of diversity in such holdings: if the bag is close enough to be reached, the search is alright though delayed, **Carrasco v. State**, 712 S.W. 2d 120 (Tex. Crim. App. 1986); a second search at the stationhouse is alright under **Chimel, U.S. v. Burnette**, 698 F. 2d 1038 (C.A. 9th 1983); delayed inspection upheld under **Belton, State v. Calezar**, 661 P. 2d 311 (Idaho 1983); search of a case after removal from the car and while defendant was handcuffed alright, **State v. Harvey**, 648 S.W. 2d 87 (Mo. 1983); briefcase opened several minutes after arrest alright, **U.S. v. Herrera**, 810 F. 2d 989 (C.A. 10th 1987); second search of wallet alright, **U.S. v. Goldfarb**, 581 F. Supp. 1141 (E.D. Mich. 1984); and **Fontaine v. State**, 2000 WL 1768681 (Md. App.). Most of these cases apply a "no harm – no foul" approach in that what could have been done at the scene was merely delayed. Others used inevitable discovery plus **Chimel** and so forth. Then you have states like New York who are more restrictive in their view. That court will allow a later search, but not as a search incident. The police must show independent probable cause to believe evidence is present. **People v. Smith**, 465 N.Y.S. 2d 896, 452 N.E. 2d 1224 (1983). This clearly limits the places that can be searched.

Whether an item was under the defendant's control was the focal point of **State v. Roberts**, 2001 WL 258445 (Neb.). A domestic dispute arose and the woman wanted the male defendant out of the apartment. The defendant was in the living room when the police arrived. He agreed to leave but said he wanted to get some things from his bedroom. A pile of books and other things were seen on the bed and the defendant said he would leave if he could take those items with him and he began to gather them.

A wants and warrants check was simultaneously completed and revealed on outstanding warrant. Roberts was arrested and when the officer went to "cuff" him the defendant asked for permission to take off his running pants and jacket that he had on over his clothing. The police said yes but heard a "thud type sound" when he dropped the items. The nearest officer escorted him from the room and another searched the clothing and found 30 to 40 tiny plastic packets inside a larger bag in the jacket pocket. Was this a proper search incident to arrest? Yes! Why? The court, agreeing with several other courts, held that the handcuffing does not extinguish "immediate control" search rights. The court firmly held that to permit an arrestee to strip and discard does not destroy immediate control and the search was sufficiently contemporaneous.

VIII. Search Incident Check List

I.   Predicate: Lawful Arrest
- A.   Not defined in terms of constitutional lawful arrest but merely as a lawful arrest.
- B.   Key Concern: Pretextual Arrest:
  - 1.   Otherwise lawful but real reason for arrest a "hidden agenda."
  - 2.   Some courts use:
    - a.   pure subjective analysis – police pretext makes arrest unlawful;
    - b.   pure objective analysis – as long as arrest otherwise objectively lawful no concern for pretext; or
    - c.   modified objective analysis – would the reasonable police officer have made this arrest absent pretext.
- C.   Scope of Search incident:
  - 1.   Very thorough search of the person as to:
    - a.   non-bodily intrusions,
    - b.   bodily intrusions (non-surgical),
      - 1.   evanescent evidence – no court order necessary *and*
      - 2.   non-evanescent evidence – many courts require an order to do more than "view," and
    - c.   bodily intrusions (surgical--requires a full adversarial hearing).

II. Mere Evidence Rule:
- A. Evidence taken is non-testimonial.
- B. Approved list:
  1. line ups, etc. (pre-adversarial),
  2. fingernail scrapings,
  3. finger prints,
  4. handwriting and voice exemplars,
  5. blood, breath, urine samples under humane techniques doctrine.

III. Search Incident: Wingspan:
- A. Not limited to person of defendant.
- B. Covers "grope" area:
  1. things and places within,
  2. defendant's immediate control, and
  3. where a weapon could be seized or evidence destroyed.
- C. A search limiting doctrine.
- D. Case-by-case regarding:
  1. defendant's abilities,
  2. even though handcuffed.
- E. Includes passenger compartment of defendant's car if arrested therein.

IV. Search Incident: Contemporaneousness
- A. A time limit imposed.
- B. Time expanded only by justifiable exigency.

IX. Booking and Jailing Inventories

A. Decisional Law

Compound the search incident contemporaneousness confusion by adding **Illinois v. LaFayette**, 462 U.S. 640 (1983) into the mix. There was a shoulder bag which the defendant could not reach that was searched at the stationhouse while he was being booked. The State of Illinois justified its search as an inventory and argued that to the Court. The Court agreed and found a valid inventory search. Inventories are a well defined exception to the probable cause requirement, the Court ruled. It is an incidental administrative step in the booking and jailing process. The community "caretaking-function," the "protection of private property from suits for theft function", the "avoidance of danger function" are all justifications for allowing inventories. That a less intrusive type of inventory could have been done is not relevant.

California has limited the inventory rule slightly. A person being "booked" for a non-jailable offense is not subject to the inventory search. **People v. Lewis**, 254 Cal. Rep. 118 (Cal. Ct. App. 1988). The only invasion right the police need in such situations is the frisk for weapons right. Indeed, this makes sense when the defendant and his or her property will not be separated.

A police officer's perusal of an arrestee's papers during an inventory was found improper by the Massachusetts Appeals Court in **Com. v. Sullo**, 532 N.E. 2d 1219 (Mass. Ct. App. 1989). The reading revealed activity of bookmaking. The police had a vague procedure, the papers did not look like a weapon or the type of things subject to theft. What this officer was doing was searching, not conducting an inventory. The court also said it was pretextual because the man had $7,500 in cash and that fact raised a suspicion of a gambling operation. What **LaFayette**, **Lewis** and **Sullo** demonstrate is that there are times when the limiting and limited search doctrine of **Chimel** runs its course. These courts also clearly indicate that not all is lost, however, because, in addition to securing a warrant the police have one more warrantless "gun" in their arsenal; the right to inventory personal effects. True, it is a less intrusive warrantless right but is powerful because it travels with plain view rights. In **Sullo**, however, the police overstepped the inventory bounds by reading the papers. They could have been quickly "fanned" to make sure no money or bearer bonds were present, but not to read each page.

Probable cause is irrelevant to such inventories. The need to protect the property, the people in the stationhouse from potential danger, and the liability for lost goods make such warrantless inventories reasonable. The Illinois court in **La Fayette** said the police should have put the shoulder bag in a sealed plastic bag. The Supreme Court disagreed and held that it is not unreasonable for police, as part of the routine procedure incident to incarcerating an arrested person, to search any container or article in his possession, in accordance with established inventory procedures. Caretaking is not the only legitimate need for an inventory.

There is a difference between a search incident to arrest that must be performed contemporaneously with the arrest and the inventory search at the stationhouse though the inventory right results from the prior arrest as a matter of the continued custody arising from or flowing from the initial arrest. The Court noted that the scope of the two search rights often vary because there may be some things that are either impractical or embarrassing that might be done at the scene (like disrobing) that might be a necessity for routine jail administrative purposes. The Court then went on to describe the scope of a proper inventory by saying: "At the station house, it is entirely proper for police to remove and list or inventory property found on the person or in the possession of an arrested person who is to be jailed. A range of governmental interests supports an inventory process. It is not unheard of for persons employed in police activities to steal property taken from arrested persons; similarly, arrested persons have been known to make false claims regarding what was taken from their possession at the station house. A standardized procedure for making a list or inventory as soon as reasonable after reaching the stationhouse not only deters false claims but also inhibits theft or careless handling of articles taken from the arrested person. Arrested persons have also been known to injure themselves – or others – with belts, knives, drugs or other items on their person while being detained. Dangerous instrumentalities – such as razor blades, bombs, or weapons – can be concealed in innocent-looking articles taken from the arrestee's possession. The bare recital of these mundane realities justifies reasonable measures by police to limit these risks – either while the items are in police possession or at the time they are returned to the arrestee upon his release. Examining all the items removed from the arrestee's person or possession and listing or inventorying them is an entirely reasonable administrative procedure. It is immaterial whether the police actually fear any particular package or container; the need to protect against such risks arises independently of a particular officer's subjective concerns. Finally, inspection of an arrestee's personal property may assist the police in ascertaining or verifying his identity. In short every consideration of orderly police administration benefiting both police and the public points toward the appropriateness of the examination of respondent's shoulder bag prior to his incarceration." (Citations omitted) **LaFayette** at 646, 647.

The justification for booking/jailing inventories is, as already noted, threefold. First, the police, etc. have a duty to properly keep and preserve a defendant's valuable property. Second, the police have a duty to themselves and to their governmental unit to protect against bogus property loss law suits. Finally, the police have a duty to themselves and the public in general to make sure that no inherently dangerous commodity gets "into the stream of commerce" so to speak.

But do police or governments ever get sued when an incarcerated defendant complains of a loss of a valuable item? Indeed they do, as illustrated by **Jungerman v. City of Raytown**, 925 S.W. 2d 202 (Mo. *en banc*. 1996). Mr. Jungerman sued over the loss of his wallet containing $1,171.00 and a gold Rolex watch. Instead of these items being placed in a property bag, they were put in a wooden box on a counter accessible to the public. No receipt was given to Jungerman. When he left the next morning the police could not find his things. The jury returned a verdict of $9,195.00 but the trial court entered a judgment NOV. Was there a submissible case? Yes, if the duty to inventory is ministerial and not discretionary. Therefore, there is no sovereign immunity. A ministerial duty arises from a public duty. The duty to secure an inventory is, in this court's view, ministerial because no discretionary function is involved and the function is regulated as noted by the existence of a written policy, training manual, and forms. The court closed by saying: "A citizen may reasonably presume that property left with the police will not disappear if the police use due care."

The duty to inventory is very limited. It only arises when a person is arrested and jailed. It only applies to property owned and/or controlled personally by the arrestee. This is illustrated by **Com. v. Knoche**, 678 A. 2d 395 (Pa. Super. 1996). Ms. Knoche was a passenger in a car operated by another. That person was arrested and the police offered Ms. Knoche a ride which offer she accepted. Before she entered the car, the officer told Ms. Knoche he would have to search her for weapons and patted her down. He then asked to examine her purse and found a marijuana pipe at the bottom of her purse. She was then charged with possession of drug paraphernalia. In her motion to suppress she argued that the pat down was illegal under **Terry** law and that she did not consent to the search of her purse. She was convicted and post-sentence she moved to have the conviction set aside upon the illegal search theories. This judge agreed and the state appealed.

The state abandoned its **Terry** and consent theories; arguing instead that the search was incident to arrest or an inventory search. No *nexus* existed connecting this passenger's purse with the arrested driver thus the appellate court did not accept this "incident to arrest" argument. **Belton** was deemed inapplicable due to Pennsylvania's rejection of **Belton**. The court then turned to the inventory argument. It properly noted that Ms. Knoche was not under arrest nor undergoing the booking function, thus the search here "...was not part of a routine administrative procedure at a police station and thus could not be classified as an inventory search."

Obviously, any arrest which necessarily leads to a jailing creates the ministerial duty to inventory the personal effects of the arrestee. For example, see **People v. Smith**, 926 P. 2d 186 (Colo. App. 1996). Mr. Smith was stopped for a traffic violation. The "wants and warrants" check revealed an arrest warrant for failure to appear in a civil case. While being booked cocaine was discovered. Smith argued that the booking inventory does not arise upon civil warrant arrests; it only arises incident to criminal arrests. Smith lost. The court simply said: "The fact that the arrest warrant was issued in the context of a civil case is of no relevance in determining the validity of the inventory search." Accord see **People v. Houstina**, 549 N.W. 2d 11 (Mich. App. 1996); outstanding civil bench warrant for failure to appear. For a like result, where the charge was domestic battery, a misdemeanor, see **State v. Julian**, 922 P. 2d 1059 (Idaho 1996). The arrest in this context was authorized by the Idaho arrest statute.

Enough facts existed for a custodial felony arrest with its attendant inventory duty. The fact that the misdemeanor number was cited was of no moment.

The duty to inventory can never arise before an arrest. This seems obvious, but one decision had to emphasize this point. In an Alabama case, the defendant-to-be was at the hospital for an overdose of heroin. The officer searched the defendant's personal effects before arresting him and the state tried to argue inventory as justification. Booking and jailing arise after an arrest, not before, the Alabama court noted. The officer also had not been delegated the hospital's inventory/safe-keeping function. However, all was not lost. The court felt that exigent circumstances justified this pre-arrest search. **Woods v. State**, 1996 WL 549085 (Ala.Crim. App.).

The booking/jailing inventory duty, like the search incident to arrest doctrine, is limited in time. The inventory can, without good cause, come too late for purposes of admissibility of the evidence. This issue was the focus of **State v. Newman**, 548 N.W. 2d 739 (Neb. 1996). Mr. Newman was arrested and his suitcases were not immediately inventoried. Instead they were stored in the police property room. Some time later, and without a warrant, the suitcases were taken from the property room and "inventoried." The standard policy of immediately searching for weapons, explosions or contraband was not followed. Instead they were officially "inventoried" as bulk property. The only saving grace was that this evidence was cumulative therefore it was harmless error to admit it.

The 48 hour rule of **County of Riverside v. McLaughlin** and the inventory doctrine came together in **State v. Riley**, 1996 WL 269948 (Wash. App. Div. 3)[unpub. op]. The defendant was arrested without a warrant. The state has 48 hours to produce such a person for a bail hearing. The right to bail and the amount are determined by a judge. Since such a person could be in jail for up to 48 hours the custodial jailing and attendant inventory were therefore appropriate.

The scope of the search often tells us whether the police intrusion was a search for incriminating evidence or a true inventory. At least four cases dealt with the "scope" issue in 1996. As have many states, New York had a case where the police read specific entries that were noted in the defendant's weekly appointment calendar. Was this a proper police precinct inventory? The police inventory policy told the officer to look at each page after shaking the book. This read or "look" direction did not pass constitutional muster because it does not further the purposes of the inventory. The important point to remember is that just because it is written in the local inventory policy does not mean it is constitutionally sound. **People v. Somerville**, 1996 WL 757173 (N.Y. Sup.). This court, therefore, agrees with the Massachusetts decision and

436

its **Sullo** case (*supra*). But we do not "throw the baby out with the bath water" when only part of the inventory was invalidly conducted. Evidence found upon an improper inventory process does not taint *per se* other evidence properly uncovered. See **D'Antorio v. State**, 926 P. 2d 1158 (Alaska 1996). This is excellent logic.

Does the inventory search policy allow officers to go back to the property in storage and take a "second look" at the items? The answer to this question should be yes as a matter of non-intrusive plain view. Can that second look exceed the scope of the first look and still be called an inventory? The answer here should be no. Can the police do a more extensive second look without a warrant? Also, no. However, from a privacy perspective should the answer be different? Kansas says the property is in lawful police custody. It then cites **U.S. v. Edwards**, 415 U.S. 800 (1974). But Kansas does not focus on the reason for the delay in the **Edwards** case and that was critical to the Court when it approved that search incident. The **Edwards** case also pre-existed the creation of the booking/jailing inventory. Kansas should read pages 804-806 of the opinion more carefully. See **State v. Copridge**, 918 2d 1247 (Kan. 1996).

The line dividing the end of the search incident right and the beginning of the more limited inventory duty is hard to define. Consider **State v. Paturizzio**, 679 A. 2d 199 (N.J. Super. 1996). The defendant was arrested but her satchel was not searched until she was placed in a holding cell. Several envelopes containing PCP, marijuana and hashish were discovered. The court mixed search incident law with inventory law in such a way as to lead one to believe that it sees them as one-in-the-same doctrine. The court cites **Belton** and **Lafayette** in tandem. It does not seem to recognize that the inventory intrusion has to be less destructive than a search incident. To be sure the prime focus of this case was on the application of **Illinois v. Gates** and its independent corroboration requirements which may account for this mixture of doctrine. However, opaque envelopes were discovered in the satchel. Under plain view this inventory was "an otherwise lawful search" and the envelopes could be opened without securing a warrant since **Coolidge v. New Hampshire** did not limit the definition of "an otherwise lawful search." The outcome is correct even if inarticulately derived.

B. Jailing Inventory Check List.

I.   Purposes to be served:
    A.   Protect defendant's property from theft;
    B.   Protect police (individually) or government entity from false claims of loss;
    C.   Protect defendant from self-injury;
    D.   Protect others from a defendant's attack;

E.   Assist the police in verifying the defendant's identity; and

F.   Promote orderly police administration which benefits both the police and the public.

II.   Scope of a Valid Inventory:
A.   Less thorough than probable cause-based search incident;

B.   "Travels" with plain view (senses) rights attached; and

C.   Must be standardized-consult auto inventory cases (**Opperman**, **Bertine**, and **Wells**),
1.   routine inventory,
2.   routinely done.

III.   Persons Subject to:
A.   Any person to be incarcerated for any crime (lawfully, of course);

B.   But not for persons to be automatically released following the booking process; and

C.   Local law governs "automatic" or "own release" decisions.

X.   Search Incident to Searches

A. Decisional Law

When police are lawfully upon premises conducting a search under a warrant, the last thing they need is people coming and going, people destroying evidence, and people threatening their lives. Some of the people they will encounter will be innocent bystanders, and others with no intimate connection with the place. Some people will be the owners, controllers, and others intimately connected with the place. In two opinions, **Ybarra v. Illinois**, 444 U.S. 85 (1979) and **Michigan v. Summers**, 452 U.S. 692 (1981) both types of persons were considered and how they could be treated would be determined. The Court, in **Ybarra**, was faced with the execution of a legitimate search of a tavern while all types of persons were present. All people present were lined up against the wall and then, under state statutory authority, they were all frisked. Ybarra, a patron who had no possessory or other apparent connection with the bar, was then searched and drugs were discovered on his person. The Court did not decide the issue of the legitimacy of the detention. They merely concluded that the police had no reason to believe that he had any special connection with the premises and that Ybarra had not made any moves that might indicate danger to the officers or the general public. They had no probable cause to believe that Ybarra was in possession of illicit drugs.

Most courts treat **Ybarra** as holding that a person's mere presence at a public place covered by a search warrant does not justify searching that person and no more. Before looking at decisions strictly construing **Ybarra,** it must be noted that keeping people from coming and going during a lawful search is a legitimate state interest which, when balanced against a "stand still" order by the police, does not appear to seriously offend the freedom of the individual in any significant way when coupled with the restrictions set out in **Ybarra;** a point made by Chief Justice Burger.

Several courts distinguish **Ybarra** when it comes to private premises. In **U.S. v. Savides**, 664 F. Supp. 1544 (N.D. Ill. 1987), the court found grounds for arresting and searching everyone present where guns, drug paraphernalia, and gambling equipment were all in view when the officers entered to execute the warrant. The notoriety of such things in open view provided probable cause to believe that the people present were engaged in unlawful activities.

The second case comes from Michigan where that court upheld arrests and searches of all persons present in what appeared to be a "controlled substance house." Why? Well, the police could have arrested everyone there for loitering at a place of an illegal business if they had desired. It distinguished **Ybarra** by saying that in **Ybarra** the bar searched did not have the reputation of being a dope house; in **Ybarra** the place was an open bar accessible to all the public; in **Ybarra,** no one ran away when the police entered; and in **Ybarra** there was no reason to believe that the patrons at the bar were involved in criminal activity. **People v. Arterberry**, 429 N.W. 2d 574 (Mich. 1988).

The California First District Court of Appeals has joined a growing list of states allowing pat downs of all present in a private residence where drugs are present. This court went one step further than Michigan since in the California case guns, drugs and money were not spread about the room. Instead the court allowed reliance upon the hypothetical case. **People v. Thurman**, 257 Cal. Rep. 517 (Cal. Dist. Ct. App. 1989). And another court appeared to apply **Ybarra** without reference to the public/private issue. A defendant, known to be a drug dealer who carried a gun, was frisked when he walked into his friend's apartment as it was being searched. Thus, apart from any investigatory concern that crime was afoot, the officer was entitled to frisk the defendant for his own and the safety of others.

Although a number of courts have limited **Ybarra** to public place searches, most of those courts allowed pat downs in the private place because drugs, weapons, *etc.*, were in plain view and the courts found that no innocents could be present in such a situation. Rhode Island has gone a step further and has held that anyone present in a private home, while a drug search under a warrant is conducted, can be frisked due to the fact that such searches are "fraught with danger." The court said the fact that the defendant was under the control of another officer at the time Detective Patterson patted him down does not render unreasonable Patterson's belief that the defendant could injure him. **State v. Alamont**, 577 A. 2d 665 (R.I. 1990).

That brings us to the Supreme Court decision of **Michigan v. Summers** (*supra*). The facts are quite simple. Officers were about to execute a warrant to search a house for narcotics in the basement, and ascertaining that defendant owned the house, the police arrested him, searched his person, and found in his pocket an envelope that contained 8.5 milligrams of heroin. Eight others were also detained. The focus for the Court was simple. Did the initial detention violate the defendant's constitutional right to be secure against an unreasonable seizure of his person? By the time police searched him they knew who he was and had a probable cause right to arrest. The balancing test had to be applied.

Key number (1), the police had a warrant and most citizens would stay to protect their own interests (except those who would flee to avoid arrest). Key number (2), the type of detention imposed is not likely to be exploited by the officer or unduly prolonged to get more information since the search will more than likely give them everything they need. Key number (3), the officers have dual interests; flight prevention and safety. Key number (4), the process often gets speeded up if occupants are present to open doors that are locked thus also preventing destruction by force. Key number (5), the connection of the occupant with the house gives the officer an easily identifiable and certain basis for determining that suspicion of criminal activity justifies a detention. The Court sums it up by saying: "If the evidence that a citizen's residence is harboring contraband is sufficient to persuade a judicial officer that an invasion of the citizen's privacy is justified, it is constitutionally reasonable to require that citizen to remain while officers of the law execute a valid warrant to search his home. A warrant to search for contraband...implicitly carries with it the limited authority to detain the occupants...while the search is conducted.

Trying to balance **Ybarra** and the implications of **Summers** has thus created a dilemma for many courts. The "no-innocents-present" formula works quite well for those already on the scene of a valid search. The dilemma arises when an outsider arrives at the scene after the search has begun. Courts are divided upon "mere-arrivals" and "late arrivals." "Late arrivals," with a known past record, are not given much in the way of rights. However, an unknown "mere arrival," without any indicia of crime involvement being displayed, has caused concern. A California court says that, without more, merely appearing nervous after being told about the search is not enough to justify a frisk. **People v. Pullar**, 270 Cal. Rep. 277 (Cal. Dist. Ct. App. 1990). In **U.S. v. Salazar**, 47 Crim. L. Rep. 1156 (S.D.N.Y. 1990), the late arrival was a man who matched a "tip" thus that court felt this was not a "mere arrival" type case. This case was affirmed on the ground that **Alabama v. White** (*infra* at **Terry** sec. XI)was satisfied. **U.S. v. Salazar**, 945 F. 2d 47 (C.A. 2d 1991).

An Arizona court decided that the police do not have an unrestrained right to stop a person who approached a place that is being searched. Where the police have no idea of whether the person is an occupant for **Summer's** purposes they must have some articulable reason for stopping such a person. In this case the defendant had never been sighted at the premises before. Besides, the court said, there was no way he could flee with evidence that is inside the house when he is outside of it. Finally, the defendant did not make any menacing overt gestures to justify **Terry-Ybarra** activity. **State v. Montoya**, 793 P. 2d 1126 (Ariz. Ct. App. 1990).

The "mere arrival" and the "late arrival" theory is well illustrated by the facts of a Florida decision. The police were conducting a search of a home when a man pulls into the driveway. The police do not recognize him. As the officer approached his car, the driver, Mr. Thomas, exited his car in a very normal manner. The police officer asked for his name and he responded truthfully. The officer then asked for his driver's license. He gave the officer his license and the police "ran" it. The report revealed that Mr. Thomas was wanted for a probation violation. The officer then searched Mr. Thomas and his car. Drugs were found in the car. He was not known to be an associate of the home occupier and, therefore, he could not be classified as a "late arrival." Even if the police had a warrant to search all vehicles present, they could not, under that warrant, search the car of a mere arrival. The arrest was lawful, however. Could they search the car incident to that arrest? No. Why? He was not stopped by the police officer for any violation of the law and the officer, while standing near the car, did not get plain view or smell, *etc.* His exit was voluntary and the police could not assume, therefore, that he exited to destroy **Belton** search incident rights. His car was not blocking traffic nor did it need community caretaking, therefore, even an inventory search would have been improper. He did not try to get back into his car, thus the police did not have **Michigan v. Long** rights to "frisk the car." Probable cause to believe the car was a repository for drugs did not exist, therefore, **Ross**, **Johns** and **Houghton** search powers did not arise. The drugs found were not in plain view thus not admissible under that theory. All in all, it was a bad day for these police. **Thomas v. State**, 761 So. 2d 1010 (Fla. 2000).

B. Search Incident to Searches: Reminders

I. Includes any search-like activity no matter how it is denominated by the police including:
   A. full-field searches;
   B. first activity; and
   C. sensory inspections.

II. Includes any lawful search
   A. warranted;
   B. exigency based; and
   C. consent based.

III. Nature of the place – critical:
   A. Public:
      1. combination lawful activity with unlawful activity location – (typical barber shop or cigar shop/bookie joint); or
      2. criminal activity only place (chop shop).

   B. Private:
      1. non-criminal activity center (son stores drugs in mom's home – no sales center) or;
      2. criminal activity center ("crack-house"/bucket shop)

IV. Rights of police when conducting lawful search:
   A. Overall – any place – any nature;
      1. right to non-interference while search is conducted;
      2. right to:
         a. issue "stand still" order; or
         b. order non-controllers to leave; and

3. *no* right to frisk non-controller unless independent **Terry** fear arises.

B. Criminal activity center:
1. no possible innocents present theory indulged;
2. at a minimum may frisk all present;
3. some states allow arrest based on probable cause derived from"no innocents present" rule – full search incident rights; and
4. arrivals during search:
   a. "late" arrivals--those who by articulable suspicion or probably cause "belong" – frisk or arrest rights arise; and
   b. "mere" arrivals – only mere suspicion or less – no rights in police other than to bar entry – a possible innocents rule.

C. Non-criminal activity center:
1. arrest known controller(s) of place when such person believed, due to probable cause, to be human source of the criminal activity;
2. may enlist arrestee(s) to aid in room-by-room coverage of the house to help minimize destruction; and
3. others – treat as in IV. A. above

XI. A Brief Look at <u>Terry</u>

Terry v. Ohio and Its Progeny

A. Time Line

Prologue: Before 1968 and as part of the so-called criminal law revolution, the Supreme Court, in a series of opinions, began striking down often used vague and ambiguous statutes that failed to tell the citizens what actual conduct was prohibited. These statutes were the darlings of police because the "usual suspects" could be "rounded up," then searched and interrogated. By 1972 vagrancy statutes were declared void by the Supreme Court. Something, however, was needed to allow police to interfere in acts of preparation and to interfere with citizens in a limited way where more than a hunch, but less than probable cause, existed in the mind of the police. The case chosen was **Terry v. Ohio**.

Terry v. Ohio 392 U.S. 1 (1968) – what it did and did not answer:

1) Gave vague recognition to the mere confrontation right, but did not spell out its definition;

2) Created a *right* to STOP a citizen on *articulable suspicion*;

3) Gave police a non-**Miranda** protected, on-the-scene, right to ask fear dispelling questions;

4) Gave police a limited right to conduct a frisk if fear not dispelled by defendant's answers to questions (or to frisk if recently committed crime is one normally thought to involve a weapon);

5) Did *not* define "brief stop" and its durational limits;

6) Did *not* spell out how much force could be used by the officer.

7) Did *not* determine if the source of articulable suspicion could come from an "outside" source such as:

   a) fellow police officer (inter or intra departmental)

   b) known informant

   c) anonymous tipster;

8) Did *not* determine if a mere hunch could rise to articulable suspicion if defendant merely fled presence of officer nor did it fully address furtive gestures.

Adams v. Williams, 407 U.S. 143 (1972):
1) articulable suspicion *can* come from a known informant;
2) **Aguilar** standard applied--now use totality under **Gates**.

Pennsylvania v. Mimms, 434 U.S. 106 (1977):
1) applied **Terry** to driver of automobile;
2) this case did not address the passengers.

Brown v. Texas, 443 U.S. 47 (1979):
1) directly addressed what is *not* articulable suspicion;
2) slowly walking away when police approach is *not* articulable suspicion;
3) no mention of faster flight.

U.S. v. Mendenhall, 446 U.S. 544 (1980):
1) fully defined a *mere* confrontation;
2) the first of the drug courier-airport stop/confrontation cases.

U.S. v. Cortez, 449 U.S. 411 (1981):
1) clarified that stop and frisk are separately based issues;
2) police may have articulable suspicion to stop *but* have no fear;
3) frisk right thus not automatic in all cases.

Ybarra v. Illinois, 444 U.S. 85 (1981):
1) fear element not automatically present when conducting a search in a *place* of *public accommodation* and *members* of *public* are present;
2) rule true even if a statute exists directing police to frisk everyone present.

Michigan v. Long, 463 U.S. 1032 (1983):

1)   allows **Terry** frisk of area of car to which driver has access if reasonable fear for officer's safety exists;

2)   not a strip search.

Florida v. Royer, 460 U.S. 491 (1983):

1)   defines difference between mere confrontation and seizure;

2)   confrontation becomes a seizure when defendant's property is withheld by police while they seek a consent and *no* articulable suspicion is present.

U.S. v. Place, 462 U.S. 696 (1983):

1)   first case to address **Terry's** "brief stop" and duration issue;

2)   if delay caused by police – the delay goes against the police.

U.S. v. Sharpe, 470 U.S. 675 (1985):

1)   second case to address **Terry's** "brief stop" and duration issue;

2)   if delay caused by defendant delay goes against the defendant.

U.S. v. Hensley, 469 U.S. 221 (1985):

1)   source of information case;

2)   articulable suspicion can come from interdepartmental police source (intradepartmental also) with no corroboration requirement;

3)   stopping officer "assumes the risk" that other officer lied, *etc.*

U.S. v. Sokolow, 490 U.S. 1 (1989):

1)   the "even a stopped clock" rule;

2)   use of profile might independently, under totality, have elements of articulable suspicion;

3)   force defined-if force is needed there shall be *no* **judicial second guessing** as to amount of force that should have been used.

Alabama v. White, 496 U.S. 325 (1990):
1)   source of information case;
2)   articulable suspicion, if corroborated even as to innocuous details, can come from an anonymous tip.

California v. Hodari D., 499 U.S. 621 (1991):
dicta suggesting that running upon sighting police may give rise to articulable suspicion.

Florida v. Bostick, 501 U.S. 429 (1991):
1)   latest case defining mere confrontation;
2)   a "close quarters" case – public bus – police in aisle – mere confrontation.

Minnesota v. Dickerson, 508 U.S. 366 (1993) proper non-manipulative frisk under **Terry** may give police probable cause to seize "thing" felt – called "plain feel."

Maryland v. Wilson, 519 U.S. 408 (1997) applies danger analysis of **Mimms** to passengers.

Chicago v. Morales, 527 U.S. 41 (1999) merely loitering does not yield articulable suspicion.

Illinois v. Wardlow, 528 U.S. 119 (2000):
1)   unprovoked "headlong" flight at sight of officers;
2)   heavy crime area (narcotics trafficking in this case);
3)   officer has articulable suspicion and may stop the "flee-er."

Florida v. J. L., 529 U.S. 266 (2000)
1)   "bare" anonymous tip (D is carrying a gun);

2)   no "insider" detail;

3)   **Alabama v. White** standards have *not* been met;

4)   no articulable suspicion.

B.   A Fresh Look at Terry v. Ohio

The major issue regarding any seizure involves the credibility of the officer's testimony. That credibility issue is even more significant in the **Terry**-stop or articulable suspicion based investigative stop. How does the judge know the difference between a hunch and articulable suspicion? The Supreme Court tells us we are to require testimony indicating the officer's training, the officer's experience and both, if necessary. The prosecution, therefore, must do more than have the officer tell "the story." The training/experience foundation must be laid. In **Terry**, Officer McFadden's basis of interpreting the facts was more experiential, as the Court emphasized his 30 or so years of "mean street" law enforcement experience. Had McFadden's experience been earned in traffic enforcement or police administration, then unless there was specific training in "joint casing," only a hunch would have been present. The rule announced in **Terry** does not appear to allow for a mystical transfer of departmental knowledge; that what one officer knows all officers know. If that were the case "training" would not have been mentioned. To be sure, even this training and experience, when matched up against articulable facts, can yield the seizure of a totally innocent person. See **Sokolow**, 490 U.S. 9 and 10. But as the Court notes, facts justifying an arrest may also net an innocent person. Those cases we never see because no guns, drugs, stolen property, or dead bodies are found during the seizure and the search intrusion permitted under the type of seizure made.

Just because an articulable reason can be proven does not mean that a reasonably trained or experienced officer would also have made that stop, let alone a reasonable non-police-officer type person. All officers are and should be suspicious of aberrant behavior. Their lives depend on being armed with heightened suspicions. To allow a Fourth Amendment intrusion requires more, however. Consider, for example, **State v. Richcreek**, 1997 WL 18221 (Ariz.). A police officer on patrol comes upon the scene of an accident. However, the driver of the car involved is nowhere to be seen. As passengers are sought, cars passing by "gawked" as is normal. The defendant also slowed, nearly stopping while he pulled over to the side of the road. However, before coming to a full stop, he quickly accelerated and left. The officer gave chase and stopped the defendant. Why? What articulable facts of criminal involvement arise from these facts? What experience or training is there to credit if the manner of driving away did not in itself violate the law? The "why" could not be credited by the Supreme

Court of Arizona though the officer was very credible in giving his story. This was a hunch that yielded a crime totally unrelated to the basis for the hunch. Clearly, stopping a car is more than a "mere confrontation or encounter "as discussed in **Mendenhall, Bostick,** *et al.*

Though police do not generally have the right to seize those who "gawk" at accident scenes, independent justifiable reasons can arise that give the police the right to make a stop. Such was the situation in **State v. Victorsen**, 2001 WL 410380 (Minn. App.). A hit and run accident had occurred and an officer was dispatched to the scene. On his way, he was told that a bumper with a license plate was left at the scene and to pick it up. As the officer neared the scene, he saw a blue pick-up truck parked on the opposite side of the street from the accident and upon his approach, that truck left the scene. Did the officer have articulable suspicion to believe that the driver of the truck may have been the "hit and run" driver who had returned to get the evidence? Both the officer and the court said yes. The officer's conclusion was reasonable.

To be sure, it is not always easy to distinguish a mere confrontation from a seizure or investigative detention. A decision from New Jersey further illustrates the difference. **State v. Rodriguez**, 765 A. 2d 770 (N.J. Super. 2001), involved what the police called a "field inquiry" at one of the local bus stations. Whether this was a consensual encounter is the key question in all of these cases. The police in this case had a tip fully describing the men who left Ocean City for Philadelphia to buy drugs and then were to return between 3:30 and 5:00 p.m. The Philadelphia bus arrived at 4:45 p.m. and the two described men got off the bus. The officers approached and asked "would they mind talking to them." The men said yes and agreed to walk back to the patrol office. The men were separated. They were asked if they "had anything they shouldn't have." A consent to search was given and a packet of heroin was found in Rodriguez's socks and another in the pocket of his shorts. Numerous bags of heroin and a needle were found in the bag he carried. The court admits that there is "no single litmus test" for these types of cases. They also realize that these types of encounters often escalate from inquiry to stop to arrest. The totality must be examined. The asking was not a demand to accompany these officers. The fact that they were told they did not have to comply with the request means that the encounter at the phone booth did not escalate into an investigative detention when the defendants entered the patrol room. The evidence was admissible.

When the hunch crosses the line into the area of a constitutional seizure is thus always a critical question. Consider the facts of **Thomas v. Com**. 1997 WL 20384 (Va. App.). A roadblock for drunk driving was set up at an interchange on I-64 in the Richmond area. Mr. Thomas entered the ramp area but stopped thirty yards before the roadblock. No effort was made by Thomas to turn around. The officer, on foot, approached Thomas' vehicle. As she approached, Thomas got out of the vehicle and walked around to the passenger side where a taller man exited the vehicle. So both were standing there when the officer arrived. The officer asked for and got Thomas' name and address. The computer said he was a "suspended habitual offender" DMV-wise. While awaiting this information, the odor of alcohol and blood-shot eyes were detected and the men were asked to do some field sobriety tests. The driver "failed" those tests and refused to take the field breath test. An arrest was made. When did the seizure occur? Thomas would like to say it occurred when he stopped his vehicle or when the officer first approached. If that were true, he would win. The hunch was there but no seizure occurred because the roadside meeting was the result of Thomas' voluntary stop. The initial meeting was a mere police/citizen confrontation at the side of the road. The hunch became articulable suspicion upon the traffic officer recognizing the articulable signs of inebriation. The seizure happened when he was commanded to do the field tests. The Virginia court said a seizure occurred when the officer approached. This is, of course wrong, under **Hodari D.** But the court saw nothing wrong with this stop and ultimately came to the right result so that the conviction stood.

The issue of articulable suspicion arises only when a crime is involved or when an emergency dictates stopping someone to keep them out of harm's way. In other words, there must be a law enforcement need to make any kind of a forced, non consensual stop. Thus, a mere articulable reason is not enough to invoke the **Terry** stop doctrine. Illustrative of this is **State v. McFadden**, 1997 WL 10138 (Ark.). Although a juvenile girl was missing it appeared she ran away, as she had done before, on her own volition. The chief and the father of the girl were riding around to see if they could spot her. The chief saw a man in a car, a man that had dated the missing or runaway girl in the past. The blue lights went on and McFadden was required to stop despite the fact that the girl could not be seen in the car; only two men could be seen. A shot gun was seen, a consent to search the driver's house was given. The shot gun was seized as it was suspected of being "sawed off." At the butt of the gun a container area was opened and methamphetamine was found. This was not a mere confrontation because a seizure had occurred. The chief admitted, on the scene, that he was not investigating a crime; "he was merely looking for a missing juvenile." The court said, and rightly so, that "there simply was no crime being investigated which would entitle the officer to stop and detain Appellee...." In accord see **Com. v. Canavan**, 667 N.E. 2d 264 (Mass. App. 1996) where the court discounted the "good Samaritan" motive where the officer stopped the defendant because he "looked lost and needed help."

However, it must be noted that a law enforcement need can arise when otherwise innocent conduct happens too often. In a case from Wisconsin, the officer saw the driver of a car cross the center line not once, not twice, but three times. The third time was the charm. The defendant was forced to stop. To be sure an inattentive driver may be quite sober but wander. But when it happens three times in a short distance the reasonably well-trained or experienced officer is going to stop the car even when "judged against an objective standard." Was this action appropriate or was it merely hunch-based? The Wisconsin appellate court agreed that articulable facts of drunk driving existed. The court noted that, "Suspicious activity justifying an investigative stop is, by its very nature, ambiguous. Unlawful behavior may be present or it may not. The behavior may be innocent. Still officers have the right to temporarily freeze the situation to investigate further." **State v. Knutson**, 1997 WL 6120 (Wis. App.).

The next case, also from Wisconsin, involved some gap in the "total" observed behavior. While on his way to work, the officer observed a car make a quick, unsignalled right turn and then twice cross (by a little) the center line. No stop was then made. While on duty, the same officer sees the same car parked at a tavern and the driver about to go into the tavern. The officer pulled over and observed the car leave the tavern lot. The officer followed it and noted that the driver overcompensated when passing a parked vehicle by going into the opposite lane and coming within 3 feet of the opposite curb. As the car pulled into the driver's driveway the officer stopped his car, got out and approached the driver. Field sobriety tests were failed and an arrest for OUI took place. A blood alcohol test revealed an 0.18% reading. The defendant said there was no articulable suspicion. The appellate court coupled, as had the officer, the separate events that had taken place within a couple of hours time span and felt there was a reasonable basis for the stop. **State v. Kister**, 1997 WL 4730 (Wis. App.).

A routine traffic stop can turn into something more, as most judges know. In a case from Colorado, the more serious problems came after the stop for a broken license plate light and failure to signal a turn at 10:30 p.m. When the driver could not produce a valid registration nor proof of insurance the police suspected the car to be stolen. Neither passenger made any attempt to claim ownership of the car. Everyone was asked for their names and the juvenile passenger gave confusing information. The officers requested all three occupants to exit the car and directed them to sit on the curb. The juvenile was handcuffed to allow the officers to conduct a possible false information charge and IDs on the others. One of the passengers was found to have an outstanding warrant. A **Belton** search incident to that arrest yielded a gun on the backseat floor board. The other adult was put in custody and the juvenile declared the gun was his. The juvenile was formally arrested for gun possession. The juvenile court declared the initial custody upon suspicion of "false information" invalid and suppressed the gun and the juvenile's statements.

The issue on appeal, of course, primarily concerned the first handcuffing episode. The initial traffic stop was proper. The suspicion of a stolen vehicle was reasonable (insufficient proof of registration at a minimum justifies further investigation). The court went on to say that "Officers may reasonably suspect that a passenger in a vehicle suspected of being stolen participated in the crime," especially where it appears that the "occupants of a private vehicle are traveling together by choice and thus may be assumed to have some personal or business association with one another." This suspicion entitled the officers to get names and addresses while everybody stands still. Obviously this juvenile played games and under **Sokolow** police may use the force necessary to achieve the basis for the stop. **People v. H. J.**, 1997 WL 27172 (Colo.).

Petty things observed always have the potential to lead to bigger things as illustrated by the prior case and a case from the District of Columbia. In **Russell v. U.S.**, 1997 WL 9976 (D.C. App.) an officer knew that a D.C. regulation required out-of-state cars to display a proper inspection sticker from the license issuing state. Mr. Russell's car did not have a Virginia sticker though it had Virginia plates. Russell was stopped and a driver's license check turned up a suspended license and Russell was arrested. The **Belton** search revealed a loaded pistol and 12 rounds of ammunition. The trial court refused to suppress the evidence on the weapons charge even though Russell argued that the District had no business stopping him for a violation of Virginia law. He argued this even in the face of the D.C. regulation. The court called his argument "ingenious" but "incorrect." There was a reasonable suspicion to stop Russell and inquire why there was no sticker and whether there was a reasonable explanation for there not being one (new windshield; newly purchased, *etc.*).

Adams, **White**, and **Hensley** teach us that the source of articulable suspicion need not originate with the stopping officer. Let us examine a few recent cases to see if these Supreme Court decisions are being properly followed.

Adams v. Williams, 407 U.S. 143 (1972) approved a **Terry** investigation and an ultimate frisk in a fear-based confrontation where the source was an informant known by the police. A recent similar case, **State v. Coleman**, 1997 WL 6299 (Ohio App. 4 Dist.), also was based on a known informant's tip. Police had a general suspicion that a man by the name of Dixon was a drug dealer. The informant told police when Dixon would be on a specific night and that Dixon was the man that drugs were "well hidden" in the car. The police stopped the Dixon vehicle which was driven by Coleman. The drug dog confirmed the presence of drugs. Only a crack-pipe was found in the car while the occupants sat on the edge of the guard rail alongside this stretch of highway. The three were arrested and taken from the scene. Five ounces of crack were found near the guard rail. Under the totality was the stop reasonable? **Adams** was cited. Yes, it was, and only an investigative stop was employed until the dog made a positive indication of drugs. The trial court thought probable cause was required for the use of the dog and, of course, if you applied that standard to the stop then it would have to be found unlawful. This court gently reminded the trial judge to use the correct standard.

In another case, the local postmaster called a deputy sheriff and told the deputy that an "apparently intoxicated person" was driving away in a blue Buick and then he gave the officer a license plate number. Thus, a known private citizen, with significant detail, gave the officer at least articulable suspicion to stop the car. However, the suppression judge found the officer saw nothing to confirm the tip, therefore, the stop was not based on articulable suspicion and that the postmaster did not give the officer more than a bare conclusion. The state took an interlocutory appeal. Prior decisions of the Iowa high court said that information from a private citizen is generally reliable. The appeals court found sufficient evidence of the informant's reliability and independent corroboration was not required. The court cited **Florida v. J. L.**,(*supra*), and **State v. Niehaus**, 452 N.W. 2d 184 (Iowa 1990) in support. **State v. Tyler**, 2001 WL 487428 (Iowa App.).

U.S. v. Hensley, 469 U.S. 221 (1985) gave approval to a stop made by Illinois officers based on a federal officer's direct observation and conclusion of articulable suspicion. The Court said the stopping officers assume the risk, however, that the transferring officer was wrong but it did not require independent corroboration by the Illinois officers. In a recent case, **State v. Kenner**, 1997 WL 13730 (N.D.), the transferred information was intra-departmental. The car was stopped based solely upon the radio transmission. The trial court suppressed the evidence. The North Dakota court reminded the judge that "where one officer relays a directive or request for action to another officer without relaying the underlying facts and circumstances, the directing officer's knowledge is imputed to the acting officer...." and the "arresting officer is entitled to assume that whoever issued the directive had probable cause." The court, citing **Hensley**, said if that standard is good for probable cause it should also be good for articulable or reasonable suspicion. The defendant argued that the suspicion focused on the driver, Deseth, not him, and the stopping officer never saw Deseth driving. The court said there was a transferred/relayed basis for the stop and the police were not required to make a positive identification of the driver, in this case, since the car was more than adequately described.

The key to reasonable reliance on police-to-police information is proof that the transferring officer had either articulable suspicion or probable cause. The officer making the stop "assumes the risk" that the relaying officer is wrong. Proof of the relaying officer's basis of information must be offered to the suppression court unless independent proper suspicion or cause arose in the seizing officer's presence. The state lost its case in **Caldwell v. State**, 2001 WL 433385 (Del.), because the relaying officer did not testify and independent articulable suspicion did not arise as the officers approached Caldwell.

Alabama v. White, 496 U.S. 325 (1990), teaches us that an investigatory stop can be based on a corroborated tip from an anonymous tipster. In fact, for articulable suspicion, the things corroborated can be wholly innocent detail. In a case accepting **White, State v. Zapata**, 1997 WL 40593 (N.J. Super. A.D.), the court upheld the judge's denial of the motion to suppress. They label such anonymous calls "the factual predicate necessary to justify an investigatory stop when there is corroboration of the information furnished." In fact, in this case, failure to stop this car after corroboration would have been a dereliction of duty, the court said. When the stop occurred the police observed the cocaine in plain view.

In a case that combines relayed information and an anonymous tip see **State v. Wilhoit**, 1997 WL 32777 (Tenn. Crim. App.). The police received a 911 call from an unknown citizen indicating that a Mercury Lynx was being operated by a "potential" drunk driver in the Roan Street area of Johnson City. The officer who received the call relayed the information to all patrols. Officer Nelson was closest to the scene and saw a car fitting the description at a nearby gas station. As the officer arrived he noticed a man standing near a phone booth. That man nodded and pointed to the defendant's car. The car started to leave but stopped, started again, and again abruptly stopped, and again a start and stop. The driver then made eye contact with the officer and the officer said he looked like "an impaired individual "a dazed look...." The officer, Nelson, decided he needed to investigate and pulled his cruiser alongside the Lynx, got out, approached the Lynx and through the open driver's window smelled alcohol. Nelson requested a driver's license but the defendant could not produce one so the officer ordered the defendant to "shut off the car" and to exit the vehicle. The defendant failed the field sobriety tests. The issue was whether Nelson's observations were sufficient for articulable suspicion. The initial encounter (through asking for a license) was a mere confrontation. The seizure happened with the demand to exit and by then enough corroboration had taken place. Proximity in time from report to arrival at the scene and the finger pointing person at the phone booth, along with the verification of other details, helped the court determine that the officer was not jumping to a conclusion. Tennessee's acceptance of **Alabama v. White** came in **State v. Pully**, 863 S.W. 2d 29 (Tenn. 1993). That court was also concerned with vindictiveness and fabrication and say these two problems must be eliminated by good police corroboration of the 1) credibility; and 2) basis of information prongs. See also **State v. Menzies**, 2000 WL 424277 (Tenn. Crim. App.) (unpub. op.).

Police and some judges do not understand that **Terry** announced two doctrines. There is the right to stop a person upon articulable, credible facts. If the answer to the officer's questions in a fear-based stop do nothing to dispel the fear of violence then, and only then, does the officer have the right to conduct a frisk. Thus the issue of the decision to stop and the issue of the decision to frisk are independent issues. One has to find the decision to stop was lawful before he or she can address the reasonableness of the decision to frisk. Even if the decision to stop is reasonable it does not automatically follow that the decision to frisk was reasonable.

For a case noting the type of inquiry required see **In re Steven O.**, 1997 WL 29315 (Ariz. App. Div. 1). The police were conducting a surveillance of a house suspected of being a drug sales point. Two youths got out of a truck that had stopped at the corner. They proceeded in a direction away from the officers until the truck disappeared, reversed themselves, and then one of them went into a house *not* under surveillance. Shortly thereafter that youth emerged from the house putting something in his pocket and he joined his companion. The police believed that a drug buy had just occurred so the youths were stopped. The detectives asked the youths if they had drugs and the reply was "We don't have any drugs, and you can't prove it." The youths began to walk away but the officers grabbed them and frisked them taking a pack of cigarettes from one of them. In that pack was a small quantity of "speed." The court acknowledged that an experienced officer, under the totality, would have a reason to stop and inquire. In fact, the prosecution proved that the lead officer had 100 hours of narcotics training and had observed more than 100 drug buys as well as having participated in a number of undercover buys. However, on the danger issue the record was too general in that the officer seemed to say that user-buyers were like buyer-seller distributors who always carried weapons. This conclusion did not "wash." Frisking is not to be seen as a simple routine police procedure. Articulable facts of an apparent danger are required by this court and, of course, the Supreme Court. These youths were not known criminals, nor was their clothing suspicious as to bulges *etc.* The encounter took place in broad daylight and there were no threatening gestures in this most public of places. The evidence should have been suppressed.

Safety concerns can evaporate and this clearly is the message of **Terry.** Whether they evaporate by the person's responses to questions, or by the facts as they unfold, it does not matter. If the safety concerns evaporate no frisk is permitted. Massachusetts had an "evaporation" case that arose from a routine traffic stop. The subject of the safety concern, of course, was the officer and the object giving rise to that concern was the passenger and not the driver. Clearly this court recognizes that the threat to the officer's safety can come from the passenger and also they clearly recognize that the officer can take control of the whole scene as held in **Ohio v. Robinette,** 519 U.S. 33 (1996). In this case the trooper approached the stopped vehicle from the passenger side. The passenger's back was facing the officer. The officer got no immediate response from the passenger and 20 more seconds elapsed. Eventually the passenger turned toward the officer. The officer asked a question or two but got no immediate response until the passenger said he spoke no English. These delayed responses coupled with an attempt to get out of the car gave rise to reasonable safety concerns. The officer asked the passenger to get out and wait at the rear of the car, which he did. No further passenger activity occurred. The driver produced his registration and license. Upon completion of his work with the driver the trooper "then turned his attention to" the passenger and got consent to look in his wallet. Since the passenger quietly waited was there any **Terry** basis for a restarted dialogue with him? Had the safety concerns, which were real, disappeared? A continued detention was not justified in this case because "any basis for further detention evaporated." The officer was no longer traveling on articulable suspicion but was operating only on a hunch.

Minnesota v. Dickerson, 508 U.S. 366 (1993), the plain feel case, finally recognized that when properly frisking a person for weapons it is possible that the officer might know immediately that the thing touched is contraband drugs and thus get probable cause to remove the items despite the fact that they do not feel like a weapon. The several state courts are combing through their cases to help find the lawful parameters of the plain feel area.

In a case from Georgia, the defendant argued that a frisk ostensibly was used not to discover weapons but only to discover drugs. If he is right, then, of course, there were no safety concerns and the frisk was totally illegal since **Dickerson** talks in terms of a lawful **Terry** frisk and the somewhat inadvertent, but hoped for, discovery of drugs. The court felt that a **Terry** stop of a known drug dealer in a high drug sales area at 30 minutes past midnight just after a sale is an episode fraught with safety concerns, thus the frisk for weapons was not improper even if the officer had hope of finding drugs. **Hill v. State,** 1997 WL 4610 (GA. App.).

Wisconsin also dealt with a case where the judge concluded that the connection between drug crimes and guns created a right to a **Terry** frisk for weapons. Like Georgia, this court noted that the officer's observation of drug-sales-like moves gave **Terry** articulable suspicion thus negating a need to ask fear-dispelling questions. Therefore, the distinction between **Terry's** crime-in-the-planning stages case and possible-crime-observed case is clearly pointed out. This Wisconsin officer frisked including the groin area and felt "little rocks" or "stones" plus folded paper. The officer retrieved 29 baggies of crack and folded money from the defendant's underwear. The juvenile judge admitted the evidence. There was proof of the officer's training and experience. There was no evidence of manipulation. The question whether groins are areas where people hide weapons was briefly addressed and the appeals court said yes, people do that too. The court said, "to suggest that police should be prohibited from conducting a pat down in a suspect's groin area flies in the face of the entire purpose of the protective pat down." **In re Jerry O.**, 1997 WL 3329 (Wis. App.).

Clearly, Wisconsin accepts **Dickerson**. But not all courts have yet accepted its rule. For example, it took Michigan three years to accept. Michigan's case is a thorough opinion. **People v. Champion**, 549 N.W. 2d 849 (Mich. 1996). The court especially focused on the hidden agenda issue only slightly alluded to by the Wisconsin court. That, of course, is the whether pure inadvertence is required. Of course, the Supreme Court decided **Dickerson** as a plain feel, plain view case which, of course, adopted **Horton v. California**, 496 U.S. 128 (1990) within **Dickerson's** reach. **Dickerson** makes clear that the safety concern must be there as required by **Terry** itself. Michigan focused on the lawfulness of the stop and the factors that gave rise to the stop. If the stop and fear factors are legitimate then **Horton** takes over. If an item, not a gun, is felt then **Horton's** "items incriminating character are immediately apparent," inquiry is made by the suppression judge. The judge must also keep in mind that **Texas v. Brown**, 460 U.S. 730 (1983), and **Arizona v. Hicks**, 480 U.S. 321 (1987), tell us that "immediately apparent" requires only probable cause, not absolute knowledge cause. Lawful access, reason to fear, fear not dispelled, and frisk permitted, non-manipulative touching are the cornerstones of **Dickerson**. Once the non-weapon item is touched the credibility of the officer's testimony regarding immediately apparent probable cause assessment is then made.

In the **Champion** case, what factor led the officer to believe that the pill bottle he felt contained contraband in the probable cause sense? Five factors supported the officer's probable cause conclusion. The court noted that: (1) the defendant got out of his car and walked away upon seeing the patrol car and uniformed officers; (2) Officer Todd recognized defendant and knew of his previous drug and weapons convictions; (3) the officers were in a high drug crime area; (4) the defendant had his hands tucked inside the front of his sweatpants while walking away from the officers and refused to take his hands out of his sweatpants after being repeatedly asked to do so; and (5) Officer Todd, having had twenty years experience as a police officer, was aware that contraband, and in particular controlled substances, were often carried in the type of pill bottle that he felt on defendant's person. The court said, "We cannot imagine that any reasonable person in Officer Todd's position, given all of the above circumstances, could have concluded that Mr. Champion was carrying prescription medication, or any other legitimate item in the pill bottle in his groin region." Clearly, this court has come to the realization that the "times they are a-changin" and that there are certain realities known and not merely guessed at.

Sometimes the "feel" of the frisk creates an ambiguity. Suppose the officer feels a hard object not apparently drugs but not necessarily a weapon? Is the officer who says it felt like a weapon and thereafter removes it only to discover a non-weapon criminally related item to be believed or disbelieved? If safety is truly the concern can there be some ambiguity that needs to be resolved by allowing the retrieval of the ambiguous but hard object? This, of course, is the whole issue of credibility. Either the judge credits the officer's testimony or does not credit that testimony. No case better illustrates the problem than **Com. v. Dedomenicis**, 674 N.E. 2d 1099 (1997). The officer properly stopped a person and properly conducted a frisk. While frisking the defendant the officer felt an object which the officer characterized as "hard." The officer inserted his thumb in the defendant's pocket and determined it was a wad of bills. Since the suspected crime was a very recent robbing in the vicinity, the officer felt he had probable cause to arrest the defendant and the money was fully removed from the defendant's pocket. The defendant argued that the intrusion by the thumb exceeded the scope of a frisk. He asked the judge to perform a personal experiment by having the judge frisk him with the money in his pocket. The judge foolishly decided to go along and decided it did not feel like a weapon. Of course the same conditions as on the day of the frisk did not exist. In fact, the judge fully credited the officer as telling the truth, but did not credit his conclusion that the money felt hard. The judge suppressed. The appeals court felt that "Having found the officer credible, the judge was not warranted in considering his own 'feel' of the wad of money in the defendant's pocket to counter the other evidence before him." The conversion of the fact finder into a defense witness was harshly criticized. The court notices the significant differences between the original encounter and this courtroom experiment. The judge's "evidence" was inappropriate. The bottom line is simple: either credit the officer's testimony or discredit it. Judges are not to conduct their own experiments. Judges are fact finders and not fact makers.

Two significant decisions by the U.S. Supreme Court indicate the balance they continue to try to achieve in the **Terry**-stop area. The decisions are **Illinois v. Wardlow**, 528 U.S. 119 (2000) and **Florida v. J. L.**, 529 U.S. 266 (2000). In **J. L.** the police received an anonymous tip that J. L. would be at a certain bus stop wearing a plaid shirt and would be carrying a gun. Without this tip the scene was just 3 guys at a bus stop; one with plaid shirt. But unlike **Alabama v. White**, no future conduct was predicted and J. L. was doing nothing wrong when he was frisked and the gun was found. Without predictive information the police had nothing against which to test the informant's knowledge or credibility. Visible attributes are not enough. The Court also said NO to a firearms exception **Terry**-tip, but left open the "he's carrying a bomb exception."

Mr. Wardlow was in a high crime area. He spotted police merely walking in his direction. He ran. They chased. He lost. He was frisked and a gun was found. As a convicted felon he should not have had that gun. The Court reminds us that mere presence in a high crime area is not enough for a **Terry**-stop. Upon unprovoked flight, however, in such an area, common sense can be used. An ambiguity arose and, as **Terry** notes, such ambiguity can be resolved.

How have the states reacted to **Wardlow**? Colorado appears to understand fully the import of the distinction between merely avoiding police and "headlong flight" as defined in **Wardlow**. A patrol stopped at a corner and the officers saw four people standing outside a bar. The officers did not know how long they had been there and did not see any "passing movements" or exchanges. When the people saw the car they began walking away. The patrol car drove onto the sidewalk and the people continued to walk. The police noticed that the defendant walked with one hand open and the other closed. The police drove back onto the street and came up side-by-side with the group. The car was stopped and the officer asked, in a conversational tone, for Outlaw to "come over to the vehicle." Outlaw approached the car with his left hand closed. He slowly made a sweeping motion with that hand and some clear plastic was seen that somehow disappeared when his hand moved back to its original position. Two baggies of crack were near Outlaw on the ground. The trial court ruled the encounter consensual and Outlaw, as a repeat offender, was sentenced to 24 years on conviction. The appeals court said the burden was on the defendant of going forward to show the unconstitutionality of the seizure. The Colorado high court said Outlaw met his burden that this meeting was not consensual; the sidewalk tailing proved that. The seizure was complete with obedience to the command to "come here." This was not a **Wardlow**-like case. It is, as they note, no crime to merely be in a high crime area. It took the officers quite some time to realize that he might have something in his hand but they had no **Terry** fear that it was a weapon. All in all this was a "bad" stop. **Outlaw v. People**, 17 P 3d 150 (Colo. *en banc* 2001).

An Ohio court also had to decide whether a consensual encounter occurred in **State v. Fleeman**, 2001 WL 243301 (Ohio App. 4 Dist.). **Mendenhall, Royer, Hodari D., Bostick**, and **Rodriguez** from the U.S. Supreme Court were all used. The trial court held that to identify oneself as an officer meant a seizure took place, which, of course, is totally wrong and is so noted by the appellate court. The court agrees with the U.S. Supreme Court that an officer can engage a citizen in a conversation. The real issue was whether a reasonable person would feel free to keep on going or to break off such a conversation. The case was remanded for the trial judge to make that analysis.

Wardlow and headlong flight was an issue in **Woody v. State**, 765 A. 2d 1257 (Del. 2001). To be sure, an person can walk away from an officer who tries to start an encounter and, the court adds, a refusal to cooperate with the officer cannot be the sole ground for a **Terry** suspicion to stop. The area in this case was a high crime area. Woody and two other men were seen standing behind a house. The officer approached the back yard. Woody turned and walked toward the front and then ran back toward the rear door after seeing the officers walking to the rear from another direction. The other two men did not move. There were no fences surrounding this yard or any other yard in the area. Woody was noticed clutching a bulge in his left front coat pocket and the police suspected a gun or a large amount of drugs. Woody did not stop upon command and he had to be tackled. A.38 caliber pistol was found. Cause for a **Terry** stop (but not an arrest) arose by Woody's flight before any attempt to detain him. His conviction was upheld.

However, there must be headlong flight before **Wardlow** can be used as analytical tool. In a Maryland case, the defendant rapidly parked his car and exited it. The officer knew a robbery had occurred around the corner some thirty minutes earlier so he put one and one together and came up with three. So the officer stopped the man and found drugs. The high court of Maryland reversed the denial of his motion to suppress. The court saw nothing more than a hunch; a hunch based, perhaps on race. Why would a robber drive around the block and park? No one seemed to know how the robber got away. Fast parking might be a traffic law problem, but the conduct is fairly inconsistent with a robbery getaway so close to the scene of the robbery. There was nothing in this case to justify the use of **Wardlow Stokes v. State**, 765 A. 2d 612 (Md. 2001).

We now have a much more complete picture of the scope of **Terry** and its progeny. A "snapshot" review of recent decisions indicates most courts are diligently trying to apply those decisions. For example, Texas faced a known informant case much like **Adams v. Williams** (*supra*). **Carmouche v. State**, 10 S.W.3d 323 (Tex. Crim. 2000). A reasonable **Terry** fear was found in **Putnam v. State**, 995 P. 2d 632 (Wyo. 2000) and in **People v. State**, 2000 WL 174606 (Ill. App. 2d).

Concerned that there are too many frisks without fear, Texas made sure their officers understand there are no routine pat-downs. The need to frisk arises only upon articulable specific facts and rational inferences drawn therefrom. It also made sure that everyone knows that the officer does not have to be personally afraid of the defendant. A routine traffic stop allows the officer to order the driver out under **Mimms**, but there must be a little more such as at night or alone on a deserted highway, *etc.* This appears to be within the reasonable understanding of **Mimms**. **O'Hara v. State**, 27 S.W. 2d 548 (Tex. Crim. 2000). Louisiana seems to have a reasonable understanding of "plain feel" as evidenced by their opinion in **State v. Small**, 2000 WL 303125 (La.), as does the Nevada court in **State v. Conners**, 994 P. 2d 44 (Nev. 2000). Appellate courts in Iowa and Illinois understand the police caused delay-defendant wins his or her case through their decisions. **Collins-Draine v. Knief**, 617 N.W. 2d 679 (Iowa App. 2000). A Nebraska appellate court also saw a prolonged detention that was unjustified. The officer could not understand the defendant's strange travel plans and prolonged the stop to ask more. **State v. McGinnis**, 2000 WL 136818 (Neb. App.). An Illinois court found flight to avoid an impending unlawful stop within the **Wardlow** rule. **People v. Thomas**, 734 N.E. 2d 1015 (Ill. App. 5 2000).

Sometimes state courts pretend to follow the Supreme Court, but at the same time misinterpret to achieve their preferred rule rather than proving that their laws, custom, history or constitution demands a more pro-defense stance. Such is the case of the Pennsylvania Supreme Court in their latest plain feel case. They give a great definition of immediately apparent plain feel but deny its use in a case because they refuse to believe that mostly drug dealers carry pill bottles in the linings of their coats and not in their pockets. Two dissenters saw the sham but it is now the law of Pennsylvania, **Com. v. Stevenson**, 744 A. 2d 1261 (Pa. 2000).

There are continuing attempts by cities and towns to regain control of their streets from gangs and drug dealers. The **Morales** decision clearly demonstrates the Supreme Court's resolve to carefully protect the right of citizens to amble or congregate, thus such ordinances are reviewed from the perspective of unconstitutionality rather than being presumed constitutional. This puts the burden where it belongs – on the government. Cleveland has attempted to create an anti-drug dealer, profile-based drug-related activity ordinance. The Cleveland ordinance allowed a **Terry** confrontation and seizure if the suspect tried to talk to another person on the street or hailed another person in an automobile. The ordinance prohibited "repeatedly stopping, beckoning or attempting to stop another person in any public or private place, or hailing, waving arms or making other bodily gestures to stop another person in an automobile with the intent to engage in drug-related activity. The ordinance was deemed unconstitutional. Those arrested were almost always Hispanic or African-American, thus suggesting racial profiling. Surprisingly, despite all the stops, very little drug evidence was found. The ordinance was over-broad because it reached ordinary lawful conduct and not criminally unique conduct. The ordinance also had a tendency to put the proof of innocence on the defendant which is also prohibited. **City of Cleveland v. Branch**, 2000 WL 33123591 (Ohio Mun.).

C.   **Terry** Checklists

POLICE-CITIZEN CONFRONTATIONS

I.   Types

    A.   Mere Confrontations

        1.   no articulable suspicion – the "shady" looking character

        2.   only a right in the officer to ask the defendant to stop and answer questions

        3.   citizen (defendant) does not have to agree – can in fact ignore the officer

    B.   Investigative stops

        1.   articulable – suspicion based stop

        2.   brief detention allowed

        3.   police conduct limited to whether the stop is:

            a.   fear-based – object=dispel danger

            b.   non-fear-based-object=consent to search

II.   Questions asked at Investigative Stops

    A.   Fear-based

        1.   to dispel fear

        2.   failure to answer – fear not dispelled

        3.   "smart" answer – fear not dispelled

               4.   reasonable answer – fear dispelled

    B.   Non-Fear based

        1.   to obtain consent

        2.   failure to answer or "no" – defendant is free to leave

        3.   "yes" as long as VKI – consent O.K.

III.   Role of Flight/Furtive Gesture in any stop case

    A.   If flight/furtive gesture deemed innocent avoidance (judge's call) then no articulable suspicion nor probable cause

    B.   If flight/furtive gesture deemed significant (judge's call) then:

        1.   mere confrontation raised to articulable suspicion

        2.   mere observation raised to articulable suspicion

        3.   investigative stop *may* rise to probable cause or non-fear-based *may* rise to articulable suspicion of fear-based

D.   Terry Check List

The Articulable Suspicion Based Investigative Stop

I.   Unusual Conduct Observed

    A.   By police officer (**Terry/Sibron/Peters**)

        1.   experience or training

        2.   leads to a reasonable conclusion

    B.   By informant

        1.   reliable & known standard – some corroboration preferable

        2.   anonymous tipster standard (**Alabama v. White**) – corroboration essential

II.   That Unusual Conduct Indicates that Criminal Activity is "Afoot"

A. Preparation (**Terry**) – preattempt conduct
1. flight/furtive gesture (more than innocent avoidance)
2. lying-in-wait
3. reconnoitering
4. enticing
5. other unusual behavior that does not appear to have a reasonable explanation

B. Perpetration (**Peters, Mendenhall, Sokolow**, *etc.*)
1. crime begun, known--actual perps not seen but only person(s) present is/are the suspect(s) (**Peters**)
2. drug courier cases (**Mendenhall, Reid, Royer, Sokolow**)

III. Such Activity Allows an Investigative Stop
A. After officer identifies himself as an officer
B. Allows reasonable questions (**Miranda** not required since "on-the-scene")
C. Limited by time (**U.S. v. Place/U.S. v. Sharpe**)

IV. Police Activity Also Limited By Which Branch Of The Investigative Stop Is Shown By The Facts
A. Fear Branch – (**Terry**)
1. ask questions
2. fear dispelled – let suspect go – do not touch
3. fear not dispelled – carefully limited search – pat-down of outer clothing (and perhaps some soft-sided container being carried by suspect-frisk incident?)
4. may remove that which feels like a weapon – (better to be safe than sorry-resolve ambiguity)
B. Non-Fear-Branch (**Mendenhall**)
1. seek consent (V.K.I. standard-**Royer**)

2.   if consent given-search

3.   if consent not given-let suspect go *unless* fear branch invoked

E.   Mere Confrontation or Terry Seizure: How To Assess the Difference

1. Police have only mere suspicion or hunch; cannot and do not try to prove articulable suspicion.

2. Officer approaches slowly and calmly

3. If in uniform gun not drawn nor does officer have hand on gun = *No* display of armed force despite fact subject can see holstered gun.

3. Plains clothed officer may have I.D. at the ready or shield on open display *but* gun cannot be seen = *No* display a mandatory seizure/armed force.

4. Tone of voice is calm and conversational; look for "excuse me" or "pardon me" = *no command* to stop thus no seizure.

5. Officer does not touch or significantly block any attempted exit of subject = *no touching*.

6. In calm conversational tones officer explains his/her concerns; need not be extended speech.

7. Officer asks to see in calm conversation tones

    a. Identification or other pertinent document (e.g., airplane ticket) and, if complied with, it is immediately returned = *voluntary consent--* look for "may I" or "would you mind showing me" type of phrases

       or

    b. Asks for the right to search/frisk

       1)   a bag, briefcase or other object or

       2)   the person in calm conversational terms = *Voluntary consent*

Note Well: The touch/command seizure analysis applies to the initial confrontation. The *consent* analysis requires the application of "feel free to leave/say no" because it requires balancing:

a) place/conditions, *and*

b) characteristics of the subject *and*

c) the conduct/demeanor of the police

Also remember that the seizure analysis no longer requires being concerned with the "feelings" of the subject--the Supreme Court intended to simplify the process by focusing only on the event and the conduct of the officer--it is not a VKI area!

F.   Abandonment/Consent
After a Terry Claimed Seizure

Remember: Abandonments and Consents must the product of the possessor's free will.

Note: If the seizure is lawful such consents/abandonments require less analysis than if the seizure was unlawful.

    1.   S. Ct. does not require subject to be told he has right to withhold consent *but* lack of such advisement *may* be used by judge-especially important when Subject *not* familiar with police practices.

    2.   Abandonment in lawful seizure cases occurs when subject disclaims control/ownership of thing (bag, etc.) *Or* surreptitiously tries to jettison something from his person.

    3.   In either one or two the most important factors are:

        a.   Characteristics of the subject and

        b.   Words of officer indicating that subject must consent or would be fully strip searched (as opposed to frisk)

Caveat: Unlawful **Terry** stop cases and consents and abandonment

    1.   Fruits of the poisonous tree doctrine fully applicable to **Terry** seizures as well as full-blown arrests.

    2.   **Hodari D.** teaches us that a seizure is a single act *not* a continuing act--look for

        a.   Unlawful seizure

        b.   No search conduct or mere frisk with no **Dickerson** discovered evidence

        c.   *True* release of subject officer observes by does not walk side-by-side

> d. Officer observed jettisoned item/picks it up/arrests subject=*abandonment*=independent source

3. Several S. Ct. cases teach us about *attenuation* of an illegal seizure.

> a. Determined if the seizure is unlawful, if so;
>
> b. Determine how soon after the seizure the consent is sought--the time span issue
>
> c. Make sure that full rights to refuse consent are given *and* that officer appeared willing and ready to accept a no
>
> d. Judge the scene-how public/private and how that might impact on a free will decision
>
> e. Judge the defendant as to
>> 1) prior police involvement and
>> 2) personal "I.Q." traits
>
> f. If a release of the subject is claimed determined the bonafides of that claim.

XII. Hot Pursuit or Some Degree

The Fourth Amendment does not require police officers to delay in the course of an investigation if to do so would gravely endanger their lives or the lives of others. If speed is essential, speed is allowed. The court must look to the exigencies of the situation. If it finds that a search without a warrant was imperative, then the fruits of that search are valid. **Warden v. Hayden**, 387 U.S. 294 (1967). In **Warden v. Hayden** an armed robbery had occurred. Within minutes the police were at a house that they thought the robber had entered. They entered with the permission of defendant's wife. They fanned out. One officer found clothing in a washing machine that fit the fleeing felon's description. Hayden was found in bed feigning sleep. Guns were found in a flush tank in a bathroom adjacent to Hayden's bedroom. Some things were found under his mattress. Since the seizure of some of these things occurred before Hayden's arrest and most were taken outside the "wingspan" doctrine of a search incident to arrest, there arose the problem of the scope of a search connected with "hot pursuit." Of course, the officer looking in a washing machine finding clothes was not looking for the fleeing felon. Could this clothing be introduced? Yes. He could have been looking for the weapon. This was justifiable because he did not know that the others had already located the weapons. Had he found the clothing after the apprehension, knowing that Hayden was already in custody, then the items would not have been admissible. The Court ruled that the permissible scope of a "hot pursuit" search must be as broad as may be reasonably necessary to prevent the danger that the suspect at large in the house may resist or escape.

Does "hot pursuit" mean a chase on and about public streets? No, said the United States Supreme Court in **United States v. Santana**, 427 U.S. 38 (1976). Hot pursuit does mean some kind of chase, but it need not be an extended hue and cry in and about the public streets. The fact that the pursuit ended almost as soon as it began did not make it any less a "hot pursuit" sufficient to justify the warrantless entry into Santana's house. "Once Santana saw the police, there was likewise a realistic expectation that any delay would result in the destruction of evidence." Here the pursuit started while Santana was standing in her own doorway. The Court concluded that a suspect may not defeat an arrest which had been set in motion in a public place by escaping to a private place. By innuendo, the Court recognized the sanctity of the home, and affirmed that sanctity in **Payton v. New York**.

The court, in **Santana**, recognizes, therefore, that grave danger to others is not the only reason for "hot pursuit." But the burden is on the state to show the existence of an exceptional situation. **Vale v. Louisiana**, 399 U.S. 30 (1970). In **Vale**, Vale ran into his house but was immediately captured. Then the police went to a back bedroom and found the "goods." The police were operating under an arrest warrant. Thus, the crime for which Vale was being pursued was not immediately fresh as in **Santana** and **Warden v. Hayden**.

The crime for which the pursuit is begun is then said to be required to be fresh. The sense of immediacy must permeate the situation. This is not to say that other exigent circumstances could not exist. But if they do, they are not "hot pursuit." Likewise the suspect must be on the move. See **Johnson v. United States**, 333 U.S. 10 (1948) and also **Chapman v. United States**, 365 U.S. 610 (1961). Though coming to the right conclusion based on **Payton** and the arrest of persons at their home without a warrant and without consent to enter, the Ninth Circuit failed to recognize the hot pursuit theory of **Santana** and made an unnecessary distinction between **Santana**, **Payton**, and the case before them. **U.S. v. Johnson**, 626 F. 2d 753 (C.A. 9th 1980).

There is no clear-cut line that designates the difference between "hot" or "fresh" pursuit and "cold" pursuit. When does the pursuit begin to cool? Can police operate under "warm" pursuit and gain admission for evidence gathered while in such pursuit? This was the issue presented in **People v. Morrow**, 433 N.E. 2d 985 (Ill. App. Ct. 1982). The rapes were eight hours old when the victims gained their release. The victims immediately went to the police who in turn immediately accompanied the victims to a garage which the victims believed to be the scene of the crime. Thus the pursuit was at best "warm." The car described by the victims was spotted through an open service door. The garage was entered and the car searched. Incriminating evidence was found in the car. Of course, the defendant complained not only of the car's search but also of the "plain view." The court recognized this as "warm" pursuit. Unnecessary delay could be fatal to this investigation. Rather than utilize "open fields" to justify the "plain view" of the car, the court chose to characterize the entry of the curtilage as a petty intrusion that yielded a brief plain view. This search was permissible under these circumstances. The search of the car was, of course, unjustified.

The temperature of the pursuits continues to decline. Consider this "lukewarm" case. Since the arrest in this case cannot be based on consent some other exception had to apply or the defendant's blood alcohol test was the result of or "fruits" of an illegal arrest. The charge was driving while intoxicated. The police came on the scene at least 15 minutes after the defendant had left the scene and more time elapsed after the officer arrived so he could get statements. This New York court readily admits that there is no possibility of hot pursuit but that this was at least "lukewarm." The evidence for this jailable New York offense would have disappeared had a warrant been sought. Therefore, "lukewarm" pursuit is alright. **People v. Odenweller**, 527 N.Y.S. 2d 127 (N.Y. Sup. Ct. App. Div. 1988).

Montana has accepted fresh or warm pursuit by its decision in **State v. Dow**, 844 P. 2d 780 (Mont. 1992). In this case the police tracked the defendant by fresh footprints in the snow some two hours after the crime. Important to the Montana was the nature of the crime, rape and robbery, thus they were willing to allow this delayed pursuit.

Three more recent cases dealt with "hot" or fresh pursuit statutes and whether they were properly observed. Those decisions may be found at **Porter v. State**, 765 So. 2d 76 (Fla. App. 4th Dist. 2000), **State v. Rideout**, 2000 WL 1643947 (Me.) and **Com. v. Sadvari**, 752 A. 2d 393 (Pa. 2000). In **Porter** the police started their pursuit in Pompano Beach and captured the fleeing suspect in Fort Lauderdale. The trial court denied the motion to suppress. The statute exempts officers from their territorial restraints. Why the debate? A prior case was deemed a fresh pursuit case. Indeed it was a "no proven fresh pursuit" or any pursuit for that matter. It was a naked "BOLO, saw his car parked" case. The **Porter** case, hoping to give some future direction, borrowed three criteria from Colorado and its decision in **Charnes v. Arnold**, 600 P. 2d 641 (1979). Those criteria are: (1) did the police have to act without unnecessary delay; (2) was the pursuit continuous and interrupted (though they may lose sight of him); and (3) was the time from crime to chase close enough to say it was fresh.? The court upheld the admission of the evidence and closed by saying that "if there is anything in our past opinions contrary to these standards, we hereby recede from it."

Maine's statute grants hot pursuit outside the officers' jurisdiction in the same manner as most, if not all, states. The problem in this case was simple. The officer was not in his jurisdiction when the pursuit started and it ended in that same jurisdiction just a few moments later. However, the crime he saw would not have been one a private citizen would recognize; driving while suspended. The chief knew this driver was suspended. Since the chief was "on-duty" in another jurisdiction for other purposes, he was not a private citizen; he was a police officer not appointed in this "foreign" municipality. Thus, he violated or got no authority from Me. Rev. State. §2557. However, since he was on duty he did have statewide authority to affect an articulable suspicion stop so the arrest was good.

Perhaps the worst case involves Pennsylvania. The pursuit started in Pennsylvania near the Delaware state line after the defendant "blew the doors" off the Pennsylvania trooper's car. They stopped the defendant in Delaware. Most states would say convict him. However, the Pennsylvania court said their police must know Delaware's law and since the arrest in Delaware did not meet Delaware standards the arrest and fruits were inadmissible. Pennsylvania officers must now learn the laws of New York, Ohio, Delaware, Maryland, West Virginia and New Jersey.

A really bad drunk driver with outstanding warrants was chased into his garage. The pursuit was "hot." "Mom" Santana's case governed and not **Welsh v. Wisconsin**, **State v. Baumann**, 616 N.W. 2d 771 (Minn. App. 2000). "Mom's" case also foiled the defendant's attempt to avoid prosecution in **State v. Flagg**, 760 So. 2d 522 (La. App. 5 2000).

The tougher issue was faced by the Wisconsin high court in **State v. Richter**, 612 N.W. 2d 29 (Wis. 2000). A police officer, in the early morning hours, responded to a burglary report in a trailer park. He met the victim and she said the burglar went into a trailer across the road. The officer approached the trailer and it showed signs of a break-in. He shone his light through a window and was let in by those sleeping on the floor. They opened the door and pointed out the owner. The officer entered, wakened the owner, and asked for permission to search, was given permission, and he found, in plain view, marijuana. The owner said the entry was illegal. If the entry was not "in hot pursuit" all of the evidence would have to be suppressed because no one invited the officer in. The trial court and the appellate court ruled there was no exigency for a warrantless entry and that the consent was not attenuated from the entry. The Wisconsin Supreme Court disagreed and said there was the exigency of hot pursuit. This was rejected by the Court of Appeals because the officer had not observed the burglar go into the trailer himself. The high court pointed out that **Warden v. Hayden**, 387 U.S. 294 (1967) does not require police observation but fresh observation from credible people. In **Hayden,** a cabby spotted the defendant who robbed a cab company run into a house. The police were notified and they entered. The U.S. Supreme Court approved the entry. The victims in this case were credible. The officer does not have to personally see the entry. He was in hot pursuit.

XIII. Enigma of Ker-Frisbie vis-à-vis the Fourth Amendment

Is it a lesser evil to seize the body of a person than to unlawfully seize evidence from that person? To this point the U.S. Supreme Court had clearly indicated that an illegal seizure or arrest of a person will cause all evidence gained thereby to be illegal "fruits of the poisonous tree." Yet has that Court given the same protection to the individual when the arrest is illegal but no evidence is obtained as a result of that seizure? If it has not, is it fulfilling the mandate of the Fourth Amendment? Consider one of the apparent puzzles of Fourth Amendment arrest law. On two earlier occasions the U.S. Supreme Court has had an opportunity to face the issue of a totally illegal arrest and its consequences where no evidence was derived from the arrest. Those cases are **Ker v. Illinois**, 119 U.S. 436 (1886) and **Frisbie v. Collins**, 342 U.S. 519 (1952). A discussion of these cases follows.

Defendant Ker was in Lima, Peru. He was kidnaped by the officer that was supposed to seek extradition, and he was forcibly brought back to Illinois. Arguing that his due process rights were violated Ker sought relief from his conviction. The Court was not very sympathetic. They, in part, said: "but for mere irregularities in the manner in which he may be brought into the custody of the law, we do not think he is entitled to say that he should not be tried at all...." **Ker v. Illinois**, 119 U.S. 436 (1886). These indeed were tough times for a defendant. The exclusionary rule of **Weeks** had not yet dawned nor were states thought to be bound by the U.S. Constitution. Nowhere in the **Ker** opinion is the Fourth Amendment discussed. Ker based his argument on the Fourteenth Amendment and the extradition treaty with Peru. Would the Court be more sympathetic later?

Defendant Frisbie did not fare much better in 1952. Frisbie was seized, handcuffed, blackjacked and thrown into a car in Illinois to be taken to Michigan. Frisbie argued that his Fourteenth Amendment Rights were violated as was the Federal Kidnapping Act. Citing **Ker** as controlling, the Court held: "There is nothing in the

Constitution that required a court to permit a guilty person rightfully convicted to escape justice because he was brought to trial against his will." Again no mention of the Fourth Amendment. **Frisbie v. Collins**, 342 U.S. 519 (1952).

Yet the Fourth Amendment says that "the right of the *people*" shall be "secure in their *persons*" against unreasonable searches and *seizures* and this right "*shall not be violated.*" The Court in **Frisbie** and **Ker** sanctioned illegal police conduct. Has the Court changed its mind in later decisions?

In **Stone v. Powell**, the Court approvingly cited **Frisbie** where they said they would not abandon the proposition. They said "judicial proceedings need not abate when the defendant's person is unconstitutionally seized." **Stone v. Powell**, 428 U.S. 465, 484 (1976). Interestingly, they label the seizure as unconstitutional yet are not concerned about providing a remedy. Even the great liberal, Douglas, apparently was satisfied with the **Ker-Frisbie** doctrine. He cited **Frisbie** in **Beck v. Washington,** 369 U.S. 541, 581 (1962) where he dissented by saying, "We there (**Frisbie**) held that forcibly abducting a person and bringing him into the State did not vitiate a state conviction where the trial was fair and pursuant to constitutional requirements." Finally, in **Gerstein v. Pugh**, 420 U.S. 103 (1975), the Court said: "Nor do we retreat from the established rule that illegal arrest or detention does not void a subsequent conviction."

How have defendants fared in state courts? Of the 36 states that have faced the issue, only one had rejected the **Ker-Frisbie** doctrine. In **Benally v. Marcum**, 553, P. 2d 1270, 1273 (N. Mex. Sup. Ct. 1976) the New Mexico court saw as the issue whether an illegal arrest was enough to divest the trial court of jurisdiction. Should the court condone illegal action, they asked? In essence they said no. The court held that, "If we are to give substance to constitutional rights, we should be ready to deter disregard of and disrespect for the law." For their support, the New Mexico court looked to the opinion of the Second Circuit in **U.S. v. Toscanino**, 500 F. 2d 267 (C.A. 2d 1974). The facts follow. Toscanino was not a nice guy. He was an Italian drug smuggler. He alleged that he was kidnapped from his home in Uruguay and brought to New York for the trial. The government, because of **Ker-Frisbie**, said: "So what?" The court was bothered that jurisdiction gained through an illegal act might still be used. It saw this as a probable reward for possible police brutality and the lawlessness of kidnapping. This court felt this was inconsistent with the trend caused by **Mapp, Miranda, Wong-Sun, Rochin** and other decisions aimed at curtailing bad police practices. If the Court would prohibit other pretrial and pre-arrest activities why not this one? They felt that **Ker-Frisbie** had to go. (Unfortunately they did not know that **Gerstein v. Pugh** would come down.) Unfortunately, this court, like so many others, did not view this as a Fourth Amendment problem. They too based their decision on due process.

The latest challenge to the **Ker-Frisbie** doctrine comes by way of **U.S. v. Alvarez-Machain**, 946 F. 2d 1466 (C.A. 9th *per cur.* 1991). The Supreme Court granted review on this case because it raised the issue whether jurisdiction is destroyed when the extradition treaty that exists is not employed. The DEA forcibly abducted the defendant from Mexico. The defendant is a Mexican national and the DEA did not invoke extradition nor did it get acquiescence from Mexico. On these facts the district court dismissed the case and ordered extradition. The Ninth Circuit, without citation to **Ker-Frisbie**, affirmed the decision saying **U.S. v. Verdugo-Urquidez**, 939 F. 2d 1341 (C.A. 9th 1991) governs. The Ninth Circuit noted that Mexico was angry and had unequivocally so stated their protestation.

The teachings of **Ker-Frisbie** are clear. Jurisdiction to try a defendant is not destroyed simply because the methods of producing the body of the defendant are criminal in nature. Just as clear, however, is the fact that international relations suffer when the U.S. courts tolerate such conduct. Of course, it is not likely Mexico would have protested had this defendant been a U.S. citizen. Less clear is their position on Mexican born resident aliens of the U.S. or others with a significant connection with the U.S. (illegal aliens). It is also not clear whether they would have protested the kidnaping of a non-Mexican national who was also not a U.S. citizen, *etc.*

The Supreme Court continued their **Ker-Frisbie** law by holding that the forcible abduction of **Alvrez-Machain** did not destroy jurisdiction to try him. What did they say about the extradition treaty issue? If the treaty has not been invoked before the abduction and if the treaty does not otherwise prohibit abductions before invocation, jurisdiction is not affected. **U.S. v. Alvarez-Machain**, 504 U.S. 655 (1992).

CHAPTER THIRTEEN

THE MOBILITY EXCEPTION: MOTOR VEHICLE SEARCHES

474

I.   Why the Mobility Exception

Theoretically, and if the words of the Fourth Amendment were to be taken literally, no search of anyone or anything could be conducted except with a warrant based on probable cause. The exact wording of the Fourth Amendment reads:

> "The right of the people to be secure in their persons, houses, papers, effects, against unreasonable searches and seizures, shall not be violated, and no Warrants shall issue, but upon probable cause

supported by Oath or Affirmation, and particularly describing the place to be searched, and the persons or things to be seized."

The more reasonable and historic position, and more realistic, is that there must be exceptions to the warrant requirement, as long as the probable cause standard is met by the law enforcement officer to conduct a search or seize the individual or thing. Limited intrusions are permitted within the confines of **Terry** and its progeny.

When police stop a car lawfully and smell the odor of burnt marijuana coming from the car, most courts say that such an odor gives probable cause. **U.S. v. Caves**, 890 F. 2d 87 (C.A. 8th 1989). As with any probable cause case, probable cause for a full search of an automobile is subject to no lesser standards even if the vehicle has a reduced privacy expectation. Thus, when police know something is amiss but are unable to identify adequately what the car carries, a search of the car is illegal. **State v. Burkhardt**, 46 Crim. L. Rep. 1161 (Mo. Ct. App. 1989).

But does a police officer have to be hyper – technical in being able to pinpoint the exact drug? Yes, but why? The **Ross** case which is discussed below at Section III. A. says that a probable cause based warrantless automobile search can be as thorough as if a warrant had been issued. With that language, the Court necessarily brought the "particularly described" requirement of a warrant to bear on the issue. The Missouri Appeals Court found that inability to be able to name the drug failed the "particularly described" test. Why? On a lawful stop for speeding, some questioning ensued as to which questions the answers were inconsistent and conflicting. The defendant appeared nervous. An auto "frisk" for weapons was conducted and none were found. Two suitcases lay in the back seat. When asked if those were making her nervous, the defendant said no. She then consented to the search of the car but not the suitcases because she did not want her "lingerie stretched up and down the highway." The officer said he would not do that and asked her to tell him where the contraband was. She then said "search it yourself because I'm not going to tell you where it's at." Ultimately, 127 pounds of marijuana were found. Because of the coerciveness issue, consent was ruled out. **Berkemer v. McCarty** would even cause the un-**Mirandized** questioning to be suspect because it was not part of the routine traffic stop. The only thing left was to determine if there was an independent source for a probable cause based search not tainted by police illegality. The Appeals Court said no because the officer had no odors or signs of a specific drug.

Disregarding this entirely and writing what appears to be a "war-on-drugs" opinion, the Supreme Court of Missouri reversed by finding probable cause based on "suspicious conduct and movements." Only the dissenter recognized the damage done

476

to the particularized description element of probable cause. Even people in automobiles have some Fourth Amendment protection, but not that day in Missouri. **State v. Burkhardt**, 795 S.W. 2d 399 (Mo. *en banc.* 1990).

The **Burkhardt** case illustrates how far some courts are willing to go to back a police officer's "hunch" by interpreting mere nervousness as enough of a furtive gesture to allow a search. In this case, the officer had no tip, reliable or otherwise. He had no independent probable cause. There were no telltale signs; no odors, no baggies, no powder residue. The court totally disregarded the possibility that any citizen is agitated when stopped even when guilty of a traffic violation. The court did not consider the fact that a lone woman might have felt some reasonable nervousness due to the fact of being alone with this armed authority figure. It also failed to consider the constant prodding of the officer to get a consent as contributing to that nervousness. The main thing the court considered was the one thing it was not permitted to do: it saw what the search produced and appeared to be blinded by that. Courts should be careful not to create rules that will be restrictive of citizens' rights because in police hands they will be used by police to test the ultimate limits.

However, when an officer at the scene confronts a driver who has run her car off a clear road into a snow bank into another person's front yard, has blood-shot eyes, slurred speech, and an appearance of disorientation, it is safe to say that the officer has probable cause to make an arrest for driving while under the influence. **State v. McDonald**, 2001 WL 498696 (Ohio App. 5 Dist.) (unpub. op), citing the lead case of **State v. Homan**, 89 Ohio St. 3d 421 (2000).

The necessity of meeting the probable cause standard is further illustrated by three Iowa cases. All three cases properly demonstrate the need by the police to establish a *nexus* or connection between the defendant, his or her crime and the vehicle. When conducting a search, as opposed to some limited intrusion (inventory or frisk), there must be more than inherent mobility, as these cases amply demonstrate.

In **State v. Kuster**, 353 N.W. 2d 428 (Iowa 1984), the defendant moved to suppress evidence taken from his truck because no warrant was used. Although the police had an arrest warrant for the defendant, they had no search warrant for the truck. The state argued in the trial court that the seizure was a legitimate impoundment under **Opperman** (*infra*); therefore, the routine inventory properly yielded the evidence. The court did not agree since the defendant was nowhere near his vehicle when arrested and the car was in no danger of vandalism where it was safely and lawfully parked. Neither **Belton** nor **Bertine/Opperman** could be relied upon. On appeal the state alternatively argued probable cause to search the vehicle. The problem was that the state developed no evidence on this theory at the trial level during the suppression hearing. The court was not willing to presume probable cause. Besides, that court went on to say, citing **State v. Aschenbrenner**, 289 N.W. 2d 618, 619 (Iowa 1980), "officers are bound by their true reason for making the stop. They may not rely on reasons they could have had but did not actually have." This is not necessarily followed in all states, by the way. Based on the **Kuster** facts, there appeared to be no facts that tied the defendant and his crime to his truck, so that the state was not only without probable cause due to a lack of *nexus*, it could not even rely on the inevitable discovery doctrine which Iowa follows.

In **State v. Lam**, 391 N.W. 2d 245 (Iowa 1986), police were given the description of an automobile that was used to effect the "get-away" from the scene of a burglary. One of two defendants was arrested. The other defendant was known to be aware of the arrest and it was probable that, with this knowledge, the car could have been removed by this free defendant. To prevent this, the police, without a warrant, towed the car to the crime scene to seek an identification. Failing that, it was then taken to a police lot. The free defendant called and asked for the release of his car. After he arrived at the stationhouse, he was asked for his consent to search the car and the defendant consented. The car was then searched, revealing some "fruits" of the burglary. The defendants argued, on appeal, that the seizure was unconstitutional. Citing **Carroll** and **Cardwell** and emphasizing the inherent mobility of automobiles even when parked, **Carney** (*infra*) was cited. Iowa again fully recognized the automobile exception. It also acknowledged the probable cause present in this case. It held that a prompt seizure was required under these circumstances because of the clear likelihood that "...the car and its contents may never have been located again."

Unlike **Kuster,** there was a clear *nexus* between the crime, the defendants, and the automobile. The automobile was clearly crime implicated as one of the tools of the crime. As clearly crime implicated was the van used in **State v. Cain**, 400 N.W. 2d 582 (Iowa 1987). In **Cain,** the police located the defendant's van parked in front of his residence while he was being questioned at the police station. A witness to the towing of the stolen tractor was brought by the defendant's house to identify the van. After the positive identification the police looked in the window and saw some bolt cutters on the passenger seat. A photo was taken from outside the van. The police went to the defendant's door and met his mother. The mother willingly gave the van keys to the police. The van was then searched, and the bolt cutters and pliers were seized. These items were then used as evidence to convict the defendant. The Iowa court labeled this vehicle "lawfully parked but fully mobile," and that finding justified the inherently exigent circumstance needed. Seeing the bolt/cutters and having a positive identification of the vehicle satisfied the probable cause requirement to search and seize the vehicle without a warrant.

Suppose a person is lawfully stopped for speeding but fails to produce a registration slip and denies ownership of the vehicle. Does the fact that a computer check does not yet reveal that the car was stolen destroy otherwise valid probable cause to believe the car was stolen? No, it does not, said a Florida Court in **Rouser v. State**, 579 So. 2d 842 (Fla. App. 1991). Clearly, in a probable cause context, there are always positive and negative facts. That is the function of the totality test. Under a totality analysis, taking everything into account, where was the balance pointing and was the officer reasonable in his or her analysis of that direction are the only questions to be asked.

Trying to sort out what constitutes an indicia of articulable suspicion creates significantly different results. In a Minnesota case, the officer observed a car with a broken side window which can be evidence of a stolen car. The officer's suspicion was genuine, but was it objectively reasonable? The car was not stolen, but the driver was drunk (.20 under anyone's standard) and a child was in the car. The officer ran a stolen car check before the stop but it did not show up as stolen. Knowing that cars can remain "undiscovered as stolen," he stopped the car anyway for that purpose, thus allowing the officer to discover the driver's condition. However, no training or experience evidence was offered by the state regarding the reasonableness of the suspicion that a broken window was "theft of car" evidence and not broken to steal contents or accidentally broken. Thus, there was no proven articulable suspicion. **State v. Britton**, 604 N.W. 2d 84 (Minn.2000).

In one Maine case, an officer saw a person whom he believed to be driving while on suspension. When he stopped the car, the driver was someone else that happened to look very much like the original target. A license check at the scene revealed that this gentleman also was operating under suspension because a state I.D. and not a driver's license was given to the officer. Was this a "hunch" or articulable suspicion? Since the car was registered to the man, Clark, who was the suspected driver and the resemblance was so close, the court found articulable suspicion. The request for identification did not exceed the circumstances justifying the initial stop. **State v. Huether**, 2000 WL 361648 (Me.). See also **State v. Gulick**, 759 A. 2d 1085 (Me. 2000), in which reasonable and articulable safety concerns arose because the defendant was parked in an empty, darkened lot of a closed emergency medical care facility at about 3:00 a.m.

The U.S. Supreme Court has repeatedly said that when an ambiguity needs resolved, the police must be able to act by way of a brief seizure. In most instances, a reasonable, non-criminal explanation will end the stop and allow the citizen to go about his or her business. Connecticut's high court fails to recognize that some areas are truly high crime areas, especially at night. The state, of course, would have to prove that point, but, once proven the "freezing" of the situation should allow the brief seizure permitted under **Terry v. Ohio** and its progeny. In **State v. Donahue**, 742 A. 2d 775 (Conn. 1999), the officer approached a car late at night and parked in an area of recent drug activity. To be sure there was no crime or violation committed in the officer's presence in this case. The officer observed lawful driving, parking, and sitting in the parking lot of a club that had closed for the evening. The officer turned on his blue lights so the driver would know who it was that parked behind him. This was found to be a seizure despite the fact there was no touching. The light was seen as a command which was obeyed because the defendant did not try to leave. The state foolishly conceded this point. The only real question was whether there was an ambiguity to resolve. The court said no, thus, the drunk driving charge could not stand because the officer did not observe any traffic violation nor any furtive conduct, and the "Wants and Warrants" check revealed nothing. The court was mainly concerned that neighborhood profiling was involved and that they would not tolerate. The dissent, however, accused the majority of overruling, by implication, their prior rule that a mere approach is not an investigative stop. The dissent felt that was the evil of the decision. The dissent also said there are provable trouble spots in every community which can be proven by statistics. Common sense is no longer tolerated, it felt. Therefore, in the dissent's view, police in Connecticut must now "simply shrug their shoulders and allow a crime to occur or a criminal to escape."

The articulable suspicion issue in **State v. Galgay**, 2000 WL 381843 (N. H.), concerned erratic driving. The driver passed the trooper but then slowed down. As the trooper attempted to pass, the driver swerved toward the left. The officer tailed the car as it made a right turn almost colliding with concrete construction barriers. Then the officer saw the driver enter a restaurant's parking lot by driving over a curb and barely missing the sign. This was articulable suspicion. The rational inferences from these facts warranted an investigatory stop.

Merely leaving the scene upon the approach or sighting of a police officer, is not, by itself and standing alone, suspicious conduct justifying an investigatory stop. No one has to stay where they are merely because an officer approaches. **Cummings v. State**, 765 A. 2d 945 (Del. 2001). It was daylight and the defendant was parked near some trash bins in a public area. The defendant safely drove away as the officer approached. This conduct in no way matched the headlong flight of **Wardlow** discussed in the **Terry** section of Chapter Twelve.

Just because an articulable reason can be proven does not mean that a reasonably trained or experienced officer would also have made a stop, let alone a reasonable non-police-officer type person. All officers are (and should be) suspicious of aberrant behavior. Their lives depend on being armed with heightened suspicions. To allow a Fourth Amendment intrusion requires more, however. Consider, for example, **State v. Richcreek**, 1997 WL 18221 (Ariz.). A police officer on patrol comes upon the scene of an accident. However, the driver of the car involved is nowhere to be seen. As passengers are sought, cars passing by "gawked" as is normal. The defendant also slowed, nearly stopping while he pulled over to the side of the road. However, before coming to a full stop he quickly accelerated and left. The officer gave chase and stopped the defendant. Why? What articulable facts of criminal involvement arise from these facts? What experience or training is there to credit if the manner of driving away did not in itself violate the law? The "why" could not be credited by the Supreme Court of Arizona, though the officer was very credible in giving his story. This was a hunch that yielded a crime totally unrelated to the basis for the hunch. Clearly, stopping a car is more than a "mere confrontation or encounter" as discussed in **Mendenhall**, **Bostick**, *et al.*

Though police do not generally have the right to seize those who "gawk" at accident scenes, independent justifiable reasons can arise that give the police the right to make a stop. Such was the situation in **State v. Victorsen**, 2001 WL 410380 (Minn. App.). A hit and run accident had occurred and an officer was dispatched to the scene. On his way he was told that a bumper with a license plate was left at the scene and to pick it up. As the officer neared the scene, he saw a blue pick-up truck parked on the opposite side of the street from the accident. Upon the officer's approach, that truck left the scene. Did the officer have articulable suspicion to believe that the driver of the truck may have been the "hit and run" driver who had returned to get the evidence? Both the officer and the court said yes. The officer's conclusion was reasonable.

Does an officer have to stop a car immediately at the first sign of bad driving, or can the officer, for five miles, follow and further observe fog line crossings, in-lane weaving, and still have articulable suspicion? A defense attorney who does not have much has to try anything. The defense lost. **State v. Loch**, 618 N.W. 2d 477 (N. D. 2000). For similar cases of "making sure," see **State v. Flanagan**, 2000 WL 763332 (Ohio App. 9), and **State v. Anez**, 2000 WL 1585073 (Ohio Com. Pl.).

Ohio has at least two cases of extended articulable suspicion. In **State v. Napier**, 1998 WL 281 368 (Ohio App. 9) (unpub. op.), the officer noticed a nervous reaction when the officer asked about money, drugs, or weapons. When asked for consent to search, the driver said it was not his car, that it belonged to Carpenter. The police now had conflicting statements of ownership. The dog was walked and it alerted when passing the open window. The dog then jumped into the car and sniffed the ash tray. When asked, the defendants said they did not have a key to the trunk even though they said their clothes were in the trunk. The trunk release button did not work. Gun, money and marijuana were found after the search. Should these men have been released after the citation was issued. No. New and independent articulable suspicion arose allowing detention until the drug dog was brought forward. See also **Ohio v. Chapel**, 2000 WL 329661 (Ohio App. 5) (unpub. op.) where, after the stop, nervousness and inconsistent stories coupled with a visible tilt to the vehicle gave new articulable suspicion to bring the dog (within 7 minutes of the original stop) for a sniff. Accord see: **Mitchell v. U.S.**, 2000 WL 2331950 (D.C.).

Strange after-stop movements by passengers to reach the back seat and a cooler located there gave at least articulable suspicion under **Long** and **Mimms** for a **Terry** frisk of the passenger compartment of the car. **State v. Ballard & Miller**, 1997 WL 531216 (Ohio App. 2) (unpub. op.).

West Virginia correctly realizes that a game officer must have at least articulable suspicion to stop a vehicle to examine it for illegally taken game. **State v. Legg**, 536 S.E. 2d 110 (W.Va. 2000).

Once one accepts the principle that some searches may be conducted on probable cause and without a warrant, can there be acceptance of a further series of exceptions? Whether the answer is yes or no, the Court has chosen to expand the exceptions for "search-like" intrusions and often without reference to the right of law enforcement to *seize* and hold as a separately recognized, less-intrusive police activity than a search. For example, a police officer may take control of something, deny access until his pre-search information has been tested by a neutral and detached magistrate. Except for the body of a person, this could have been accomplished in most, if not all, "houses, papers, and effects" cases. People have been and should be held in higher esteem and not subject to unreasonable restrictions. What we have seen, despite law enforcement complaints to the contrary, is an expansion of warrantless intrusions, with an attempt to maintain the delicate balance necessary to keep a free society from becoming a police state.

One of the major exceptions to the plain language of the Fourth Amendment is the so-called "automobile exception" or as it is labeled here, the mobility exception. The first major pronouncement of the mobility exception came in **Carroll v. U.S.**, 267 U.S. 132 (1925). In **Carroll**, the Court said, yes, there are privacy interests in an automobile and those interests are constitutionally protected. **But**, the ready mobility of the automobile justifies a lesser degree of protection than persons, papers, houses, and other effects. Mobility is the principal, but not the only reason advanced, however. The Court also acknowledges a lesser exception of privacy with respect to the automobile. **South Dakota v. Opperman**, 428 U.S. 396 (1976). That reduced expectation of privacy arises from the tremendous amount of regulation, controls, (some states require inspections) and, of course, licensing by the various governmental units. See also **State v. Cain**, 400 N.W. 2d 582 (Iowa 1987). However, a lesser degree of protection does not mean a lesser degree of probable cause. See **Acevedo** (*infra*). Therefore, law enforcement officials are given greater intrusion rights where motor vehicles are concerned. The nature, types and limits of those intrusions will make up the bulk of this chapter. The types of intrusions to be examined are:

1. Full-field strip searches;
2. Exigency or emergency beyond mobility searches;
3. Search incident to arrest;
4. Terry-type intrusions;
5. Inventory intrusions;
6. "Plain view" searches;
7. Consent searches.

As with all intrusions, however, there are correlative doctrines that may affect the admissibility of incriminating evidence found. The following section discusses those related concepts that impact upon automobile searches or intrusions.

II.   Related Applicable Doctrines or Rules

A.   Standing

The first doctrine or concept to be considered is that which the courts label as standing. Simply put, in order to complain one must prove that his or her privacy was invaded. The Court has said that the Constitution protects persons and not places. A person cannot assert the violation of another person's privacy; a right that is not to be vicariously asserted.

The case that most clearly illustrates this concept also happens to be an automobile search case. In **Rakas v. Illinois**, 439 U.S. 543 (1976), the Court held, in essence, that only those with control or some degree of control can object to an illegal search. The Court does not require a showing of title, ownership, co-ownership, or other standard level of rightful possession as taught to lawyers in law school. Control, the right to come and go in a car, the right to direct the driver in his coming and going, sharing in the cost of operating the vehicle and more, may be enough to establish control. In any event, whether there is control depends on the facts of each case and is governed by considering the totality of all the circumstances. As one court held, merely being the boyfriend of the owner-driver does not create standing in the boyfriend. **Munson v. State**, 458 P. 2d 324 (Okla. 1988). That same court earlier held that mere ownership by one's common law wife is not alone enough. **Cooks v. State**, 699 P. 2d 653 (Okla. 1985). But if one is permissibly driving another's car, there is standing. **State v. Pena-Lora**, 1998 WL 94785 (R.I.).

In summary, who can complain about an unlawful search and seizure? Obviously, the person must have been the victim of the search. To be a victim one must demonstrate two factors: *First*, it must be shown that the victim had some legitimate interest in the automobile, other than being a mere passenger; and, *second*, it must be shown that a personal expectation of privacy was invaded. For example, a mere passenger who puts counterfeit cash beneath a floor mat does not have standing to complain when it is found. **U.S. v. Paulino**, 850 F. 2d 93 (C.A. 2d. 1988). Accord see: **State v. Earley**, 2000 WL 840506 (Ohio App. 9) (unpub. op.).

Does a person who is driving a car with the consent of the owner-passenger obtain the **Rakas** protection? Is a person endowed with both dominion and control plus a privacy expectation or is such a person no more than a mere passenger? The Tenth Circuit felt that being a driver when the owner is present does not establish the kind of dominion and control required in **Rakas**. Therefore, the driver did not have a reasonable expectation of privacy by merely taking a turn at driving. It was unwilling to indulge in an "on-again, off-again" privacy rights analysis; that he had none when not driving but had rights when driving. This certainly is a very strict interpretation of **Rakas**. **U.S. v. Jefferson**, 925 F. 2d 1242 (C.A. 10th 1991), but not an improper conclusion.

Arkansas, however, takes a different view. The court indicated that passengers who agree to share the driving and place luggage in the car are "more than passengers *qua* passengers." It found such persons to be in joint possession of the car. **State v. Villines**, 801 S.W. 2d 29 (Ark. 1990). Ohio agrees with this position. See

State v. Hamilton, 701 N.E. 2d 717 (Ohio App. 2d), rev. denied 687 N.E. 2d 295 (Ohio 1997).

Perhaps the "control" language of **Rakas** and the "mere passenger" language of cases like **Paulino** need to be reexamined due to the Supreme Court's decision in **Minnesota v. Olson**, 495 U.S. 91 (1990), where a mere overnight household guest acquired standing in the host's home. **Rakas** was cited in **Olson,** but it was not overruled. The Court talked about control but not in the automobile context but rather seemed to be stressing the unique qualities of the house as a refuge. The car, on the other hand, shares none of those qualities. The Court will, however, have to resolve this issue ultimately if the states begin to "muddy the waters."

In **State v. Eis**, 348 N.W. 2d 224 (Iowa 1984), for example, the Iowa court held that all lawful occupants of motor vehicles have an expectation of privacy in stopping a vehicle. This was specifically not seen as a rejection of the **Rakas** case because it was the search and not the legality of the stop that was challenged in **Rakas**, according to Iowa. Rather, it said that **Delaware v. Prouse** governed and that **Prouse** made no distinction between passengers and drivers. It then held that an illegal stop of a vehicle effectively constitutes a seizure of the car's occupants. Therefore, if the stop is illegal, evidence seized as a result is fruits of the poisonous tree. But where was the evidence found? If found on the passengers, then this court is correct. But if found in the trunk or on the floor board or even in the glove box, where do mere passengers get standing? Following up on this theme, the Iowa Court of Appeals held that when the police act on nothing more than speculation, conjecture, or surmise such a stop, being illegal, invokes the fruits of the poisonous tree doctrine making the evidence gathered inadmissible. **State v. Losee**, 353 N.W. 2d 876 (Iowa App. 1984).

This small flurry of judicial activity indicates a general dissatisfaction with the **Rakas** rationale. What these courts faced were the basic questions of why police and the state should be allowed to benefit from otherwise clearly illegal activity merely because a person is a passenger and not a controller. In essence, these courts seem to prefer an automatic standing rule but do not want to curtail all illegal police activity that such a rule generally demands. The stop in **Rakas** was illegal. Nothing in **Rakas** permits the search of the passenger based on such an illegal stop. In fact **Rakas** does nothing to expand the search incident doctrine when an illegal seizure takes place. What **Rakas** says is that the automobile, as a container, is not a protected area for such a passenger unless that passenger can show the element of a right to control even in the smallest way. Mr. Rakas had one legitimate argument regarding the drugs found at his feet and attributed to him. Rakas should have argued that at the time of the stop those drugs were things on his person or intimately connected with him. Then he would have argued that his unlawful removal from the car forced him to be parted involuntarily from the intimately connected (under his immediate control) item, thus the seizure of the drugs was illegal in that his personal standing was violated.

This issue has been clarified by the U.S. Supreme Court by their decision in **Wyoming v. Houghton**, 526 U.S. 295 (1999). There the Court found that probable cause existed to believe that the car was a repository for drugs and that included all containers including Ms. Houghton's purse wherein the drugs were found. However, the stop in this case was totally justified.

If a court wants to reject **Rakas** they should have the courage to do so under their own constitution and institute an automatic standing doctrine. If a court wants to accept **Rakas** they must make clear that the search incident doctrine is the key point of analysis regarding the search of any individual and those things within his immediate control. In so doing they will focus on who was searched and not what was searched.

On the surface the **Eis** decision (*supra*) logic makes initial sense when compared to **Hodari D.** A seizure under **Hodari D**. takes place when the person is touched or the person accedes to the command of the police. Certainly a person who stops his car when ordered has been personally seized as has his car been seized. However, whether there is seizure of the individuals in the car after the stop requires some additional analysis. If the car is seized, its contents are seized and passengers at that point are contents, at least. If the police ask passengers to stay in the car truly it can be said they then are personally seized if they obey that command. However, they still only have standing as to their persons and those things intimately connected to them. The car does not appear to be something they possess without a showing of **Rakas** control. And this is a risk the police take. If the police permit the passengers to leave the car, the initial seizure is over. **Hodari D.** makes clear that seizure is a single act and not a continuing act. Evidence voluntarily left behind by the passenger is an act of abandonment and its subsequent seizure, while the passenger is free, would constitute no Fourth Amendment violation under the **Hodari D.** rule. A subsequent seizure of the passenger would not be fruits of the poisonous tree.

Therefore, the logic of cases like **Eis** must now be tested against **Hodari D.** For example, if the police order the passengers out of the car and tell them to leave personal belongings, obedience to this command would apparently constitute a seizure if the passengers are told to "stand by." Whether allowed to leave or ordered to stand by, the "leave belongings" order that is obeyed would not constitute an abandonment of those belongings, thus the expectation of privacy continues in those goods. In any event, the passengers under **Rakas** do not have standing in the car or its trunk at that point as we are taught by **Rawlings** (*supra* at Chapter One).

Suppose the officers order passengers out of the car, allowing them to take their belongings and indicate the passengers are free to go. Is there now a seizure? Unfortunately, it may depend on the locale. Telling a passenger he is free to leave in the middle of a town as opposed to the middle of the desert are two entirely different options. This points out that totality and common sense work both for and against the police. Suppose the free-to-go directive is coupled with an offer by the police to secure transportation or to provide a ride and the passenger turns down the option even in the middle of the desert. The turn-down would be an act of free will, thus the desert factor would lose its impact. This scenario could be stretched further. However, all that need be said is that *all* the facts and circumstances and *all* the cases must be taken into account.

Does a member of a drug importation conspiracy have standing in a car illegally stopped and searched merely because he is a member of a conspiracy? The Ninth Circuit felt there was standing in one defendant even though he could not satisfy any of the **Rakas** tests. The U.S. Supreme Court vehemently disagreed and completely rejected, once more, vicarious standing. See **U.S. v. Padilla**, 508 U.S. 77 (1993).

South Dakota indeed understands who has standing and when that standing exists when it comes to the automobile. In **State v. Ramirez**, 535 N.W. 2d 847 (S. D. 1995), the defendant and his passenger were removed from the lawfully stopped vehicle and placed in the rear seat of the patrol car while the officer received the results of a "wants and warrant" check. Unbeknownst to both, a secret tape recorder ran while they conducted a very incriminating conversation. The lawfulness of detaining them was upheld. The defendants argued that the tape recorder invaded their privacy. The court, *per* Justice Konenkamp, held that since these defendants had no standing in the rear seat of the police cruiser there was no reasonable expectation of privacy in that rear seat. Konenkamp did not praise secret recordings – indeed he said they "may offend individual sensibilities" but there still was no objective reason to expect privacy in the patrol car.

B.   State Action Requirement

Only governments or their agents are prohibited from violating rights. **Burdeau v. McDowell**, 265 U.S. 465 (1921). The Fourth Amendment was intended as a restraint on the activities of government agents and was not intended to be a limitation on private activity. If the record shows that no governmental official had anything to do with the wrongful seizure, then the defendant cannot complain that the evidence acquired was "fruit of the poisonous tree." See also **Stanfield v. State**, 666 P. 2d 1294 (Okla. Crim. 1983), in which this court said a store security guard is a private citizen when the state is not directly or indirectly involved in the search and detention of the defendant.

The problem in applying **Burdeau** centers on whether the person taking the evidence was acting as an agent for the government. A person can become a police agent without being paid for his or her activity. The critical question is whether the private person was directed by police, controlled by them, or motivated by them. See **Perez v. State**, 614 P. 2d 1112 (Okla. Crim. 1980). If such direction, control, or motivation is found, the fact that the police did not do the taking does not relieve the police of improper conduct. However, as **Perez** notes, evidence brought to police without police order or suggestion should be seen as a private taking.

The real test is: Does it appear that the police were trying to accomplish indirectly, by using a citizen, that which the police could not do directly? This was the conclusion reached by a California court. A police officer accompanied a burglary victim to the suspect's car. The police did not get near the car but stood some distance away while the victim entered the car to search for his property. The court viewed this as state action giving great weight to the motives of the private citizen. **People v. North**, 629 P. 2d 19. (Cal. Dist. Ct. App. 1980). See also **State v. Barrett**, 401 N.W. 2d 184 (Iowa 1987) (purely private action) and **State v Campbell**, 326 N.W. 2d 350 (Iowa 1982) (government got too involved in the search).

C.   Abandoned Property

It is a basic property law concept that people can abandon their personal property. That is, they can throw it away, giving up all their rights to ownership, custody, and possession. Abandoned property may be picked up by anyone, and it is theirs to do with as they wish. Applying this concept to the criminal law, police have as much right to take control of abandoned property as any other person. They may keep it, destroy it, use it, and search it. If they search it, establish criminality, and connect it to the prior possessor or owner, that prior possessor or owner cannot complain. Why? The act of abandonment is a surrender of all expectation of privacy. **Harrigan v. State**, 566 P. 2d 139 (Okla. Crim. 1977).

Can an automobile be abandoned? Yes. Whether it has been abandoned or not depends on all the surrounding circumstances of the case. No two cases will necessarily demand the same result. An Oregon court applied the abandoned property doctrine to an automobile. The defendants were trying to elude the police who were lawfully chasing them. They fled into a dead-end alley. They got out of the car and ran

488

away from it. The police took custody of the car, and thoroughly searched it and all its contents. In the trunk was a closed sack which the police opened. A gun was discovered. Since this car was abandoned, the police did not need a warrant. **State v. Green**, 605 P. 2d 746 (Or. App. 1980). See also **Henderson v. State**, 695 P. 2d 879 (Okla. Crim. 1985), where leaving the car after a chase and shoot out was held to be an abandonment.

In one of South Dakota's recent abandoned automobile cases, the defendant left the accident scene and left his keys in the car. The police were told he left just before they arrived. One of the officers entered the car to get the registration or other proof of ownership. He found a "roach" and a "roach clip." The defendant was found, arrested, and a second search was conducted whereupon more drugs were found. The court said that though some standing remained in Anderson, he lost, by his conduct, a justified expectation of privacy (one which society is willing to protect). Citing **Henderson** (*supra*) and cases from Arkansas and Indiana, the answer was he did not have a reasonable, societally protected interest in the car regarding police search activity.

In one case, police observed two men get out of a van at a truck stop, jog into a building, speak with a cashier, and then seem to disappear. After 20 to 30 minutes of observation the police went to the cashier to ask about the men and were told they "had left the area." The police assumed abandonment. Did this conduct present "clear, unequivocal, and decisive" evidence of abandonment? No, said the Iowa Supreme Court in **State v. Baldwin**, 396 N.W. 2d 192 (Iowa 1986). They were unwilling to find an abandonment so easily just because the object was a motor vehicle. Citing, with approval, cases where defendants fled from vehicles after high speed chases and longterm non-use in public areas, the Iowa court felt those cases were markedly different from the conduct in this case. A lawfully parked, vacated vehicle involving no police chase, from which the keys have been removed and the doors closed, is not abandoned.

The real problem in this area is whether the abandonment must be voluntary in the sense that it was not physically caused by illegal police conduct. Obviously, therefore, knocking something out of someone's hand is not an act of abandonment and is not the question raised here. What if the police chase in the case discussed above was totally illegal? Could the Court still find an abandonment? This is one of those areas in which courts do not agree. Some courts, like New York, say you judge whether the action of abandonment was spontaneous or whether it was deliberate. The more time between the beginning of the illegal police activity and the forsaking of the object would aid in finding deliberate abandonment rather than spontaneous reaction. **People v. Boodle**, 391 N.E. 2d 1329 (N.Y. 1979). This is tantamount to applying the philosophy of the attenuation doctrine.

Florida, on the other hand, does not make such an analysis, but comes to the same conclusion. They said a person's otherwise voluntary abandonment of property cannot be tainted or made involuntary by prior police illegality. **State v. Oliver**, 368 So. 2d 1331 (Fla. App. 1979). The Federal Fifth Circuit Court disagrees and says that an abandonment must be freely done in order to be effective. Thus, where the abandonment is a product of police misconduct, that relinquishment cannot be said to be voluntary. **U.S. v. Morin**, 665 F. 2d 765. (C.A. 5th 1982).

These, then, are the three major views on judging the effect of illegal police activity. The Supreme Court long ago recognized that even when police are trespassing they can seize abandoned property, **Hester v. United States**, 265 U.S. 57 (1924), and have only adjusted the geographic area of protection given to private property (**Oliver v. U.S.**, 466 U.S. 170 (1984)). This is fully discussed in the chapter on Abandoned Property. The Supreme Court case of **California v. Hodari D.**, 499 U.S. 621 (1991), held that no seizure takes place until the defendant is touched or the defendant submits to the police command. Thus, **Hodari D.** indicated that an abandonment before seizure was, in fact, a free act of the defendant and indicated the legality of the attempted seizure was to play no role in the admissibility of the evidence. A prior Oklahoma decision appears to be in agreement with this rationale. See **Jackson v. State**, 654 P. 2d 1057 (Okla. Crim. 1982). In the **Jackson** case, a pursuit for speeding was characterized by the defense as a subterfuge and by the prosecution as lawful. The trooper testified that although he had heard information about a Honda, he did not connect this speeding quarry with that Honda. The trooper said he was only out to stop someone who was going 60 miles per hour in a 55 mile per hour speed zone. During this pursuit a green garbage bag full of marijuana was jettisoned from the car. The Oklahoma court addressed the subterfuge issue and held that the contraband was not obtained by the use of an illegal search or seizure. They found the property to be abandoned. This decision appears to fit well within the rule announced in **Hodari D.**

Courts that had been forced to find legality of police conduct to justify the admissibility of such abandoned property must now reexamine those policies. Before **Hodari D.**, Iowa found that flight from police was enough to justify an attempted seizure thus justifying the seizure of abandoned property. **State v. Bumpus**, 459 N.W. 2d 619 (Iowa 1990). Whether that court will continue "a seizure as having begun" analysis or the adoption of **Hodari D.'s** analysis is not clear from reading **Bumpus**. The **Bumpus** position appears to be that abandonment during an attempt at any lawful seizure is done at the defendant's risk. This, of course, is not the policy of **Hodari D.** The question left open on **Hodari D.** was answered in **Illinois v. Wardlow**, 528 U.S. 119 (2000). Wardlow fled at the mere sighting of the approaching police. This unprovoked flight in an area of heavy narcotics trafficking created reasonable suspicion of involvement in criminal activity. Wardlow's seizure was justified. Common sense, the Court said, does not have to be disregarded. An ambiguity had to be resolved.

D.   Statutory Forfeiture

The states and the federal government provide that certain items of personal property are forfeited to the government if the item was used in certain criminal activity. Of course, this would apply and often specifically applies to motor vehicles of all kinds. It is also obvious that not all criminal conduct requires forfeiture. For example, no state requires forfeiture of the car for reckless driving. The standard motor vehicle forfeiture statute involves the use of the vehicle to transport drugs, illicit alcoholic beverages, or other contraband. Forfeiture is akin to abandonment and many states say that the forfeiture takes place and privacy rights are lost when the prohibited criminal conduct occurs. At the moment the police seize such a vehicle, there can be no standing to complain. Some do not think this is rational, however, it does appear to be the general rule. LaFave and Israel, Criminal Procedure, St. Paul, MN. West Publishing Company (1985) at page 169.

The Third Circuit takes a more restrictive view of rights to search when an automobile is seized, and they refused to recognize the search incident to forfeiture that LaFave says is the general rule in this country. In U.S. v. Salmon, 944 F. 2d 1106 (C.A. 3rd 1991), the defendant's car was seized from the parking lot where the drug transaction was to take place because it was used to facilitate the drug deal. The vehicle was searched and a gun held in violation of federal law was seized from a bag in the trunk. The warrantless seizure was upheld by the Third Circuit because it found there was ample probable cause for the Pennsylvania police to believe it was used to "facilitate" the crime. However, they had no probable cause to believe that the car contained further contraband or weapons. The court said, however, that the search without a warrant could not be justified under the so-called "search incident to forfeiture" doctrine. Without proof of a standardized inventory policy regarding such vehicles this search was denominated an investigative and not an inventory search. Therefore, a warrant was required.

The Third Circuit acknowledged some language in Cooper v. California, 386 U.S. 58 (1967) that suggested the "search incident to forfeiture" exception to the warrant requirement. It rejected a broad reading of the following language from Cooper as clearly creating the exception: "would be unreasonable to hold that the police, having to retain the car in their custody for such a length of time, 'four months'... had no right, even for their own protection, to search it. Under the circumstances of this case, we cannot hold unreasonable the Fourth Amendment the examination of a car validity held by officers for use as evidence in a forfeiture proceeding." Looking at the Pennsylvania forfeiture statute, which differs from the federal forfeiture statute, the court said that Pennsylvania does not strip the owner of all privacy rights, noting that title does not pass until a court hearing has occurred. Next, it held that **Cooper** did not establish an exception by the above cited language. What was established was not a right to search but only a right to do an inventory. Therefore, the court ruled that the inventory right recognized in **Cooper** must meet the **Opperman-Bertine** standards of 1991.

What is not discussed in **Salmon** is whether the local police were totally without an inventory policy or whether they were missing only a subject-to-forfeiture inventory policy. If the former, the decision makes sense. If the latter, the court missed the "lawfully in police possession" feature of **Opperman-Bertine** and the court has created a standard requiring a series of inventory policies not required by the U.S. Supreme Court.

Perhaps the best and toughest cases of forfeiture is set out in **Com. v. Crosby**, 568 A. 2d 233 (Pa. Super. Ct. 1990), in which that court upheld the theory of the forfeitability of a drunk driver's vehicle. Using the doctrine of common law forfeiture, the appellate court upheld the trial court's theory that the truck in this case was derivative contraband because it was used in the perpetration of a crime. But the court said, just because it is forfeitable does not end the inquiry. Mandatory forfeiture does not follow. There must be notice and a hearing. At such a hearing the impact on innocent family members must be weighed. Once considered, it is within the discretion of the trial court to order forfeiture and how to direct the proceeds. It will be interesting to see if the Pennsylvania Supreme Court will agree. In any event, prosecutors should not feel bound by using only statutory forfeiture if their state still recognizes common law forfeiture.

Florida's statutory forfeiture act permitted seizure of an automobile believed to have been involved in criminal activity but the statute did not require a warrant or other judicial act to allow the seizure. In **White v. State**, 1998 WL 79060 (Fla), the police seized White's auto, searched it and found crack cocaine. The Florida court said the issue under the Fourth Amendment centered on the warrant requirement absent some additional exigency. They said a warrant was required where the arrest took place totally removed from the car's location. The car was safely and properly parked. They felt this would be stretching the auto exception too far. **Carney** and **Chambers** were cited.

The **White** case was accepted for decision by the U.S. Supreme Court. The rule of the case is simple. If there is probable cause to believe a car is forfeitable contraband, a warrant is not required to seize it if it is located in a public place. **Florida v. White**, 526 U.S. 559 (1999). With this decision cases from the Third,

Tenth, Second and Ninth Circuits were abrogated. The public place, in this case, was either a parking lot or city parking space near White's place of employment. Since it was not at his home or in his garage, no personal right of privacy was violated. Therefore, the **Salmon** case from the Third Circuit is no longer the law.

III.   Gaining Access to the Moving Vehicle

Subject to the abandoned property exception, it is generally stated that the stop of a moving auto must be lawful. Here it is to be assumed that the person properly possessing the auto has not fled the car. There are several rules applicable to the question of the legality of the stop.

A.   Lawful Even Though Pretextual Stops

The first rule is that the stop must be lawful. Suppose an officer has a hidden motive for the stop. Does the pretextuality or hidden motive cancel an otherwise legal stop of the car? No, not according to **Whren v. U.S.**, 517 U.S. 806 (1996). If the stop *could have* been lawfully made that is all that is needed. Whether all police officers *would have* made the stop is not to be used under the Fourth Amendment. Dual motive stops are not subject to condemnation. See also **State v. Bjerke**, 697 A. 2d 1069 (R.I. 1997); **State v. Predka**, 555 N.W. 2d 202 (Iowa 1996) – agreeing with **Whren**; **Buffington v. State**, 492 S.E. 2d 762 (Ga. App. 1997) – exhaust system stop not primary reason for stop; **Holland v. State**, 696 So. 2d 757 (Fla. 1997) – "would have" test jettisoned in favor of **Whren**; **Burris v. State**, 954 S.W. 2d 209 (Ark. 1997) – flopping licence plate stop o.k.--**Whren** approved; **State v. Aderholdt**, 1996 WL 133250 (Iowa) – seat belt violation stop that led to inventory – upheld inventory – did not cite **Whren** but conforms to **Whren** reasoning; **State v. George**, 557 N.W. 2d 575 (Minn, 1975) – unlawful stop but reasoning of **Whren** accepted in fn. 1; and **State v. McBreairty**, 697 A. 2d 495 (N. H. 1997) – accepts **Whren.**

Despite the fact that the Arkansas Supreme Court approved the use of **Whren** in a floppy license plate case, it appears to have two rules regarding pretextual stops. Without citation to their 1997 decision in **Burris** (*supra*), the Court found that police stopping a person going 40 m.p.h. in a 35 m.p.h. zone was merely a pretext to arrest and conduct a search incident. It relied on previous local cases from 1986 to 1993 and **U.S. Lefkowitz**, 285 U.S. 452 (1932). This indeed will cause consternation among trial judges; joy among defense attorneys, sorrow to prosecutors and total disbelief if an average citizen ever finds out. Sometimes, consistency is *not* the hobgoblin of small minds. **Arkansas v. Sullivan**, 16 S.W. 2d 551 (Ark. 2000).

For some reason the Arkansas Supreme Court thought that **Whren** did not mean what it said. It felt it was mostly *dicta*. Therefore, it found that an officer who stopped a car knowing it belonged to a non-law abiding citizen did so unconstitutionally under the U.S. Constitution. That person, Sullivan, was stopped for speeding and an improperly tinted windshield. The officer, upon receiving Sullivan's license, said it was at that point that he knew of Sullivan's reputation regarding narcotics. A rusting roofer's hatchet was seen on the floor of the car. The formal arrest took place and the car was searched and drugs were found. He successfully moved for suppression alleging the arrest was a pretext and a sham. The Arkansas high court affirmed the suppression. A rehearing was requested and the Arkansas court said, "we do not believe that **Whren** disallows...." such a suppression.

However, Arkansas was wrong. In a *per curiam* opinion the Court reversed the Arkansas decision as "flatly contrary to this Court's controlling precedent." The opinion goes on to cite: **Atwater v. Lago-Vista** (the seat belt arrest case); **U.S. v. Robinson** (the full field search on a misdemeanor arrest case); and, of course, **Whren**. The Court also soundly criticized the Arkansas court for saying that it could interpret the U.S. Constitution more liberally than the U.S. Supreme Court had interpreted it. The concurring justices noted the Arkansas concerns and felt there could be an exponential growth "like an epidemic of unnecessary minor-offense arrests." The Court hoped that would not happen but, if it did, it also hoped "the Court will reconsider its recent precedent." **Arkansas v. Sullivan**, 121 S. Ct. 1876 (2001).

B. Random Stops Prohibited

The second rule is that random stops are prohibited. A random stop is one that occurs when there is no crime committed in the officer's presence, and no warrant or independent probable cause exists for the arrest of the individual or seizure of the car, nor is there articulable suspicion of drunk driving, *etc*.

Citing cases from Alaska, Utah, and Washington, Idaho approved a temporary roadblock set up to catch a fleeing felon. Such is permissible as long as the police have probable cause to believe a serious felony is being or has recently been committed, and that the officer reasonably believed the perpetrator is using the highway or streets. Such a roadblock is independent of any statute or administrative regulation governing drunk-driving roadblocks and its notice-to-the-public provisions. **State v. Gascon**, 811 P. 2d 1103 (Idaho Ct. App. 1989). Such a case can be justified under **Cady** (*infra*).

In a Virginia case a brutal murder had occurred and police decided to set up a "traffic canvassing detail" to see if any driver had traveled by the house where the murder occurred during the suspected time of 7:00 p.m. and 11:30 a.m. the next day. The soon-to-be arrestee, Mr. Burns, was stopped. He was the son-in-law of the victim. He was told what happened and was asked to speak to another officer. He was escorted to a police cruiser where he sat in the right front seat. He was given the Miranda rights, and proceeded to deny he was in the house that night; that he only turned around in the driveway. This put him at the scene within the time of the murder. He was asked and he agreed to go to the sheriff's office where the convicting evidence was obtained. The roadblock was challenged under a lack of discretion, control, plan, and other neutral criteria.

The court says that three criteria are to be used to judge a roadblock: (1) gravity of the public concerns served by the seizure; (2) the degree to which the seizure advances the public interest; (3) the severity of the interference with individual liberty citing **Simmons v. Com**. 380 S.E. 2d 656, 658 (Va. 1989). The court then ruled that these criteria were met. To be sure, border policing and road safety were not the concerns here. They also felt "its purpose...." was not "simply to investigate ordinary wrongdoing...." This road block was created "specifically to investigate a particular murder that had occurred in the area...." of that murder. This was an exigent circumstance and would likely be recognized as proper by **City of Indianapolis v. Edmond,** 121 S. Ct. 447 (2001). **Burns v. Com.**, 541 S.E. 2d 872 (Va. 2001).

There are several reasons for a lawful stop not related to legal violations or articulable suspicion. High among them are safety justifications. Thus, when a defendant proceeded through an intersection on a clear night by driving through the right-turn-only lane, the officer's decision to stop the defendant and tell him to obey such lane markings justified the officer in making the stop. The defendant's subsequent arrest for drunk driving was not fruits of the poisonous tree. **State v. Pinkham**, 564 A. 2d 318 (Me. 1989).

In a like vein, consider **State v. Gerrish**, 815 P. 2d 1244 (Ore. 1991). Here the police knew a robbery had occurred just a few minutes before the complained-of stop occurred. The police positioned themselves at the motel's only exit for the purpose of seeking witnesses. Emergency lights were flashing. The defendant drove past this point without stopping and then was ordered to stop. The officer asked about the robbery. When asking that question the officer noticed the defendant appeared to be drunk. Before the field sobriety test was the defendant illegally seized? Citing **Hodari D.** (*supra*), and their own constitution, the Oregon court found no significant interference in the defendant's movements. This was a mere police-citizen confrontation, the environment was not psychologically intimidating, no threats were used, and no ordinary citizen, though annoyed, would feel that his freedom of movement was significantly restricted. The "crime scene" protection interest was the significant factor in this encounter.

By their decision in **Delaware v. Prouse**, 440 U.S. 648 (1979), the Supreme Court held: "except in those situations in which there is at least articulable and reasonable suspicion that a motorist is unlicenced or that an automobile is not registered, or that either the vehicle or the occupant is otherwise subject to seizure for violation of law, stopping an automobile and detaining the driver in order to check his driver's license and the registration of the automobile are unreasonable under the Fourth Amendment." In that same paragraph the court nominally approved 100% roadblocks where all cars are stopped allowing for no discretion in the law enforcement officer. The rule thus announced approved the decisions of Delaware, New York, Arizona, Pennsylvania, the Eighth, Sixth, and D.C. Circuits as well as West Virginia. The decisions disapproved the determinations of Nebraska, North Carolina, Texas, the Tenth and Fifth Circuits. The decision carefully protects the border search case of **U.S. v. Martinez-Fuertes**, 428 U.S. 543 (1976). Yet random "games" were not permitted under **Brignoni-Ponce**.

South Dakota was one of the first courts to interpret **Delaware v. Prouse**. Roadblocks of all cars to check for illegally taken game is alright under **Delaware v. Prouse,** held the South Dakota Supreme Court. They said the probable cause standard would not work. The game belongs to the public and the only effective way to implement the hunting statutes is by use of roadblocks. They said that since hunting is a licensed privilege there is tacit consent by the hunter to the inspection of any game in his possession. The intrusion into the uninterrupted travel of the non-hunter is slight as compared to the greater public interest in the management and conservation of wildlife. **State v. Halverson**, 277 N.W. 2d 723 (S. D. 1979). However, no issue of immediate public safety seems to appear in this case and that fact makes this decision very suspect.

C.   Articulable Suspicion Stops

Outside the valid 100% roadblock scenarios apparently approved, the **Delaware v. Prouse** decision is most important for its recognition that a car can be stopped on less than probable cause. The police officer must have at a minimum **Terry**-type articulable suspicion to make such a stop. Mere suspicions or hunches will not suffice. This concept is illustrated by the following cases.

The first is **State v. Frisby**, 245 S.E. 2d 622 (W. Va. 1978), where the officer observed a strange license plate not commonly known. The West Virginia Supreme Court held that a citizen could be stopped to explain such a license. The second case comes from Georgia. In **State v. Carter**, 242 S.E. 2d 28 (Ga. 1978), the officer observed a light-colored van at 1:30 a.m. exiting a school parking lot. The officer knew that a nearby school had been burglarized recently several times. A radio report had earlier informed him to watch out for such a van as the men were cruising and acting suspiciously. The court upheld the detention since the detention was used to ask for an explanation. They felt an ambiguous situation needed to be resolved.

Certainly, observation of a safe but an unusual driving pattern will catch the eyes of the police. But does it give the officer articulable suspicion? Not necessarily, and certainly, there must be more. In a Vermont case, the officer observed someone he knew and knew he was proceeding in the direction of his home. But the driver, after two miles, stopped and turned into a driveway, stayed there a few minutes, then proceeded, once more in the direction of his home. A second stop was made a few minutes later and again, after a short time, the defendant again drove toward his home. The officer decided to make the stop because he thought the driver was trying to avoid him. The defendant was DUI, but other than these stop and go episodes, nothing else indicated DUI. What the officer had was "an inchoate and unparticularized suspicion or hunch." **State v. Warner**, 2000 WL 333031 (Vt.).

These cases demonstrate the need for a reasonable relationship between the conduct observed and the justified, objective, and reasonable suspicion that needs to be explained by the driver. For an example of *mere* suspicion consider the case of **Brooks v. State**, 240 S.E. 2d 593 (Ga. App. 1977). A police officer saw the defendant, in broad daylight, peer through a car's open window and then get in another car whose motor was running, and then drive off. Because the officer considered this suspicious, the officer chased and stopped the defendant. The court found this an impermissible intrusion upon the rights of the citizen. They held this, even though the subsequent search produced all manner of violations. The Missouri Supreme Court could learn much from this case.

Another decision illustrates the difference between mere suspicion (called a hunch) and articulable suspicion. The car that was ultimately stopped had been parked in an unusual place late at night. As the occupants returned and drove off in a normal manner, the observing officer followed. The officer subsequently stopped the car; thinking that a hunch was enough for the stop. The court said that the fruits of the search of the car should have been suppressed. The officer was not able to give specific details that backed his hunch. **Walker v. State**, 398 A. 2d 801 (Md. Ct. Spec. App. 1979).

Another case illustrating a bare hunch or a mere suspicion and the stopping of a motor vehicle is **Ozuna v. State**, 315 S.W. 2d 738 (Tex. Crim. 1979). The police heard these comments on a C.B.: "Look out, there is smoke," and later "red Ford, turn at the red light." Their interest peaked, the officers began searching for a red Ford and spotted a red and white Ford with a C.B. antenna and stopped it. Marijuana odor wafted from the car and this led to a search which yielded 285 pounds of marijuana. Worried about the connection between a red Ford and the car they stopped, the court spent more time on the fact that what was heard were not necessarily messages of illegality. They said hunches, good faith, and inarticulate suspicion will not justify a temporary detention.

Noting that there is a difference between an abrupt U-turn to avoid a police roadblock which gives articulable suspicion, and a lawful turn at a street before reaching a roadblock which does not give articulable suspicion, the Virginia appeals court reversed the defendant's conviction. A lawful turn without other indicia such as erratic driving gives the police nothing upon which to act. **Murphy v. Com.**, 384 S.E. 2d 125 (Va. Ct. App. 1989). Utah, on the other hand, says that the mere fact that a motorist turns around just before reaching a police roadblock and drives off in the opposite direction does not in itself create articulable suspicion to justify a stop. **State v. Talbot** 792 P. 2d 489 (Utah Ct. App. 1990).

Can a person lawfully avoid a roadblock? The answer is, of course, yes. But what is lawful avoidance? Making an illegal turn of any kind creates in the police a right, independent of the road block, to stop the violator and the stop carries with it all of the officer's plain senses and, of course, the ability to make the "wants and warrants" check through the electronics available to the officer. But does anyone have to proceed to the check-point? Can they make lawful turns or stops to avoid the road blocks? Most, if not all courts, would say yes. If the turn, stop, *etc.* is lawfully executed then no articulable suspicion exists for a lawful stop.

This point was forcefully brought "home" by the Virginia Supreme Court in **Bass v. Com.**, 525 S.E. 2d 921 (Va. 2000). The facts are quite simple. About 500 feet from the check point, the defendant lawfully executed a lawful turn into a gas station parking lot and exited, without stopping, going in the opposite direction. The "chase officer" determined this to be "avoidance" and he pursued and stopped Mr. Bass. Bass was DWI. Should his conviction stand? No, reversed and final. Why not? The command to stop does not extend over a distance of 500 feet and one intersection beyond the checkpoint in question. Second, a traffic checkpoint is not a "traffic control device," thus the law that prohibits the use of private or public property to avoid a traffic control device was not violated. Finally, a mere, lawfully executed U-turn does not give rise to articulable suspicion. They also noted the turn was not "headlong" flight as discussed in **Illinois v. Wardlow**, 528 U.S. 119 (2000).

Can the articulable suspicion come from a source other than the direct observation of the police? This question would be answered in two cases. The first case is **U.S. v. Hensley**, 469 U.S. 221 (1985), where the Court held that an articulable suspicion stop can come from another police department's "wanted flyer." The Court held that objective reliance on that flyer justified the other police department's reliance. The stop will be justified if the issuing department has articulable suspicion. The stop will not be justified if the issuing department did not have the requisite articulable suspicion, however, a defense to a civil suit against the stopping officers exists if those officers relied in good faith on the apparent quality of the information spelled out in the flyer. The only loss in the latter case is the loss of evidence gathered through plain view on the authority of **Mimms** and **Long**.

Oklahoma cited **Hensley** approvingly in **Peters v. State**, 725 P. 2d 1276 (Okla. Crim. 1986) but in the **Peter's** case the articulable facts were directly observed by the stopping officer, however the officer also knew of the description of a car recently used in a robbery. That second-hand information appears to have come from within the same department. Likewise, in **Moody v. State**, 738 P. 2d 943 (Okla. Crim. 1987), the conduct was directly observed by the officer. Once again **Hensley** was cited with approval. However, the most convincing evidence that Oklahoma would follow **Hensley's** secondhand information premise is **Coulter v. State**, 777 P. 2d 1373 (Okla. Crim. 1989), where articulable suspicion came by way of a non-anonymous tip given by a respectable citizen.

South Dakota has also reacted to the "assumption of the risk" doctrine used in **Hensley** in **State v. Richards**, 1998 WL 905068 (S. D.). Their case, unlike **Hensley**, involved an intra-departmental request for other local officers to make the stop. Also, unlike **Hensley**, the requesting officer did not, by flyer or even radio communication, inform the officers why the stop was being made. The stopping officer was told merely to make a "traffic stop" with his marked, lighted, and "sirened" vehicle. The stop was made, and the requesting officer arrived rather quickly after the stop. As to the "flyer" issue the court said the real issue was the articulable suspicion or probable cause that existed in the requesting officer prior to the stop and not the form of that knowledge. Imputation of that knowledge (good or bad) is transferred to the stopping officer. It felt, and rightly so, that "in aid thereof" was a real part of law enforcement (a proper and often necessary part). In fact in **U.S. v. Sharpe**, 470 U.S. 675 (1985), a duration-of-the-**Terry**-stop case, no justice was concerned that a DEA agent used South Carolina police to stop a suspect and hold him until the DEA agent arrived. More important was the continued recognition of the "collective knowledge doctrine" which applies intra- as well as interdepartmentally.

Until 1990, the Supreme Court had not decided whether articulable suspicion could come from an anonymous tip. The Court in **Gates** (*supra*) (discussed in Chapter Three) had decided that a corroborated anonymous tip could yield probable cause for the issuance of a warrant. Would the Court extend the basic corroboration principles to warrantless investigative stops of automobiles? The answer was yes. The case chosen was **Alabama v. White**, 496 U.S. 325 (1990). There were a growing number of cases like **U.S. v. Alvarez**, 889 F. 2d 833 (C.A. 9th 1990) that upheld stops based on anonymous tips that were corroborated under **Illinois v. Gates** standards. Even courts that found specific stops illegal did so because the corroborated details were innocent details not because the tip was anonymous. **People v. Garcia**, 789 P. 2d 190 (Colo. 1990). Would the Supreme Court agree? Yes, a corroborated anonymous tip can yield articulable suspicion to stop a vehicle.

Alabama had decided that there was not enough articulable suspicion to stop the car. Recognizing the split on this issue in the U.S., the Supreme Court combined **Adams v. Williams**, 407 U.S. 143 (1972) and **Illinois v. Gates**, 462 U.S. 213 (1983) to hold that such a tip can be corroborated and yield enough articulable suspicion for a stop. A "totality of the circumstances" must be taken into account. The Court did say this was a close case but held that what was corroborated exhibited sufficient indicia of reliability to justify the investigatory stop. It felt there was enough "inside information" in this case to believe this was not casual street rumor. As for the corroboration the Court said: It is true that not every detail mentioned by the tipster was verified, such as the name of the woman leaving the building or the precise apartment from which she left; but the officers did corroborate that a woman left the 235 building and got into the particular vehicle that was described by the caller. With respect to the time of departure predicted by the informant, Corporal Davis testified that the caller gave a particular time when the woman would be leaving, App. 5, but he did not state what that time was. He did testify that, after the call, he and his partner proceeded to the Lynwood Terrace Apartments to put the 235 building under surveillance, id., at 5-6. Given the fact that the officers proceeded to the indicated address immediately after the call and that respondent emerged not too long thereafter, it appears from the record before us that respondent's departure from the building was within the time frame predicted by the caller. As for the caller's prediction of respondent's destination, it is true that the officers stopped her just short of Dobey's

Motel and did not know whether she would have pulled in or continued on past it. But given that the four-mile route driven by respondent was the most direct route possible to Dobey's Motel, 550 So. 2d at 1075, Tr. of Oral Arg. 24, but nevertheless involved several turns, App. 7, Tr. of Oral Arg. 24, we think respondent's destination was significantly corroborated. The **Alabama v. White** decision will most likely be followed by those states that have already chosen to follow **Gates**. However, states that have chosen to stay with **Aguilar** and its "two-prong" test will not likely follow the **White** decision.

The key issue for South Dakota is whether the anonymous tip supplied sufficient information as required by their decision in **State v. Kissner**, 390 N.W. 2d 58 (S.Dak. 1986). Kissner and other cases were those "insider only knows" type of cases much like **Alabama v. White**. However, in **Graf v. State Dept. Commerce**, 508 N.W. 2d 1 (S. D.1993), the information was general and no attempt to corroborate was made. Thus they reversed Graf's conviction. The most recent anonymous tip case in South Dakota is **State v. Olhausen**, 1998 WL 850343 (S.Dak.). A "possible drug transaction" tip came in describing the car, its license plate number and location. The police did a "wants and warrant" check and a positive result occurred also giving the description of the owner. Was the car lawfully stopped based on this information? Yes. There was sufficient corroboration for his stop.

One state, Massachusetts, which had rejected the **Gates** totality test, had already decided that **Aguilar** should apply to **White** anonymous tip-articulable suspicion cases. **Com. v. Lyons**, 409 Mass. 16 (1990). In **Lyons** the police received the following anonymous tip: "At or about 1:15 a.m. on September 10, 1988, the State police received an anonymous telephone call stating that two white males, one of whom was named Wayne, had just purchased narcotics in Chelsea and would be heading for Bridgton, Maine. The caller said they would be driving in a silver Hyundai automobile with Maine registration 440-44T." **Lyons** at 17. The police then set up surveillance on the two main roads that led to Maine. They did not attempt to call Maine to determine the registration of the vehicle. A car meeting the description and having inside two white males appeared and was stopped. The car was being driven in a lawful manner so there was no independent reason to stop the car. The car was being driven by a Wayne; Wayne Lyons of Bridgton, Maine. But this they did not know until after the stop and production of the license. The car contained in plain view a rolled up dollar bill and known to be a "bill-straw" for snorting drugs as well as a brown tray with white powder on it. This too was not known until the stop. The court, in rejecting **White**, said this tip did not have sufficient articulable facts for this investigatory stop under **Aguilar**. Why? There was no information regarding the informants' reliability or basis of knowledge. Car, license, race, gender, and direction do not signal illegality, the court noted. These were obvious details and not "nonobvious details," **Lyons** at 21, and that was all that was corroborated. Of course, had the police corroborated nonobvious details the result would have been different. The tip would and could only be a starting point. Independent police investigative corroboration was needed to reduce the chances of the tip being a prevaricating tale, mere street rumor or vengefully motivated.

Using common sense, the D.C. Court of Appeals upheld a threshold **Terry/Mendenhall** confrontation upon an anonymous tip that was not as detailed as the one in **Alabama v. White**. On a cold December evening police received an anonymous tip that drugs were being sold from a car in a specified alley in Washington, D.C. The police approached the alley and saw two darkened cars with passengers. The police had ample proof that this was a notorious drug dealing area. The court said that it was highly unlikely that these people were conducting a social visit in this weather at this hour. **Gomez v. U.S.**, 597 A. 2d 884 (D.C. Ct. App. 1991).

The Wyoming Supreme Court faced the **White** issue in **Buckles v. State**, 2000 WL 223757 (Wyo.). A confidential informer called the police. The chief deputy knew the informant. The deputy was told that Buckles and another were on their way to Denver to buy marijuana and speed. He said that they left on 15 December and would return late on the 16th. The informant said he overheard a conversation between Buckles and a third person. A BOLO for a red 1989 Dodge Daytona and descriptions of the occupants of the car was issued. An officer in Gellith, Wyoming, tailed the car out of a convenience store parking lot to make sure it was going in the right direction. It made the northerly turn. This officer radioed ahead to another officer who saw the car and confirmed its license plates. The car was stopped. Buckles consented to a search and two large bags of marijuana were found. The corroboration done in this case was praised by this court and held that under the totality there was reasonable articulable suspicion.

D.   Pre-Sitz/Post-Prouse Road Block Cases

The final problem of articulable suspicion and the automobile involves the nature of the intrusion. The stop is a seizure. To search that which is seized does not always automatically follow as illustrated by recent constitutional interpretations. Search incident, for example, has a time limit and will be discussed later. All of this is important since a significant effort has been mounted to rid the highways of drunk drivers. States have determined that one of the best ways to do that is to target high-incident periods such as holidays and to set-up road blocks. As long as the states stay within the rule of **Delaware v. Prouse**, their efforts were not likely to be stopped as violative of the Fourth Amendment.

The District of Columbia, however, had instituted a drug enforcement program it called "operation clean sweep." As a part of that program a roadblock for the ostensible purpose of traffic enforcement was set up. It seems that drug dealers caused traffic jams with their street corner and curbside service. The defendant was stopped when police got plain view of drugs in his car. **Texas v. Brown**, **U.S. v. Martinez-Fuerte**, and **Delaware v. Prouse**, were the base cases upon which this road block was upheld. The court said all the factors legitimizing this road block were present: (1) a legitimate state interest was present; (2) the checkpoints served to promote the state interest in a sufficiently productive manner; and (3) the check point was minimally intrusive in that, (a) it was clearly visible, (b) it was part of a systematic procedure that strictly limited the discretionary authority of the officers, and (c) the detentions were no longer than necessary to accomplish the purposes. The issue of pretext or subterfuge was dismissed by the court saying that police officers are not required to ignore evidence of other crimes while conducting legitimate roadblocks **U.S. v. McFayden**, 865 F. 2d 1306 (C.A. D.C. 1989). This was a clear linkage of **Texas v. Brown** (*supra* at Plainview). Decisions like this would ultimately lead the Court to react.

The Maryland Court of Special Appeals would not agree with the District of Columbia's way of doing things. The police "sealed off" a neighborhood and stopped everyone. Calling this a "para military operation," the court invalidated the evidence seized saying that this was not like a sobriety checkpoint operation and was not minimally intrusive. **Brown v. State**, 553 A. 2d 1317 (Md. Ct. Spec. App. 1989). Massachusetts also does not agree with the District of Columbia at least with regard to using the minimum intrusion or less intrusive means test for upholding a checkpoint roadblock for enforcing their drunk driving laws. Instead it said reasonableness is determined by balancing the need to search or seize against the invasion that the search or seizure entails. The court was more concerned about the limits placed on the discretion of the officers. The constitutionality of roadblocks is based in large measure, it noted, on the lower expectation of privacy traditionally accorded to the motoring public. **Com. v. Shields**, 521 N.E. 2d 987 (Mass. 1988).

Vermont, on the other hand, felt that balancing the means of intrusion against privacy is the test to be employed. In addition to the three points made by the Court of Appeals for the District of Columbia, Vermont added a specific reference to the roadblock's use in a non-random manner. It did agree that "less intrusive" is not the controlling factor, but only one of many to be utilized. **State v. Record**, 548 A. 2d 422 (Vt. 1988).

Virginia was less concerned about the absence of a detailed plan than any of the three foregoing jurisdictions. The roadblock in this case was to check licenses and vehicles for safety concerns. A substantial interest was found which was advanced by the roadblock. The severity of the interference was slight as compared to both objective and subjective intrusions. They stopped all vehicles as the *dicta* in **Prouse** suggested. The problem was that no supervisor told these officers to do this at this time. The court felt there was no consequence to this. **Simmons v. Com.**, 371 S.E. 2d 7 (Va. Ct. App. 1988).

Should a check point that allows the stop of the first car that could be safely stopped once the previous stop was concluded be classified as a random stop procedure declared illegal in **Delaware v. Prouse** or should it be seen as the equivalent of a 100% roadblock? That was the issue presented to the North Dakota court in **State v. Wetzel**, 456 N.W. 2d 115 (N. D. 1990). The police called this the "stop the next available vehicle when safe" procedure. The check point in this case was a safety-inspection checkpoint. The defendant was found to be driving without a valid license and contested the validity of the stop. The North Dakota Supreme Court upheld this procedure and found it in compliance with **Prouse**. This court felt that since it was fixed in position, visible to motorists, and systematic enough to limit the police discretion it was more like a 100 percent roadblock.

A Missouri Court liked the idea of a plan that included the choice of location based on statistics. All other criteria normally required by most courts were met. **State v. Welch**, 755 S.W. 2d 624 (Mo. Ct. App. 1988).

Arizona approved a roadblock because sufficient advance notice was given the public and said they were more effective than traditional patrols. It, too, thought that a unique governmental interest was shown and that the intrusion was minimal. **State v. Super. Ct.**, 691 P. 2d 1073 (Ariz. 1984). Kansas had also approved roadblocks for drunk driving, citing the enormity for the drunk driving problem. The court stressed the advanced notice to the general public and the advance warning given to the motorist by the clearly marked checkpoints. The police were careful to observe safety conditions. **State v. Deshins**, 673 P. 2d 1174 (Kas. 1983).

Though some states indicate they would approve them, a few courts have turned down some checkpoints. For example, Texas found that the one it was faced with was a subterfuge in that it was set up to check licenses, but the real purpose was to catch drunk drivers. The roadblock was set up at the discretion of the officers and there was no proof that this road was any problem. **Hiqbie v. State**, 723 S.W. 2d 802 (Tex. App. 1987) aff'd 780 S.W. 2d 228 (Tex. Crim. 1989).

Minnesota said a balancing test has to be applied. It will look for the presence or absence of publicity as to whether the state can carry the burden of production on whether the checkpoint advanced the public interest. The officers must be well trained as to what to say and do. The state, when it selects a location, must show why it was chosen in regard to safety concerns by showing the level of incidents. Warning signs and advanced notice are required. The site has to be rationally selected and there must be a detailed administrative plan. None of these factors were present in **State v. Muzik**, 379 N.W. 2d 599 (Minn. App. 1985).

As to the public notice issue the cases should be carefully reviewed to determine whether such was *dicta* or judicial imperative or constitutional imperative. New Jersey, for example, had taken the position in one of its earlier cases, suggesting, by way of *dicta*, the requirement of advanced public notice. Subsequently, however, it determined that though such advance notice might have some deterrent effect, such notice was not a constitutional imperative. It labeled advanced notice "heightened effectiveness" only. **State v. DeCamera**, 568 A. 2d 86 (N.J. Super. Ct. App. Div. 1990) explaining **State v. Kink**, 202 N.J. Super. 28 (N.J. Super. Ct., App. Div. 1985).

Another group of states demonstrated no real interest in accepting roadblocks. In **State v. Koppel**, 499 A. 2d 977 (N.H. 1985), the New Hampshire court said that the state failed to show that roadblocks produced sufficient public benefit to outweigh the intrusion. In fact, roving regular patrols produced more arrests than did this roadblock on this same date.

The Michigan Court of Appeals upheld a trial court's injunction enjoining the state police from conducting roadblocks. It said, "While the goals of the sobriety program are laudable, the program fails to qualify as a reasonable seizure under the Fourth Amendment." The court agreed with the trial court that they were not effective nor did they have any long term deterrent effect. **Sitz v. Michigan Dept. of State Police**, 429 N.W. 2d 180 (Mich Ct. App. 1988).

Alabama rejected the "success of apprehension" approach in upholding drunk-driving road blocks that were operated pursuant to an objective and neutral plan, using brief stops of all traffic. They, however, also approved field officers making the decision when and where to set up such roadblocks rather than requiring supervisory personnel to make that decision. They felt departmental policy saying who to stop sufficiently restricted their discretion. **Cains v. State**, 555 So. 2d 290 (Ala. Crim. 1989). Virginia also rejected "success of apprehension" in **Crandol v. City of Newport News**, 386 S.E. 2d 113 (Va. 1989).

E. Sitz, The U.S. Supreme Court, and Drunk Driving Road Blocks

With all of this activity, the Supreme Court chose the **Sitz** case from Michigan to determine the Fourth Amendment validity of such road blocks. The Court, by a six to three decision, speaking through Chief Justice Rehnquist upheld the use of sobriety checkpoints. Brief, minimally intrusive, discretion-limited stops to protect society against the background of the major societal problems caused by drinking drivers do not violate the Fourth Amendment. **Michigan Dept. of State Police v. Sitz**, 496 U.S. 444 (1990).

What points did the Court make beyond the balancing test/minimal intrusion analysis? With regard to the effectiveness issue, whether roving patrols or checkpoints were more effective, the Court said that is a local political decision selecting one of two reasonable alternatives. The only unreasonable alternative was the random stop alternative prohibited in **Prouse**. The Court was impressed with the guidelines and said, "All vehicles passing through a checkpoint would be stopped...." Does this mean that anything less than 100% stoppage is prohibited? This opinion does not address that issue nor the "stop-when-safe-to-the-next-car" policies as in the **Wetzel** case (*supra*).

Doubt was cast on the "U-turn" and "turns-to-avoid-the-checkpoint" cases. In talking about the Michigan record of proceedings, the Court said, "This was so because the record failed to demonstrate that approaching motorists would be aware of their option to make U-turns or turnoffs to avoid the checkpoints." One cannot say that it adopted "the right-to-avoid-without-penalty" rule because the discussion at this point was centering on the "generation of fear or surprise" and police discretion. One cannot even say that this is *dicta* to serve as the base for a new rule to come. The question thus remains unanswered though it appears to approve the **Murphy** and **Talbot** cases (*supra*). What it approved was the system employed by Michigan. An examination of that system is needed. As noted in the Michigan opinion the guidelines required that there be: (1) Site selection; (2) Publicity; and (3) Operational limitation. 429 N.W. 2d 180, 181 (Mich. Ct. App. 1988).

It appears then that the site selected had to bear a reasonable relationship to the drunk driving problem. The public was to be notified of the use of roadblocks, however, it is not clear from either opinion whether a general or specific notice was required. The restraint on police activity took two paths. First, all cars subject to safety considerations were to be stopped. Second, unless sobriety was at issue, the driver was to be allowed to leave (subject, of course, to unrelated plain view issues.) Where sobriety was at issue the driver was to pull over to a "safe spot" where a license, registration, and field sobriety check (including breath analysis) could be conducted. If sobriety did not appear in doubt the driver was to be released (unless plain view or license registration problems arose). If sobriety was at issue the arrest would be made.

Is the Court saying that this is the only form of sobriety program allowable? The case cannot be read that tightly. However, any program with less than these points is questionable which will require the Court to address the legality of the other alternative programs. The District of Columbia faces an uphill fight with their "clean sweep" operation. Virginia's approval of random selection of the site without supervisory approval is of doubtful worth. The whole idea of advanced notice needs to be specifically resolved. Is it constitutionally mandated or merely a "reasonable alternative?"

F.   Post-Sitz Road Block Decisions

After the foregoing paragraph was written the District of Columbia Court of Appeals took a second look at "Operation Clean Sweep" and on April 30, 1991, found that operation unconstitutional. Citing **Sitz**, the D.C. Court in **Galberth v. U.S.**, 590 A. 2d 990 (D.C. Ct. App. 1991), held that police may not use a roadblock to seek evidence of drug-related crimes. However, they acknowledged that such road blocks could be used for license and registration checks and the case was remanded to address that issue. The D.C. case thus raises the possibility that a roadblock may have mixed multiple purposes; some legal, some not. The D.C. case appears to approve such roadblocks as long as there is a legal purpose for the process. Will all courts agree? Time will tell, but at least one other court reads **Sitz** very broadly. This also tracks the "mere hope" language of Supreme Court plain view cases addressing inadvertence.

In **State v. Everson**, 474 N.W. 2d 695 (N. D. 1991), a checkpoint was set up at the site of a week-long motorcycle rally. The main reason was to look for evidence of drug possession. The court took the position that a checkpoint is not unconstitutional because its true purpose is to enforce the criminal laws. The North Dakota court addressed directly the subterfuge issue thus it must have been set-up under another purpose; and it was – safety inspections. Brushing the subterfuge issue aside, the court said drug trafficking is as much a societal harm as drunk driving. The court then went into the discretion - limited process that was used. Therefore, the consents to search that were secured were not the fruits of a poisonous tree. Thus North Dakota appears to agree with the D.C. court.

After **Sitz,** the Court of Appeals of Utah held that **Sitz** implicitly requires that sobriety roadblocks must be legislatively authorized. Thus it held a police initiated roadblock, even though approved by a departmental superior officer, was invalid since there was no statutory authorization. The court carefully noted that other types of roadblocks had been authorized in the past for livestock importation and game law enforcement. It also noted that three other western states had come to the same conclusion prior to **Sitz** citing **State v. Henderson**, 756 P. 2d 1057 (Idaho, 1988), **Nelson v. Lane County**, 743 P. 2d 692 (Ore. 1987), and **State v. Smith**, 674 P. 2d 562 (Okla. Crim. 1984). Thus, Utah said the consent to search the car which yielded a kilo of cocaine was "not sufficiently attenuated from the illegal stop...." **State v. Sims**, 808 P. 2d 141 (Utah Ct. App. 1991).

For more recent cases on road blocks see: **State v. Boisvert**, 671 A. 2d 834 (Conn. App. 1996) – roadblock o.k. and seen as a "modest intrusion on individual driver's rights;" **State v. Miller**, 1996 WL 75344 (Tenn. Crim.) (unpub. op.) – traffic roadblocks may not be used as a subterfuge to search for other crimes – license checkpoint stop for drivers avoiding other drunk driving road block – this second stop area not legitimate; **Sieveking v. State**, 1996 WL 29204 (Ga. App.) – u-turn case – police stopped Defendant and he smelled "of alcohol" – stop not challenged by Defendant or by court.

In **State v. Claussen**, 522 N.W. 2d 196 (S. D. 1994), the police set up a road block near a residence where juveniles were observed drinking alcoholic beverages. The observations were made after responding to "loud party" complaints by neighbors. They stopped *all* vehicles that left the residence but not others not connected with the residence. Does this conduct meet the requirements of **Sitz**? No, *but* the observed activity reasonably justified the police stopping all those from the party and did meet the standards of **Delaware v. Prouse** and **Terry v. Ohio.**

A second rule that comes into play when stopping a vehicle is that any crime committed in the officer's presence by the driver or occupants can justify the stop of the car. It does not matter, of course, that the crime is a misdemeanor. **Gustafson v. Florida**, 414 U.S. 260 (1973) and **U.S. v. Robinson,** 414 U.S. 218 (1973).

A third rule that applies concerns the articulable suspicion or **Terry**-type delay rule. In this instance the police have more than a mere hunch but less than probable cause of a crime committed in their presence. How long can such a stop last?

That question was answered in **Michigan v. Long**, 463 U.S. 1032 (1983). **Terry**-type delays must be reasonable as to the length of time; or, as the courts call it, no "bright line." This, of course, was affirmed in **Sitz**. In this type of case the court is to apply a "totality of the circumstances" test. The court is supposed to judge the purpose to be served by the stop and then ask if the police acted diligently and did they reasonably pursue a means of investigation to confirm or dispel the suspicions quickly. The police are not required to pursue the perfect means. If they did not act diligently and reasonably, then, any evidence uncovered during the delay would be inadmissible.

In **Michigan v. Long** (*infra* at sec. V. C.), the police saw a car run into a ditch and stopped to investigate. Long was already out of his car. After he was asked a second time Long produced his driver's license. When asked to produce the registration slip Long did not respond. Again he was asked and Long began to walk toward the open door of the car. The officers followed, saw a hunting knife and did a frisk of Long at that point. The immediate area of the car was "frisked." Nothing more was found then. The police decided to impound the car because the officers felt Long was "on something." The police opened the unlocked trunk and found "75 pounds of marihuana." Here there was no unreasonable delay in the frisk of the passenger compartment. When the danger element arose (seeing the knife in the car) the police did not delay in their process. The delay in getting to the car was caused by the failure of the defendant to respond and not by some police stalling tactic.

If a valid drunk-driving roadblock is set up, can police ask for a driver's license and proof of insurance after it is determined that the stopped driver is not drunk? Does not the reason for the stop end with a "not-drunk" determination? At least three courts do not adhere to the "no-justification-end-the-police-rights" theory. Citing the New Jersey case of **State v. Coccomo**, 427 A. 2d 131 (N.J. 1980) and Oregon's **State v. Tourillott**, 618 P. 2d 423 (Ore. 1980), Hawaii also approved the practice of asking for licenses, *etc.*, after a "no drunk" finding. **State v. Aquinaldo**, 782 P. 2d 1225 (Haw. 1989). It felt this was of no concern. Certainly, after **Thomas,** continued delays after dispelling the reason for the stop should raise a **Michigan v. Thomas** argument.

Whether this conduct comports with **Sitz** should be determined. **Berkemer v. McCarty** and **Sitz** both recognized this type of stop as a seizure. But **Sitz** does talk about time limitations especially where no reason to question sobriety arises after the brief interruption of travel. Asking for the license, *etc.*, after determining no reason for a continued sobriety stop it is not "the associated preliminary questioning and observation by checkpoint officers..." approved in **Sitz**. The Court approved only the detention for "more extensive field sobriety testing..." when individualized suspicion occurred. Unless reasonable suspicion as to license, insurance or registration issues independently arose or existed, the continued detention after a "not drunk" determination should be found to be an illegal detention under the Fourth Amendment. However, there is a possibility that **Delaware v. Prouse** could save such extensions.

G.   The Supreme Court Reaction to Non-Drunk Driving Road Blocks

It is clear that many states and the law enforcement community have used the **Sitz** drunk driving road block decision to approve other road blocks for purposes such as fish and wildlife road blocks, safety inspections, and, more importantly, drug transporting interdiction. There is no doubt that all highways are being used to move large and small quantities of drugs to all points of ultimate consumer sales.

To address this issue, the U.S. Supreme Court chose a case from Indiana to set the record straight. In **City of Indianapolis v. Edmond**, 121 S. Ct. 447 (2001), the city had been using road blocks to stop all cars to interdict unlawful drugs. In four months, of the 1,161 vehicles stopped 55 were found to be transporting drugs and 49 persons were arrested for non-drug-related offenses. This represents a 9% "hit rate." A five-minute stop limit was imposed and site selection criteria were set. The officers were carefully instructed on how to conduct the confrontation. All of this was, of course, an attempt to work within the **Sitz** drunk driving interdiction guidelines.

Justice O'Connor succinctly reminds us that **Sitz** was approved to help reduce the "immediate hazard posed by the presence of drunk drivers on the highways...." She added that "there was an obvious connection between the imperative of highway safety and the law enforcement practices at issue..." in the **Sitz** case. She also notes that even in **Delaware v. Prouse,** a vital interest exists regarding highway safety where the issue of mechanically safe vehicles and safe operation were at issue and the court condemned random, discretionless stops. But **Prouse**, as she further notes, said stolen cars and general law enforcement goals were not clearly safety issues. Thus it was clear that the drug interdiction program was *not* a highway safety issue but rather it was predominately a general law enforcement issue. The Court has, in her words, "never approved a checkpoint program whose primary purpose was to detect evidence of ordinary criminal wrongdoing." The Court was unwilling to raise drug transportation to the emergency level. But what of other types of roadblocks? Not much is said. However, one sentence is important. She writes, "While we do not limit the purposes that may justify a checkpoint program to any rigid set of categories, we decline to approve a program whose primary purpose is ultimately indistinguishable from the general interest in crime control." The opinion reconfirms legitimate sobriety and border checkpoints. The Court condemns general crime control checkpoints. The Court also reminds us what was truly in the mind of the individual officer at the scene and what he really hoped to find is not germane and courts are not to "probe the minds of the individual officers acting at the scene." For this they cite the **Whren** case. See **Whren v. U.S.**, 517 U.S. 806 (1996).

H.   Post City of Indianapolis Reactions by the States

Obviously, any of the decisions cited in these materials which predates the **City of Indianapolis** that were not safety based are without constitutional support. Of course, cases decided in the year 2000 that tolerate a general law enforcement criminal detection purpose now also have to be reexamined.

One decision from Massachusetts, however, also came to the same conclusion as the U.S. Supreme Court. Its case, **Com. v. Rodriquez**, 722 N.E. 2d 429 (Mass. 2000), also involved a drug trafficking road block. It also focused on emergency or imminent threat to lives and safety as did the U.S. Supreme Court. Thus, absent, at a minimum, an issue of articulable suspicion any road block outside the **Sitz** public safety concern is without constitutional authority.

An Oklahoma case focused on a safety-check road block that yielded a transporter of marijuana. The plain smell alerted by a drug sniffing dog was, of course, no constitutional violation. Since the U.S. Supreme Court cites approvingly to the **Prouse** dicta on 100% road blocks for safety purposes, Oklahoma seems to be on firm constitutional grounds. **Crowell v. State**, 994 P. 2d 788 (Okla. Crim. Ct. App. 2000).

New Jersey's appellate court, however, is on the wrong path. Their decision was a stolen car road block. However, before being stopped for that purpose, the defendant committed a traffic violation which gave independent grounds for his seizure. The *dicta* that such a road block does not violate the Fourth Amendment must now be disregarded. **State v. Flowers**, 745 A. 2d 553 (N.J. Super. 2000).

Utah's case was a pure **Sitz**-type road block, thus the defendant had no U.S. grounds to fight his drug possession conviction. However, the Utah court saw all that was approved in **Sitz** as a pretext and in violation of the Utah constitution as certain statutory safe guards were not scrupulously followed. Thus Utah judges are going to have to read Utah Code §77-23-104 very narrowly and carefully. **State v. DeBooy**, 2000 WL 126749 (Utah).

In a Georgia case the defendant did not challenge the driver's license and insurance checkpoint. The court also avoided the issue, but as requested by the defense, focused on the urine test methods. He lost. **State v. Coe**, 2000 WL 320720 (Ga. App.).

Ohio, through one of its appeals court, also faced a driver's license check point case. The state lost at the suppression level because the municipal court said the checkpoint was unconstitutional under both state and federal constitutions. Since Ohio's Supreme Court had not addressed the exact issue, the court of appeals looked for direction from other states and, of course, the U.S. Supreme Court. The trial judge, like the U.S. Supreme Court in **City of Indianapolis,** focused on the general law enforcement versus danger analysis to strike down the road block in this case. Despite that, this court of appeals reversed the judgment by focusing on **Sitz** and Ohio's need to keep unlicensed drivers (the too young, the too old and the suspended scofflaw) of Ohio's road. They saw a danger base and not a general law enforcement base. **Ohio v. Smith**, 2000 WL 20882 (Ohio App. App. 2 Dist) (unpub. op).

To some extent the **City of Indianapolis** decision calls into question other driver-related roadblocks. Ohio, as noted above, is one of those states that has permitted a driver's license check-point program to be used by its cities. These were challenged in **State v. Orr**, 745 N.E. 2d 1036 (Ohio 2001). Despite their reluctant acceptance of **Robinette** as decided by the Supreme Court, the Ohio court fully justified their state's driver's license roadblock program. The program stopped every car unless traffic was too heavy in which case "the next car when safe" process discussed above. The court noted acceptance of this type of program in Georgia, Maine, and North Carolina. The court also distinguished **City of Indianapolis** in that license checks were not stops to detect drug trafficking. It held that the intrusion on privacy was not great because advance notice was given, most stops only lasted 45 seconds, pamphlets were handed out, and those without licenses were detained for about 10 minutes. The interest in having only qualified drivers on the roads reduces the threat posed by unqualified drivers. Roving patrols were found not to be satisfactory since there are no signs of the unlicensed status. Effectiveness statistics from Dayton, the city challenged in this case, noted that of 2,110 drivers stopped, 224 were cited (but not all for license violation). As an aside, two months prior to this decision an Ohio appellate court upheld safety check stops in **State v. Stoneking**, 2001 WL 273641 (Ohio App. 7 Dist.). The defendant was cited for driving under a suspended license. **Delaware v. Prouse** (*supra*) and **State v. Goines**, 16 Ohio App. 3d 168 (1984) were cited in support, and **Sitz** was cited as not addressing the issue.

However, what neither of these cases addresses is whether the police were told to keep their senses open to and to target drug violations. These instructions doomed Virginia's driver's license check-points. **Trent v. Com.**, 544 S.E. 2d 379 (Va.. App. 2001). Emphasizing the "plain senses" had a tendency to raise the subterfuge issue.

There was no doubt that **City of Indianapolis** would encourage defendants to challenge drunk driving road blocks as "general law enforcement" stops. Such was the case in **Wrigley v. State**, 2001 WL 204243 (Ga.App.). The court found that the primary purpose was not to detect ordinary crime. The defendant was convicted for DUI. The court noted that the officer was trained to detect drunk driving and had ten years of such experience. This satisfied Georgia's concern about the issues raised in **City of Indianapolis** which had been addressed in **LaFontaine v. State**, 497 S.E. 2d 367 (Ga. 1998) by the Georgia Supreme Court. In accord see **Com. Yastrop**, 768 A. 2d 318 (Pa. 2001) , accepting the distinction made by the Court and that it "sufficiently protect[s] citizens form untoward results...." The court did note that Rhode Island was concerned that such a process could "overwhelm the right of privacy," but Pennsylvania felt their constitution was different than Rhode Island's. See **Pimentel v. Dept. of Transportation**, 561 A. 2d 1348 (R.I. 1980). The Pennsylvania court also gave approval to registration, licensing, and equipment roadblocks by approving **Com. v. Blouse**, 611 A. 2d (1992) and **Com. v. Talbert**, 535 A. 2d 1035 (1987).

An "informational roadblock" was condemned in **People v. Lidster**, 2001 WL 379039 (Ill. App. 2 Dist.). The roadblock was set up to pass out flyers about an accident in the hopes that someone had witnessed the incident and could provide information. Mr. Lidster almost hit the officer and when the officer approached him after the stop the officer detected the odor of alcohol use. The defendant was arrested. The roadblock was challenged. The court said this was a general law enforcement case and not a road safety case. It was seen as an unbridled checkpoint and the courts are not to accept all police justifications. No "effectiveness statistics" were offered to say this process was more effective than general law enforcement techniques.

Utah was asked to decide whether administrative highway checkpoints for eight different reasons were reasonable under both the state and federal constitutions. In a decision that predates the **City of Indianapolis** opinion of the U.S. Supreme Court, the Utah majority found wanting such a multipurpose checkpoint/road block plan for primarily the same reason the "drug-stops" were condemned in **City of Indianapolis**. It said: "When many legal violations are searched for, the purpose of the check point becomes less a highway safety measure, and more a pretext to stop all vehicles to search for any and all violations of the law that might be apparent. The generalized stop and search, of course, occurs without any individualized suspicion of a crime having been committed, much less probable cause." **State v. DeBooy**, 996 P. 2d 546 (Utah 2000).

I.   Border/Checkpoint Stops

Finally, there can be no discussion of correlative rules without mentioning the motor vehicle and border searches. Border search stops are different. They are subject to the broad policy of **U.S. v. Martinez-Fuertes**, 428 U.S. 543 (1976), as limited by **U.S. v. Brignoni-Ponce**, 422 U.S. 873 (1975) and **Almeida-Sanchez v. U.S.**, 413 U.S. 266 (1973) and other cases.

The question is, what is a border? Is a border a line or a zone? If it is a zone, how far does it extend? These were the questions presented in **Almeida-Sanchez v. U.S.**, 413 U.S. 266 (1973). A federal statute, the Immigration and Nationality Act, allowed searches of automobiles within a reasonable distance of the border. A federal regulation established that reasonable distance as 100 miles from any U.S. boundary. The search in the instant case took place 25 miles from the border on a road that did not directly connect with Mexico. The Court recognized the border was not a line but did not establish a zone theory either. Rather, the Court recognized that searches may be made at the border or its functional equivalent. **Almeida** at 272. As examples of functional equivalents, they cited a station near the border where two or more roads extending from the border met or the instance where a non-stop flight from Mexico City landed in St. Louis. These are functional equivalents, they said. If a search takes place outside the functional equivalent, it must meet normal Fourth Amendment standards.

In 1975, the Court was faced with the Border Patrol's use of roving patrols near the Mexican border which was supposedly forbidden in **Almeida.** Because of bad weather, a standard checkpoint was closed. Two patrol cars, with lights on to illuminate passing cars, saw Brignoni-Ponce's car and pulled it over. Illegal aliens were discovered. The Court of Appeals said this was a roving patrol, thus prohibited. The issue in **U.S. v. Briqnoni-Ponce**, 422 U.S. 873 (1975) was, can a roving patrol stop a vehicle in an area near the border and question its occupant when the only ground for suspicion is that the occupants appear to be of Mexican ancestry? **Briqnoni** at 876. Since roving patrols must operate within the Constitution, the patrol must have at least reasonable (articulable) suspicion to make the stop. Thus, the random stops on mere suspicion are prohibited. Standing alone, looking like a Mexican, is not grounds for reasonable suspicion.

On that same day, the Court announced its opinion in **U.S. v. Ortiz**, 422 U.S. 891 (1975). The issue was: can the government set up a checkpoint some 62 miles from the border and say this it is a functional equivalent? The Court said no. At traffic checkpoints removed from the border and its functional equivalents, officers may not search private vehicles without consent or probable cause. **Ortiz** at 897. Would that be the end of the checkpoint question? No. The following year, the Court handed down their opinion in **U.S. v. Martinez-Fuertes**, 428 U.S. 543 (1976). In fact, it was the very same checkpoint that was involved in **Ortiz**. **Ortiz** prohibited searches but reserved the question whether such devices were permissible for a limited stop and question procedure. Arbitrary and oppressive interference cannot be allowed. What is arbitrary must, however, be weighed against the public interest. **Martinez** at 554. The inquiry into residence status is a modest interference, said the Court. No doubt these stops are seizures within the Fourth Amendment. The flow of traffic at these points is too heavy to require reasonable suspicion for a limited stop to answer one or two basic residence questions. In such a stop, there is no search and the visual inspection is limited to what can be seen without a search. **Martinez** at 558. Finally, the Court said, a warrant is not required to set up such checkpoints for the limited purpose of stop and question as here authorized. **Martinez** at 567.

J.   Stops of Boats and Trains

The rationale of **Delaware v. Prouse** and its prohibition of random stops has been taken to the sea. The Ninth Circuit Court of Appeals held that random stops of boats at night for safety checks were forbidden by the Fourth Amendment. **U.S. v. Piner**, 608 F. 2d 358 (C.A. 9th 1979).

The Supreme Court, however, had a totally different view which they expressed in **U.S. v. Villamonte-Marquez**, 462 U.S. 579 (1983). About noon one day, Customs officers and Louisiana state policemen were patrolling the river ship channel some 18 miles inland from the Gulf of Mexico when they sighted a sail boat anchored near the channel. They boarded the boat. A state trooper looked down an open hatch after smelling burnt marijuana, and he saw burlap wrapped bales that were marijuana bales. In fact, 5,800 pounds of marijuana were discovered. Was such a random boarding reasonable in light of **Brignoni-Ponce, Martinez-Fuerte** and **Prouse**? Yes, water is different than asphalt. Checkpoints are impractical on water. Boats can move in any direction at any time. In water providing ready access to the seaward border, checkpoints are not feasible. Perhaps for inland waters, rivers, canals, and such, the roadblock approach might be feasible, but not in this instance. A ship or boat may never come to port or harbor. License plates and stickers are so much a part of automobiles, trucks and other motor vehicles. Boat owners paint the identifiers on their vessels. In this case the markings indicated Swiss registry but it carried French documentation. The intrusion to check documentation is limited and requires only a brief detention. Neither the vessel nor its occupants were searched and the visual inspection was limited to what can be seen without a search. The government has a valid interest in assuring compliance with our documentation requirements and the need to stop smugglers is substantial. So, document and safety inspections are permitted by federal law to occur without suspicion. Interdiction only requires reasonable suspicion.

Reasonable suspicion can arise when the master of a vessel denies a request for permission to board. **U.S. v. Reih,** 780 F. 2d 1541 (C.A. 11th 1986). Flying no flag and having an easily removable name plate (not permitted) gave reasonable suspicion in **U.S. v. Pringle**, 751 F. 2d 419 (C.A. 1st 1984). Likewise, when the captain is taking the vessel in a direction opposite to what he has reported over the radio also raises reasonable suspicion. **U.S. v. Del Prado – Montero**, 740 F. 2d 113 (C.A. 1st 1984). Refusal in "customs" waters to obey an order to stop gives rise to a pursuit right and reasonable suspicion. **U.S. v. Berriel-Ochoa**, 740 F. 2d 883 (C.A. 11th 1984). Document check cases have been upheld even where the customs people suspected criminal activity. **U.S. v. Troise**, 796 F. 2d 310 (C.A. 9th 1986). Safety checks allow entry into engine rooms and holds because these are not private areas. **U.S. v. One Blue Lobster Vessel**, 639 F. Supp. 865 (S. D. Fla. 1986). Boats on inland or non-customs waters are treated in the same way as automobiles. **U.S. v. Lauchli**, 724 F. 2d 1279 (C.A. 7th 1984) and **U.S. v. Maybusher**, 735 F. 2d 366 (C.A. 9th 1984).

IV.   Mobility Not Use Governs

Until 1985, there was some question as to whether a vehicle used also as a home was entitled to the greater protection afforded homes or the lesser protection afforded motor vehicles. In 1985, the Supreme Court answered the question by their decision in **California v. Carney**, 471 U.S. 386 (1985). The issue was: Is a warrantless search of a fully mobile motor home located in a parking lot proper under the "automobile exception" if based upon probable cause? Yes, said the Court. This parking lot was not a place regularly used for residential purposes. Yes, the motor home had some attributes of a home. However, the Court was not willing to carve out an exception to the exception. The Court said it could not ignore the fact that a motor home lends itself easily to use as an instrument of illicit drug trafficking or for other illegal activity. Footnote 3 of the opinion should also be considered. There the Court stated: "We need not pass on the application of the vehicle exception to a motor home that is situated in a way or place that objectively indicates that is it being used as a residence. Among the factors that might be relevant in determining whether a warrant would be required in such a circumstance is its location, whether the vehicle is readily mobile or instead, for instance, elevated on blocks, whether the vehicle is licensed, whether it is connected to utilities and whether it has convenient access to a public road." Thus the Court recognizes that there may be times when such a vehicle can be classified as a residence for which a warrant would be required if no other exigency or other exception exists. The **Carney** case would open the flood gates. Courts would find that the exception would apply in a broader range of cases.

The first such case came from the Sixth Circuit. In **U.S. v. Markham**, 844 F. 2d 366 (C.A. 6th 1988), the court held that an unattended motor home in a private driveway, locked and having out-of-state tags, was also covered by **Carney**. This is the most far reaching **Carney** case involving motor homes so far. Oregon does not agree with the "unattended" part. They go their own way and hold that after a driver leaves his car and walks away the mobility exception leaves with him. **State v. Vaughn**, 757 P. 2d 441 (Ore. Ct. App. 1988). This is an obvious misreading of the exception.

Things other than cars and motor homes have been brought within the exception because of **Carney**. A houseboat navigating in open waters at night was more like a boat than a house. Ready mobility was the key for the Tenth Circuit in **U.S. v. Hill**, 855 F. 2d 664 (C.A. 10th 1988). A train roomette was held to be more like a car than a hotel room in **U.S. v. Whitehead**, 849 F. 2d 849 (C.A. 4th 1988); in accord see **U.S. v. Trayer**, 701 F. Supp. 250 (D.C. Dist. Ct. 1988) and **U.S. v. Tartaglia**, 864 F. 2d 837 2308 (C.A. D.C. 1988).

Some states have had a very restricted mobility rule. **Carney** has caused some changes. Wisconsin, for example, has finally, through **Carney**, accepted the mobility exception by its decision in **State v. Tompkins**, 423 N.W. 2d 823 (Wis. 1988).

V.   Types of Intrusions Permitted

A.   Full-Field Strip Searches

1.   Pure Probable Cause Searches

It has been said that the power to search is the power to destroy. If the search of an automobile has been authorized by a judge upon probable cause, or if an automobile is searched without a warrant under the guidelines of **U.S. v. Ross**, 456 U.S. 798 (1982), discussed below, then the only limitation is whether the thing sought is small enough and perhaps, in some cases, indestructible enough to be where the searcher searches. If that means the car has to be torn apart, then so be it. In the movie, "The French Connection" (starring Gene Hackman), Hackman obtained a warrant for drugs and literally cut the car to pieces. Since drugs of the nature of heroin come in powder form, the possibility that they could have been placed almost anywhere in that car made the type of search conducted in that movie reasonable. Hence the title "full-field strip search." In fact, if the car were acquired by a forfeiture statute such search could be even more destructive (if possible) since the forfeiture statute vests both title and possession in the government. For a case illustrating a search that was too destructive, see **Bailey v. Lancaster**, 470 N.W. 2d 351 (Iowa 1991) holding that the scope of a search may be unreasonable if the destruction done was not necessary to effectively execute the search warrant.

The major question settled by **U.S. v. Ross,** as mentioned in the preceding paragraph, was if the police had probable cause to search a car, do they need to secure a search warrant or would the mobility exception allow them to conduct the search without a warrant? The Court held that they could conduct a warrantless search that would be as thorough as a judge could authorize by warrant. In fact, upon such probable cause, they may search every part of the vehicle and its contents, including all containers and packages that may conceal the object of the search. The scope of the search is defined by the object of the search and the places where such object could be found. In the **Ross** case, it was established upon probable cause that the car was intimately connected with and a significant part of the crime of transporting drugs which could have been concealed anywhere. The Court said if the object searched for was illegal aliens for example, then a standard suitcase could not be searched.

What then is probable cause? First, it is not good faith; that is not enough to constitute probable cause, **Ross** at 808. The probable cause determination has to be founded on objective facts that could justify the issuance of a warrant by a judge or magistrate, **Ross** at 808. It must be cause sufficient enough to overcome the right of free passage that people within this country enjoy. The standard definition of probable cause was quoted by the **Ross** majority in footnote 10 as follows: "the facts and circumstances within [the officers'] knowledge and of which they had reasonably trustworthy information were sufficient in themselves to warrant a man of reasonable caution in the belief that..." (a crime had been committed or was being committed).

Thus probable cause is not based on guesses or hunches (many of which are good guesses); it is based on trustworthy facts and circumstances (not street rumor) and all this information would lead a reasonable man (not trained to be suspicious and adversarial) to believe that which the officer believes. Probable cause does not need to be as strong as that which is needed to convict (proof beyond a reasonable doubt), but it does have to point reasonably to a specific crime and not to general suspicions of some crime or crimes. See also **U.S. v. Barrett**, 890 F. 2d 855 (C.A. 6th 1989). That is why the Missouri Supreme Court's decision in **Burkhardt** (*supra* page 2, this chapter) is faulty.

An Ohio officer made a lawful stop of a vehicle and got permission to search the passenger compartment and discovered evidence of a theft. He sought permission to search the trunk but was denied. But his experiences as a mall cop told him there was more in the trunk of the car so he searched it and it was there that he found the evidence of theft (shoplifting). Citing **Ross**, the Ohio court found that the officer did have probable cause to search the trunk thus a consent was not needed for the trunk. **State v. Payne**, 1999 WL 441776 (Ohio App. 12) (unpub. op.).

2.   Good Faith Reliance in Auto Search Cases

With **Ross**, the probable cause rules of other areas, of course, apply. Particularly important are the sources of probable cause. Whether directly observed by the police, or from an inherently reliable source such as a fellow police officer or non-criminal citizen, or upon the corroborated anonymous tipster, or the information of a reliable but criminally involved known informant, in most cases the searching officers generally have complete information at their disposal to make an independent probable cause determination.

Four years after **Leon** was decided South Dakota got its first chance to react to **Leon** and its "good faith" reliance rule. The case involved the search of the defendant, his house, and his truck. The suppression judge found the warrant "bad" but upheld admission of the evidence under the **Leon** theory. The court agreed that punishing bad police work and not bad judging by an otherwise neutral and detached magistrate was the goal of the exclusionary rule. The court praised Judge Warren Johnson for the structure of his findings. **State v. Saiz**, 427 N.W. 2d 825 (S. D. 1988).

However, what if the searching officer stops and searches a vehicle solely on the word of another police jurisdiction as to probable cause without personally knowing the underlying facts and circumstances? Is such a search valid? One court that addressed this issue is the Seventh Circuit. In **U.S. v. Celio**, 945 F. 2d 180 (C.A. 7th 1991), federal officers asked the Illinois State Police to stop and search a truck for drugs. Based strictly on this message and without independent corroboration, the stop and search took place. The defendant argued that the state police were without probable cause even if the federal agents did indeed have probable cause. The search was upheld by the Seventh Circuit by borrowing from and extending **U.S. v. Hensley** (*supra*), which they categorized as a "collective knowledge" case. It held that if the originating jurisdiction has probable cause and requests help, that knowledge becomes the knowledge of the acting jurisdiction when the search is conducted. Why? The court said drugs, mobility, and resulting drug networks, to be stopped, require a common sense approach that reduces the volume of information to be transmitted and enables police in one jurisdiction to act promptly in another. The risk run, of course, is that the acting department could be held liable in a civil suit if the originating jurisdiction did not have probable cause and the acting jurisdiction acted without good faith. This is the core of the assumption of the risk doctrine adopted in **Hensley**.

During the routine traffic stop the police will conduct a "wants and warrants" check on the car and its driver. The modern era connects the officer with a computer data bank that will yield information that contains all forms of warrants that are outstanding and this will not be limited to vehicular crimes. Suppose an officer gets information indicating that an outstanding arrest warrant exists as to the driver. Is the officer justified in making the arrest and conducting the search incident of both the arrestee and the passenger compartment of his car? If the warrant was and remains valid the answer is yes. However, what is the result if the warrant was no longer valid? The answer is that the arrest was unlawful and, therefore, the search incident is unlawful. Can the "good faith" doctrine of **Leon** be applied?

The **Leon** "good faith" issue presents a more difficult problem. Maryland's highest court addressed this issue and they provide a well-reasoned answer. They felt that **Whiteley v. Warden**, 401 U.S. 560 (1971), as applied through **U.S. v. Hensley**, 469 U.S. 221 (1985), provides that answer. As it noted, **Whiteley** held that "an arrest predicated on a warrant of which the arresting officer learned by radio was invalid because the warrant was not supported by probable cause" and that **Hensley** says the arresting officer acts at his own risk whether the information he relied on was valid and that **Whiteley** was not affected by **Hensley**. In the Maryland case a valid warrant indeed had been issued. However, it had already been served and the problem was cleared up before this arrest. The police had failed to "clear" the warrant from the computer database. That, however, was not the end of the problem. Reality is a part of the process. The reality is that there will be gaps in processes. When can it be said that an officer is negligent in relying on the radio or computer report? When can it be said that the department becomes negligent in failing to remove such information? The Maryland court recognized these realities. The state put on no evidence that this seven-day delay was required or, at least, not negligent. The court cited a case from the District of Columbia where a four-day delay (with a two day weekend) was not negligent and **Leon,** therefore, applied. **Ott v. State**, 600 A. 2d 111 (Md. 1992). See also **Childress v. U.S.** 381 A. 2d 614 (D.C. Ct. App. 1977).

The Supreme Court addressed the computer issue in **Arizona v. Evans**, 514 U.S. 1 (1995). The defendant was lawfully stopped for a traffic violation. The "wants and warrants" check was run and indicated an outstanding misdemeanor warrant. The arrest was made and the search incident revealed a bag of marijuana. However, the warrant had been quashed 17 days before this arrest. Unfortunately, the court personnel responsible for updating computer records had not removed the "warrant" from the database. The Supreme Court, through Rehnquist, held the police cannot be faulted for this breakdown in the data maintenance. This database was controlled by the court and not the police. The exclusionary rule was intended to deter police misconduct and not misconduct by the court personnel. Thus, this case joins **Leon** in limiting the state action doctrine to police misconduct. This point was the "bone of contention" noted in the dissents of Stevens and Ginsberg. The Court did say, however, that the rule applied to those officers *reasonably relying on data banks controlled and maintained by non-police actors*. Data banks under the control of police might demand a different result. In that event, the judge should consider using the **Ott** decision from Maryland cited above. It is not a good faith case. It relies on the understanding of the law of negligence and all that word implies.

3. Containers and Probable Cause-Based Searches

Minnesota has placed a limit on **Ross** that not many courts will recognize. In this case drugs and paraphernalia were found in the front seat of a car. The police then searched the duffel bag of a back seat passenger. Raising a *nexus* requirement, the court said unless the police can show that the front seat probable cause can be attributed to the passenger, that item cannot be searched. This is a proper use of **U.S. v. Dire** (*supra*) discussed in Chapter Two. This is also a case where the container is definitely not the property of the car's owner, however, regular scope search cases allow the search of visitors' containers. Therefore, Minnesota's "no innocents" analysis is not germane when postured against **Ross's** scope policy (as broad as a magistrate may allow). **State v. Bigelow**, 451 N.W. 2d 311 (Minn. 1990). Iowa, on the other hand, fully accepted the **Ross** case in **State v. Eubanks**, 355 N.W. 2d 57 (Iowa 1984), as did Oklahoma in **Coulter v. State**, 777 P. 2d 1373 (Okla. Crim. 1989).

The broad language of **Ross** would seem to indicate that if police have probable cause to believe a car contains evidence of a crime the car, and all packages therein, may be searched. However, in **Ross,** the probable cause arose after the package was placed in the car. If the probable cause as to the package's contents arose before being placed in the car do the police have a right without a warrant to open the package that has been placed in the car? If **Ross** overruled **U.S. v. Chadwick**, 433 U.S. 1 (1977) the answer is that a warrant is not needed. But if **Chadwick** was not overruled by **Ross** then the answer is that a warrant is indeed needed.

In **Chadwick** the probable cause arose before the footlocker was placed in the car. The car was stopped, the footlocker was secured, the defendants arrested and the footlocker search was conducted more than an hour after the defendants were in custody thus destroying search incident rights. The Court announced what was to become the "closed container" doctrine. The government did not attempt to call this an automobile search thus the role of the car in transporting evidence of a crime was not argued. This point truly distinguishes the holding in **Ross** from that of **Chadwick**.

In any event, confusion existed after **Chadwick** and the Court tried to clear the confusion by its decision in **Arkansas v. Sanders**, 442 U.S. 753 (1979). The car in **Sanders** was stopped and searched for contraband. The probable cause arose before the suitcase was put in this taxi at the Little Rock airport. The seizure of the suitcase was not at issue. The Court indicated that a suitcase taken from a car is still imbued with a privacy expectation. The Court held that "the warrantless search of one's personal luggage merely because it was located in an automobile..." is not justified under **Carroll** and, therefore, may not be searched without consent, warrant, exigency or other exception.

Assuming that Sanders was properly arrested on a probable cause base, the fact that the suitcase was in the trunk meant that search incident rights did not arise because the suitcase was not in his immediate control. Also, since the suitcase was in the trunk no **Belton** passenger compartment search incident rights arose. Since the car was a randomly chosen taxi, no **Ross** probable cause search rights arose (assuming, as we must, that **Ross** did not overrule **Sanders**).

In **Ross**, the car as a container for drugs was known by the police in the probable cause context simultaneously with the fact that the drugs were in containers in the car. Therefore, they did not first know of the containers and then watch them be put in the car. The Court mentioned **Chadwick** primarily as holding that footlockers are not cars and a footlocker does not become a car merely because it is placed within a car. **Sanders** was also discussed and both **Chadwick** and **Sanders** were distinguished from **Ross** in that in those cases probable cause did not exist as to the whole car whereas in **Ross** such probable cause did exist for the whole car and any containers in it.

With this history in mind a California Court held that where the probable cause arose before the bag was placed in the car, the car was not inextricably linked with the criminality and that **Ross** did not apply but rather **Chadwick** applied. It said any other interpretation would allow warrantless searches merely by police allowing the container to be placed in the car and that result could only be so if **Ross** overruled **Chadwick**, which of course it did not. **People v. Acevedo**, 265 Cal. Rep. 23 (Cal. Dist. Ct. App. 1989).

Other courts have wrestled with the issue of allowing police to "get around" the **Chadwick-Sanders** holdings and to let them enjoy the breadth of **Ross**. In a First Circuit case, the prearranged use of a get-away car after a bank robbery led that court to hold that **Sanders** was truly distinguishable. Unlike the car in **Sanders** (a taxi; any taxi) was coincidental. But in this case the court said this car "was scarcely coincidental" and therefore it "contributed to probable cause as an instrumentality of the crime. It was not simply a repository for contraband." The case, wisely decided and distinguished, is a recognition that **Chadwick-Sanders** were not affected by **Ross**. **U.S. v. Maguire**, 918 F. 2d 254 (C.A. 1st 1990).

Because of the confusion caused by **Chadwick-Sanders** (*supra*) and **U.S. v. Ross** (*supra*) the Supreme Court in **California v. Acevedo**, 500 U.S. 565 (1991), held: "The police may search an automobile and the containers within it where they have probable cause to believe contraband or evidence is contained." In **Ross,** the police had probable cause to search the entire car but the Court left open the question whether a warrant would be required when the police lacked probable cause to search the whole car but did have probable cause to search one place or area in the car; in this case the trunk. They answered that question in this case and concluded a warrant is not required under the **Carroll** doctrine. The Court acknowledged that the **Chadwick-Sanders** rule provided only minimal privacy protection and could have said, illusory protection. They specifically noted the **Belton** search incident rule and, of course, the **Opperman-Bertine** inventory rule. The Court said the Fourth Amendment does not compel separate treatment for an automobile search that extends only to a container within the vehicle. Saying that **Chadwick-Sanders** "is the antithesis of a 'clear and unequivocal' guideline..." it said one clear-cut rule should govern automobile searches. The Court thus eliminated "the warrant requirement" for closed containers set forth in **Sanders.** It did reaffirm the principle that probable cause to search the trunk does not by itself justify a search of the whole car. The Court also said it is clear, in this case, that the probable cause in this case only went to the trunk.

This decision is totally in line with the general limits placed on the scope of all sorts of searches whether warranted or not. It makes more sense than having two lines of authority that the Court noted was highly criticized in the academic legal community and confusing to lower courts. States like Oklahoma that carefully followed **Chadwick** as noted in **Castleberry v. State**, 678 P. 2d 720 (Okla. Crim. 1984) must now rethink their positions. South Dakota also recognized the confusion caused by **Chadwick-Sanders** but came to a conclusion ultimately in line with **Acevedo**. See **State v. Anderson**, 316 N.W. 2d 105 (S. D. 1982).

One of the first courts to rethink its position was Vermont's Supreme Court. In **State v. Savva**, 616 A. 2d 774 (Vt. 1992), that court rejected **Acevedo**. The container in **Savva** was a brown paper bag which was opened by the officer revealing plastic bags of marijuana. They looked at recent developments and decided to follow **Sanders** and **Chadwick** rather than **Acevedo** under Vermont's constitution. The court held that a container that can be seized and held awaiting a warrant, must be held unless there is a true exigency and not the "makeweight" exigency of the automobile search policy. It also clearly protected plain view case law and indicated no warrant would be required in the distinctive package cases. The court felt that the officer could and should have given the defendant a choice-consent or await the warrant issuing outcome.

Courts must keep one very important factual distinction in mind when doing a **Ross** type case. If the police only have probable cause to believe the owner of the car committed a crime, there is no justification for the warrantless seizure and search of the car on that *nexus* alone. **Ross** is to apply only when probable cause exists that the car itself is an instrumentality of crime and that can arise independent of the owner-possesor's activity. See **U.S. v. Cooper**, 949 F. 2d 737 (C.A. 5th 1991).

Whether the police may conduct a **Belton** or a **Ross** search may turn on the reason for the seizure and the statutory violation involved and not on whether the state court accepts the U.S. Supreme Court's decisions. In an Oregon case the police stopped a defendant for having an open container of alcohol in his car. Upon the stop and seizure of the defendant and the can of beer, the police did a further search for more open containers. During that search drugs were found. The Oregon court said the drugs had to be suppressed because there was no independent probable cause and the statute only authorized the taking of what was necessary to properly charge the offense. Since they already had the one container necessary to make the charge, further searches were not authorized. **State v. Porter**, 817 P. 2d 1306 (Ore. 1991). The case is correctly decided on the **Ross** issue but it is suspect on the **Belton** issue. However, it appears that the officer was not seeking a weapon but was only seeking further evidence of the charged offense. In that case the officer eliminated the "weapon reaching" aspect **Belton/Chimel** by his own testimony.

The U.S. Supreme Court has put a "no warrant required" exclamation point on **U.S. v. Ross** and **Acevedo** by its decision in **Pennsylvania v. LaBron**, 518 U.S. 938 (1996). They emphasized that probable cause coupled with ready mobility permits police to search a vehicle without more. The Pennsylvania's reaction was to look to their own constitution which required an exigency beyond mere mobility. **Com. v. Gelineau**, 696 A. 2d 188 (Pa. Super, 1997).

The debate whether **Ross** or **Belton** or a limited search right exists only to the driver's property when probable cause exists came to a head in **Wyoming v. Houghton**, 526 U.S. 295 (1999). Houghton was a passenger in a car that was legally stopped for two traffic violations. The officer noted a hypodermic needle in the shirt pocket of the driver and had the driver exit the car and place the needle on the hood. The driver admitted to using "speed." The officer called for help and the car was searched including all containers. One of those containers was Ms. Houghton's purse. That purse contained the drugs. She argued that her personal property was outside the probable cause scope thus her conviction was unlawful. The Supreme Court said that when police have probable cause to search a car, they may search every part of it *and* its contents. That means *all* containers found in the car, including personal containers of passengers. Individualized probable cause for each container in a car does not have to be shown. This was a 6-3 decision.

Finally, in a 7-2 concurring decision, the Court rebuffed Maryland and its decision in the **Dyson** case. Maryland felt that even though the police had "abundant" probable cause to search Dyson's car, the general automobile exigency was not enough to authorize a warrantless search. This, of course, went against the clear precedent of the U.S. Supreme Court. The Court tersely revisited the **Carroll** towing doctrine of 1925 through the 1996 **LaBron** case (*supra*) and abruptly and firmly stated that the "automobile exception does not have a separate exigency requirement." If a car is readily mobile and if there is probable cause, the police can search it without more. **Maryland v. Dyson**, 527 U.S. 465 (1999).

Nevada also appears to take a restrictive view of **Ross-LaBron**. In **State v. Harvisch**, 1998 WL 84570 (Nev.), it held that if the defendant is in no position to move the car, probable cause without additional exigency required a warrant under the Nevada constitution.

Ohio has weighed in on the auto probable cause issue through the **Moore** case. Moore ran a red light and was stopped. As he opened his window a strong odor of marijuana was detected. Moore was asked to get out of the car and when searched drug paraphernalia was found. The vehicle search yielded a burnt joint. Was this evidence lawfully gathered? The trial judge said no; the appeals court said yes, it was, saying: "We find no reason why a trained and experienced officer, in the detection of marijuana, should be prohibited from relying on his or her sense of smell as it pertains to the establishment of probable cause for a warrantless search of a motor vehicle." **State v. Moore**, 1999 WL 770216 (Ohio App. 5) (unpub. op.). A discretionary appeal to the Ohio Supreme Court was taken. The high court also fully recognized the training and experience of this police officer. The auto search was not seriously questioned. Instead they talked about needing a warrant to search the person but noted the high probability of losing the defendant while a warrant is sought. Whatever happened to search incident to an arrest? Somehow they got off into a **Schmerber** analysis and exigency. How they got on that track I do not know. There was probable cause to arrest Moore and that automatically gave rise to a non-life threatening search incident to that arrest. The outcome is correct; the reasoning is off-base. **State v. Moore**. 734 N.E. 2d 804 (Ohio 2000).

Other Ohio cases on probable cause are of interest. For instance, does a BOLO support probable cause? Yes, under these circumstances. "As an identified citizen informant, Oswald provided Officer Tuttle with specific details of criminality and the circumstance surrounding her knowledge of them. Therefore, upon independent examination, the court finds that this detailed and credible information, which precipitated the police dispatch relief upon by Trooper Brock, established probable cause for the search of defendant's motor vehicle." **State v. Arnez**, 2000 WL 1585073 (Ohio Com. Pl.) (unpub. op.).

Does seeing a person take a box from a house and put it in his van and start to drive off just before a warrant to search the house is to be executed give the officers probable cause to stop the van and search it? Coupled with information that the house was a major drug distribution center, the answer was yes. **Ohio v. Pitchford**, 1998 WL 827606 (Ohio App. 8) (unpub. op.).

B.   Contemporaneous Search – Under Probable Cause – Warrant Not Required

How soon after the police take possession to search do they have to conduct the search? Must the search be contemporaneous with the seizure or can there be a delay? It was established in **U.S. v. Johns**, 469 U.S. 478 (1985), and **Michigan v.**

Thomas, 458 U.S. 259 (1982), that when the government is entitled to seize a vehicle and the packages therein, the government does not have to conduct an immediate search. Basically, the limit on the time in which to search is governed by and subject to each jurisdiction's rule, statutes, constitution, or regulation. Police, must, in common terms, "fish or cut bait," but whether that action must come one, three, or ten days later is subject to local rules. This is so because the car, *etc.*, itself is an object of criminality; part of the crime and not incidental thereto.

Thomas was a *per curiam* opinion and the defendant urged that once the car was immobilized the exigency ended, thus the continued search of the car after finding the drugs during the inventory was not contemporaneous. As to this the Court said: "It is thus clear that the justification to conduct such a warrantless search does not vanish once the car has been immobilized; nor does it depend upon a reviewing court's assessment of the likelihood in each particular case that the car would have been driven away, or that its contents would have been tampered with during the period required for the police to obtain a warrant."

In **Johns** the packages were found three days after the trucks were taken into custody. The Court said this was not unreasonable. The police did not have to immediately open these packages. The police cannot indefinitely postpone a search, the Court noted. Of course there is always the possibility that a delay could otherwise adversely affect a defendants "privacy or possessory interest" opined the Court, but that was not the case here. For their authority the Court cited other delay cases such as **Cooper v. California**, 386 U.S. 58 (1967); **Cardwell v. Lewis**, 417 U.S. 592 (1974); **U.S. v. Edwards**, 415 U.S. 800 (1974); and, of course, **Thomas** (*supra*).

Independent probable cause that arises after a vehicle has been left in a parking lot while the defendant is taken away to be booked justifies the search of the car long after the defendant is removed from the car and is no longer able to drive it, said the Colorado Supreme Court in **People v. Romero**, 593 P. 2d 365 (Colo. 1989). The officer in **Romero** overheard the defendant talking to a bail bondsman and learned that there may be guns in the car. The officer had the car impounded after she flashed her light in the car and saw the butt of a gun. She unlocked the car and found the gun. A warrant was obtained and another gun and some ammunition were found. Although the Court based its decision on **Carney** (*infra*) this case more closely approximated the emergency that existed in **Cady v. Dombrowski** (*infra*). In any event, unless a car is on blocks, its mobility is only very slightly impaired if one does not have the keys. Thus in **Romero,** there is the mobility of **Carney** and the underlying emergency of **Cady,** under either theory the search was proper.

For other cases discussing what constitutes probable cause to search a car under **Ross -LaBron** see **People v. Reyes**, 1998 WL 112857 (Colo. *en banc*.) – articulable suspicion plus canine alert equals probable cause to search a trunk of a stopped car; **State v. Longs**, 1998 WL 85310 (Conn.) – driver consented to search but owner of bag search said no – court says that probable cause due to odor of drugs overcame any consent issue and courts cites **Ross**; **State v. Guzman**, 959 S.W. 2d 631 (Tex. Crim. 1998) – disagrees with Pennsylvania and says P.C. plus auto exigency is all that is needed; no additional exigency required when D no longer in control of car; **Callaway v. State**, 1998 WL 85602 (Wyo) – a proper search is not over when some but not all stolen items are found thus plain view of other items found before final stolen item is located is admissible; **State v. Ireland**, 1998 WL 76228 (Me.) – odor of burnt marijuana plus furtive gestures gave police P.C. to search car and when none found in passenger compartment then P.C. existed to search the trunk; and **Kenner v. State**, 703 N.E. 2d 1122 (Ind. App. 1999) – officer's detection of scent of marijuana was sufficient cause to detain the auto until the dogs arrived and dog's alert gave P.C.

C.   Emergency Beyond the Mobility Exigency

There are times when the police have no probable cause, there is no apparent crime, and they do not have lawful custody of a car, yet a true need could arise that demands that the police gain access to a car. Can a limited intrusion be permitted that can, by inadvertence (at least not pretexually), produce admissible incriminating evidence? The answer is yes, and best illustrated by the case of **Cady v. Dombrowski**, 413 U.S. 433 (1973).

Dombrowski was an off-duty Chicago police officer in Wisconsin on a holiday. He wrecked his rented car, turned himself in, and explained who he was. A quick check of the passenger compartment did not reveal the revolver that police were sure he was required to carry at all times. No further search was made and the car was turned over to a private towing company to be towed to the private garage where it was stored without police guard. Dombrowski had to be taken to a hospital whereupon he lapsed into a coma. The gun was not among his personal belongings. The police thought the gun must be in his car. They went to the private garage, opened the trunk and found evidence of the homicide for which Dombrowksi was convicted.

Although this case is normally placed with the inventory search cases, it is not quite clear, though it could be assumed, that the police were still in possession of the car. If they were not, and the Court wrestled with this, saying the police did not have actual physical custody, although the towing and storing were done at their direction, then could they conduct this search for the revolver thus giving them plain view (to be discussed below)? The Court said, "These officers in a rural area were simply reacting to the effect of an accident – one of the recurring practical situations that results from the operation of motor vehicles and with which local officers must deal every day."

Therefore, properly viewed, this case represents a situation that does not fit neatly under any other car intrusion category. It should not have to. The principle of emergency should be applied sparingly and only where no pretext for the search appears. The practicalities, under the totality of the circumstances, are limited by reasonableness.

A California court also recognized that **Cady's** function is that of a "safety of the community" case that may be based upon an emergency need for police action. In **People v. Holzworth**, 265 Cal. Rep. 557 (Cal. Ct. App. 1990), police arrest a man on an outstanding warrant after an articulable suspicion stop based on a potential homicide case. Prior information said that the defendant carried a gun in his jeep. Police asked Holzworth what he wanted to do with the car and he said it did not lock but leave it where it is. The police decided to act on the prior information and found the gun that led to his conviction as an ex-felon in possession of a firearm. The reasonable belief standard of **Cady** is not a probable cause standard if it is to serve the public protection function there recognized. See also **Lamphere v. State**, 348 N.W. 2d 212 (Iowa 1984). However, it should be kept in mind that once the exigency is over, it is over. **Lucas v. State**, 704 P. 2d 1141 (Okla. Crim. 1985). In **Lucas,** the initial stop was based on articulable suspicion that the woman in the car was being assaulted or at least seriously threatened. After confronting the people in the car, the police determined that there was no threat. However, the defendant made a few furtive gestures. The court said these gestures were not enough to give police the probable cause necessary to search the car. The gestures created no more than mere suspicion. Since the lawful intrusion had come to an end, the fruits of the continued search were poisonous under **Wong Sun**.

D.   Inventory

1.   Decisional Law
a.   Opperman – the base-line case

There are times when the police are required by law or good sense to take an automobile into custody when there is no probable cause to believe that the car is an instrument of a crime. The police have to perform a caretaking function. Once they have possession, are they required to ignore it? No. Can they search it? Not fully, but they can inventory the personal property found in the car. Why? The purpose is to: (1) Protect the defendant's property; (2) Protect the police from lost property claims (the liability issue); and (3) Protect all citizens from the potential danger of hidden weapons or explosives from falling into the wrong hands. The police who have lawful custody of a car may conduct a routine inventory (established by departmental policy) routinely done (not just for some cars) so as to avoid the claim of pretextual searches. The scope of an inventory is non-destructive and can be done in a manner that proves a caretaking function and not a disguised search function. Therefore, if evidence of a crime is found through a routine inventory, routinely done, that evidence would be admissible. This inventory intrusion right was established in **South Dakota v. Opperman**, 428 U.S. 396 (1976).

The facts are simple. Opperman's car was parked on a public street at 3:00 a.m. It was ticketed for a parking violation. At 10:00 a.m. it was ticketed again. Later the car was towed away and impounded on the city lot. Some valuables were seen in the car. The police entered the car and searched for valuables by following the procedures set out on their standard inventory form. A plastic bag filled with marijuana was found. The property was removed and placed in the police station for safekeeping. The defendant came by later and was arrested on a possession charge. The Court said there is a difference between automobiles and homes or offices. *First*, the car has mobility and this creates a practical exigency. *Second*, there is a lesser expectation of privacy in a car. In the interests of public safety and as a part of what is called the community caretaking function, automobiles are frequently taken into police custody. When impounded, local police generally follow a routine practice of securing and inventorying the car's contents. The Court said that inventories pursuant to standard police procedures are reasonable. The Court went on to say that "intrusion into automobiles impounded or otherwise in lawful police custody where the process is aimed at securing or protecting the car and its contents" is reasonable. The facts and circumstances of each case must be examined.

b.   Reaction to Opperman

The issue of "lawful custody" giving rise to an **Opperman** inventory has become a most controversial issue. Several police departments have taken the position that they are not required to deliver the car into the hands of an otherwise qualified and sober driver selected by the vehicle's arrested driver, nor do they feel that they are bound to allow a towing company of the arrested driver's choice to take possession of the car. Over such objections the police have taken the car, impounded it and then conducted the **Opperman** inventory. To this conduct, several states have reacted negatively.

New Jersey, for example, says the defendant must be given the option of parking and locking the car or to summon someone to take possession of the car. **State v. Slockbower**, 397 A. 2d 1050 (N.J. 1979). New Jersey continued its policy by its decision in **State v. Lark**, 2000 WL 233325 (N.J.). The option whether to arrest a driver for being unlicensed does not, in New Jersey, carry a search incident right. So if the police want to search the car they must have lawful possession. In this case the driver, though unlicensed, had proof of ownership and was accompanied by a sober licensed driver. Thus, the decision to impound and inventory the car was unlawful and the cocaine found was inadmissible. The District of Columbia Court of Appeals would appear to agree. **Schwasta v. U.S.**, 392 A. 2d 1071 (D.C. Ct. App. 1978). Louisiana would also require the officers to give the driver the option. **State v. LaRue**, 368 So. 2d 1048 (La. 1979). Florida provides a waiver of liability form which allows the driver the leave the car at the site if it presents no danger to the motoring public. **Gordon v. State**, 368 So. 2d 59 (Fla. App. 1979). The State of Kentucky requires that alternatives are to be sought before impoundment can occur. **Wagner v. Commonwealth**, 581 S.W. 2d 352 (Ky. 1979). Missouri has held that where the car is parked on a residential street and locked thereby necessitating no further safety measures, it is improper to impound it. **State v. Peterson**, 583 S.W. 2d 277 (Mo. Ct. App. 1979). In Georgia, the police cannot reject the owner's reasonable plan for securing the car. **State v. Ludvicek**, 259 S.E. 2d 503 (Ga. App. 1978). This also is the rule of Minnesota. **State v. Goodrich**, 256 N.W. 2d 506 (Minn. 1977).

On the other hand, Oklahoma says the police officer has no mandatory duty to advise an arrestee of non-impoundment options. **State v. Shorney**, 524 P. 2d 69 (Okla. Crim. 1974). In **Shorney** the defendant was charged with possession of marijuana. After the pursuit for traffic violations had begun, the defendant's car ran out of gas. The defendant legally parked his car on the city streets. He was arrested by the police. His three passengers, all licensed drivers, were told to leave the scene. The officer informed the defendant that his car was going to be impounded. The car was impounded. The defense argued that the failure to let one of the others take possession of the car was fatal. The defense felt it was the officer's duty to inform the defendant of this option. The Oklahoma court approved impoundments upon a lawful arrest and said no duty exists to advise an arrestee of other options. The case does say that other options exist. The court seems to be saying that the citizen must present those options with the innuendo being that the officer might have to accept such other, reasonable options. It is a care-taking function after all.

Kansas takes the position that when a car is legally parked, an able owner or driver of the car is to be given the option of police impoundment or to provide for the care of his car on his own. Only when there is a justification for impoundment can the police withhold this option. Thus the unattended illegally parked car or the car in the possession of a person incapable of or unwilling to give the officer his decision may be impounded. **State v. Teeter**, 819 P. 2d 651 (Kan.. 1991).

The immediate reaction to **Opperman** by the South Dakota Supreme Court, was to some, unexpected. It was one of the first cases by that court clearly expressing an adoption of the "new federalism" approach to search and seizure decisions by the U.S. Supreme Court. Thus under its own Constitution the South Dakota Court said towing a car, though lawful, *does not* give police the right to an invasive search, only a "plain view search" and seizure for safekeeping purposes. **State v. Opperman**, 247 N.W. 2d 673 (S. D. 1976). There was no examination of the community care taking function, no discussion of "sham law suits" nor that the towed car could be a rolling bomb or arsenal. They just felt the search was unreasonable when towed for such a "minor" purpose.

But they did not totally reject **Opperman** for all purposes. Twelve years later in **State v. Flittie**, 425 N.W. 2d 1 (S. D. 1988), the stop involved drunk driving and the inventory included the opening of a locked trunk. In **Flittie**, the court finally talks about the three prongs of the community caretaking responsibility. **Opperman's** plain view limitation was explained away but the court nowhere overruled the remanded **Opperman** opinion. But what it does do is follow the routine inventory – routinely done philosophy of **Colorado v. Bertine** except for illegally towed vehicles – or does it? Time will tell.

A footnote in the U.S. Supreme Court's **Opperman** opinion indicated that the inventory was not unreasonable in scope. This is the only mention of a distinction between an inventory and a full-field search. No distinction was made in this case as it was in the **Dombrowski** case that the impounding lot was or was not under 24-hour police guard. That really should make no difference since things can be stolen from guarded places as well.

As to the difference in the scope of the search, it would not be unreasonable for the police to check under mats (for keys or other valuables that are there), in the cracks of seats (wallets, checkbooks, and credit cards have a tendency to get in these places), under the dash for a magnetic key box (many people have these), and an unlocked glove box (this case so held). The question remains as to whether trunks and glove boxes that are locked can be accessed. In **Dombrowski,** the search for the service revolver positively answers the more recent **Opperman** case. Since vandals could easily remove the glove box or "pop" the lock, such openings would appear reasonable. Besides, in **Opperman,** the police had to unlock the car to gain access to the unlocked glove box.

An inventory policy that prohibits opening trunks and locked glove compartments sounds properly protective of privacy rights. However, it negates a genuine caretaking function. Cities will be held liable for negligent keeping of cars that are broken into and from which valuables are taken. In order for the city or other governments to properly protect themselves from such claims locked trunks and glove boxes should be opened and the contents inventoried and listed. The lesser expectation of privacy in the car balances against the community caretaking function. The caretaking function should win. This was the conclusion drawn by Massachusetts in **Com. v. Garcia**, 569 N.E. 2d 385 (Mass. 1991). After citing the three purposes of inventories as found in **Opperman**, that court noted the strong likelihood that valuables will be stored in a trunk and they found that locked trunks are only somewhat more secure than locked passenger compartments. In reality, they are no more secure. They also raised the possibility of false claims. The "best approach" they said is to have a non – investigative inventory policy that "reasonably includes opening a locked trunk."

After those items and areas are checked, then it would be questionable whether a look under the hood would be reasonable in scope. Removal of hubcaps is unreasonable unless all hubcaps of all cars are removed and stored for safekeeping. Removal of door panels is a part of a full-field search as is removal of seats, seat covers, stuffing and the like. Dismantling the car in any manner is a full-field search and not an inventory.

The second problem involves the question of whether an inventory is reasonable if the impounding lot is under 24-hour security. It made a difference in **Dombrowski,** but it was not raised in **Opperman**. Since things are stolen from secure areas of society, it should not make a difference. Even some policemen have stolen items from impounded cars. To look at all the facts and circumstances; that is the only guideline to be followed here.

Another question arises. Suppose a citizen is arrested for a traffic violation and taken to the police station and his car is then inventoried while the booking function is taking place. Could the police inventory that car? From the Court in **Opperman**, these words: "**Cady** distinguished **Preston v. United States**, 376 U.S. 364 (1964), on the ground that the holding, invalidating a car search conducted after a vagrancy arrest, stands only for the proposition that the search challenged there could not be justified as one incident to an arrest...." **Preston** therefore did not raise the issue of the constitutionality of a protective inventory of a car lawfully within police custody. Practicality should dictate no inventory right in the brief detention type cases. These are usually either non-jailable offenses or ones for which some form of standardized bail provisions apply.

There has been considerable reaction to the **Opperman** decision. In one 1978 case a man had illegally double-parked and was asked to pull around the corner. A check was made and the computer revealed the defendant's license had been suspended. The defendant was arrested. The officer noticed some "furtive" actions while the computer check was being made. The defendant was driven to the station and the arresting officer drove the defendant's car to the station. At the station, a brown bag protruding from under the seat was checked. It contained contraband. Upon this evidence the defendant was tried. The court held this was not an inventory search because the state failed to prove that the defendant was unable to provide for the car's safekeeping or incapable of making that decision as required by local police regulations. Thus the police did not have lawful possession of the auto as required by **Opperman**. **Arrington v. U.S.**, 382 A. 2d 14 (D.C. Ct. App. 1978). This case well illustrates the need by the defense to secure the local inventory policy.

Indiana recognizes that not all criteria for impounding a vehicle can be spelled out in any departmental inventory policy. To control the discretion of police officers, the Indiana Supreme Court had given police a list of factors to be considered when the policy does not address every exigency. This major concern was the hidden desire by police to conduct an investigatory search. They say to determine the following: (1) Does the vehicle constitute a hazard; or (2) Is the property upon which the vehicle is located subject to the defendant's control; and (3) How long will the car be unattended thus the car itself is in danger; or (4) Is the owner of the property upon which the car is located asking that it be removed. See **Fair v. State**, 627 N.E. 2d 427 (Ind. 1993). The dissent in **Fair** made some telling observations. The majority failed to point out that gun shots had been fired so this might not have been a mere intoxication case at the time the officer made the impound decision. The car was a rental car thus the owner's rights were being protected. And finally, this judge says the car was not on the defendant's own property but was parked in a tenant parking lot while the defendant visited friends.

Local inventory policies coupled with restrictive local decisional law must be carefully considered as illustrated by five Oklahoma cases. One line of cases focuses on who may conduct the inventory and the other addresses the inventory list prepared. The lead Oklahoma inventory case is **Gonzales v. State**, 507 P. 2d 1277 (Okla. Crim. 1973). That case held that a police inventory can only be conducted by a police officer.

Thus a garageman is not a police officer and therefore cannot conduct an inventory. Where a non-police officer conducts an inventory, the contraband discovered is inadmissible and any subsequent police inventory is a subterfuge and *void ab initio*.

The court followed up on this theory in **State v. Shorney**, 524 P. 2d 69 (Okla. Crim. 1974). In **Shorney** the officer instructed the tow truck driver to do an inventory. A hole cut in the quarter-panel was noticed by the tow truck driver, the officer was summoned and the marijuana was seized. The state argued that Oklahoma City Code, Art. 19§ 34-280 et seq. governed. The provision said that an inventory must be conducted "by the authority of a police officer." The court was unwilling to back – down from **Gonzales** and said such inventories must be conducted by the police.

A second line of Oklahoma cases deals with the inventory list prepared by the officer. The lead case is **Magann v. State**, 601 P. 2d 123 (Okla. Crim. 1979). To accomplish an inventory's lawful objectives, an inventory sheet showing the contents of the vehicle must be filled out appropriately. The court then said that anything less than that points to the possibility that the inventory was a subterfuge – a pretextual search. In **Magann** there was conflicting evidence as to why the trunk was searched. Items of value were not listed and the glove compartment was not touched. Thus the court had ample evidence to hold that a routine inventory, routinely done, was not in fact done in this case. The procedure in this case was held to be a search and not an inventory.

Limits on the broad language in **Magann** would come through two subsequent decisions. The first case is **Wheeler v. State**, 751 P. 2d 198 (Okla. Crim. 1988). Bobby Dean Wheeler was convicted of weapons and drug possession charges that arose as a result of the inventory of his car. He argued that the failure to list one item of value on the inventory sheet made this a pretextual search. In this case an answering machine found in the car was not listed. The Oklahoma court noted that things can be overlooked without requiring an automatic find of a pretext. Thus human error can be tolerated. The defendant also argued that a failure to look into the spare tire compartment also proved it was a search and not an inventory. The court refused to consider this point. Why not? Since substances were found on the defendant **Ross** search rights existed. Otherwise this may have been more like **Magann** where the glove compartment was overlooked.

The third "inventory sheet" case is **Hall v. State**, 766 P. 2d 1002 (Okla. Crim. 1988). Hall, who was alone when driving his car on a suspended license, had no grounds to complain of this impoundment. In fact in such a situation the "standard policy" required impoundment. Drugs were found during the inventory. The defendant argued pretextual search because the officer failed to fill out an inventory sheet properly under **Magann**. Rather than using the official departmental inventory sheet the officer used a regular sheet of paper. Substance and not form rules, thus the "piece of paper" argument had to fail. The court said the purported inventory in **Magann** was a narrowly tailored search rather than the space by space inventory conducted in this case. To save **Wheeler** as a decision, the court added that when a proper inventory is conducted the discovery of contraband gives probable cause to conduct a **Ross** search.

The key to the finding of a valid inventory policy is whether the scope has been adequately defined and, therefore, if adequately defined, the officer's discretion will be limited so that general searches cannot be conducted under the guise of an inventory search. This issue was faced by Oregon in **State v. Willhite**, 824 P. 2d 419 (Ore. Ct. App. 1992). The inventory policy in question was founded on a brief, 52-word memorandum. Did this satisfy the "standardized criteria" of **Bertine**, Oregon asked. No, it did not, they held. A policy that is too general is not a discretion-limiting policy. Too much room was left for personal experience and thus individual discretion.

The New Jersey Superior Court, Appellate Division, accepted the **Opperman** decision as long as the inventory procedure is not a pretext concealing an investigatory police motive. **State v. Roberson**, 384 A. 2d 195 (N.J. Super. Ct. 1978). The Supreme Court had already made that point clear.

How does a judge know when an inventory was pretextual even when the impounding is otherwise lawful? An Indiana case provides some clues though. In the case of **Fair v. State**, 627 N.E. 2d 427 (Ind. 1993), the impoundment itself was also unreasonable. What raised their suspicions? The court noted that: (1) the inventory was conducted at the scene and not at the impoundment lot; *CAVEAT*: some states require inventories at the sight; (2) an investigatory officer and not an inventory officer conducted the inventory; (3) inventory sheets were not completed; (4) only contraband items were noted not other personal effects; and (5) no official record of impoundment existed. The court said, "collectively, these facts are very harmful to the state's position." Therefore, the state failed "to carry its burden of establishing that the search was reasonable and not a mere pretext."

One of the questions which was not answered in **Opperman** is whether a car properly parked in a public or private place, which is not a threat to people's safety, may be impounded and then inventoried. The Fifth Circuit provides one answer that was not addressed in **Cardwell v. Lewis**, (*supra*). Two defendants were arrested at a shopping mall for passing counterfeit money. Their car was lawfully parked in the mall parking lot. The car was inventoried and towed. The inventory yielded more counterfeit money. The court said that the fact that the car is legally parked does not necessarily negate the need to take the vehicle into protective custody. These two defendants were from out-of-state and had no friends or relatives to whom they could entrust the car. Because of the crime, there was a reasonable expectation that the men and their car would be separated for some time. (No bail?). The court found an appreciable risk of vandalism thus raising the community's caretaking function. The seizure was lawful. **U.S. v. Staller**, 616 F. 2d 1284 (C.A. 5th 1980). This case applies correctly the "totality" analysis that must be done in all such cases.

Whether the custody of the car is lawful is a matter of some dispute as can be seen. A Fourth Circuit case represents one of those decisions where the officers do not have to follow other alternatives to impounding. The defendant claimed that the officer should have let one of his friends take the car or merely should have left the car in a parking lot. The Court held that since the man had been arrested for drunk driving the officer was not required to accept any of these options. **U.S. v. Brown**, 787 F. 2d 929 (C.A. 4th 1986).

Formal impoundment is not required under **Opperman** and **Bertine** but lawful police custody is the minimal requirement. Agreeing with this, the Nebraska court held that rather than towing the car, they would store it, at the suggestion of the defendant, at a nearby farm. By so agreeing the police were assuming the community caretaking function. **State v. Stalder**, 438 N.W. 2d 498 (Neb. 1989). For a different view consider a recent case from New Jersey. The lawful police possession that gives rise to the community caretaking function means that the police have actually taken custody and care of the car. If that process is jumped over, the entry of the car to do an inventory is no good. Such was the outcome in **State v. Hill**, 557 A. 2d 322 (N.J. 1989). The car in question was illegally parked. Before it was towed and while awaiting information whether it was stolen, the officer broke in and searched an open zippered bag wherein drugs were found. Since no impoundment had taken place the court held this an invalid inventory search. The court did not address the inevitable discovery doctrine which could possibly have been applied.

In another case the defendant was arrested more than two blocks from his car. The Court did not allow the inventory because it did not want police combing the streets to find cars of arrestees. **U.S. v. Vidal**, 637 F. Supp. 327 (S.D. N.Y. 1986). This decision places a proper limit on police activity. This was obviously a "search" and not a caretaking case. See also **State v. Kuster**, 353 N.W. 2d 428 (Iowa 1984).

In yet another case, a driver asked the police to let him have his car towed a short distance to his home. They denied his request despite the fact that the only thing they observed was a minor traffic violation. The failure to consider the alternatives to impounding and inventory was fatal said the Connecticut Appeals Court in **State v. Murphy**, 505 A. 2d 1251 (Conn. App. 1986). Obviously these police were acting pretextually. The crime observed was a non-jailable offense where bail is automatic or recognizance used automatically.

If the vehicle is parked on private property not easily subject to vandalism there is no justification for a **Opperman** impoundment and inventory. The court would not uphold a written policy of police requiring the impoundment of all vehicles of arrested persons to include those whose cars do not need caretaking. **U.S. v. Pappas**, 735 F. 2d 1232 (C.A. 10th 1984). Some written policies can be unconstitutional.

Normally, when the car of an arrestee is parked in a public lot, it would not be subject to impoundment and inventory. However, the Tenth Circuit said there are exceptions and found one in **U.S. v. Kornegay**, 885 F. 2d 713 (C.A. 10th 1989). In this case the defendant's true identity was not known, they did not know where he lived, no one was there to take his car, his future prompt release was doubtful and leaving it in this lot made it vulnerable to vandalism or theft. This, they said, made it reasonable to impound the car. The real problem was that he was nowhere near his car when he was arrested making its taking appear more like a seizure for criminal investigation purposes. Only the dissenter recognized these factor. The court felt compelled to distinguish **Pappas**, cited above, thus leaving one to wonder which is the rule and which is the exception. However, on balance, one cannot say the "totality" test was abused.

What can be gleaned from these divergent approaches are attempts by courts to curtail runaway pretextual searches. The easy cases are those where necessity demands taking charge of the car. Thus, where all occupants of a car are arrested, police are often put in a "no choice but to impound" position. **LMOC v. State**, 744 P. 2d 1271 (Okla. Crim. 1987). The clearly pretextual search case is at the other end of the scale. Most cases fall somewhere in between these two extremes.

Frankly, a judge could, and probably should, suspect an ulterior police motive in every case. But a hope of finding evidence and a subterfuge are two different postures. Courts should always suppress pretext in this limited context. One question that therefore should be asked by the court in trying to determine whether the impoundment was lawful is how much in the way of police resources would have been needed to provide an alternative to impoundment. A ten-minute wait for the defendant's wife to arrive is quite different than a one- hour wait. A wait beside a dangerous roadway is different than a wait on a safe, well-lighted side street.

Accepting the rationale of **Opperman** approved inventories, there would seem to be, when coupled with **Cady v. Dombrowski**, no reason for police to avoid locked trunks. Yet some courts which have accepted **Opperman** are quite bothered by entry into the locked trunk. Consider the decision by the Texas Criminal Court of Appeals in **Gill v. State**, 625 S.W. 2d 307 (Tex. Crim. App. 1981). The Texas court appears to base inventory rights only on custodial/negligence rationale. It indicated that since substantial force would be needed to open a locked trunk, police would not be held liable for losing items stolen from a locked trunk. For some reason, and for their own purpose, they find trunk opening requires probable cause. This is good logic but disregards the three-point rationale approved as a reason for an inventory in **Opperman**. In essence, Texas, like West Virginia, is holding **Opperman** to its facts as to place of search within the car. This choice is, of course, left to the individual police department in the first instance subject to review by the courts. Above all there must be a policy to review.

c. Clarifying Opperman – Colorado v. Bertine and the States

Many commentators felt that if the Rehnquist Court reconsidered inventory intrusions they would probably loosen their standards. Instead of loosening the standards of **Opperman**, the Court in **Colorado v. Bertine**, 479 U.S. 367 (1987) re-emphasized the requirement of "routine inventory routinely done." If any new element was added, it was the fact that under a well-drawn, standardized criteria, the Boulder police had the option of impounding the vehicle or locking it in a public parking place. Such discretion when limited by specific standards, as noted in footnote 6, is permissible. Here the discretion related to the feasibility and appropriateness of parking and locking a vehicle. There was also no showing that the police chose impoundment in this case as a ruse to search. This decision was no victory for unrestrained search under the guise of inventory.

If the police do not have a standardized policy, an inventory attempted is no good. But when police also fail to perform the community care taking function for four days, the delay is fatal. Both problems were present in **Boyd v. State**, 542 So. 2d 1276 (Ala. 1989). Fortunately, for the state, there was independent probable cause to search the car under **U.S. v. Johns**, which saved the fruits of the abortive inventory.

The lack of an inventory policy by a local police department spoiled a federal prosecution in **U.S. v. Salmon**, 944 F. 2d 1106 (C.A. 3rd 1991). Local officers seized the car under the state forfeiture statute and conducted an investigatory search that yielded evidence from a container in the trunk. The federal government's argument that this was in essence an inventory failed because of a lack of a policy governing inventories. The court was also unwilling to accept a search incident to forfeiture theory which was advanced by the government. This aspect of the case is discussed in the forfeiture section of this chapter. What is not discussed in **Salmon** is whether the local police were totally without an inventory policy or whether they were missing only a subject-to-forfeiture policy. If the former, the decision makes sense. If the latter, the court missed the "lawfully in police possession" feature of **Opperman-Bertine** and this court has created a standard requiring a series of inventory policies not required by the U.S. Supreme Court. The fatal point is that the government proved *no* policy of any kind.

A California court held that the guidelines for inventory do not have to be written. The court argued that unreasonable procedures could be written but they would not be standard. **People v. Steeley**, 258 Cal. Rep. 699 (Cal. Dist. Ct. App. 1989). However, the best practice is to have them in writing. Written procedures tend to be more credible and limit the discretion of the officer. **Bertine** seems to prefer, if not demand, written policies.

Although it has been said that an inventory policy need not be in writing, it is difficult to imagine being able to prove a departmental policy that is not in writing especially when the object is to show limits on police discretion. Strange as it may seem the Internal Revenue Service has no policy, written or unwritten. They tried to argue that they were operating under the policy of the local police. They failed because they could not prove they were even aware of the local policy or its contents. The Fifth Circuit felt there was a total lack of nexus between the I.R.S. conduct and a standardized policy in the case before them. They held that inventory was conducted as if no standardized procedures governed their conduct. **U.S. v. Hahn**, 922 F. 2d 243 (C.A. 5th 1991).

We have begun to see the impact of **Bertine** in the last few years. Oklahoma adopted **Bertine** and rejected their old rule in **Johnson v. State**, 764 P. 2d 530 (Okla. Crim. 1988). South Dakota eased their rules and now allow a broader search than under their own past rule and has now come more in line with the U.S. Supreme Court. **State v. Flittie**, 425 N.W. 2d 1 (S. D. 1988). See also **State v. Mesa**, 717 N.E. 2d 329 (Ohio 1999).

Utah, on the other hand, has taken a more restrictive approach. They say that no discretion whether to inventory will be allowed. The police procedure must mandate inventories in all cases. **State v. Shamblin**, 763 P. 2d 425 (Utah Ct. App.

1988). This is a clear recognition by this court that police, for the most part, only inventory cars possibly connected with general criminality.

Florida, in looking at the procedures adopted, has held that because the police did not have an inventory procedure mandating the opening of closed containers, the evidence gained by the inventory was not admissible. **State v. Wells**, 539 So. 2d 464 (Fla. 1989). That same state had also addressed the issue of legitimate custody. They held that of course an inventory may be conducted prior to towing if the vehicle is already in legitimate custody. However, the defendant in this case asked police for help in getting a tow and the Court said the police did not get possession and the owner did not relinquish control. **Caplan v. State**, 531 So. 2d 88 (Fla. 1988).

Finally, the Third Circuit had a case demonstrating that the police inventory policy had been adequately established. **U.S. v. Frank**, 864 F. 2d 992 (C.A. 3rd 1988). Frank was arrested in his vehicle that was parked in the parking area of the motel where he was staying. The charge of interstate fugitive felon was the cause of his arrest. The F.B.I. impounded the car. This custody was determined to be lawful. Frank said they were really investigating and not inventorying. The court said, "The mere fact that an inventory search may also have an investigatory purpose does not, however, invalidate it." **Frank** at 1001. There was strong proof at the suppression hearing of a routine inventory routinely done. The testimony demonstrated that the policy was a combination of written and oral procedures and regulations. This was found to be adequate under **Opperman** and **Bertine** standards.

Since **Opperman** announced that inventories that are routinely done in a routine manner are alright and since **Bertine** emphasized standardized criteria limiting the officer's discretion one would think that all issues are settled. They are not. Courts are beginning to split on the scope of such inventories. The inventory search is not a crime generated probable cause intrusion. It is, as already noted, an intrusion based on the community caretaking function. As such there are two scope issues.

First, when does a caretaking search end and crime search begin? For example, if a full-field strip search is done as already described, the police are not caretaking. Of course, that extreme will not be what most often will be judged. Removal of hub-caps, air cleaners, tires from wheels and removal of the car seats are what will be encountered. Are these caretaking or crime searching activities? It may depend. If the tires are taken off the wheels, even in all cases, the activity "smells" like a crime search. If the hubcaps are taken off only to be put right back on then a crime search has occurred. If, however, the department requires all hubcaps to be removed, bagged and stored for safekeeping then an inventory has occurred. If plain view yields criminal evidence in such a case then so be it. Looking under the hood could be a crime search unless the police are directed to see if a magnetic box containing a key is present that could aid in the theft of the car; then a court could find routine inventory routinely done.

The interrelationship of the inventory doctrine and the plain view doctrine is well illustrated in **U.S. v. Khoury**, 901 F. 2d 948 (C.A. 11th 1990). Police had lawfully seized Khoury's car and conducted an inventory. A notebook was found. The police officer thumbed through it but apparently there was no "immediately apparent" evidence of the crime. At that point the inventory of the notebook was over and plain view rights thus ended. The officer later returned, took out the notebook and carefully read it. This was not a part of the inventory but was a search for criminal evidence. Since the second look was not an inventory the plain view gathered was illegal and the evidence gathered was inadmissible.

The second scope area concerns closed containers found in an impounded car. How detailed should the policy be or does it need to be detailed at all? If one looks at this from a property perspective *vis-à-vis* the caretaking function one could argue that detail is not needed; all containers are subject to opening. Why? Bailees of goods have been held liable for the loss of extremely valuable goods even though they had no reason to believe that such a container held such valuable goods. For example, in **Shamrock Hilton Hotel v. Caranas**, 488 S.W. 2d 151 (Text Civ. App. 1972), the hotel was liable for valuable jewelry in a purse that a guest left in the dining room. The hotel took possession of the purse and lost it. They had no idea of the contents. Other cases have held to the contrary but the potential for such a finding of liability should dictate that police are being reasonable in opening containers. Besides, if the police also have a protection function for being permitted inventories, how are they going to conclude that explosives or guns are not present unless they open such containers? Some common sense logic should be applicable.

One department's policy failed to tell officers what to do with closed containers. In **U.S. v. Frank**, 864 F. 2d 992 (C.A. 3rd 1988), the officer opened and made a list. Of course, he came across incriminating evidence. The Third Circuit did not see as fatal a lack of written policies on the subject of opening containers.

In a Michigan case, the police gave chase seeking a speeding motorist. The defendant "lost" the police and abandoned her car, leaving her purse behind. The police found the car and entered it. They opened her purse to determine the owner/driver's address. The purse had cocaine in it. The officer then impounded the vehicle and conducted an inventory. Were the officer's actions reasonable? Yes, said the court in **People v. Russell**, 435 N.W. 2d 487 (Mich. Ct. App. 1989) under either a probable cause theory: (instrumentality of the crime of speeding); or inventory (no police officer would leave a purse in an unlocked car in these circumstances). The fact that he could have determined the address by less intrusive means as a matter of hindsight should not rule the circumstances here; he was not going to violate the community caretaking function in any event. The officer's actions were reasonable and the evidence should not have been suppressed.

Utah, on the other hand, said a lack of such standardized police procedures was fatal. **State v. Shamblin**, 763 P. 2d 425 (Utah Ct. App. 1988). Arbitrary action is prevented by such written procedure. Standardized procedures prohibit "fishing expeditions" and promote equality of treatment. It did not help in this case when the officer was asked about containers when he said in response to "Pretty much up to you?", "Pretty much so, yes." The court did not use a bailor-bailee analysis.

The next procedure is what is a container? That was the issue in **U.S. v. Judge**, 864 F. 2d 1144 (C.A. 5th 1989). DEA guidelines require the opening of all containers while conducting an inventory but fail to define what a container is, leaving that to the discretion of the officer. The agent in this case felt that a backpack was a container and drugs were found. Did this satisfy **Opperman** and **Bertine**? Yes, the inventory search was proper said the court. They felt that what constitutes a container is inherently discretionary and that all forms of police discretion are not condemned. The real issue was caretaking versus evidence seeking. Here they found the container was one likely to hold valuables (or explosives). This was not an impermissible use of discretion. The Fifth Circuit was willing to go into the issue of mixed motives by looking into the police officer's "heart of hearts." Utah, on the other hand, would prefer not to have to be faced with this type of dilemma. Yet another state court overruled their earlier decision and began to allow all container inventories. **Johnson v. State**, 764 P. 2d 530 (Okla. Crim. 1988).

With the container/inventory problem receiving such diverse treatment the Supreme Court chose the **Wells** case, discussed earlier, from Florida, to tell states what the Fourth Amendment permits. The locked suitcase in the trunk was opened revealing a garbage bag of marijuana. There was no evidence that the police had any form of "closed containers" policy within their standard inventory policy. The entire Court agreed that the lack of any policy prohibited the opening of any closed containers found within the car. The Court split on what would be a valid container policy. Five members of the Court said there are three viable possible policies. *First*, the police can have a "no-containers-to-be- opened" policy. *Second*, they can have an "all-containers-to-be-opened" policy. Even Stevens and Blackman would agree with this "all-or-nothing" stance. Thus seven agree on that point. Brennan and Marshall think exigency or consent are needed in all events. The major point of disagreement of the four is that the five said the police can have an "open-container-whose-contents are-not-ascertainable-from-the-exterior" policy. They feel (the four) this is the same as no policy. The five disagree. **Florida v. Wells**, 495 U.S. 1 (1990).

How soon does an inventory have to be conducted? Clearly, if the purposes of **Opperman** and **Bertine** are to be achieved, the sooner it is done the better it is. Delays in the process, unless properly explained, have a tendency to raise the issue of pretextual search. In **Rudd v. State**, 649 P. 2d 791 (Okla. Crim. 1982) there was a delay. The case involved a marijuana possession charge brought due to an inventory performed on the trunk of the defendant's automobile following a fatality producing accident. The inventory was found reasonable in this case. The car in **Rudd** was impounded at 2 a.m. and the inventory was conducted at 10 a.m. The police officer who ordered the impoundment conducted the inventory as required under Oklahoma law. The defendant argued that the eight-hour gap created the possibility of a "dropsy" case in that he alleged poor security at the impounding lot. The officer said that since he had to pry open the trunk with a crowbar the possibility of a "plant" was low. The officer went on to explain that the delay was due to problems in identifying the deceased.

The Oklahoma decision makes good common sense especially under the general delay philosophy expressed by the U.S. Supreme Court in its search incident case of **U.S. v. Edwards**, 415 U.S. 800 (1974), where a ten- hour delay of the search incident of an incarcerated defendant's clothing was upheld as reasonable under the factual circumstances. If the police cannot explain the reason for the delay, the fruits should be suppressed. If the delay is reasonable, the state must then demonstrate why, in their view, no tampering with the car was possible. The officer in **Rudd** clearly demonstrated both. Had this car been impounded with an unlocked trunk in an area where anyone could have gained access then it stands to reason that the evidence would have to be suppressed.

One of Ohio's more recent inventory decisions arose out of a midnight stop for weaving outside the driving lane. The officer's testimony was very detailed and not general as those condemned in two cases from the 1990s. Thus the stop was valid. An arrest and impound decision was made by the officer, an inventory followed revealing a concealed weapon. For that conviction the defendant argues that the inventory was invalid. The Nelsonville Police inventory policy was introduced and the trial court found just cause to impound. The defendant argued that the inventory that was done at the scene was "too early" and that it should be done after it arrived at the impound lot.

The court noted that earlier inventories "often better serve" the interest of all. In fact, as an aside, many states require that the inventory be done only by the arresting (impounding) officer and at the scene. Unlike several other states, Ohio does not require the officer to utilize alternatives to impoundment. So the defendant lost on this ground. The defendant next argued that the officer failed to do a complete inventory as required. He did miss one or two spots and overlooked several dollars in loose change in a pouch on the side door. But the trial court found substantial compliance and the appellate court agreed. Both courts agreed this was not a pretextual search because he continued the inventory even after finding the gun. **State v. Goodin**, 2000 WL 134733 (Ohio App. 4) (unpub. op.). Accord: see **Com v. Ellerbe**, 723 N.E. 2d 977 (Mass. 2000); **Butler v. Com.**, 525 S.E. 2d 58 (Va. App. 2000). Nebraska's case featured a policy that failed the **Bertine** guidelines but the fruits of the search were admissible because of the search incident law of **Belton** since the drugs were found in a backpack discovered in the passenger compartment of the car. **State v. Ray**, 9 Neb. App. 869 (2000).

2.   Auto Inventory Summary

An inventory is not a general crime search but it is a carefully limited search doctrine that arises out of the bailment law and the necessity for observing the bailee's duty to provide reasonable care. The bailee's duty as it applies to governments is called the community caretaking function which arises in all cases where the government comes into possession of goods that have not been abandoned. The search right created under this function arises only when lawful governmental seizure occurs.

The caretaking function protects three key interests:
- the duty to protect the bailor's property from theft or destruction;
- the duty to protect general society from dangerous instrumentalities that might be taken from such bailed goods; and
- the duty to protect the pocketbooks of the police and the taxpayers from specious lost or destroyed or damaged property claims.

Thus the law allows an inventory search upon a lawful seizure if based upon a routine policy and conducted in a routine manner:
- all cars bailed; and
- all limited in scope.

Evidence of a crime thus seized is fully admissible. Even when police illegally seize the caretaking function exists but the evidence seized may not be used in the state's case-in-chief though it may be admissible for impeachment purposes.

There are four critical steps to be considered when testing any claimed inventory invasion.

STEP ONE: <u>Lawful Access</u>:

Access to the defendant and his or her car must be initially lawful – no "poisonous trees" are allowed.
Lawful police possession of the car due to the fact that the defendant and the car will be separated for a significant time (real and not pretended potential). The guides to be considered are:

- the nature of the crime and the existence of standard prompt release from custody says that no potential lengthy separation exists thus no inventory right arises;
- the nature of the crime, though automatically bailable on recognizance, coupled with an inability of the defendant to safely drive the car may raise a potential for a legitimately significant time giving rise to an inventory right;
- the nature of the crime as a felony and the "48 hour rule" creates a potentially significant time in felony cases giving rise to the inventory right; and
- the possession in police independent of any crime where circumstances indicate a potential for a significant time giving rise to the inventory right.

A *nexus* between the defendant and the need to protect the car must exist:

- the locus of the car at the time of an arrest or other custody at the time of the arrest or other custody must yield a need to protect;
- the ability of the defendant to waive caretaking or otherwise provide for its protection should be considered; and
- clearly the mere fact that a defendant owns an automobile does not automatically establish a *nexus* for the imposition of the caretaking functions.

STEP TWO: <u>Contemporaneousness</u>:

Upon lawful governmental possession, if the caretaking function is to have any meaning, a prompt, limited invasion of the car must be undertaken. This is the contemporaneousness requirement:

- unless good cause is shown for any delay, the inventory should be started immediately: – if it is to be privately towed under police control to a private holding or storage facility.
- unless good cause is shown for a delay, the inventory should be started as soon as possible (prioritizing human life and safety concerns); – if it is to be towed by the government to a government holding or storage facility.
- Conditions at the scene, safety needs, *etc.*, are always legitimate excuses for some delay (credibility is the issue).

The duty to inventory appears to be non-delegable to private parties due to the "routine" requirement. Some dispute exists whether the power can be delegated to non-possession taking police officers.

STEP THREE: Caretaking Conduct:

Since this is a limited, special purpose search doctrine based on caretaking needs and not a probable cause, the officer's intrusion must not appear to be general – crime--search like.

- a policy and an inventory sheet should be present to guide and limit the officer's discretion
- the places and things invaded should be limited to areas and things easily accessible and to things easily removable
- note: plain senses travel with the officer while conducting the inventory
- the process of protecting loose items found indicates clearly whether a crime search or an inventory took place – things of value not otherwise criminal left in the car "speak loudly."
- were the items secured in a secure holding facility that was not accessible to the general public, or were valuable items returned to the car – completeness of the inventory indicates whether it was a *bona fide* inventory – "striking for the jugular vein" and only going through the trunk and its contents, for example, says general crime search and not routine inventory, routinely done.

STEP FOUR: <u>Arisen Probable Cause</u>:

If probable cause arises during the inventory suggesting the need for a more complete search, the police could rely on **Ross** and conduct the more thorough search, but the better practice would be to:

- remove the car to a high security general search facility
- guard the car
- secure a warrant
- do a complete "full-strip" search.

E.   Search Incident Doctrine

When a person is arrested the police have a right to conduct a search incident to that arrest. The limits of a search incident are to the person of the defendant and the immediate area surrounding him where the defendant could reach a weapon or destroy evidence. This limit is called the "wing-span" doctrine and was announced in **Chimel v. California**, 395 U.S. 752 (1969). The purpose of the decision was to prohibit whole-house searches that were being conducted after an arrest.

A search incident to the arrest of a driver or passengers of a car was approved in **Gustafson v. Florida**, 414 U.S. 260 (1973) and **U.S. v. Robinson**, 414 U.S. 218 (1973), even in misdemeanor situations. The only question that was unanswered was whether, under **Chimel**, police should be limited to the search of the person arrested or could they search the car or any part of the car as an area immediately surrounding the arrestee? The answer came in **New York v. Belton**, 453 U.S. 454 (1981). In an attempt to clarify the concept of a search of an automobile incident to an arrest for a traffic violation or other lawful stop, the Court decided the **Belton** case. We knew such a search could be conducted while the defendant was still in the car and felt it could be when transporting the defendant in his car to the stationhouse due to the "seize weapon or destroy evidence" language of **Chimel**. But are these the only instances?

Belton and others in the car were stopped for speeding. It was apparent that none of the occupants owned the car, that there was the odor of burnt marijuana, and that an envelope on the floor probably contained "pot." All were asked to get out of the car. They were arrested for possession of marijuana. The passenger compartment of the car, including an unzipped jacket, was searched. In the zipped pocket of the jacket cocaine was found. For this, Belton was convicted.

Was the search lawful? On the theory that a lawful custodial arrest justifies the infringement of any privacy interest, the search of the passenger compartment and closed containers therein was upheld. Citing **Chimel** and its rule that the scope of a search must be "strictly tied to and justified by the circumstances," the Court said each case stands on its own facts. It also noted that they had no straightforward rule in this type of case. The Court felt that such a rule was now needed so the policeman will know the scope of his authority. The Supreme Court held: "when a policeman has made a lawful custodial arrest of the occupant of an automobile, he may, as a contemporaneous incident of that arrest search the passenger compartment of that automobile." The Court went on to say that the police may also examine the contents of any containers found within the passenger compartment, because if the passenger compartment is within the reach of the arrestee, containers in the car will also be within his reach.

There are two important *caveats* in **Belton** as spelled out by the Court in footnotes 2 and 3 of the opinion. First, footnote 2 tells us that: "The validity of the custodial arrest of Belton has not been questioned in this case." That is addressed in detail in the materials on arrest. More important is footnote 3 which, in essence, tells the courts not to read this case too broadly. It says: "Our holding today does no more than determine the meaning of **Chimel's** principles in this particular and problematic context. It in no way alters the fundamental principles established in the **Chimel** case regarding the basis of the scope of searches incident to lawful custodial arrests." The Court knew they had expanded the "wingspan" doctrine of **Chimel** in this context and they wanted to restrict that expansion to automobiles only.

Though **Belton** allows as part of the search incident the inspection of closed containers found in the vehicle's passenger compartment, it did not, as a case, set a time limit on what constituted "incident thereto." This was the subject of **People v. Riegler**, 168 Cal. Rep. 816 (Cal. Dist. Ct. App. 1981). Packages were taken from the car upon arrest and put in a police car. Five hours later and 100 miles from the site of the arrest the packages were opened and the hashish discovered. The court said this delay was fatal to the **Belton** right. The **Belton** right is exercisable only where the search incident is contemporaneous with arrest. A five-hour delay is not contemporaneous. Do not confuse this with the contemporaneous search rule discussed at III. D of this chapter. The scope of **Belton** would, of course, become a serious question. The Seventh Circuit says **Belton** applies even after handcuffing of the defendant and he thus has been reduced to police control. They read the facts of **Belton** correctly. **U.S. v. Karlin**, 852 F. 2d 968 (C.A. 7th 1988). But Washington disagrees somewhat. It says that **Belton** right ceases after the defendant is transported away from the scene. This court based its decision on the local constitution. **State v.**

Boyce, 758 P. 2d 1017 (Wash. Ct. App. 1988). Finally, the rear of the station wagon, because it is reachable from within the passenger compartment, is within the scope of **Belton** said the Sixth Circuit in **U.S. v. Pino**, 855 F. 2d 357 (C.A. 6th 1988), and Connecticut has held that the hatchback area of an automobile is a part of the passenger compartment, **State v. Delossantos**, 559 A. 2d 164 (Conn. 1989).

Washington decided that **Belton** applied even though the arrested defendant was handcuffed and placed in the back seat of a police cruiser before her purse was retrieved from the car and searched. **State v. Fladibo**, 779 P. 2d 707 (Wash. 1989). Since the car was likely to have been impounded the car inventory would have yielded the same result. There certainly was a community caretaking function here. See also **State v. Calovine**, 23 Conn. App. 123 (1990).

Once the police have **Belton** rights, the contents of the passenger compartment may be searched no matter to whom they belong. This is so even if the officer does not have probable cause to arrest the passenger in the vehicle whose property inside the passenger compartment was searched. **People v. Prance**, 277 Cal. Rep. 567 (Cal. Dist. Ct. App. 1991).

Wisconsin clearly recognizes the difference between a seizure and an arrest. Without a lawful arrest there can be no search incident rights in the police. If all they have are frisk rights then a more extensive invasion of the clothing can only be done upon an arrest lawfully accomplished. **State v. Swanson**, 475 N.W. 2d 148 (Wis. 1991). In the **Swanson** case, the defendant was stopped upon articulable suspicion of drunk driving. Before the sobriety test the officers conducted a search and not a frisk. Since the defendant was only detained (seized) in a **Terry** sense, the fruits of the search had to be suppressed.

Of course, once the search incident to an arrest is conducted and ended, there may be no further search under that justification. Any further search of the automobile by that or any other officer must be justified upon another theory or the evidence taken during the subsequent search is inadmissible. In an Iowa case the arresting officer conducted the search incident and found only a homemade pipe. The officer left the car with others who were assigned to tow it. A second officer who knew of the prior search proceeded to conduct a second search under the search incident theory. This was not approved. Had the second officer known of the homemade pipe, the court felt that the second officer may have had probable cause to do a **Ross** search. Alas, he did not know and the court felt compelled to suppress the evidence. Obviously they did not feel a necessity to apply a principal-agent knowledge analysis; that what one officer knew in the department everyone knew. **State v. Derifield**, 467 N.W. 2d 297 (Iowa Ct.

App. 1991). Otherwise Iowa accepts **Belton** as noted in **State v. McGee**, 381 N.W. 2d 630 (Iowa 1986).

That there is a time limit to **Belton** searches is without dispute. That courts may disagree on when to draw the lines is also beyond dispute. The better reasoned decisions would appear to draw the line when the defendant or his car is removed totally from the scene. A broad reading of **Belton** suggests proximity and not real ability of the defendant to reach the car. As one California court said: "The rule effectively changed the **Chimel** actual grabbing area for a *hypothetical* grabbing area." **People v. Stoffle**, 3 Cal. Rptr. 2d 257 (Cal. App. 3 Dist. 1991) (emphasis added). The immediacy of the search is a concern, but as long as the delay is only that which is necessary to secure the defendant and to address other exigencies that may be present, most courts will find (and should find) contemporaneousness.

A more significant problem was raised by the **Stoffle** case. **Belton** requires the arrestee to have been an occupant or recent occupant of the auto search. Does this mean the police must be the cause of the defendant's removal? Do the police have to see the arrestee in the vehicle in order to get **Belton** rights? Those were the facts of **Belton**. Stoffle was outside the car and a full-car length away from the car when the police came upon the scene. The police knew Stoffle was connected with the car because as the police approached Stoffle leaned through the open window of the car. A "wants and warrants" check revealed grounds for arrest. Stoffle was arrested, handcuffed and put in a patrol car. A search of the passenger compartment revealed cocaine. The California court upheld the search because of the bright line drawn in such cases. It felt the hypothetical grab rule of **Belton** was designed to eliminate case-by-case decision-making by police. The court held that if the police can establish that, at the moment of arrest, the defendant had a close association with the car, then **Belton** search powers can be exercised.

However, the District of Columbia views **Belton,** in this context, somewhat more restrictively than California. In **U.S. v. Lewis**, 632 A. 2d 383 (D.C. Ct. App. 1993), they said **Belton** does not apply when an arrestee parks and locks his vehicle and walks some distance from it. The charge was a missing front license tag. When confronted, the defendant bolted but was arrested. While awaiting a paddy wagon ten people came up to the officer and asked for the keys. The officer knew or suspected these ten people were drug users. The car was searched by the officer and 100 bags of heroin were found in the glove box. Was this indeed a valid search incident? The D.C. court said this man was a pedestrian when accosted and not an occupant as were the facts in **Belton**. The search was, therefore, unreasonable.

Does **Belton** grant a search incident right when the defendant pulls into a private driveway and exits his car only to discover the police are conducting a search of the premises and when the police approach and ask for identification, he gives them his name and the police, five minutes later, discover he is wanted on a probation arrest warrant and is immediately arrested? Florida said no. Why? A person who leaves his car voluntarily in a situation not connected to a forced police stop but who is subsequently arrested cannot have his car searched under **Belton**. The U.S. Supreme Court took certiorari but ultimately decided that it was not a final judgment in the case of **Thomas v. State**, 761 So. 2d 1010 (Fla. 2000) and sent it back to Florida. Does the "removed from" language of **Belton** govern? Florida was not concerned about that because it felt a driver who is stopped cannot defeat **Belton** that easily. No, the rule relied upon by the court comes from a Sixth Circuit case that makes **Belton** inapplicable when the person exits his car when there is no police initiated contact. See **U.S. v. Hudgins**, 52 F. 3d 115 (C.A. 6th 1995). The Sixth also has a rule that **Belton** is not defeated by an early exit after a police stop.

The debate on the Florida court centered on the following language from **Knowles v. Iowa**, 525 U.S. 113 (1998): "Here we are asked to extend 'that bright-line rule' (referring to Belton) to a situation where the concern for officer safety is not present to the same extent and the concern for the destruction or loss of evidence is not present at all. We decline to do so." Justice Wells, who concurred in part and dissented in part, said **Knowles** was the case to follow since, "In this case there was not a reasonable basis to search Thomas; (when he first exited his automobile) nor was there an arrest made related to the vehicle." His dissent says that "**Belton** does not add as a conditions 'where the law enforcement officer initiates contact with the defendant either by actually confronting the defendant or signaling confrontation with the defendant.' "Justice Wells is probably correct in one very important context. Suppose when Thomas drove up and got out of his car police could see weapons, contraband, or explosives. The requirement of police initiated contact created that day by the Florida court could be interpreted to mean that the plain view probable cause is negated. Hopefully, it does not mean that by the announced rule. What all courts must realize is that the rules are not always "clean-cut" but operate in practical terms that balance privacy against public and personal safety. The words "reasonable under the circumstances" have to play a part in the decision- making process.

In this case, nothing about the defendant being a probation violator said he was armed or dangerous and he did not act that way. His arrival at the scene of the search aroused no reasonable belief that he was connected to the criminal evidence sought by the warrant for the house. The police did not know who he was, thus, he was a "mere arrival" and not a "late arrival." The officer's plain senses did not give the officer independent probable cause. Nothing in **Knowles** was intended to limit any independent constitutionally based rule: **Knowles** was intended to prevent searches incident to non-criminal behavior – no more, no less.

Sometimes the search doctrines are dependent, interdependent and independent. Consider for example **Gonzales v. State**, 507 P. 2d 1277 (Okla. Crim. 1973). If the initial stop of the car had been illegal in **Gonzales,** all attempts at searches thereafter would have been *dependent* on that illegality thus fruits of the poisonous tree. The stop in **Gonzales** was determined to be legal and the search incident was found by the Oklahoma court to be illegal. However, due to the nature of the crime an impoundment of the car was required. The plain view of certain evidence was not tainted by the illegal search incident. The plain view produced evidence that was *independent* of the illegal search but *dependent* on the legal stop. Because of local law, the inventory done in this case was invalid, therefore, what was found during the inventory could not be used to support the subsequently issued search warrant. But the fruits doctrine was applied only to those things taken or seized during the illegal search and if sufficient evidence of probable cause existed the warrant could be upheld because the search principles that arose in this case were *not interdependent.*

South Dakota was asked to reject **Belton** on state constitutional grounds. In **State v. Rice**, 327 N.W. 2d 128 (S. D. 1982) a lawful arrest of the defendant from an automobile took place. The immediate search was seen, however, as a "logical extension" of this arrest and thus was reasonable under Art. VI, §11 of the state constitution. Accord see **State v. Peterson**, 407 N.W. 2d 221 (S. D. 1987) in which the driver was lawfully stopped. The officer smelled alcohol on the breath that led the officer to believe an open container was present. The container was found and the glove box was searched revealing more evidence.

In **Gustafson, Robinson** and **Belton** the Court approved full field searches of the driver and the passenger compartment of his or her car whenever a lawful custodial arrest occurred. None of these cases created an auto search independent of an arrest. That type of search, not incident to arrest, was approved only "where police have probable cause to believe contraband or evidence is contained." **Acevedo** (*supra*).

Trying to keep these two lines of cases separate is not always easy as illustrated by **Knowles v. Iowa**, 525 U.S. 113 (1998). The Iowa police stopped Knowles for speeding – no pretext at all. The officer has two choices: (a) arrest the defendant or (b) issue a citation of this bailable offense. Iowa Code Ann. §805.1 (1). The officer chose not to arrest Knowles and instead gave him a citation. However, an §805.1 (4) allows the officer to conduct a search incident to citation. This officer searched Knowles under this statute since there was no arrest. All Iowa courts upheld this search that produced marijuana and a pot pipe. He was then arrested for controlled substances violations and convicted upon this evidence. No independent probable cause (under **Acevedo**) arose at the scene, thus only **Gustafson**, **Robinson**, **Belton** were available for possible use. Likewise no facts were presented for the police to rely on **Terry**, **Mimms**, **Long**, **& Wilson** (the "frisk" cases). The U.S. Supreme Court thus held that **Robinson** *et al's* "bright-line rule" was violated thus violating the Fourth Amendment. The case was remanded to the Iowa court.

F.   Consent Search

1.   General Theory

One form of the warrantless search approved by the courts is the consent search. Any citizen may make a voluntary, knowing and intelligent waiver of the right to privacy and give permission for a police search of his or her automobile. The basic tenets of consent search are set out in too many cases to be cited here. However, consents gained by some trick or ruse are generally not voluntary; consents given while under an illegal arrest are suspect, and unless an attenuation is found, they are illegal; consents given by some third person who also controls or shares the item are usually good; and consents given by persons suffering the D.T.'s, drug withdrawal, some form of retardation, and very young children are usually invalid. The consenter is not entitled to a warning that he or she can withhold consent. A consent obtained after an illegal search has begun is no good. Attention must be focused on coercion in all its forms and whether the will of the consenter was overridden. See, for example, **State v. Erickson**, 362 N.W. 2d 528 (Iowa 1985) and **State v. Garcia**, 461 N.W. 2d 460 (Iowa 1990), where Iowa fully adopted the totality test for consents. Accord: **Kennedy v. State**, 640 P. 2d 971 Okla. Crim. 1982) and **Sullivan v. State**, 716 P. 2d 684 (Okla. Crim. 1986) and **Lumpkin v. State**, 683 P. 2d 985 (Okla. Crim. 1984).

2.   Controlling the Scope of the Consent

The scope of the consent search is the same as that for a full-field strip search. The consenter can limit his consent as to scope and area but if he or she does not, the only limit that will be applied is the "reasonableness" test. Consider these two cases. The Third Circuit found that the police could justifiably rely on the consent of the driver of a rental car even when the lessee is present but fails to object. This comports with good **Rakas** reasoning but does call into question the "silence-is-not-waiver" portion of **Bumper**. All in all it is a good decision where contraband is concerned. **U.S. v. Morales**, 861 F. 2d 396 (C.A. 3rd 1988). The Florida Supreme Court had issued a scope of consent case. They held that consent to open a trunk was not consent to open the locked luggage. **State v. Wells**, 539 So. 2d 464 (Fla. 1989); see the discussion of **Wells** (*supra*) under the inventory section of this chapter.

This was to become a "hot" topic for the Supreme Court during the 1990-91 term. In **State v. Jimeno,** 564 So. 2d 1083 (Fla. 1990), that court decided that nothing in the U.S. Supreme Court's decision in **Wells** affected Florida's prior scope of consent rule and held that consent to search a vehicle was not consent to search closed containers in the vehicle. Because of the conflict among several jurisdictions on this point, the Supreme Court granted certiorari on the **Jimeno** case. Though more fully discussed in the chapter on Consent Searches, **Jimeno** decided that a consent to search "the car" reasonably could allow the officer to search not only the surface of the car's interior but also brown paper bags and other unlocked containers. The duty is on the consenter to limit the search, the Court held. **Florida v. Jimeno**, 500 U.S. 248 (1991). Apparently agreeing with the **Jimeno** case, Iowa holds that the failure of a defendant to limit the scope of consent allowed the search of a jacket strapped onto his motorcycle. **State v. Harman**, 470 N.W. 2d 369 (Iowa 1991).

The latest consent issue that arose from the automobile context came by way of the **Ohio v. Robinette**, 519 U.S. 33 (1996) opinion. In that case, the officer at the end of a routine traffic stop, asked for and received consent to search the trunk of the car. The officer found contraband. The defendant convinced the Ohio Supreme Court that the failure of the officer to tell the defendant that he was free to leave violated the consent. The U.S. Supreme Court, in light of the **Schneckloth** case and its progeny, once again stressed that no bright-line rule existed that required the police to tell a defendant (as in **Miranda**) of his or her right to refuse to give a consent. They said, once again, that reasonableness, in this context, must be judged on all the surrounding facts: the totality of the circumstances.

Nebraska has accepted the **Robinette** totality analysis through their decision in **State v. Ready**, 565 N.W. 2d 728 (Neb. 1997). Colorado used the **Robinette** case to determine that an encounter with citizens in a parked car was not a seizure but was, instead, a consensual encounter. Thus the request for an I.D. was not a seizure but more like an airport encounter. Colorado says police do not have to tell people in parked cars that they have the right not to surrender their IDs. **People v. Paynter**, 1998 WL 112858 (Colo. *en. banc.*).

In all suppression issues, the U.S. Supreme Court uses the preponderance standard for admission of evidence – even confessions. However, South Dakota, in consent cases uses the clear and convincing standard to review the validity of a consent. In a **Robinette**-like case the state trooper told the defendant in **State v. Dreps**, 558 N.W. 2d 339 (S. D. 1996), that the citation part was over, but then asked for permission to search for guns, drugs, or contraband. The defendant first said he had to get on down the road. The officer said it would not take long and the defendant said o.k. Drugs were found and Dreps was arrested. The court first notes that probable cause is not needed for consent. It then said that Dreps was free to leave and that his consent was voluntary. Whether they fully accept **Robinette** is still up in the air as far as the **Dreps** decision is concerned. However, they did not fully address the officer's comment that it would not take long. Did the defendant ask how long the search would take? Was the defendant's comment that he had to get on down the road really a no? These issues should be addressed when the defendant's response is equivocal.

Perhaps, as already noted, one of the most significant cases on consents to search automobiles is **Ohio v. Robinette**, 519 U.S. 33 (1996). The officer lawfully stopped a car for a violation and issued the ticket. After issuing the ticket, the officer asked for consent to search the car. The defendant consented and contraband was found. Ohio took the position that the officer was required to tell the driver that he was free to leave and free to refuse to consent. The U.S. Supreme Court accepted certiorari wherein it repeated the oft-stated principle that no "bright line" exists in the Constitution that requires the police to tell a person that they have a right to leave after receiving a traffic ticket and, of course, that they have the right to refuse consent.

On remand to Ohio, that Supreme Court *appears* to reject the Fourth Amendment rule and now *seem* to require an announcement of a free to leave/end of ticketing process statement and a right to refuse consent. **State v. Robinette**, 685 N.E. 2d 762 (Ohio, 1997). Let us examine exactly what Ohio said. First the court said the officer was justified in briefly detaining Robinette in order to ask him whether he was carrying any illegal drugs or weapons. But was the detention after this lawful, the court asked. Not really, because no articulable facts or suspicion arose. Thus, the officer was *not justified* in detaining to ask for and execute a search. But the consent was given so can we say it was voluntary under the circumstances? The court then turned the totality of the circumstances rule (it's a question of fact rule). The facts indicate that Robinette was told he was free to go @ p. 769; and that Robinette felt he was free to go @ p. 770, but that he was shocked by the search request @ p. 770. The court felt this made the circumstances "impliedly coercive... and the consent was involuntary." But they positively state that the Ohio and U.S. Constitution are not at odds. Only one Ohio justice felt the right rules were applied to reach a wrong result. It is perplexing.

How have other states reacted to the Supreme Court's **Robinette** decision? It is clear, even without citation, that courts feel driven to do a better factual analysis of the consent and whether it was free and voluntary. Consider, for example, **People v. Ruffin**, 734 N.E. 2d 507 (Ill. App. 2000). In **Ruffin,** the defendant was stopped for 22 minutes before permission to search was sought. The stop was seen as a subterfuge to get evidence of a crime. The license check took only four minutes with five minutes to write the ticket. The remaining 12 or so minutes was used to "rattle" the driver so he would consent. The consent was not voluntary. Maine fully recognizes that a bare request for a consent to search does not need to have anything to do with the reason for the stop as long as that stop had a lawful basis. **State v. Kremer**, 754 A. 2d 964 (Me. 2000). But a New Jersey appellate court disagrees with Maine and holds that articulable suspicion is required to request a consent to search. Why? The New Jersey constitution gives greater protection than the U.S. Constitution. See **State v. Carty**, 753 A. 2d 149 (N.J. Super, 2000) and footnote 3 at page 153.

Several courts have also struggled with consents arising out of routine traffic stops. In a Pennsylvania case the traffic stop was over and while the officer began to walk to his cruiser, the officer turned and asked the owner if he had anything illegal in his car. The owner said no and the officer asked if he could look through the car. The owner hesitated and the officer said, "You don't have to say yes, you know," and then asked him again. The owner consented. A marijuana smoking pipe was found and the arrest for paraphernalia followed. The Pennsylvania high court said that this case offers an example of the blurring between a legal detention and an attempt at consensual interaction. This is what bothered Ohio in **Robinette I.** Ohio wanted a clear break that could be understood by any citizen. This, of course, was rejected by the U.S. Supreme Court in **Robinette II.** This court agrees with Ohio in **Robinette III** that there is a possibility of a mere encounter following a traffic stop which would give rise to a totality inquiry. It then looked at the local case and noted a prior lawful detention with some "degree of coercion (geography and the lateness and flashing lights). But the court also saw a calm restrained officer – laid back even for a traffic stop. Language, tone, absence of gun waiving, were all set out in the record. How did they assess the consent seeking event? No words were used that flavored the officer's words as directives; the officer did not touch the defendant, nor did he direct the defendant's movements. The court summed it up as follows: "Although the officer did not make the end point to the lawful detention an express one, there was an end point nonetheless; moreover, the officer confined his subsequent conduct and conformed his requests in a manner consistent with a consensual encounter and expressly advised Strickler of his right to refuse consent." Therefore, the evidence found upon this consent was admissible. **Com. v. Strickler**, 757 A. 2d 884 (Pa. 2000).

The Arkansas high court faced a consent that the defense urged was coerced because the owner felt the officer would not let him and his wife leave until the search was over. The record indicates that was not the case, rather the defendant said, "Yes, but I want to get on down the road." The officer said, "If I find nothing you will be on your way in 5 minutes." The owner then said o.k. The owner also said he did not consent to a trunk search only the interior. This argument also went down in flames since the officer asked to search the car and the defendant did not limit the scope of the area of the proposed search. **Miller v. State**, 27 S.W. 3d 427 (Ark. 2000). The fair import of this case is that the officer did not talk the owner out of a "no" stance.

In a Colorado case the defendant argued that his consent was not valid because he was not given his **Miranda** warnings. This argument did not work. Somehow the trial court got this point wrong. In fact, the U.S. Supreme Court had never encouraged using **Miranda** beyond its intended purpose, and has continuously refused to attach a "right to refuse consent" advisement to the consent area. **People v. Garcia**, 11 P. 3d 449 (Colo. *en banc* 2000). How did the trial judge get it so wrong? The Supreme Court of Colorado raised this issue in an earlier case by way of *dicta* in **People v. Redderson**, 992 P. 2d 1176 (Colo. *en banc* 2000), even though later in the same opinion they state the rule ultimately re-announced in **Garcia**.

Although Nevada understands the voluntariness issue well, it appears they may be having difficulty with the scope of consent when given. The U.S. Supreme Court said years ago in **Bumper v. North Carolina** that a search is a search, and more recently in **Florida v. Jimeno**, that if the defendant wants to narrow the search, the duty is on the defendant to say so. Only the two dissenters in **State v. Johnson**, 993 P. 2d 44 (Nev. 2000), understand this point and unless Nevada's constitution gives a defendant more rights, the court has misinterpreted the U.S. Supreme Court decision.

What then is the bottom line on this consent to search issue? Are Ohio and Pennsylvania correct in looking for a new or continued detention when the officer seeks a consent to search when trying to follow the Supreme Court's consent law? They both may be wrong. Why? To be sure an unattenuated illegal seizure yields an invalid consent *but* even an attenuated illegal seizure can yield a good consent. The **Bostick** case clearly points out that the officer can always ask for a consent and needs no probable cause to seek it. From **Bumper v. North Carolina** to date, the Supreme Court does not require the subject to answer because silence is a resounding NO. In the

Ohio and Pennsylvania cases all these drivers had to do was to start their cars and leave. But, after all, these two courts went to great lengths to try to fit their decisions in under existing case law and they used the totality to determine voluntariness since that was suggested by the **Bostick** decision on remand to the Florida court even though the Supreme Court held Mr. Bostick was not seized at the time. Neither officer in Pennsylvania and Ohio appeared to try to argue their quarry into a consent. Both officers "took a shot" and both were successful. Neither officer held onto some item (registration license *etc.*), while asking for the consent, so coercion was not present in either case. Nor did these officers suggest by any means that the defendants were *not* free to leave. Both defendants probably believed that if they said yes, that would be the end of it (the "I have nothing to hide ploy").

South Dakota faced a **Robinette** issue in **State v. Ballard**, 617 N.W. 2d 837 (So. Dak. 2000). After giving Ms. Ballard a ticket, the officer told her she was free to leave. The officer then asked for consent to search the car. She said no. But instead of letting her go, the officer forced her to stay to await the arrival of a drug-sniffing dog. Noting that no new suspicions arose after the ticketing, this continued seizure was without a valid Fourth Amendment foundation. Without citation to **Robinette,** the court found the search unconstitutional. An unattenuated illegal seizure cannot yield consent as illustrated by **State v. Vanderhoff**, 665 N.E. 2d 235 (Ohio App. 3d 1995) app. den. 656 N.E. 2d 951 (Ohio 1995). This has always been the law.

In a Nebraska case a police officer completed the traffic stop, told the defendant he could leave, but asked for a consent to search. The driver asked if he was only going to look in the passenger compartment and the officer said no, that he was going to search the trunk also. The defendant said no to the consent issue. The officer felt that the nervousness shown and the staring ahead while answering questions, plus a bulging neck artery, were sufficient to hold the defendant and his car until the "dog" arrived. Drugs, of course, were found. The Nebraska high court found that nervousness was not sufficient to constitute articulable suspicion to detain this motorist, thus the continued or new detention was an unlawful seizure that had not attenuated, and thus the evidence was inadmissible. **State v. Anderson**, 605 N.W. 2d 124 (Neb. 2000). This is a reasonable conclusion.

G.   Terry-type Intrusions

Some years ago the Court approved a limited search of persons known as the "frisk" or "pat-down" of outer clothing to determine if the suspect had a weapon on his or her person. The right could only be exercised when a trained officer had a reasonably based articulable suspicion (more than a hunch) that the suspect was armed and dangerous. On those articulable facts, the officer was given the right to "stop" (not arrest) the person, and ask a few questions to see if the fear suspected could be relieved. If the answers did not relieve the "fear" the right to "frisk" arose. This is known as the "stop and frisk" doctrine.

The question left unanswered was whether, in a non-arrest situation, a similar type of intrusion could be permitted within the passenger compartment of a car? The issue was resolved in **Michigan v. Long**, 463 U.S. 1032 (1983), which will be discussed below. The Court had already applied the "stop" theory of **Terry** in **Adams v. Williams**, 407 U.S. 143 (1972). In **Adams** the court said, "a brief stop of a suspicious individual, in order to determine his identity or to maintain the *status quo* momentarily while obtaining more information, may be most reasonable in light of the facts known to the officer at the time."

In both **Adams** and **Pennsylvania v. Mimms**, 434 U.S. 106 (1977) the Court emphasized the dangers confronting the police officer during the average automobile stop. The Court approved, in **Mimms**, the police order to the driver to get out so that the driver could be frisked where there was a reasonable belief that the driver was armed and dangerous. In fact, in one study cited by the Court in **Adams**, 30% of police shootings occurred when a police officer approached a suspect seated in an automobile. **Adams** at 148, n.3, citing Briston, *Police Officer Shooting--A Tactical Evaluation*, 54 J. Crim. L.C. and P.S. 93 (1963). Thus, the stage was set for the Court's decision in **Michigan v. Long**.

Long's car went into a ditch. The police observed this and pulled up to the scene and stopped to investigate. Long was out of his car and the driver's side door was still open. Long met the police at the rear of his car. The police wanted the vehicle registration. The police followed him to the door and saw a hunting knife on the floor-board. The police stopped Long, grabbed the knife and made a pat down search for other weapons discovering marijuana under the front seat arm rest. Was this pat down or "sweep" lawful? Yes, said the Court. Why? **Terry** does not restrict the preventative search to the person suspected. The rule announced in **Long** goes as follows: "the search of the passenger compartment of an automobile, limited to those areas in which a weapon may be placed or hidden, is permissible if the police officer possessed a reasonable belief based on specific and articulable facts which, taken together with the rational inferences from those facts, reasonably warrant the officer in believing that the suspect is dangerous and the suspect may gain immediate control of weapons," **Long** at 1032. Accord see: **Spenner v. City**, 580 N.W. 2d 606 (S. D.1998) and **State v. Ashbrook**, 586 N.W. 2d 503 (So. Dak. 1998).

The "furtive movements" problem involving the automobile, as previously noted, does cause the courts some concern. The Indiana Court of Appeals had held that making a U-turn ostensibly (from the police point of view) to avoid a sobriety checkpoint justifies the police in making an investigative stop. The court reasoned that to properly deter such drivers, people cannot flagrantly avoid the roadblocks. **Snyder v. State**, 538 N.E. 2d 961 (Ind. App. 1989). As noted, this matter needs to be resolved by the U.S. Supreme Court since they indicated, by dicta, a contrary view in **Sitz** (*supra*).

Utah, on the other hand, had a case where the driver was lawfully stopped for speeding. As the officer approached the car, the passenger bent over in the front seat, acted fidgety, and looked from side to side. Not suspecting danger the officer only suspected that the passenger was trying to hide something, thus **Long, Mimms** and **Adams** were not implicated. The court held the intrusion was, therefore, a non-probable cause-based search and **Ross** could not be used. **State v. Schlosser**, 774 P. 2d 1132 (Utah 1989). For a full discussion of furtive movements see Chapter Two.

It was a foggy night and an unknown and unrecognized truck pulled out of a shopping center parking lot at 1:00 a.m. The area had been plagued with a number of recent acts of burglary and vandalism. The officer stopped the truck, but recognized the driver as one of the area businessmen. The problem was, however, he was drunk. The Nebraska Supreme Court properly held that this was a proper use of the **Terry**-type stop. **State v. Kavanaugh**, 434 N.W. 2d 36 (Neb. 1989).

New Jersey has placed limits on **Mimms, Long** and **Terry,** and rather than accept the fact that auto stops inhere with danger, they require their officers to spell out articulable suspicion of danger in each specific case. **State v. Lund**, 573 A. 2d 1376 (N.J. 1990). Iowa had decided to limit **Mimms** to drivers of automobiles only. Police in Iowa must have articulable suspicion independent of the auto stop to order a passenger out of a car. **State v. Becker**, 458 N.W. 2d 604 (Iowa. 1990). Otherwise Iowa approves **Mimms** and **Michigan v. Long**, see **State v. McGee**, 381 N.W. 2d 630 (Iowa 1986).

At "first blush," **Com. v. Gonsalves**, 711 N.E. 2d 108 (Mass. 1999), seems to be an anti-**Mimms** decision. However, it appears the Massachusetts police were requiring all drivers to exit their cars even if there were no furtive gestures. The frisk that occurred in these cases was the evil that most bothered the court, however, and not the order to exit. The court felt that citizens should not be "subjected to unjustified exit orders during routine traffic stops." They join New Jersey, Hawaii, Oregon, and Iowa and require a reasonable suspicion standard as opposed to the "statistical suspicion standard" of **Mimms**. There is an excellent appendix to this decision on pages 124-129. This appendix is a complete survey of **Mimms** decisions as to both drivers and passengers.

In two more recent cases it is clear that **Ohio** also understands and properly applies both **Mimms** and **Long**. See **State v. Cullers**, 695 N.E. 2d 314 (Ohio App. 3d 1997), and **State v. Miller**, 1997 WL 531216 (Ohio App. 2 1997) (unpub. op.). Oklahoma generally approves both **Mimms** and **Long** by their decision on **Coulter v. State**, 777 P. 2d 1373 (Okla. Crim. 1989). In **Coulter,** the court approved a stop because it was based upon articulable suspicion that had come from information given by a respectable citizen. The case involved some pre-stop "gun-pointing" and gun possession issues. The court said the risk to the officers and community justified this type of limited intrusion under **Long, Mimms** and **Terry**. Likewise where police know a burglary has been committed and have articulable suspicion to stop a car, such a defendant who gets out of the car with a bulge in his coat can expect a **Mimms-Terry** pat-down. **Loman v. State**, 806 P. 2d 663 (Okla. Crim. 1991).

The Michigan Court of Appeals says there is no real difference between a passenger and a driver in the **Mimms** context, therefore, an officer can order a passenger to get out of a car. The safety concern is equally applicable to anyone in the vehicle as long as there is a justifiable safety concern. **People v. Martinez**, 466 N.W. 2d 380 (Mich. Ct. App. 1991).

Why courts appear to assume that only the driver of a car might kill or seriously injure the officer makes no sense as pointed out in the Michigan case cited above. Yet courts, as already noted, had negatively reacted to the expansion of **Mimms** to passengers. The D.C. Court of Appeals said that without independent articulable suspicion on the part of the passengers, those passengers must be treated as innocent bystanders. They felt the only order that could be given by a police officer is the "keep your hands in sight" order. Is such a court disregarding, as the dissent in the D.C. case indicates, the officer's safety, in this high crime area, late at night? The dissent says that **Mimms** teaches us that the officer's safety interest is substantial. In this case, one officer was talking to the offending driver in the officer's car while the remaining officer was outnumbered two-to-one. See **Cousart v. U.S.**, 50 Crim. L. Rep. 1078 (D.C. Ct. App. 1991); aff'd 618 A. 2d 96 (D.C. Ct. App. *en banc.* 1992).

Louisiana has joined those states that read **Mimms** as allowing an officer to order passengers out of a car upon a routine traffic stop. It thus overruled **State v. Williams**, 366 So. 2d 1369 (La. 1978) with their decision in **State v. Landry**, 588 So. 2d 345 (La. 1991). The court was quick to point out that the right to order passengers out of the car does not entitle the officer to frisk or search those passengers. That will be determined from subsequent conduct of the passengers. However, there is a significant safety risk upon such a stop and the officer has a right to get everyone out where they can be observed.

A Florida court, looking at the reasonable fear theory of **Mimms**, upheld the admission of a weapon taken from a passenger in a car who was ordered from the car because some bystander said, "My brother thought there was a gun in the car." As the passenger emerged from the car the gun was taken from his arms. The Court said the primary rationale of **Mimms** was safety. The court said this was not a stop case because the car was already at a standstill due to the accident which the officer was there to investigate. The Court held "...a report concerning a firearm in a vehicle which is not plainly without foundation on its face, is sufficient to justify ordering the occupants to leave the car." Fortunately, the outline of the gun was seen because the court had some doubt whether the officer could "pat-down" the individuals since the information was not sufficiently detailed. **State v. Williams**, 371 So. 2d 1074 (Fla. App. 1979).

If a passenger can be ordered to get out of a car for the officer's safety under **Mimms**, can an officer order a passenger to get back into a car for the officer's safety? An Arizona court answered this question in the affirmative even though this was a routine stop for a minor traffic violation. While obeying this command the passenger "dropped" some drugs which were picked up by the officer. The court saw **Mimms** as a safety case and not as direction case. In any event, drugs dropped during submission to a lawful command constitutes lawfully acquired evidence during a lawful seizure. **State v. Webster**, 824 P. 2d 768 (Ariz. App. 1992).

The answer to the issues presented in the foregoing decisions lies within the Supreme Court's policy announced in **Ybarra v. Illinois**, 444 U.S. 85 (1979). That case explained what could and could not be done to apparent innocents while a lawful search was being conducted on the premises. Without independent articulable suspicion, the innocents present were not subject to frisks for weapons. The court clearly rejected a "coincidental search of innocent persons" rule. Citing **U.S. v. Di Re**, 332 U.S. 581 (1947), the Court noted that a passenger does not, by mere presence in a car, lose his or her immunity from searches.

Justice Burger's dissent points out that police are not required to ignore everyone else that is in the place and that they do present, by mere presence, a form of danger to the officers. That point, as far as it goes, is not disputed by the majority. Rehnquist in his dissent points out that there are required in such situations some incidental seizures in order to allow the police the right to do their job. See footnote 1 at 252 (dissenting opinion of Rehnquist). His position is that, at least as to a stop order or a stay in the car order or get out of the car order, a limited seizure to allow the officer to do his or her job must be permitted. He, of course, would personally allow a greater intrusion. He says the police can freeze the area as a minimum. His minimal intrusion theory was adopted in **Sitz**. Clearly, the votes were on the Court to allow police a limited control of passengers.

To what extent the "stop and frisk" rationale can be taken beyond the limits of Terry v. Ohio and Pennsylvania v. Mimms is illustrated by a unique case dealing with very common and recurring facts. Federal law and most states prohibit pedestrians and hitchhikers on limited access highways. When an officer comes upon such a hitchhiker is the officer required to merely issue a ticket and leave the hitchhiker there to continue his offense? Is it not the duty of the officer to remove the offender from the highway by placing the offender in the patrol car and at least drive the offender to a road where such conduct is not an offense? If the state had rejected Gustafson and Robinson, there could be no full-field strip search because of such a minor violation. If the offender has demonstrated no dangerous propensities as required by Terry even a pat-down would seem to be eliminated. This was the dilemma faced by the Michigan Court of Appeals. An officer had issued a citation. Before placing the offender in the patrol car a frisk was conducted. The frisk produced a weapon. The Michigan court refused to assume that all hitchhikers are armed and dangerous. Yet the court found that the officer's pat-down was reasonable under the circumstances. They noted that, unlike Terry, an offense was committed in this officer's presence. The Court did not say why it was reasonable even though it was noted that there were several instances of suspected foul play by hitchhikers or pedestrians. The court also noted that the officer could not have made a full-blown arrest in this instance. **People v. Otto**, 284 N.W. 2d 273 (Mich. Ct. App. 1979). The Otto case does demonstrate the compromise that states rejecting Gustafson and Robinson will have to make.

The Court, although clear about the circumstances allowing the frisk of a driver of a car following a routine traffic stop, were not as clear in Mimms regarding what conduct to tolerate from police concerning the car's passengers. The preceding state cases demonstrate the problems caused by lack of Fourth Amendment guidance. Only a few decided the issues involved were decided by the state courts under their own state constitutions. The Court decided to address some of the issues left unsettled by Mimms by choosing Maryland v. Wilson, in which Judge Moylan, a leading lecturer in search and seizure law, had upheld the suppression of evidence taken from a passenger who was ordered from the car because he "appeared nervous" despite the fact that speeding caused the stop of the car. Moylan said Mimms does not allow the police to order passengers from the car. The Maryland high court refused to review Moylan's opinion. Continuing their emphasis on the reasonableness requirement of the Fourth Amendment, the Supreme Court per Justice Rehnquist reversed the Moylan position and held that "an officer making a traffic stop may order passengers to get out of the car pending completion of the stop." **Maryland v. Wilson**, 519 U.S. 408 (1997). The Court stressed the nervousness exhibited by the passenger (sweating and fidgeting) as the cause for the exit order. Cocaine fell to the ground and Wilson, the passenger, was arrested. This led the Court to discuss officer safety and the logical conclusion that passengers could kill or injure the officer – that the threat comes from all sources present. That in 1994 5,762 officers were assaulted and 11 killed during traffic stops was specifically set out in the opinion and not as a footnote. In fact they noted that "danger to an officer from a traffic stop is likely to be greater when there are passengers in addition to the driver in the stopped car."

What the Court did not specifically address was whether the officer could require the passengers to stay in the car. This was the point of debate in **Dennis v. State**, 693 A. 2d 1150 (Md. 1997). The Court of Special Appeals had affirmed the Dennis conviction, the high court of Maryland reversed that decision, then the U.S. Supreme Court vacated and remanded the high court decision at 117 S. Ct. 40. On remand to Maryland's high court, it was to use **Whren v. U.S.**, 517 U.S. 806 (1996). However, the Maryland court did not see **Whren** as dispositive, and did not address **Whren.** They concluded that the unarticulated reason to force the passenger to stay in the car cannot justify this man's conviction, therefore, they reversed the conviction. Subjectivity not objectivity governed their view.

What have other courts said in reaction to **Wilson**? Connecticut accepts **Wilson** as being consistent with its state constitution. **State v. Wilkins**, 692 A. 2d 1233 (Conn. 1997). Idaho fully accepts **Wilson** and says that facts may be present to justify requiring exit at gun point as a proper **Terry**-based stop. **State v. DuValt**, 961 P. 2d 641 (Idaho 1998). This is certainly consistent with **Sokolow.** The Superior Court of Pennsylvania also accepts **Wilson**. **Com. v. Rodriguez**, 695 A. 2d 864 (Pa. Super 1997). Handcuffing a passenger for the"officer's personal safety" was upheld under **Terry** and **Mimms-Wilson** by the Court of Criminal Appeals of Texas. **Rhodes v. State**, 945 S.W. 2d 115 (Tex. Crim. 1997). Utah also approves the use of **Wilson**. **State v. Shepard**, 955 P. 2d 352 (Utah App. 1998); see also **Welshman v. Com.**, 502 S.E. 2d 122 (Va. App. *en banc* 1998), South Dakota in **State v. Tilton**, 561 N.W. 2d 660 (S. D. 1997) also cited **Wilson** approvingly.

As already noted, however, the next battleground involves requiring passengers to stay in the car or requiring them to return to the car. In addition to the

Dennis case cited above, three other states addressed the issue – Illinois, Montana and Washington. Articulable suspicion justified the Illinois officer in stopping the passenger who was walking away from the lawfully stopped car. **Terry v. Ohio** was the key along with **Mimms**. **Wilson** was used to stress the danger of routine traffic stops. **People v. Gonzalez**, 689 N.E. 2d 1187 (Ill. App. 2d Dist. 1998).

In the Montana case the officer ordered Mr. Roberts, who attempted to get out of the car, to stay in the car. The car was stopped because the police believed there was an outstanding warrant for the driver. A second officer ordered Roberts to stay and asked for I.D. A warrant check revealed a valid warrant for Roberts. The Montana court broadly read **Wilson** as saying that an officer may control a passenger's freedom of movement by requiring the passenger to get out of a car pending completion of the stop. It saw this as a *non-exclusive rule* that would prevent "stay in" orders. **State v. Roberts**, 943 P. 2d 1249 (Mont. 1997).

Washington has one case involving a passenger. It is a "get back in the car" case. The passenger refused and he was charged with "obstruction." **Terry** and **Wilson** were used. However, this particular police department has a single policy, that all passengers must stay in the car. This was not seen as unreasonable and reasonableness is the "touchstone" of seizure analysis. The court said, "We conclude the benefit of increased police protection outweighs the intrusion to passengers. We hold the police lawfully ordered Mr. Mendez to remain in the car." **State v. Mendez**, 947 P. 2d 256 (Wash. App. Div. 3 Panel 5 1997).

Like other states, South Dakota has wrestled with the passenger issue *vis-à-vis* routine traffic stops. In **State v. Ashbrook**, 586 N.W. 2d 503 (So. Dak. 1998), the police observed "furtive gestures" by a passenger as the police signaled the car to stop. The police asked the passenger about the movements. She said she was moving her purse and admitted she had a pocket knife. Concerned for his safety, the officer ordered her out so he could search under the seat. A stack of drug pouches were found. Was this police conduct objectively reasonable? **Long** and **Wilson** were cited in support of the action as being reasonable under the circumstances.

In another case, **State v. Tilton**, 561 N.W. 2d 660 (S. D. 1997), the passenger was ordered out of the car at a sobriety checkpoint because the officer needed to move the seat forward to see the floor boards in the rear because the driver consented to a search of the car. The reluctant passenger caused safety concerns in the officer's mind. Fearing a weapon, the officer asked the passenger to empty his pockets but the passenger refused to remove his hand from his pockets. A scuffle ensued and drugs were found. **Wilson** was cited approvingly.

Suppose a set of circumstances requires an officer to check a suspicious registration form against the VIN number on the dash. Would it be reasonable to require the passenger to exit the car? Suppose when the passenger gets out the officer sees a type of pipe used most often to smoke marijuana and psilocybin mushrooms. Note that the reason for the initial stop, speeding, was eminently reasonable. This happened to the passenger who was prosecuted and convicted of drug charges in **State v. Shepard**, 955 P. 2d 352 (Utah App. 1998). Citing **Wilson**, they felt that language in the **Wilson** decision did not require any threatening behavior on the part of the passenger. It quoted the following: "An officer making a traffic stop may order passengers to get out pending the completion of the stop." Therefore, this Utah officer did not exceed the scope of a routine traffic stop by ordering the passenger out.

The Texas high court for criminal matters addressed a **Wilson** issue in **Rhode v. State**, 945 S.W. 2d 115 (Tex. Crim. 1997). In the Texas case the officer handcuffed the passenger out of concern for his own safety (dark area, high crime locale, car chase, single officer). The court said that in evaluating the police conduct and the reasonableness of the detention the courts must use common sense and ordinary human experience and not rigid criteria. Reasonableness, at the time, not hindsight, must be used to judge the quick decision under "tense, uncertain and rapidly changing circumstances." It also cited the "pending completion of the stop" language of **Wilson**.

The intermediate appellate court of Pennsylvania agrees with **Wilson** and noted they have been allowing the **Wilson** practice for years. It also said that the officers are not required to articulate a "specific concern" for the "get out of the car" order. **Com. v. Rodriguez**, 695 A. 2d 864 (Pa. Super 1997).

Like Texas, Idaho also dealt with an unhappy handcuffed passenger in **State v. DuValt**, 961 P. 2d 641 (Idaho 1998). Idaho says one must judge the totality of the circumstances to reach the right result; look not to unparticularized suspicions or hunch *but* to specific reasonable inferences the officer may draw from the facts in light of his experience. There were five suspects; it was late at night, three occupants were suspected of drug activity and they displayed uncooperative behavior. This made the cuffing in this case reasonable.

Totality also meant a great deal to the Connecticut court in **State v. Wilkins**, 692 A. 2d 1233 (Conn. 1997). In this case, the driver and passenger were removed from the car at gun point. Why? Their car nearly hit the officer. When the officer made his U-turn, they sped off and pulled into an apartment complex parking lot. As the officer approached their car they were "scrunching down" or "laying down" in the front seat of the car "as if trying to avoid detection." The occupants disobeyed repeated orders to keep their hands in sight. The officer thought they were trying to reach weapons. Both were ordered from the car so that the officer could call for backup and he ultimately locked them in the cruiser. Was this reasonable? Yes.

Virginia's **Wilson**-based case did not involve a car but rather an in-the-neighborhood possible drug sale context. To arrest the two suspects and to minimize danger to the officers and the neighborhood, the police, at 8:25 p.m., in front of a notorious crack-house where shots had often been reported, ordered everyone to lie flat on their stomachs with their arms extended. One did not fully comply and a pat-down was conducted and crack was immediately felt. Citing **Wilson** this court emphasized and cited the following: "the reasonableness of an officer's actions depends on a balance between the public interest and the individual's right to personal security free from arbitrary interference by law officers." **Wilson** at 519 U.S. 411 (1997). These officers were justified in their conduct when 5 officers were facing a group of 8 people. There was a reasonable fear for the officers' safety.

Maryland reluctantly accepts **Wilson** but notes that the officers cannot force the passenger to stay in the car since the U.S. Supreme Court specifically left that question open for another day. Thus a conviction for disorderly conduct was reversed for refusal to follow the "stay-in" order in **Dennis v. State**, 693 A. 2d 1150 (Md. 1997). Cert. Den. 118 S. Ct. 329; prior history **Maryland v. Dennis**, jud. vac. for consideration in light of **Whren v. U.S.**, 517 U.S. 806 (1996).

By remanding to Maryland, the Supreme Court was saying to use **Whren v. U.S.** and its "objective reason" theory. The majority, because of the difference in factual issues, totally refused to understand why they were to consider **Whren**. In fact, they said they could not understand why any police officer would feel safer with the passenger in the car. One must assume (without knowing) that none of the justices had ever been a police officer and faced the potential of being attacked by a roaming compatriot. In fact, on the day of the **Robinette** decision, an Ohio State trooper's camera captured the sight of a passenger getting out of a truck and shooting at the second officer standing at the cruiser while the first officer was gathering the registration information from the driver. Fortunately no one was hit by the flying bullets. The Ohio stop was a very ordinary traffic stop. Only the dissent by Justice Baker in the **Dennis** remand understood that, objectively, this officer is allowed to control the scene without reference to his subjective reasons; a reason that may even be infirm.

A panel of the Court of Appeals of Washington disagrees with the position of Maryland in **Dennis**. **State v. Mendez**, 947 P. 2d 256 (Wash. App. Div. 3 Panel 5 1997). Ms. Mendez was a passenger in the lawfully stopped car. Both the driver and Mendez got out of the car but the back seat passengers stayed in. Mendez started walking away causing the officers to order him back into the car but he disregarded their command. The driver obeyed, but Mendez began to run. He was caught and placed under arrest for "obstructing." The search incident revealed evidence of paraphernalia. Convicted of both counts, Mendez appealed the failure to suppress. The appellate court, despite agreeing with Mendez that he appeared to present no real threat at the time, said his conduct increased the objective potential for danger. The court then said, "We conclude the benefit of increased police protection outweighs the intrusion to passengers." It held the police order lawful, thus a reasonable cause for arrest arose giving the police the search incident right. It must also be noted that in May of 1997 the Washington Supreme Court abolished the right of their citizens to resist unlawful arrests. **State v. Valentine**, 953 P. 2d 1294 (Wash. *en banc* 1997). But since this arrest was deemed lawful the evidence was admissible; if found unlawful the only real cost is suppression and not the officer's life.

H.   Plain View

The eye cannot trespass. Whatever can be seen without undue acrobatics, without physical trespass, without ultra sophisticated devices (not generally available to the public) cannot be said to be clothed in privacy. Upon this basis the doctrine of plain view was based and framed in Coolidge v. New Hampshire, 403 U.S. 443 (1971). Though the eye cannot trespass, the head that holds those eyes (and nose) can trespass. Thus, when a police office sticks his head in the open window of a car and penetrates the air space of the interior there has been a search. See **U.S. v. Pierre**, 943 F. 2d 6 (C.A. 5th 1991). However, the case was reheard en banc and the search was found reasonable in this case. **U.S. v. Pierre**, 958 F. 2d 1304 (C.A. 5th en banc 1992).

Although many authors would like to make plain view more complicated than it is, it is not a very difficult rule to apply, especially with the automobile. There are two branches to the rule. The first branch involves the police while conducting a lawful search, either by way of warrant or under the guidelines of **U.S. v. Ross** which was discussed earlier, or while lawfully executing some other intrusion discussed above. In these instances the police are where they have a right to be. If, while conducting the lawful search, the police come across, inadvertently, an object that is contraband or other immediately apparent evidence of another crime (more on this later), the police may seize the item even though it was not something they were seeking. The item seized is admissible.

If this were the only justification for plain view, however, it would have been placed in Section II above as a related applicable doctrine. There is a second branch of the plain view doctrine. This branch is totally related to the "eye cannot trespass" theory of search law. This second branch also requires the lawful positioning of the police officer at a place not prohibited by decisional law. For example, policemen may get plain view if they trespass on another's land as long as they do not violate the curtilage protection of **Oliver v. U.S.**, 466 U.S. 170 (1984), which limited the area of the "open fields" that was announced in **Hester v. United States**, 265 U.S. 57 (1924). The plain view so acquired generally required no artificial viewing aids such as binoculars or infra-red scopes. Eyeglasses are not prohibited. However, recent decisions have lost sight of these limitations and it is not clear how much the naked eye can now be aided. In fact, if the device is available to the public, police efficiency should not suffer. Thus the use of a flashlight to peer into a car is plain view and not a search. **Dick v. State**, 596 P. 2d 1265 (Okla. Crim. 1979).

In fact as noted in Chapter Seven on Plain View, the Supreme Court has repeatedly said since **Coolidge** that they would not "equate police efficiency with unconstitutionality." It has approved the use of cameras, beepers, airplanes, and helicopters. The standard followed by most courts is, as stated in Chapter Six, whether the device used is generally available to the public, thus potentially only foreclosing national security devices that are available only to the government.

If while lawfully viewing (as described above) the police non-pretextually see an object that is an immediately apparent criminal object, the officer has arrived at the moment of probable cause. In a "non-automobile" context and without proof of an exigency, the officer is generally required to secure a warrant to search the item. However, under the guidelines of **U.S. v. Ross**, it appears that the mobility exigency will allow the immediate search of the car. It was said that the view had to be inadvertent.

The inadvertence requirement deserves comment. The purpose of this requirement was to discourage pretextual intrusions. However, total surprise, such as shock and dismay, is not required. Police, after all, are trained to be suspicious and adversarial. All the inadvertence requirement tried to do is keep them honest. The properly trained officer should be observant to fulfill his peace-keeping and crime detection duties. Therefore, when an officer walks by a car and looks in and sees evidence of a crime the inadvertence requirement should have been met. Despite the fact that most states adhered to the inadvertence requirement, the Supreme Court in **Horton v. California**, 496 U.S. 128 (1990), held that inadvertence was not required by the Fourth Amendment. States are free to interpret their own constitutions as requiring inadvertence.

One troublesome aspect of the plain view doctrine is the requirement that the object seen must be immediately apparent as a criminally involved object. What exactly does that mean? The issue has been somewhat resolved in two Supreme Court Decisions.

The first decision is **Robbins v. California**, 453 U.S. 454 (1981). The court implied that in the proper case the contents of a package could be inferred from its size, shape and packaging method. Unfortunately, the record in **Robbins** did not establish such a permissible inference. The more conclusive and direct decision defining immediately apparent came in **Texas v. Brown**, 460 U.S. 730 (1983). The Court saw the issue whether "immediately apparent" meant a high degree of certainty. Its answer was no. The Court called the use of words "immediately apparent" an "unhappy choice." Basically, "immediately apparent" means probable cause to believe the object is incriminating. A "practical non-technical probability is all that is required." Thus common sense, experience, and training come into play. The exact impact of **Arizona v. Hicks**, 480 U.S. 321 (1987) and its effects on automobile searches is not fully known yet. **Hicks** established the **Brown** rule as a majority rule which must be followed when making decisions under the U.S. Constitution. In **Payne v. State**, 744 P. 2d 196 (Okla. Crim. 1987), that court fully accepted Justice Rehnquist's position on immediately apparent as being probable cause based. This, of course, became the majority position of the U.S. Supreme Court in **Arizona v. Hicks**.

Finally, plain view is really a misnomer. The doctrine is not limited to merely the sense of sight. In any number of cases courts have recognized that the other senses may be trusted to arrive at probable cause. Thus, in the proper circumstances, the teachings of plain view may be satisfied by smelling, hearing, tasting, and even touching the non-pretextually discovered object.

In the nature of a "plain view" case, consider the Court's opinion in **New York v. Class**, 475 U.S. 106 (1986), where the Court found no reasonable expectation of privacy in the VIN number that is required to be placed at a viewing position at the base of the windshield. Class had committed a traffic offense and he was stopped. The VIN number was obstructed by items on the dashboard. The officer reached in the car and moved the objects. When he reached in he saw the butt of a gun protruding from under the driver's seat. The possession of the gun led to his arrest and he was ultimately convicted. The Court held that the VIN number is important and without a privacy right and the defendant does not create a privacy right by obstructing its view.

The intrusion by the officer to remove the obstacles was reasonable and permissible. The Court was quick to point out that had this VIN number been viewable from outside the car as intended, then no intrusion would have been permissible.

There are a number of numbers required by state and federal law. One is the gross vehicle weight tag. If **New York v. Class** approves moving objects to view the VIN, do the police have the same right to open a truck door to get at the gross weight tag (GVWR)? No, said an Illinois court. The weight tag is not required by law to be visible from the exterior, held the court. This seems to be restrictive of the purpose of such acts to regulate overweight vehicles, but it does strictly construe the statute. **People v. Anderson**, 531 N.E. 2d 116 (Ill. App. 2 Dist. 1988).

There is a significant, inherent limit to **Class** and VIN numbers, as illustrated by a decision from the Ninth Circuit. In **U.S. v. $227,000 U.S. Currency**, 49 Crim. L. Rep. 1436 (C.A. 9th 1991), the police suspected that a car parked on private property was stolen. To confirm their suspicions they went onto the property and lifted an opaque cover that obstructed the view of the interior and the VIN. The factual distinction of this case from **Class** was found to be important and controlling. In **Class** the vehicle was being illegally operated on the road. The court felt that **Class** was factually driven and did not create a right to uncover VINs without probable cause when not being operated upon the highways.

Should police be permitted to open a car door to view a second VIN number when the first VIN observable through the windshield was not obstructed? This was the issue faced by the Utah Supreme Court. That court took the opportunity to criticize the U.S. Supreme Court's relaxation of the warrant requirement. Using their own constitution they felt there was no exigency in this case, thus they felt the officers should have obtained a warrant before opening the car. This case is not only an attack on **New York v. Class** but upon **Carroll Towing** and the **Ross** cases as well. **State v. Larocco**, 794 P. 2d 460 (Utah 1990).

VI. Conclusion

The Court, in order to balance the rights of privacy of the individual against the need to deter crime and aid in its investigation, has chosen to limit the privacy rights one can expect with regard to the high mobility of vehicles. The wisdom of this choice may be subject to debate and criticism, but it is nonetheless the current policy of the Court which will probably continue as long as rapid personal transportation devices exist.

CHAPTER FOURTEEN
ELECTRONIC INTRUSIONS: WIRETAPS, *etc*.

I.   Surreptitious Surveillance: Introduction

Before **Katz,** the prime concern about whether the Fourth Amendment was violated centered on the place and if the place had been penetrated. Katz was a professional gambler who made his calls from a glass phone booth where he could be seen by the whole world (at least by those who passed by). The obvious reason for using a phone booth was to avoid any "taps" that might be on his private line. His mistake was that he used the same public phone booth every time he made his illicit calls. The FBI attached a listening device and recorder outside phone booth. On the information collected, Katz was tried and convicted.

The Court abandoned the purely physical intrusion rule and added to it an expectation of privacy rule that is personal to the defendant. Wherever a man may be, the Court said, he is entitled to know that he will remain free from unreasonable searches and seizures. **Katz v. U.S.,** 389 U.S. 347 (1967). But this is not a general right of privacy. The Fourth Amendment protects people but not all places. However, what the person seeks to keep private even in a public area may be constitutionally protected.

Government attorneys urged that the Fourth Amendment protects only tangible items because it is limited to persons, houses, papers and effects. Of course, the U.S. Supreme Court, which uses a historical argument when it upholds border searches but abandons it at other times, was not willing to "buy" this limitation. Earlier in **Silverman v. U.S.**, 365 U.S. 505 (1961), it said that the Fourth Amendment governs not only the seizure of tangible items but extends as well to the recording of oral statements. **Silverman** prohibited the warrantless use of a "spike mike" in a wall. Thus the fact that the device used in **Katz** did not penetrate the phone booth had no constitutional significance.

The Court, having determined that a search had taken place in violation of a reasonable expectation of privacy, turned to the issue of probable cause and the warrant requirement. The government wanted a new exception to the warrant requirement. Without some proper demonstration of a real exigency, which the Court was not ready to admit could exist, it rejected the government's plea. The Court ruled that omission of an authorization by a magistrate bypasses the safeguards provided by the objective predetermination of probable cause. The specter of after acquired information being used to justify the search at a suppression hearing loomed large.

Just before the **Katz** decision, the Court addressed the issue of the constitutionality of New York's eavesdropping statute. Did it meet the requirements of the Fourth Amendment? No. The New York statute permitted a warrant to issue upon the reasonable belief that evidence of a crime may be obtained by the eavesdrop. What was sought and what crime was involved need not have been shown under the ill-fated New York statute. The Court characterized this legislative scheme as a broadside that reinstituted general searches that were detested by the colonists. **Berger v. New York**, 388 U.S. 41 (1967). Too much was left to the discretion of the police officer. Too much time was allowed for the gathering of evidence. New information was not required for renewal. Thus, the Court held, the statute's blanket grant of permission to eavesdrop was without adequate judicial supervision or protective procedures.

Bugs and wiretaps, however, can be used when constitutional safeguards are observed. Obviously, the government does not always go to the trouble of applying for permission to intrude into the privacy of an individual. What recourse does the defendant have when he suspects that the evidence gathered was the result of illegal wiretapping or bugging? In this situation the government is not using the poisoned tree but rather the fruits thereof.

The Ohio Supreme Court was faced with a secret taping of the defendant's side of the telephone conversation with his attorney. The defendant urged a violation of the Sixth Amendment right to counsel while the state argued no reasonable expectation of privacy under **Katz**. The court focused on the right to counsel issue and whether the defendant was given the opportunity to freely discuss his case and defense with his attorney. The court correctly found a violation of the constitution and turned their attention to the remedy. The state argued for mere suppression whereas the defendant sought outright dismissal which he said was required on a *per se* basis. The Ohio court opted for the case-by case approach and adopted the test of **Weatherford v. Gursey,** 429 U.S. 545 (1979) which requires balancing all the factors and puts the burden on the state to demonstrate that information gained was not prejudicial to the defendant. **State v. Milligan**, 533 N.E. 2d 724 (Ohio 1989).

Fruits of the poisonous tree was one of the prime issues in **Alderman v. U.S.**, 394 U.S. 165 (1969). After the conviction of the defendants, it was discovered there was illegal governmental electronic search activity. Alderman sought discovery of the transcript of surveillance to see if he was entitled to a retrial. The Court held that all records of illegal electronic surveillance to which any defendant has standing to object must be made available to such defendants without any prior judicial screening. The Court concluded that the adversary process, though not perfect, would provide the necessary scrutiny the exclusionary rule demands. Of course, the defendant can get only the conversations to which he was a party. Additionally the defendant and his counsel could be put under orders not to share the information through unwarranted disclosures.

The use of illegally seized evidence to obtain an intercept order would, of course, invoke **Wong Sun** and the "fruits of the poisonous tree" doctrine. Suppose, however, the evidence used was lawfully gathered but an intercept order was issued that was otherwise substantively defective. Would such an order be the poisonous tree for any extensions filed, thus making the extension derived evidence "fruits?" The answer, according to **U.S. v. Giordano**, 416 U.S. 505 (1974) is yes. The Court said:

> "It is urged in dissent that the information obtained from the illegal October 16 interception order may be ignored and that the remaining evidence submitted in the extension application was sufficient to support the extension order. But whether or not the application, without the facts obtained from monitoring Giordano's telephone, would independently support original wiretap authority, the Act itself forbids extensions of prior authorizations without consideration of the results meanwhile obtained. Obviously, those results were presented, considered, and relied on in this case.

Moreover, as previously noted, the Government itself had stated that the wire interception was an indispensable factor in its investigation and that ordinary surveillance alone would have been insufficient. In our view, the results of the conversations overheard under the initial order were essential, both in fact and in law, to any extension of the intercept authority. Accordingly, communications intercepted under the extension order are derivative evidence and must be suppressed." **Giordano** at 533.

Sections 2515 and 2518(10)(a) of the federal act address the standing issue when the statute has not been followed. These sections incorporate the fruits of the poisonous tree doctrine and prevent illegal interceptions from being used in any trial, hearing or proceeding in any court, or before any agency, including grand jury proceedings. In order to utilize these sections, however, the defendant (aggrieved person) must present "some credible evidence that the prosecution violated the law before ponderous judicial machinery is invoked..." according to Justice Douglas. Douglas said the burden of the aggrieved person is that of probable cause at a minimum. **Russo v. U.S.,** 404 U.S. 1209 (Douglas as Cir. Just. 1971).

The matter was ultimately addressed by the entire Court in **Gelbard v. U.S.,** 408 U.S. 41 (1972). The defendants refused to testify before a grand jury saying they had the right to challenge whether information used to question them was based on illegal wiretaps. Contempt proceeding had begun because of their refusal to testify. Was the refusal to testify "just cause" to preclude a finding of contempt? The Ninth Circuit said this was not "just cause" and the Third Circuit said it was "just cause."

Five members of the Court said it was "just cause" with four members dissenting. The five felt that "...Congress simply cannot be understood to have sanctioned orders to produce evidence excluded §2515," at p. 51. Justice White, in concurring, said such a challenge is available only when there has been no order authorizing the "tap" or interception. His point, of course, is that grand juries may hear suppressible evidence to determine probable cause and he concluded Congress did not intend to interfere with traditional grand jury processes for arriving at probable cause and also did not intend to expand the rights of criminal defendants regarding avoidance of testifying at grand jury proceedings.

II.   Statutory Reaction to Katz and Alderman

Katz and **Alderman** would move the Congress to act. Title III of the Omnibus Safe Streets and Crime Control Act of 1968, 18 U.S.C. Sec. 2510, *et.seq.*, also known as the Federal Electronic Surveillance Statute as now amended, was its response. When enacted, the statute was aimed at "bugs" or the planted listening devices and "taps" or interception of wire communications. By amendments in 1986 brought about by the Electronic Communications Privacy Act of 1986, the statute now covers wire, electronic and oral communications. Definitionally this would now include data transmissions, video teleconferences, electronic mail, and wire communications by wire, cable or other "like connection."

As for oral communications the statute defines these as "any oral communication uttered by a person exhibiting that such communication is not subject to interception under circumstances justifying such expectation." Will that include car telephones and other "wireless" phones? Any number of courts before 1986 found that the use of portable phones did not create a reasonable expectation of privacy since the unit usually comes with a clear warning that transmission may be intercepted and in fact can be heard over regular F.M. airwaves. That being so, no court order was necessary to properly intercept the conversation. See **State v. Howard**, 679 P. 2d 197 (Kas. 1984). The Kansas court limited the interception without judicial approval only to the party using the cordless phone. If the other person was using a regular phone, then Title III would have to be satisfied.

Cordless phones and cellular phones are not "hard-wired" or land - wired devices. No physical intrusion is required, nor is any attachment device required to intercept these transmissions. Until 1994 the Congressional act did not protect these forms of devices. In fact cordless phones were specifically excluded from protection under the act. The amendments to 18 U.S.C. Sec. 2510 clearly now extends protection to these devices as well as communication through the use of computers. Thus Congress has created a reasonable expectation of privacy where none existed before 1994.

Many cases must be read to determine if the interception occurred before the 1994 amendments. Intercepts before enactment are governed by the old law and not the new. Fugitives from justice who, by their absence, have tolled the statute of limitations and will get no relief in federal courts. See **McKamey v. Roach**, 55 F. 3d 1236 (C.A. 6th 1995), where the conversation on a cordless phone by one person erased the protection of the land-line user.

A number of states reacted more quickly to protect wireless phone users. Some have not amended their statutes but they are bound by the "greater rights" doctrine of the federal preemption doctrine. A state may not give lesser protection to its citizens under this doctrine but may give them greater rights. Michigan found a way around its statute's silence on the subject by construing the primary goal of its statute. Thus the words "private conversation" would be nullified if wireless phones were not included in the statute's protection. **People v. Stone**, 621 N.W. 2d 702 (Mich. 2001). The appeals court reversed the trial judge's decision by finding an expectation of privacy in the former wife's conversations that had been intercepted by the former husband. Michigan affirmed the appeals court decision saying that, as a matter of law, it was not unreasonable for her to believe her conversations on her cordless phone were private. States like Georgia were quick to correct their old statute. See the discussion in **Barlow v. Barlow**, 526 S.E. 2d 857 (Ga. 2000).

Judicial approval is the crux of the statute. The hope is that all other means of getting the information have failed and have been exhausted before such eavesdropping will be permitted. Probable cause standards have to be met. Whether that standard is the **Gates** standard or the **Aguilar** standard in state statutes is a concern, but clearly the federal agents must follow **Gates** which is less restrictive than **Aguilar**. See **State v. Ross**, 481 A. 2d 730 (Conn. 1984) saying **Aguilar** applies and **U.S. v. Tufaro** 593 F. Supp. 862 (S.D.N.Y. 1984).

The order can also issue even if other regular means have not been exhausted. If the government can prove that other methods would either be futile or dangerous, then an order may issue. Thus where the government shows that regular investigative techniques were only somewhat successful the court could authorize a wiretap where it was shown that the informants were afraid to testify and the government demonstrated that they were unable to recruit new informants since the defendant only dealt with people he had known for a long time. **U.S. v. O'Connell**, 841 F. 2d 1408 (C.A. 8th 1988). Likewise where they show only limited success and demonstrate that other regular techniques would also be unlikely to be productive because they involve a high risk for safety, a wiretap warrant may issue and will be overturned only if the issuing judge abused his or her discretion. **U.S. v. Zamrana**, 841 F. 2d 1320 (C.A. 7th 1988). See also **Com. v. Wilson**, 405 Mass. 248 (1989) that a showing that other investigative techniques were not likely to succeed as sufficient to issue a wiretap order. **State v. Knight**, 995 P. 2d 1033 (N. Mex. 2000) in accord.

What the judge is supposed to insist on is basic probable cause law plus strict compliance with the statute. Certainty of result is not required which, of course, is true for other probable cause based searches. A difference of judicial opinion is not enough to invalidate an order. The government does not have to prove that all other techniques have been tried. The government merely shows what steps have been taken and then shows why it would be difficult to place an informant or maintain continuing surveillance. **U.S. v. Alfano**, 838 F. 2d 158 (C.A. 6th 1988). If the government can demonstrate that a prosecutable case cannot be achieved under standard investigative techniques, then it should get an order. In **U.S. v. Leisure**, 844 F. 2d 1347 (C.A. 8th 1988) the government demonstrated that physical surveillance, pen registers, telephone records and unwilling informers all had created an un – prosecutable case. However, each application must stand on its own. The court cannot put a series of applications together to determine necessity. Each application must satisfy the requirements. And, each application must at least spell out what had been done by the government before the application. **U.S. v. Carneiro**, 861 F. 2d 1171 (C.A. 9th 1988). In **Carneiro,** a "guilt by association" approach was taken. Thus a valid affidavit was used to bolster an invalid independent affidavit. This cannot be done.

Are there any circumstances under which the authorities may eavesdrop without an application in writing or a written order? In other words can there be a warrantless interception akin to the exigent circumstances doctrine tolerated in general search law? At least four states by statute provide some form of an exigency exception.

Maryland, for example, provides for the hostage and barricade situations by allowing certain designated officers to conduct an interception without first contacting a judge in Md. Code Cts. and Jud. Prac. §10-413. Pennsylvania has a very similar statute.

Since exigency has long been a fully recognized, well-defined exception to the warrant requirement, there would seem to be no reason for emergency actions as contemplated by these statutes. They do, however, create an orderly process, provide for the assignment of responsibility and establish immunity from civil damages for those that exercise or rely on those who exercise this power.

New York, New Jersey and Pennsylvania also provide relief in other emergency situations. In these statutes, the relief is in the form of allowing a judge to issue an oral order to intercept, etc., upon an oral application. See: New Jersey Stat. Anno. 2A:156A-13, McKinney's New York C.P.L, and 18 Pennsylvania C.S.A. §5713.

Broadly, these statutes recognize that there are times when emergencies arise in which time is of the essence. All three allow verbal approval by the court upon verbal application. All three also place a time limit on the validity of the order. By implication, if not expressly, all three do not envision extension of such orders. By implication, if not expressly, immunity from civil rights actions inhere in the statutes for properly invoking the emergency provisions.

The foregoing statutes represent the primary principle of search and seizure: reasonableness. Even when seizing words by way of surreptitious surveillance, reasonableness should be the key. **Katz** and **Alderman** should not be read or applied to undo constitutional guarantees. A balance should be struck between the rights of individuals and the right of society to deter and ferret out crime.

Nevada, through Nev. Rev. Stat.707.340, specifically provides for an exigent circumstances exception. The "911" provision of this statute is a clear application of the "person in need of help" branch of the exigent circumstances doctrine and thus no written request to the utility for assistance is required. However, only trap and trace devices are allowed; no wiretapping is permitted under this section.

There is one other exception to the use of judicially approved telephonic interceptions and that involves consent of the owner of the receiving phone. Two fairly recent cases illustrate this. The first is from Georgia; it involved a statutory rape and child molestation of J.C., child of Cherrie Collins. J.C. and her mother agreed to tape incoming calls from the molester, Malone. Malone called and their conversation was recorded. The local statute, as most do, permit parties to record such conversations with J.C.'s consent. Malone argued that J.C. could not give consent. The court disagreed. **Malone v. State**, 541 S.E. 2d 431 (Ga. App. 2000).

The next case is from Missouri. It too involved sexual misconduct with a child; the stepdaughter of the defendant was the victim. The stepdaughter lived with her grandmother. The grandmother consented to tape-recording the conversation between the defendant and the victim that took place on the grandmother's telephone. This too was upheld due to the child's consent. The child was examined by the judge regarding the consent issue, and he found her capable of giving consent. **State v. Barrett**, 2001 WL 168057 (Mo. App. 2001), citing **State v. Holt**, 592 S.W. 2d 759 (Mo. *en banc* 1980), a case on very similar facts.

Orders issued under the statute are limited in time and scope. If the time limit expires, the intrusion right ends unless the government makes application for an extension of the original order. The statute specifically governs. Sometimes an officer does not know whether an extension is needed. Suppose the extension is not filed in a timely manner because the agents were having a difficult time getting translations into English of the transcripts they had taken under the prior order. Should the police be penalized when they come at the earliest possible time after securing the translations? No, said one district court judge in **U.S. v. Ragusa**, 586 F. Supp. 1256 (E.D. N.Y. 1984). This decision makes practical common sense.

Under the statute an initial order may only issue for certain stated categories of federal crimes. One of the questions often raised is whether an amended order may include crimes not included on that list. The Second Circuit has concluded that Congress only intended the list to apply to the initial order and not to amended orders. They said, "We hold that 'other' offenses under Section 2517(5) may include offenses, federal as well as state, not listed in Section 2516 so long as there is no indication of bad faith or subterfuge by the federal officers seeking the amended surveillance order." **In re Grand Jury Subpoena Served on John Doe**, 889 F. 2d 384 (C.A. 2d 1989). When there is an adequate necessity showing, the listing of a misdemeanor with a proper list of felonies will not be enough to render the order improper. **U.S. v. Savaiano**, 843 F. 2d 1280 (C.A. 1st 1988). This comports with the severance doctrine that is applied to the general law governing regular search warrants.

Normally, a wire tap authorizes the surveillance of a specific telephone line and no other. Amendments in 1986 to the wire tapping law allows the order to cover any phone the target is using. A district court judge in California held this does not violate the Fourth Amendment; thus "roving wiretaps" can be approved if the government can show the target as one who had "evidenced an intent to thwart interception of his or her communication." **U.S. v. Silberman**, 732 F. Supp. 1067 (D.S. Cal. 1990). See **State v. Matthews**, 5 P. 3d 1273 (Wash App. Div. 2 2000) (statutory language did not limit the territory within which the call may be made).

One problem not specifically anticipated by most of the electronic surveillance statutes concerns a phone number change caused by the target or perhaps the phone company. The issue was ably addressed by the high court of New York. The court agrees that the Fourth Amendment and statutory requirements were satisfied when the police applied for the wire tap. The only problem was that the telephone number for the residence was changed between the date of issuance and the date of installation. Did this change go beyond the warrant's explicit terms thus requiring suppression? No. Why not? The same line was used and it was the only line that went into the house. Besides, the statute does not require that a wiretap application or warrant designate a *particular* telephone number. This is also true of 18 U.S.C. Sec. 2518. The court said, "'Strict compliance' does not entail hyper – technical or strained obedience, nor is common sense its enemy." Thus, the change in the number of the only phone in the house had no bearing on the established probable cause. **People v. Darling**, 720 N.Y.S. 2d 82 (N. Y. 2000) [unanimous opinion].

When addressing the issue of scope, the warrant says seek evidence of Crime A only. While listening, the agents get information involving unknown and unsought crimes. What should happen with this "windfall" evidence? Is there a "plain hearing" exception like the "plain view" rule of **Coolidge v. New Hampshire**? Sec. 2517(5) requires prior judicial approval before the government can use "windfall" evidence. If a judge approves progress reports and extends the warrant, is that tantamount to judicial approval? Yes. **U.S. v. Van Horn**, 789 F. 2d 1492 (C.A. 11th 1986). Courts can also interpret whether the evidence is windfall or just part of the genre of crimes already approved to be sought. **U.S. v. Young**, 822 F. 2d 1234 (C.A. 2d 1987). Sometimes an officer thinks that he or she is hearing more about the same crime and only later, upon close analysis, is it discovered that a windfall has occurred. If believed by the court, a late filing of the amendment application will be excused. **U.S. v. Southard**, 700 F. 2d 1 (C.A. 1st 1983).

Windfall evidence shares what was thought to be the inadvertence requirement of plain view. The issue is whether the police concealed from the judge a high likelihood that evidence of other crimes would be revealed. If so, that would be bad faith. However, where there is a mere belief in other crimes, a failure to reveal them does not justify a conclusion of bad faith. **U.S. v. Levine**, 690 F. Supp. 1165 (E.D.N.Y. 1988). Since this inadvertence requirement is statutorily mandated, it was not changed by the Court's decision in **Horton v. California**, which abandoned the inadvertence requirement for plain view cases.

There are other scope issues as well. For example, in **U.S. v. Borch**, 695 F. Supp. 898 (E.D. Mich. 1988), the defendant did not place the phone properly on its cradle. The police overheard the conversation that took place in the room and said it was covered by the wiretap that had been authorized. The court held this was not a wire communication that had been authorized; thus, it suppressed the conversation. However, in another case, the court held that reading telephone numbers on a "pager" was not an "interception" under Title III. **U.S. v. Meriwether**, 917 F. 2d 955 (C.A. 6th 1990).

The Sixth Circuit joined other courts by applying plain hearing to evidence gathered during a lawful wiretap when the phone was left off the hook allowing the officers to overhear a conversation in the room where the telephone was located. The court analogized such conduct to the plain view doctrine and called it a "lucky break." **U.S. v. Baranek**, 903 F. 2d 1068 (C.A. 6th 1990).

The federal government wanted to use the product of a Florida authorized wiretap in **U.S. v. Nelson**, 837 F. 2d 1519 (C.A. 11th 1988). The wiretap was authorized by a state judge under the Florida Statutes. The circuit court judge issued it, but when the "tap" was put on, the intercept was sent into another judicial circuit for recording. The defendant said that this was outside the issuing judge's jurisdiction and order. The court disagreed and said the intercept occurs where the communication is initially obtained regardless of where it is ultimately heard.

Other state versus federal scope issues also exist. States may not grant the state more rights but it can give the defendant more rights. What if the state attempts either? What can the federal government use?

If a state shrinks state rights to wiretap, but the state issues an order to cover crimes permitted to be covered under the federal act, the federal government may use the evidence gathered. Thus a district court in **U.S. v. Sanchez**, 675 F. Supp. 445 (D. Conn. 1987), held that the government may use the fruits of such a search in the federal prosecution. See also **U.S. v. Glasco**, 48 917 F. 2d 797 (C.A. 4th 1990).

Though states may give the defendant more protection from wiretaps, they cannot diminish the reach of the federal act and allow wiretaps for crimes not dangerous to life or limb gathered by the state for use in the federal courts. Thus evidence derived from the state's broader act cannot be used by the federal government in a tax evasion case according to the court in **U.S. v. Millstone Enterprises**, 684 F. Supp. 867 (W.D. Pa. 1987).

Finally, on this point, the Eleventh Circuit had a case in which prior wiretaps involving this defendant had been attempted, but the police did not inform the Florida state judge of the disposition of these wiretaps. The federal government does not make this fatal to the issuance of the order. In Florida, however, such failure is fatal. This more rigorous rule must be used according to the Eleventh Circuit, since the state procedure was used to issue the wiretap. The court felt bound under these circumstances to apply state law. **U.S. v. Brown**, 862 F. 2d 1482 (C.A. 11th 1988). This appears to be contrary to **Sanchez** and **Glasco**, cited above.

Once an officer has satisfied the court that an eavesdropping is needed does the court have to specify the manner, or approve in advance the manner in which the device is to be installed? No. The lower court held that because there was no prior approval of a covert entry to install the "bug," the entry was no good and invalidated the electronic surveillance. The Supreme Court did not agree. Neither statutes nor the constitution prohibit the covert entry. Congress was silent on the issue thus it is apparent that they recognized that the use of "bugs" would require surreptitious entries. The Court concluded by saying:

> "It would extend the warrant clause to the extreme to require that...the court must set forth precisely the procedures to be followed by the executing officers... the manner in which a warrant is executed is subject to later judicial review as to its reasonableness...." **Dalia v. U.S.**, 441 U.S. 238 (1979).

For the most part, the states appear to follow the rule of **Dalia**. Some have codified this principle. For example, see the provisions from West Virginia and Maryland. Pennsylvania appears to take a more restrictive approach in 18 Pa. C.S.A. §5712(g). Most states, however, are more concerned with immunizing from suit those persons needed to assist law enforcement in the installation, use, and removal of such devices. Consider, for example, So. Dak. Code §23A-35A-8. See also: Cal. Pen. Code §629.40; N. D. Cent. Code §29-29.2-03; Vern. Mo. Stats. Anno. §542.408.7 and.8; La. Stat. Anno. R.S. 15§1316; and 18 Pa. C.S.A. §5712(f).

As with regular warrants, a return must be made; but in this case Sec. 2518(8)(a) calls for the presentation of the tapes for sealing. Officers are not always as diligent as they should be. How much leeway do the courts allow? There is no uniformity. See **U.S. v. Mora**, 821 F. 2d 860 (C.A. 1st 1987). The concern, of course, is the issue of tape alteration. The First Circuit said if the proof shows no alteration, and there is no harm to the defendant and no advantage to the prosecutor, then the delay should be excused. **U.S. v. Donlan**, 825 F. 2d 653 (C.A. 2d 1987). For other cases permitting some leeway see: **U.S. v. Badalmenti**, 794 F. 2d 821 (C.A. 2d 1986);**U.S. v. Morgan**, 646 F. Supp. 1460 (S.D.N.Y. 1986);**U.S. v. Venuti**, 625 F. Supp. 1460 (S.D.N.Y. 1986);**U.S. v. Rodriguez**, 786 F. 2d 472 (C.A. 2d 1986); and **U.S. v. Masino**, 784 F. 2d 153 (C.A. 2d 1986).

The tapes must not only be returned they must also be sealed. Sometimes there is a delay in the sealing. Is that fatal? No, it is looked upon as ministerial and the defendant must show prejudice. In one case there was a five-day delay in sealing due to administrative delay. The court felt this was justifiable. In the same case a delay of 15 days to check for "leaks" that might endanger the lives of government informers was also found to be permissible. **U.S. v. Squitieri**, 688 F. Supp. 163 (D. N.J. 1988). In **U.S. v. Kusek**, 844 F. 2d 942 (C.A. 2d 1988) an eight-day delay between termination and sealing was approved despite the fact that the Delaware statute was used which said such delay was fatal. The court held that this material was usable in the federal prosecution because, unlike the Eleventh Circuit in **U.S. v. Brown** (*supra*) federal law would apply as long as there was no bad faith, tampering, or prejudice to the defendant shown.

The United States Supreme Court decided to resolve the issue concerning the sealing statute caused by decisions like **Kusek**, (*supra*). To the Court, the statute means it when it says; immediate sealing is required unless there is a satisfactory explanation, *not just* an explanation. It agreed that the presence or absence of a seal does not ensure that the tapes were not tampered with, but immediate sealing limits the government's opportunity to alter the recording. The Court was unwilling to accept the argument that any delay in sealing is acceptable as long as the government proves non-tampering. Likewise, they said proof of non-tampering is not a satisfactory explanation. In fact, the Court had its doubts about tampering being detectable in all cases. Thus, if there is a delay in sealing, the government must show why the delay is excusable. Without such a showing the tapes must be suppressed. **U.S. v. Ojeda-Rios**, 495 U.S. 257 (1990). Accord: **State v. Cain**, 670 So. 2d 515 (La. App. 4th Cir. 1996).

Unsealed tapes are used for a variety of purposes, not all of which are approved. Defense attorneys have not had a great deal of success in suppressing the tapes or getting indictments dismissed. In **U.S. v. O'Connell**, 841 F. 2d 1408 (C.A. 8th 1988) disclosure of the tapes to secretaries and an intelligence analyst (though both were improper) did not give the court grounds to throw the tapes out. In **U.S. v. Vest**, 842 F. 2d 1319 (C.A. 1st 1988) playing the tapes to a grand jury violated the act but that was not found to be the kind of misconduct to require dismissal of the indictment.

Once the tapes are sealed it requires a judicial order to unseal them. When unsealed the government must show there has been no tampering or alteration for tactical gain. A court has the inherent power to unseal them for the legitimate purpose of audio enhancement without affecting the integrity of the tapes. **U.S. v. Angiulo**, 847 F. 2d 956 (C.A. 1st 1988).

The tapes are usually resealed after their use in a trial to preserve their integrity should they be needed again either in another case or in a retrial. They do not have to be resealed until the proceeding in which they are used is concluded, however. Thus their use in another proceeding, while the first proceeding is still underway, satisfactorily explains the absence of a seal in the second or subsequent proceeding. **U.S. v. Scopo**, 861 F. 2d 339 (C.A. 2d 1988).

As a predicate to admission of the contents of the tapes, Sec. 2518(9) requires that copies of the application and order must be delivered to each party at least 10 days before the proceeding. The Second Circuit says the prior delivery requirement was applicable to detention hearings under the Bail Reform Act. **U.S. v. Salerno**, 794 F. 2d 64 (C.A. 2d 1986) cert. granted 107 S. Ct. (1986) (as to other issues) but, unless prejudice occurred to the defendant, suppression would not be ordered. The prejudice issue was the key. **U.S. v. Berrios-Berrios**, 791 F. 2d 246 (C.A. 2d 1986).

As to who is entitled and when, consider the Tenth Circuit's position in **In re Grand Jury Proceedings**, 735 F. 2d 1230 (C.A.10th 1984). It held that a grand jury witness whose conversations have been intercepted is entitled to a copy of the application, affidavit and court order.

Once a person receives the notice, is that person always entitled, forthwith, to get everything that involves them? In **Stoddard v. U.S.**, 710 F. 2d 21 (C.A. 2d 1983), the court denied such discovery on the basis that the government had adequately established that disclosure would jeopardize ongoing investigations. Accord: **In re Warrant Authorizing The Interception of Oral Communications**, 708 F. 2d 27 (C.A. 1st 1983).

The defendant is not necessarily entitled to the originals, especially when good duplicates are made, or the prosecutor offers to allow the originals to be heard in the prosecutor's office. **U.S. v. Terry**, 702 F. 2d 299 (C.A. 2d 1983). Are the defendants entitled to know the location and type of equipment used? No, that is privileged information and disclosure would only serve to educate criminals about the government's methods and techniques. **U.S. v. Van Horn**, 789 F. 2d 1492 (C.A. 11th 1986).

In the general search warrant context, some matters are of constitutional proportions while other matters, time of the search, for example, are ministerial concerns. Constitutional concerns require the application of the exclusionary rule of **Weeks-Mapp** (*supra* at Chapter One). Where a ministerial provision has been violated, the evidence need not be suppressed unless the defendant can show prejudice. Is there room for such a distinction under the electronic surveillance statutes? The answer is apparently yes as illustrated by **U.S. v. Donovan**, 429 U.S. 413 (1977). In **Donovan** there was a failure to send a post-intercept notice to two of the defendants. However, the government made everything available to these defendants including transcripts of the intercepted conversations. The Court found that there was no prejudice to the defendants by failing to include them in the original post-intercept notice. In the absence of a clear order by the legislature requiring suppression for a failure to observe a ministerial directive, the **Donovan** case should be used as a guide.

Another ministerial concern was addressed by the Court in **U.S. v. Chavez**, 416 U.S. 562 (1974). In **Chavez**, an executive assistant to the Attorney General, under the Attorney General's personal order, authorized an application for a wiretap order. This executive assistant was not *the* Attorney General nor was he an Assistant Attorney General. The statute requires approval by the Attorney General or an Assistant Attorney General designated by the Attorney General for that purpose. In all other respects the order that was issued was valid. The defendant felt the evidence should be suppressed. The Supreme Court disagreed because this provision was not a substantive violation of a substantive part of the statute.

III. Pen Registers and Trap and Trace Devices

The 1986 amendments added two new devices to the list of "court-approval-required" electronic items. The law now includes pen registers and "trap and trace" devices. They may be approved upon application by any government attorney who can demonstrate that such surveillance is relevant to an ongoing criminal investigation. The 60-day order, subject to extension, must list the crime, telephone listing name (if known), the person who is subject of the investigation, and the number and physical location of the telephone line to which the device will be attached.

The U.S. Supreme Court approved the warrantless use of the pen register on telephones. **Smith v. Maryland**, 442 U.S. 735 (1979). A witness to a crime was receiving threatening phone calls from the suspect of the crime. The police went to the phone company and secured permission to register the phone numbers that the suspect called. The register indicated calls to the witness' home. With this and other information, the police obtained a warrant to search the suspect's home and came up with incriminating evidence. The Court held that the defendant did not have a legitimate expectation of privacy in the numbers he dialed; only in the conversations he conducted. All telephone users must know that the numbers they dial could be recorded. Such users assume the risk of disclosure to third parties of information they voluntarily surrender to others. Thus no warrant was required for the use of the pen register, see also **U.S. v. N.Y. Tel. Co.**, 434 U.S. 159 (1977).

As can be seen, the 1986 amendments to Title III now create at least a shadow of a right but not a full Fourth Amendment right. Idaho feels pen registers are subject to a full Fourth Amendment probable cause determination and thus a prior warrantless use of a pen register and the information gathered cannot be used to obtain a wiretap warrant. **State v. Thompson**, 760 P. 2d 1162 (Idaho 1988). Florida says permission to use a pen register is required and will be granted on articulable suspicion standards. **Shaktman v. State**, 553 So. 2d 148 (Fla. 1989). The federal standard in 18

U.S.C. §3123 is "information likely to be obtained" that is "relevant to an ongoing criminal investigation." This statute also provides for order-less emergency pen registers to be used, §3124.

As already noted, the Congress does not require probable cause for the use of a pen register. Relevance is the issue. At most this would be articulable suspicion; at least it would be merely announcing the fact of an on-going but otherwise legitimate investigation. What Congress wanted more than anything else is a "paper trail" coupled with judicial intervention. Congress, therefore, does not appear to disagree with the Supreme Court regarding the lack of an expectation of privacy.

Since the federal act is supreme regarding the minimum rights afforded a defendant, the states were required to amend local wire-tap laws. Most appear to have adopted the federal language without question. One such state is Texas. The Texas provision and the whole theory of **Smith** was called into question in **Richardson v. State**, 865 S.W. 2d 944 (Tex. Crim. App. 1993). The state, in **Richardson**, applied for and received permission to use a pen register. The information gathered was used to support an application for wiretaps and search warrants. The defense argued that without probable cause the court-approved use of a pen register was indeed a search and thus in violation of the Texas Constitution. The intermediate appellate court disagreed and relied on **Smith**. The Court of Criminal Appeals disagreed with their appellate court and the U.S. Supreme Court and said a person may well have an expectation of privacy in numbers dialed that is both reasonable and one that society is willing to protect. If so, probable cause is needed to issue a pen register order because it is a search. The case was remanded to determine these issues.

The pen register merely gives authorities the numbers called by the person using an already identified telephone line. The second known telephone is the receiver's phone. Some concerns arise, often in emergencies, when the identification of the location of a calling phone is important. Emergency calls to crisis centers, for example, and 9-1-1 calls often demand finding the source of the call to provide needed assistance. Caller I.D. will satisfy that need unless the caller has some sort of "block" that terminates such a call.

In a law enforcement context, police are not dealing with a call to a crisis enter but still need to know the source of the phone's location. This is the function of the "trap and trace" operation. Does the caller have a Fourth Amendment expectation of privacy that prohibits unauthorized "trap and trace" operations? How do they differ from the use of pen registers? Since both do not record the conversation but only identify non-conversational information, there appears to be no invasion of privacy in that context, since only location is revealed. The pen register identifies numbers called while "trap and trace" locates the source of calls; facts already revealed to the phone company.

Smith v. Maryland, 442 U.S. 735 (1979), was the decision that approved the warrantless use of pen registers and should be used for the "trap and trace" issues as well (unless the state has a statute on the subject). The recording of electrical impulses is the key to both operations. In **Smith** the Court said there was no reasonable expectation of privacy in those impulses. Since the telephone company cannot bill without recording, the primary interest in such information is not protected. As a Texas court has said: "The Fourth Amendment protection extends only to the content of a telephone conversation and not the fact that a call was placed or that a particular number was dialed. **McArthur v. State**, 1 S.W.3d 323 (Tex. App. 1999). But how does this court get around the **Richardson** case cited above? Note that the **Richardson** court *did not say* the pen register *was a search* but said it *may be a search* and remanded the case. The distinction in **McArthur** was that McArthur was not using his own phone, but that of his employer, thus if a privacy interest was invaded it was not one that McArthur possessed. It seems, by the way, that there is no definitive answer in Texas as yet on the issue left open in **Richardson.**

In any event, the key is to consult local decisional and statutory law to determine the electronic impulse issues of the devices. For example, in New Jersey the reaction to **Smith** came by way of a statute that only allows pen registers upon a probable cause based warrant. See **State v. Mollica**, 554 A. 2d 1315 (N.J. 1989) where the court noted the legislative reaction to **Smith**. As an aside the **Mollica** case gave birth to the "reverse silver platter doctrine" discussed in Chapter One.

Although pen registers may require a warrant or articulable suspicion, "trap and trace" may have an emergency need; thus in kidnapping or hostage cases, the exigency of the situation will allow bypassing any warrant or application process in most if not all cases. Pen registers were the subject of two other decisions; one from Louisiana and one from Ohio. The phone records in the Ohio case were obtained by subpoena and not by using a warrant. The defense argued that the warrant process should have been used. The defendant argued that today's technology means that **Smith** is "no longer persuasive." The court disagreed saying the reasons stated in **Smith** "remain valid today." Users still realize that they must convey phone numbers to the telephone company and the company still keeps records of calls made and customers still receive lists of long distance phone calls made when they receive their bill. Since Ohio follows **Smith** as noted by **Ohio Domestic Violence Network v. Pub. Util. Comm'n of Ohio**, 638 N.E. 2d 1012 (Ohio 1994), this court did not accept this defendant's challenge to **Smith**. **State v. LeMaster**, 1998 WL 27937 (Ohio App. 4 Dist.) (unpub. op.).

In the case from Louisiana the issue was whether the application for the pen registers complied with the "oath or equivalent affirmation requirement." This was a statutory administrative requirement. But is exclusion the remedy for this failure to comply with the statutory requirements? The court reasoned that since the constitution is not implicated in the gathering of pen register information, the failure to observe the statute in this case did not require exclusion of the evidence. Why? The court points out that the act "does not include a specific exclusionary rule for violating the statutory requirements for obtaining a pen register" as it does for the issuance for wiretap warrants. Since **Smith** does not extend Fourth Amendment protection to pen registers, use of them does not constitute a search. The court then cites **U.S. v. Thompson**, 936 F. 2d 1249 (C.A. 11th 1991). In a footnote the Louisiana court says that since 1979, the use of caller I.D. means that the Court was correct in finding no legitimate expectation of privacy in numbers called. They also cite **State v. Fakler**, 503 N.W. 2d 783 (Minn. 1993) indicating a lack of statutory sanction meant there would be no exclusion of evidence when the officer had sufficient information to include it in his application. The Louisiana court closed this section of the opinion by analyzing the state constitution. The word "communication" is included in their "Fourth" but since numbers dialed are not communications the defendant also lost that argument. **State v. Cain**, 670 So. 2d 515 (La. App. 4th Cir. 1996).

Are there any other classes of electronic equipment subject to Title III? Yes, there is at least one other device. Some courts hold that video surveillance is covered by Title III. **U.S. v. Crevas-Sanchez**, 821 F. 2d 248 (C.A. 5th 1987); and **People v. Kalchik**, 407 N.W. 2d 627 (Mich. App. 1987). Contra see: **Ricks v. State**, 520 A. 2d 1136 (Md. App. 1987) and cases cited therein and **People v. Heydenbeck**, 430 N.W. 2d 760 (Mich. Ct. App. 1988) public area of restrooms ok. See also **Com. v. Price**, 562 N.E. 2d 1355 (Mass. 1990) where undercover agents used video in a hotel room the state rented. The tape was used to convict the defendant. Although a warrant was used it did not matter.

There are courts that have expressed a hostility toward video surveillance at a pure privacy right level. Consider two decisions by the Oregon Court of Appeals issued in 1988. Both cases apparently involved non-court approved installations of cameras in public restrooms but that is not the sticking point. Both cases involved masturbation that could have been viewed by any member of the public passing by; but that was not crucial to their decisions. One defendant did his deed in a stall without a door while the other did his act in the public area. Both were found to have had their

Fourth Amendment right to privacy violated. They found the surreptitious surveillance was a search that invaded privacy. This was an impairment of the people's freedom from scrutiny; this surveillance, they say, people do not anticipate. They couched their decisions on state constitutional grounds. **State v. Casconi**, 766 P. 2d 397 and **State v. Owczarzak**, 766 P. 2d 399 (Ore. Ct. App. 1988). A California Appellate Court put limits on a consented-to video surveillance requiring the consenter to be present when the videotaping takes place. **People v. Henderson**, 270 Cal. Rep. 248 (Cal. Dist. Ct. App. 1990).

There are a few other matters when considering the application for and use of electronic surveillance orders. First, all such applications are subject to a **Franks v. Delaware** (*supra* at Chapter 5) analysis. The court may reject one if it was issued upon a deliberately false or reckless statement. However, the defendant must do more than make bare allegations of falsity. He must offer proof on the issue. **U.S. v. Leisure**, 844 F. 2d 1347 (C.A. 8th 1988). The **Franks** issue is not possible, according to the Sixth Circuit, where the issuing judge did an exhaustive examination of the affiant and otherwise established the veracity of that witness. **U.S. v. Giacalone**, 853 F. 2d 470 (C.A. 6th 1988). In **U.S. v. Valdez-Pacheco**, 701 F. Supp. 775 (D. Ore. 1988), the court said that false statements in an affidavit that were the product of negligent checking or recording of facts did not make the affidavit vulnerable to attack. In addition, failure to mention a wiretap in another state did not constitute a material omission and where an omission does not go to the heart of probable cause, a **Franks** hearing does not have to be held.

Even if the evidence is gained by a bad wiretap it may still be of some use. **U.S. v. Kusek**, 844 F. 2d 942 (C.A. 2d 1988) held that a tape which had been suppressed could be admissible to refresh the defense witness' memory on cross-examination. It can be used to impeach a witness.

Some problems can occur during the collection of the information. In one case the agents temporarily disconnected the apparatus to avoid detection by an electronics expert that worked for the conspiracy. Such a disconnect did not terminate the authorization for the wiretap so as to require a separate authorization from the court for re-connection. **U.S. v. Leavis**, 853 F. 2d 215 (C.A. 4th 1988).

In **U.S. v. Gerena**, 695 F. Supp. 1379 (D. Conn. 1988) the F.B.I. listened without recording everything. This is called "live monitoring." The court held that the failure to record everything does not render the electronic surveillance unlawful thus suppression is not required. Only two of the 64 agents involved did this occasionally. The court felt this did not taint the monitoring as a whole.

IV.   Other Electronic Intrusions

This section covers other electronic intrusions such as: beepers, microwave sensing devices, magnetometers, x-ray, and fluoroscope units. The microwave sensing device is used by a number of stores to detect shoplifting. Magnetometers and x-rays are used at airports by security guards to screen for weapons and explosives. Assuming some form of state action is involved, are these intrusions reasonable?

Any intrusion must be measured against the need to search. Thus, in using the microwave sensor what governmental interest is served? Shoplifting poses a serious economic problem. Its effects are passed along to paying customers in the form of higher prices. Therefore, the need for some intrusion has been found necessary, e.g., **Lucas v. U.S.**, 411 A. 2d 360 (D.C. Ct. App. 1980). If a need exists, the question is whether the intrusion is the minimal amount necessary to pass constitutional muster without the oversight of a neutral and detached judge. This device, the microwave sensor, does not generally scan everything. It does not reveal the property of the person scanned. It merely determines whether the subject has left the store with merchandise of that store from which the sensor tags have not been removed.

As for the use of magnetometers and x-rays at airports, no court now doubts the reasonableness of such intrusions. Consider this Florida decision, **State v. Baez**, 530 So. 405 (Fla. Dist. Ct. App. 1988). Citing the leading Florida case on the subject, **Shapiro v. State**, 390 So. 2d 344 (Fla. 1980), the court addressed the traveler's Fourth Amendment rights in the alternative. First, this type of security search does not constitute an invasion of the air traveler's reasonable expectation of privacy; thus the Fourth is entirely inapplicable or even if the Fourth applies, such a security search is entirely reasonable based on an implied consent and balancing rationale thus satisfying the Fourth's reasonableness standard. The **Baez** court thus called the x-ray and magnetometer searches of this defendant perfectly legitimate airport security checkpoint searches. In upholding the poorly motivated, but properly grounded, field search of this defendant this court said: "The Fourth Amendment is not a suicide pact and does not require airline security personnel to...[ignore the alarms]. To do so, the court held, would be reckless conduct with airline passengers safety."

Another electronic device that has received judicial scrutiny is the beeper. This inaudible sound transmitting device is used to trace the movements of people and property. It changes signal when something to which it is attached is opened. All you need to do is "pop" one of these things on a cache of contraband and it will lead you to its owners. Does the surreptitious use of a "beeper" constitute a search? Prior to two major decisions on beepers by the Supreme Court, the other courts of the U.S. were all over the place. Before those decisions I had written these words in 1977:

> None of the courts issuing opinions in the area admit the problem of stealth, sneakiness or dirty tricks which is the real issue. Instead the expectation of privacy plus search are the cornerstones. Yet when the agents get to where the "beeper" leads them they are "still on the outside looking in." At this point, hearing no conversations and seeing activity which most often the reasonable man would not find criminal, they would still need arrest and search warrants or probable cause plus exigent circumstances to use that "beeper" found location.

In some cases the "beeper" is planted in property once in the lawful possession of the police, **U.S. v. Perez**, 526 F. 2d 859 (C.A. 5th 1976) or by the permission of the true owner of the property before possession is given to the defendant, **U.S. v. Curtis**, 562 F. 2d 1153 (C.A. 9th 1977) and often it is stealthfully placed on, in or under the defendant's vehicle when the defendant is not looking, with a warrant, **U.S. v. Pretzinger**, 542 F. 2d 517 (C.A. 9th 1976) or without one in a public parking lot or street, **U.S. v. Holmes**, 521 F. 2d 859 (C.A. 5th 1975) or in a private garage, **U.S. v. Hufford**, 539 F. 2d 32 (C.A. 9th 1976).

The circuits appeared to be headed for hopeless conflict on this issue. The Fifth Circuit considered the attachment of a "beeper" without the owner's consent or the vehicle having been in the lawful possession of the police as an illegal search which uncovered the incriminating evidence **(Holmes).** The Ninth Circuit, on the other hand, in **Hufford**, said that monitoring the "beeper" as the vehicle passed along the road was not a search because there was no expectation of privacy. The Fifth Circuit reconsidered their position on a beeper installation to a vehicle parked in a public place. Finding the placing of the beeper a minimal intrusion the court saw no unreasonable violation of the expectation of privacy. The court was unwilling to say that this was not a search as some members of the court urged. It further noted that the beeper only aided the agent's ability to perform their lawful surveillance while the car traveled public roads exposed to public view. The surveillance was lawful because it was based on reasonable (articulable) suspicion. **U.S. v. Michael**, 645 F. 2d 252 (C.A. 5th 1981).

Although a person does not expect to be followed he often is if he is a suspect. What is the difference between being followed by an officer or being traced through an electronic device in regard to a privacy expectation? The operative fact is the privacy expectation and not the following, which is not bad unless done in private confines and even then is limited by **Hester** and "open fields."

This point brings up the utility of the "inevitability" doctrine: that the evidence gained through the use of the "beeper" would have ultimately been discovered anyway. Some call this the "hypothetical independent source exception." By whatever name, the doctrine requires that normal police procedures would have produced that same evidence. Some courts require proof that an actual independent source did exist. **U.S. v. Bergdoll**, 412 F. Supp. 1323 (D. Del. 1976). Other courts require only a "could have" finding (**Hufford**). Inevitable discovery is discussed in Chapter One.

There is no doubt that the entry onto private property to place such a "beeper" is a "dirty trick" and should require prior court sanction. Likewise, an argument can be made that following a "beeper" is a search but it is also an observable event to which all people are subject. If stealth is the problem the courts should recognize it as such and deal with it directly. Any illegal activity needed to plant the "beeper" should be barred. But no attempt should be made to twist search and seizure principles further. **Why**? When the destination is found what often occurs will take place not in an open field or in plain view. The officer will have only mere suspicion and not articulable suspicion because one cannot be convicted for being with a known criminal. Criminal profiles may not be used to parlay probable cause from the profile's generalities.

Assuming the strength of the logic that continuous tracking of a person moving a container with a planted beeper is not a search, does this logic extend to the situation where the trail is lost and the item not relocated until it has come to rest? The Eighth Circuit said that when the signal was lost its subsequent rediscovery came when the item was moved into a sphere of privacy and thus a violation of the Fourth Amendment. **U.S. v. Knotts**, 662 F. 2d 515 (C.A. 8th, 1981). This is a proper reading of **Knotts**.

The Georgia Court of Appeals in **Dunivant v. State**, 273 S.E. 2d 621 (Ga. Ct. App. 1980) held that the installation of a beeper did not violate the Fourth Amendment. It was a question of first impression for Georgia. Citing **U.S. v. Holmes**, 521 F. 2d 859 (C.A. 5th 1975) and **State v. Hendricks**, 43 N.C. App. 245, 258 S.E. 2d 872 (1979) as holding this conduct as a search, the court noted that the First Circuit rejected such a conclusion in **U.S. v. Moore**, 562 F. 2d 106 (C.A. 1st 1977). The court relied heavily on the rationale of **Moore** in that the public has a right to expect protection from illicit drug flow thus there is no expectation of privacy in contraband. They felt the better rule to be that the installation does not violate any rights as long as no trespass is involved and there exists probable cause to believe that a crime is intended.

The stage was thus set for Supreme Court action. Two separate cases were needed to give the lower courts direction. Those cases are **U.S. v. Knotts**, 460 U.S. 276 (1983) and **U.S. v. Karo**, 468 U.S. 705 (1984). What did these two cases hold? Did the Court answer all the questions that would settle the considerable disagreement among the circuits? Not really.

The first case to give the Court an opportunity to pass on "beepers" was **U.S. v. Knotts**, 460 U.S. 276 (1983). Chloroform used in the manufacture of illicit drugs when not purchased by laboratories and pharmaceutical companies or other legitimate enterprises was at the heart of this case. On such suspicion a "beeper" was placed in a container that was stolen by a man named Armstrong. Armstrong took the container and after 3 days of tracing by both "beeper" and standard visual surveillance it came to rest at Knott's cabin. The police secured a search warrant and the illicit lab for making "uppers" was discovered. The Eighth Circuit called this illegal "beeper" monitoring. The Supreme Court reversed. The true owner had consented to the "beeper's" placement thus no issue of warrant was therefore implicated. It is hard to imagine a right of privacy arising in a criminal with regard to goods he has stolen. Coupling that with the consent of the true owner, **Katz** was not violated. Following a car on highways falls into the mobility exception which is more fully discussed in the search of automobile materials. In any event the Court says one hardly has an expectation of privacy with regard to his movements upon the public roads from one place to another. One voluntarily conveys to the whole world his direction, speed, and ultimately his final destination.

Knott's expectation of privacy in his cabin is not implicated by the mere arrival of the car, with the chloroform, at his address which could be visually observed. "Nothing in the Fourth Amendment prohibited the police from augmenting the sensory faculties bestowed upon them at birth with such enhancements as science and technology afforded them in this case," the Court held and further said, "We have never equated police efficiency with unconstitutionality and we decline to do so now." The most important *caveat* came at the end of the opinion. Rehnquist narrowed the scope of the holding by saying, "But there is no indication that the beeper was used in any way to reveal information as to the movement of the drum within the cabin or in any way that would not have been visible to the naked eye from outside the cabin." So there was no search and seizure problem here. Oregon has restricted **Knotts** and the use of beepers under their constitution. **State v. Campbell**, 759 P. 2d 1040 (Ore. 1988).

The Wisconsin intermediate appellate court has approved the use of "beepers" on automobiles by their decision in **State v. Haas**, 2001 WL 388930 (Wis. App.). The police attached an electronic tracking device to a vehicle registered to the defendant's companion. Haas had been driving the vehicle and was a suspect in several burglaries. Two more burglaries were committed and the police, having tracked him to and from those locations, stopped him. He fled on foot. Goods were found in the vehicle that were identified as having been stolen in the two burglaries. The trial court refused to suppress and relied on **Karo** and **Knotts**. No error was found by the appellate court in applying these decisions. A warrant to attach these was needed under Wisconsin law.

Still there existed many unanswered questions. Without consent can a "beeper" be placed? Did the Court mean what Rehnquist said in his *caveat*? Would prior judicial approval be needed even though "beepers" are not included in Title III? Would any of these questions be answered in **U.S. v. Karo** 468 U.S. 705 (1984)? In **Karo** the defendant purchased the goods and the police got both a court order and the consent of the seller to "beeperize" the container of ether that was, according to the informant-seller, to be used to extract cocaine from imported clothing. Karo picked it up and visually and by "beeper" traced it to his house. They traced it as it is moved within the house and then to another house. This the "beeper" also told them. The ether wafted through the air. Again it was moved to another house. Again moved, but this time to a commercial storage facility, but where no one knew. Again it moved, but not until they installed an alarm device on the locker in which it was stored. Rather than use the court order, they obtained consent of the manager of the locker facility to install a video camera aimed at the locker. The stuff finally came to rest whereupon the police, using all the previously gathered information, obtained a search warrant for the final resting place. The Circuit Court held a warrant was required to install the beeper originally and to monitor it at its several stopovers. Since a warrant had not been obtained, the ultimate warrant was tainted. The warrant issue was to be addressed by the Supreme Court.

As to installation, the Court held that no Fourth Amendment interest of the defendant was infringed by the installation of the "beeper." Any impairment of privacy came through the monitoring. Indiscriminate monitoring was seen as "far too serious a threat to privacy interests...to escape entirely some sort of Fourth Amendment oversight." A warrant requirement "will have the salutary effect of ensuring that use of beepers" will not be abused. The Court was quick to note the protection of the "time exigency" rule. Any search of a house, absent other applicable doctrines of exemption, requires a warrant.

That these two cases did not settle all issues is evidenced by subsequent decisions. The Fifth Circuit says an extended use "beeper" requires a warrant. **U.S. v. Butts**, 710 F. 2d 1139 (C.A. 5th 1983). A mailman has no expectations of privacy in the mail he is to deliver. **U.S. v. Emmanuel**, 572 F. Supp. 1215 (S.D. Tex. 1983). One thief thought it was totally unfair of the police to monitor a beeper placed in the deposit bag by the owner of the bag. It led police to the motel room where the defendant and his cohorts were arrested without warrants. The court tried to figure out how such thieves could expect privacy in a bag they could not possess without stealing it. More important was the potential **Karo** issue. Yes, a motel room can indeed be a private residence. But the court felt that **U.S. v. Jones**, 31 F. 3d 1304 (C.A. 4th 1994) made sense. In **Jones**, a post office employee stole a bag of mail with a beeper in it. But the Fourth Circuit said, "The mail pouch with the beeper found its way into Jones van only because Jones stole the pouch and hid it in his van himself." Personal property protected by the Fourth is not stolen property and thus the rule of **Karo** was not violated. The California court went on to note that the beeper in **Jones** was placed in that bag by the police but in their case the victim placed the beeper in the bag and it, too, was a stolen item. They felt this made their case even stronger than the monitoring approved in **Jones. People v. Erwin**, 63 Cal. Rep. 2d 617 (Cal. App. 3d Dist. 1997).

By requiring a search warrant for the use of a thermal imaging device, the Court continued the rule of **Karo**. The key for the five member majority (led by Justice Scalia) is the exploration of "details of the home that would previously have been unknowable without physical intrusion." Therefore, as in **Karo**, the surveillance, even without the police personally intruding, was a search. **Kyllo v. U.S.**, 2001 WL 636207 (U.S.).

V. Conversation Monitoring: Body Wires, Hidden Tape Recorders, etc.

One final Title III issue must be addressed concerning the acquisition of information. Can one party consent to "interception" by some electronic form that can be used against the other participant? Yes, Title III permits consent to being overheard. The consent must meet all voluntary and knowing standards – **U.S. v. Koloqziej**, 706 F. 2d 590 (C.A. 5th 1983); **U.S. v. Yonn**, 702 F. 2d 1341 (C.A. 11th 1983), and must not be done for a criminal or tortious purpose (on the part of the consenter and of course by implication the police) – **U.S. v. Vest**, 813 F. 2d 477 (C.A. 1st 1987) – **U.S. v. Underhill**, 813 F. 2d 105 (C.A. 6th 1987). Finally, the Second Circuit held that where a sign tells a prisoner that conversations are monitored and the defendant has signed a form noting this, the prisoner had consented to the taping. **U.S. v. Willoughby**, 860 F. 2d 15 (C.A. 2d 1988).

The only strange cases in the consent area are represented by **U.S. v. Passarella**, 788 F. 2d 372 (C.A. 6th 1986), and **U.S. v. Ordonez**, 722 F. 2d 530 (C.A. 9th 1983). While lawfully executing search warrants the phone rang and the officers answered and, without identifying themselves, carried on defendant incriminating conversations. Both courts held since the officers were each a party to the conversations, Title III consent applied. In the Ninth Circuit case the owner of the apartment did not want the police to answer the phone. It did not matter. See also **U.S. v. Sangineto-Miranda**, 859 F. 2d 1501 (C.A. 6th 1988).

All of the discussions thus far have centered on the federal decisions and not on the states. Why? First of all, by Congressional preemption the federal act is the linchpin. The states may enact their own Title III types, but they cannot decrease a defendant's rights, though they can expand them. For state case see: **People v. Schulz**, 501 N.Y.S. 2d 12, 492 N. E. 2d 120 (N.Y. 1986); **People v. Sporleder**, 666 P. 2d 135 (Colo. 1983); **People v. Crowson**, 190 Cal. Rep. 165, 660 P. 2d 389 (Cal. 1983); **People v. Ingram**, 648 P. 2d 243 (Colo. 1984); **People v. Basilicato**, 484 N.Y.S. 2d 7, 424 N.E. 2d 215 (1984); **Bashaw v. Com.** 675 S.W. 2d 376 (Ky. 1984); **Com. v. Brachbill**, 555 A. 2d 82 (Pa. 1989); **People v. Corr**, 682 P. 2d 20 (Colo. 1984); **State v. Howard**, 679 P. 2d 197 (Kan.. 1984); **Com. v. Hashim**, 525 A. 2d 744 (Pa. Super. 1987); **People v. Kalchik**, 407 N.W. 2d 627 (Mich. App. 1987); **State v. Hume**, 512 So. 2d 185 (Fla. 1987); **Com. v. Blood**, 507 N.E. 2d 1029 (Mass. 1987); **Com. v. Blystone**, 541 A. 2d 81 (Pa. Ct. 1988); and finally, **Com. v. Fini**, 531 N.E. 2d 570 (Mass. 1988) that absolutely bans one party consent in the home.

The use of body wires, tape recorders, and the like are often used by both police and private citizens. This section will focus on the proper and improper use of such listening/ recording devices and the consequences that flow from their use.

Many, if not all, police cars are equipped with tape recorders that capture the conversations of arrestee and suspects while they sit in the rear seat of the police vehicle. There are no warning signs posted. Do such persons have a reasonable expectation of privacy that society is willing to accept in these circumstances? Most but not all courts agree with the conclusion reached in **State v. Morgan**, 929 S.W. 2d 380 (Tenn. Crim. 1996). They felt that the expectation is unreasonable. The court relied on a decision of their own high court denying a "reasonable expectation" to a jail cell conversation and they felt that rule was applicable here. See **State v.**

598

Williams, 690 S.W. 2d 517 (Tenn. 1985). They also found supporting decisions from California, Florida, Louisiana, Michigan, and Oregon.

The issue in **State v. Poyson**, 7 P.3d 79 (Ariz. en banc 2000), was whether the defendant consented to his interrogation being taped. He did and this "shot down" his claim that he was not read his **Miranda** rights. Otherwise, there would have been a violation of the Illinois eavesdropping law where the interrogation took place.

The "body wire" issue came up in at least three cases in 2000. The first came from Oregon. The state requires an *ex parte* order before a body wire can be used. Police with probable cause are excused from the criminal penalties, but do they lose the evidence? Whether to suppress or not depends on application of the "taint removers" discussed in Chapter One and in particular the independent source doctrine. The judge failed to determine if what was overheard by wire was also heard by others who could give first-hand testimony. If such persons exist then suppression is not required. **State v. Cleveland**, 16 P3d 514 (Ore. 2000). Police, however, should not take a chance by avoiding the *ex parte* application process. This was the lesson learned by Oregon police in yet another case. **State v. Fleetwood**, 16 P.3d 503 (Ore. 2000).

In another case the detective who posed as a drug buyer was to testify. The defense tried to allege a **Brady** violation because the state failed to allow discovery of this fact. The tape revealed no exculpatory information, thus there was no **Brady** discovery violation. **State v. Williams**, 752 A. 2d 951 (R.I. 2000).

The private violation cases involve criminal charges and fines and imprisonment. In **State v. Lombardo**, 738 N.E. 2d 653 (Ind. 2000) the defendant secretly taped his wife's telephone conversations. The major issue centered on how to charge him. The court said the state must charge this as a specific intent crime and prove that intentional conduct. The defense also argued that the words "by means of any instrument device or equipment" are vague and ambiguous those words do not notify citizens of the types of devices prohibited. The court tersely dismissed that argument.

In a Florida case the police enlisted the help of the defendant's fiancé. They wanted her to encourage him to talk about the crime. She agreed and during her visit with him at the jail he incriminated himself. He claims this violated his right to counsel. However, he was in jail on an unrelated crime thus he had no Sixth Amendment right to counsel on the charge discussed that day in the jail. **Jones v. State**, 756 So. 2d 243 (Fla. App. 5th 2000). The body wire she wore yielded usable information.

In **Com. v. Fetter**, 2001 WL 128443 (Pa. Super), the state "planted" a wire on a juvenile to obtain recorded statements from the defendant while the juvenile was in the defendant's home. No counsel rights had attached at the time of the recording. Defendant's belief that the child was old enough for consensual sex, of course, did not matter. Pennsylvania has a one party consent statute. Though the district attorney did not have physical possession of the tapes, she retained total control of access in a secure location and the defendant could show no signs of evidence of tampering. No error arose from the recording of the conversation nor from the preservation procedures after acquired.

Massachusetts found that their wiretap statute also covered the defendant' acts of making secret, unconsented-to tape recordings of oral communications between himself and his attorneys. His mistake was not excusable as a crime due to the attorney-client privilege. **Com. v. Hanedanian**, 742 N.E. 2d 1113 (Mass. App. 2001).

When a law enforcement officer, for personal purposes, violates the law, he or she must suffer the consequences. Such was the fate of the defendant in **People v. Lesslie**, 2000 WL 1509867 (Colo. App.). This deputy sheriff "wired" a bathroom in a bar and hid its presence. He wanted to pick up conversations about narcotics. The owner of the bar found the device and reported. The investigation led to the sheriff and the deputy. The sheriff (without a court order) ordered it and the deputy followed orders and installed it. Under Colorado law there is no immunity without such an approved order. There was no mistake of law defense to help this deputy.

One final point has to be made. The government wanted to be exempted from Fourth Amendment requirements in domestic surveillance cases involving subversion. The Supreme Court rejected the argument making clear that the executive branch of government is subject to the Fourth Amendment warrant procedures in domestic surveillance cases even if it involves subversion or the overthrowing of the government. **U.S. v. U.S. District Court**, 407 U.S. 297 (1972).

VI. E-MAIL and Chat-Room Conversation Monitoring

How should conversations on the Internet be treated? Cases have begun to appear in the appellate reports. In **State v. Townsend**, 20 P.3d 1027 (Wash. App. 2001), the private Internet conversations between the defendant and a fictitious 13-year old girl (created by the detective) were recorded. The defendant said he did not consent to the recording. Did these recorded conversations violate the Washington Privacy Act? No. Does the fact that the victim was not "real" make a difference? No. His acts were a substantial step (perpetration and not preparation) toward the crime of second degree child rape by enticement to meet him and engage in sexual intercourse. He appeared at the door to the motel room selected for the tryst. Defendant knew his communications would be recorded on the fictitious girls's computer. The software manufacturer pre-warned on this possibility. The attempt law focuses on criminal intent and not on the possibility of completing the crime.

In a case of first impression for Pennsylvania, the court held that the victim's act of forwarding chat-room conversation did not violate the wiretap act. The court held there is no expectation of privacy in e-mail and Internet chat-room conversations. Therefore, the corruption of a minor conviction was upheld in **Com. v. Proetto**, 2001 WL 294027 (Pa. Super.).

TABLE OF CASES

INDEX

names from, 258

Plain view and lawful presence of police, 259

Police cars equipped with hidden tape recorders, 597

Public restrooms and videotaped evidence, 259, 589–590

Shredding documents as an act of privacy, 312

Students and schools, privacy expectations, 332

Surgery to remove evidence, 422

Telephone of drug dealer answered by police after drug raid telling callers to come over, plain hearing, consent and privacy issues, 258

Tenant unlawfully holding over, effect on landlord's consent to police searches, 208–209

Video surveillance, 589–590

Private Citizens

Conversation monitoring, use of body wires, hidden tape recorders, 596–599

Exclusionary rule, state action requirement, 31–38

Fire alarm company with keys to apartment, effect of company employee calling police into apartment, 207

Mobility exception, motor vehicle searches, private citizen's actions directed, controlled, or motivated by police, 487

Taping of conversations by

private citizens, penalties for violation of electronic surveillance law, 598–599

Tips by citizens. See **Informants**

Privileges

Attorney-client privilege. See **Attorney-Client Privilege**

Informer's privilege, 150–152, 181

Marital privilege. See **Marital Communications Privilege**

Self-incrimination. See **Self-Incrimination, Privilege Against**

Probable Cause

Affidavits

Spinelli affidavit, 105–109

Sufficiency of affidavit, 109–110

Veracity challenges to affidavit under *Franks* standards, distinction between omissions, mistakes and lies, effect on probable cause, 151–152, 177–193

Arrest

Describable crime, 103

Distinction between probable cause for arrest and probable cause for search, 108–109

Entry to make arrest, 392

Felony/misdemeanor arrests, 79, 101–103, 414–416

W

NOTES